Whaur Extremes Meet

Whaur Extremes Meet

Scotland's Twentieth Century

CATRIONA M. M. MACDONALD

First published in Great Britain in 2009 by
John Donald, an imprint of Birlinn Ltd

West Newington House
10 Newington Road
Edinburgh
EH9 1QS

www.birlinn.co.uk

ISBN: 978 1 906566 08 1

The publishers acknowledge subsidy from the

 Scottish
Arts Council

towards the publication of this volume

British Library Cataloguing-in-Publication Data
A catalogue record for this book is available on request from the British Library

Typeset by IDSUK (DataConnection) Ltd.
Printed and bound in Great Britain by MPG Books, Bodmin

Gu Dòmhnull Ailig Mhurchaidh Aonghais Thàilleir

Contents

Acknowledgements

I am indebted to a great many scholars whose names people the footnotes of this book, and whose research provided the inspiration for this study. Without the work of generations of historians and commentators who have sought to record the progress of Scotland in the twentieth century, a work of this nature would, frankly, be impossible. I hope that this work honours their legacy.

In addition to the sources credited in the text and footnotes, I am grateful to copyright holders for permission to reproduce extracts from the following: **Robert Crawford:** 'The Declaration of Arbroath' from *Talkies* (Chatto & Windus, 1992); **Lavinia Derwent:** from *Beyond the Borders* (Hutchinson, 1988); **Douglas Dunn:** from 'Tay Bridge' from *Northlight* (Faber & Faber, 1998); **Archie Fisher and Bobby Campbell:** from 'The Shipyard Apprentice' from *Folk Music Revival in Scotland: The Democratic Muse*, edited by Ailie Munro (Scottish Cultural Press, 1996); **Hamish Henderson:** from 'Freedom Come Aa Ye', © 1960 Hamish Henderson; **Tom Leonard:** from 'Ghostie Men' from *Intimate Voices* (Galloping Dog Press, 1984), © Tom Leonard, and 'Dripping with Nostalgia' from *Outside the Narrative* (Etruscan Books/ WordPower, 2009), © Tom Leonard; **Liz Lochhead:** from *Mary Queen of Scots Got her Head Chopped Off* (Penguin Books, 1989); **Hugh MacDiarmid:** from 'A Drunk Man Looks at the Thistle', and 'Glasgow is Like the Sea: A Hebridean Speaks' from *Complete Poems* (Carcanet, 1993, 1994); **Aonghas MacNeacail:** from 'gleann fademach'/'glen remote' from *an seachnadh agus dain eile. The avoiding and other poems* (Macdonald Publishers, 1986); **Edwin Muir:** 'Carlin' from *Scottish Journey* (Heinemann, in association with Gollancz, 1935); **Thea Musgrave:** from *The Decision: An Opera in Three Acts* (J & W Chester Music, 1967); **Catherine Smith:** lines from Dundee song, reprinted in *Songs and Ballads of Dundee*, edited by Nigel Gatherer (John Donald, 1985); **Iain Crichton Smith:** from 'You Lived in Glasgow' from *Selected Poems* (Carcanet Press, 1985); **Joan Ure:** from 'Something in it for Cordelia' from *Joan Ure, five short plays* (Scottish Society of Playwrights, 1979). Every effort has been made to trace or contact copyright holders prior to publication. If contacted, the publisher will be pleased to rectify any omissions or errors at the earliest opportunity.

Thanks must also go to my academic and administrative colleagues for their support and encouragement during the writing of this book. Financial support from Glasgow Caledonian University for the reproduction of illustrations was also very much appreciated, and two semesters on sabbatical leave made the whole project possible. My students, as ever, offered nourishing food for thought, and Professor Chris Whatley (University of Dundee) provided invaluable help and instructive criticism throughout. (I hope I managed to decipher his handwriting correctly!)

Finally, Hugh Andrew, Mairi Sutherland and the team at John Donald were patient and supportive throughout the writing process, even when pregnancy and motherhood caused me to focus on another 'production' – Thomas – who will only come to know the twentieth century in history books. I hope I offer him enough here of which to be proud as a Scot and sufficient challenges as the heir of an old century to make up for the occasions when history rather than toys occupied his mother's thoughts.

The past's an experience that we cannot share.
Flat-capped Glaswegians and the Music Hall.
Apples and oranges on an open stall.
A day in the country. And the sparkling Clyde
splashing its local sewage at the wall.
This April day shakes memories in a shade
Opening and shutting like a parasol.
There is no site for the unshifting dead.
You're buried elsewhere though your flickering soul
is a constant tenant of my tenement.

'You Lived In Glasgow'
Iain Crichton Smith (1928–98)

Preface

The luxurious touch of the velvet collar of her new green coat suited the novelty of her situation. She had left Stornoway at midnight on the *Loch Seaforth* – the biggest ferry of David MacBrayne's fleet, it dwarfed anything she had ever seen dock in Tarbert. Away from home for the first time in her thirteen years, she had then arrived in Mallaig, with trepidation and excitement equal to that of any explorer, to be met with the sight of a train – the first she'd ever seen (except for those that appeared out of focus and accompanied by the whirr of a turning film reel courtesy of the touring film van at the village hall). To Edinburgh!

A group of Hebridean children, on the invitation of Uist man and Moderator of the Church of Scotland, the Right Reverend Alexander Macdonald, were making the long trip to the country's capital for the General Assembly of 1948. Siblings and classmates back home were jealous. They had learned much of Scotland's cities during the war and a trip without parents made the prospect of city streets and tramcars all the more enticing. And the weather that May was good. Edinburgh looked its best in the spring sunshine and windows, recently dressed in the widow's weeds of blackout curtains, blinked in the bright light of peace. For the children, it merely served to make the Moderator's request that they each bring a peat from home all the more perplexing. Indeed, Joey felt it was an incongruous parcel to be carrying to the metropolis and quite out of keeping with the newness of her coat.

Years on, she would remember little of the stern debates in the Assembly but would smile at recollections of the pranks her student chaperones had got up to. She would remember the kindness of the McPherson family who had shared their home and rations with her and her classmate Bella and recollect the sight of penguins in the zoo with the delight of her first visit undiminished.

And yet, had she concentrated on the speeches that May, she would have had a glimpse of a future that would soon challenge the values at the heart of her Hebridean childhood and ideas that would anticipate some of the major themes of life in post-war Scotland. On 19 May the Assembly accepted an overture from the Presbytery of Lochaber to set up a Commission to inquire into the disinclination of Gaelic-speaking ministers to serve in the Gàidhealtachd – twenty-nine charges were vacant, awaiting the arrival of a Gaelic minister, and in none of the four theological colleges was a Gaelic-speaking student proceeding for licence that year. Meanwhile, that same day Mrs Coutts of St Fillans, the convener of the Women's Home Mission Committee, pressed the case for female ministers in the kirk, though she eschewed chaining herself to the Moderator's gallery to make her point. Some two days later, the Assembly would pass a resolution that communism constituted a menace to liberty and the Christian faith and yet, on 24 May, the Assembly embraced another 'ism' – nationalism – when it recognised the necessity for a greater measure of devolution by Parliament of legislative and administrative power in Scottish affairs. But who was listening? As the applause of the assembled churchmen faded and George MacLeod rose to his feet on 25 May, this latter-day follower of Columba warned of 'a first-class crisis of the nature and content of mission to-day'.

For the girl who first saw an elephant in the week she first travelled by train, Scotland in 1948 was a country of promise and anticipation, of wonderment and surprise. Yet it was a Scotland she had encountered safe within the embrace of familiar values and the stern discipline of a church that was about to embark on a period of dramatic decline.

The story of this girl, my mother, and one week in an erstwhile uneventful island childhood offer insights into the contradictions at the heart of most twentieth-century Scottish lives – comedic moments and soaring drama; technology meeting tradition; unpredictability kissing convention. The smell and taste of lives lived and the unexpected leaps when events create a before and after offer a very human authenticity to any attempt at history but such snapshots are not equal to telling the nation's story.

In what follows, I have rejected a chronological narrative – a straightforward biography of Scotland – as the most appropriate approach for this stateless nation in the twentieth century. Neither the reigns of successive British monarchs nor the terms of office of each prime minister; neither war nor interludes of peace; not even the unrelenting predictability of the Kirk's annual gathering offered patterns quite equal to the task of plotting and measuring this country's most recent rites of passage.

Instead, by theming the century and breaking it into economic, social, political and cultural fragments, I have sought to make my interventions in this history more transparent and, in doing so, present competing voices of Scotland's past in order to avoid the convention of privileging one voice in the search for a storyline.

By unpicking the narrative of history, much is to be gained. The past emerges as a place resistant to order and closer to the messy nature of life as it was lived and we become more alive to multiple ways of understanding the country. But other insights are lost. The pretence of the 'big picture' is seen for what it is – the chronicler's trick – and we are denied the reassuring balm of uncontested knowledge. We must leave the girl in the green coat to walk on Edinburgh cobbles in her memory in old age and deny her the right to walk these pages. That is the gamble. And yet it is tempered by the wish that she may yet find traces of May mornings in these pages and perhaps come to understand them in new ways.

Catriona M. M. Macdonald

Introduction: 'Whaur Extremes Meet'

LA CORBIE: Country: Scotland. What like is it?
It's a peatbog, it's a daurk forest.
It's a cauldron o' lye, a saltpan or a coalmine.
If you're gey lucky it's a bricht bere meadow or a park o' kye.
Or mibbe . . . it's a field o' stanes.
It's a tenement or a merchants' ha'.
It's a hure hoose or a humble cot.
Princes Street or Paddy's Merkit.
It's a fistfu' o' fish or a pickle o' oatmeal.
It's a queen's banquet o' roast meats and junkets.
It depends . . . Ah dinna ken whit like your Scotland is.
   Here's mines.
National flower: the thistle.
National pastime: nostalgia.
National weather: smirr, haar, drizzle, snow.
National bird: the crow, the corbie, le corbeau, moi!
         Mary Queen of Scots Got her Head Chopped Off (1987)
                         Liz Lochhead (1947–)

Scotland's landscape is the place where the nation is most powerfully itself; here it is most marked by the passage of time but, then again, most resistant to the changes wrought by modernity. Through it, identity emerges only to be unravelled by the contradictions of different localities; and it is here that Scots are made and make their country. Place and the past have combined to shape the landscape of Scotland, and in the twentieth century – perhaps more than at any time – it offered access to a time when Scotland appeared more sure of what it was and what it could become. History seemed to mark each gradient on its map and tradition set its borders – the very place appeared to exist as an expression of its past.

The writings of travellers in this landscape affirmed its debt to history. In 1880, William Fyfe left his native Dundee for a tour of the Highlands, passing through Stirling en route:

> A fine view as we enter Stirling is obtained of the town and castle. We are now on classic, as well as historic ground, for [Walter] Scott has with his enchanter's wand peopled this district with the heroes of bygone centuries.[1]

A decade later, the American writer and drama critic William Winter (1836–1917) visited Edinburgh and took in the view from Calton Hill.

> A thousand years of history are here crystallised within the circuit of a single glance, and while you gaze upon one of the grandest emblems that the world contains of a storied and romantic past, you behold likewise a living and resplendent pageant of the beauty of today. Nowhere else are the Past and the Present so lovingly blended.[2]

Similarly, in Fife, in 1910, an imaginary tourist – conjured into being in the interests of railway tourism – would write home, saying, 'As you will see we are now in Dunfermline, the home of kings – ancient and iron – Malcolm Canmore and Andrew Carnegie.'[3]

In the Highlands this impulse was probably at its most profound. In 1931, writer and photographer Alasdair Alpin MacGregor (1899–1970) published *Wild Drumalbain* and cautioned his readers that they:

> must never lose sense of the reality that we are wayfarers in a glorious country, and are treading along the tracks known so well to the warriors of old, when in the days of wrath and oppression and vengeance they sped with the sure-footed fleetness of the fallow doe, bearing erect the Fiery Cross to apprise their kinsfolk of imminent danger, and to summon their clansmen to arms.[4]

This blend of nature and antiquity proved a valuable commodity in the twentieth century and inspired luxurious prose even in the most mundane publications. In the interwar years, MacBrayne's description of their one-day steamer excursion to Iona illustrates what happened when poetry was twinned with profit:

> Iona, the holiest place in Scotland, lies within half an hour's sail from Staffa. Here the spirit of Columba still hovers over those grey

stones, and those sands like mountain drift stir memories of the ruthless Viking massacre of martyred monks when their silvery sheen was stained with blood. It is a hallowed island of dreams, an oasis in the desert of ocean whose myriad voices seem stilled in this sacred endroit. The wild spirits' wrathful storm throughout the centuries have left Iona its tranquillity, and the tourist will find that his visit evokes an expression of the upward longing of the human heart.[5]

And all for 27s 6d, including breakfast, dinner and a plain tea.

Yet some places were resistant to both poetic and commercial imperatives – at least for a while. Through long railway tunnels, William Fyfe entered Glasgow as if 'through the bowels of the earth' and, in the 1930s, for Elgin's John Gray, two hours spent in Glasgow – an interruption in a Highland sojourn – 'were too much'.[6] In 1894, *Bonnie Scotland: A Handbook for Visitors* recommended that '[f]rom the purely pictorial point of view, there are only two things worth the attention of the visitor in Glasgow – the old Cathedral and the new University'.[7] The only hope for the city seemed to be in reliving its past. In 1907 the historian and travel writer George Eyre-Todd (1862–1937), in a piece entitled 'St Mungo's City', suggested that Glasgow in the twentieth century would only emerge from the vulgar commercialism of the age if it 'came into touch again with its character during the Middle Ages as the great lamp of spiritual and scholarly light in western Britain'.[8] And yet, at the time he wrote these words, less than half of Glasgow's five-year-olds attended school, a great many children entered work at the age of twelve and the provision of free secondary education was extremely limited.[9]

In many areas across Scotland and in the borderlands, the present was only scornfully recognised by visitors when it encroached on the remnants of the past. William Winter – this time in Berwick-upon-Tweed – reflected in 1890 that '[t]he present indeed, has marred the past in this old town, dissipating the element of romance and putting no adequate substitute in its place'.[10] Meanwhile, by the 1930s, Culloden – scene of Jacobitism's ultimate demise – supported 'two tea-houses and a filling station' and 'rude advertisements for oil and petrol shriek[ed] their vulgarity to the sky'.[11] At its best, the present was a pale reflection of a nobler bygone age, at its worst an unwelcome intrusion.

Present and past collided in Scotland's landscape and served to ground the 'now' in contradiction and paradox. Scotland was either becoming or it had already been; it was either to be remade or preserved; it was both memory and myth; the vision of visitors and the creation of native sensitivities. Scots typically did not dwell on such dilemmas on a daily basis but their culture and national aspirations had to make their way in this landscape.

SCOTLAND – 'NAE HAUF-WAY HOOSE'

> I'll ha'e nae hauf-way hoose, but aye be whaur
> Extremes meet – it's the only way I ken
> To dodge the curst conceit o' bein richt
> That damns the vast majority o' men.
>
> *A Drunk Man Looks at the Thistle* (1926)
> Hugh MacDiarmid (1892–1978)

Scotland has always occupied a contradictory temporal and material place in the modern world – it is a place of extremes more resistant to the typical conceits of history than most. In order to make sense of this state, perhaps more so than at any other time, Scotland in the twentieth century was styled in opposition to that which it was not – England – that which it had been – independent– and that which it could have been had earlier Scots possessed the imagination to seize the future. Yet the creation of contemporaneous, historic and futuristic 'others' against which Scotland could be defined too often took place in the realm of caricature and, as a result, engendered prejudices in the present, myths of the past and alternating unrealistic hopes and fears regarding what lay ahead. It is the historian's job to try to avoid these pitfalls.

Time has yet to grant the historian of the twentieth century the valuable perspectives that come with posterity – we have not yet reached 'the end of history' or, arguably, the twentieth century. The spirit of the new age is yet to assert itself and the old is still to relinquish its call on our sympathies. Nevertheless, it is reasonable to assume that, in the processes that shaped the last century – whether or not they have reached their conclusions – something of Scotland's history will be revealed.

Four principal themes emerged in the writing of this book as being salient to any understanding of Scotland in the twentieth century: change and continuity; identity; the Union relationship; and globalisation. As one might expect, none of these is freestanding and nor did they influence all aspects of life in Scotland to the same extent or in the same way. Together, however, they encouraged extremes: they allowed the contemporary imagination to soar, while calling it back to tradition; they encouraged homogeneity, while privileging difference; they determined the challenges which Scotland faced and the parameters within which Scotland could respond; and they recast the world in which Scotland sought its place.

Change and Continuity

One would be surprised if little had changed in the course of a hundred years so the novelty in a study such as this is often to be found in the survival of that which remained pretty much the same. The historian's choice is not great – the economy was transformed, society reinvented the family, politicians sought and secured a new legislative environment and culture deliberately distanced itself from the literature of the century's opening decades.

We have to look more closely. When we do, change often appears more apparent than real – traditions tended to absorb 'the new' rather than abandon their place entirely and custom accommodated novelty rather than stepping aside. For the most part, Scotland was reluctant to abandon 'old ways' simply to follow the whims of fashion. We see this in the economy, in the perpetuation of heavy industry's dominance in the manufacturing sector; we see it in politics, in the nation's 'traditional' Labour vote; and we see it in culture's debts to Scotland's past artistic achievements. For all its cherished radicalism, Scotland could be a conservative country.

Identity – A Fragmented Thing

Scottish identity exemplified these dynamics of change and continuity but was further complicated by its very nature: identity posed as a unifying force when, in reality, it was fragmentary; it posited characteristics peculiar to Scots but, for most Scots, their sense of belonging was an intensely personal 'thing' which hardly lent itself to explanation, far less generalisation.

At the end of the century, political scientists and sociologists went some way to confirming traditional assumptions regarding Scottish identity by suggesting that Scots tended to prioritise national welfare in their attitude to the state – 'the commonweal'. Others confirmed the rhetoric of Liberal and Labour platforms through the years by identifying a radical trait in the national psyche and still others focused on traditions of Scottish democracy and civic participation. But 'being Scottish' was only partly understood in these terms. Even Scottish culture offered little relief from such confusion – respected commentators referred to it as 'distorted' (Tom Nairn, 1932–), while others saw futility in any search for a singular Scottish identity or a national culture worthy of the name (David McCrone). Such homogeneity, it was claimed, simply did not exist.

The evasive nature of identity and a tendency (among intellectuals at least) to be overcritical of Scotland's cultural products, nevertheless, failed to make Scottishness less meaningful. Belonging was powerful even though at times faintly ridiculous. Take author and journalist Iain Hamilton's (1920–1986) early love affair with Scotland:

> I enjoyed the curious pain which the landscape aroused in me, a quickening, enlivening discontent with the present time, place, and order of things.
>
> A romantic idea of Scotland began once again to obsess me, as it had obsessed me long before in infancy, and gradually I fell in love with it just as I might then fall in love with a girl, vaguely and to no purposeful end, treasuring the emotion for its own sake and keeping it to myself like a secret.[12]

We might not understand it but we know what he means – this is the way with many expressions of Scottishness that eschewed academic realism for emotive honesty in the twentieth century. Only 'conceit' – to use MacDiarmid's phrase – would lead us to question their authenticity, although we must beware of making too much of them.

The Union – Neighbours, Partners, Rivals

The apparent logic of topography and the legacy of Unions, monarchical (1603) and parliamentary (1707), premised and continues to inform the writing of Scotland's history as at once part of and distinct from that of the United Kingdom. No understanding of Scotland's twentieth century is possible without an appreciation of the Union relationship and an understanding that neighbours who were constitutional partners could also be rivals. Sketching the differences between the countries is relatively straightforward – the following pages highlight such contrasts across the economy, society, politics and culture – but appreciating how difference was accommodated is a different matter.

Again change and continuity mark this relationship. Scotland, until the interwar years, was relatively content with her place in the Union settlement – in the nineteenth century, Scots had benefited from Britain's imperial mission and, at Westminster, were partners in a democracy that proved remarkably stable during war and responsive to social change in peacetime. The nationalism which animated the smaller nations of Europe in the early decades of the century found only faint echoes in Scotland. By the end of the century, however, the Empire had all but gone and, between 1979 and 1997, Westminster was dominated by a party that repeatedly failed to secure a Scottish mandate. The welfare state and nationalised industries that had sustained Scottish unionism, as imperial promises receded, also suffered in these years. Is it any wonder that Scotland began to re-assess her constitutional marriage?

The solution to the Union's midlife crisis was, given a new global environment, less predictable than the series of events that had made Scotland question her place in it. In the 1990s, the nation state was increasingly being seen as 'too small for the big problems of contemporary social life and too big for the small problems'.[13] The creation of a separate Scottish legislature may have seemed the obvious answer (it was more obvious to those who were out of office at the time, than those who held power). But global change – the pre-eminence of international bodies in foreign policy, the worldwide reach of corporate giants and changing modes of communication – seemed to point to the obsolescence of the nation state, just as Scotland was claiming its own.

Devolution, therefore, failed to resolve Scotland's place in the world and created an asymmetry in the Union relationship, which, till then, had operated relatively smoothly partly as a result of a commitment to – or, at least, the appearance of – equality of treatment across the member nations.[14] Globalisation had consolidated the Union (in the form of imperialism) but, at the end of the twentieth century, seemed to be un-making it.[15] Nation-state status was an understandable goal for a country that felt deeply excluded and misrepresented – even more so when history seemed to ground such desires in legitimate claims to autonomy.[16] But one got the feeling that Scotland had secured this prize just at the time it was losing its ultimate value.

Globalisation

For generations of Scotsmen, war and military service mediated their engagement with the world beyond the country's borders. Foreign travel in peacetime was familiar only to those who could afford both the luxuries of time and expense or for those who never intended to return home. In this, the early twentieth century was to be no different. Yet, in the era of 'total warfare', neither geography nor gender, neither age nor conscience would limit the reach of the war machine. Industry, agriculture and leisure were mobilised alongside the regiments that had led the imperial campaigns of the past. And, though they appear on no memorials, among the casualties of war were family firms, rural ways of living and a certain innocence that had honoured loyalty in ways that, to later generations, seemed at best naive and at worst foolhardy. For many twentieth-century Scots, war – whether the World Wars of 1914–18 and 1939–45 or the neglected campaigns in Korea (1950–1953), Suez (1956) or Northern Ireland (1968–98) – divided their lives into a 'before' and 'after', establishing a fault line which, while shared with many other citizens worldwide, was intensely personal.

War drew Scotland into the world but how the nation came to understand the experience remained distinctive. When the guns stopped firing or the mushroom cloud dissipated, the peace was still to be won. This Scots typically achieved in civilian garb, owing much to traditions which even the collapse of empires and the Cold War failed to destroy. Nevertheless, the later twentieth century was to find Scots fighting a different war – ostensibly a war of words.

Throughout the late twentieth century, global media were widely criticised as a force making for the 'Westernisation' or 'Americanisation' of contrasting national cultures. But the homogenisation towards which globalisation tended was 'never absolutely complete, and it [did] not work for completeness'.[17] Rather, globalisation is best understood as a framework through which differences were articulated, reproduced and absorbed – as an agency conducive to variety and diversity and, in many respects, resistant to hegemony.[18] Global culture was not 'given' but, as Tony Spybey makes clear, it was 'developed precisely by means of its continual reproduction in local scenarios, and in the process it [was] transformed'.[19] As a result, rather than disabling minority nations, cultures and voices, globalisation in the late twentieth century made marginality a 'powerful space'.[20]

What distinguished this global phenomenon from the internationalism of world markets and alliances encouraged by the imperialism of an earlier age were less the channels through which it operated than its autonomy – it was detached from nation-state control. New interests – environmentalism and gender, for example – evolved and they owed little to nation-state orthodoxies or, indeed, to established territorial patterns. But interests and ethnic groups whose claims for self-determination could be expressed territorially were especially empowered by the particularising tendencies of globalisation – Scotland is a case in point.[21] Nation states were weakened but nationality and nationalism . . .? Now that's a different thing.[22]

Just as British imperialism had thrived on the perpetuation of a distinct sense of Scottishness within the UK and beyond, so globalisation encouraged a sense of Scottish nationality that sought articulation in international forums (for example, the European Community) and through supra-national media (such as film) within the context of a global economy.[23] Scotland has always existed within a global nexus in which her partnership with her southern neighbour has been qualified by independent – and sometimes more significant – relationships with other nations. In this regard, globalisation reveals little new. Yet, in stressing that Scotland is as much made by as revealed in its engagement with the world, globalisation highlighted the importance of external influences on Scotland's twentieth century.

The memories inherent in Scotland's landscape were as important at the century's close as at its dawn – global landscapes have no popular memory and beyond recognition elicit few feelings of belonging.[24] But global media made it more possible for Scots to *be* a nation and to feel part of that nation. The interface between the individual and the nation became more complex in the twentieth century – by the 1990s, Scots could readily come closer to moments and experiences which marked the nation's history without being physically present at 'great events'. National newspapers, sound recordings, 'talking' films, television and latterly the World Wide Web successively widened the individual's 'experience' of nationhood. But they did so without demanding much personal effort in return and privileged selective views of the nation in action. Whether Scotland was more or less 'Scottish' by the end of the century is open to debate. What is clear is that, by its close, one came to know Scotland in different ways – this history is but one of them.

PART ONE

In the Shadow of the Crane – Scotland's Economy

Prologue

Many Palaces

Five miles of them – the loveliest exhibition the world has ever known – a city where colour and artistic form delight the eye at every turn. The majestic highways are surfaced with red asphalt and chips of white Skye granite and pink mica-veined Banffshire granite, so that they look like avenues gay with the dawn.

Pastel shades of cream and rose, steel greys and steel blues, warm creams and light reds, plum, yellow and emerald – all the colours of the rainbow light up the façades of the palaces across the breadth of these 170 acres, which, not many months ago, formed a recreation ground and golf course.

'Souvenir Guide' (Empire Exhibition, 1938)

Glasgow's Empire Exhibition grew out of the creative collision of three worlds: the past – rose-tinted by the faded memories of passing years; the present – known, familiar and haunted by the recent experience of economic and social tragedy; and the future – hidden, alien and falling between optimism and the fear of history repeating itself, came together in the make-believe palaces of 1938. The armistice concluding the Great War was approaching its twentieth anniversary when Bellahouston Park hosted this celebration of Scotland's role in Britain's age of Empire and the premier, who would only too soon declare a second war to end wars, blessed Scotland's faith in its future. Neville Chamberlain, an Honorary President of the Exhibition, noted:

Scotland has in the past made a notable contribution to Imperial development. In her present effort I see an earnest resolve to add to that contribution. I see in it also, and I hope our visitors will see, a sign of her own vigour, and her resolve to keep, in the twentieth century, the notable place in world affairs which she won for herself in the years which went before.[1]

The Exhibition looked both backwards and forwards – a recreated Highland clachan shared the site with a Palace of Engineering and decorating the Scottish Pavilions were statues of Wallace, Burns, Scott, Carlyle, Livingstone and Watt.[2] Automobiles and aeroplanes, telephones and radios, dams and bridges pointed to a revolution in global transport and communications but the UK Pavilion gave pride of place to industries born in the age of Victoria – working models of mines and blast furnaces and the fully-equipped bridge of a liner proved its centrepiece attractions.

This was, nevertheless, a distinctively Scottish celebration. The advertisements dominating the 'Official Guide to the Exhibition' offer an insight into the economic geographies of early twentieth-century Scotland. The three Dundee jute and tarpaulin manufacturers, Low and Bonar Ltd, J. T. Inglis & Sons Ltd and Baxter Brothers, frugally shared a single page to publicise their goods. Harris tweed manufacturers protected their products and reputation by explaining the 'orb' mark to customers. The Outram Press (Glasgow) and D. C. Thomson & Co. Ltd (Dundee) represented Scotland's regional press barons. And the presence of the Carron Iron Company (Falkirk) and William Baird & Co. Ltd (Coatbridge) suggested that the advance guard of Scotland's industrial revolution were still very much part of the contemporary scene.

A year thence, however, Bellahouston's palaces appeared little more than the naive imaginings of a country that should have known better. The relative prosperity of 1938 had, after all, been a by-product of military expenditure in a country preparing for war. The optimism the Exhibition engendered was stillborn. The power of the past and the regional economies of Scotland survived the war years to influence the future of the nation after 1945. With the end of Empire, however, it would be some time before Scotland would allow herself to dream again.

ONE Scotland in Context – Coincidence and Contrasts

The progress of the Scottish economy in the twentieth century shared many of the characteristics of other western nations, particularly her southern neighbours – with two world wars, the emergence of a global economy and the rise of the multinational corporation, one would be surprised had it been otherwise. At various times during the twentieth century, this caused many commentators to doubt the notion of a Scottish economy as a 'useful unit of analysis' and to identify Scotland's economic problems in the post-1945 period in particular as, in reality, 'more extreme manifestations of British problems' rather than substantially different dilemmas.[1]

However, in 1954, Scotland's foremost economic chronicler, A. K. Cairncross (1911–98), whilst acknowledging that the English–Scottish border was 'but a line between two segments of a single economy', identified significant and persistent features of autonomy within the northern infrastructure. He noted that 'there is a sufficient degree of segregation from the rest of the economy, and a sufficient diversity within Scotland, to allow one to speak of a Scottish economy, functioning as a unit and with an independent momentum'.[2] It was a position that was re-affirmed by government (or, at least, the Scottish Office) and was supported by both capital and labour (at least in the north). But it was not to last (at least not in the same form).

The Scottish experience was one marked by internal regional peculiarities. One might even suggest that 'Scotland was not one specialised region but a complex web of specialised regional and local economies'.[3] Towns and counties were easily identified at the turn of the century by their 'trademark' manufactures: Dundee – jute; Kirkcaldy – linoleum; Falkirk – iron; Aberdeen – fish – and so on. Throughout the century, however, the industrial and increasingly urban Central Belt dominated industrial production and employment in financial and legal services and, when male employment reached its peak of almost 1,600,000 following the First World War, it was the Central Belt that absorbed most of this active labour.⁴ Yet, the southern, northern and island regions are misrepresented as an agricultural 'fringe' to this industrial core. For most of the century, Aberdeen boasted engineering works, paper manufactures and woollen textile enterprises as well as fishing, and Scotland's distilleries – a great many of them located in peripheral rural areas – numbered 150 and employed thousands at the turn of the twentieth century. Foyers was producing aluminium from as early as 1896 and iron ore and barites (barium sulphate) were mined in Raasay (an island just off Skye) and the isle of Arran respectively. At times the regions also contributed significantly to prestige projects typically associated with the west and the Central Belt. In the 1930s, for example, the A1 Electric Welding Appliances Company of the Rose Street Foundry in Inverness gained the contract to weld the flanges on the main steam pipes of the liner, the *Queen Mary*, and would claim, in the 1950s, that 80 per cent of all British wheels were spoke-welded by machines produced at its Highland works.⁵ While some of these industries ultimately failed to stand the test of time, in general, the dogged persistence of regional specialisation and the clustering of ancillary industries that facilitated this were salient features of Scottish distinctiveness up until the 1970s at least.⁶ The subsequent timing and nature of declining national economic autonomy were ultimately a consequence of decline at this local level.⁷

Nevertheless, it is, perhaps, in the analysis of Scotland's economic performance relative to that of England that the country's peculiar progress within the Union is most readily made apparent. Partners or rivals or simply neighbours? At various times and for various reasons, Scotland both benefited from and suffered as a result of her southern partnership and was alternately inspired and discouraged by a friendly rivalry with English business. Generally, however, the imperatives of geography and the historical legacy of two centuries of shared economic transformation encouraged a neighbourly accommodation or, at least, mutual sufferance throughout the twentieth century.

COINCIDENCE

Indeed, in two principal aspects, the Scottish economy mirrored general trends in the rest of Britain in the twentieth century – in the chronology of boom and recession which patterned the years following 1918 and in the changing proportional share of industrial sectors, the Scottish experience was similar to the UK 'norm'.

Scotland entered the twentieth century as a mature industrial economy, matching if not exceeding English performance according to a variety of economic and industrial indicators. Thereafter, like her Union partners, Scotland experienced increased foreign competition in the years before 1914 and shared the dislocation of the Great War. Flush with victory, she approached the post-war environment with the confidence of a veteran, only to become a casualty of a new economic conflict of global proportions.

The slump that was experienced by English industry after 1922, following an initial short-lived post-war boom, was mirrored in Scotland, as, of course, was the devastating impact of the worldwide depression which followed the Wall Street Crash of 1929. In 1931, Sir Eric Geddes (1875–1937), himself an Indian-born son of Scottish parents and Chairman of the Dunlop Rubber Company, was far from optimistic: 'Whenever men meet today in this country, there is a consciousness that we are suffering from an industrial malaise – our depression has been longer, and seems more deep-seated and permanent, than the depression in other countries.'[8] Scotland, like elsewhere, suffered terribly through the late twenties and early thirties but thereafter benefited from the demand which rearmament injected into the economy and enthusiastically met the demands of wartime production. Nevertheless, once again, despite the hopes of Scots who greeted victory in 1945, the post-war world was not to herald a new economic dawn.

Evidence of Scotland's economic performance vis-à-vis her southern neighbour is more readily available for the second half of the twentieth century and, though the issue is by no means resolved, most would agree with a recent commentator that 'the economic record of Scotland in the twentieth century, while rather undistinguished, is neither different from nor worse than most other regions of the United Kingdom'.[9]

In the decade or so after 1945, post-war reconstruction prolonged the increased demand for Scottish products which rearmament had initiated and, until 1954, industrial output recorded an annual rate of growth of around 4 per cent.[10] Consequently, from 1950 to 1957, Scotland's gross domestic product (GDP) rose at roughly the same rate as that of the rest of the UK and stood at 9 per cent of the UK as a whole, with per capita GDP at around 90 per cent of the UK average.[11] But, as in many English regions, the so-called 'years of affluence' masked worrying trends in Scotland's economic infrastructure. Walter Elliot (1888–1958), a former Secretary of State for Scotland, was right when, in 1948, he told the students of the University of Glasgow that 'this is a hard century into which we have been born'.[12]

From around 1958, demand for Scotland's traditional manufactures began to decline and the rate of growth in Scotland's GDP seriously lagged behind that of the rest of the UK. By 1960, per capita GDP north of the Border stood at less than 88 per cent of the UK average.[13] Internally, the nations of the Union showed subtly contrasting fortunes but these were, in reality, merely variations on the theme of overall decline in relation to the rest of the world. Between 1955 and 1977, while Scotland recorded a per annum growth rate in manufacturing output of 2.6 per cent in comparison to the UK average of 2.2 per cent, Italy, France, the Netherlands and West Germany all recorded growth rates of over 5 per cent and Japan, in the same period, recorded a growth rate of 10 per cent.[14]

In 1961, the Toothill Report[15] confirmed that Scotland was merely exhibiting an acute form of an economic malaise that was afflicting the whole of the UK.[16] The cure – at least for the surface ailments – was identified as regional assistance which, coinciding as it did in the 1960s with the discovery of North Sea Oil, did much to encourage greater growth in the economy. By the early 1970s, aggregate GDP in Scotland grew at a significant rate vis-à-vis her southern neighbour and, in per capita terms, reached a peak in 1976.[17] Such success, however, failed to lift British fortunes worldwide – between 1960 and 1980, the UK recorded growth rates of only 2 per cent per annum in industrial production.[18]

In 1981, James Johnstone, having recently resigned as the Chief Executive of the Scottish Council (Development and Industry), reflected in his St Andrew's Day Lecture on BBC Radio Scotland, that, as Scottish industry declined, 'only the world of footballers, pop stars and television personalities seem[ed] to be waxing more strongly every year'.[19] De-industrialisation was the principal feature of British regional economies in the 1980s and 1990s, as the final demise of old industries and the rise of the service sector transformed the dynamics at the heart of the economy.[20] But even for Scotland's celebrities, this 'new world' held little promise, in the short term at least. GDP per capita in comparison to the UK average actually fell in the 1980s and only came close to matching the UK as a whole in the mid 1990s.[21] This did not mean than Scots were immune to a growing consumer culture. In Daniel Wight's study of 'Cauldmoss' – a fictional name for a real community experiencing 30 per cent male unemployment in the early 1980s – the unemployed felt compelled to consume at levels beyond their income. As one young man noted, 'Without a car or a good job, it doesn't matter if you look like Robert Redford.'[22]

By the nineties, there was less to distinguish the structure of the Scottish economy, in comparison to its southern neighbour than there had been fifty years before.[23] As in the rest of the UK, the distribution of employment in Scotland over the course of the twentieth century illustrated the increasing importance of the service sector (financial, legal, health, education, leisure, transport and communication providers) in comparison with and partly at the expense of the older manufacturing industries. Services even had a dramatic impact on family budgets. Excluding rent, rates and water charges, expenditure on services rose to 31 per cent of consumer spending in 1988 – it had been about 16 per cent in 1948.[24] This was a phenomenon common to most advanced capitalist economies in these years and, by the late 1980s, services contributed over 50 per cent of Scottish employment.[25] By 1997, the service sector accounted for 35 per cent of the whole Scottish economy and, of the top twenty companies in Scotland, half were in financial services.[26]

By comparison, whilst manufacturing largely 'held its ground' until the 1970s, from employing around 35 per cent of Scots in 1921, its share of the employed population had declined by around 10 per cent by 1981.[27] Yet, even within manufacturing itself, change was evident. As in England, from the 1920s onwards, 'new industries' began to make an impact on Scotland. In 1930, 9 per cent of Scotland's net output was generated by 'new industries', rising to 11 per cent five years later. Over the same period, England recorded a similar rate of growth in 'new industries' but, by 1935, this sector accounted for a far greater proportion of net output overall (21 per cent).[28] Nevertheless, trends in the growth of new industries were comparable and, by the 1980s, the sectoral imbalance in the Scottish economy in favour of heavy industry was largely a thing of the past. Restructuring, however, came at a cost. Between 1966 and 1981, around one third of industrial employment was lost across the UK.[29] Speaking in the Commons in 1982, Eric Varley, Labour's spokesman on employment, noted that '[p]ractically every family in the land now had some direct or indirect experience of unemployment. From Scotland to the South East its tentacles stretched out, affecting areas that had never had it worse even in the 1930s'.[30]

CONTRASTS

A coincidence of general trends and outcomes can clearly be identified across the regional economies of the UK over the century but one ought not to conclude that the processes and particular chronologies of change were either linear or identical in their impact. In Scotland, the legacy of the nineteenth century; the export-driven nature of manufacturing industry and the relatively small size of Scottish markets; the role of distinctive 'Scottish' institutions and their 'place' in the UK; the changing nature of devolved administration and the priorities of governments; the contradictory impact of globalisation, together with depleting indigenous resources and advancing technologies; the changing sympathies of native and foreign capital; and the shifting character of the labour market all determined marked differences in the Scottish experience to that suggested by UK 'norms'. Certainly, Scotland's place within the UK state and the interdependencies which had developed between British producers determined the parameters within which her response to global economic change could differ from that of the other nations within the Union state. But, that aside, Scotland was simply different. Explaining how and why this was the case demands that we revisit Britain's economic development and look beyond apparent similarities. Let us retrace our steps.

Whether in the years of austerity following the end of the Second World War, in the aftermath of the nationalist revival soaked in the promise of North Sea 'crude', in the depths of the eighties' economic recession or in the throes of a constitutional re-awakening on the eve of a 'new millennium', Scottish commentators found much to admire in the 'Indian summer' of Edwardian Scotland.[31] Then, surely, Scotland faced the challenge of modernity and won handsome victories. Scotland launched around one fifth of the world's ships, constructed thousands of locomotives, dominated the world jute industry and in sewing thread, beer and spirits boasted some of the world's major producers.[32] This 'economic vitality', however, hid a complex of factors that would ultimately determine the severity of post-war decline in the 1920s.[33]

Looking more closely at the Edwardian experience, premonitions of tragedy are evident, not least in the trade depressions of 1904 and 1908–09. A depression in shipbuilding resulted in applications for assistance to the Glasgow Charity Organisation Society in 1904 rising by 728 in comparison to the previous year's demand. The Society's president, the Duke of Montrose, was despondent, saying, '[S]hipbuilding could not always remain on the same plane. It fluctuated up and down, and, perhaps out of no fault of his own the workman who was employed in these industries found his labour and his wages taken from him.'[34] Yet the hardships of 1904 paled into insignificance in 1908. As *The Scotsman* recorded in September of that year, 'From Glasgow to Coventry, all the chief industrial centres of the country are ringing with the bitter cry of the unemployed.'[35] No area of Scotland was immune. While the Baltic and continental trade of Dundee's docksides remained steady, jute spinners introduced short-time schemes as prices fell and demand for yarn declined; the foundries were far quieter at the end of the year than at its opening; and preserve and confectionery manufacturers felt the consequences of falling market demand, as unemployment hit industrial areas across the UK.[36] In Kirkcaldy, looms were silent at the weekends and, during the week, they were operational for shorter periods.[37] Problems persisted well into 1909. Edinburgh engineering, building, metal and shipbuilding trades recorded precious little improvement in conditions over the course of that year during which unemployment levels for masons and plasterers averaged somewhere in the region of 44–54 per cent and the unskilled persons on the Distress Committee's books numbered some 2,000.[38]

Aside from the instability rooted in the economy's reliance on foreign markets and investments and the experiences of individual industries that will be discussed later, many features common to various branches of the Scottish economy read now as ill omens. The overwhelming predominance of the 'family firm' and the relatively small size of individual concerns were hallmarks of the regional economies of Scotland. In small-town Scotland, locally owned and managed family businesses were generally the norm until the 1950s. While in the early part of the century they imbued industry with the claims of service and loyalty, their persistence into the second half of the century burdened many businesses with aging directors more reliant on established practice than emboldened by modern challenges, and with low capital enterprises that were not well placed to survive the interwar depression and were generally unable to fully exploit the new opportunities of the post-imperial world.[39] The dominating influence of Sir William Bilsland (1847–1921), for example, compromised the diversification of his baking empire in the years following the Great War, although Robert McAlpine and Sons, the successful Scottish builders, do not seem to have been held back by a surfeit of family members – around forty McAlpines worked for the firm in the 1930s. Nevertheless, further difficulties were evident in some firms' reliance on labour-intensive means of production and higher transport costs for Scottish producers in comparison to their southern competitors. There was also a dependence on increasingly costly indigenous fuel resources and raw materials, and increased foreign competition in key sectors from Germany and the USA. Together with a declining home market and falling profit margins, all these features boded ill for the future.

However, 1914 brought economic challenges of a nature none could have predicted in the heady days of Edwardian economic confidence. As in the rest of the UK, the Great War heralded the unprecedented intervention of the state in the Scottish economy, particularly following the passing of the Munitions Act in 1915. The Admiralty assumed control of the shipyards; enforced dilution altered the gender composition and skill hierarchies of various engineering works; recruitment and conscription decimated the male labour force; agriculture experienced its first real taste of state subsidies and control; and, generally, the objectives of industrial production became more collaborative than competitive. Scottish firms were also to the fore in many strategic innovations – William Beardmore (1856–1936), for example, was influential in the development of the tank and his company made all the pedrail shoes for every British tank built.[40] In a broad sense, there was little in this to distinguish the Scottish economy from that of the rest of Britain or indeed the other Allied powers.

However, Scotland's contribution to the wartime economy *was* distinctive and the long-term consequences of these four years were profound. War stimulated employment in heavy industrial manufacture where established skills or manual dexterity were at a premium; war reinforced the existing dominance of the Central Belt in the Scottish economy; and war fostered the suspicions of major engineering producers towards investment in new technologies and new products by creating fresh demand for Scotland's traditional manufactures. While some sectors certainly benefited from war-driven demand, others faltered. Disruption to world trade caused difficulties for the eastern coalfields and the east-coast ports. Pig iron manufacture declined despite the increase in steel production. Government intervention in the wool and linen industries cut supplies for fancy-goods producers already struggling with the loss of markets to cotton. Dunfermline's linen industry, one of the leading sectors in that area's industrial revolution in the eighteenth century, was crippled during the war years – its lucrative American markets were lost (prior to 1914 over 50 per cent of its goods crossed the Atlantic) and the cost of fine linen yarn rocketed in price. By 1933 only three factories were still in operation.[41] Scotland's primary producers were also seriously affected – the Scottish fishing industry, for example, suffered tremendously as a result of the loss of crews, boats and markets.

Peace was to bring little relief to those who had suffered under the conditions of war and, indeed, made casualties of many of those who had profited from wartime demand. As Anthony Slaven has noted, while the war effort 'strained the regional economy and its labour force', the period of peace that followed 1918 'almost drove it to breaking point'.[42] An immediate post-war boom (1919–1920), offered re-assurance to those whose optimism in the future of Scottish heavy industry had been strengthened by the country's war effort. But the demand for shipping in these years, for example, was initially premised on making good the losses of war and, with competitors in the wings, would not last long. The overcapacity in Scotland's traditional industries which had been encouraged by wartime demand was cruelly exaggerated by this brief period of prosperity, which merely postponed the learning of some painful lessons and perpetuated a reliance on old plant and outdated methods. Farms that had been inefficient in the pre-war years had merely been given a brief respite during the war as inflation increased the price of foodstuffs. But profits made in the war years were soon exhausted in the difficult climate of the 1920s. Regional specialisation in Scotland meant that areas would suffer the consequences of the victorious war at different intervals after 1920 and in different ways. Dundee's jute manufacturers, for example, while sustained during the war by high prices and restrictions on foreign (principally Indian) competition were, as a result, arguably less well placed to meet the challenges of the global marketplace in the twenties.

It took some time for Scotland to acknowledge and respond to the long-term impact that war had had on an already vulnerable economy. When the travel writer H. V. Morton toured Scotland in the interwar years, he reflected:

> I went to the offices of a Clyde shipyard to meet a friend and I was shown into the waiting-room. It was a dignified, solid, polished mahogany room from which all knowledge of world chaos had been carefully concealed. The room was living in the bright prosperity of the Edwardian Age when a man in a silk hat might drop in on the spur of the moment to order a couple of liners. At least that is how it impressed me. It impressed me also as a fragment of a world that was vanished. Nothing in our world is quite so solid and assumed as the waiting-room of a Clyde shipyard. Even the clubs of Pall Mall, to which this room bears a distinct resemblance, have subtly changed with the times, but here beside the Clyde, now so tragically silent, this rich, confident room lingers on in a condition of suspended animation.[43]

One might question which era is most reflective of Scotland's true economic potential in a century moving from the age of Empires to a period of truly international production and exchange, when the economic vitality of nation states was determined less by their self-sufficiency than by their strategic position in a global trading network. Was the late Victorian and Edwardian period an atypical interlude and were the interwar years a more realistic measure of Scotland's place in the world? Or was the momentum of economic success before 1914 cruelly dissipated by a global tragedy which no one – least of all the long-term achievers – could have anticipated? While some commentators still style fin de siècle Scotland 'a power house of the global economy', others caution us against viewing the interwar years from the 'commanding heights of late-nineteenth-century industrial success'.[44] Still, it cannot be denied that, in the 1920s and early 1930s, Scotland experienced economic hardships, industrial disasters and social catastrophe of a nature and on a scale unprecedented in her post-Union history.

Scotland's relative position within the UK economy was seriously weakened in the 1920s and early 1930s. In general terms, while Britain's interwar growth rate was relatively better than that of the Edwardian years, Scotland's contribution to such improvement was minimal. Indeed, estimates at the time indicate that total activity in the Scottish economy fell by around 20 per cent in the years 1929 to 1932 and experienced only a mild recovery before the mid thirties.[45]

Such slow growth in industrial production in Scotland over a relatively long period clarified that Scotland was not merely experiencing cyclical depression, as she had done on various occasions in her industrial history, but that there were serious impediments to success and even survival in her economic structure. The causes and consequences of Scotland's poor performance in the interwar years are, at times, difficult to distinguish from one another and together they involve a reliance on increasingly inefficient and relatively unprofitable industries, the slow growth of 'new industries', falling demand for Scottish products and high unemployment. The interrelatedness of these factors generated a vicious circle that proved difficult to break.

In the mid thirties, Scotland contributed over 18 per cent of the UK's workers in iron and steel foundries, 26 per cent of workers in shipbuilding and 11 per cent of coalmines' employees.[46] But between 1913 and 1937, output from these industries in the north fell by between 40 and 60 per cent, with predictable consequences for profits and jobs.[47] One should not be surprised, therefore, that established businesses were cautious about investing in modernised plant and technologies. The Fife-based paper manufacturers Smith, Anderson & Co. Ltd had the same three paper machines in 1920 as in 1910 and, after 1911, no new investments in plant were recorded until the purchase of a new bag-making machine in 1933.[48]

Overcapacity in coal, steel and shipbuilding, alongside heavy engineering, jute and others, was generally not effectively addressed by streamlining and rationalisation. There are, of course, exceptions. Facing a dramatic decline in demand due to global depression and American prohibition, the numbers of Scottish distillers were decimated. By 1936, Distillers Co. Ltd controlled around 70 per cent of Scotland's whisky producing capacity and reduced production to match demand. Yet the ethos of the family firm and a lack of innovative management impeded many other attempts at effective amalgamation and reform in other industries. Even where amalgamations were successfully brokered, over-capacity was not always adequately addressed. In 1920 seven Dundee family firms came together to form Jute Industries Ltd and, four years later, the Low and Bonar partnership was secured. Yet, in 1937, a study conducted for the Scottish Development Council noted, 'Dundee has too many of her eggs in one basket and it is a basket liable to be upset by Asiatic competition coming from within the Empire.'[49] Even after rationalisation, Dundee jute was still vulnerable.

For those who forsook the scepticism of the times and invested in new production methods, the Depression proved modernisation was often no safeguard for future prosperity. Those whose businesses directly related to the growing consumer markets in the more prosperous south did reasonably well. A case in point is Michael Nairn & Co. Ltd, Kirkcaldy linoleum manufacturers. This business grew in the interwar years as the suburbs flowered around London and the English Midland towns.[50] Meanwhile, to meet the literary appetites of the suburbs' affluent, literate and news-hungry commuters, William Hope Collins (1903–1967) invested over £100,000 in American printing and binding equipment at the height of the Depression, giving this Glasgow publisher undoubted competitive advantages in the years that followed. Indeed, in the 1930s, the Dundee press barons of D. C. Thomson also experienced a period of unprecedented expansion, capturing a new chil-dren's market with titles such as the *Hotspur* (1933), the *Dandy* (1937) and the *Beano* (1938). At much the same time, 'modern' cookers in coloured enamels went into production in the factories of Allied Ironfounders Ltd in the Falkirk district while, not too far away, Mitchell, Russell & Co. Ltd branched out of domestic goods into cinema seats. More worryingly, in the late 1930s, the Perth manufac-turers of Rodine rat poison embarked on the production of a liquid inhalant for treating nasal catarrh!

Other companies beset by declining markets and more dependent on the struggling heavy industries for either custom or raw materials were often not as fortunate. Archibald McMillan & Sons Ltd (shipbuilders, Dumbarton) were taken over by Lamport & Holt Ltd in April 1918. During the following year, six new tower cranes were erected in the yard, only to be sold off fourteen years later – two years after the yard's last ship (a barge, *Caledonia*) was launched. In the north, Thomas Young Cleghorn invested in a new suction gas plant at the Holm Woollen Mills when he took over the business from the Chisholm family in the 1920s. Such plant required superior Welsh anthracite to operate successfully. While not the whole story, it is no coincidence that soon after supplies were disrupted in the period leading up to the General Strike of 1926, Cleghorn went bankrupt and the Inverness mill lay idle.[51] Perhaps the most spectacular tale of thwarted ambition, however, is that of William Beardmore (Lord Invernairn from 1921). At the end of the First World War, Beardmore's industrial dreams were almost limitless, encompassing the production of passenger vessels, tankers, steam locomotives, marine steam and oil engines, buses, lorries, taxies, aeroplanes and airships.[52] But the times did not favour industrial dreamers. In 1930, the Duke of Montrose – prompted by the recent announcement of the closure of Beardmore's Dalmuir works – wrote to the *Glasgow Herald* in defence of Beardmore's management of Scotland's foremost engineering and shipbuilding empire.

> [He] was constantly thinking in what way his great organisation would take a leading part in the prosperity of the Clyde and the trade of the country. Hence, it was that William Beardmore and Company 'dashed in' and took a lead in ordnance manufacture, submarine building, aircraft manufacture, and the making of railway plant, motors and steel houses etc. Indeed, anything that was up-to-date found a sympathetic and courageous supporter in Lord Invernairn.[53]

After 1920, nearly all Beardmore's departments and subsidiaries were losing money and, by 1926, the company was, to all intents, bankrupt. Beardmore himself, following a committee of investigation into the affairs of the company, was ousted from executive control of the company in 1927.

The failure of such endeavours made others increasingly sceptical of abandoning old ways. And arguably Scotland felt the impact of depression all the more keenly because such thwarted attempts to interpret the challenges of the times as opportunities seemed to confirm the wisdom of retrenchment and the inescapable inevitability of decline.

Such rigid defensiveness in the industrial structure of the nation was further emphasised by Scotland's small share of 'new industries', namely light engineering products, chemicals, electrical goods and consumer articles.[54] While early successes had been notable – in car manufacture, for instance – by the 1920s, many producers had retreated to the comfortable familiarity of more traditional manufactures. Peak production at the Arrol-Johnston Car Company was reached before the First World War and Albion Motors ceased production of motor cars (focusing instead on commercial vehicles for the overseas market) in 1913.[55] Richard Saville describes the outcome of such neglect for the wider Scottish economy:

In 1935 Scotland still produced virtually no electrically powered generators, and a small fraction only of UK output of electric motors, power transformers, and switch gear. No lighting accessories or fittings were produced, no wireless sets, telegraph or telephone apparatus, sound reproducers, radio gramophones, valves or batteries. The electrical engineering industry, such as it was, was tied up with shipbuilding, ship fitting and mining equipment, and nearly a quarter of the meagre total of net output was accounted for by repair work and maintenance.[56]

Had demand for the products of Scotland's traditional industries been buoyant, the nation's reliance on such sectors would have been relatively unproblematic in the short term at least. However, as Neil Buxton explains, by 1933, 'export markets upon which Scotland so heavily depended had virtually collapsed, and the volume of exports through Scottish ports had fallen dramatically'.[57] Scotland – more reliant than her southern neighbour on exports – was extremely sensitive to changes in the global marketplace and, after 1929, would feel the impact of Depression immediately and severely. By then, hopes prevalent in the 1920s that a revival in world trade would re-invigorate the Scottish economy appeared naive, if not otherworldly. In November 1930, Leith Chamber of Commerce recorded 'a continued premium on pessimism, procrastination and timidity', while markets declined and profits tumbled.[58]

Like elsewhere in Britain, some sections of the Scottish labour force survived and indeed improved their standard of living in these difficult years but these predominantly middle-class wage earners never grew at a rate in Scotland sufficient to develop a domestic market for goods which would have gone some way in persuading Scottish producers of the compelling logic of innovation. Only Edinburgh (or at least parts of the capital) did well during the Depression years – more new buildings were evident here than in Glasgow and industries such as printing thrived as marketing, advertising and the service industries weathered the storm. (Employment in printing, bookbinding and photography in Edinburgh increased by 19 per cent in the 1920s.[59]) Brewing – one of the capital's most successful interests – also enjoyed years of growth in the 1930s, particularly after Youngers and McEwan & Co. Ltd came together in 1931 as Scottish Brewers Ltd. Yet even here, in the Edinburgh of Muriel Spark's fictional protagonist, Miss Jean Brodie, the relative wealth of the novel's central characters only becomes apparent through their contrast with the Old Town and its residents.

A man sat on the icy-cold pavement, he just sat. A crowd of children, some without shoes, were playing some fight game, and some boys shouted after Miss Brodie's violet-clad company, with words that the girls had not heard before, but rightly understood to be obscene. Children and women with shawls came in and out of the dark closes. Sandy found she was holding Mary's hand in her bewilderment, all the girls were holding hands, while Miss Brodie talked of history.[60]

Rising real incomes among this privileged minority were more than offset by high levels of unemployment.[61]

Scottish unemployment averaged 14 per cent in the years 1923 to 1930 and 21.9 per cent from 1931 to 1938 when the comparable figures for the UK were 11.4 and 16.4 per cent respectively.[62] Looking at the regions, local unemployment frequently outstripped national averages. In Ayrshire, the proportion of insured workers registered as unemployed in the period 1929 to 1932 rose from 12 to 25 per cent; in Lanarkshire, from 14 to 33 per cent; and in Dunbartonshire, from 10 to 50 per cent.[63] Even in the Scottish Borders, it was recorded in 1935 that 'all the traditional Border courage is required to maintain a feeling of confidence in the face of persistent adversity', as mills closed and hours were cut.[64] For many, the experiences of these years would stay with them for life. Margaret Jamieson was a young girl in Paisley in the 1930s. In 1981 she reflected on these years:

Daddy didn't seem to be at his work, and he wasn't ill. Then the piano was sold. Great tragedy. Mind you, I hated it, and wouldn't practise, but I didn't like the degradation of it being carted out of the house and the whole neighbourhood watching.[65]

Soon after this humiliation, her mother went back to work.

In the 1920s, a distinctive Scottish response to unemployment had been emigration. Between 1921 and 1931, nearly 400,000 Scots emigrated, transforming the high natural increase recorded in the population in 1931 to a net decline of 40,000 and further impeding the regeneration of the domestic market.[66] In Kilbirnie, travel to the United States was so common in the 1920s that the Atlantic Ocean was referred to as the 'herring pond'.[67] By the 1930s, however, awareness of the global nature of economic depression proved a disincentive to potential emigrants who kept hold of their Savings Bank deposits and stayed home, either in the hope of better times ahead or in fear of worse times to come.

The lasting economic consequence of this brief interlude of peace was the identification of a 'Scottish Problem' and the official recognition of this state of affairs in increased government intervention and the beginnings of a corporate approach to planning the country's way out of recession which would influence government policy throughout the second half of the twentieth century.[68] But all of this was in the future.

Work was suspended on Hull 534 at John Brown's shipyard in Clydebank in December 1931. An ex-soldier rhymed it into poetry:

> Well do I remember
> The dark and dreary day
> When all work was cancelled
> And we put our tools away.
> The workers were down-hearted
> As they heard the siren roar;
> They heaved a sigh, and bid goodbye
> To the famous 534.[69]

Work was not resumed until April 1934. At the eventual launch of the vessel that became the *Queen Mary*, some five months (and ten million rivets) later, something of a renaissance was anticipated. The *Queen*, after all, was the largest vessel launched in Britain since the *Aquitania* in 1914.[70] Ultimately, however, it was rearmament that secured Scotland's short-term future and saved the Scottish economy from reaching a state of total paralysis. Scotland's surplus industrial capacity of the interwar years – both in terms of men and machines – became essential active agents in Britain's preparations for total war. And the region's long history of specialisation in heavy engineering and the extractive industries, instead of a liability, became a vital base on which to build an economy making ready for conflict.

As in the rest of the UK, industry in Scotland proved adept at meeting the demands of warfare: steel production increased from an average of 1.5 million tons per annum in the 1930s to 1.9 million tons in the early 1940s; pig iron production rose from 409,000 tons in 1938 to over 659,000 tons in 1940; and the tonnage launched on the Clyde rose from an average of 322,000 per annum in the years 1934 to 1939 to 493,000 per annum between 1940 and 1944.[71] Even more remarkable were the contributions of industries that were relative strangers to the demands of the armed forces. In addition to waterproofed textiles, Nairns of Kirkcaldy produced aircraft fittings, food containers and even torpedoes during the war.[72] Caldwell and Young's Lochwinnoch factory switched production from exquisite silks to parachute cloth.[73] In many ways, the war years disprove theories that Scottish businesses either could not or would not diversify when new markets emerged. What they do indicate, nevertheless, is the level of compulsion that was required to effect shifts in production and the guarantees of custom that were necessary to alleviate concerns about the risks attached to innovation.

Full employment, which was reached around 1944, and the 25 per cent rise in real incomes, that was achieved by 1945, began to dispel the gloom of the interwar years.[74] Moreover, Scottish producers never had to cope with the degree of war damage to plant experienced by industrialists in the south of England. Rolls-Royce's new presence in the Hillington Industrial Estate near Glasgow suggested a promising future for innovative aeronautical engineering in the post-war years and Ferranti's arrival in Edinburgh signalled the beginning of Scotland's electronics industry. In the north, twentieth-century 'military roads' further integrated Highland communities with centres of production and, following the Hydro Electric (Scotland) Act of 1943, a (quite literally) brighter future for northern areas seemed guaranteed.

Yet there were worrying portents of future decay. In the Scottish coal industry, output declined from 30.5 million tons in 1939 to 21.4 million tons in 1945 and productivity slumped by around 80 tons per man during the war.[75] Still, the steel and iron industries had not been integrated effectively and, by the end of the war, in terms of employment, Scotland's reliance on heavy industry had actually increased, with one quarter of the insured population working in that sector. Abroad, lucrative Scottish interests had been seriously disrupted – for example, in 1942, the Burmese assets of the Burmah Oil Company (a Glasgow company founded in 1886) had to be demolished due to the imminent Japanese invasion.

Nevertheless, the boost which wartime demand granted to Scottish heavy industry was largely carried over into the 1950s. In 1953, the coronation year, the Scottish Council (Development and Industry) proudly detailed the exports of the new Queen's most northerly kingdom.

Clydeside ships, Kilmarnock shoes, Edinburgh sealing wax, head-squares for the sheiks of Araby, clay tobacco pipes for West Indian sugar cane cutters, jute looms for Pakistanian weavers, whisky for Chicago convention roisterers, lager for Singapore merchants, hydro-electric power plant for North Canadian pioneers, carpets for New Zealand newly-weds, ice-cream cabinets for Argentinian purveyors, kippers for Australian sheep farmers, bicycles for Malayan rubber growers, horse leather for German glove makers, industrial belts for Dutch engineers, perfume bottles for Californian chemists, Edinburgh crystal-ware for Canadian collectors, cantilever cranes for Egyptian dockers, lignum vitae bowls for Australian sportsmen, sewing machines for Jugo-Slavian garment makers, rolling mills for Turkish steel makers, clothes wringers for Portuguese hotel keepers, tweeds for German countrymen, footballs for Danish pig-breeders, golf clubs for South American miners, paper-making plant for Swedish manufacturers, alarm clocks for Swiss mechanics, firebricks for Japanese foundrymen, locomotives for Greek railwaymen, wrist-watches for Norwegian transport managers, cash registers for Indian shop-keepers, Christmas cards for French peasants, screw nails for South American carpenters, typewriters for Brazilian stenographers, adding machines for New York actuaries, bronze propellers for Dutch boat-builders, razor blades for Belgian textile operatives, refinery machinery for West Indian plantation owners, domestic refrigerators for Canadian house-holders, even brass coffin furnishings for deceased Italians.[76]

As noted earlier, until 1958, Scotland was reasonably successful in maintaining her share of GDP.[77] But such apparent success masked serious problems in the pace of economic growth north of the Border. As Gavin McCrone made clear, 'total growth between 1954 and 1960 was only nine per cent compared with 18 per cent for the United Kingdom'.[78] In the first years of this new Elizabethan age, it was slowly becoming apparent that the relative health of Scotland's post-war economy was declining and that the demand for her traditional heavy industries was seriously ebbing away. Even nationalisation (coal, 1947; rail and electricity, 1948; iron and steel, 1949) failed to solve the familiar problem of overcapacity in declining sectors and merely added substance to claims from Nationalists, amongst others, that, while Scotland had helped win the war, England – through the centralisation of industry and the southward drift of economic control – was benefiting most from the peace.

North of the Border, government intervention – emboldened by wartime experiences – was identified as the solution and Scotland, variously styled a 'special' or 'development' area, embarked on a range of regional planning initiatives during the 1950s and 1960s in an attempt to accelerate the 'glacial slowness' of structural change that had been evident in Scottish industry since 1900.[79] The Forth Road Bridge – at its inauguration the largest suspension bridge in Europe – was finally completed in 1964 and, one year later, the Highlands and Islands

Development Board was established to encourage industry and discourage population decline in this fragile area. The Tay was straddled by a road bridge in 1966 – the same year that the UK government identified Caithness as the site for a new prototype fast reactor (Dounreay) and, two years later, the Invergordon aluminium smelter was built. Largely as a consequence of such policies, the growth of public sector employment and other incentives offered to firms 'locating' in Scotland, public expenditure in Scotland was 20 per cent above the British norm by the end of the decade.[80] But, despite such efforts, the rise in aggregate GDP in the UK continued to outstrip Scottish levels; income per head in the north increasingly slipped behind UK levels and Scottish unemployment rates grew relative to both the position of the previous decade and the experience of her southern neighbour.[81] Once again, many Scots sought in emigration the traditional escape route from economic hardship.

Geology rather than government policy and foreign investment rather than native entrepreneurship came to Scotland's aid. The discovery of oil in the North Sea in 1969 stimulated growth and encouraged the restructuring begun in the early 1960s, and foreign investment had, by 1973, developed to such an extent that nearly 60 per cent of Scots in manufacturing industries worked for companies based outwith Scotland.[82] For a time 'aggregate GDP north of the border began to increase at a significantly faster rate than in the rest of the country' and employment was stimulated.[83] Looking back, the 1970s appear a period of optimism – an uneasy calm before the storm.

Three dynamics characterised the transformation of the Scottish economy in the last three decades of the twentieth century – deindustrialisation, the rise to dominance of the service sector and the withdrawal from 'planning'.

Despite the boost from oil-related activities, the expansion of industrial output in the 1970s was markedly lower in Scotland than in the UK as a whole. In Dundee alone, over six thousand jobs in engineering were lost in the first half of the 1970s.[84] On the other hand, growth in services in this decade seemed to offer some consolation. Yet the years between 1979 and 1981 proved to be a painful period of transition. In these years, manufacturing in Scotland lost 20 per cent of its jobs, heralding a period of dramatic decline, referred to by one historian as the 'holocaust' of Scottish manufacturing.[85] In the 1980s, losses to male employment in the productive sector amounted to 20,000 jobs a year and, across the board, Scotland recorded significant losses in manufacturing capacity.[86] Even the dynamism of the service sector could not accommodate such a haemorrhage and unemployment soared. In 1985 unemployment in Scotland reached 15.6 per cent, in comparison to a UK average of 11.8 per cent.[87]

By 1994, the number of Scots in manufacturing had declined by around 250,000 in comparison to 1979 and over 40 per cent of Scottish exports were being derived from electronics manufactures predominantly controlled by foreign firms.[88] Government policy played a major role in such a transformation. From the early 1980s, the priorities of the Conservative government elected in 1979 sought the removal of restrictions on competition and an end to the planning agenda characteristic of the 1960s that was so heavily dependent on central government resources. Finally, it seemed, the restructuring anticipated and encouraged by generations of Scottish economists had been inaugurated (though not perhaps in the way they had either hoped or envisaged). It was to be a costly process in terms of jobs, status, economic control and national pride and it contributed significantly, if unintentionally, to the re-awakening of demands for constitutional reform in the late 1990s.

On the eve of a new millennium in 1999, the Scottish economy was certainly very different to the one that greeted the dawn of the twentieth century. Unmistakably, Scotland's experience had much in common with the rest of the UK but, in the timing, intensity and cost of economic transformation, there was much about Scotland that was distinctive. At the close of the twentieth century, it was clear that Scotland had responded to global change in various different ways and with varying degrees of immediacy and success. Why this should have been the case is best explained by a closer look at the industries which dominated the Scottish economy and the influence of government on Scotland's economic fortunes.

TWO   Manufacturing Scotland –
Traditional Industries

Each member of the ruling family was 'heid bummer' (boss) of a
section defined by a letter of the alphabet: A, B, C, D, etc. His
consent had to be procured before any big decision in the department could be made; and anxious heads of sections were forever
seeking a rendezvous with 'my Director' to get an OK and so avoid
a hold-up in their department's work.

Beyond the Borders (1988)
Lavinia Derwent (1909–1989)[1]

Global trends certainly interacted with the balance of heavy industries
in Scotland to influence the relative longevity of traditional manufacturing sectors in comparison to other western powers. Yet it would be a
mistake to surrender responsibility for Scotland's economic destiny to
the caprice of impersonal commercial forces. The conservative nature
and prejudices of capital investment in Scotland to a large extent guaranteed such continuity with the past. Whether due to the impediments
of declining profits, the disincentives to change characteristic of family
firms, a legacy of industrial militancy (the myths of which lasted longer
than its reality), the inadequacies of Scottish technical education or a
complacency resulting from the artificial sustenance of the public purse,
Scottish industrialists, as much if not more so than others, were the
arbiters of Scotland's future and failed to free her from the more regres-
sive features of her industrial inheritance.[2]

At the start of the twentieth century, the leaders of Scottish industry
were typically self-made men or the sons (or grandsons) of company
founders who had 'learned the ropes' through apprenticeships of various
sorts. For example, David Colville (1860–1916), son of the founder of
what would become Scotland's last and greatest steel company, was sent
as a third hand melter to the Steel Company of Scotland after he finished
his schooling at Glasgow Academy. Sir William Arrol (1839–1913)
worked as a bobbin maker in his father's mill before being apprenticed to

a blacksmith. He was to become one of Scotland's most famous engineers as the builder of the iconic Forth Rail Bridge.

In a period of high profits, Scottish businessmen bemoaned the quality of elementary education in the Edwardian years but they rejected the need for commercial education. They frequently resisted specialised day classes for their workers (as was common in America and Germany) in favour of on-the-job training due to the dislocation of production and services that absences would cause. Scotland, industrialists of the time argued, would be put at a commercial disadvantage vis-à-vis her southern neighbour if the Scottish Education Department made release for attendance at day classes compulsory in the north. Ambitious workers paid the price. A former laboratory assistant at the Glengarnock works near Kilbirnie, taken over by Colville's in 1916, recounted his experience during the First World War:

> The nearest college providing classes in chemistry was in Paisley but attendance was interfered with by shift work as the Company allowed no time off on the afternoon shift. Intending students had to make what arrangements they could with one or other of their 'mates' in order to cover the awkward afternoon shift as well as a slightly late arrival on night-shift class nights.[3]

Out of 4,043 students at Edinburgh's Heriot Watt College in 1900 only 157 attended day classes.[4]

Perhaps the greatest form of short-sightedness is to presume that the next generation will not require that which you did not have yourself. Excuses are hard to find – it is not good enough to suggest that, in a period of economic vitality, it was understandable that industrialists chose to let the future look after itself while, in the period of recession which followed, it behoved industrialists to concentrate on the job in hand. One cannot have it both ways. Put simply, the instincts of Scottish industry to rely on tradition as a guide to the future were dangerous. Even Andrew Carnegie (1835–1918) could offer little in the way of direction at a time when Scotland, with hindsight, certainly needed it. 'One rule I have often suggested to youth,' he told the students of the University of Aberdeen in June 1912, 'remain teetotallers until you have become millionaires.'[5] It is hardly surprising that, in the interwar years, Scottish industry was often ill equipped to meet the new challenges of a more sophisticated and less forgiving global economic environment.

As the previous chapter revealed, in the twentieth century, decline in the traditional industries that had been the leading sectors of the early phases of the industrial revolution was an experience shared by the economies both north and south of the Border. In the UK, while the staple industries contributed 37 per cent of net output in 1924, by 1930, this had declined to 29.6 per cent and stood at 27.8 per cent on the eve of the Second World War.[6] In 1954, 42 per cent of the UK workforce were still employed in manufacturing sectors of the economy, but by 1960, manufacturing's share had fallen to under 40 per cent and dropped to 31 per cent in 1979, when the primary industries – agriculture, forestry, fishing, mining and quarrying – accounted for only 3 per cent of the workforce.[7] Scotland contributed to this trend but decline was slower and the proportionate share of heavy industry within manufacturing remained higher for much of the century.

In 1935, the staple industries still accounted for 36.8 per cent of Scotland's net output. Thereafter, in the 1950s, Alec Cairncross would lament that Scotland's dependence on heavy industry had 'grown rather than diminished'.[8] In 1961 the influential Toothill report reflected that there 'is still a relatively heavy representation of long-established industries for the most part no longer characterised by prospects of expansion'.[9] And still, in the 1970s and beyond, Scotland 'remained more committed to traditional industries, agriculture and fishing, coalmining, textiles, shipbuilding and heavy engineering than the rest of the UK.'[10]

Until the late 1980s, the speed of decline in the old industries was not matched by the growth of the new, hence the reliance on traditional sectors was perpetuated at a time when their profitability was diminishing. Indeed, declining profits in established industries arguably made technological innovation and diversification more difficult than it would have been under 'normal' conditions and encouraged firms to 'struggle on for as long as possible in [their] accustomed path'.[11] In the second half of the century, for example, equipment that had made its first appearance at the Ardrossan shipyards before the Great War was still being used.[12] Scotland appeared the victim of a cruel riddle. Decline, however, was neither a linear nor an irreversible process, at least in the short term, and it afflicted industries at different times and with varying degrees of debilitating power. A keener understanding of their individual experiences partly explains how the riddle was worked through, if not entirely solved.

COAL

> 1st Miner: Twenty years now the coal's black face
> has grinned at me, mocked me, gritted the stink
> of its breath against me.
> 2nd Miner: You say the same thing every night.

But it's pointless to complain.
The likes of us were born to suffer.
The Decision: An Opera in Three Acts (1965)
Thea Musgrave (1928–)
(Libretto by Maurice Lindsay)

Musgrave's opera sings the tale of John Brown, a sixty-year-old Ayrshire miner who was trapped for twenty-three days in Kilgrammie pit in the Girvan valley in 1835. In 1979, the last coal-mining venture in the Girvan valley closed.[13]

The Scottish coal industry made a significant contribution to Scotland's early industrial pre-eminence in the nineteenth century and grew steadily as other industries came to depend on 'black gold' as their principal source of energy. Between 1870 and 1913 both output and employment doubled and, on the eve of the Great War, Scottish coal reached its peak production of 42.5 million tons, representing nearly 15 per cent of total UK output that year.[14]

In the years that followed, however, Scotland's coal industry faced fundamental problems in demand, competition and supply. Declining domestic consumption, particularly amongst coal's greediest early clients (for example, pig iron manufacturers), and increased competition from foreign and UK firms compounded problems caused by markets lost or seriously eroded as a result of the disruption to trade caused by war and its aftermath. By 1914 Scottish colliers had already exhausted the most profitable and economic of the nation's coal seams and high costs and a proliferation of small firms in the north resulted in serious decline in the interwar years.

The slump in demand hit hard in the interwar period and numbers employed in the Scottish coal industry declined from 155,000 in 1920 to 81,000 in 1933.[15] By the mid 1920s, the selling price of Scottish coal per ton did not even cover the cost of extraction and, as time went on, Scottish producers lost the advantage they had enjoyed by their early adoption of mechanised extraction and conveyance. James A. Hood (1859–1941), Chairman and later Managing Director of the Lothian Coal Company, had been a pioneer in the mechanisation of the extraction process, introducing such machines to the Newtongrange colliery from as early as the 1880s. In 1924 this head start was reflected in the statistics – the proportion of coal that was cut mechanically in Scotland was 48 per cent, compared with only 19 per cent in England. By 1937, however, this advantage had narrowed – 79 per cent of Scottish coal was mechanically cut, whereas 57 per cent of English coal was cut with the aid of machines.[16]

Poor industrial relations in the 1920s certainly did not encourage optimism for the future. During the 1921 miners' strike, first the Black Watch then the Marines were called on to bring order to the Fife coalfields and the Riot Act was read in Cowdenbeath.[17] Thereafter, the flooding of mines resulting from the lack of maintenance during the dispute added to company expenses, and the setting of a minimum wage compromised employers' abilities to cut costs in a heavily labour-intensive industry. Further disruption and damage to property as a result of the General Strike in 1926 merely exacerbated an already desperate situation for both workers and management. It pays to be reminded that, while other workers returned to their posts after little more than a week in May 1926, the miners stayed out until November.

Encouraged by government interest in this strategic industry – Westminster had exercised control over the industry in one way or another since the Great War – the interwar years brought some rationalisation and the increasing concentration of ownership but at a cost. In the Dunfermline area alone in the 1920s, the Fife Coal Company closed several loss-making mines, among them Blairenbathie, Lassodie, Blairadam and Oakley (Kinnedar); Wilson and Clyde closed Lethans No 1 (Saline) in 1925; and, by 1931, Lassodie Nos 4, 10 and 11 had been closed by Thomas Spowart and Co. Ltd. Altogether, between 1929 and 1939, the number of active pits in Fife fell from thirty-two to fifteen, with an associated loss of manpower of around 4,000 men.[18] Productivity increased in these years – despite the loss of labour, output fell by only 0.5 million tons in Fife in the decade 1929–39. But prices fell too, adding to coal-masters' problems. In the west, Lanarkshire collieries experienced similar re-organisation – in the 1930s, coal mining in Motherwell was reduced to three large collieries owned by one combine.[19] Mining communities paid the price of such modernisation – unemployment levels in the Scottish coalfields were amongst the highest in the country.

The Second World War saw both output and productivity slump – an ominous record for an industry that would be amongst the first to be nationalised (1947) by Clement Attlee's Labour government.[20] By the early 1950s, paid annual leave and the reduction of hours for face workers – however commendable in terms of occupational health and safety – further added to the expenses of an industry now facing stiff American competition. Nevertheless, until 1956, the industry and its new leaders enjoyed a brief honeymoon period, as growing demand necessitated by post-war reconstruction even made the thought of expansion a realistic ambition. However, the fresh hopes recorded memorably in the National Coal Board's (NCB) *Plan for Coal* (1950), were not to be realised. The plan envisaged a 27 per cent increase in Scottish output between 1948 and the mid 1960s and new sinkings were to go ahead at Rothes and Glenochil. By 1959, however, rationalisation was back on the agenda as demand had fallen and overcapacity again posed major problems. The closure of the Rothes colliery – a state-of-the-art white elephant according to many – was announced in 1962, just five years after its inauguration. It was estimated that Rothes boasted 183 million tons of workable coal reserves. But geological difficulties, wedded to a centralised management for whom Rothes was only one project among many, meant that it never met its projected output.[21]

The NCB were to record an operational deficit in Scotland every year after 1950 and, while the labour force was halved in the decade 1958–68 and the number of active pits fell from 166 to 21 over the period 1958–76, Scottish coal still struggled.[22] A regional surcharge applied to the pit-head price of Scottish coal in 1962 and again in 1966 raised revenue in the short term but, in the end, it overpriced a commodity that was facing stiff competition from alternative fuel sources (mainly oil, gas and electricity). In 1969, 50 per cent of Scotland's coal output was consumed in the power stations.[23] But even the guaranteed market of the Scottish electricity generators could not ensure a bright future for this ailing industrial monolith. As Peter Payne has recorded, 'During the sixties, Scotland was responsible for almost half of the total deficiencies recorded for the operating Divisions of the NCB.'[24] By 1966, for example, the Glencraig colliery in Fife was losing £1 for every ton of coal produced.[25] And, by the 1970s, it was clear that *none* of Scotland's pits were economic – in 1983–84, the operating loss per ton of the Scottish collieries was almost £14. Further closures were inevitable.

The Coal Industry Act of 1980 that followed the victory of Mrs Thatcher's Conservative Party in 1979 set a deadline of 1983–84 for the NCB to become self-supporting. A year later, the National Union of Mineworkers (NUM) threatened industrial action over industry plans to cut uneconomic capacity. This time, the government backed down and made some strategic investments in the sector. But confrontation was guaranteed, particularly after the fiery Arthur Scargill succeeded Joe Gormley as NUM president and Ian MacGregor was appointed NCB Chairman with a political mandate for drastic reform. It was to be as much a clash of philosophies and cultures as it was an industrial dispute.

The miners' strike of 1984–85 that followed was the most violent and passionate industrial dispute of the late twentieth century, tearing communities apart and demonising the leaders of both sides. Miners at Scotland's Polmaise colliery (earmarked for early closure) were among the first to strike and, by the end of the dispute, 200 Scottish miners had been sacked. At the Cartmore Industrial Site in Lochgelly, 133 pickets were arrested over the course of just two days.[26] 'We were fighting for our communities, a way of life and the fabric of British society,' reflected Neil Valentine from Ayrshire nearly twenty years after the miners returned to work – the stakes were high.[27] The strike was called on 12 March 1984 and officially ended on 5 March 1985.

In retrospect, 1984 stands as the last fighting breaths of a dying industry. Between 1947 and 1987, the number of jobs in the Scottish industry fell by about 80,000 and, in the 1980s alone, the number of active pits in Scotland fell from fifteen to just two. Thereafter, Monktonhall in Midlothian closed in 1998 and, by the end of the century only one deep mine, the Longannet complex in Fife, remained, only to be closed in 2002. Following privatisation in 1994, the Scottish Coal Company would directly employ around 1,500 in an industry dominated by opencast extraction and, in 1997–98, Scotland produced around 40 per cent of UK opencast coal. But, in an age of cheap imported coal and alternative sources of power (many, like nuclear and solar energy, not even requiring coal as a raw material), Scottish coal could simply not compete. Economic forces did not necessarily, as before, privilege nations with indigenous coal supplies. This fact, together with a developing environmental agenda, encouraged many to question the efficacy of 'preserving' the coal industry.[28]

By the 1990s, the Scottish coal industry simultaneously entered a new opencast age and the history books and, like the death of handloom weaving and the passage of the age of the ploughmen some hundred years before, offered little but inspiration for poets. Geddes Thomson reflected:

> In Ayrshire now the pit bings
> Are covered with grass and trees.
> Those bings are mysterious
> As ancient burial mounds
> To the children who play there,
> Whose grandfathers would pull
> Bunches of fresh sweet grass
> For the ponies under the ground.[29]

IRON AND STEEL

> Firing the blast furnace, bursting the sky,
> Flame in a pillar of smoke shoots up

And like the magic fires of Autumn, as witched-leaves dancing,
The fire plumes play within a wraith of smoke.
Bright red dust sparks, light stars, glinting,
Midges rising on the shooting air,
Stars themselves exploding in their dizzy motion,
Light's last nebulae to red death sinking,
Smould'ring softly as their sisters dance.

Extract from *Deserto Rosso: Ravenscraig*,
'(3) Nec Tamen Consumebatur'[30]
John Roy

The Monklands, reducing and recreating scrap and ore and bringing them to life as steel, evidenced at various times in their modern history both the creation story and the hell of Scottish industry. For most of Scotland's industrial past, towns such as Motherwell and Coatbridge confirmed the nation's debt to the riches which lay beneath its feet. By the 1990s, however, they epitomised how, as world demand changed and indigenous ores diminished, such an inheritance, by itself, simply was not enough.

Scottish pig iron production was faltering even in the late Victorian period, as producers became increasingly reliant on imported ore – indeed, imports of iron ore doubled in the Edwardian years.[31] Rising costs, poor economies of scale due to the high number of small units of production and increasingly outdated and inefficient furnaces meant that the price of Scottish pig iron rose, relative to its main competitors. As a result, between 1870 and 1913, Scottish exports declined by half and many Scottish customers even sourced their iron from England and abroad.[32]

The interwar years confirmed iron's troubled position, as continued lack of investment in new technologies perpetuated the inefficiency of production methods at a time when the industry's reliance on expensive English coke increased. Iron manufactures also failed to meet the changing priorities of their main customers – Scottish steel manufacturers – and continued to produce haematite pig iron when steel interests were increasingly requiring basic pig iron.[33] As a consequence Scottish pig iron output fell by around two-thirds between the two World Wars.[34]

By contrast, the Scottish steel industry had much more recent roots – the first Scottish steel company was founded near Glasgow in 1871, although there are records of steel production in Calder from as early as 1805 and cementation steel production at the Cramond works from the 1790s – but its relative youth was no guarantee of success.[35] In the early years, Scottish steel production rested overwhelmingly in the hands of local iron manufacturers. Nevertheless, the economies of scale and production advantages that such a relationship suggested were rarely exploited. Only two steel works – Merry and Cunninghame and the Glasgow Iron and Steel Co. – were fully integrated with iron foundries and, as a result, businesses in this highly labour-intensive industry faced further costs in terms of transport in particular.[36] Technical innovation from the late 1870s and price fixing in the Scottish industry from 1886 went some way to securing markets and retaining traditional customers into the 1900s but, even by 1913, many Scottish industrialists were importing their steel from England and elsewhere – German steel 'dumped' on British markets in 1913 cost 20 shillings less per ton than the native equivalent.[37] Nevertheless, in the two decades of European peace preceding the Great War, Scottish steel was booming, increasing output nearly threefold in response to the growth of Scottish ship-building, its principal client.[38]

Scottish steel effectively met the demands of the war economy between 1914 and 1918 and, under the direction of its new Chairman, John Craig, David Colville and Sons increased its ingot steel output by about 250 per cent. From employing 2,800 at its Dalzell works in 1914, by 1920, Colville's employed 18,000 at its collieries and plants across the west of Scotland.[39] The company was one of Scotland's industrial giants but, in 1918, it was not alone in its interest in enlarging its steel capacity. Shipbuilders, anxious about supplies of steel to meet the requirements of plump order books, bought out steel manufacturers. But this buoyant marketplace would not last. The miners' strike of 1921 severely disrupted production just at the time it was becoming apparent that the post-war boom was coming to an abrupt end. With steel production stagnating in the 1930s, Scotland's share of UK production declined.[40] Native iron producers proved increasingly incapable of meeting steel's demands so Scottish steel manufacturers were forced to rely on imported pig iron. As a result, in a period of declining demand, costs increased. Shifting to basic steel production (as opposed to the acid steel preferred originally by shipbuilders and their insurers) allowed some steel producers to diversify their markets. But such measures alone were not going to solve steel's problems.

In the thirties, ownership became increasingly concentrated as steel interests sought to streamline production and reduce overcapacity – ultimately Colville's controlled over 90 per cent of Scotland's steel-making capacity in 1936.[41] But problems persisted. Amalgamation schemes, first from Lord Invernairn in 1923, then from the accountant Sir William Plender, came to nothing. The proposals of Lord Pirrie

(1847–1924), the chairman of the shipbuilders Harland and Wolff, for a 'mammoth holding company' died with him in 1924.[42] And the recommendations of the Brassert Report (1929) for a modern integrated coastal site on the Clyde following the American model, while attracting supporting murmurs from Colville's, the government and even banking interests, grounded on the rocks of 'parochial jealousies and antagonisms'.[43] The final words of the Brassert consultants' covering letter to Lord Weir of Cathcart (1877–1959), the chairman of the engineering firm G. & J. Weir Ltd and government industrial advisor, were ominous:

> If the rehabilitation of the Scottish iron and steel industry is not undertaken in the broad spirit which we have assumed and by concentration of its basic production in the most favoured location, the Clyde, we believe that it is doomed, sooner or later, to failure.[44]

In the end, it was protection that ensured that steel's problems were not more acute in the short term at least – a tariff was placed on imports of steel into the UK in 1932 – but, for many in steel's heartland, it had come too late. The registered unemployed in Motherwell numbered 4,100 as early as March 1921 and, in 1933, 53 per cent of the population of Wishaw and 49 per cent of Motherwell's population was 'on the dole'.[45] A *Scotsman* reporter recorded that Bellshill in 1935 was a town suffering from 60 per cent unemployment, following the transfer of Stewarts & Lloyds to Corby and the short-time working at the Universal Plate Mill:

> The tragedy of Bellshill is that, despite its numerous advantages as an industrial district, it has been waiting in vain for a revival of the industries which have hitherto supported the population. What this means in human values has got to be seen in close perspective to be properly appreciated. The spectacle of veterans of industry thrown on the scrap heap is sad enough, but to see concentrated numbers of youths, as you do here, for whom beginnings are not available, is sadder still and disquieting.[46]

War and the demands of post-war reconstruction brought much-needed modernisation and investment in the industry in the 1940s, and production increased. By 1952, pig iron production had risen to 886,000 tons and 2.1 million tons of steel were produced.[47] By the time the industry was briefly nationalised in the early 1950s, therefore, Scottish steel appeared confident of a bright future. In November 1948, Sir Andrew Duncan (1884–1952), the Scottish MP for Westminster and the iron and steel Controller during the early months of the Second World War before becoming President of the Board of Trade, announced to the House of Commons that the steel industry was 'doing well, very well'. He saw little need for further government intervention in an industry that was fully aware of its own limitations and opportunities and warned, 'There is an onus on the Government to show that under any change they can do better.'[48] Initially politicians met such cynicism with remarkable self-confidence and, in 1954, embarked on plans to invest £34 million in the Scottish industry and establish a fully integrated iron and steel works at Motherwell (Ravenscraig was operational from 1957). Indeed, the popularity of the industry was perversely most evident when, on denationalisation in 1955, shares in Colville's attracted 160,000 applications (twelve times the number of shares actually available).[49]

The year 1958, however, was to be a turning point when it was announced that a new cold reduction plant would open at Gartcosh, and, under enormous pressure from government, Sir Andrew McCance of Colville's was reluctantly 'persuaded' to build a new strip mill at Ravenscraig (commissioned in 1963).[50] As a consequence of such developments, Scottish production increased to 2.7 million tons in 1960 and continued to grow throughout the 1960s.[51] But Scotland's share of UK output was declining. A world surplus of steel and a recession in manufacturing meant that the future of Scottish steel became the focus of wide attention. To say the least, matters were not helped by persistent industrial disputes in the north – between 1 May and 30 September 1964, no fewer than thirty-two strikes took place in the Ravenscraig-Gartcosh complex alone.[52]

In 1967, Scottish steel was nationalised for the second time in less than twenty years and, over the next decade, faced serious restructuring and modernisation. In 1973, work started on a new ore and coal terminal at Hunterston which was to be enhanced soon after by the completion of two direct reduction plants on an adjacent site. Hopes for the future, however, were soon dashed as industrial action at Hunterston, increases in the price of natural gas (an essential energy source in the modernised industry) and low levels of demand pointed again to overcapacity in the industry and Scotland's vulnerable position within the British Steel Corporation (BSC) vis-à-vis other areas. In 1976–77, BSC's Scottish Division was losing £50.5 million and, by 1979–80, was recording losses of £96 million.[53]

In 1974, nearly 27,000 workers were employed in the Scottish steel industry; by 1982, this had fallen to a little over 12,000; and, by 1991, the figure stood at less than 3,000.[54] For iron, the story was much the same – between 1969 and 1983, the number of workers in iron foundries across Scotland fell by 60 per cent.⁵⁵ The Glengarnock works were closed in 1985 and, a year later, Gartcosh closed its doors. It seemed only a matter of time before Ravenscraig – already identified as a marginal plant among BSC's integrated steel works – would meet the same fate. In December 1982, the Committee on Scottish Affairs abandoned its measured prose when it assessed the consequences the closure of 'the Craig' would have for the North Lanarkshire area:

It is . . . estimated that the closure of Ravenscraig would result in an increase in the number of unemployed in the District of over 7,000, raising the total to over 20,000. Since a high proportion of BSC employees in particular live in the inner urban areas of Wishaw and Motherwell, unemployment rates in those areas would be exceedingly high and the social consequences, when combined with the loss of morale that would inevitably follow in a community which has traditionally been based on steel making, would be extremely grave.⁵⁶

In the end, while closure of the Motherwell plant was postponed for a time in the early 1980s – largely for political reasons – it finally ceased operations in June 1992 and, in doing so, broke the mould in Scottish industrial history by failing, not through its timidity, but as a result of early overambition.⁵⁷

The numbered 'findings and conclusions' of a consultant's report for the Scottish Development Agency in 1991 summed up steel's problems:

1. The overall climate for steel investment in Scotland is not attractive.

Steel demand is flat in Europe and worldwide, and over-capacity in the European steel industry will continue beyond 1995 . . . Scotland is not well placed to compete. The Scottish markets for most steel products are not large enough to justify economically sized plants, and in total account for less than 5% of UK consumption. Moreover, Scotland has no local raw material resources, relatively poor access to the rest of the UK and no significant cost advantage to address EC markets.

2. New technology is not a panacea for steel in Scotland.

New technology is not likely to create major new opportunities for steel in the next decade.⁵⁸

Predictably, the Scottish Trades Union Congress was at odds with these findings, although the miners' strike in 1984 had shown the futility of resistance and the folly of self-sacrifice. While admitting that there were no 'magic formulas or quick fixes', it pleaded for rather than identified a profitable way forward: 'We . . . firmly believe that steel-making has an important place in a modern economy and even now a credible future course for the industry could be charted with active Government intervention.'[59]

Peter Payne concluded in 1995, however, that the Scottish steel industry had 'succumbed, a victim of the economic realities . . . shaping the global steel industry'.[60] But there was something else. Mediating this relationship between global demand and national production was Scotland's relationship with her 'partners' in the Union. Between 1967 and 1988, when steel was once again privatised, Scotland's steel industry had been part of a much larger *British* industry and decisions on the fate of distinct regional components were determined by their impact on the network of interests that comprised the whole. Scotland's steel industry was thus caught in the unenviable position of being both a partner and rival of English and Welsh producers. Nationalism intro-duced unpleasant sympathies – you had to be careful what you wished for when protecting Scottish jobs could threaten the future of other British regions. The author James Kelman (1946–) was right when he shared the 'harsh truth' with Scottish steelworkers in 1990 that 'it isn't their industry at all, it is part of the property of British Steel.'[61] Scotland had no claim on it either.

SHIPBUILDING

In the catalogue for the September 1946 Scottish Industries Exhibition at the Kelvin Hall in Glasgow, 'shipbuilding' appeared between 'sewing machines' and 'souvenirs' in the list of featured industries, as if fate was conspiring with the alphabet to predict its future ignominious decline. Nevertheless, a little over twenty years later, the launch of the *Queen Elizabeth II* from John Brown's shipyard in Clydebank in 1967 seemed to point to the longevity of shipbuilding's vitality in Scotland. The Cunard flagship, the QE2 as she became known, was, however, to be the last of the great Clyde-built trans-Atlantic liners. In the same year, the *Queen Mary*, the older regal daughter of the Clydebank yard that had seen war service as a troopship, arrived in Long Beach, California, to begin life as a tourist attraction and air travel had won the battle for the trans-Atlantic routes. When, in 1972, the *Alisa*, the last ship to be built at John Brown's was launched, bringing over a hundred years of shipbuilding in Clydebank to a close, it was clear that 'the great ships [had] outlived the industry'.[62]

Scottish shipbuilding was especially sensitive to changes in demand on a global scale, despite the custom it received from the British merchant fleet and the Admiralty. What is more, its production of highly specialised non-standard vessels and the development of individual practices across the multitude of family firms which comprised the industry in 1900 meant that its response to the vicissitudes of world trade in the first half of the twentieth century was often piecemeal and unimaginative. In the first two decades of the twentieth century, however, Scottish shipbuilding was booming. Between 1909 and 1913, Clyde launchings averaged 565,000 tons a year and, on the eve of war, the Clyde yards recorded their highest production, as over three-quarters of a million tons were named and baptised in the Clyde's waters.[63] Small yards elsewhere in Scotland were also doing well in these years – in Ardrossan, demand was such that a new yard was being planned in 1916 (completed in 1920) and, in Kirkintilloch, the buoyant canal trade was filling the order books of J. & J. Hay's yard in the years before 1918.[64] War brought more business – in Aberdeen, the Alexander Hall shipyard built thirty-five steel drifters for the Admiralty and Yarrows on the Clyde produced twenty-nine destroyers, sixteen gunboats, three hospital ships, a floating workshop and a submarine to power allied efforts in the war at sea.[65] Between 1914 and 1920, the capacity of the industry increased by 40 per cent. Then, perhaps, more than any other Scottish industry, shipbuilding benefited most from the immediate post-war boom and, between 1918 and 1920, annual average Clyde launchings amounted to over 600,000 tons, as world demand coincided with Scottish specialities – cargo ships and passenger liners.[66]

But perhaps it was more than the whimsy of fate that ensured that the Clyde's greatest warship of these years would see its first active service in the domestic industrial 'wars' of the 1920s rather than in a heroic naval encounter. Ship 460, HMS *Hood*, was launched from John Brown's Clydebank yard in August 1918 – too late to see active service in the Great War. Still, flag-waving crowds crammed the Greenock piers to bid adieu to the most graceful battlecruiser of the fleet, as she sailed to Rosyth for her first sea trials. Less than two years later, however, her crew would form shore parties under cover of darkness to protect essential services from the anger of local striking miners in the Cowdenbeath area – midshipmen would train as bus drivers to ensure Fife workers would reach their employ on time and seamen would challenge striking miners to a game of football in an attempt to calm a tense industrial situation. More worryingly (at least for those in charge), two able seamen seemed to have been radicalised by the experience and decorated the seamen's mess with red bunting. Although little time had passed, the world into which the *Hood* had been launched would have been unrecognisable to those Edwardians who had commissioned her in 1915 when the crowned heads of Europe sat comfortably on their thrones and the Clyde rang confidently to the sound of the labours of the riveting gangs.[67]

By the 1930s, the merchant fleet was beset by overcapacity, demand fell and production on the Clyde declined. Many of the shipping and tramp-steamer companies that had been among Scotland's most reliable clients had amalgamated in the Edwardian period to effect efficiencies in their services but this did not guarantee their survival. The Cunard Steamship Co. had taken over the Anchor Line in 1911 and the Anchor and Donaldson Lines came together as early as 1916. In 1935, however, Anchor Donaldson Ltd was liquidated.[68] For those who remained independent, only exceptional local businesses – like Hogarth and Sons of the Baron Line – maintained their building programmes in these years of global depression.[69] While the shipbuilding industries of Scotland's competitors were sustained through these difficult years by state subsidies, between 1931 and 1933, over 80 per cent of all berths in Scotland were idle and, between 1934 and 1938, only around 56 per cent of Scotland's shipbuilding capacity was being used.[70] From Glasgow to Greenock, 'many a forest of gaunt poles and many a company of tall cranes stood above an emptiness which in good times [held] the skeleton of a ship.'[71] The return to the gold standard in 1925 had not helped competitiveness and, increasingly, yards were forced to accept orders at cost price until rearmament again generated new projects on companies' books. But even bargain-basement prices did not guarantee custom. In 1921, Yarrows submitted a £25,000 tender for a ship for British owners. It was the lowest price from a British yard and would not have yielded a profit for the firm but, in the end, the order went to a Dutch yard at a cost of just £19,000.[72]

In part, this lack of global competitiveness was the result of stiff competition for contracts between yards in Scotland. The need to beat competitors on delivery encouraged individual businesses to retain labour that could not be fully employed at all stages of construction and this overmanning simply added to overheads.[73] But the experience of falling demand had encouraged some rationalisation and modernisation in the Scottish industry. Many, like Sir James Lithgow (1883–1952) believed that a 'fundamental and painful process of readjustment was inevitable'.[74] Capacity on the Clyde was cut by at least 19 per cent in the 1930s. Between 1930 and 1933, a new consortium of shipbuilders, National Shipbuilders Security Ltd, financed the closure of seven Clyde yards and mothballed two others. In total, 1.3 million gross registered tons of berth capacity in the UK were purchased and closed (35 per cent of the 1930 total) at a cost of £2,519,000, of which £724,000 was spent on closing yards in Scotland.[75] In Ardrossan, the new yard at the Inches was dismantled in 1930. In the end, however, rationalisation did not go far enough. By 1938, forty-nine shipbuilding companies still remained active in Scotland and no serious transformation had occurred in ownership patterns – twenty-four companies remained private limited companies, each generally under the control of one family group.[76]

Yet, elsewhere, innovation was evident. While shipbuilding on the Clyde and the Dee declined between 1920 and the mid 1930s, the tonnage launched on the Tay and the Forth in 1936 outstripped pre-war production levels.[77] At the Burntisland Shipbuilding Co. Ltd, standardisation was the watchword and production was streamlined with as much construction work as possible being carried out by steel manufacturers.[78] Clyde yards themselves had invested heavily in their works in the years immediately following the Great War, although this strategy left some of them – for example, Fairfield's and Lobnitz & Co. – short of capital during the depression years.[79] In 1933, Clydeside's William Denny & Bros. became the first shipbuilders in Britain to produce an all-welded ship – the ferry, *Robert the Bruce*. But the Clyde failed to produce its own diesel engine and, for some, this telling omission represented a major loss of technical initiative.[80]

By 1925 weeds bloomed in the berths of the Grangemouth Dockyard which, as recently as 1918, had launched a series of vessels in the flower class – *Lilac*, *Clematis*, *Carnation*, *Hibiscus* and others.[81] The response of the state to the problems of the Scottish industry was slow. It was not until 1934 that the policy of 'scrap and build' was adopted. Under this scheme, British ship owners were encouraged with subsidies to scrap old vessels and place orders with British yards for new craft. The Dunlop fleet in Glasgow was almost entirely renewed under this scheme but nationally such support was too little too late and did not lead to lasting change.[82] Lithgow's at Port Glasgow would ride out the storm by building 'on spec' and they encouraged customers such as the Lyle Shipping Co. to build in slack times by contributing to the cost of the ship themselves in exchange for shares in the completed craft.[83] But, with war clouds gathering in 1938, merchant ship orders on the Clyde generally were only a third of the 1937 figure and, in 1939, only 15 per cent of Fairfield's contracts came from private interests.[84] It was only in 1939 that the government introduced a shipping loan and grant scheme – a scheme which, within months, war made obsolete.

In later life, Arthur Mitchell, Yarrow's shipbuilding director between 1922 and 1962, reflected on shipbuilding during the Second World War:

> In some ways it was easier to build ships during the war than it had
> been before. It was certainly very much easier than it became after
> the war when steel was scarce. You had the feeling that everyone
> was trying to help you. Any material you needed, any job you
> wanted done, you had only to ask.[85]

Yarrows attracted large Admiralty orders for 'C' class and 'Hunt'
class destroyers and, between 1939 and 1945, built fifteen destroyers,
eight sloops and four gunboats, besides boilers, turbines and recipro-
cating steam engines.[86] Of all the Scottish yards, it was possibly the best
placed to exploit wartime conditions and, like others, was fortunate not
to suffer more severely from enemy bombing. On 13 March 1941, while
two bombs and a land mine fell on the yard killing forty-seven men,
work was only temporarily suspended.[87] Similarly, in Aberdeen, only
one major raid on 12 July 1940 seriously affected production. Most
remarkably, when the blitz razed much of Clydebank to the ground on
13 and 14 March 1945, John Brown's shipyard was comparatively
untouched. Even war clouds could have silver linings.

The year 1945 ushered in a period of considerable demand for new
vessels that required speedy delivery and the refitting and repair of vessels
that had seen war service. The Baron Line of Glasgow had lost twenty
ships out of a total fleet of forty-one during the war and Cunard's estimated charges for the reconditioning of the *Queen Elizabeth*, the *Queen
Mary*, the *Mauretania* and the *Britannic* alone were £7,600,000.[88]
Shipbuilding had never had it so good nor – with hindsight – could the
industry have anticipated it would get as bad as it did within twenty years.

> These were the days when the sun shone on the shipbuilding
> industry as it had never shone before, days when overtime in the
> yards became a way of life. The order books were filled five years
> ahead and no yard could attract the labour it needed without
> offering work on Sundays at overtime rates. In 1950, there was war
> in Korea to prolong the demand and, before that tapered off, the
> Egyptians blocked the Suez Canal and more ships were needed for
> the long haul round the Cape.[89]

The straitened conditions of the post-war years of austerity, when
many raw materials remained in short supply and regulated by government, encouraged a reliance on old working practices and marketing
strategies and a general complacency about modernisation. More immediate concerns dominated the pre-occupations of Scottish manufacturers – a lack of ship steel, a shortage of skilled labour and increasing
industrial disputes. Lack of investment in marketing, new plant and new

technology, however, merely reinforced outdated Scottish operations in comparison to the competition – for example, Japan, America and Germany – at a time when the credit schemes offered to potential buyers elsewhere in the world made Scotland a less attractive option for foreign clients. In many ways, Scottish yards were too focused on meeting British demand to the detriment of their place in the global marketplace. But even Scottish fleets were not necessarily 'buying British'. By the 1960s, Hogarth's were placing orders with Scandinavian shipbuilders – the *Baron Ardrossan*, the *Baron Maclay* and the *Baron Wemyss*, names reminiscent of Scotland's long industrial past, were being launched by Scotland's competitors.[90] As a result, while Scottish yards were experiencing a period of relative prosperity that would last until 1960, their share of world tonnage was deteriorating. In 1950, when UK producers launched 1.3 million tons of merchant tonnage, representing around 38 per cent of world production, the Clyde contributed a third to overall UK output. By 1960, while world merchant tonnage stood at over 8 million tons, the UK contributed less than 16 per cent and the Clyde's share of this dismal total had dropped by around 5 per cent.[91]

Where investment did occur in these years, it was often directed at disappearing markets. Barclay Curle & Co., Alexander Stephen & Sons and Fairfield's re-equipped in the early 1960s but, by 1965, Barclay Curle's yard was closed and Fairfield's was approaching bankruptcy. It was not long before Alexander Stephen & Sons' independent life ended in 1968 with its absorption into Upper Clyde Shipbuilders (UCS). The Clyde yards that had dominated world shipbuilding in the early twentieth century, through their production of the iconic passenger liners of those days, were less suited to the production of tankers, which became the dominant staple of the 1970s. Such simple shapes and finished craft no longer placed a premium on high skill levels in the labour force and a high-spec finish. It was a phenomenon that, by then, should have come as no surprise. As early as 1931, Sir Eric Geddes, First Lord of the Admiralty at the end of the First War, had noted that 'the skilled craftsman is passing in reproductive industry, as the bowmen and knights in armour have passed in war.'[92] One may be forgiven for thinking that, in this instance, like so many others in Scotland's modern industrial history, the defence of a skilled workforce and pride in a quality product were simply consolation for the disturbing fact that manufacturers were just not making what customers wanted.

In such changing circumstances, Scottish producers revisited the unfinished business of interwar rationalisation – there were still sixty shipbuilding yards in Scotland in 1953 – and turned to the government for support. Between 1960 and the mid 1970s, the number of Clyde yards fell by around 80 per cent, in the process erasing some famous industrial names. Harland and Wolff, Simons-Lobnitz and William Denny became casualties of the new industrial environment in 1963 and were joined, a year later, by the Blythswood Shipping Company and William Hamilton's.[93]

In 1966, the report of the government-sponsored inquiry into ship-building (the Geddes Report) recommended the further concentration of ownership on the Clyde and elsewhere in an attempt to meet the changing character of global demand.[94] By 1968, two large combines had emerged on the Clyde – Scott Lithgow, established in 1967, and Upper Clyde Shipbuilders, established in 1968. Within months, jobs were cut – between August 1969 and the end of 1970 just over 2,000 shipyard workers were made redundant by UCS although this was far fewer than the projected 5,500 cull management desired initially.[95] Yet problems continued. Yarrows opted out of the UCS combine in April 1970 and UCS called in the receivers in 1971. A trade union work-in to preserve jobs in 1972 made the headlines but it made little impact on the ultimate fate of the industry. As a result of union action, four yards were saved in the short term and another sold to the Texas oil giants, Marathon Manufacturing, with a £12 million sweetener.[96]

Persistent late delivery of orders, low productivity, trade union disputes and overpricing, not helped by inflationary trends in the general economy, dogged the industry. Fifteen trade unions operated in UCS and rivalry was often intense. This was nothing new. As early as 1942, Sir James Lithgow, in a letter to the Earl of Elgin, bemoaned the 'worship of the status quo' among the craft unions and reflected on how it had 'frozen out at their source most efforts to adopt modern methods'.[97] Twenty years later, restrictive practices meant that, in 1968, there were no fewer than 500 pay grades in the yards and 20 per cent of all hours worked were at over-time rates. This was no way to run an industry and paints neither managers nor trade unionists in a favourable light.[98] Despite significant government investment, Clydeside's position continued to deteriorate. By 1976, UCS and its offspring Govan Shipbuilders, established in 1972, had received £80 million from public funds but much of this had gone to meet losses rather than develop plant and technology.[99] In April 1975, Govan Shipbuilders announced an anticipated loss of £15 million on existing contracts and expected no profit until 1978.[100]

Nationalisation in July 1977 failed to transform the industry and, indeed, half of British Shipbuilders' losses by 1980 were attributed to Scottish yards.[101] Redundancy payouts rather than wage packets there-after maintained the economy of Clydeside's communities in the 1980s for a while at least. But research indicated and time confirmed that neither youth nor skill protected workers looking for employment in a continuing recession as 'no industrial sector . . . provided a completely safe haven after redundancy'. [102] By the 1990s, shipbuilding on the Clyde rested uneasily in the hands of three major interests – Yarrows, Kvaerner and Ferguson's. In Aberdeen, the Hall Russell shipyard, which had been taken over by A. & P. Appledore in 1986, closed its gates for the last time in 1992. As in the thirties, there was a silence – 'a silence in which men draw the dole and talk politics at street corners'.[103]

By 1980, the UK produced less than 2 per cent of the world's merchant tonnage.[104] It could, therefore, be argued that Scottish decline simply reflected a wider UK phenomenon. But, in Scotland, the decline of shipbuilding caused greater social and industrial dislocation than bare statistics would suggest, largely due to the industry's dominance in the manufacturing sector and the demand it generated for other products. Its destruction also deeply affected Scottish pride and seemed to mark the end of an era at a time when there seemed little in the future to encourage optimism.

SPECIALISATION AND INTERRELATEDNESS

The interdependence that had developed between the coal, iron, steel, engineering and shipbuilding industries in Scotland determined that all sectors would feel the impact of decline on associated manufacturers. The close relationships that guaranteed the perpetuation of heavy industry's commanding influence in Scotland into the second half of the twentieth century would also determine the totality of its eventual eclipse.[105]

Problems in the interrelatedness of Scotland's heavy industries had been evident since the early years of the twentieth century and were thereafter exacerbated by acute problems of overcapacity, lack of competitiveness, the obsolescence of plant and archaic management techniques. Iron manufacturers' early ownership of steel plant and, in the 1920s, shipbuilders' investment in steel companies consolidated this industrial pattern which was further reinforced by a 'series of interlocking directorships' amongst the Scottish industrial and financial elite.[106] At various times, the fragility of the structure was apparent to all but it took the onset of recession in 1957–58 before the true dimensions of the tragic consequences of this state of affairs were appreciated.

Interrelatedness eventually became mutually destructive when both end points of the chain of dependency began to fail and it became evident that the relationships that sustained interdependence were resistant to newcomers. Declining economic coal resources and iron ore deposits, unsuited anyway to changing patterns of demand, destroyed the premise on which the chain had been founded – that is the economies of scale resting on an adequate, cheap supply of processed native raw materials and fuel. Thereafter, when the period of growth in Scottish shipbuilding ceased and the industry eventually went into decline, the 'artificial' expedients that had sustained relationships across sectors – for example, imports of foreign coal, ores and scrap – were thrown into sharp relief. Over the years, it had become apparent that no other industry could match shipbuilding's position and generate the levels of domestic demand needed to sustain the coal and steel industries and little effort had been invested in encouraging alternative custom. Then, despite support from the public purse, which ensured social obligations on industrial managers as well as those of profit and efficiency, the chain broke. The west of Scotland is still living with the consequences.

All of the industries considered here in some depth were nationalised and privatised at some stage in their development over the course of the century. Nevertheless, efficiency, profitability, productivity and modernisation were seldom as important as political dogma when it came to the decision to bring them into public ownership. Nor were imaginative approaches to their long-term future necessarily to the fore after 1979 when quickly ridding the country of 'lame ducks' appeared the essential first step on the road to a free market economy for a Conservative Party who had abandoned full employment as a worthy economic goal. Throughout, the majority of Scots were too apt to see nationalisation as a panacea for their ills, rather than the quack remedy it so often turned out to be. At the end of the day, the transfer to public ownership of the major industries of a mature western economy was little less than one of the most ambitious industrial experiments of the century. There could be no guarantees. Too often, in the years that followed, commercial folly sustained by state subsidies – the Rothes colliery, the new strip mill at Ravenscraig, Upper Clyde Shipbuilders – led to regret but, ultimately, little in the way of real change. At times, nationalisation also seemed to work against the long-standing economic geographies of the industries concerned – both the NCB and the BSC overturned decades of industrial practice to impose artificial regional structures and targets on their UK units that they were often ill equipped to survive. Similarly, in 1966, the government ignored the complaints of the board of Yarrow & Co. who questioned whether it was 'sound policy to merge a number of widely differing shipyards on the Upper Clyde simultaneously and expect a profitable organisation to emerge'.[107] Nationalisation was not the solution to Scotland's long-standing industrial problems but this does not mean that privatisation, as it was effected in the final decades of the century, was necessarily the best way out.

Throughout Scotland, patterns of dependency across industries similar to those in the west developed organically in the first half of the twentieth century. They emerged from the distribution of natural resources and the bias of industrial sectors in the country rather than from state direction but, nevertheless, they carried risks. In Dundee, Paisley and the Borders for example, local engineering enterprises sustained by the jute, cotton thread and woollen industries either diversified or went under after 1950. In the north, fish curers and processors suffered as a result of the herring industry's demise after 1918. Coal, metal and engineering interests in the west of Scotland were affected as much as locomotive manufacturers in Springburn and Queen's Park when, variously, foreign competition, bus services, diesel engines, nationalisation and electrification challenged the supremacy of steam locomotives on the railways of the UK and India and the railroads of North America. In the 1950s, the North British Locomotive works were forced into liquidation.[108]

Over the course of the second half of the twentieth century, regional specialisations that had grounded Scottish economic distinctiveness were challenged. In October 1953, Walter Elliot, speaking to receptive audiences on both sides of the Tay, described Dundee as 'one of the cantilevers of Scotland – of the Western World'.[109] At that time, jute employed around 20 per cent of the city's workforce and the Tay Valley Plan promised a renaissance in local industry. Forty years later, the city was characterised by 'a more inchoate economic structure' – new industries that had challenged jute's dominance in the 1960s had closed down by the 1980s and the service sector was one of the few growth areas.[110] It was a post-industrial city and, according to the historian Chris Whatley, it was still looking for a 'distinctive role for the future'.[111] In Fife, Kirkcaldy's reliance on coal, linen and linoleum was under threat by the 1960s. In the south-west of the county the numbers employed in the coal industry had fallen by 14,500 in the course of the decade and fishing, once a major employer along its coast, was employing only 230 – mainly in Anstruther, Pittenweem and Crail – by 1970.[112] As in Dundee, science-based industries and services were seen as the way forward, encouraging one optimistic commentator in 1966 to style Fife 'the California of Scotland'.[113]

In the course of the century both industrial and regional patterns of interrelatedness gave way to more complex relationships less bounded by geography and native entrepreneurship. Through this process, distinctive features of Scottish industry came under attack, regional as well as national autonomy diminished and Scottish identity was transformed.

WORKING WITH MOTHER NATURE

Given the high proportion of Scotland's land mass devoted to agriculture, its rich inshore waters and experienced seafaring workforce, it was perhaps inevitable that the agricultural and fishing sectors retained a higher profile in the north in comparison to the rest of the UK in the twentieth century. The proportion of Scots employed in agriculture did decline steadily throughout the century, from 12 per cent in 1901 to 7.4 per cent in 1951, then to 1.5 per cent in 1990. However, in 1951, the comparable British figure was over 1 per cent below the Scottish proportion and had sunk below 2 per cent of the employed workforce at least a decade before Scotland.[114] In fishing, we see similar trends – while the numbers involved in the industry halved over the course of the century, even in 1978, 46 per cent of the UK's fishing catch was landed by the Scottish fleet and, in the 1980s, the 600,000 tonnes per annum caught by the Scottish fleet represented 78 per cent (by weight) of the fish landed in the UK.[115]

Such statistics suggest that the experience of Scottish agriculture and fishing in the twentieth century cannot be explained solely by recourse to general UK trends. Nor can such a strategy explain the primary sector's role in Scotland's wider industrial development and the regional dynamics that shaped the industries. According to the National Farmers' Union of Scotland, as late as 1999, one in ten Scottish jobs were dependent on farming.[116] And, in 1993, Grampian Region alone boasted a third of the Scottish fishing fleet, with 5,800 additional jobs in associated activities from boatbuilding to haulage.[117] Scottish agriculture clearly boasted many features that distinguished it from the sector south of the border, as did the Scottish fishing fleet.

Agriculture

Making money from Scottish agriculture has always been a challenging prospect. More than any other industry, farming must work with the landscape – whatever its limitations – and Mother Nature still has success in her gift. As early as 1905, Mrs Helen Beaton, writing as 'A Farmer's Wife', suggested that farming did not pay under existing circumstances and warned that '[a]t the present time there is no room for the drone farmer nor the Mistress Maclaurties who "canna be fashed" '.[118]

Seven years later, A. D. Hall wrote in the *Times* of the plight of the smallholders in Aberdeenshire:

> It is the small holder entirely dependent on his farming who tends to disappear, and the cause is really the rising standard of living and the opportunities emigration offers. For this reason the loss is

not entirely to be deplored. Away in the hills, not only in the Highlands, but south of the Forth also, may be seen traces of old crofts where only sheep and the grouse abide; the men who tilled them worked as no slaves ever work for a bare subsistence, always hovering on the brink of starvation. The history of these deserted holdings is to some extent being repeated now; the old men persist in the old homes, but their sons will not face the life, and it is not to the interest of either agriculture or the state to try and hold men to such ill-remunerated toil.[119]

The flight from the countryside was still a cause for concern in the 1920s. The Scottish Liberal Federation reported on their inquiry into the state of Scottish rural areas in 1928. Their observations were all too familiar. In Banffshire, '[t]he population of some of the small villages has decreased greatly during the past year or two and in some cases nearly all the young men, most of them agricultural workers, have emigrated'. In the Rhynie district of Aberdeenshire, '[t]he population . . . has decreased during the past 50 years. Many of the hamlets surrounding [the] village have entirely or almost disappeared'.[120] In the Highlands, '[s]chools which had one hundred children twenty and thirty years ago have now not more than about twenty or thirty on the average'.[121]

Forty years later, the sociologist James Littlejohn would suggest that rural depopulation reflected a 'rejection of the status of working-class countrymen' and, in particular, he observed that shepherding was regarded less favourably in the Borders than it had been in the past.[122] Yet it would be wrong to assume that Scottish agriculture was an industry for those who could think of or do little else. When Hall visited the Lothians in 1910, he 'had not imagined that the management of arable land could reach such perfection' and, in Perthshire, he was struck by the 'enlightened opportunism' of its mixed farming practices.[123] The story of Scottish farming in the twentieth century is a complex one and far from a tale of unremitting decline.

Throughout the century Scotland's agriculture differed from that of its southern neighbour in five significant aspects: the proportion of the land mass devoted to temporary grasses and rough grazing; the lower profile of wheat as a principal crop; the continued importance of livestock and dairy; the size and ownership patterns of productive units; and its slower moves towards mechanisation.

On the eve of the First World War, Scottish farmers were less reliant on purchased feedstuffs than their English competitors and, as a result, proved more adaptable to the restrictions of wartime conditions.[124] During both world wars, the Scottish acreage under grain crops rose to meet the increased demands of the home market – a peak tillage acreage of 2,121,000 was reached in 1943. But, with the return to peacetime conditions, the relative importance of rotation grasses, permanent pasture and rough grazing reasserted their holds.[125] Between 1920 and 1926, for example, the total area of land under crops fell by 58,000 acres.[126] In 1952, 47 per cent of Scotland's arable land was devoted to temporary grass, in comparison with 27 per cent in England and Wales, and, despite the growth in cereal production in Scotland after 1945, in 1980 1,126,800 hectares or 67 per cent of the total area of crops and grass were devoted to grazing, conservation and fodder crops.[127]

Twentieth-century Scottish agriculture inherited a cropping pattern very different to that of England. In addition to having 71 per cent of Britain's rough grazing in 1908, Scottish farmers grew significantly more oats, potatoes and turnips and significantly less wheat than growers in England and Wales.[128] In 1950, the area of land under oats and mixed grain was still over eleven times greater than that under wheat and, while the production of oats declined thereafter, the rise in cereal production at the end of the century was carried by barley, another Scottish staple of long-standing, rather than by wheat.[129] Yet, in other ways, Scottish arable farming exploited new conditions in a similar manner to its southern neighbour. Wheat acreage expanded in the 1970s and, in the 1980s and 1990s, Scottish producers, like those in England, benefited from the set-aside policy of the European Community (EC), intended to reduce surplus arable crops. In 1991, 2 per cent of arable land in the Scottish Borders had been set aside and, across Scotland, in 1994 alone, 225 farmers received £1.68 million under the scheme.[130]

Differences in the character of arable production are only partly explained by the topography of the Scottish land mass. Rather, as Houston noted in the 1950s:

> A study of land utilisation points at each stage to the main feature of Scottish farming, the emphasis on livestock production rather than crop sales. There is a similar emphasis in Britain as a whole, but it is more pronounced north of the Tweed.[131]

Such a state of affairs was further confirmed by changes in the last quarter of the twentieth century. While about 600,000 tonnes of hay and 298,000 tonnes of silage were produced in Scotland in the 1950s, 1,034,000 tonnes of hay and 3,390,000 tonnes of silage were produced in the five years to 1979.[132] Agricultural production has long been dominated by livestock in Scotland and, between 1870 and 1952, the number of cattle in Scotland increased by 60 per cent.[133] Thereafter, in the north-east, numbers of beef cows increased from 140,000 in 1951 to 480,000 in 1980 and, in the south-west and elsewhere, milk production increased from around 830 million litres to 1,258 million litres.[134] Despite declining ewe numbers, production of sheep meat also rose significantly in the later twentieth century (largely due to new breeding techniques) so that, by the early 1980s, livestock and livestock products together accounted for around three-quarters of the value of gross farm output in Scotland.[135] Scottish expertise in livestock production and sheep rearing earned farmers an enviable reputation for much of the twentieth century and served to ensure the traditional balance of Scottish husbandry. By the 1980s it was clear that the continued prosperity of cattle and sheep was of 'vital importance' to Scottish agriculture.[136]

The last two decades of the twentieth century, however, were to bring crises in the farming sector. In the 1980s, farmers' debts rose and prices failed to keep pace with the cost of production. Advances from Scottish banks to farmers increased by over 200 per cent between 1977 and 1981 and, while farm output prices rose by 6 per cent in 1980, input costs rose by 14 per cent.[137] These straitened circumstances encouraged the acceleration of operational trends in Scottish farming that had been evident much earlier. In the late 1980s, the number of full-time regular male farm workers in the Borders fell by a third, as farmers sought to cut costs by increasingly relying on subcontracted or seasonal labour. Part-time farming also grew in these years. By the 1980s, farmers (and farming families) in the hill and upland areas of the Borders were forced to diversify – forestry, tourism and jobs in the public sector were among the activities that would supplement the agricultural incomes of these often reluctantly part-time farmers.

The years 1986 and 1996 were to bring further unpredictable challenges for Scottish agriculture. In 1986, the Chernobyl nuclear reactor's disastrous demise affected farming across Europe, as animal sales in affected areas were either prohibited or subject to restrictions. Even at the end of 1994, forty-five farms in Scotland remained subject to statutory restrictions on movement and slaughter due to high levels of radioactivity in sheep and, in that year alone, the Scottish Office paid out over £100,000 in compensation.[138] Further challenges from the East had to be faced after 1990–91, when the fall of the Berlin Wall and the collapse of the USSR ushered in a period of declining prices that was much exaggerated in the UK due to the strength of sterling.[139] Then, in March 1996, the link between BSE (mad cow disease) in cattle and a new variant of Creutzfeldt-Jacob disease (vCJD) in humans was identified. A selective cull was undertaken and the carcases of older animals (those thirty months old or over) were removed from sale. Almost immediately, the

European Union banned all exports of British beef. It was a ban that would only be lifted (in part) in November 1998, though the French government proved intransigent, maintaining the ban on imports until 2002. It is, perhaps, still too early to assess the *full* implications of the BSE crisis of the 1990s, which influenced a downswing in domestic beef consumption and disrupted exports for a considerable time. Needless to say, the outbreak of Foot and Mouth Disease in 2001 merely added to farming's woes, and threatened to undermine the health of an entire industry that was just beginning to reassert its position after the challenges of the nineties. In total, over one million animals were culled in 2001–02, costs rose (particularly for sheep farmers), exports once again were curtailed and the tourism on which an increasing number of Galloway and Border farming communities relied was severely undermined.[140] Many farming enterprises simply did not survive.

Throughout the century, Scotland differed from her southern neighbours in the size and character of ownership of her productive agriculture units. Leaving aside the unique nature of crofting tenure in the north-west (the particular experience of the crofting counties will be addressed later), in 1908, over one half of holdings in the lowland counties were below 50 acres and just over 5 per cent were over 300 acres.[141] By 1947, there were 77,500 agricultural holdings in Scotland of which only 32,000 were classified by the Department of Agriculture as 'full-time' farms. At this time, the average size of holding in Scotland was 57 acres, ten acres less than the UK average.[142] However, Scotland also boasted a considerable proportion of large interests. Estimates from 1977 indicated that 87 per cent of the Scottish land mass was in private ownership and that, of this, estates of 1,000 acres and more accounted for over 72 per cent.[143] As early as mid century, almost half the total net income of farmers in Scotland could be accounted for by the production of 9,000 holdings, each over 150 acres, and owner-occupied farms over 300 acres accounted for 41 per cent of the Scottish acreage under crops and grass.[144] After 1950, the control of Scottish agriculture was marked by a further process of concentration. In the thirty years up to 1980, 20–25,000 holdings either went out of production or were amalgamated within bigger concerns.[145] The steadings abandoned by former farming families were now ripe for renovation by property developers and, between January 1985 and September 1990, seventy-eight farm steadings in the Borders Region alone were given planning permission principally for housing conversions. It was a trend that would grow in popularity.

The designer homes of the 1980s, however, were a world away from the typical housing of the Scottish rural community at the start of the twentieth century. Then, bothies and chaumers housed generations of single male workers, their kists territorially lining the walls and their Sunday suits hanging like curtains on either side of small windows.[146] For the families of farm servants, conditions were, if anything, often more desperate. The Scottish Board of Health, in 1925, estimated that the shortage of houses in rural districts amounted to 20,989.[147] And the housing that was available was often very poor. 'Farm Servant' wrote to the *Scottish Farmer* in October 1927:

> For six months I lived in an old house which used to be used for cattle, and was cleaned out prior to my arrival. This was on a particular farm in Fifeshire. The tiled roof leaked like a sieve, and the bed (which, by the way, had mice in the tick) was at the further end under the better portion of it.

Poor housing was not just an urban phenomenon but reform took time. Is it any wonder that many chose not to wait?

Due in part to the smaller size of average holdings, the importance of hill grazing, lower labour costs and the dominance of livestock production, Scottish agriculture was relatively slow to engage with the developments which led to the mechanisation of agriculture. In 1917, the Board of Agriculture for Scotland (BoAS) estimated that there were only 162 tractors north of the border, compared to 135,418 horses operating in the industry.[148] Yet, a year later, Robert Munro, the Scottish Secretary, declared confidently, in the first edition of the *Scottish Journal of Agriculture*, that '[t]he motor tractor has come to stay'.[149] The influence of motor traction took time to emerge – between 1919 and 1938, the number of horses for agricultural purposes declined to 105,000 but, even by the end of the 1930s, it has been suggested that tractors contributed less than one quarter of the motive power on Scottish farms.[150] War was to change all this. The Second World War saw the numbers of privately owned tractors in Scotland rise significantly to 19,000 and, additionally, government-owned tractors ploughed almost 120,000 acres in 1942 and 1943.[151] In a BBC broadcast in March 1942, Walter Elliot described such changes in memorable prose: 'Tractors – climbing like beetles along the slopes of hills, or chug-chugging through the haughs like very large mechanical turtles'.[152]

After a sluggish start, mechanisation continued apace in Scotland in the second half of the twentieth century. By 1970, there were only 1,402 horses for agricultural purposes on Scottish farms; by 1961, there were 60,000 tractors in operation; and, in the 1950s and 1960s, innovations in labour-saving harvesting and milking machines – alongside new scientific methods encouraged by the Rowett Institute (established in 1920), the Macauley Institute (established in 1930) and others – succeeded in altering for ever, the character and culture of Scottish farming.[153] For one former female farm servant (bondager) from the Borders, progress had come at a cost. Jean Leid, in conversation with the oral historian, Ian MacDougall, reflected:

> Well, ah wis sorry tae give up ferm work, ah wis, right enough, because ah liked it. But, ah mean, there's naething tae it now – mechanisation. They've spoiled it a'. They were the happy days then, ah mean, ee wis a' . . . When ee wis on the ferms then ee a' kent yin another. But nowadays, ee see, it's a' this contract work. There are nae workers, hardly any workers left.[154]

In 1921 there had been 21,772 female farm workers employed in Scotland. At mid century only 5,874 remained.[155]

Fishing

> In the 1930s, Aberdeen's fish market rang with the early morning noises of thousands of fish being slapped on a stone floor, with the crying of hungry gulls, with the creak of derricks, the stammer of steam winches, and the hoarse sirens of trawlers trying to get out from the stern-to-stern and port-to-starboard crush at the quay-side.[156]

The scene would have been familiar to older generations of Scotland's fishing communities, but in many ways much had changed even since 1900. Over the course of the twentieth century, Scotland's fishing industry responded – sometimes profitably and sometimes to its disadvantage – to changes in world demand for its catch. This can be seen most clearly in the decline of the herring fisheries, the technological advance of the industry and the regional concentration of the industry and its ancillary trades.

On the eve of the Great War, nearly 33,000 fishermen contributed to the 90,000 workers in the Scottish fishing industry as a whole, and the value of the herring alone landed at Scottish ports amounted to over £2 million, around 80 per cent of which was destined for European markets.[157] By the 1920s, however, the disruption caused by war (in terms of boats requisitioned by government or sunk or damaged as a result of enemy action), the loss of key eastern European markets and frequent coal shortages left the herring fleet a shadow of its former self.[158] By 1926, it was estimated that fewer than 67,000 were involved in the fishing industry as a whole and declining prices for herring, combined with the protection of foreign markets in the 1930s and the challenge of ring netting, meant that both output and employment in the industry fell. In 1937, Russia and Japan together exported fish to the value of £3.3 million to Britain while at least seventy trawlers were laid up at Aberdeen.[159] For the herring fishermen, average earnings had fallen from £51 in 1929 to about £12 in 1933.[160] As early as 1930, Peter Anson recorded:

> No boys or lads can be persuaded to go to sea, when, as they say, the fishing has so little to offer them . . . If you ask an old fisherman of Stonehaven why the young lads of today will not go to sea, he will shake his head and tell you that it's because they will na' work, and prefer to live on the dole: they are a different breed to their forefathers. Whatever may be the cause, the fishermen's quarter of Stonehaven gives one the impression of tragic decay.[161]

White fish sales faired better in these years but, even in the demersal sector, competition from English ports such as Hull challenged the Scottish market share. Many fishermen sold their vessels to work as waged seamen for a larger interest, bought smaller boats to focus on the shellfish market or held out as best they could until seine netting in the 1940s and 1950s went some way to reviving trade. In 1950, for the first time in Scotland, the seine netters out-fished the trawl fleet.[162] But war had had serious consequences for this ailing industry – 671 Scottish boats were requisitioned and around 17,000 fishermen served in the navy or the merchant marine during the Second World War. In the Scottish fishing villages, old men and boys kept the industry alive.[163] Peace was to bring little in the way of a reprieve and, in the later 1940s, the herring catch stagnated, amounting to around 2 million hundredweight.[164] Thereafter decline was dramatic. Landings at Peterhead of the 'silver darlings' fell from 108,900 crans in 1952 to under 7,000 in 1964, as inshore waters were effectively fished out, and Scottish boats faced the dual challenge of Norwegian vessels with their effective purse nets.[165] By 1960, fishing and its ancillary industries employed around 30,000 but, by 1986, this figure had dropped to 16,000.[166]

The challenge from technology, for the most part, was met effectively by the Scottish fleet as far as its resources and ownership structure would allow. Sailing drifters still made up around 72 per cent of the fleet in 1914 but steam-powered vessels soon came to dominate the industry. In 1911, Scotland boasted 783 steam drifters and, by 1913, 218 steam trawlers operated out of Aberdeen alone.[167] In 1929, John Grierson's film documentary, *Drifters*, confirmed this change. It recorded, 'The herring fishing has changed. Its story was once an idyll of brown sails and village harbours – its story is now an epic of steam and steel.' But, by the eve of the Second World War, the Scottish fleet was aging – in 1939, the average age of the Scottish trawlers in Aberdeen was about twenty-one years and 108 of the 277 vessels in Aberdeen were twenty-five years old or over. In Hull at the same time, only fifty-four out of 330 vessels were more than a quarter century old.[168] The Scottish Home Department's film of 1947, *Caller Herrin'*, while emphasising the support of government and the value of scientific research for the industry, was in stark contrast to the optimism of Grierson (1898–1972) less than twenty years before, noting, 'Many boats are old and their gear is wearing out.'

Oil-fired engines made their first appearance in Scotland around 1906, though real changes only arrived with diesel-powered vessels that came to dominance in the 1950s. John Robb from Newhaven started fishing in 1947 and remembered the impact of the first diesel trawlers that fished out of Granton:

> One diesel trawler could probably catch as much as three steam trawlers. They were more efficient. On an old steam trawler, if the steam went back, the boat was just bobbing up and down, but with the diesel engine everything was steady power, faster. They used the same nets but they were more efficient and more powerful. As the price of fish went down and the price of coal rose, the diesels cost less to run. The last steam trawler here was the *Fort Rannoch* in about 1957. If the steam trawler went home with 500 or 600 boxes the diesel would be bringing in 1,000. And it was cleaner, with no coal to shovel and no ashes to haul up.[169]

In the following decade, Scottish fishermen, like their competitors, were not slow to appreciate the value of changes in hull construction (notably the use of glass reinforced plastic), labour-saving devices such as modern mechanised winches and the arrival of navigational aids and echo sounders. Even the herring fleet was modernised in the late 1970s and, by 2002, this thirty-three-strong fleet was generating average gross earnings of £98 million.[170]

Regional concentration and amalgamation also marked the ever-changing fishing fleet in the twentieth century but not in like measure – ownership patterns remained stubbornly individualistic. The east coast ports landed around three-quarters of the herring catch in 1913 although, by the end of the century, Ullapool had become the base for the pelagic sector. Meanwhile, in the east, smaller ports were eclipsed by Aberdeen and, latterly, Peterhead as the foremost market places for the industry's goods and services in Scotland. Aberdeen had been manufacturing artificial ice from as early as the 1890s and boasted special rail and motor vehicle services to get its catches to the consumer ahead of the competition.[171] Certain ports held out for some time – in the 1950s, for example, Fraserburgh alone boasted thirty-one curers, twenty-one kipperers, seven boatbuilders, seven marine engineers, four fish-salesmen, three barking stations, a fishmeal factory, a ship-repair company and a barrel factory.[172] But by the end of the century, along the northern, eastern and island coasts, all that remained of earlier remote curing stations and a vibrant processing industry were ruins and dim memories. By contrast, the ownership patterns of the first half of the century largely withstood the travails of the industry and were still evident in its closing decades. The Scottish tradition was for owner skippers or joint ownership among crew members. This contrasted sharply with the English pattern from as early as the interwar years when 52 per cent of the Hull fleet was owned by twelve companies with over nineteen vessels each while, in Aberdeen, only 9 per cent of the local fleet was owned by twenty-eight companies with around nine vessels each.[173] On the positive side, this bred an individualistic spirit in Scotland which encouraged many to persevere in an industry that, at times, was a cruel master. But the system had its problems – it meant that owners had limited resources for improvements and experimentation, especially when most boats were funded by personal bank loans, and, when catch quotas were introduced, it limited the individual fisherman's chances of making sizeable profits to reinvest in his craft even more. From the 1920s, various governments had encouraged amalgamations in the industry to little avail. In 2004, the Royal Society of Edinburgh still saw the need to encourage the industry to consider the case for reforming into a corporate structure where efficiencies would more easily be achieved in an increasingly regulated market.[174]

CONCLUSION

In the second half of the century, the development and relative prosperity of the agriculture and fishing industries was largely determined – or at least circumscribed – by government policy and the priorities of supra-national trading bodies, such as the European Community, which few could have anticipated in the period up to 1939. (We will return to this in due course.) This meant that, like the nationalised industries, socio-political as well as – and sometimes as much as – economic concerns were allowed to influence their direction. Being industries that also doubled up as the guardians of the nation's natural heritage, this is perhaps not surprising – Scots were prone to thinking of them as holding the country's resources in trust. What is more surprising is the extent to which characteristics normally associated with the heavy industries discussed earlier were also evident in the history of Scotland's primary producers in the twentieth century. Regional specialisation, the persistence of family ownership in an economy being sculpted by corporatism, the loss of foreign markets that had sustained these sectors at their height in the earlier part of the century, the relatively slow uptake of technological improvements and failure to match foreign competition on price were all evident for long enough periods in the course of the century to give one the impression of an endemic Scottish disease in industry from which even the traditional sectors were not immune. Similarly, the consolation typically sought in high quality products and skilled workers betokened little more than desperation, especially after the emergence of BSE and growing public concern regarding over-fishing in the post-war decades. It was surely little more than short-sighted snobbery that encouraged one commentator at the height of the interwar depression in Scottish fishing, when boats and crews lay idle, to scoff that 'the fish and chip shop has no use for good quality Scottish fish'.[175]

The lasting importance of the heavy industries in Scotland and the continued higher profile of agriculture and fishing point to important structural features of the Scottish economy which influenced its direction throughout the course of the twentieth century. Innovation had to evolve within and through this structure, regardless of what was happening elsewhere in the world. As C. E. V. Leser noted in the 1950s, this had important implications for any new ventures:

> The predominance of heavy industry in Scotland has a significance extending beyond the vexed question of stability and vulnerability. It means, for example, a predominance of mechanical engineering over electrical and chemical engineering; a comparative absence of mass production techniques; a corresponding demand for skilled men and above all for *manual* skills; a demand also for heavy metal products, particularly steel plates.[176]

This was the environment in which the 'new' willed itself to survive, far less thrive; these were the interests with whom new industries had to negotiate; this was the culture in which new ideas sought their place. Scottish industry in the late twentieth century could not simply leave the past behind.

THREE The Novelty of the New

In the early 1950s, economists noted the 'comparative indifference of Scottish industry to advances in technology, to new equipment, new knowledge, and new opportunities for development' and 'an inability or reluctance' to use new materials.[1] A decade later, attitudes appeared to have changed little. Burns and Stalker in 1961, for example, highlighted a 'general apprehension' on the part of Scottish industrialists towards the amalgamation of electronics technology within the engineering industry and a suspicion regarding 'long-haired types [who] amble[d] about in white coats'.[2] Such anxiety, often mixed with hostility, proved somewhat short-sighted as markets for traditional manufactures contracted.

In a more fundamental sense, such conservatism also meant that the new industries that *did* establish themselves in Scotland did so without significant input from established manufacturing interests and thus, not fully integrated with existing producers, failed to spur the restructuring of the economy that had become a necessity by the 1960s.

NEW INDUSTRIES AND NEW APPROACHES – CHARACTERISTICS

In 1935, 'new industries' accounted for 11 per cent of net output in Scotland.[3] Between 1939 and 1945, employment in the production of motor vehicles, cycles and aircraft rose to nearly three times its 1939 level – from 18,340 to 52,260.[4] Chemicals increased their share of the workforce from 7,890 to 11,510 between 1939 and 1947 and, by 1948, the net output from this sector accounted for 4 per cent of Scottish industrial production.[5] New industries were clearly contributing more to the Scottish economy by the end of the Second World War than hitherto. However, comparison with similar developments in the rest of Great Britain is illuminating.

Between 1925 and 1935, employment in the fastest growing new industries in Scotland rose by only 20,000.[6] By 1948, the net output of

Scotland's aircraft manufacturers accounted for only 4.7 per cent of the British total and occupied only 5.5 per cent of workers in that sector in Great Britain.[7] The manufacture of electrical wires and cables in Scotland employed only 2.4 per cent of the British workforce and the net output of electrical engineering, in general, north of the Border accounted for only 2.6 per cent of the British total.[8] A similar state of affairs was evident in other growth sectors – pharmaceuticals, light machine tools and, particularly, motor car manufacture, which employed only 1 per cent of British workers in that industry north of the Tweed. The country that prided itself on its inventors was clearly falling behind.

In 1928, it cost £385 to buy a 15.9hp Scottish-made Arrol-Johnston motor car when a Morris Oxford tourer cost £315 and a Model-T Ford cost £150. Scotland certainly produced a high-quality product, but this was the age of the mass market and price mattered. By this time the Argyll Motor Co. (est. 1899), whose grand Alexandria site had the capacity to manufacture 2,000 cars a year as early as 1905 (though it never did), was little more than a dim memory. In a single day in 1913 at the Brooklands track in Surrey, an Argyll had broken thirteen world records but the company itself was liquidated in 1914 and the works turned over to munitions production during the Great War.[9] Quality meant little if no one was prepared to buy.

From the mid 1950s, a widening gap opened up between Scottish and UK indices of production and productivity. The Toothill Report of November 1961, which indicated that around 62 per cent of Scottish employment was concentrated in slow-growing industries, merely confirmed a state of affairs that had been evident for some time. In 1965, the economist Gavin McCrone urged that '[p]riority needs to be given to investment which will generate growth of output and result in higher employment'. Coal and shipbuilding, he warned, 'cannot do this, and one needs to look to the newer industries where an expansion in the market may be expected'.[10] One wondered if anyone was really listening.

Infrastructural improvements in the Scottish economy in the second half of the twentieth century did much to attract new industries but there were still problems. By 1954, Scottish electricity providers had been organised into two generating and supply bodies and, following nationalisation in 1957, could guarantee power to 2.3 million customers across Scotland by the 1960s.[11] But transport could still pose difficulties. By 1960, Scotland boasted over 28,000 miles of public roads but, in Glasgow, congestion had already begun to assert its influence and average speeds, at 8mph, were the slowest in the country.[12] In the north, no trunk road in the Highlands was wider than 18 feet and average train speeds between Inverness and Edinburgh were around 30mph.[13] In 1971, British Leyland would attribute a significant proportion of the deficit recorded by their Scottish interests to the £4.6 million per year they spent on transport in the north.[14]

Perhaps most serious of all was the character of the labour market. While a survey in 1911 discovered that over 60 per cent of Scottish ship-yard workers were skilled men, the skills demanded by the old heavy industries were frequently not suited to the 'new'.[15] In the 1960s, the Scottish car industry repeatedly suffered from a lack of operatives experienced in assembly-line techniques.[16] At other times, problems connected with industrial relations would eventually offset the earlier counter-attractions of a skilled workforce. In 1973, for example, 841 man-hours were lost at Chrysler's Linwood car plant as a result of industrial disputes.[17] In the 1950s, many new companies in Scotland co-operated, if reluctantly, with trade unions but, by the 1970s, Scotland's reputation for industrial militancy and a non-union culture in incoming corporations made some employers more sceptical of Scottish labour's merits and more resistant to recognising trade unions in the day-to-day operations of their Scottish factories. In 1954, the Amalgamated Engineering Union (AEU) had only fifty members in the 400-strong workforce at the Greenock plant of International Business Machines (IBM) and its shop stewards reported, 'Vicious industrial relations, regimentation of workpeople by management amounting to terrorism. Discharged on the slightest pretext and flimsiest reasons without notice – even for divulging your wage rate.'[18] In the 1990s, not one semiconductor plant in Scotland had ever been unionised.[19]

The industrial revolution of the late eighteenth century had been marked by internal investment and many home-grown innovations but the 'new' revolution of the period after 1945 drew Scotland into a precarious reliance on foreign capital, research and enterprise. Scottish producers continued to invest abroad but proved exceedingly disin-clined to finance ventures in the new industries and the growing non-financial service sector at home. When Roy Thomson (Lord Thomson of Fleet, 1894–1976) sought Scottish partners to tender for the new independent television station in Scotland in 1954, he came face-to-face with this reluctant elite:

> Starting at the top, I began to write to all the dukes and lords and heads of clans; I presented my proposition to law-lords and heads of Scottish businesses; I turned to the noble chairmen of insurance companies and banks; I came down the scale to provosts and

well-to-do shopkeepers; and I eventually even approached the Scottish Co-operative Society and the Labour Party . . .

Many excuses were offered – other commitments, a dislike of TV, a conviction that the losses being suffered by the TV companies in England would certainly be incurred in Scotland, a willingness but no wherewithal, 'my company would not like my connection with this enterprise' and so on . . .

It is ironic to look at those refusals, to think of the money those men, some of them shrewd in business and affairs, could have made. Among them were Lord Bilsland, Lord Rosebery, Sir Ian Colquhoun, George Outram & Co. (publishers of the *Glasgow Herald*), Hector McNeil MP, Sir Hugh Fraser, Sir A. B. King (the Glasgow cinema owner), Lord Elgin, the Duke of Hamilton, the Mackintosh of Mackintosh, Sir Harold Yarrow, Admiral Dalrymple-Hamilton, Sir Will Darling . . . the Earl of Crawford, Lord Weir, Brendon Bracken and Lord Beaverbrook.[20]

In the end, a personal loan (admittedly from a Scottish banker) provided the capital for Thomson's project.

Scottish capital had been investing abroad for generations – 'Scotland revels in foreign investment', noted *Blackwood's Edinburgh Magazine* in October 1884.[21] The favoured investment mechanisms were typically Trusts and all Scotland's major cities boasted such companies, with Dundee being particularly successful in this regard. While North American mortgages and railroads soaked up a vast quantity of this wealth, on the eve of the Great War investment further afield was also notable. The Scottish Mortgage Investment Trust has its origins in the Straits Mortgage and Trust Company (est. 1909), which invested heavily in the rubber industry of Malaysia and Ceylon, and the British Investment Trust had £1.1 million in Latin American railroads in the Edwardian period.[22] In the years that followed, profits made from industrial mergers and amalgamations in the interwar years provided a lucrative source of wealth for the Trusts to exploit, despite the onset of a global depression. As a consequence, the relative importance of the investment sector in Scotland in these years of economic instability actually increased, although comparatively little capital was being invested at home.[23] By the 1970s, despite the interruptions to trading caused by the Second World War and the disappearance of some of the smaller Trusts after the 1950s, Scottish investment companies remained a profitable undertaking and were beginning to invest – if at one remove – in the native merchant banking sector and the North Sea oil industry. The total assets of the largest investment group, Bailie Gifford, amounted to

£224.8 million in 1976, for example. Yet, as Stephen McKendrick and others wrote in 1985, such success masked failure elsewhere in the economy, most notably in native industry. Ironically, 'the roots of Scotland's decline are to be found in a "surfeit of imperialism" rather than, as is so often made out, the country's position of clientage or dependence'.[24]

Quite simply, in the 1940s and 1950s, indigenous enterprise was slow to seize the initiative in new areas of production. In his study of the west of Scotland, Anthony Slaven notes:

> Ten American companies had set up by 1949, and 41 by 1960, five other companies were in joint Anglo-American control and four had been taken over by American interests. These 50 concerns employed 25,000 people and occupied six million square feet of factory space.[25]

By 1964, direct investment by US companies was supporting 52,000 Scottish jobs – 7.2 per cent of total manufacturing employment.[26] And, between 1950 and 1968, employment in the manufacturing sector dependent directly on US firms rose fourfold.[27] In Dundee alone, National Cash Registers (NCR), who arrived on the banks of the Tay in 1945, had nine factory complexes in the city by 1969, covering over a million square feet of space and employing 6,000 people. The dollar shortage of the early post-war years was clearly one determinant encouraging initial American investment, as were later US concerns about access to the markets of the European Community – in 1982, the EC represented 18–20 per cent of the world market for semiconductors, for example.[28] However, the trend for inward investment also included a strong English presence. Of the 218 incoming firms between 1937 and 1950, a majority came from the rest of the UK.[29] By the 1970s 40 per cent of manufacturing labour in Scotland was employed by English-owned firms.[30] 'Increasingly', wrote Neil Buxton, 'the level of Scottish economic activity came to depend on the policies and performance of incoming firms whose headquarters remained firmly based either in England or abroad'.[31] It was a trend that was only accelerated by Britain's entry into the EC in the seventies: the number of units owned by continental European companies rose from 30 in 1973 to 73 in 1981.[32]

Many incoming firms were multinational in their operations and interests. Their Scottish investments were simply one part of a much larger whole and native Scottish expectations frequently proved incidental to their development strategies. The Singer Manufacturing Company of Clydebank is a case in point. Singers established a presence in Glasgow as early as 1867 and moved to the Kilbirnie plant – then, the largest sewing machine factory in the world – in 1885. Demand for the Clydebank machines secured the jobs of the Clydebank workers until the 1940s but then post-war competition (especially from Japan) led to a drop in company profits in the 1950s of around 25 per cent. Retrenchment became the watchword and job losses were initiated – the numbers employed in Clydebank fell from around 10,000 in 1945 to 7,000 in 1970. By then, the Clydebank machines were old-fashioned and expensive when compared to the models of competitors and the factory had developed a reputation for poor labour relations and high production costs. In 1978, the Clydebank factory was operating at only 35 per cent of its capacity. At a time when the company was expanding elsewhere in Europe (for example, in Italy and Germany), they were running down their Scottish operations and, in 1980, the Clydebank factory closed.[33]

Regardless of the evident risks involved, the momentum behind attracting foreign investment was hard to resist. In October 1963, for example, Michael Noble (1913–1984), the Secretary of State for Scotland, flew to the USA to attract firms to 'the old country', with the Scottish Council (Development and Industry) preparing the way by sending out over 2,000 letters to prospective US business partners.[34] Still, in 1997–98, Scottish government agencies were investing great time and effort in attracting foreign business and, in that year alone, eighty-seven inward investment projects were secured, involving the creation or retention of around 18,000 jobs.[35] Whether such firms, and others like them, were as committed to the Scottish economy as it was to attracting them remains to be seen. Certainly, the historical record fuels a suspicion that Scottish interests were seldom prioritised when global markets declined.

NEW INDUSTRIES AND NEW APPROACHES – CONSEQUENCES

Four principal consequences derived from the origins and nature of development characteristic of the new industries in Scottish manufacturing that would have repercussions for the wider economy throughout the second half of the century and beyond. These were: firstly, the loss of 'native' control over the direction of some of the fastest growing areas of industry: secondly, low levels of new firm formation and impediments to entrepreneurship; thirdly, persistent high levels of unemployment and relatively low levels of growth; and, fourthly, the un-integrated development of new industries within the manufacturing sector.

In 1948, a Scottish Socialist Party pamphlet exhorted its loyal Scottish readers to 'FREE THEIR COUNTRY FROM ALIEN CONTROL SO

THAT THE DEVELOPMENT OF SCOTLAND'S GREAT RESOURCES MAY
ENRICH THE WHOLE OF THE SCOTTISH PEOPLE'.[36] In 1957, the
Scottish National Party (SNP) published an economic review in which it
detailed, at length, the decline of native business and the encroachment
of English firms north of the Border.[37] Seven years later, a Fabian
Society author seemed to share the nationalists' concerns when he
bemoaned the 'remote control' of Scottish industry and the 'erosion of
local responsibility'.[38] In the second half of the twentieth century,
foreign investment in and control over Scottish manufacturing enterprises merely reinforced a trend towards increasing external control,
epitomised in the first fifty years by English takeovers of Scottish
companies.[39] This dynamic was a source of concern for politicians of
nearly all political colours and was reinforced by the centralising
tendencies of nationalisation in the 1950s and 1960s. Nevertheless,
until the downturn in the economy from the late 1950s, fears that
Scotland no longer shaped her own economic destiny and could no
longer safeguard national prosperity appeared unfounded and unduly
pessimistic.

By the 1970s and 1980s, however, the material – as opposed to the
theoretical – dangers of this state of affairs were made manifest when
many large interests withdrew from Scotland. Thirteen hundred redundancies were announced at Talbot's Linwood automobile plant in May
1980; East Kilbride's BSR record player factory, employing 1,700, closed
a month later; Ayrshire lost 750 jobs when ICI closed its chemical works
there in October; and, in February the following year, Talbot's production in Linwood finally ceased with the loss of a further 4,800 jobs.[40]
Such dislocation was also felt outwith the Central Belt when, for
example, in 1982, the British Aluminium Company's Invergordon
smelter closed, with the direct loss of around 890 jobs and a further 360
indirectly dependent on the smelter.[41] With bewildering regularity,
closures and redundancies in industries that had been hailed as Scotland's
industrial future were announced and there seemed little Scottish
industry and government could do to stem the tide. The Scottish novelist,
James Kelman, summed it up in 1990, saying, 'For hundreds of thousands of people throughout Great Britain the last decade or more has
been a form of nightmare . . . we are inured to bad news.'[42]

For a time, the Scottish renaissance in electronics manufacture
appeared to promise a way forward. By the end of the 1950s, Ferranti,
NCR, Honeywell and IBM had a presence in Scotland. In the 1960s, they
were joined by National Semiconductors and Motorola and, despite a
period of recession in the 1970s, new Japanese investments in these years
ensured that electronics manufacture in Scotland grew significantly. In

the 1980s alone, around 150 new electronics companies were set up in Scotland and, by 1992, 50,000 Scots were employed in the industry, with an additional 4,000 involved in software development.[43] Five years later, Scotland's electronics industry accounted for 35 per cent of the European market and 10 per cent of world personal computer output.[44]

However, a pre-occupation with external investment had a pernicious affect on new-firm formation and entrepreneurship. Even before the emergence of Japanese manufacturers, nearly half of Scotland's electronics workers were employed by foreign firms and a large proportion of employees of UK firms worked for companies whose headquarters were located south of the Border.[45] By the 1980s, it was clear that 'the degree of external ownership and control of Scottish industry' acted as a 'brake' on new-firm formation which, by the 1990s, was described as 'laggardly'. At this time Scottish companies employed only 17 per cent of the electronics workforce in Scotland[46] and many English regions were outstripping Scotland's economic performance – a trend partly explained by a 'lack of entrepreneurial culture' in the north.[47] Investment from outside did little to address these areas of concern and the relatively low profile of research and development (R&D) in the branch plants of corporate firms in Scotland failed to nurture local talent in a way that might have fostered independent initiatives. In 1982, around 40 per cent of the US plants in Scotland undertook no research and development work at all and only around half the R&D that was undertaken had significant developmental potential.[48] Even Scottish economists bemoaned university environments that failed to reward the speculative interests that had been the hallmark of earlier generations.[49] Amongst the small firms that did emerge in some areas, a marked lack of ambition was evident and economic leaders, in vain it seemed, urged Scotland to retain her 'renegades, optimists and achievers', as many of 'Scotland's finest' continued to seek more lucrative prospects elsewhere.[50] Emigration rose significantly in the late 1950s and, by the 1960s, between roughly thirty and forty thousand Scots left on an annual basis. While the number of emigrants fell in the 1970s, net emigration remained higher than the levels of natural growth in the population in the seventies and eighties, causing the overall population to decline. It would not be until the opening years of the twenty-first century that native Scottish enterprises would go some way to quelling the impulse to leave – Edinburgh- and Dundee-based computer and video-game designers established a reputation for innovative software technology and world-class biotechnology and genetic advances developed by the Roslin Institute and others whispered of a promising future for these areas.

Nevertheless, the rise to prominence of new science-based industries in the late twentieth century failed to match the speed of decline in the old manufacturing sectors. The new industries also demanded resources and labour (typically young female labour) underutilised by older industries and hence could neither fully exploit nor totally absorb the redundant plant and workforce discarded by heavy industry. Unemployment in Scotland, as a consequence, remained higher than the national average and impeded growth in the domestic market for the very consumer durables that the new industries were manufacturing.

As we have seen, in Scotland, new industries were not effectively integrated within the wider industrial structure, largely as a consequence of low levels of native investment in their futures and their failure to influence the processes and product range of established interests. Such a state of affairs became even more apparent as the century progressed. New industries generally failed either to exploit local manufactures in their own production processes or alternatively, if local products did not meet their demands, bring about sufficient demand to encourage the creation of new firms. Rather, corporate interests in electronics tended to source products and components within their own company or from established manufacturers with whom they had 'an understanding'. From the beginning, NCR, Honeywell, Burroughs and IBM had set the trend by importing American components simply to be assembled at their Scottish plants.[51] Thirty years later, little had changed – Scottish manufacturers provided only around 12 per cent of the annual purchases made by foreign-owned electronics firms in 'Silicon Glen' and the products supplied tended to be easy-to-manufacture items.[52] Even Scottish subcontractors were not guaranteed new custom – in 1979, only 30 per cent of subcontracted work was sourced locally.[53] By 1990, Scotland boasted 'islands of automation and excellence' but these were isolated in terms of the wider economy and offered 'limited opportunities for technology transfer'.[54] By the end of the century, electronics, like many of the 'new industries' that had emerged earlier in the twentieth century, by failing to develop substantial and durable local multiplier effects, had been unable to effect necessary structural changes in the Scottish economy. In 1994, Scottish Enterprise, the nation's principal development agency, itself acknowledged that one of its major challenges was to 'strengthen the links between foreign-owned and Scottish-owned companies'. It admitted that '[s]uch linkages are weak, and the Scottish economy is fragmented as a result'.[55]

'SCOTLAND'S OIL'

In 1964, the North Sea was divided into national sectors for the purposes of oil exploration, with the largest share (62,500 square miles) of the UK Continental Shelf (UKCS) technically falling under the jurisdiction of Scots Civil Law. This represented around one third of the North Sea area as a whole and over 20 per cent more than that allocated to the Netherlands.[56] Early UK exploration focused on gas resources in the southern areas of the British sector off East Anglia but signs of Scotland's eventual role in the oil industry were already evident. The first survey ship to dock in Aberdeen harbour arrived in 1964 and, in 1965, Shell became the first oil company to set up a permanent office in the city when they located to Market Street.[57] Five years later, British Petroleum (BP) discovered oil in the Forties Field around 100 miles north-east of Aberdeen, in the 'Scottish sector', and, within three years, the Brent and Ninian Fields were discovered. These were among the richest finds in the North Sea and, from its small beginnings, 19,000 Scottish jobs were attributable to the oil industry by 1975, with 7,000 of these in the north-east.[58] By 1980, the UK was self-sufficient in oil and, a year later, UK oil production exceeded 87 million tonnes, contributed £9.8 billion to the UK's GNP, fed the Treasury with annual taxation in the region of £6 billion and, in terms of international competition, was ranked seventh in the world.[59]

In the 1970s, oil lubricated a cultural and political renaissance in Scotland and promised much for an economy marked elsewhere by stagnation and decline. Over the next thirty years, however, the hopes of the 1970s proved illusory and the stimulus they gave to nationalism elsewhere in Scottish society failed to generate an enduring legacy, other than despair and a determination to learn a lesson from the experience. Oil could not withstand many of the pressures that challenged the older industrial sector and, in the end, proved just as incapable of resisting the corporate dollar and the allure of foreign investment as Scotland's new industries. Indeed, in one enterprise, oil illustrated several of the features of Scotland's twentieth-century economic metamorphosis we have already encountered. In its reliance on global trade, its regional concentration (this time in the north-east), the dominance of foreign interests, the relatively limited nature of spin-offs from the industry secured by Scottish firms and the significant role played by government, oil reflected the experience of the wider economy.

Peaks and troughs in the global oil market, as one might expect, had serious consequences for the exploitation of the North Sea. In the winter of 1973–74, partly as a consequence of the Yom Kippur War and changes in the policies of the Organization of the Petroleum Exporting Countries (OPEC), the price of oil quadrupled; again, in 1980, the Iran–Iraq War influenced an escalation of 150 per cent in the price of oil; and, in 1991, the Gulf War again disrupted production and gave rise to a further short-lived peak in oil prices. Such sharp increases artificially stimulated the extraction, processing and retail arms of the industry at various points in their history, only to be followed invariably by periods of declining prices when production had, once again, to be adjusted. The North Sea – a high-cost producer at the best of times, due to the inhospitable conditions in the area and the depths at which finds were made – often struggled to meet such changing circumstances. In the late 1990s, however, Scotland's oil producers instituted more collaborative working practices to keep the North Sea competitive in a period of price reduction worldwide. Styled the Cost Reduction Initiative for the New Era (CRINE, established in 1993) it was hoped the efficiencies it would bring would guarantee the future for the North Sea in an increasingly competitive worldwide market. New subsea technologies were also developed and the more sophisticated use of computer applications facilitated the evolution of smaller, more economic fields. By 1998, project capital and operating costs had been reduced by 30 per cent.

While clearly responsive to global stimuli, the Scottish oil industry also had a local dynamic. In February 1964, the *Glasgow Herald* identified a need to restore the vitality of Scotland's most northern city, Aberdeen.

Traditional industries are declining. The granite city is importing nearly all of its granite from Scandinavia and only a little can be quarried commercially from Rubislaw . . . Generally . . . wage rates are lower than in other parts of the country. A longer and a broader vision is necessary in the context of Aberdeen's now no longer isolated position. If it is not forthcoming, the vicious circle of the contraction of traditional industries and the consequent migration of skilled labour could become a spiral. More goods are imported into Aberdeen than leave the town and it is difficult to see how Aberdeen's service industries can close the gap indefinitely . . . Whether the new industry that Aberdeen needs will come from organic renewal within or outside is not clear.[60]

Three months later the *Herald* got its answer – the government approved the exploitation of oil and gas reserves in the UKCS. The newspaper announced, 'NORTH SEA MAY BE BRITAIN'S "TEXAS"'.[61] Although it was not immediately apparent, Aberdeen was to be the principal beneficiary of this offshore oil rush.

By the 1990s, the oil industry was an established feature of the economy of the north-east Scottish mainland and an unexpected boon to the communities of the Shetland Isles. Between 1971 and 1981, the population of Aberdeen grew by 30,000 and average earnings rose by nearly 20 per cent, to exceed the UK average.[62] By 1985, 50,000 jobs in Grampian Region were attributable to the oil industry.[63] During periods of high prices such as 1980, Aberdeen could take on the character of the Klondike. But, in turn, the north-east suffered in terms of jobs and property values when oil prices dropped – in 1986, for example, six thousand offshore and 22,000 onshore jobs were lost in the oil industry.[64] The industry itself was also not without real risks and, in July 1988, explosions and fire on the Piper Alpha platform killed 167 workers. Crisis shook the industry and regional confidence was seriously undermined.[65] At the close of the century, however, recovery had been effected and, while Aberdeen City recorded only half the GDP of Glasgow, its growth rate was the highest in Scotland.[66]

With the Brent Field and the Sullom Voe oil terminal in their vicinity, Shetlanders also benefited from oil exploration and extraction. Jonathan Wills, a former editor of the *Shetland Times*, has reflected:

> Lots of people got very rich very quickly ... Taxi drivers made money. Truck drivers. Bus companies made money. Up to 7,000 temporary workers arrived, and while a lot of goods and services to keep them supplied were imported, there was an enormous demand for local labour and local services, and quite rightly people who'd been working for a pittance for the same employer for 20 years, and taking a lot of stick as well, told them to stuff it. They went. They walked out and went to work for the oilies.[67]

In the longer term, the 1973 Zetland Act brought order to the early urgent bedlam of North Sea development for local islanders and ensured lasting returns. The Zetland County Council (later the Shetland Islands Council) was given significant powers to influence the policies of the oil giants on its doorstep and established a trust fund to safeguard its future and protect it from a downturn in the industry. The legislation also offered protection, unknown in the rest of Scotland, from unforeseen challenges of a political nature. Jonathan Wills, again: 'As a result of oil, Shetland was able to create, right in the middle of the Thatcher holocaust, the hurricane of Thatcherism, a miniature welfare state of Scandinavian proportions.'[68] By 1980, unemployment in the islands, which had stood at about 123 per cent of the UK average in the early seventies, had fallen to 45 per cent of the UK rate, school rolls were more buoyant than they had been for many years and car ownership had nearly doubled.[69] Oil had transformed the Shetlands.

With high oil prices in the early seventies, encouragement from governments demanding the speedy exploitation of their new-found wealth and a comparative lack of expertise in Scotland and the UK as a whole in oil extraction, rig and platform construction and onshore processing, US firms came to dominate Scotland's oil industry.[70] In the early days, American companies and US–UK consortia were major players in rig and platform construction but, while the UK's contribution to the offshore market rose to over 70 per cent by 1980, Scottish companies made up only 20 per cent.[71]

During the last thirty years of the century, the Dutch economic base benefited far more from offshore developments than Scottish interests, despite Scotland's far larger North Sea sector.[72] Two years after the discovery of the Forties Field, *all* the rigs constructed to exploit the UK's resources had been constructed outwith Britain.[73] Even by the mid 1980s, while the oil from the UKCS was piped ashore in Scotland, only 16 percent of that oil was refined in Scotland and 40 per cent in the UK as a whole.[74] Despite construction efforts in Ardsier, Nigg Bay, Loch Kishorn, Ardyne Point and Methil – supplemented by smaller yards in Dundee and Stornoway – by the mid 1990s, Scottish industry had contributed less than 30 per cent to the development of its own oil and gas reserves.[75] There was very little that was Scottish about Scotland's oil.

Scotland's thwarted dreams were summed up in the character and songs of 'Texas Jim' in John McGrath's political 'romp' through Highland history of 1974, the popular play *The Cheviot, the Stag and the Black, Black Oil*:

> There's a many a barrel of oil in the sea
> All waiting for drilling and piping to me
> I'll refine it in Texas, you'll get it, you'll see
> At four times the price that you sold it to me.[76]

In 1993, similar American characters turned up in Bill Forsyth's film *Local Hero*, intending to buy up land and properties in the fictional Furness area for the site of an oil refinery and storage base. The local inhabitants could 'smell the money' – 'We've been invaded by America. We're all going to be rich. We won't have anywhere to call home, but we'll be stinking rich.' They even mused on the relative merits of roomy Rolls-Royce and sporty Maserati motor cars – 'I can just see you getting four winter rams and a box of mackerel into the back of a Maserati.' In the end, however, the oilmen's legacy was ambiguous as it became increasingly obvious what the community would lose when they found riches.

The oil and gas coming ashore in Scotland was not counted as part of Scotland's regional product and, as a consequence, it is somewhat diffi-cult – beyond a consideration of employment growth, for example – to assess the true value of 'Scotland's oil' to the Scottish economy.[77] Indeed, theoretically this is a non-question as this disaggregated value does not exist – at least in administrative or fiscal terms. The entire output of the UK sector of the North Sea was attributed by governments to the UKCS, not to component nations. Scotland's place in the UK therefore had a fundamental impact on the way in which oil reserves were considered and accounted.

Oil was political. The role of changing governments had a major impact on the oil industry. In their initial desire for quick returns to address balance of payments difficulties and ease the public-sector borrowing requirement (PSBR), in their creation of the British National Oil Corporation in 1974 and its successors as the agents of public control, in their changing licensing and tax regime and their wider foreign policies, British governments determined the speed, character and profitability of North Sea oil in a fundamental way.[78] But oil revenue was largely considered at the level of macro-economic policy. Its potential role in the regeneration of *Scottish* industry was, if not incidental, at least secondary to wider UK interests. Yet again, Scotland's position within the UK state determined the extent to which industry could respond in its own interests to international stimuli and to the bounty lying offshore. Even the seabed was subject to the legacy of 1707.

New industries frequently had to address the suspicions of 'the old' north of the Border; new technologies had to find their place in the customs and traditions of a mature industrial nation and older dreams of industrial supremacy would not easily fade to reveal new visions of Scotland's economic future. Throughout, by its action and its inaction, the state was, directly and indirectly, instrumental in shaping Scotland's economy.

FOUR   Interests, Institutions and
        Interference

In the nineteenth century, free trade in world markets and minimal government intervention in the Scottish economy were identified as intrinsic to the nature and success of Scottish industry. The experience of global depression, structural unemployment, the loss of British colonies and the trauma of two World Wars, however, challenged such attitudes and signalled major changes in Britain's economic role on the world stage. At the end of the twentieth century, government intervention, economic and regional planning and British membership of international trading bodies had changed the economic culture inherited by Scotland in 1900 beyond all recognition. This was by no means unique to Scotland. The rest of the UK was also transformed as state and capital, alternately and in concert, dictated the direction of economic policy and shaped regional infrastructures for economic and social ends.

But Scotland *was* different. The maintenance of the quasi-independent legal and educational systems in part enshrined in the Union settlement of 1707; the persistent operation of other distinctive Scottish institutions, such as banks and local government bodies; increasing administrative devolution and the existence, from 1999, of a separate legislative assembly in the north; and the peculiar nature of Scotland's economic profile vis-à-vis her Union partners – these factors all dictated that the character and consequences of government intervention north of the Tweed would, in many ways, be distinct from elsewhere in the UK.

INTERESTS AND INTEREST RATES

The Scottish banking network inherited from the nineteenth century usefully illustrates how, in a union state, certain features unique to individual nations managed to thrive and dictate distinctive development patterns. As a successful service industry in the 1990s, it also offers a useful counterpoint to the tale so far which has, at times, been marked by near unremitting gloom. Scotland's banks had a long lineage – the

Bank of Scotland was established in 1695 and the Royal Bank in 1727 – and, despite failures, affiliations, amalgamations and mergers, eight Scottish clearing banks survived the first half of the twentieth century. Their individual histories were marked by periods of growth, diversification and changing relationships with their southern rivals but a number of themes across the Scottish sector in the twentieth century are evident.

Initially Scottish banks maintained an almost exclusively Scottish branch network but, with early forays into London and then the north of England before overseas offices became common in the 1960s, Scotland's banks expanded their geographical profile. Typically the English branches of Scottish banks had greater success than branches of English banks in the north, which, even at the close of the century, remained few in number. Yet the Scots were not to have it all their own way. At the beginning of the twentieth century, banks and average bank deposits were larger in Scotland than in the south. 'The ten Scottish banks had average deposits of £10.7m compared with the 67 English banks with average deposits of less than £1m.'[1] But the size advantage did not last long in the new century – by 1918 English banks numbered twenty, with average deposits of £98 million, while the remaining eight Scottish banks retained average deposits of only £35 million.[2]

Amalgamations were inevitable, though not always entirely popular if they threatened regional identity and local economic autonomy. When the Bank of Scotland took over the Caledonian Bank of Inverness in 1907, local letter writers to the press were aggrieved and one wrote, 'Inverness sleeps while it is being strangled for premature burial.'[3] Similarly, the Aberdeen offices of the North of Scotland Bank felt increasingly marginalised following its merger with the Clydesdale some forty-three years later.[4] But mergers and affiliations such as these generated efficiencies in the sector in the North that made it more able to withstand the challenges of the century. In 1920 the British Linen Bank (established in 1746) became affiliated to Barclays and, at much the same time, the Clydesdale Bank (established in 1838) announced its merger with the Midland Bank. Scottish banks similarly absorbed English interests – in 1924 the Royal Bank of Scotland took over Drummonds Bank and, six years later, took over William Deacons Bank, which boasted 200 branches in the north of England, before assimilating another private bank, Glynn Mills & Co.[5] Amalgamation was also marked in the insurance industry in these years. Scottish Union took over the City of Glasgow Company in 1913, at much the same time as Norwich Union absorbed Scottish Imperial and, five years later, the Commercial Union took over Edinburgh Life. A second intensive period of banking mergers took place in the 1950s and 1960s. In 1950, the Clydesdale Bank and the North of Scotland Bank merged; in 1955, the Bank of Scotland took over the Union Bank (established in 1830); and, in 1958, the Commercial and the National Bank came together as the National Commercial Bank. By 1969, after the merger of the Royal Bank with the National Commercial Bank and the Bank of Scotland with the British Linen Bank, Scotland's 'big three' remained – the Bank of Scotland and the Royal Bank of Scotland (each under the influence of minority share holders from the south) and the Clydesdale Bank (owned by the Midland Bank from 1950, then sold to the National Australia Bank in 1987). When, in 2000, the Royal Bank took over the Nat West at a cost of £21 billion, Scotland could boast the fifth largest bank in the world.

Concentration of ownership was matched in these years by the rationalisation of branch numbers. In 1951, Scotland, with one branch for every 3,000 of her population, had a banking density significantly above that of England and Wales. Twenty years later, Scottish branch numbers had fallen by around 200 and the country's branch to population ratio had consequently declined.[6] Efficiency was a prerequisite for survival in a changing marketplace and, as agreements and restrictions on borrowing and lending rates ended, banking services became more competitive.

In 1910, the Edinburgh Trustee Savings Bank held an international 'Thrift Conference' that attracted over 300 delegates from around the world. The savings bank movement was particularly successful in Scotland, where account holders consistently made up a higher proportion of the population than south of the border.[7] By the end of the twentieth century, however, the Trustee Savings Bank (TSB) in Scotland would have been unrecognisable to the early pioneers who had valued thrift for its own sake as much as for the returns it could yield. Restructured in 1975 to ensure its competitiveness, in 1986, the TSB was privatised and, in 1995, the TSB Group merged with Lloyds Bank to create Lloyds TSB Scotland.

By the 1980s, the TSB was operating in a very competitive market, as Scottish deposit accounts failed to match English rates of growth. This new environment was epitomised by an increasingly innovative range of services and 'products' offered by the clearing banks. The Clydesdale Bank was to the fore in many of these initiatives and was the first British bank to introduce a mobile banking service in 1948. In 1958, Scottish banks developed schemes for personal loans and, in 1972, the Royal Bank became the first British clearing bank to introduce a house purchase loan scheme. In 1964, the Bank of Scotland opened its first drive-in bank and, by 1980, the Royal Bank's 'Cashline' ATM system was the busiest in the world. With further innovations in telephone and internet banking and diversification into other insurance and financial services, Scottish banks were frequently pioneers across a range of services.

With changes in merchant and wholesale banking activities, increased Scottish interests in and collaboration with banks overseas, the continued high profile of Scottish life insurers and investment trusts and the integration of Scottish stock market activity with the London stock exchange from the 1970s, business and banking interests in the course of the late twentieth century certainly kept pace with international developments and represented a very modern success story.[8] But success had its price in the shape of declining Scottish financial independence. This, to a certain extent, was inevitable but that did not necessarily make it any more palatable. The Monopolies and Mergers Commission went some way to acknowledging this in 1979 in its report on the proposed merger of the Standard Chartered Bank, the Hong Kong and Shanghai Bank and the Royal Bank of Scotland:

> We believe that an important factor in Scotland's economic diffi-culties has been the progressive loss of morale which the taking over of large companies has caused; and we accept that this is damaging to Scotland. Entrepreneurial spirit and business leader-ship depend critically on self-confidence, and we believe that such self-confidence has been weakened.[9]

In the traumatic conditions of global recession in 2008–09, such wise words had a haunting relevance when the takeover of the Bank of Scotland (then part of HBOS) by Lloyds TSB appeared the Scottish bank's only hope for survival and the government became the largest shareholder of the Royal Bank of Scotland (RBS), as shares in this banking monolith crashed. Time has yet to grant the historian the neces-sary space for reflection on such recent events. In November 2008, Sir Tom MacKillop, the out-going chairman of RBS, told the press that 'a new chapter in the RBS story must now begin' – many doubt it will have a happy ending.

Elsewhere in the economy, other institutions and relationships unique to Scotland exerted distinctive influences throughout the century, though their force changed over time. Trade unions and industrial inter-ests frequently organised themselves in bodies distinct from, if not inde-pendent of, English groups – the National Farmers' Union (Scotland), established in 1913, and the Scottish Fishermen's Federation, estab-lished in 1973, are cases in point. The Scottish Trades Union Congress, established in 1897, was frequently at odds with its southern brethren over the course of the century, even though, by the 1930s, many individual Scottish unions had merged with UK-wide general unions. The Confederation of British Industry in Scotland regularly asserted priorities that were out of line with southern business and various professional bodies, organised territorially, would customarily acknowledge that the Scottish case was simply 'different'. Notable here were the Law Society of Scotland, established in 1949, and, of course, the Faculty of Advocates, dating back to the sixteenth century, the Chartered Institute of Bankers in Scotland, established in 1875, and the Institute of Chartered Accountants of Scotland, established in 1854. A commitment to informal networking in these groups and interlocking directorships on the Boards of Scotland's major companies consolidated this Scottish nexus, and corporate approaches to policymaking in the Scottish Office (and later the Scottish Executive) confirmed the influence of these various Scottish lobbies.

At the turn of the twentieth century, out of 108 Scottish companies studied by John Scott and Michael Hughes, 85 per cent were connected through interlocking directorships and, in the interwar period, this network tightened up around a 'financial core' of insurance companies and investment trusts. While connections between industrial companies were less dense in the 1950s than they had been and there was a continued decrease in the amount of clustering across the entire network by the 1960s, Scott and Hughes concluded that, even in the 1970s, the 'Scottish business system must be seen as the outcome of overlapping shareholdings, interlocking directorships and the bonds of kinship.'[10] Mutual self-interest, as much as nationalism, protected the last vestiges of Scottish economic autonomy at the end of the century. It had always been thus.

GOVERNMENT WITH A SCOTTISH 'TWIST'

It is perhaps in the operation of devolved administration and in the state institutions charged with wedding Scotland tighter to common UK goals that, paradoxically, the strongest influences making for Scottish difference and divergence are to be met. Throughout the twentieth century, the economic policies of various governments were generally served with a Scottish 'twist' north of the Border. Treated alternately as a region of the British economy and, less often, as a distinct economic totality, Scotland occupied a unique position in British governments' attempts at economic planning after the Great War. This meant that the way in which the Scottish economy responded to global and national pressures in the twentieth century was frequently different from the economies of England and Wales, despite apparently uniform policies emanating from Westminster and, indeed, Brussels.

A British Region?

Between the wars, government economic policy north of the Border was dominated by concerns to attract the new industries which were thriving in the south of England and alleviate the unemployment and social dislocation which was crippling much of the west-central region. This combination of economic and social objectives remained at the heart of government intervention in the economy of Scotland until the 1980s.

By the end of the 1930s, the Special Areas legislation of 1934, 1936 and 1937 had granted many Scottish areas government funds to attract new businesses and establish public works schemes. Significantly, such activities were co-ordinated by a Scottish Commissioner who worked closely with the Scottish Development Council (SDC, established in 1931), a body that counted the foremost members of Scotland's industrial aristocracy – Lord Bilsland (1892–1970), Lord Elgin (1881–1968) and Sir James Lithgow – among its promoters. By 1937, however, only £2.48 million had been spent on the Scottish special areas, with the majority of this going on public works to alleviate unemployment rather than inducements to new firms.[11] In 1936, at the instigation of the Scottish Commissioner, a Scottish Economic Committee (SEC) was established. This proved to be an influential body, promoting the Empire Exhibition (1938), Scottish Industrial Estates (1937) and the Scottish Special Housing Association (SSHA), and quickly attracted the suspicions of Whitehall.[12] In its paper, 'Scotland's Industrial Future: The Case for Planned Development' (1939), the Committee recommended 'a measure of planned development aided, where desirable, by Government assistance . . . during . . . [this] difficult period of transitional character' and the creation of a centralised planning unit for Scotland.[13] This was a radical proposal which, despite the intervention of war, established the vocabulary of Scottish interests which would frame much post-war policy.

The significant autonomy granted to Tom Johnston (1881–1965), a Labour MP who was Churchill's Secretary of State for Scotland from 1941, and the specifically 'Scottish' agencies that were established during the war were further re-affirmation that there would be a distinct Scottish voice in post-war reconstruction. As Graham Walker has noted, 'Johnston was intent on preparing Scotland for the post-war era on its own terms . . . His was a fervent patriotism directed at practicabilities and the milking of opportunities.'[14] In 1941, Johnston set up the Advisory Council of Ex-Secretaries of State on Post-war Problems in Scotland in an attempt to harness the collective sentiments of the wartime political consensus to prepare for the future. However, as an advisory body, it was more important for the active subcommittees that it spawned than for its own initiatives.[15] In 1942, the Scottish Industrial Council was established, which drew together the insights of industrialists, trade unionists and the local authorities. It was later joined by a Scottish Distribution of Industry Panel, the Scottish Physical Planning Committee and the Scottish Building Committee. In terms of the physical planning achieved in these years, the activities of the Clyde Valley and the Central and South-East Scotland Regional Planning Committees (established in 1943) built on the earlier successes of Scottish Industrial Estates Ltd and signalled the arrival of the types of regional planning ventures which would mark the policies of the 1960s and beyond.[16] The Scottish Office in wartime, however, did not solve Scotland's economic problems. Rather, it conducted a 'holding or a salvage operation', the aims of which were often narrowly defensive. Johnston highlighted the plight of Scottish female munitions workers sent compulsorily to the Midlands to support the war effort and ensured that Scottish firms appeared on government lists so that they could tender for government contracts. But war itself left a challenging legacy for those he had helped survive the years of hostilities and, in peacetime, government offices seldom had the freedom and influence they had exploited during the war.[17]

In 1946, the Scottish Industrial Council became the Scottish Council (Development and Industry) – the SC(D&I). With representation from local authorities, trade unions, industrialists and the Scottish banks, it proved to be, in the words of one senior civil servant, 'the most effective pressure group in Great Britain', at a time when government intervention in the economy, following the passage of the Distribution of Industry Acts (1945, 1950) and the Town and Country Planning Act (1947), was reaching new heights.[18] That did not necessarily mean it wanted radical reform. The outlook of industry leaders brought in by the government could often simply perpetuate traditional pre-occupations. The words of Sir Steven Bilsland – a key player in the Scottish Committee of the Council of Industrial Design – in 1947 were telling. While acknowledging that a 'wider diversification of industry' was required, he emphasised that 'Scottish heavy industries – steel, shipbuilding and engineering – *have been and must remain the backbone of her employment.*'[19]

By 1950, largely as a result of the government's regional policies, factory floor space in Scotland had grown eleven fold, the average size of factory had trebled and the Scottish Development Area (established in 1945) had attracted over 13 per cent of all new industrial building carried out in Britain.[20] The industrial estates set out to break with the conventions of the factory production of the past. Bilsland enthused:

> The Industrial Estate factories are of modern design, and are bright, warm and well ventilated. They are laid out in attractive surround-ings along roads bordered with trees and flowering shrubs, providing an atmosphere and amenity which helps to create a good spirit amongst all who work in them.[21]

By 1954, 46,000 workers were employed on government industrial estates in Scotland.[22]

The recession of the late 1950s in Scotland signalled the intensification of government interest in regional planning as it became obvious that new industries were not moving north in sufficient numbers to stem the tide of decline in localities hit by industrial crisis.[23] In 1959 the Cabinet Economic Committee on the Future of the Shale Oil Industry admitted that 'there was a marked reluctance on the part of industry generally to undertake new projects in Scotland. This was no doubt due, in part, to the difficulty of persuading key personnel to move there.'[24] Steps were taken to modernise steel production and encourage the development of a Scottish motor car industry – particularly the Rootes (later Chrysler) plant at Linwood and the BMC Corporation (later British Leyland) truck and tractor works at Bathgate. The 1960s reinforced this trend and, by the end of the decade, Development Areas encompassed the whole of Scotland except for Edinburgh and its environs.

By 1966 five New Towns had also been built – East Kilbride, Cumbernauld, Glenrothes, Livingston and Irvine. The impetus behind such innovation was to be found in the Clyde Valley Plan of 1946, which sought to facilitate massive slum clearance in Glasgow by re-housing citizens in new communities around Glasgow, and in the delib-erations of the interdepartmental New Towns Committee, established in 1945 and chaired by Lord Reith (1889–1971).[25] With higher than average home- and car-ownership and a lower age profile than the rest of Scotland, these towns proved attractive to industry and sought in their very architecture to assert their novelty.[26] Funded by the Development Corporations that oversaw the growth of Scotland's New Towns until 1996, sculptures too adorned these planned communities and memorialised faith in central planning. The crocodiles at Pitcoudie in Glenrothes, the stone water lilies at Calderglen Country Park, East Kilbride, and 'The Windvane Family' at Livingston's Boulevard

Roundabout were sculptural expressions of optimism and a self-conscious desire to break with the past.[27]

In similar fashion, the creation of the Highlands and Islands Development Board (HIDB) in 1965 promised a renaissance in Highland industry and society and the success of the Dounreay nuclear power station seemed to point to the positive effect modern industrial investment could have at grass-roots level even in the Highlands. In 1967 the population of Thurso – the nearest town to the reactor – was nearly three times that of the 1950s and more than two thirds of wage earners were employed at the plant.[28]

The co-ordinating role of the Scottish Office in implementing central government initiatives had increased throughout the first two post-war decades and was substantially enhanced in the 1970s. In 1974, the Scottish Office took over the administration of the Regional Development Grants introduced under the Industry Act of 1972; the Scottish Economic Planning Board, established in 1964, was eclipsed by the Scottish Economic Planning Department (SEPD) – later the Industry Department for Scotland – in 1973; the Scottish Development Agency (SDA) – Scottish Enterprise from 1991 – was established by the SEPD and made its appearance in 1975; and, in 1976, the Scottish responsibilities of the Manpower Services Commission were transferred to the Scottish Office. Between 1960 and 1976, it has been estimated that jobs created by regional policies in Scotland numbered 90,000 and, by 1980, regional policy measures north of the Border cost £198 million a year.[29]

The victory of the Conservative Party in the 1979 general election, however, signalled a change in regional policy. The priorities of the SDA almost immediately came to focus on inward investment and commercial development, with employment coming a poor second. Then, in the early 1980s, the creation of Locate in Scotland placed the emphasis firmly on attracting outside capital. The closure of the SDA in 1988 and the subsequent creation of a network of Local Enterprise Companies (directed by private business) highlighted the abrupt end of government's love affair with planning. Board membership of these companies was dominated by private businessmen, with local authorities playing little more than a supporting role.[30] Between 1986 and 1990, regional preferential assistance fell by 34 per cent and the subsequent years, marked by the collapse of earlier government-sponsored industrial initiatives, served to challenge the distinct features of Scottish development and economic control which had become increasingly associated with the Scottish Office.[31] Yet Conservative schemes to encourage small businesses failed to generate much interest north of the Border and contributed little to economic growth, despite the obvious, if ironic, impact they could have had in re-energising Scots' control of their own economic destiny. Instead, the relatively higher profile of the public sector north of the Border meant that the consequences of the retreat from public initiatives, particularly in terms of jobs, were felt more acutely in Scotland than elsewhere and there was little to cushion the blow.[32]

In the 1990s, the activities of Locate in Scotland partly served to make amends – in the year 1989–90 alone, they were successful in attracting £853 million of inward investment.[33] But the experiences of the 1980s had severely undermined the economic devolution that had been partially achieved a decade earlier. Many in the 1990s hoped that the new Scottish Executive would reclaim this lost ground while, in the run-up to devolution, others feared rising business costs would come with Scotland's devolved powers to raise income tax (the 'Tartan Tax'). In the end, policy on a macro-economic level was still created in Whitehall after 1999 (albeit, in the short term, under Scottish Chancellors) and the first coalition administration in Holyrood predictably sought to reassure business interests that they had nothing to fear from the new Executive.[34] Indeed, there was much that was familiar in the coalition's aims to use economic growth for social improvement – The Executive's 'Framework for Economic Development in Scotland' (2000) emphasised that its vision 'is that economic development should raise the quality of life of the Scottish people through increasing economic opportunities for all, on a socially and environmentally sustainable basis'.

Whether they will have more success than their forebears remains to be seen, yet the first years of the new devolved administration re-introduced a familiar cause for alarm – growing dependence on the public sector. In 2006, David Bell estimated that, while the private sector had grown by 12.8 per cent since 1998, the public sector had increased by 19.3 per cent.[35] Such evidence resurrected fears that evoked Thatcher's first years in office of a bloated public sector crowding out private initiative. (In 2004, nearly 24 per cent of Scots were employed in public sector jobs.) That the level of public spending as a proportion of GDP (at around 50 per cent) remained lower than other small-sized European countries offered scant consolation – it was still 6 per cent above the UK average and the rest of the UK was recording higher levels of private sector growth than Scotland. It seemed far-fetched to believe that this was simply a coincidence.[36]

Throughout the twentieth century, Scots had dangerously high expectations of the state when it came to the economy and, between 1939 and 1979, its rhetoric of planning did little to discourage this. 'Planning' presumed that success could be easily defined and measured, that most economic goals were necessarily complimentary and that the economic environment was – in some senses at least – predictable. Yet the goal of the planned economy evolved in an environment marked by rapid change and intense international competition. There were bound to be victims.

Government intervention in the economy after 1930, however, had been predicated on twin economic and social visions and, until 1979, the goal of full employment was one shared by parties of all colours. Social and political considerations meant that governments would inevitably be seen as the natural guardians of Scotland's traditional industries, just as much as midwives to the new. Indeed, they had set the precedent themselves in the 1930s. But protection could be taken too far – successive administrations invested in failing enterprises for the sake of communities that would inevitably have to cope with their ultimate demise. The nationalised industries were perhaps the most obvious examples of such subsidised decline. In the 1990s, the legacy of this strategy – as much as that of seventeen years of Conservative rule – was only too apparent in the massive wasteland that had once supported Ravenscraig's blue towers. The loss of traditional industries in the 1980s felt worse because of the long-drawn-out deaths to which they had been condemned and the energies that had been expended in their final futile battle for life.

A European Region?

Britain's entry into the Common Market in 1973 brought economic restrictions and rewards – while limits were set on investment subsidies offered by British governments, the UK, like her partners, qualified for grants and loans from various European funds. Nevertheless, after entry, membership became the focus of controversy – Scottish exports to European Community markets rose by 10 per cent in the six years after entry but, even in 1978, it was estimated that Scotland had paid considerably more into EC coffers than it had received in return.[37] Scotland's place within the European Union (as the EC became in 1992) was contradictory as Scotland had no independent representation within the EU's Council of Ministers but, either in whole or in part, was frequently treated in isolation from the rest of the UK. (For example, after 1991, Scotland was represented in the 200-strong Committee of the Regions.) Nevertheless, between 1975 and 1983, Scotland was awarded £340 million from the European Regional Fund – monies that were invested in projects ranging from the construction of the Scottish Exhibition and Conference Centre in Glasgow to tourist attractions on

Culloden Moor.[38] By 1998, European Structural Funds, amounting to more than £200 million per year, affected 85 per cent of the Scottish population and, in key local areas, European finance contributed to industrial renewal. In Dundee, for example, funds from the European Social Fund were invested in training programmes in consumer electronics and, through the Millennium Link Project, icons of Scotland's Victorian past were redeveloped as the Forth and Clyde Canal and the Union Canal were restored. Of the industries most directly affected by Britain's new economic status within Europe, however, agriculture and fishing felt the change most immediately and dramatically.

By the 1970s, Scottish farming was very familiar with government intervention. Until 1912, government interest in Scottish farming concentrated mainly on the crofting counties. In that year, however, the Board of Agriculture for Scotland (BoAS) was established before becoming the Department of Agriculture for Scotland (DoAS) in 1929. Its initial role focused on the land settlement reforms instituted by the 1911 Small Landholders' (Scotland) Act but, despite additional powers granted in 1919, progress was slow. While nearly 20,000 applications for new holdings were lodged with the Board between 1912 and 1925, only 1,571 new holdings were established and 894 holdings were enlarged.[39] During the depression of the 1930s, however, attention turned increasingly to production issues. In 1931, the government guaranteed a minimum price for wheat under the Wheat Act of that year but, due to the rather insignificant role of wheat in Scottish arable production, such protection had little effect. It was not until the Agriculture Act of 1937 that price guarantees were offered for oats and barley – Scottish staples.

War thereafter greatly increased government intervention in agriculture. In June 1940, it was announced that an additional 260,000 acres of tillage were required in Scotland for the next year and that the number of livestock would have to be adjusted to meet the demands of the nation's food policy.[40] Compulsory cropping notices and special acreage payments were successful in increasing the output of essential crops and the rationing of feedstuffs after 1941 successfully cut the number of livestock. Grants for liming and fertilisation contributed to the increased productivity of the arable sector and, over Scotland as a whole, net agricultural output increased by a quarter.[41] But at what cost? In 1942, it appeared to a former Scottish Secretary that:

> The Agricultural Committees are now the real masters of the land ... To plough, to sow, to reap, and to hoe, are operations conducted nowadays under the watchful eye of the committee-man

supervising on behalf of the County Committee the work of his neighbours . . . In fact, if you were to ask what is the chief country-side change in changing Scotland, I should say not 'The Plough', but 'The Committee'. A Committee rules even at the auction marts where the fat beasts come stumping in.[42]

As in the rest of the UK, the history of Scottish agriculture since the Second World War has been 'inextricably bound up with government'.[43] Following the 1947 Agriculture Act and the 1948 Agriculture (Scotland) Act, government support for British agriculture became part of the post-war political consensus and a habitual political pre-occupation. In Scotland, however, the changing position of the DoAS within the Scottish Office and the expanding role of the European Community since the 1970s in many instances resulted in distinct patterns of change.

The Scottish Office, through the BoAS, had assumed responsibility for agriculture (except animal health) in 1912 and, in 1939, following the Reorganisation of Offices (Scotland) Act of that year, the DoAS became one of the four 'new' Scottish Office Departments. It was to become the principal milch cow of Scottish farmers.[44] By the end of the 1960s, Scotland received proportionately more in agricultural subsidies than any other region of the UK and around 9 per cent more than her share of the value of UK agricultural output.[45] This growing dependence on government loans and subsidy was common across the UK regions in these years and into the 1980s, but it left a challenging legacy for the new Scottish Executive in the late 1990s which sought to develop a joined-up policy on agriculture in a new department combining Environment and Rural Affairs and end the perceived elite privileges that were enshrined in antiquated land laws that were supported by the power of the big estates. It was not surprising that land reform would be high on the agenda of the new Scottish Parliament.

In the early years after Britain's entry to the European Community, initial allowances were made for the obvious differences between British and European agricultural policies. Despite this, Scottish agriculture subsequently suffered and succeeded in turn, along with the rest of the UK, in this new market environment. In Scotland, membership of the Community encouraged 'significant structural change', particularly in traditional cropping patterns.[46] As Gavin Sprott has noted, many farmers, encouraged by European grain subsidies, abandoned livestock altogether and took the 'one-way ticket' of pure arable.[47] European grain surpluses by the 1980s, the disastrous harvest of 1985–86 and changes to the Common Agricultural Policy in the 1990s highlighted the dangers of this strategy.[48] Nevertheless, Europe's subsidy expenditure in Scotland was notable. In 1978, Scotland received nearly £10m from the EC's Agriculture Guidance and Guarantee Fund; in 1983, Scottish agriculture was awarded £160 million of direct financial assistance to stimulate improvements in industrial efficiency and marketing capability; and, in 1994, direct subsidies from Europe were as high as £332 million and contributed significantly to the resources of Scotland's farming families.[49] Money also came into Scottish agriculture via the EU's Structural Funds which targeted infrastructural improvements and diversification in the rural economy, not just in areas designated 'Objective 1' up to 2000 (largely Highland areas, with per capita GDP of less than 75 per cent of the wider union) but also the 'Objective 5b' areas – areas where economic development was lagging behind the EU average in terms of income and employment which included Dumfries and Galloway, the Borders and large areas of the former Grampian, Tayside and Central Regions.[50]

A new geography had been superimposed on Scottish farming as a result of EU membership that had little, if anything, to do with political borders – regions were now defined by topography, resources and development opportunities.[51] This had obvious merits but what, then, of *Scottish* farming? Many wondered if this new geography was indeed as suited to modern demands as it first appeared – in any case, with the imminent expansion of the EU in the new century, few believed that Scottish regional distinctiveness would be quite as liberally endowed in the future.

The Scottish fishing industry has always had problems getting itself heard. In part, this is down to its distance from centres of political power – in 1935, for example, a Herring Board was created to assist the industry but this was housed in London offices. (After devolution, Holyrood, at times, did not appear to be that much closer either.) It is not surprising, therefore, that the Scottish fishing community's relationship with Europe was marked by tension and suspicion from the beginning. The Common Fisheries Policy (CFP) was agreed by existing EC members on the night of 30 June 1970. This was the day that negotiations for the accession of the UK, Ireland, Denmark and Norway were due to begin and it was clearly an attempt to settle, in advance, the new environment in the fishing industry that the expanded Community would create. But it was not to be so simple – the new entrants demanded exclusive rights for their own fleets within a 6-mile limit round their coasts and restricted foreign competition between 6 and 12 miles out. With a few amendments, a 12-mile cordon sanitaire around individual EC members would be the norm until the end of the century.[52] However, impediments to fishing in Icelandic waters in the

1950s had already offered Scotland's fishermen a first taste of international conflict that made them suspicious of diplomatic agreements. Thereafter, further restrictions in the 1970s around Iceland and the Faroes signalled new challenges for the industry and, within the EC, problems were already emerging. A herring ban in 1977 signalled the Community's serious intentions of preserving declining fish stocks particularly in the North Sea and, in 1983, a conservation policy was included in the CFP which introduced quotas and 'Total Allowable Catches' for vessels. In 1992, under the Seafish (Conservation) Act, the British government went one step further by empowering its offices to impose a limit on the number of days which every vessel over 10 metres in length could spend at sea. This was supplemented with additional regulations on mesh sizes and a £25 million decommissioning scheme. William West, a retired fisherman, recorded views that many shared at the time, when he commented, 'There's terrific strain and stress with these new rules. All this they're up against now. Some of the rules are sensible but the most of them are made up by men who don't know what they're speaking about.'[53] Politicians and fishermen both believed that stocks had to be conserved but few could persuade the fishing communities of Scotland's north-east coast that the CFP was doing anything other than killing them slowly. In 1988, quotas for Grampian's north-east fleet were cut severely – cod landings were to be reduced from 70,790 tonnes to 45,340 tonnes, and only 77,620 tonnes of haddock, instead of 128,580 tonnes, were to be landed.[54] As Grampian Regional Council admitted, only the 'cushioning effect' of the oil industry served to mask the serious problems of the area's coastal communities.[55]

Governing bodies, regional, national and supranational, had a determining influence on many aspects of Scotland's economic development. On very few occasions, however, was the outcome of policy uniform across the territories subject to shared governance. Policy worked on, in and through unique local institutions and was influenced by contrasting economic geographies and histories and the bias of existing interest groups. Scotland's experience in the twentieth century confirmed that not only the governed but governments and states would be changed in this process.

Conclusion

Scotland's economic leaders adjusted to new and emerging economic environments throughout the course of the twentieth century but they were frequently too late, too hesitant and too conservative in their response. This record can be partly explained by the nation's integration within a larger UK state that, on occasion, restricted the range and scope of Scotland's choices. But many more answers are to be found within Scotland itself.

Scottish industrialists concentrated too intensely and for too long on markets in which foreign competition was to become overwhelming and on too narrow a range of products which all too often failed to address the demands of a developing consumer society. Crystal balls at the time could not have necessarily predicted when this precarious reliance would eventually become a liability but failure to diversify was costly. The perpetuation of relationships between industries no longer sustained by profitability and economies of scale further prolonged the life of industrial sectors for which there was eventually little in the way of a financial logic. Thereafter, the nation as a whole had unreasonably high expectations of experiments in public investment and ownership to rejuvenate heavy industry and, with hindsight, a somewhat naive faith that, come what may, Scottish industries would be protected under the umbrella of UK-wide state operations. This bred an over-reliance on Scottish government offices which, while growing increasingly sophisticated, were ill-equipped to deliver national economic renewal and, in turn, vested too much hope in corporate approaches to planning that were too dependent on keeping faith with established interests to effect the radical changes needed. Similarly, new industries, unconnected to Scotland's traditional manufactures, and foreign investment, no matter how impressive, did not solve structural impediments to growth in the Scottish economy or, necessarily, encourage its modernisation. Oil did not – and, arguably, could not – have rescued the situation without significant reform elsewhere in the economy. But it was not, as many would have it, that the crisis eventually 'cam wi' a lass' (Mrs Thatcher) in 1979 – creating political scapegoats is too easy, although it makes our past easier to live with. Rather, Scotland had been living with crises throughout the century that the nation (industrialists, trade unions, governments, economists and the citizenry in general) had failed to resolve. Perhaps the real tragedy of the recession of the 1980s was that history had already given Scotland plenty of warnings of its arrival and many had seen it coming for decades. By the late 1990s, no one wanted to turn the clock back – neither the New Labour government of 1997 nor the Scottish Executive after 1999 unpicked the Thatcher legacy. Yet it boded ill for the future that the recovery effected in the late 1990s was led by a public sector that had grown partly at the expense of private initiative and a service sector over which Scots could assert little control.

PART TWO

'These Various Scotlands' – Scottish Society

Prologue

Throughout the twentieth century, changes in the urban profiles of Scotland's foremost cities, and comparisons made between them, high-lighted the diversity at the heart of Scottish society and the prejudices upon which regional types were based.

Edinburgh's architecture tended to dominate most descriptions of the capital. A native of the place, Norman MacCaig (1910–1996) regularly revisited its wynds in his poetry throughout a long literary career. In 'Edinburgh Spring' (1955), 'Slatternly tenements wait till night / To make a Middle Ages in the sky' and on the High Street 'Tombs and monuments / pile in the air', while MacCaig himself walks a 'paint-box suburb'. Five years later, even the summer sunshine fails to entice the capital's citizens out of doors – in 'Edinburgh Courtyard in July':

> Hot light is smeared as thick as paint
> On these ramshackle tenements.
> Stones smell of dust.

By comparison, Glasgow's built environment, largely shrouded in smog and dressed in the sooty deposits of industry until the 1960s, tended to take second place to its citizenry in descriptions of the place. In the last decade of the century, the novelist, William McIlvanney (1936–), considered 'humane irreverence' to be Glasgow's greatest export and placed its more colourful inhabitants at its heart:

[T]he quizzical starers, the cocky walkers, the chic girls who don't see a phoney accent as an essential accessory of attractiveness, the askers of questions where none was expected, the dancers on the train, the strikers-up of unsolicited conversations, the welcomes of strangers, the deliverers of deadly lines in the most unlikely places, the people fighting decency's rearguard action in Possil, the unpre-tentious, the unintimidated. Glasgow belongs to them.[1]

In this Glasgow – largely a product of its people – the city's 'emotions [were] nearer the surface' than in Edinburgh.[2] As a consequence of this intimacy, Glasgow's problems readily came to the fore in most accounts and were often written about in the imagery of disease and decay affecting the civic body. In 1934, the novelist Lewis Grassic Gibbon (1901–1935) personified Glasgow as a corpse, upon which 'the maggot-swarm . . . [was] fiercely alive'.[3]

Meanwhile, authors such as Edwin Muir (1887–1959) suggested that Edinburgh hid her dirty secrets behind a 'proud display', making the capital a 'city of extraordinary and sordid contrasts'. Here, the poorest endured life 'cribbed, cabined and confined in infernal dens' – 'a disgrace to a city with such pretentiousness'.[4] For many, Edinburgh stood as something of an enigma – 'This Edinburgh's just a bag o tricks/filled tapsle-teerie baith bi Gode an Deevil,' wrote the local poet, Robert Garioch (Sutherland) (1909–1981) in 1940. It was a riddle resolved by commentators in conflicting ways. For the Conservative politician Walter Elliot, speaking to an Edinburgh audience in 1951, the city was 'always fertile; always like the good earth, bringing forth life when men most suppose her dead'.[5] But, for others, the promise was false – 'Edinburgh is a handsome, empty capital of the past,' suggested Muir.[6] Such emptiness, moreover, might hide more sinister features. Hugh MacDiarmid suggested, in the 1930s, that Edinburgh was 'demoralised', 'dependent' on other places for her creativity and home to an 'emasculating' spirit which rendered imaginative and spiritual activity impossible.[7] This was the Edinburgh of Robert Garioch's 1954 'Masque', 'owre-valued Edinbro, yon cauld-kale toon'.[8]

Glasgow's apparent transparency allowed the observer to sketch its form more easily – though it is less clear whether, as a consequence, the city was better understood. The austere silence or the ghostly whispers of the eastern city are replaced with noise, action and personalities that strain within the confines of even the most accommodating prose style.

> Glasgow contains such a number of things: thousands of families living in harmony or in dissension, comfortably or poorly, in anything from one small room to twenty large ones: slums, villas and turreted mansions, varying in comfort, but alike in ugliness: factories, at work or silent: socialist societies and YMCAs: churches, Catholic chapels and Orange halls: cinemas, dance-halls, tea-rooms and hotel lounges: literary societies: brothels: graveyards: trains and tram-cars where a whole population seems to be in migration: Labour Exchanges with queues waiting before the doors: streets of prostitutes: young men waiting for young women at a thousand corners: football matches: gymnasiums: Salvation Army bands: fathers and mothers beating their

children in cold suburban parlours: bands of misguided or desperate youths . . . roaming about the slums: professors: drinking clubs: street fights: black-coated congregations dispersing from a thousand churches, Catholic, Protestant, Baptist, Wesleyan, Unitarian: unemployed men walking about in a vacuum represented by one or two or five or ten years: boxing matches and theosophical lectures: luxurious shops and shebeens: curtains discretely raised and lowered in suburban streets: bun-fights: Band of Hope concerts: bridge drives: law courts: schools: prisons: official receptions: and a thousand things more which paralyse the mind when it tries to number them.

The author Edwin Muir concluded that a 'modern city is strictly inconceivable'.[9]

Distinctions between the two cities were generally explained by the contrasting legacies which industrialisation left for their citizens – Edinburgh's industry, like her poor, was largely hidden to the superficial tourist gaze while, for long enough, Glasgow *was* her industry. Yet, even about this, there were disagreements. In the midst of economic depression, Muir considered Glaswegians the victims of industrialisation – a process which 'set its mark on several generations of the men, women and children by whose work it lived, in shrunken bodies and trivial or embittered minds'.[10] However, facing the grim realities of de-industrialisation more than fifty years later, McIlvanney saw Glasgow as a 'gallous lion tamer with a chair', having domesticated the industrial beast and 'made it part of [its] way of life'.[11] As a consequence of industrialism's uneven impact and its ready accommodation in parodies of regional difference (Edinburgh – middle-class – aloof; Glasgow – working-class – gritty), by the 1990s at least, a self-conscious inverted snobbery marked many accounts of Glasgow vis-à-vis her eastern neighbour. Tom Leonard's 'Dripping with Nostalgia' sums up how a Glasgow, reinvented as a City of Culture while its industry died, championed her working-class roots:

> While the judges
> in the Snottery Weans Competition
> were still licking clean
> the candidates' upper lips
>
> the 'Dear Aul' Glesca' Poetry Prize
> for the most heart-warming evocation
> of communal poverty
> was presented to the author of
>
> 'The Day the Dug Ate ma Ration Book'[12]

It was hardly surprising that the eastern metropolis would lampoon Glasgow's self-righteousness and seek to expose its extravagance. In Irvine Welsh's 1993 novel, *Trainspotting*, set in Edinburgh, we encounter the following sarcastic aside: 'Ah've never met one Weedjie whae didnae think that they are the only genuinely suffering proletarians in Scotland, Western Europe, the World. Weedjie experience ay hardship is the only relevant experience ay it.'[13]

Clearly, too much can be made of contrasts between Scotland's great cities. Indeed, in 1949, the author Moray McLaren (1901–1971) was 'continually puzzled by the fact that two places [Edinburgh and Glasgow] can be so essentially the same yet so different on the surface'.[14] But differences mattered. Within cities and counties and across regions, it was mainly through difference that twentieth-century Scots came to know their country and, in turn, themselves. Both Edinburgh and Glasgow grew during the course of the twentieth century by absorbing small towns and conurbations in their hinterland. For example, Leith was incorporated into Edinburgh in 1920 and Govan and Partick lost their separate burgh status to Glasgow in 1912. But the fierce community loyalties of these areas and others that had nestled uneasily alongside these western and eastern capitals persisted for as long as they remained meaningful. In 'Lesson', Robert Garioch walks the streets of Leith and is reminded how, while 'Leith's moistly rubble nou', 'a century sinsyne' confident merchants talked business in 'weill-appyntit pubs'. But now 'Leith crined in Embro's grup'. In the west, meanwhile, Govan citizens supported a lively community culture until the gloomy prediction of its burgh motto *Nihil sine labore* (Nothing without work) was realised with the closure of engineering shops and shipyards in the second half of the century.

Scotland's other great cities also clung to identities forged in the days of Victorian confidence. The strength of Aberdeen, the 'Granite City', was easily transposed into human qualities by the author Paul Harris in 1988, though the outline of an earlier music-hall stereotype was still evident:

> isolated and isolationist but cosmopolitan in international connections centuries before the arrival of the relative youngster the oil industry; measured and reserved in response but warm and hospitable before long; matter of fact and dry of wit, sometimes seeming to border on cynicism but solid and reliable in judgement; and an apparent conservatism which belies remarkable regenerative qualities.[15]

By contrast, for the authors of an architectural guide in 1993, late twentieth-century Dundee was struggling to realise a new identity since the collapse of jute and the death of the poet William McGonagall (1825–1902) made its two previous appellations (the 'Women's Town' and the 'ancient City of the silv'ry Tay') somewhat anachronistic and faintly comic. 'The task facing twentieth-century Dundee', they wrote, 'has been how to create a city of permanence and prosperity from a city with a small, nearly obliterated core, swathed by hastily erected and unplanned shanty towns.'[16] Instead of waiting for the organic emergence of a new identity, 'City of Discovery' was eventually chosen by councillors towards the end of the century to rebrand this city still searching for a way out of the debris of its industrial past.

Beyond the principal cities, small-town Scotland was the convenient (if hardly sympathetic) shorthand that commentators used to frame local identity in areas unclaimed by either city or countryside and boasting too few historians to make a claim on the country's conscience. Such towns were rarely allowed a distinctive voice in their country's modern history and their presence in literature reaffirms callous generalisations that, by denying each town its name, largely denied the unique experiences of their inhabitants. Many towns, like Strathaven, were said to 'diet on shadows' of an earlier more vibrant past; and others, like Kirkcaldy, were styled as places young inhabitants waited for years to leave.[17] For those who remained, life (in every sense) was bounded by local horizons. In 1982, the poet Tom Pow (1950–) reflected on the life of a woman in small-town Scotland:

> A tedious job, a place; a person lost
> and never returned to:
> these are what hardened her
> and fastened her meditations
> to the knot of time she had.
> Though outside there are stars, blossoms,
> chestnut trees a child might paint,
> she has bound herself to circumstance;
> so how can she be saved?[18]

Industrial dislocation and the concrete dreams of post-war town planners conspired to bolster the tendency to view small towns en masse – high streets were restyled with 'identikit' shops occupied, in turn, by chain stores and charity retailers. Many shared the fate of Falkirk when, in the 1980s, both the Falkirk Iron Company and the Carron Company closed their doors:

Few developers were prepared to invest in new enterprises and, as derelict foundry buildings all over the district crumbled, the very heart of the old town itself began to fall apart. Empty buildings covered in tattered posters, abandoned shops, dirty and un-mended streets and the graffiti of idle hands – that was the Falkirk of the early 1980s.[19]

But this is only part of the story – Scotland's towns contributed in unique ways to Scotland's history in the twentieth century. The decline of cotton manufacture could be read from the townscape of Paisley; the fate of the woollen trades was reflected in the smashed window panes of Galashiels's mills; the renaissance in Gaelic culture partly explained Inverness's belated city status; while the relative quiet of the Clyde's coastal resorts whispered of changes in leisure. It pays to be reminded that how small towns were understood from the outside or by those who chose to leave them does not necessarily match the view from within.

Regional differences – exaggerated or otherwise – raise important questions about Scottish society as a whole. If local identities still mattered throughout the twentieth century, what – if anything – bound Scottish society together? Iain Crichton Smith, growing up on the island of Lewis, 'didn't think much about Scotland at all. It was a vague lump on the horizon, not of great importance to [him]'.[20] Did 'Scottish society' actually exist?

Two principal strategies were regularly employed by commentators wishing to 'rescue' Scottish society from parochial debates and regional rivalries or otherwise colour the bland homogeneity suggested by Scotland's apparent embrace of English mores, corporate industry, urbanisation and consumerism. Firstly, attempts were made to isolate expressly Scottish social characteristics and, secondly, contrasts were made with England and English 'ways'. That some of these analyses bordered on ethnic or racial stereotyping is significant – they point to many commentators' reliance on the past or on caricature when making their case. It is dangerous territory for the historian.

Thrift, doggedness, Sabbath observance, humour, passion, love of liberty – at one time or another, throughout the twentieth century, such values and qualities (and many others besides) were taken to be characteristics of Scottish society. Yet, once identified, with a deft sleight of hand, commentators, through the years, readily mourned their passing or recorded their final days as if, in each decade, another final breath was being exhaled. Even as early as 1901, 'A Tramp' mused that the 'unmistakable and long-recognised characteristics of Scotchmen are becoming less pronounced each decade' and he feared that the 'characteristic Scotch virtue' of 'living within one's means' was being eroded.

Now, he claimed, 'extravagance is more seen among the Scotch working class than their equals in England and Ireland'.[21] Yet, others acknowledged that, however much such a state of affairs was to be regretted, it had been Scottish qualities themselves that had guided the nation to such a time. Edwin Muir bemoaned the apathy and resentment which he met among fellow Scots in the 1930s but noted that 'the Scotland of the present day' was only the 'inevitable result of the Scottish spirit, and its sole extant expression'.[22] Scottish values were not invariably valuable. Ian Rankin's fictional detective Rebus, standing in the Hogmanay crowds outside Edinburgh's Tron Kirk, considered that:

[t]he best and the worst of the Scots came out as another New Year approached: the togetherness, the sharpness, the hugging of life, the inability to know when to stop, so that the hug became a smothering stranglehold. These people were drowning in a sea of sentiment and sham.[23]

In and of themselves, Scottish characteristics did little to establish the persistence of Scottish society. As part of an Anglo-Scottish comparison, however, they seemed more potent. Muir himself identified in the Scottish character 'a thoroughness . . . an inability to know when to stop, which is rarely found in Englishmen, who make a virtue of compromise'. Walter Elliot, in his rectorial address at the University of Aberdeen in 1934, echoed similar sentiments in a rousing celebration of Union:

Have we not here great assets in our hands at home? To the Scottish power of work is added the English power of tolerance. I should not like to say which will be more essential in the days to come. At least as a Scot, I know what we lack as well as what we have. Tolerance, fair-play, forbearance – these were never the marks of our furious race . . . The danger of England is that she should be too tolerant, too terribly anxious to play the game, too forbearing both to herself and to others. I look to the grim traditions of Scotland, to our harsh and salt humour, to correct that excess. We can never be by instinct as tolerant as the English, as fair as the English, as forbearing as the English. We must make . . . our special contribution from our special qualities – industry, fury, romance.[24]

But not everyone agreed. In 1995 the writer, Alasdair Gray (1934–), considered the limits of this romantic sense.

The Lowland Scots suspect the creative imagination. John Knox, the man we love to hate, is usually blamed for this, but the cause is poverty. The English middle-classes know that imagination can be a way of managing things ... But where there is little wealth respectable people fear the future and are sure that only carefulness will help them survive it. They feel that an active imagination excites the passions, especially sexual ones, and breeds discontent and extravagant actions. And indeed, for those with low salaries and positions, unimaginative carefulness is a way of avoiding pain, in the short run. In the long run it makes us the easy tools of people with high salaries and positions, and when they have no use for us they drop us in the shit.[25]

Many others were not so inclined to lapse lazily into national carica-ture. The playwright, James Bridie (1888–1951), acknowledged a Scottish tendency of 'yapping and howling and complaining that the English don't understand them' but, in the same volume, his sharp commentary cut with precision when he drew attention to the limits of Scottish sentiment by saying, 'The Scotsman's adoration for ruins he does nothing to preserve and for traditions he only keeps to vulgarise sometimes makes an intelligent Englishman laugh. It is not for Scots to complain.'[26]

. Characteristics, cultural values, social mores, traditions and tenden-cies all prove engaging but unreliable traces of evidence to establish something we might call 'Scottish society' in the twentieth century. They suggest that a more virile national community was superimposed on regional distinctions but, resting on little more than assumptions and impressions, they too readily point in opposite directions and, being fluid, changeable, contradictory and imprecise, they tell us little of the life experiences which together made up society as a whole.

Without a legislative state apparatus coinciding with its borders for all but the last year of the century and sharing a language and an impe-rial past with a southern neighbour, Scotland's claims to a society that was, in at least some ways, distinctive within the UK would have appeared somewhat irrelevant (or, at most, an interesting aside) at the beginning of the twentieth century. By its end, however, an altered acad-emic climate allowed the sociologist, David McCrone, to emphasise in 1992, that Scotland lay at the heart of the postmodern dilemma in his discipline. In the closing decades of the twentieth century, sociological studies shattered conventional appreciations of society as being coter-minous with nation states and asserted the significance of compound identities that reside within, between, among and across individuals and groups living inside and outside national borders. National parameters, it seemed, no longer dictated the limits of postmodern societies. Despite (or because of) the absence of a Scottish state, despite (or because of) similarities in English and Scottish social structures and social mobility and despite (or because of) increasingly similar economic structures, McCrone argued that, since 1707, 'if anything, a sense of difference and identity has grown rather than diminished' in Scotland.[27]

'Difference' and 'identity', however, threaten to throw us back on the attempts at national caricature that earlier offered little in the way of authoritative guidance on Scottish society. Yet they point to an essential reality, namely that what was necessarily distinctive about Scotland's society in the twentieth century was not always what happened to it or within it, but how it was understood and made part of existing lifestyles, relationships and communities. It is clearly possible to identify something called 'Scottish society' in the twentieth century that was at once part of the wider UK and international community but, in many aspects, retained important differences. Such differences, moreover, are revealed not simply through a comparison with Scotland's 'significant other' south of the border but also through internal contrasts within Scottish society itself – regional disparities, class and ethnic differences and gender distinctions. There were various Scotlands.

FIVE Health and Hearth – Scotland's
People

By the late twentieth century, Scotland's population was over four times
that of 1707.[1] This represented one tenth of that of England and Wales
whereas, in 1801, the Scottish population had been over 15 per cent of the
British total and, at the time of the Treaty of Union, it had numbered nearly
one fifth of that of her southern neighbour.[2] In Scotland and elsewhere in
the British Isles, the nineteenth century had brought rapid population
increase but that came to an abrupt end after 1918. Between 1911 and
1971 (when Scotland's population reached a census peak at 5.23 million),
the population had grown by less than half a million.[3] In contrast, between
1911 and 1988, the population of England and Wales had grown by nearly
40 per cent.[4] Slow internal growth was thus twinned with decline in
Scotland's relative position within the UK over the twentieth century.

Of the constituent countries of the UK, Scotland was the least densely
populated, with 66 people per square kilometre in 1995, compared with
a UK average of 241. Yet, as one might suspect, the population was not
distributed evenly across the Scottish land mass – the Glasgow area
recorded a population density of 3,533 per square kilometre at this
time, while the Highland Council area was the lowest in Scotland with
just 8.[5] Scotland was, then, a land of stark contrasts. And, in this regard
at least, little had changed since mid century when evacuated mothers
sent to lonely Highland shooting lodges to escape the ravages of the
blitz bemoaned, 'At nicht it wis hills, jist hills! And in the mornin' it wis
hills again, hills and hills.'[6] Many of these Scots had been removed from
tenement landscapes squeezing nearly 200 persons to the acre.

Overwhelmingly, the Scots were an urban people, with over 80 per cent
of the population residing in conurbations by the 1950s.[7] In 1991, the
four principal cities of Glasgow, Edinburgh, Aberdeen and Dundee
together absorbed nearly 28 per cent of the entire Scottish population.
But, even in the century's final years, the majority of Scots were of
the small-town variety – over 50 per cent of Scots in 2000 lived in conurbations of less than 100,000 folk. United by little more than demographic

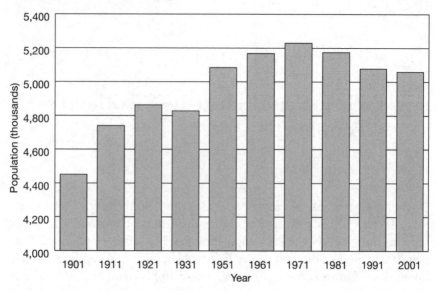

Figure 5.1 Population of Scotland, 1901–2001
Source: *Annual Abstract of Statistics, 2006* (HMSO, 2006), p. 29

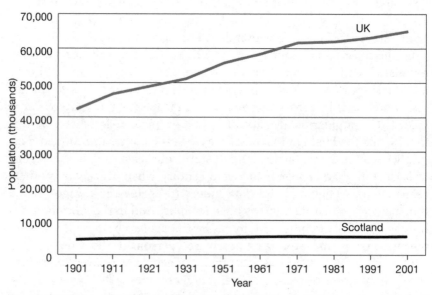

Figure 5.2 UK population compared with Scotland's population, 1901–2001
Source: *Annual Abstract of Statistics, 2006* (HMSO, 2006), p. 29

concentration, the towns certainly do not present a picture of uniform and uninterrupted growth over the course of the century – the health of Scotland's small towns reflected the contrasting regional economies of the areas within which they were sited. By way of contrast, the experience of Scotland's rural areas is more easily summarised. As Michael Anderson has made clear, 'decline was endemic and often profound'.[8] Only the traditionally prosperous farming areas of the north-east, areas within commuting distance of larger conurbations and areas adept at exploiting their tourism capacity managed to resist the flight to the towns.

Nevertheless, Scots – no matter where they lived – were living longer. Expectation of life at birth rose from 45.9 years for males and 49 for females in 1900–02 to 64.1 and 67.8 respectively in 1948–50. Yet, figures for England and Wales show even better improvement, with male life expectancy rising from 45.9 to 66.3 and comparable female figures rising from 49.8 to 71.[9] With improvements recorded in levels of infant and maternal mortality, health reforms following the foundation of the National Health Service (NHS) in 1948 and a general rise in the standard of living, the second half of the century brought further improvements in Scotland. By 1990, expectation of life at birth had increased further north of the Border, with male and female figures being recorded at 71.1 and 76.9 years respectively.[10] But not all Scots lived to see seventy birthday candles. At the end of the century, Glasgow men could expect to live to only 69 – the lowest life expectancy rate for males in Scotland. Comedians would joke that Glaswegians spoke faster than other Scots as they died sooner, but the laughter that greeted them was tinged with tragedy and those outside the 'Dear Green Place' had no reason for complacency. In the second half of the twentieth century, Scotland's relative position within Europe had worsened – in 2004, Scottish women had the lowest life expectancy in the European Union and men the second lowest.[11]

Those wishing to share their relatively longer lives with a partner were delaying 'wedded bliss' by the end of the century, in comparison to earlier newly weds. Scots, as well as the English, were marrying later towards the end of the century, with the mean age at marriage increasing from 28.9 for males and 26.2 for females in 1901–1910, to 32.5 and 30.3 in 1995.[12] (The rise was consistent apart from a dip in the 1960s and early 1970s.) Marriage, indeed, was not always seen as the only or most appropriate union for Scottish couples. Divorce rates rose dramatically in Scotland from the 1960s (10,631 couples untied the knot in 2001) and at much the same time the numbers of cohabiting couples and illegitimate births increased significantly – around 40 per cent of births at the end of the century were out of wedlock.

The size of households that would eventually emerge from these various types of union also changed as the century wore on. The fertility of Scottish women remained higher than the rest of the UK into the 1950s, resulting in larger families in these years – despite the rise in the age of first marriage.[13] Thereafter, family size was consciously limited to an extent not realised before. Married women aged between twenty and twenty-four in the mid 1940s were likely to have no more than two or three children, in comparison to their forebears who, in 1911, could have expected to have around six children.[14] The greater availability and reliability of artificial contraception encouraged this trend. By 1988, only 14 per cent of Scots women's potential fertility was being realised and, a decade later, the average age at motherhood was touching thirty.[15] This was despite growing numbers of teenage pregnancies – the schoolgirl conception rate increased from 6.6 to 8.7 per 1,000 girls aged thirteen to fifteen between 1984 and 1997 while, among sixteen- to nineteen-year-olds, the rate peaked in 1991 at 77.8 per 1,000 females in this age group, declining to 68.2 by 1995.[16]

Overall, Scotland's demographic regime in the twentieth century became increasingly marked by the consequences of medical intervention, personal choice and the environment. The span between the Scottish cradle and the grave widened as the century progressed, as the mortal power of serious childhood diseases declined due to widespread immunisation and vaccination, the development of professional surgical practice and a growing awareness of prevention and what made for healthier lifestyles. While nearly 16 per cent of Scottish boys and 13 per cent of Scottish girls aged zero to five died in 1921, less than 2 per cent of boys and less than 1 per cent of girls of the same age group died in 1988.[17]

Regional demographic distinctions remained, however, and, at times, statistics spoke loudly of national and personal trauma. The Highlands, for example, had a larger proportion of its population in older age categories throughout the century and, in this area, women in their early twenties were less likely than their southern sisters to be married in the 1930s.[18] In many Highland areas, the First World War had virtually wiped out a generation of young men and, for those who returned, the lack of opportunities and available land north of the Highland Line did little to encourage confidence far less thoughts of marriage. Class would also at times combine with the happenstance of one's place on the planet to dictate demographic peculiarities. At the end of the century, for example, the mortality rate in the ten most deprived neighbourhoods in Scotland was a third higher than in the most prosperous 50 per cent. And, more specifically, the six parliamentary constituencies recording the highest levels of premature mortality in the UK were all located in Glasgow.[19] Nevertheless, across the nation, life generally seemed more predictable, the future more assured and the present less of a biological game of chance.

For some Scots, however, such improvement failed to counter the impulse to leave. In the 1940s, an SNP pamphlet warned 'BEWARE OF EMIGRATION' and recorded that 'nothing has sapped the life of Scotland more in the last 150 years than mass emigration'. It implored, 'Remember, it is the young and enterprising, the skilled craftsman and the handyman crofters, the backbone of industry and the fathers and mothers of the next generation, who go.'[20] Cultural commentators similarly reflected on the Scottish migrant tradition and what it revealed about the emigrant's home. The novelist Eric Linklater (1899–1974), a decade before, grimly observed that 'no country can nurture a national culture when its cultural instincts express themselves in flight'.[21]

As we have seen elsewhere in this volume, the Scottish diaspora – Scotland's proudest boast and Scotland's greatest loss – reveals in its history the rhythm of Scotland's social and economic transformation in the twentieth century. Net loss by migration, either overseas or to the south, totalled 217,000 in the years 1881–91 (43 per cent of the natural increase) and, having fallen in the years 1891–1901, rose again to 254,000 in the first decade of the new century.[22] A peak year was recorded in 1911 when 88,852 Scots left the country but the 1920s were to have a more long-term impact as the net loss to Scotland's population of migration was 392,000 – a figure that represented 111 per cent of the natural increase.[23] (In the same period, the population of England rose by 6 per cent.[24]) With the imposition of immigration quotas in the USA and the deterioration in overseas opportunities because of the impact of the Depression, the early 1930s recorded smaller numbers leaving Scottish ports or heading south. Thereafter re-armament and the gathering clouds of war encouraged others to stay home, at least 'for the duration'. Nevertheless, between 1931 and 1951, Scotland still recorded a net loss of population by migration of 220,000.

Even in 1951 migration amounted to 90 per cent of the natural increase, and in the subsequent decade the net loss by migration totalled 286,000.[25] Thereafter, the level of migration in the 1960s was 16 per cent higher than in the previous decade, and among those leaving was a significant number of service sector workers – ironically employees in one of the few growth areas in the Scottish economy.[26] Immigration from south of the border and elsewhere failed to offset such losses: while 41,000 'economically active' persons migrated north into Scotland between 1961 and 1966, 91,300 Scots left.[27] Thereafter, between 1972 and 1986, on average 15,000 Scots emigrated every year.[28]

In his last novel, published posthumously in 1944, Frederick Niven (1878–1944), himself an immigrant in British Columbia, described the dreams of one prospective fictional Scottish emigrant – Robert Wallace, a railway engineer from Glasgow:

> [T]here was enough of the boy left in him . . . to cause him to pretend to himself when surveying a siding – let us say to a coal mine in Lanarkshire – that his chief there was really Palliser or Hector looking for a way through the Rocky Mountains, and that the cows in the smoke-smirched fields nearby were buffaloes or bears.[29]

Emigration did much to solve the problem of blighted personal ambitions in Scotland and the emigrants, in the process of leaving Scotland, did much to shape its image. Yet it is impossible to measure what the loss of citizens on this scale meant for Scotland in the long run. Arthur Herman, who in 2001 would claim that the Scots of an earlier age had invented the modern world, regretted that the Scotland of the late twentieth century had lost its earlier sense of direction and inspiration.[30] But that is surely not the whole story. Regret is certainly the most common response to the exodus, even though, with hindsight, it is a sentiment rarely matched with suggestions of what would have offered migrants a compelling reason to stay. The poet Edwin Morgan (1920–) lists as 'Flowers of Scotland', 'lads o' pairts that run to London and Buffalo without a backward / look while their elders say Who'd blame them'. It is clear that, of these twentieth-century exiles, the majority chose to leave. Scotland has yet to come to terms with the fact that many only stayed because they simply had no choice.

Statistics clearly take us only so far in understanding Scottish society. Demographic trends showed important comparisons and contrasts with the rest of the UK throughout the twentieth century. But what do they *mean*? Those who left Scotland could be counted but what did it mean for them and what did it say about the nation they left behind? Manifest statistical similarities can mask complex qualitative issues. Here we will address two of the most basic necessities. Health could be measured but how was it sustained? Housing could be quantified but what did Scots expect of home?

SCOTLAND'S HEALTH – 'THE VOYAGE OF LIFE'

In 1907, Thomas Cunningham, chairman of the Greenock Provident Bank, expressed a common scepticism among Scots regarding the moral and cultural impact of the social reforms of the Liberal government elected in 1906[31]:

While it would be a disgrace on the nation if it had not made provision to succour the weak and helpless and to extend relief to those who, buffeted by fortune, have stranded on the voyage of life, I venture to say it is almost as dark a stain upon our vaunted civilisation to have members of society who recklessly are living lives by which they will eventually become a burden upon their plodding, hard-working and frugal neighbours.[32]

The ethos of self-improvement and personal responsibility was alive and well in Edwardian Scotland, where savings banks, charities and the efforts of the voluntary hospitals anticipated many of the benefits which the Liberals' insurance schemes and, later, the welfare state were to provide. But the change to state-sponsored provision involved a change in outlook as well as a change of provider.

'Fellow Scots!' exhorted the Secretary of State for Scotland in a leaflet from 1948:

I am confident that 5 July will be an important milestone on the road to better health for Scotland. But the help of all of us is needed. We should know what our Health Service will be able to give us and, of course, we must know how to get it.[33]

In these words, anticipating the institution of the National Health Service, responsibility is summed up in a thorough awareness of personal entitlement and rights. Health in Scotland had become a national rather than a personal concern and comprehensive medical provision was now considered a matter of pride – a privilege won alongside martial victory in 1945 – rather than a state-sponsored folly encouraging 'reckless lives'.

Less than a decade later, however, some were to show doubts about the new system. T. T. Paterson, of the University of Glasgow, noted in 1954:

It may be objected that in these days sick people do not die so readily as before because they are molly-coddled by the expert therapeutic skills of the general practitioners and the care of hospital staffs: that the Scotsman is no healthier than he was, but is kept by science and government from dying earlier.[34]

Improvements in services certainly did not guarantee improvements in lifestyles or, for that matter, the health of every Scot. The Gorbals doctor, George Gladstone Robertson, was sceptical about medical attitudes to illness and public attitudes to health after the foundation of the NHS:

> In medicine there is little thought devoted to errors in the lives of the people, crying out for correction, when they complain of the wind in their stomachs, their sickness in pregnancy, their running noses, their bronchitis, asthma and rheumatism.
>
> All the emphasis is on the search for the break-through, the new 'wonder drug' – anything that will forgive them their sins, the magic that will permit the finger to be kept in the fire without being burned.
>
> Let me smoke my forty cigarettes a day! It is the duty of the doctor and the state to produce the drug to cure me.[35]

So much for self-improvement!

At the start of the twentieth century, state provision of health services did not reach much beyond the basic treatment of the poor and the mentally ill. However, as imperialism demanded healthy soldiers and fertile mothers, concerns for the health of the nation led to the introduction of medical inspections in schools from 1908 and school medical services for necessitous children from 1913. Health and unemployment insurance was operational nationwide from 1911, maternity and midwifery services were improved in Scotland from 1915 and medical services in the Highlands and Islands were given fresh encouragement in 1913 with the introduction of Treasury subsidies.[36] In 1919, the Scottish Board of Health (SBH) was established as an umbrella organisation for health services then co-ordinated by the Local Government Board, the Scottish Education Department, the Scottish Insurance Commissioners and the Highlands and Islands Medical Services Board.[37] But attempts at the extension of national health insurance services and the co-ordination of provision across local authority and voluntary hospitals came to little in the interwar years. Instead, the role of the municipalities was greatly enhanced after 1929 when – as part of local government re-organisation – responsibility for the major health and hospital services was passed from parish and district committees to the county councils. In 1929 the SBH was replaced by the Department of Health for Scotland, but otherwise little changed in the interwar years: by 1936 only Edinburgh, Dundee, Aberdeen and the County of Bute had converted Poor Law infirmaries into general hospitals, for example, and in 1939, 10,398 hospital beds in Scotland were still being provided by the voluntary sector, that is about a third of Scotland's patient provision.[38]

War, however, was to speed up reform and persuade sceptics of the need for a co-ordinated service free to all. The Emergency Medical Service (EMS), established in 1938 in anticipation of high civilian war casualties, encouraged the development of new specialist facilities and co-ordinated the various types of hospital provision on a regional basis. With civilian casualties mercifully less than expected, the EMS began to absorb client demand on the voluntary sector and allowed the Scottish Office to assert its influence on national health in a decisive manner – by 1945 the EMS had treated nearly 33,000 voluntary hospital patients.[39] Indeed, during the Second World War, the number of Scottish hospital beds rose from 35,331 to 48,101.[40]

As elsewhere in the UK, the publication of the Beveridge Report (Report of the Inter-Departmental Committee on Social Insurance and Allied Services) in 1942 inspired Scots to will the seemingly impossible – a free national health service, supporting every citizen from 'cradle to grave'. Families that had relied on traditional remedies, quack cures advertised as miracle restoratives in popular newspapers and the wisdom of peers who had seen or survived more than their own fair share of infectious diseases and accidents could look forward to a time when calling the doctor would no longer generate debts that may long outlast the medicine prescribed. In May 1947, preparations began as the National Health Service (Scotland) Act was passed and a Scottish scheme – influenced in its early development by Tom Johnston and controlled largely by the Scottish Office (as opposed to local authorities, as in England and Wales) – was instituted.[41] Hospitals in Scotland were now to be administered by five Regional Boards and GP services were to be administered by twenty-nine Executive Councils.[42] (This structure lasted until the NHS (Scotland) Act of 1972 created regional health boards.) Over the years, new forms of treatment and surgery developed at a faster pace than ever before.[43] Across Scotland, free general practitioner services and prescriptions signalled the end of generations of concern and anxiety for many poor families. Indeed, the early demand for ophthalmic and dental services overwhelmed the new system – demand for ophthalmic services alone was five to six times greater than had been expected.[44]

During the following decades, growth in NHS services seemed relentless. Between 1965 and 1974, there was a 38 per cent increase in the number of hospital doctors in Scotland (rising to 4,417) and a 40 per cent increase in hospital nurses (to 44,642).[45] Despite cutbacks from the late 1970s, by 1990, spending on the NHS in Scotland amounted to nearly £3,000 million, rising to nearly £4,500 million by 1997.[46] At this time, nearly 4,000 doctors operated as general practitioners for the

Service (there had been just 2,806 in 1965) and 275 hospitals (with 7,500 doctors and dentists) provided care for around one million in-patients alone.[47] Growth in personnel, however, was matched elsewhere by rationalisation. In 1985, around 57,000 staffed beds were available in Scotland's NHS but, by 1997, this number had declined to 40,950 – less than the 1945 total.[48] Reforms in practice, a changing patient profile and new recuperative regimes dictated that the average patient spent less time in hospital than at mid century. But such arguments failed to calm the fears of patients who equated a reduced number of beds with a reduced service. Indeed, the ideal of free care in all aspects had been compromised as early as 1951 when prescription charges and the cost of spectacles had to be met (at least in part) by many patients. From an early date, therefore, the ideal of care in terms of quality and level of provision was qualified. Throughout the century, medical professionals were compelled to assess the cost-effectiveness of new treatments as much as their impact on health. But what of the standard of health itself?

By the end of the century, the survival of Scottish babies into adult-hood was confidently predicted by the majority of mothers, rather than being the subject of chance, luck and prayer as it had been at the beginning of the century. In 1901–05, the Scottish infant mortality rate stood at 120 per thousand live births (129 in the principal towns) and even in 1914 infant deaths stood at 109 for every thousand live births. By 1950, however, this figure had fallen to forty.[49] The statistics clearly improved but that did not make infant death any easier to cope with. In July 1940, the author Naomi Mitchison (1897–1999) lost her newborn daughter:

> I at least cannot change pain into love. And all the little things hurt, hurt, hurt, and there is nothing to be done. Nor is it fair to speak about them to others; nor indeed, would the others understand one's minding so much. But she was part of me, and wanted, all these months, and warm, and one said what a nuisance, but lovingly, and now the whole thing is ended: the love has no object. I had dreamt so often of the sweet warmth and weight of a baby at my breasts and now my bound breasts ache. If I get all drowsy I begin to expect someone to bring the baby in, and that's hell. One has to keep awake.[50]

By 1900 improvements in sanitation and hygiene, a greater awareness of public health issues and the effective implementation of a long-standing vaccination programme had virtually wiped out many of the major killer diseases of the nineteenth century – smallpox, typhus and cholera, for example – but Scots still faced other potential killers. Having survived the Great War, many Scots met their deaths in the Spanish flu outbreak of 1918. While official figures record 17,575 deaths in Scotland, recent research would seem to indicate that the real figure was somewhere in the region of 27,641 to 33,771, the majority of victims being from the young adult population which had so recently and so cruelly been decimated already in the trenches of Europe.[51] Other diseases lingered longer.

In September 1913 Housing Commissioners visited Embo in Sutherland:

> At one spot, on an open space, stood a tuberculosis shelter, with one inmate. The patient slept there overnight and had the company of her girlfriends during the day. There was no indication of unwillingness to occupy such a place, nor was there the slightest indication that the rest of the people regarded such a structure as odd or abnormal.[52]

Tuberculosis was a fact of life (and death) – a very real presence in the social landscape. TB annually killed over 200 Scots in every hundred thousand between 1901 and 1910 and, despite direct government intervention to eliminate it, the disease killed nearly eighty Scots in every hundred thousand on the eve of the Second World War.[53] In 1945, cases of TB reached a peak of 7,316.[54] Victory over this national enemy appeared secure after the mid century as mass X-ray campaigns were introduced in 1957 and the BCG vaccination was developed against the disease but, at the dawn of the twenty-first century, the re-emergence of cases among the poor and ethnic minority groups in urban Scotland aroused fears that TB was yet to be conclusively defeated.

In the mid 1930s, a study by the Rowett Institute of the University of Aberdeen indicated that 'the diet of nearly one-half of the population, though sufficient to satisfy hunger, is deficient for health'.[55] It is hardly surprising then that, until the 1940s, children regularly succumbed to scarlet fever, whooping cough, diphtheria and croup. Together, these diseases annually killed seventy Scots in every one hundred thousand in the first decade of the twentieth century and remained potent threats to young lives in the thirties when, on average, twenty-four in every hundred thousand lost their lives to them every year.[56] By the 1950s, however, heart disease, cancer and cerebral haemorrhage were the major causes of adult deaths, claiming around 747 lives per 100,000 of the population and accounting for nearly two thirds of all deaths.[57] The destructiveness of this unholy trinity persisted until the end of the century, when heart disease killed nearly 8,000 males and around 7,000 females in 1995 alone, and cancers, which affected one in three Scots, claimed the lives of over 15,000.[58]

The writer, Alan Bold (1943–) felt compelled to admit in 1983 that:

> The typical Scot has bad teeth, a good chance of cancer, a liver under severe stress and a heart attack pending. He smokes like a chimney, drinks like a fish and regularly makes an exhibition of himself. He is a loser and he knows it. He is forever trying to cover up the pathological cracks in his character.[59]

Improvement in care was not always matched by comparable improvements in health, and personal choices still had a profound impact on the nation's well-being. But few seemed willing to point the finger of blame inwards. The NHS alone could not solve the health problems attendant on conditions of poverty and ignorance outwith its control and nor, when health wisdom was shared with patients, could health professionals assume with confidence that many would act upon it. Damaging changes in diets and lifestyles, resulting from higher sugar and alcohol consumption over the course of the century, and the smoking habits of the nation required the active participation of individual families to correct them. But the evidence would suggest that many Scots preferred to take their chances in beating the statistician rather than changing their ways. After all, in comparison to their forebears, they had less to lose. 'Reckless lives' were now generally less costly to the individual as the nation bore many of the financial consequences – respiratory disorders would be treated at no charge even though patients smoked, and social security benefits would be paid virtually regardless of how they were spent. Over the course of the century, the nation had clearly taken responsibility for its ailing citizens but many of those failed to take responsibility for their own health. While care was free, health cost money, and many were unwilling to pay the price. The universal benefits of the NHS in the second half of the twentieth century are obvious but, by the 1990s, the system was nursing as many bad habits as patients. Scotland may have benefited from an NHS that maintained a distinctive Scottish dynamic but that wasn't enough to cure its ills.

SCOTTISH HOUSING – 'DESPERATE FOR A BIT OF GRASS'

> 11 March 1914: Calderbank Square, County of Lanark.
> In this old Square, there are four outside privy middens. The conditions of filth were such as could not be described in decent language. So far as this and a large number of other conveniences

in this County are concerned, the Public Health Acts might as well not exist . . .

12 March 1914: Craighead Rows, County of Lanark.
A house of two rooms, taken rent of 2s.8d. per week. A beautiful infant of less than one year old was having his morning bath in the kitchen. Even this small performance was a severe test of the available space.

4 June 1914: Coatbridge.
One group of houses is regarded as exceptionally insanitary. One house is built practically over an open sewer, which takes the sewage of about 30,000 people . . . the aggregation of iron work blasts has resulted in keeping the town practically always under a pall of smoke. The only thing that can be said in favour of the soot is that it is sterile.[60]

On the eve of a war that would claim millions of lives, poor housing in Scotland was claiming the health of the nation. These were the homes to which heroes returned.

Urban myths and faded childhood memories would have us believe that the tenement lifestyles of millions of Scots and the cramped miners' rows of colliery districts bred a community spirit strong enough to triumph over the squalor from which it emerged. We see it in drama, for instance. Alan Spence's play *Changed Days* contains the following exchange between its Edinburgh characters:

2nd Actor: There was a warmth about the place. Folk looked out for one another. They were sociable.
1st Actress: Never a house you couldnae go into. And none of this locking your door.
1st Actor: My father used to say our kitchen was like an Irishman's parlour. Everybody talking and nobody listening![61]

But, for many, the urban landscape failed to support even the simplest pleasures. Ellen McAlister remembered her childhood in the Gorbals:

We were desperate for a bit of grass in our back courts so we used to go to the old graveyard in Rutherglen Road now known as the Rose Garden. We would dig up divots of grass and try to grow them. We would go eagerly to the back court next morning to inspect them but, alas, they never grew.[62]

In 1908, 12.6 per cent of Scotland's urban population lived in one-roomed dwellings and 49.5 per cent of urban Scots lived in homes with more than two persons per room.[63] Rent strikes during the war succeeded in limiting – at least for the duration – the rents that families paid for such overcrowded accommodation (Rent Restriction Act, 1915). But little in the way of real housing reform was attempted until the interwar years. The Royal Commission on Housing which reported in 1917 found that 47.9 per cent of the Scottish population lived in one- or two-roomed houses, compared to only 7.1 per cent in England and Wales. It also highlighted important regional differences in standards.[64] In 1911, 66.4 per cent of Glasgow's housing stock consisted of dwellings of one or two rooms, which accommodated 62.6 per cent of its population.[65] However, while the Commission recommended that at least 250,000 new houses were needed in Scotland, by 1923 – largely as a result of the central government finance offered by the House, Town Planning (Scotland) Act (the Addison Act) – only 25,500 houses had been built.[66] With pitched roofs, rough-cast walls, inside conveniences and often generous back gardens, these early houses met the aspirations of many tenants lucky enough to be offered one and sufficiently well-off to afford it. They were never meant for Scotland's poor. Across the country, many like mill-worker Mary Brooksbank (1897–1978) in Dundee simply had to make the best of what was available. As a newly married young woman in October 1924, she moved into a cramped garret in Foundry Lane of that city. 'I draped my "bonny wee windae", as I came to call it, with light spotted muslin, and tied it with bows of blue ribbon,' she recalled.[67]

Further legislation in the 1930s reduced the generous subsidies offered by the Wheatley Act of the first Labour government (1924) although it was successful in establishing a responsibility on councils to provide adequate housing for local residents. But was adequate housing a laudable aim? Between 1919 and 1939, 272,000 houses had been built in Scotland with the aid of government subsidies (337,000 in total), yet even by 1935 overcrowding in Scotland was still around six times higher than in England.[68] Increasingly, corners were being cut – traditional materials were being replaced by concrete and, for the sake of speedy results, councils were building tenements again. Much can be gleaned about a society from the buildings officials deem suitable for their fellow citizens to call home. And, in the interwar years, we find dangerous precedents were set that would prioritise quantity over quality in the years that followed.

In the short term, however, war brought most building to an abrupt halt in 1939 and, in the immediate post-war years, despite the need for an estimated 500,000 houses in Scotland, shortages curtailed many building ventures.[69] By 1946, desperation had driven 1,500 families to squatting in empty Glasgow properties and, at various times, 'churches, hotels, mansion houses, former warden's quarters at Barlinnie Prison, the Glasgow Press Club and a hospital' were commandeered.[70] Squatters also took up residence for a while in Aberdeen's Balmoral and Willowbank Hotels. In response to such clamant demand, priority was given to the provision of council houses and 144,000 houses (amongst them prefabricated homes) were completed between 1946 and 1951.[71] Thereafter, both Labour and Conservative governments in the 1950s and 1960s continued to identify the provision of council housing and the improvement of existing stock as a priority. Indeed, outbidding the opposition in terms of the number of public sector completions parties would promise became something of a political pastime. The future would caution later administrations to be careful what they wished for.

Across urban Scotland, demolition was the first tangible sign of change. After all, the planners surely could not do worse than what was there already, could they? In Anderston in Glasgow, the population plummeted from 31,902 in 1951 to just 9,265 in 1971 as people were removed to make way for ring roads – a very modern kind of clearance.[72] Gap sites punctuated long rows of tenements and, on gable ends, bright wallpapers exposed the last occupants' tastes to the public. In Dundee, Catherine Smith set the experience to music:

> Come pull doon the chimneys and close a' the mills,
> Demolish the fact'ries where-er ye will,
> Remove the West Port and soon ye will see,
> There's nauthin' at a' left o' Bonnie Dundee.[73]

Jim Reid, meanwhile, mused on the particular fate of Catherine Street in the same city:

> The demolition squad's been there,
> An every stick an' stane they cleared.
> They said the hooses were nae fit,
> For modern families tae be reared.[74]

While England recorded a rise of 62 per cent in private house building in the decade 1954–64, Scotland's rate – while trebling – amounted to only 20 per cent of completions in these years.[75] It was a trend that was to continue. Public provision came to dominate the character of house building and the nature of tenancy in the housing market in Scotland to an extent unknown in England. (Less than one thousand (4 per cent) of the houses built in 1950 were for private owners.[76]) By 1977, 53 per cent of Scottish households were in accommodation provided by either local authorities or the Scottish Special Housing Association (SSHA).[77]

Council housing had a profound effect on Scottish society. The provision of local authority dwellings certainly improved housing standards for a huge number of Scots in a relatively short time period and at great cost to the public purse but, for the tenants of this monolithic system, there was precious little reward for their loyalty over the years and few means of escape.[78] The 'points system' for allocating council tenancies limited the choices available to tenants and the private rented sector provided only 6 per cent of all housing tenures in 1992 – this was even lower than in Communist East Germany.[79] Andrew Gibb was unforgiving in this description of council housing in 1989:

> Building designs totally unsuited to the Scottish climate and to the mass incarceration of humanity were symptomatic of the lack of architectural conception and commitment, producing built environments of stultifying insensitivity and monotony. Flat roofs failed to shed heavy rainfall and acted as reservoirs for rain-water which percolated through inadequately sealed joints to the dwellings below – cladding slabs were secured by ferrous pins which rusted rapidly in the moist climate and in the worst cases gave way entirely, hurling their half-ton burdens hundreds of feet to shatter on the paving slabs below . . . Steel-framed windows which no amount of painting could protect from corrosion, and which acted as reservoirs for condensation, thin interior divisions which transmitted the slightest noise, and uninsulated exterior walls which permitted expensive heat to drain away were but a few of the basic structural drawbacks.[80]

Scots were both the beneficiaries and the victims of state housing schemes designed to meet political targets and chase prestigious architectural acclaim rather than the needs and aspirations of the families that lived in them. High-rise buildings, for example, retained high populations in urban centres that were haemorrhaging citizens to the more desirable New Towns and suburbs and were seen as prestige symbols for both architects and councils.[81] Once up, however, scant attention was paid to lifts that were continually out of order, long corridors regularly bereft of light and windows as high as eagles' eyries that lacked safety catches.

The 1980s were something of a turning point. In 1980, the Housing (Tenants' Rights etc.) Act introduced the tenants' 'Right to Buy' their council houses at very favourable rates but, thereafter, change emerged relatively slowly. In 1987, 49.2 per cent of Scottish households – compared to 24.2 per cent in England – remained public sector tenancies.[82] It was only after 1986, when terms governing the purchase of council flats were improved – a large proportion of Scottish housing stock – that sales took off.[83] By 1991, over 250,000 public sector houses had been sold in Scotland and, in 1991 alone, Scottish sales amounted to over 20 per cent of sales across Great Britain.[84] In East Kilbride, house sales reached almost 50 per cent of the existing New Town stock by 1991 and similarly, in Cumbernauld and Kilsyth, sales were above 40 per cent. Even in the local authority ranked lowest in terms of council house sales during this period (Motherwell), sales approached 14 per cent.[85] A silent revolution was under way and it was matched by the transformation of the private sector and declining public sector investment in housing. In 1990, the private sector accounted for 82 per cent of new house completions, in comparison to 64 per cent in 1979 and, while the public purse financed 8,000 dwellings in 1979, less than 2,000 completions in 1990 were accounted for by the public sector.[86]

Changing tenurial arrangements and the growth of tenant-run housing associations complete the picture of a housing market in Scotland transformed in the final decades of the century. Altered government priorities, personal desires to own one's home and the realisation that the optimism of the building boom of the 1950s and 60s had failed to address the desires of more affluent Scots just as it had failed Scotland's poorest made Scotland more receptive than some care to admit to the prospect of a 'property-owning democracy'. Between 1981 and 1991, the number of dwellings in Strathclyde owned by their occupiers rose by 16.4 per cent and, in Tayside, a rise in owner-occupation of 18 per cent over the previous decade meant that the majority of houses in this region were in the hands of home-owners.[87] Scots were keen to remove themselves from the shackles of Labour-controlled housing departments even if they did not embrace the ethos of the Conservative government that made this possible.

But it tended to be the most desirable council properties that were sold to tenants. What was left often became a burden on councils that struggled to find paying tenants and increasingly found central government grants cut or withdrawn altogether. Many Scots continued to live in substandard accommodation. The 1991 Scottish House Condition Survey showed that 94,000 dwellings (almost 5 per cent of the occupied housing stock) were below tolerable standards and 13 per cent of Scottish homes suffered dampness – a state of affairs that led to illness and low attainment in their occupants.[88] In Edinburgh in the early

1990s, a social worker remembered 'talking to this wee girl [who] said that she always felt that her clothes smelt damp and she was ashamed' – it wasn't just health that suffered in these circumstances.[89] For others on council house waiting lists – and in Edinburgh alone these numbered around 25,000 in the late nineties – the prospect of homelessness was a very real fear. In 1985, more than 23,000 families had applied for help under the Homeless Persons Act and, a year later, it was estimated by the charity, Shelter, that one Scottish family in every hundred was home-less.[90] By the late nineties, conditions had worsened and the number of households making formal homelessness presentations to Scottish local authorities reached an all-time high of 43,100 in 1997–98.[91] At the same time, it was estimated that between 8,400 and 11,000 individuals had slept rough on at least one occasion during that year.[92] In John Cathcart's 1988 short story, 'One Completed Day', the central protagonist leaves a night shelter in Glasgow:

> I was heading for Bridgeton Library . . . I never found any mental ease or comfort walking that straight road along Argyle Street amidst nicely dressed early morning city workers. Everyone always appeared to be in a hurry – to get somewhere! I was, and felt I was, going nowhere. And always the fear inside myself that I would be recognised for what I secretly hoped I was not, A DOSSER.[93]

At the same time as many Scots became the first generation in their family's long history to own their own home, thousands had nowhere to call home. It is more than hindsight that permits the historian to condemn a century of housing policy in Scotland – its legacy is to be found in the boarded-up windows of council properties, the ill-health of generations rocked to sleep in damp houses and the shame of individuals who quite simply have nowhere to go. For good reasons, both public and private enterprise were limited at various times in what they could achieve but surely, after one hundred years, one could have expected more?

SIX   Living in Scotland

At times the big picture, revealed with the gift of hindsight and refined by the historian's craft, is deceptive. Eric Linklater, in 1935, drew attention to this dilemma, and is worth quoting at length:

> Half a millennium hence historians may write of 1935 as a village on the slope of a smoking volcano. They may say that all Europe was an armed camp, and the threat of war occluded all other thought. They may speak of the millions of men who were unemployed and had no hope of employment. They may describe our desperate race to re-arm, and our futile conferences to keep the peace. They may quote statistics to show that children were undernourished, and most of their parents cancerous. They may see the Class Struggle as we see the Wars of the Roses, and with horror discuss our miseducation, our music, and our mass hysterias. But what will they know, these grave historians, of our sweet pillow-whispering and our dinner-tables, our love of Garbo, our joy in sailing-boats, our excursions in charabancs, our winning shillings on the Glasgow Rangers? Nothing at all.[1]

We *know* that some *Scotsman* readers in 1935, like W. R. G. Moir of Kinnear Road, Edinburgh, were sufficiently concerned about German rearmament in the aftermath of the Saar's overwhelming vote in favour of reunification with Germany to write letters to the editor.[2] We *know* that unemployment was the concern of many Scots in the same year – Katharin Wells complained to the same newspaper of a scheme to relocate 200 Scottish boys for work in the English Midlands.[3] We *know* that childhood diets were occupying the concerns of health visitors at their annual conference in Stirling. We *know* that chromium candlesticks, tall white chrysanthemums, bonbon dishes and a fine linen tablecloth were the preferred decorative flourishes of middle-class dining tables for Christmas 1935. We can deduce with some confidence that Garbo fans would have queued to see their screen goddess in March that same year when she appeared in *The Painted Veil* and can muse that, for at least a while, the Skye Holiday Agency of Portree would have satisfied chara-banc travellers with 'Marvellous Thrills' during their tours of the 'Land of the Far Coolins'.[4] But was it Rangers' win against Partick Thistle on 31 August, the Ibrox side's blistering performance against Celtic in the Glasgow derby of 12 October, the Blues' difficult game against Hamilton Academicals on 16 November or perhaps another game that won Linklater's everyman a shilling?

In what follows, consumerism, poverty, crime, multiple deprivation, education and changing gender roles will be explored in an attempt to draw the parameters within which life was lived in Scotland and identify typical instances and features of Scottish lives. Certainly, as Linklater suggests, there are more cherished vehicles for the remembered whispers of past generations than in history's pages and feelings alive in memory rarely survive transcription. Yet we can seek to understand what Scottish lives meant and how each generation changed with the times, even if we cannot hear their pillow talk.

WAGE EARNERS AND CONSUMERS

> Your main food then was soup and porridge. My mother used tae tell us, 'There's a shillin' which was quite a lot then. You went down to the butcher's and asked them for either a marry bone or a sheep's heid to make the soup with. And with the sheep's heid you always told him tae keep the eyes in to see you over the weekend! If you got a marry bone, which was good as well, then you went over to Dunsmore and got thruppence worth of mixed vegetables . . .
>
> John Webster (1919–, Edinburgh)[5]

Scottish tastes have frequently reflected the limits of poverty and the restraint of thrift more than free cultural or epicurean predilections. At the interface of needs and wants, ability to pay exerts a most powerful influence and working Scots typically operated in a low-wage economy that was beset, in the early decades of the century at least, by cyclical unemployment and short-term work.

Partly as a consequence of the earlier availability of cheap Highland and Irish labour, the relatively slow growth of mass trade unionism and the sluggish development of new industries at a time when traditional industries were shedding employees, Scottish average incomes generally remained lower than those of England and Wales throughout the twentieth century. In 1924, average income per head in Scotland stood at £83, declining to £67 in 1932 with the onset of the Depression, before rising to £97 on the eve of the Second World War and £166 at the war's end, when it represented around 90 per cent of the English average.[6] And yet significant improvements were recorded subsequently, when the average male manual worker's real wage rose dramatically in the 1960s and early seventies.[7] Due mainly to the economic boost offered by North Sea oil, per capita income in Scotland by the 1970s rose to a level close to the UK average, though the cost of living remained about 5 per cent above the UK average.[8] Homes had to be heated longer each year in Scotland and food and consumer goods incurred greater transport costs en route to the north. Scotland also represented a relatively small marketplace for retailers, so competition was not as marked and nor did it bring about prices as low as those to be found elsewhere. All this added further strain on families when the 1980s ushered in a period of relative decline, as Scottish wages fell from 99 per cent of the UK average in 1980 to 93.5 per cent a decade later.[9] In 1995–96, when average weekly disposable income per household in the UK stood at £306.80, the Scottish figure was £275.11.[10] Thus, while Scotland clearly shared in the increased standard of living that was common to most western European countries throughout the century, in comparison to her southern neighbour, growth started from a lower level, generally proceeded at a slower rate and failed to reach the same heights.

Judging from the table of a traditional Aberdeen high tea in the 1930s, however, you would hardly realise it:

> [T]he order of it is this: First, one eats a plateful of sausages and eggs and mashed potatoes; then a second plateful to keep down the first. Eating, one assists the second plateful to its final home by mouthfuls of oatcake spread with butter. Then you eat oatcake with cheese. Then there are scones. Then cookies. Then it is really time to begin on tea – tea and bread and butter and crumpets and toasted rolls and cakes. Then some Dundee cake. Then – about half-past seven – someone shakes you out of the coma into which you have fallen and asks you persuasively if you wouldn't like another cup of tea and just *one* more egg and sausage.[11]

In the Scottish diet, we see an important aspect of consumption that was resistant to change – or, more particularly, improvement – and reflected traditional tastes in their most literal sense. Up to 1914, oatmeal was still the basis of the rural Scottish diet although, in the towns, bread and other wheat products had largely taken its place.[12] In a study of twelve Glasgow families in 1922, bread was the staple. More worryingly, milk was nearly absent from their diet, butter had been replaced by margarine and fruit formed no part of their food intake whatsoever.[13] One can muse that low incomes, life in small over-crowded tenement apartments and the exhaustion of mothers with large families did much to encourage such a state of affairs, but the persis-tence of these problems into more affluent times is more difficult to explain. In general, by the 1930s, Scottish households tended to spend more on bread, cakes, cereals, butter, jam, eggs, sausages and biscuits than their southern counterparts and less on milk and vegetables. Rationing, which persisted into the post-war years, ultimately did little to change this overall pattern – even in 1949, the Scots spent nearly 4 per cent less on fruit and vegetables than the British average.[14] There was little now to distinguish country areas from the towns and the soci-ologist James Littlejohn regretted the changes he saw in the Borders in the early 1960s:

> Porridge twice a day made from local meal is now a thing of the past (the mill itself is now in ruins); cereals have replaced it on the breakfast table. Sheep which die on the hill are rarely eaten. A supply of meal is no longer part of the bargain between farmer and servant. Shop-bought bread is eaten as much as home-baked scones, and processed foods like semolina and creamola are as popular here as elsewhere.[15]

Changes in diet even affected the most remote Scottish areas. Naomi Mitchison's poem 'The Talking Oats' is set in the Western Isles:

> In the old days we lived on porridge and mutton
> Now we can shop with the best: Argentine beef,
> Canadian flour, good quality, white and dry,
> New Zealand butter and Californian peaches,
> South African apples.[16]

By the 1990s, despite the introduction of some new national favourites such as curries and pasta, the Scots still clung to the old staples and were now more able than ever before to satisfy their appetite for the sweet things that had been denied to earlier generations. They spent one quarter less than the English on vegetables and ate 48 per cent more chocolate biscuits than the national average.[17] What this meant in real terms was staggering – by 2001, Scots consumed around 9lbs less fruit and 38lbs less

vegetables per household per year that the rest of Britain.[18] As a consequence, by the end of the century, the diet of Scottish children was judged
to be worse that that of those in England and other major European
countries – in 1998, almost three quarters of boys and three fifths of girls
were drinking sugared fizzy drinks on a daily basis in Scotland.[19] Was it
any wonder that, by the late nineties, despite consuming less food than
others in Britain, 62 per cent of men and 54 per cent of women in
Scotland were either obese or overweight?[20]

Increasingly sedentary lifestyles, encouraged in part by rising car
ownership and the greater availability of home entertainments, did little
to counter the effects of Scottish cuisine. Until the 1920s, 'motor cars and
buses were rarely seen . . . and the aeroplane was unknown' in rural
Lanarkshire – it was still 'the age of the horse'.[21] For the young Alec
Cairncross, 'the world outside Lesmahagow and certainly the west of
Scotland was known to me almost exclusively from books'.[22] Even in
more cosmopolitan Edinburgh, the diplomat, nationalist and author Paul
Scott (1920–) recalled that, in his youth, 'before the days of wireless and
talking pictures in the cinema, few of us had much experience of English
or American voices' and 'social habits and celebrations were little influenced by what happened elsewhere'.[23] But that was soon to change. The
revolution in private travel and communications in the early part of the
twentieth century was facilitated by the car, the cinema, the wireless, the
telephone and, later, the television, but the significance for the average
Scot went beyond the mere ownership of such consumables – they represented new geographic, associational and cultural horizons.

In 1905, 2,697 cars and 2,430 motorcycles were registered in Scotland.
At around the same time, despite a speed limit on Scottish roads of twenty
miles per hour, the new Scottish Automobile Club adopted the motto
'Gang Warily'.[24] Given the state of much of Scotland's road network, the
high cost of the early vehicles, the limited leisure time of the bulk of
Scottish workers and the provision of public transport by local authorities
and private companies throughout Scotland, it was not until after the
shortages and austere economic conditions of the late 1940s that motoring
took off. The number of cars per thousand Scots increased from eighty-
six in 1961 to 171 in 1971 although, reflecting Scotland's lower average
incomes, the comparable UK figures were larger at 116 and 223.[25]
Nevertheless, by 1994, 62 per cent of Scottish households boasted the
regular use of a car and, three years later, Scottish expenditure on motoring
was higher than the UK average.[26] Scots no longer had to restrict their day
trips to the established seaside resorts and Highland towns that boasted
railway or motor coach access, and commuting to work by car was easy
as the reach of new dual carriageways and motorways increasingly

extended into the very heart of Scottish cities. However, by the end of the century, pollution, congestion and gridlocked city traffic was the price that had to be paid for such convenience.

Radio, television and telephones similarly had both positive and negative consequences for the domestic environments of Scots. Television sets north of the Border increased from 41,000 in 1952 to 1,119,000 ten years later.[27] And, by the early 1970s, over 92 per cent of Scottish families owned a television set and over 36 per cent had a telephone.[28] In 1991, television ownership amounted to 98 per cent of the Scottish population, by which time 75 per cent owned a landline telephone.[29] Chapter 13 explores many of the consequences that the expansion of media and communications had for Scotland. Suffice to say here that these trophies of an emerging consumer age were not without their critics. While many Scots eagerly crowded round the wireless to hear big band sounds and Scottish dance music in the 1930s, others mourned the passing of a pre-electric age when entertainment required some effort. In 'Then', Naomi Mitchison recalls:

> Oh the evenings of songs and dancing,
> Brush of the kilt and touch of partners–
> Dust on the pipes and the dancers dumb.
> Now I twist the knob of my programme,
> Cold as fairies the voices come.[30]

Others were less apt to decry the benefits that electrical power brought. For the Scottish housewife – the 'new man' in Scotland was still in his infancy even as the century closed – electric washing machines from as early as the late 1920s came to revolutionise heavy laundry work, electric suction carpet sweepers became popular from the 1930s onwards and the invention of electric cookers (the first Baby Belling made its appearance in 1929) brought to an end the era of the work-intensive kitchen range.[31] Canning, freezing, refrigeration and the development of plastics and effective cleaning agents similarly made housework easier, if no more enjoyable.

The temptations of modernity were also brought closer to home as advertising, modern retailing, mobile shops and catalogue and online shopping made consumption both more attractive and more convenient for Scots across the country. Even the most remote areas participated in this trend and, in the late 1930s, the Irish poet Louis MacNeice (1907–1963) wrote, when considering the contents of the contemporary Hebridean home, 'I reflected that the parlours of the Hebrides could stock all the fun fairs in the world with vases and bijoux to be won by throwing darts or hooplas or rolling balls into holes. They are also the place to go for clocks with eccentric chimes.'[32]

In 1909, Scotland hosted its first 'Modern Homes Exhibition' and, thereafter, domestic furnishings and fashions spoke colourfully of the impact of consumerism on the everyday lives of Scots. Glasgow District Council, the proud sponsors of the 45th Exhibition in 1975, drew attention to the emergence of a 'vast and discriminating public' that welcomed 'the opportunity to compare prices, quality and design'.[33] And in 1994, fashion designer Lex McFadyen commented in that year's exhibition catalogue, that people 'are constantly amazed by what comes out of Scotland, how fashionable we are.'[34]

To Ethel Kilgour, growing up in the late 1920s, the Woolworth's store on George Street, Aberdeen, sufficed – it was 'quite an Aladdin's cave'. There was also a dizzying choice of merchants across the city:

[T]here are Raggie Morrison's and the Equitable, where good bargains were to be found on all manner of things ranging from artificial silk stockings to sheets, enamel pails and basins. At Reid & Pearson's could be bought such things as hats, artificial flowers for weddings, ladies' lingerie, and fully fashioned silk stockings . . . There were the Mascot and Parkinson's dress shops, Coopers for dairy foods, the fruit bazaar, then in Loch Street, the 'Copie' with its comfortable arcade.[35]

By the end of the century, however, the age of the independent shop-keeper had been eclipsed. In 1980, 'multiples' accounted for 48 per cent of shops in Stirling's town centre.[36] Superstores were also by then a familiar sight in or on the edge of most of the larger towns in Scotland. Grocery superstores alone numbered eighty in 1995 – a sixteen-fold increase on the number of such outlets in 1970.[37] Meanwhile, malls (Glasgow alone had four by 1974) were corralling shoppers in sheltered corridors and away from high streets. The Co-operative retailing movement, typically offering the shops of choice for the majority of Scots in the first half of the century, survived these challenges until the 1960s, whereupon suburbanisation and the creation of peripheral housing schemes, the lure of out-of-town centres and the popularity of self-service shop-floor layouts made the 'Co-op' appear old-fashioned, despite the promise of an annual dividend. By the 1990s, the independents had either been taken over or were generally restricted to specialist, exclusive or corner-shop services. In 1994, for example, Dundee's William Low grocery empire was sold to Tesco after thirty-six years of independent trading.[38]

For some Scots, debt was the ultimate consequence of satisfying consumer impulses. The pawn shop or 'tick man' was a familiar feature in many Scottish towns in the first half of the century, though many customers chose to hide their patronage of such services due to the shame attached to both poverty and living beyond one's means. Borrowing, however, typically did not finance luxuries in these years and, for many, it was simply a way of getting by in the short term. Roddy McMillan's play, *All in Good Faith* (1954), is set in a Glasgow tenement apartment and contains the following exchange between the mother and daughter of the Bryson family:

> Rena Bryson: This coat's seen it's day. Time ah had a new yin.
> Mrs Bryson: Oh aye, it's time we a' had somethin' hen.
> Rena: Nae chance o' another credit line fae oul Baird yet?
> Mrs Bryson: No till the last yin's cleared Rena. He's a patient sowl for a tick-man, but he's no' gein' us lines fur the good o' his health.
> Rena: How much is there to pey on the last line yet?
> Mrs Bryson: Too much tae start thinkin' aboot a fresh yin.
> Rena: Ach.[39]

The debts incurred by Scots in the latter decades of the century were of a different magnitude. By 1995, it was estimated that 1 per cent of all Scottish households were facing multiple debt problems and inquiries to Citizens' Advice Bureaux on financial matters had increased more than threefold in the decade from 1985 to 1995.[40] There was little reason to doubt that Scotland made a significant contribution to estimates of UK debt that showed an increase of between 40 and 50 per cent in consumer credit in the mid 1980s.[41] Borrowing to finance a more comfortable lifestyle was no longer seen as shameful but that did not make it any less dangerous. Debts still had to be repaid and incomes were not rising as fast as Scottish aspirations.

POVERTY – 'SORE ENOUGH, EVEN IN ITS MILDER FORMS'[42]

The spoils of the new age were widespread but they were not equally divided and took some time to reach those in the tenements of Maryhill in Glasgow. In the twenties, Roderick Wilson (b. 1917), the son of an unemployed shipwright, 'flitted' to number 72 Braeside Street. He reflected in later life:

> As far as I can remember our wealth of furniture and fittings, care-fully scraped and saved for over years, was a wardrobe, chest of

drawers, two tables, four chairs, a shaving mirror, crockery, cutlery and ridiculous things like a goldfish bowl and Aunt Marian's soup tureen.[43]

Others in the same city had far less.

Charity and official poor-relief agencies in the first decades of the twentieth century offered little to those cast adrift by family or workplace and generally assisted only the poorest and most helpless members of society. The Scottish Poor Law still operated for nearly a hundred years after its partial modernisation in 1845. And, despite changes in its administrative boards and its treatment of the unemployed in the 1920s and '30s, it maintained an uncompromising attitude to its claimants and a conservative attitude to their relief. Emphasis was placed on the obligations of wider kin networks to assist claimants in times of hardship. The children 'looked after' in Stobhill Hospital, a Poor Law facility in Glasgow, in 1910 knew the system's limits, as they literally lived within its bounds.

> There are no pictures on the walls, no ornaments, and no plants. The fires are never lighted, and the rooms are very imperfectly heated by the hot water pipes . . . The children go to church in the grounds and practically never go outside until discharged . . . some of the children have been in the hospital for years.[44]

In the second half of the twentieth century, the welfare state, which emerged after the Second World War, acted as protection for many Scots against much of the distress caused by recurrent economic recessions and the break-up of family units. But 'the system' neither prevented poverty nor cured its ills.[45] There was more than a glimmer of truth in McIlvanney's observation that 'the Welfare State has become less a panacea for the poor than Valium for the rich, more concept than reality, more psychic palliative than physical cure'.[46]

As a country apt to take pride in its early global mercantile reach, its Victorian economic successes and its industrial magnates, Scotland proved reluctant to acknowledge that such proud boasts were not acquired without victims. There was, therefore, a shameful tendency in the twentieth century for poverty to be 'rediscovered' by each generation and greeted with horror and surprise. Clearly, over the course of the century, progress was made in tackling rates of pauperism in the north. But the persistence of high levels of poverty into the twenty-first century and the overwhelming reliance on government and social services to pacify rather than embolden the victims of capitalism and circumstance suggest that, in Scotland, the legacy of misplaced pride was subsidised failure.

In the 1980s, the Scottish Trades Union Congress (STUC) publication, *Scotland – A Land Fit for People*, concluded:

> Scotland in 1987 is a land of vivid contrasts. The bleak, damp-infested high-rise towers, tenements and council estates in our cities are carefully segregated from the fine Georgian and Victorian terraces and villas. The lifestyles of the people who inhabit them contrast even more strongly than the architecture.[47]

This was hardly news – it had always been so. Nevertheless, between 1947 and 1972, the number of means-tested social security payments made in Scotland rose from 91,000 to 324,000 – figures which represent a rise in those dependent on such payments from 150,000 to 536,000 (10.3 per cent of the population).[48] In 1975, the historian, Ian Levitt, observed that 'a new class of poor has been created – and because we have been blinded by outward manifestations of growth, the new poor have been ignored'.[49] By 1977, 9 per cent of Scots relied on supplementary allowance, pension and family income supplement payments.[50] Fourteen years later, 487,000 Scots claimed Income Support (IS) from the Department of Social Security and, in 1994, 42,000 Scots were recipients of Family Credit.[51] Moreover, of the 555,000 IS claimants recorded in 1995, 324,000 (over 58 per cent) had been claiming this benefit for two years or more.[52] Labour Party figures from 1993 recorded that 'as many as 1.25m people, a quarter of the population, may be living in poverty in Breadline Scotland'.[53] In particular areas across Scotland, whole communities were dependent on the state – between 70 and 80 per cent of the population of Greater Pilton in Edinburgh in the early nineties, for example, depended wholly or in part on state benefits.[54] By 1998, with Labour in power, little had changed – nearly 45 per cent of the Scottish workforce earned below the low-pay threshold of £5.89 per hour and, in 2000, poverty affected 45–47 per cent of households in Glasgow.[55] If we are to judge Scotland by the way it treated its poor, the record is hardly edifying.

High unemployment rates in the interwar years and again in the 1980s reminded Scots that no one had immunity against poverty and, for a while at least, drew attention to the personal (as opposed to the statistical) consequences of being out of work. In both periods, as we have seen, Scotland – like many northern English counties – suffered the effects of unemployment disproportionately. At the height of the Depression in 1932, nearly 28 per cent of Scotland's insured population was unemployed, compared to a UK average of a little over 22 per cent.[56] Similarly, while around 10 per cent of the population of the English south-east were unemployed in 1982, nearly 16 per cent of Scots were without work.[57] Between 1967 and 1979, Scottish unemployment doubled and doubled again in the four years to 1983.[58] Within Scotland, there were also regional and sectoral disparities. While the service trades of Edinburgh did comparatively well in the interwar years, industrial Lanarkshire suffered acutely. Again, in 1980, when 35 per cent of males of working age in Glasgow's Provan district were out of work, in rural Gordon less than 4 per cent experienced unemployment.[59]

No matter where or when it struck, however, for those affected, unemployment had similar consequences that were not readily eased by doles and benefits. In the interwar years, Walter Elliot observed, 'The unemployed man, given a dole which will keep him alive, even given a vote by which he can change a cabinet, does not feel himself fully a man.'[60] Research by the Carnegie UK Trust in the late thirties also suggested that few among the unemployed cared much about wider political concerns:

> Unemployment due to conditions of world trade, or technological changes in industrial organisation meant nothing to them. Such explanations left them cold. What mattered to most of them was that they were fit for work and wanted it badly, not so much as an end in itself as a means to an end. They needed the money, their homes needed the money, and it would be money earned by their own effort. One young wife put it thus: 'Somehow when it's money that your man has worked for, it goes further.'[61]

Edwin Muir reflected on the fate of the unemployed in interwar Glasgow: 'Their life now is a long and dreary Sunday; their hands have grown useless, their skill has dropped from them; their days have turned into an unending, inconclusive dream.'[62] Many Scots in the 1980s would share such a dream and, for some, the nightmare is yet to end.

Social Security was the principal area of social policy in which the breach with Scotland's past and Scottish tradition was perhaps most acute after the mid century. By then, parish and local authority administration and funding of poor relief were a thing of the past – policy was made at Westminster. In the process, control became far removed from Scottish communities and an arm of government on which increasing numbers of Scots were reliant also became one over which few Scots had any real influence. While the administrative responsibilities of the Scottish Office grew in the course of the century and Scottish solutions to Scottish social problems became recognised as the way ahead for the economy, this fundamental feature of social policy was stubbornly controlled by Whitehall. In terms of benefits and allowances, Scots were treated the same as necessitous citizens elsewhere in the UK and this was clearly a principle worth defending. But a blind commitment to equality – defined financially, resistant to cultural differences and filtered through a myriad of civil service forms and definitions – failed to take account of the distinctive character of the Scottish economy and Scottish society over the years and failed to address fully the relationships between social security and areas of health, housing and education that were simply different in the north. Scotland's poor clearly benefited from the Social Security safety net created after 1945 but, even at the end of the century, Scottish poverty still awaited a Scottish solution more attuned to the peculiar geography of disadvantage that mapped the country, and more in keeping with the traditions of discrimination and individual responsibility that had always marked poor relief in Scotland.

CRIMINAL SCOTLAND

> There were several cases of drunk and disorder that a minute or two's examination disposed of. Then a woman was called and charged with attempted suicide: she had drunk a bottle of spirits of lemon for no other reason, it seemed, than to attract the waning attention of her husband, and her neighbours. She was bound over to keep the peace and released under her husband's recognizances. She had succeeded in arousing his interest. Then an old man, handsome in a Roman way, white-haired and dignified, was accused of cruelly ill-treating his grandchildren: he was remanded for further examination.
>
> *Magnus Merriman* (1934)
> Eric Linklater

Magnus Merriman's fictional view of a Monday morning courtroom in thirties' Edinburgh confirms that crime, like poverty, is seldom as impersonal as the official statistics suggest.

Over the years, the scale, nature and impact of crimes and offences in Scottish society changed in ways rarely explained simply by economic, moral or cultural shifts. The privations of the interwar period certainly had an impact on rates of offending in these years but it was somewhat contradictory – for example, recorded crimes and offences actually increased after rearmament began to ease the burdens of unemployment. War also made an impression – driving offences plummeted, as did breaches of the peace during the Second World War as potential offenders were compelled to leave their cars at home during blackouts and fuel famines and find more patriotic outlets for their aggressive energies in the armed forces. But, overall, recorded crime actually increased during the period of hostilities.

In the 1950s, it was said that the Scots were 'statistically more wicked than the English' but, from an end-of-century perspective, the early post-war years appeared a time of relative tranquillity.[63] Recorded crimes and offences rose from around 200,000 in 1950 to 955,000 in 1995.[64] The rate of growth was particularly marked in the decade following the mid 1950s and, from the early 1970s, crimes began to grow at a faster rate than offences. (Thefts dominated crime statistics – 43 per cent of recorded crimes in 1995 were thefts.) Reported crimes levelled off from 1992 onwards but substantial increases in violent crimes and sexual assault since the 1950s left little room for complacency and appeared to reaffirm popular perceptions that Scotland was more crime burdened than in earlier years.[65] In comparison to England and Wales, however, Scottish criminality had grown at a slower pace – 'the increase in notifiable crimes in England and Wales between 1950 and 1993 was by a factor of ten, compared with a 7.3 times increase in Scotland.'[66] Looking at homicides, however, comparison casts Scotland in a darker light – homicides in Scotland increased fourfold over the post-war period (there were 133 in 1995) while England and Wales saw homicides double.[67]

High-profile cases regularly dominated newspaper headlines. There were plenty of bogeymen to people the nightmares of twentieth-century Scottish children, from 'Bible John', killer of three Glasgow women in the late sixties, to Thomas Hamilton, the perpetrator of the Dunblane Primary School massacre of 1996 during which sixteen children and their teacher were shot dead. In some communities, criminality was simply part of a way of life. Glasgow's gangland culture of the 1930s has attracted particular attention. Gangs like the Billy Boys of Bridgeton Cross numbered 200 by 1927 and even boasted a junior wing, the Derry Boys, for youths aged fourteen to twenty-one.[68] Thieving, protection rackets and even dances and lotteries raised money to pay the fines of gang members who got on the wrong side of the Glasgow constabulary. Clashes between rival gangs were marked by violence as territory and a sinister interpretation of honour were defended. Guns were not unknown but a domestic arsenal was more common – 'hammers, hatchets, bayonets, sticks filled with lead, huge metal bolts attached to waxed cord and used like an Argentinian bolas, razors of all sorts, broken bottles, shotguns (home-made and stolen), revolvers, swords'.[69] For the young men of Glasgow communities like the Gorbals, membership of street gangs offered them considerable 'cultural capital' and, for older unemployed men in the thirties, they were a way of affirming their status and virility in an economic depression that denied them much else.[70] Into the 1940s and beyond, the popular memory of such street fighters remained strong and continued to influence the outlook of later generations. 'They were put on pedestals by us,' remembered Gorbals boy Jimmy Boyle, himself incarcerated in Barlinnie Prison for murder at the age of twenty-three.[71]

Throughout the century, youth crime was a persistent focus of public interest. As early as the 1930s, delinquency among the nation's youth was a concern. From accounting for around a third of proven crimes in the 1920s, under-seventeens in Scotland were responsible for over 40 per cent of crimes in the 1930s – rising to 44 per cent by 1951.[72] By 2005, 43 per cent of all crimes and offences in Scotland were attributed to young people but the statistical consistency hides the fact that, as the number of crimes and offences had grown considerably over the course of the second half of the twentieth century, the number of crimes committed by children had grown proportionately. In the 1980s, children were the focus of over 26,000 initial police reports annually and, despite some improvements recorded at the close of the decade, worrying indicators of future social problems were evident in a rise in serious assaults, car theft, indecency and drugs offences.[73]

In other respects, youth crime had changed little since mid century. In 1946, a spate of vandalism in Edinburgh's schools was proving a cause for concern. For example, on 10 June, pupils arrived at Blackhall School only to find their classrooms in chaos. 'Cupboards, chairs, and other furnishings had been broken or damaged and ink had been smeared over the walls. The school radio set and a gramophone had been thrown down the stairs, and were found smashed to pieces.'[74] Youngsters were blamed for this 'sheer wanton damage'.[75] In West Pilton, two months later, window smashing was similarly causing problems and the entry of new tenants on this housing estate had to be delayed due to the vandalism of local children. The *Scotsman* recorded:

> It is estimated that within the past few weeks, on the latest scheme, over 500 windows have been broken, and during the past twelve months, over 1000. Just about a year ago, over 1100 new panes had to be fixed at one block, consisting of 32 houses . . . In other places, plugs, pendants for electric lights, 'pulley' ropes, and parts of grates have been taken away. Outside galvanised ventilators – which are at present in very short supply – have been kicked in and smashed.[76]

As these incidents suggest, we clearly have to be wary of offering rose-tinted views of the first half of the twentieth century but it is obvious that youth offending grew massively after those years. By 2005, it was Scotland's youth that was responsible for the majority of offences in the following categories: fire-raising, vandalism, motor vehicle theft, theft from lockfast places, handling offensive weapons and housebreaking.[77]

Much was achieved through the introduction of a Children's Hearing system in Scotland (operational from 1971) to tackle the offending behaviour of children outwith the traditional courts. Persistent high levels of youth offending even after this time, however, pointed to serious failures in contemporary parenting and social policy. A 1995 survey indicated that more than 40 per cent of child offenders came from single-parent households, that nearly 50 per cent of these children's families were on benefit and that 65 per cent of these children were unenthusiastic about school.[78] Crime was clearly part of much wider social problems in Scotland.

Policing in Scotland echoed changes in Scotland's administrative structures and responded positively, if somewhat belatedly, to techno-logical innovations, although it was arguably slower to reflect the changing fabric of Scottish society. In 1945, there were forty-nine forces in Scotland, by 1969 amalgamations brought this total down to twenty and, following local government reform in the 1970s, the number of Scottish forces was reduced to eight.[79] By the 1990s, these forces employed 14,000 officers. Over the years, policing had changed dramat-ically. Police boxes and radio cars had made their first appearance on Glasgow and Edinburgh streets in the 1930s and radios revolutionised communications from the late 1950s. Still, in the North Division of Glasgow in 1969, however, there were only two police cars. And, while women officers had been employed in Scottish forces from the 1930s, it took time for the female presence to make its mark – in 1932, there were less than twenty policewomen in the whole of Scotland, none of whom were uniformed and all of whom had to resign their appointments on marriage.

Popular perceptions of policing were profoundly influenced by the activities and personalities of local constables and, like elsewhere in the UK, the image of the 'common sense' beat cop, who at times flouted political correctness and the shuffling of paperwork to get his man, was generally rendered sympathetically and occupied a special place in urban mythology. 'Big John' served in the notorious Saracen area of Glasgow after a spell with the Royal Navy in the Second World War:

> You, as a cop, were supposed to protect the public and we did just
> that. We sorted the neds out. No mercy, pick out the biggest of them,
> pick out the leaders, hit them hard and give them a good tanking

and show them who was boss. If anybody caused trouble anywhere on our beat we would find out who they were and we'd go after them. When we did we showed no mercy, we gave them a tanking they'd never forget and made sure they knew what it was for. We didn't bother to run many of them in, unless it was for something really bad, a slashing or a stabbing or something like that.[80]

Flexibility in the application of the law was a constant feature of Scottish enforcement bodies throughout the century. We can see it most notably in the treatment of drunkenness – the vast majority of those arrested for drunkenness were males, as women tended to be dealt with informally. Moreover, in the 1980s, many police officers considered punishment and the use of the criminal law in particular an ineffective and inappropriate response to drunkenness. Older officers were apt to adopt a flexible response when coming across such antisocial activity.[81]

Not surprisingly, then, the operation and effectiveness of the criminal justice system were far from uniform across the country and are not entirely reflected in official statistics. Policing as much as criminality had a regional dynamic. In Dundee, in the 1950s, on average 104 crimes were 'known' per thousand of its population annually and nearly 62 per cent of crimes were cleared up, whereas, in Aberdeen, while there were only around twenty-two known crimes per thousand, less than 43 per cent were cleared.[82] Even in 1990, 63,767 crimes and 134,528 offences became the subject of the courts' attention but there were still marked variations in practice across the Scottish forces.[83] The rate of children referred to the procurator fiscal ranged from two per thousand in Grampian in 1989 to seventeen per thousand in Central Region. And, of the 743 women convicted of offences relating to prostitution in 1995, only five were convicted in Edinburgh, while 642 were convicted in Glasgow.[84] Stirlingshire's children and Glasgow women were no more inherently prone to crime than their Highland and Edinburgh counterparts. But their circumstances were different and the system treated them differently.[85]

In 1995–96, the Scottish prison population numbered 5,632 with an additional 718 in young offenders' institutions – an increase of some 1,739 since 1979.[86] Crimes and criminals had changed significantly over the course of the century – drug-related crime in the last two decades had mushroomed. In 1998, 8,290 Scots were convicted for the possession of illegal drugs with intent to supply and a further 22,500 for straightforward possession.[87] No region was immune. Although drug-related offences were highest in the major Scottish cities and their hinterlands,

Above. **Ships that made the Clyde:** Here John Brown's workers on Cunard's *Carinthia* in the early 1950s show scant regard for personal safety as they construct one of the Clyde's iconic trans-Atlantic liners. © The Scotsman Publications Ltd. Licensor www.scran.ac.uk

Left. **Marching through Motherwell:** A child joins the miners' strike of 1984. The dispute tested the inter-generational loyalties of communities built on the coal industry almost to breaking point. © The Scotsman Publications Ltd. Licensor www.scran.ac.uk

'The Craig': Although little now remains but traces in the landscape, photographs and memories testify to the scale and grim majesty of the Ravenscraig Steelworks. © Scottish Media Newspapers Ltd. Licensor www.scran.ac.uk

M. Nairn & Co Linoleum Works, Kirkcaldy, c.1954: Women were styled as the consummate consumers of the paraphernalia of the modern age, but they also played a major role in the manufacture of the decorative and practical components of many 'ideal homes'. © The Scotsman Publications Ltd. Licensor www.scran.ac.uk

Glasgow Stock Exchange, 1964: Computerisation, the consolidation of London's role as Britain's financial capital, and Edinburgh's dominance in banking services, eroded the regional geographies of Scotland's financial sector. © Newsquest (Herald & Times). Licensor www.scran.ac.uk

'Silver Darlings': Scotland's fishing fleet changed dramatically over the course of a century, from sail to steam to diesel. Modernisation alone, however, was seldom a guarantee of profitability in the fast-changing economic context that determined the future of Scotland's fishing communities. The scene here shows a Banff steam drifter discharging its herring catch c.1904. © Moray Council (Elgin Library). Licensor www.scran.ac.uk

Haymaking on Eriskay, 1934: Crofting regularly employed the labour of the whole family, and – due to the size and character of holdings and the relative poverty of Highland communities – only slowly embraced mechanisation in arable cultivation. © University of Edinburgh Department of Celtic and Scottish Studies. Licensor www.scran.ac.uk

Life in chains: Workers at Hughes microelectronics factory in August 1975 were chained to their work-benches to reduce the build-up of static electricity. The electronics industry was identified as Scotland's greatest hope for the future as industrial monoliths of a former age shed their workforce in the second half of the twentieth century. Scotland, however, could never boast the productive or research capacity of Silicon Glen. © The Scotsman Publications Ltd. Licensor www.scran.ac.uk

Hillman Imp Deluxe motor car, 1973: Despite building some of the fastest British cars during the Edwardian period, Scotland's car industry would be remembered for less illustrious products and an unenviable reputation for poor labour relations. © National Museums Scotland. Licensor www.scran.ac.uk

'The Hydro Boys': These men were the human face of the hydro-electric schemes in the years following the Second World War. Here the two gangs of the Loch Sloy tunnel meet after two years of drilling from opposite sides of Ben Vorlich. © Newsquest (Herald & Times). Licensor www.scran.ac.uk

One of her Majesty's subjects in Glasgow's Trongate in the year of her Silver Jubilee, 1977: Despite numerous welfare initiatives, the lives of many Scots throughout the century were blighted by periods of homelessness. © Newsquest (Herald & Times). Licensor www.scran.ac.uk

Above. **A capital view:** The elegance and grace of former times still marked the skyline of Edinburgh in the late twentieth century. © James Gardiner. Licensor www.scran.ac.uk

Right. '**Small town Scotland**' was a useful, if wholly insufficient, short-hand for the countless lives lived in towns such as Kirkcaldy. Here and elsewhere, the apparent absence of metropolitan sensitivities encouraged many to neglect and under-value the industrial and cultural achievements of such communities. © Scottish Motor Museum Trust. Licensor www.scran.ac.uk

Nether Street, Kirkcaldy.

'The ties that bind': Four generations of Kate Robertson's Perthshire family in 1910 celebrate the baptism of the youngest member. © National Museums Scotland. Licensor www.scran.ac.uk

D.I.V.O.R.C.E.: While the lengthy divorce proceedings of the 11th Duke and Duchess of Argyll were unusual (and scandalous) enough to encourage newspaper headlines between 1959 and 1963, by the century's close most Scottish families had direct experience of the impact of divorce on couples and their children.(Margaret, Duchess of Argyll, is shown here arriving at court in 1959.) © The Scotsman Publications Ltd. Licensor www.scran.ac.uk

A pearl fisher and his itinerant family make their way between camps in the 1930s. The Scottish family changed dramatically over the course of the century. © National Museums Scotland. Licensor www.scran.ac.uk

Will ye no come back again? Emigrants wave to friends and family as they leave Greenock in April 1967. © The Scotsman Publications Ltd. Licensor www.scran.ac.uk

Right. **At your service:** District Nurse Dunsire cares for a patient from the Dunbar area at home in 1960. © The Scotsman Publications Ltd. Licensor www.scran.ac.uk

Below. **Life in one room:** This Glasgow apartment was home to a family of eight in 1964. Overcrowding remained a problem in Scotland, particularly in the first half of the century. © Newsquest (Herald & Times). Licensor www.scran.ac.uk

F.W. Woolworth & Co Ltd, 119 Union Street, Aberdeen, 1937: Renowned for its cut-price goods, 'Woolies' boasted two Aberdeen branches by the late 1920s, where they joined a plethora of independent retailers that were eclipsed only in the final decades of the century by the growth of national retailing 'giants' and franchised stores. © Aberdeen City Council, Arts and Recreation department, Library & Information Services. Licensor www.scran.ac.uk

Millennium doom: Multiple deprivation in Easterhouse in 1999 meant many expected little from the new century. © Newsquest (Herald & Times). Licensor www.scran.ac.uk

A proud heritage? A classroom scene from the 1940s, typical of many schools across Scotland. © Newsquest (Herald & Times). Licensor www.scran.ac.uk

Sex and sexuality: Civil Scotland took some time to come to terms with more liberal attitudes to homosexuality. Here members of the International Gay Rights Congress demonstrate outside the *Scotsman* offices in Edinburgh in 1974. © The Scotsman Publications Ltd. Licensor www.scran.ac.uk

Left. 'The Dundee Suffragettes on the Warpath', by Tom Ross: Militant suffragism left its mark on Scotland in the years before the First World War, but it was war service that secured women the vote in 1918. © Dundee Central LIbrary. Licensor www.scran.ac.uk

A new constituency: It took time for female enfranchisement to effect change in the representative political offices of Scotland. However, in 1988 the two most senior positions in the local authorities governing Glasgow and Edinburgh were occupied by women. Eleanor McLaughlin was Edinburgh's Lord Provost, while her Glasgow counterpart was Susan Baird. © The Scotsman Publications Ltd. Licensor www.scran.ac.uk

Above. **On the site of Calton jail:** The building of St Andrew's House in Edinburgh in 1939 affirmed the growth of the administrative offices then required to support the work of the Scottish Office and its enhanced ministerial team. © The Scotsman Publications Ltd. Licensor www.scran.ac.uk

Right. **Sir James Gunn's 1950 portrait of Labour's Thomas Johnston,** Secretary of State for Scotland in Churchill's wartime cabinet. © Scottish National Portrait Gallery. Licensor www.scran.ac.uk

rural areas also experienced the horrors connected with such crimes. Drug-related offences in Highland Constabulary's area, for example, stood at 1,296 in 1999.[88] The mother of a Fraserburgh heroin addict recounted her experience of a family under siege around this time:

> Eventually at some point down the line as the habit grows money becomes a major problem.
>
> By this time the addiction has become so powerful that morals and any scruples go out the window . . .
>
> Soon nothing is safe to be left unattended . . .
>
> You end up sleeping with your purse under your pillow, and taking your purse and credit cards etc. with you even just to go into the next room.
>
> Washing windows becomes impossible, as you cannot do that with your handbag under your arm.
>
> Unless something is nailed to the ground it is likely to get stolen.[89]

Criminal behaviour in the home seldom went reported but it sentenced many to what amounted to imprisonment.

Despite the changing profile of Her Majesty's guests, the atmosphere as much as the architecture of Scotland's aging prisons in the late twentieth century was little altered in the course of a century. Boyd Keen, imprisoned in Barlinnie for drug smuggling – a very modern form of piracy – offers us this insight into prison life in the 1980s:

> Permeating everywhere is the smell peculiar to all prisons. A heavy miasma that consists of unwashed bodies and unbrushed teeth. Of damp sweaty jail clothing and the cabbage based flatulent emissions of almost three hundred sphincters which – along with hawking and spitting – seems to form the most popular activity amongst the cons. A smell mixed with the cloying sweetness of the cheap pine disinfectant slopped everywhere that adds to, rather than dispels, the atmosphere. A smell that is redolent of despair and frustration, and the pheromones of violence and fear emitted by the bodies of the caged male animal.[90]

Over the years, the provision of radio sets, televisions, educational programmes and billiard tables did little to civilise these cages.

Gender played its part in the sociology of crime. Boys made up the majority of young offenders throughout the century and, in 1998, 88 per cent of those convicted for drugs offences were men. But women accounted for around 90 per cent of the victims of domestic abuse towards the end of the century and, as always, women dominated the prostitution statistics. Around 1,400 women were believed to be involved in street prostitution in Scotland in 2004.[91] And a study of female Glasgow prostitutes at the end of the twentieth century showed that around one quarter had become involved in prostitution aged eighteen or under.[92] The following testimony comes from one of the ten to fifteen women believed to have been involved in street soliciting in Dundee in 2004.

> I was in and out of foster homes. I practically brought my sisters up, till I got taken into a home. Once I was taken into a home they got taken into foster care as well and that's why I ended up blaming myself. I've been sexually abused by about eight different people. When I was growing up my uncle sexually abused me for eight years from the age of 2 to 10, and the thing is my parents know about it but because they were alcoholics they just ignored it.[93]

This young woman enters her country's history as a crime statistic, yet she – and, regrettably, many more – may equally be considered manifestations of wider social problems prevalent across Scotland in her time. Crime was personal but society, through the whimsy of birth and environment, too often selected the criminals and they too could be victims.

The high proportion of young offenders emerging from Scotland's broken homes, the overwhelming proportion of homicides committed by the unemployed (78 per cent in 1994) and the rise in crimes of dishonesty from the late 1980s (including housebreaking, theft and shoplifting), as other Scots borrowed their way to affluence, all suggest that wider social forces influenced the pattern of Scottish crime. The same acquisitive culture that led to consumerism led to burglary. Given what we know of Scottish social conditions in the twentieth century, it is hardly surprising that social injustice and personal tragedy readily expressed itself in crime. These are not excuses – just part of an explanation. Failed by the system or having failed themselves, it was easier for some to believe that they owed little or nothing to the society that helped bring this about and even less to the laws that governed such disadvantage. In Scotland, the maintenance of a distinctive legal system did not cure the nation of its criminality. It is an unsettling conclusion, repeated in other areas of social policy, that those who should have known Scotland best were not always best placed to effect radical change. Bringing law making closer to home did not, of itself, guarantee progress.

MULTIPLE DEPRIVATION – 'A SENSE OF HOPELESSNESS'

Between the 1940s and the 1980s, local authorities found that planning lent itself most readily to problems easily distinguished by location and bounded by recognisable communities, even though social ills seldom seemed to stop at ward boundaries or contain themselves within specific postcode areas. Nevertheless, at various times over the course of the century, Scotland's cities were to be divided into 'project areas' and 'schemes' as generations of social reformers sought to unravel the causes from the consequences of multiple deprivation. In the brutal prose characteristic of such policies, a Strathclyde Regional Council document of 1976 attempted to itemise and list the problems associated with communities residing in areas of multiple deprivation. It is worth quoting at length.

a) sense of hopelessness: lack of knowledge and access to established machinery
b) increasing sense of dependence on outside agencies, linked often with frustration at lack of control over own affairs
c) lack of leadership to form groups among the community, organise self-help etc.
d) incidence of crime, particularly juvenile delinquency and vandalism
e) patterns of long spells of unemployment
f) truancy, underachievement in schools and general lack of sympathy for educational system
g) very limited horizons, particularly affecting the young
h) sense of anonymity and irresponsibility arising from breakdown of older communities with redevelopment and population movement, from housing policies, from the concentration of disadvantaged groups like one-parent families
i) ill-health – incidence of poor health and handicap
j) feeling of stigmatisation – loss of sense of worth and identity
k) indifference to, if not estrangement from, councillors and members of Parliament.

This list of problems quoted is by no means exhaustive.[94]

The problems of environment had become personal; the stigma of 'place' had become self-fulfilling. In 1998, Erica would recount:

I dread to think what the future holds for my kids if I don't get away from Easterhouse soon while they are still young. I know in my heart that they will either turn to drugs or end up in prison. My kids keep asking to move.[95]

In the 1940s, 700,000 people lived on the 1,800 acres comprising the central Glasgow area – an average density of 400 per acre. Seen another way, here, one seventh of Scotland's population was concentrated into three square miles.[96] Glasgow's population peaked at 1,055,017 in 1951. Thereafter, central Glasgow's population slipped below one million in 1966 and then to a little under 900,000 in 1971, when the population of the city's core represented little more than 50 per cent of the Glasgow conurbation as a whole.[97] In the subsequent decade, a fall of 22 per cent set Glasgow city's population at around 766,000 – somewhere between the size of the metropolitan districts of Manchester (448,000) and Birmingham (1,007,000).[98]

Glasgow's city fathers were initially alarmed by the city's declining share of the population in the Central Belt and at least until the late 1950s attempted to retain the maximum number of productive citizens within the city's bounds. By the 1960s, however, a surplus population had been identified in Glasgow's city centre that came to be known as 'overspill'. The council had little option but to accept that the solution to Glasgow's housing problems – overcrowding, unsanitary dwellings and a preponderance of 'single-end' tenements – lay in rehousing its surplus population outwith the city's bounds. It was social engineering on a grand scale with families being sent as far away as Stranraer and Wick. But this did not solve the problems of the inner city.

In 1954, an inner city Development Plan identified twenty-nine Glasgow neighbourhoods as comprehensive development areas – areas where just about everything was to be demolished and rebuilt.[99] The Gorbals and Hutchesontown on the city's south-side were the first to come under the developers' gaze – by 1957, at a cost of £13 million, the number of shops was reduced from 444 to fifty-seven and pubs from forty-six to nine and just about any trace of industry was to be found only in the memories of the few south-side families who decided to stay.[100]

Glasgow was not alone in its attempts to reshape the urban environment. Over the next twenty years, addressing multiple deprivation within Scotland's city centres took various forms. In 1968, urban aid programmes sponsored by government subsidies encouraged local councils to embark on community development projects and, ten years later, the Inner Urban Areas Act set out funding opportunities to strengthen inner-city economies, improve the built environment and address social problems.[101] Deprivation was to be addressed through *re*-generation, creating a convenient fiction that something valuable had been lost by deprived communities which the very local authorities that had overseen decline could *re*-form.

In 1976, eastern Glasgow – an area comprising the Calton and other districts – became the focus of an ambitious area renewal scheme called Glasgow Eastern Area Renewal (GEAR).[102] Public money and initiative poured into an area whose population had declined by 37 per cent in the fifties and sixties and where de-industrialisation had made its mark at an early stage as firms sought the more attractive facilities and financial packages offered in new industrial estates.[103] By 1981, however, despite successes in improving the housing and physical environment of the area, the Calton still had its problems. Over 26 per cent of the economically active population of the GEAR area was recorded as unemployed or temporarily sick and, two years later, a survey showed that around 70 per cent of east-end residents had no academic qualifications.[104] Glasgow's city centre makeover as the Merchant City in the late 1980s grabbed newspaper headlines and attracted the upwardly mobile into areas which, for generations, had appeared more alive on history's pages than on the streets. But problems clearly persisted.

Thirty years before, the great hope of city planners across Scotland looking outwith city boundaries for solutions to the nation's post-war housing crisis had been housing estates on the peripheries of the major towns – communities were to be formed where the town met the country.

> Here indeed was paradise. A shining new house, running hot and cold water and a bath – luxury indeed! A little strip of garden where my father grew roses and won prizes in the local garden competition. Great stretches of fields in front of the house over which we ran daily to the little red brick school, built on the banks of Niddry Burn and named after the ancient mill which for centuries had graced its banks.[105]

Here is a picture painted as quaintly as anything the Kailyard School could produce but this is Craigmillar, a housing estate on the edge of Edinburgh, designed in the 1930s, which, alongside West Pilton and Wester Hailes, ranked as one of the three main areas where deprivation was concentrated around the heart of the capital by the 1980s. Alongside Glasgow's peripheral housing schemes, Barlanark, Drumchapel, Castlemilk and Easterhouse, Dundee's Whitfield, Paisley's Ferguslie Park and Aberdeen's Middlefield and Northfield estates, these areas represented the major concentrations of multiple deprivation in late-twentieth-century Scotland. They had been planned with scant regard for the social needs of the new communities that would live there – schooling was inadequate in the early years at least, shopping and leisure facilities were insufficient for the numbers involved, the churches seldom caught up with parishioners that moved to the schemes and going to work could mean a long commute on unreliable public transport. After all, few residents could afford cars. Overall, there was little to sustain these communities when unemployment afflicted thousands of residents from the 1970s onwards. In estates containing thousands of families, the loneliness was strangely tangible. By 1975, over a quarter of the tenants of Glasgow's peripheral estates had requested transfers out of these areas.[106]

Paisley's Ferguslie Park exhibited all of the symptoms of an estate suffering the acute effects of multiple deprivation. Increasing numbers of dwellings over the years remained unoccupied and fell into disrepair, making them the object of vandalism and the haunts of drug users; a high proportion of single-parent families dependent on Social Security benefits were housed in the estate; and, in the mid seventies, large numbers of homeless people were allocated houses in Ferguslie Park.[107] While Paisley suffered 8 per cent unemployment in 1971, nearly a quarter of Ferguslie Park residents were unemployed and many of these were among the long-term unemployed.[108] Similarly, the proportion of children receiving free school meals in Ferguslie Park was more than double the rate in Paisley. At the end of 1971, there were at least 300 houses standing empty in Ferguslie Park and there was a strong feeling amongst its residents that they were stigmatised simply because of where they lived.[109]

Across Scotland, multiple deprivation had very real consequences for the life chances of those affected. In the early nineties, infant deaths were 50 per cent more likely in deprived areas and low birth-weight babies were twice as common; there were higher rates for both lung and cervical cancers; young people were at an increased risk of suicide and schizophrenia; and coronary heart disease and mortal strokes were more common in the under sixty-fives in these areas.[110] In response, planners increasingly sought the solution to the problems of the periphery in an integrative approach to housing, social care, employment and education – a 'partnership approach' involving the local community in decision making. Schemes such as the 'New Life for Urban Scotland Initiative' (1988–1998), which invested £485 million in Castlemilk, Ferguslie Park, Wester Hailes and Whitfield, were lauded as a success, raising 'residence satisfaction' with the estates by 27 per cent over the course of their operation.[111] Their more long-term impact and sustainability, however, is still to be judged.[112]

Multiple deprivation was nothing new to Scotland in the second half of the twentieth century – only the language had changed. In the past, reformers would have been more open to calling a slum a slum than the more politically correct professionals of the generations that followed who, after all, were usually the employees of the same agencies that had erected them. They had also identified connections between poverty, crime, health and housing problems as early as the late nineteenth century without the statistical apparatus of the modern sociologist, making it all the more to Scotland's shame that, a century later, problems of such magnitude remained. Scots of the twentieth century, at times, proved more adept at reforming their language than the environments of the poorest citizens but renaming and quantifying old problems did not solve them. A multiplicity of approaches had been tried over the years in numerous short-term projects but these were big problems that demanded long-term solutions and straight talking. During a century when most relevant policy areas (bar Social Security) lay in the hands of the Scottish Office and Scottish local government, it took decades for effective multi-agency approaches to multiple deprivation to be devised. The Scots had only themselves to blame.

SCOTTISH EDUCATION – ELEMENTARY

Education has long been identified by commentators as a Scottish child's most obvious way up the social ladder and out of poverty, suggesting at once a ready acceptance that poverty would 'aye' be with us and a propensity for styling education as social welfare. However, for those growing up in houses with few books and a solitary table that supported food preparation, dining, ironing and card games as much as study, a trade, the armed services, boxing, billiards, betting or the music hall may all have appeared more likely (and far more attractive) contenders. Regardless, the supposed open access to education enshrined in John Knox's Reformation settlement, enhanced by the activities of dominies and schoolmasters throughout Scotland in the nineteenth century, was said to have ensured the health of a world-class system of education based on egalitarian principles and personified in the figure of the 'lad o' pairts' (note its masculine gender). In 1928, John Wilson, a school inspector himself in later life, recalled such young men during his years at Aberdeen Grammar School in the 1870s:

> I knew young men of twenty who every morning entered the class-room in a state of perspiration. They were come of poor parents who could not afford to pay for the education of their sons. But the lads themselves were pushful, and determined to rise in the world. Accordingly, they rose with the lark and earned money by labouring in local granite quarries for some hours every morning before

hastening to studies in the Grammar School. Oatmeal, butter, eggs and the inevitable bag of potatoes were their chief sustenance. On such food some of them became brilliant classical scholars. This, however, is a tale of the past, at which the pampered young student of today is apt to smile with incredulity.[113]

On the eve of the twentieth century, many asked, with Shakespeare's Macduff, 'Stands Scotland where it did'?

In 1890 Professor Patrick Geddes (1854–1932), hailed as the father of town planning, spoke in a closing address at University College, Dundee, of the needs and aims of Scottish universities but they were concerns that could quite easily have been applied to every level of Scottish education. 'Here we are divided between two exaggerations – one, that of a legendary superiority in almost every conceivable respect to almost all conceivable people; the other of excessive self-depreciation, as if we had no nationality worth the name.'[114]

The twentieth century resounded to cries that important traditions were being compromised and that, in some intangible way (research did not seem to prove it), standards and the quality of provision were declining. However, beyond such popular perceptions – frequently based on little more than myth and rose-tinted childhood memories – the reality was far more complex. Scotland clearly shared in the widening educational opportunities encouraged by nationwide twentieth-century reforms, yet the system in the north held to meritocratic principles which confined many opportunities only to those identified as academically gifted. In Robert Garioch's poem 'All Prizes, No Blanks', the merits of such competitive individualism are questioned (if not overturned) as teachers enter grades on end-of-year report cards:

> They enter rows of figures, theirs not to reason why–
> In tables fourteen columns wide and forty spaces high;
> They add, and work percentages until their heads are sore,
> I suppose you find this tiring too, and so I'll say no more.
>
> So somebody will go up Dux, and someone gets the Spoon,
> With all the rest of them sized up, like squaddies in platoon.
> Reports go out in envelopes, addressed and sealed with care,
> With comments, tense with self control, from 'Excellent' to 'Fair.'
>
> Now, if God made all men equal, as religious people say,
> It would seem that those percentages are leading us astray;
> We are surely doing wrong, in giving someone a reward
> Just because he is cleverer, and is keen on working hard.[115]

Circular 374 of the Scottish Education Department (1903) emphasised that a principal aim of education in the north was the production of 'useful citizens' in the broadest sense.[116] But evidence would suggest that paper-based assessment was integral to the learning process at almost every juncture. Mary Liverani, educated in Glasgow in the 1940s, recalled:

> There was little rest. Play was never simply play, nor learning simply learning. You were always being tested. Tested in the morning for tables and whack with the pointer if you were too slow. Tested for the names of capital cities and dead kings, tested for writing, up light and down heavy so that your fingers clawed in cramp from the strain of controlling your pen, tested for spelling, tested for the dozen rule, tested for the score rule, tested every Friday so that your fingers trembled independently in anticipation when you sat down at your desk.[117]

It is surely not surprising that such a system generated – but, for long enough, failed to address – serious gaps between pupils' abilities, their vocational interests and the demands of the examination system.

Elementary education became compulsory in Scotland in 1872, eight years before it was enforced in England. Thereafter, two years before England, in 1889, primary education was made free to all in Scotland. In 1901, seventeen years before its universal application across England, the school leaving age in Scotland was raised to fourteen years and, in 1918, free secondary education in Scotland was made available. In 1901, 95 per cent of Scottish children aged between six and twelve attended school and, with the expansion of secondary schooling after 1918 and the rise in the school leaving age to fifteen years in 1947, the number of children in secondary education per thousand of the population in the late forties was forty-six.[118]

The apparently uniform and unrelenting nature of such reforms, however, hides a contradictory legacy. Hamish Paterson noted that:

> far from embodying an abiding concern for the education of 'the whole people', the Scottish school system was designed to neglect the education of the bulk of the population in favour of a few children with a narrowly defined range of talents.[119]

Despite rising school roles, meritocracy frequently overwhelmed democracy as the guiding principle of education in the twentieth century.

As early as the late 1890s, Advanced Departments had been added to the upper end of primary school provision to accommodate children not continuing into the secondary school.[120] By the 1920s, these had become the Advanced Divisions based at primary, 'omnibus' and secondary schools, where a broad curriculum encompassing academic and vocational subjects led to the award of Day School Certificates, either 'Higher' (after three years) or 'Lower' (after two years). By 1932, sixty-seven of Scotland's 251 recognised secondary schools offered advanced courses and three years later, out of the 2,898 primary schools in Scotland, 1,550 taught advanced courses.[121] For children in the secondary schools – those who passed the Qualifying Exam – their ultimate goal remained the Leaving Certificate, an award focusing on a heavily academic curriculum, despite some innovations in the early 1920s. In 1936, however, the Advanced Divisions – offering little more than a 'diluted form of the secondary school curriculum' – vanished. (The merits of a more specialised two-tier approach had been pushed since before the First War.) The secondary schools that emerged were divided into two groups – those offering five-year courses leading to the Leaving Certificate (generally known as 'senior secondaries') and 'junior secondaries' providing three-year courses offering no ultimate award.[122]

The inadequacies of this system were acknowledged by many at the time but few radical reforms were attempted. Scotland boasted the first educational research institute in the British Empire – the Scottish Council for Research in Education, established in 1931 – but even its concerns were not always addressed.[123] In 1931, it noted:

> It is an interesting commentary on our Scottish system that our present highly organised secondary education is directed almost exclusively to preparation for professions engaging only 2.75 per cent of the male population and seven per cent of the female population in employment.[124]

The nature of the post-primary curriculum was clearly failing to meet the needs of the majority of young Scots. While the Qualifying Examination was intended to be taken by children at twelve years, many primary schools often retained pupils who failed first time and encouraged them to try again. (In Edinburgh in 1927, over 28 per cent of those who passed the Qualifying Examination were over thirteen years of age.[125]) Furthermore, in the 1930s, a significant proportion of children in secondary schools were failing to complete the five-year course leading to the award of the Leaving Certificate. In session 1937–38, while there were 35,118 pupils in the first year of secondary education, there were only 5,950 in the fifth.[126]

The attitude of the Scottish Education Department (SED), increasingly operating from Edinburgh rather than Whitehall in those years, was summed up by George Macdonald (later Secretary of the SED) when he wrote in 1920, accepting the inevitability of such 'wastage', 'The school population falls into two parts – the majority of distinctly limited intelligence, and an extremely important minority . . . who are capable of responding to a much more severe call.'[127] It was a common perspective.

Between 1921 and 1966, elite members of Scottish education policy networks were drawn overwhelmingly from a body of male professionals whose experience in education had been principally drawn from a career in rural and small-town Scotland.[128] Such experience, it has been suggested, blinded the educational Establishment to the inequalities inherent in the system which, to a certain extent, were being perpetuated through its reliance on a model of Scottish society that was losing its relevance. Put simply, the so-called 'Kirriemuir Careers' of the men at the top established restrictive parameters within which innovation could take place.

World War Two, however, was to disrupt the relative stability of the system, as schools lost and gained pupils through evacuation and faced fresh objectives in their efficient co-ordination of many public service activities. During the war years, the number of permanent exemptions issued to children below the official school leaving age rose dramatically – from 2,989 in 1939 to 7,010 in 1942 – as pressures on family budgets encouraged many parents to put their children out to work.[129] Yet the number of entries and awards for the Senior Leaving Certificate also increased, sparking worries about declining standards. Still, there were some notable movements making for reform. In 1943, the Association of Directors of Education produced a significant report, *Education in Scotland*, and, in the same year, the teachers' union, the Educational Institute for Scotland (EIS), produced *The Scottish School* – their suggestions for reconstruction. This was to be the background to the 1945 Education (Scotland) Act.[130]

The 1945 legislation made it a statutory obligation that all educational provision in Scotland was to be divided into primary, secondary and further education and obliged all educational authorities to offer adequate provision in all three areas. But it attempted no reform of the curriculum and examination structures which had proved woefully inadequate on the eve of war. In 1947, the school leaving age was raised to fifteen years but the courses offered to many of these young adults continued the traditions of the 1930s. The Inspectorate noted that, in the 1950s, many junior secondaries were simply offering courses which were 'pruned or diluted versions of an academic course'.[131] For many teachers in this sector, they appeared to be fighting a losing battle. James Inglis, speaking at the AGM of the EIS Lanarkshire branch in 1953 noted:

> The job is too big for human endurance and the better the teacher the more he puts into it and the more exhausted he becomes . . . These schools have no prestige among parents and they have generated no affection among their pupils whose one ambition is to leave and get work. Discipline is a constant, almost unbearable problem.[132]

In 1959, following the report of a working party on the curriculum, it was recommended that an ordinary grade certificate be introduced. In 1962, Scottish children sat Ordinary ('O') Grade examinations for the new Scottish Certificate of Education for the first time. Operating within a new climate, symbolised by the introduction of comprehensive education and a greater focus on 'child-centred learning' in the primary schools from 1965, the new 'O' Grade Certificate proved to be a significant improvement. While 18,562 pupils had been presented for the Scottish Leaving Certificate in 1961, in 1965, 68,937 pupils sat the new examination and the proportion of school leavers gaining certificates rose from 27 per cent in 1964 to 66 per cent in 1974.[133]

The raising of the school leaving age to sixteen in 1973, however, increased pressure on the system, as did declining opportunities for young people in the job market of the 1980s. More and more pupils were staying on and increasing numbers of less able students were being presented for the O Grade examination to which they were far from suited.[134] Following the recommendations of the Munn Committee (1977), the O Grade was replaced by the Standard Grade in the 1980s, the principal goal of which was 'certification for all'. Between 1985 and 1995, the proportion of Scottish school leavers with no qualifications fell dramatically from 25.2 per cent to 7.9 per cent.[135]

Conservative policies in the 1980s, which included the popular introduction of the statutory right of parents to choose their children's school (1981), nevertheless had only a limited impact on Scottish educational traditions. But further curricular reforms in the late eighties and nineties seemed to signal important changes in Scottish education, as the interface between primary and secondary became mediated by the '5–14' model of progression and the Higher – that bastion of Scottish traditionalists – was finally stormed (albeit not entirely successfully) through the Higher Still programme. More radical proposals to encourage parental involvement in the management and policy of schools, however, were roundly rejected – a report in 2004 concluded that 'the belief in the teachers' professional expertise and commitment remains strong'.[136] Almost despite itself, from among the 850,000 Scottish pupils who attended school in the mid nineties, the Scottish education system would produce modern 'lads o' pairts' (many of them female) in excess of anything 'maisters' and 'dominies' of the nineteenth century could ever have anticipated.[137] This was bound to have a profound impact on the Scottish universities.

By 1910, most of the fundamental characteristics of Scottish higher education (HE) in the twentieth century were in place. From 1889, entrance was generally restricted to those over eighteen years of both sexes passing an entrance exam, a BSc degree supplemented traditional Arts provision and an Honours degree programme was establishing itself. While no 'constitutional' relationship existed between government and the universities at this stage, University Commissioners had played a major role in reforming university governance in the nineteenth century and state support for universities was increasing and attracting wide approval.[138] A University Grants Committee, established in 1919, did little to refine this ambiguous relationship between the state and academia and, until mid century, most government bodies supported a non-interventionist stance in the curricula of higher education establishments, despite substantial financial investment in the sector. War, however, highlighted an apparent failure on the part of universities to produce graduates suited to the demands of the new technological age and – in tune with successive governments' desires to plan the post-war environment – by the 1950s, state grants frequently brought with them higher and increasingly prescriptive expectations of the universities. By 1960–61, recurrent grants from government represented nearly 70 per cent of British universities' income and special payments (for expenditure other than revenue expenses) increased from £1,553,000, between 1920 and 1939, to £44,007,000 between 1945 and 1963.[139] At this stage, universities were growing at a faster rate than ever and so were student numbers. In 1901, the ratio of university students to total population was 1.4 per thousand; by 1951, it was 2.9 and, by 1991, it was 10.8.[140]

Until 1956, Scottish students relied largely on personal income (if they had any), bursaries, grants from the Carnegie Trust and local authority stipends to fund their way through university. Following the introduction of state grants, administered by the SED from 1956, however, numbers depending on this source of finance rose dramatically and at a rate three times that experienced south of the Border. By 1961, 84 per cent of Scottish students relied on state grants for their fees and living expenses.[141] State support for students would change dramatically in the 1990s, as loans replaced grants, but student numbers continued to rise.

By 1989–90, there were 131,598 students in HE in Scotland. By 2000–2001, this figure had risen to 262,913, when over 50 per cent of Scots under twenty-one years attended higher education courses in UK institutions.[142] If students (both full- and part-time) in further education (FE) institutions are brought in to the calculation, a total figure of over 660,000 persons in the tertiary education sector at the end of the century is derived.[143] By this stage, Scotland boasted forty-three FE colleges and twenty HE institutions.[144] Over the years, the number of mature students had risen significantly in response to increased opportunities for non-standard entrants and the decline of traditional well-paid jobs in manufacturing industry – from comprising just 23 per cent of entrants to full-time undergraduate courses in 1984, students over twenty-one made up 37 per cent in 1993.[145] Women were also to be found in increasing numbers in Scotland's universities – 43 per cent of full-time entrants in 1980 were female, rising to 49 per cent in 1993, and women became vitally important on part-time courses, making up 43 per cent of entrants in 1993.[146] Change was also evident in the social class profile of the typical university student in Scotland. Between 1980 and 1994, while the proportion of school leavers entering university whose fathers were in professional and managerial occupations grew (from 27 per cent to 32 per cent), such growth was dwarfed by the rate of growth of entrants from skilled working-class backgrounds whose numbers more than doubled (from 14 to 30 per cent) and students from skilled manual, semi-skilled and unskilled working-class families whose presence rose from just 4 per cent in 1980 to 15 per cent fourteen years later.[147] The student profile of the nation had clearly changed and so had its universities.[148] The state was now far more interventionist and universities were no longer kept at one remove from the social and economic goals of successive governments – indeed, they were prime vehicles ensuring their attainment. The persistence of wide academic support for the universities' civic role in Scottish life also meant that they were more readily inclined to meet the demands of devolved government after 1999, although many feared that greater social inclusion was gradually being secured at the cost of academic excellence.[149]

Scottish education, caught between reflecting the values of a former age and anticipating future change in both the economy and culture of the nation, negotiated the twentieth century as effectively as one could have realistically anticipated, given the nature of devolved administration, the changing priorities of Westminster and the transformation of the populace which it sought to instruct. In many ways, it was an area of social policy, unlike those addressed earlier, where it was easier to effect change and respond in a co-ordinated fashion to the transformation of society. Broadly speaking, one profession, namely teaching, dominated primary and secondary education throughout the century and the majority of its members received their professional training in one of only four education colleges. One professional body, the Educational Institute for Scotland (EIS), claimed most Scottish teachers as its members. One examination board governed certificated examinations in Scottish schools, making a common approach to teaching, if not a common curriculum, easier to effect. The persistence of local government control over state schools and the distinctive governance structures of Scottish universities also ensured that wider Scottish opinion was readily felt in the operation of education at all levels. Education planning in Scotland was also comprehensively addressed within the wide remit of the Scottish Office alone and relied less on the goodwill and co-operation of other Whitehall departments as was the case in England where, for far longer, educational reform was dependent on the passing of local by-laws for effective implementation.[150] Even at the century's end, education in the north was still very different from that of its southern neighbour and the democratic traditions of an early age were still starkly apparent in a secondary school environment strongly resistant to selection and in the ethos governing widening access to tertiary education.

HAPPY FAMILIES?

Mary Ogilvie was the tenth of eleven children born to a local solicitor and his wife in Dundee in 1859. In later life she recalled her childhood:

> I did not know my father very well. He used to play with me some-times, and had a wonderful trick of making half a crown go through the table, (of course it went through for I heard it fall into the cup below!) but I should have welcomed more tokens of affection. Children should grow up lapped in love.[151]

The Scottish family changed remarkably in the twentieth century though attitudes, conventions, customs and gender roles were harder to break and remake.[152] In Joan Ure's play *Something in it for Cordelia*, we encounter the following exchange between a wheelchair-bound and tartan-clad King Lear of Scotland and his dutiful daughter at Edinburgh's Waverley railway station:

Cordelia (eagerly): Oh father, give me a cuddle.
Lear: I don't know if I know how.

Cordelia: You put your arms around me; it's easy. And I nestle nearer to you. Oh, father, you're bigger than me. You were always bigger than me. I thought it was significant somehow. I thought, 'There will be one day when I need to cry. One day when I'll think it worthwhile crying, for my father will gather me into him closely.' Only, you never did.

Lear: Oh I must have nursed you once or twice when you were a baby.

Cordelia: No. There was a girl I know. Her father was a foreigner. He used to bounce her, balanced on his foot. And it made a swing. Oh I missed not having a father who was a . . . foreigner!

Lear: I must have told you stories though, when you were small.

Cordelia: No, you were always drilling your soldiers.

Lear: Nonsense.

Cordelia: You never told any of us stories.

Lear: Well, it would just be that I don't approve.

Ure (1918–78) knew her audience would recognise the type.[153] The inference is clear – Scottish men, like their aging king, had a lot to learn about family.

In Govan, it was said that men were rarely seen in food shops in the 1950s, were 'never seen wheeling a pram, and would look ridiculous if they had to carry home a bunch of flowers'.[154] It was not the same everywhere – high levels of female factory employment in Dundee meant working-class men in that city regularly took on domestic chores – and, anyway, no two fathers were clearly alike. But social expectations tell us a lot about common perceptions of family roles. Alexander McRobbie grew up in Glasgow in the 1930s:

From the age of five, I never dreamt of kissing my mother, nor can I remember her kissing me. Kissing was reserved for babies or very wee bairns. At five and going to school, I was a 'big boy', especially as I was the oldest child. Big boys didn't cry, suck their thumbs, or expect to be kissed or praised for their small successes.[155]

Unlike most other areas of Scottish society, women were central to the operation of the family. Males, by comparison, appeared to contribute remarkably little to discourses on family life. But that silence is important. It might either denote a dismissive attitude to the family, marking it out as female territory and hence unimportant, or it simply reflects that men remained in control of what was considered really important – the public world outwith the home. Even political parties in the immediate aftermath of full female enfranchisement (1928) identified women's role as mothers as their chief concern as new voters. A National Party of Scotland (NPS) pamphlet from 1929 implored:

> SCOTS WOMEN
> Vote First for Your
> CHILDREN
> Scots Women Vote Nationalist
> AND SAVE THE SCOTS CHILDREN[156]

During the century changes in women's role recast family structures but change was also conditioned by domestic imperatives – female education and female employment frequently had to find their place in family environments which undervalued their significance. The home may have remained the woman's sphere and empowered females in household decisions but, at times, it circumscribed her ambitions and restricted her horizons. Mary Brooksbank worked at Thompson and Shepherd's mill at Hawkhill in Dundee: 'I never liked the mill, but very early I learned the habit of self-discipline. My wishes, desires, hopes, ambitions were dutifully suppressed in the interests of those I loved, my father, mother and brothers.'[157]

A study in 1969, which considered the educational experiences of pupils born in 1936, concluded that the 'intelligent boys seemed to find the pathway to higher education and hence to corresponding employment distinctly easier than the girls'.[158] This was nothing new. An oral study of Scots born between 1896 and 1905 highlighted a similar state of affairs among an earlier generation.[159] Until the latter decades of the century, girls tended to participate in formal education in smaller numbers, attended school, on average, for a shorter period, experienced a curriculum which emphasised their future roles as wife and mother and left without qualifications equivalent to those awarded to their male classmates. For many, domestic responsibilities from an early age compromised their childhoods.

By the 1990s, however, in many aspects, girls were out-performing boys – on average, more girls than boys achieved four or more Standard Grades (at levels 1–4) and their scores in these assessments tended to be higher than their male counterparts. By 2000–01, over 50 per cent of students in higher education were female.[160] But educational reforms which opened the doors to increased female participation did not guarantee that opportunities stayed open after graduation. Despite legislative support through the Equal Pay Act (1970), the Sex Discrimination Act (1975), the Employment Protection Act (1978) and the Employment Rights Act (1996), women occupied a larger proportion of lower grades rather than higher grades in the professions in Scotland and gender stereotyping was commonly identified as a major impediment to female promotion and advancement.[161]

As in the rest of Britain, increasing numbers of women entered the job market in Scotland in the twentieth century, particularly after the 1930s, and women's experience of employment came to resemble more closely that of other UK nations as the Scottish fertility rate waned after the post-war baby boom.[162] Between 1951 and 1981, spurred on, in part, by their experience of diverse work environments during wartime, the number of economically active women in Scotland rose by 38 per cent and women came to represent around a third of the Scottish work-force.[163] Thereafter, at the beginning of the twenty-first century, two thirds of Scottish women aged sixteen to sixty-four went out to work.[164]

But what of married women in particular? In 1911, a mere 5.3 per cent of the employed female labour force was married and, by 1951, this had increased to 23.4 per cent, yet, by 1991, a startling 60.4 per cent of women in employment in Scotland were married.[165] In comparison to England, however, married women in Scotland had entered the labour market at a slower rate.[166] For the most part, this can be explained by the comparative longevity of higher fertility rates, Scottish industry's emphasis on heavy manufactures that in any case paid relatively good wages to skilled men and, of course, the marked opposition across classes to the notion of the working mother. A marriage bar was operational in many occupations, which meant that, regularly if not invariably, women left work for good as soon as they found a husband. 'The Spinner's Wedding', a Dundee song, contains the following lines:

> The gaffer's looking worried, the flett's a' in a steer
> Jessie Brodie's getting mairit an' the morn she'll no' be here.[167]

The nature of married female employment was distinctive – part-time employment was prominent among married women. While only 7 per cent of males aged sixteen to sixty-four worked part-time in 2002, the comparable figure for women of the same age group was 43 per cent and married women and women with older children made up much of this number.[168] The service sector absorbed a significant proportion of such female labour. In 1951, women in personal service and commercial occupations, together with clerks and typists, made up over 56 per cent of the occupied female workforce – a similar proportion to those who, fifty years before, had worked in textiles, clothing and domestic service.[169] Opportunities had certainly broadened but choices were often remarkably few.

Economic change gradually destroyed the pre-eminent position of traditional industries but the conspicuous masculine culture which they had privileged was slower to recede. Domestic demands and poor pre-school care provision for young children only partly explain women's restricted position within the labour market at the end of the century. Social attitudes still prioritised the woman's role in the home, still laid the principal duties of child care on her and still adopted gender stereotypes that impeded successful female careers. 'Let's face it,' wrote the editors of the short-lived Scottish feminist magazine *Harpies and Quines* in 1992, 'being a Scottish woman is often an uphill battle.'

Being a man, however, was not an easy ride either. At the end of the century, while the plight of women torn between conflicting roles was generally acknowledged, many men felt changes to their gender identity were being ignored. A character in Tom Leonard's sequence *Ghostie Men* sums it up:

> its awright fur you hen
> at least your oppresst
> yi know wherr yi urr
>
> no mahtr whuts wrang way yi
> yi kin looknthi mirrur
> nsayti yir sell
>
> I am a wummin
> naw
> I am a persn
> who ztreatid izza wummin
> by thaht basturd therr
> niz imperialist cock
>
> but ah luknthi mirrur
> nasayti ma sell
> ahv goat a cock
> a canny help thaht
>
> I am a man
> naw
> I am a persn
> who happnz tay be a man
> but ahm no iz bad iz summa thim
>
> its no thi same[170]

Scottish cultural values were changing and they were transforming family life. The increasing availability of artificial contraception, particularly from the 1930s onwards, gave couples greater control over family size and, for many, changed perceptions of the role of sex within and outwith marriage. A 1982 survey indicated that, while less than 10% of Scottish women in their sample born between 1926 and 1930 had had pre-marital intercourse by the time they were twenty, the corresponding figure for women born between 1961 and 1965 was about 60 per cent.[171] Contraception certainly played a major role in facilitating this change although, in some areas, sex before marriage had, for a long time, simply been accepted as a fact of life. In parts of the rural north-east, a doctor commented that pre-nuptial conceptions were 'almost socially acceptable':

> I have a positive rash of young girls from a village not five miles from here who all became pregnant in the last few months. They're all getting married, every single one of them. It seems to me that there they jog along quite happily until the girl gets pregnant and then they decide to marry.[172]

Family planning services were particularly well advanced in Aberdeen from a very early stage, mainly as a response to high rates of maternal and foetal mortality. Indeed, the local authority took over the operations of the progressive charity, the Constructive Birth Control Clinic, as early as 1946. In 1967, advice and contraceptive supplies were given free of charge and, in 1968, the clinic opened its services to unmarried women for the first time.[173] Until 1964, the vaginal diaphragm was typically recommended by north-east clinics and others like them across Scotland that were by this time also offering a domiciliary service, but the oral contraceptive pill became the method of choice for many women in subsequent decades. Sterilisation was also increasingly common, particularly among married couples who had completed their families and, more particularly, after publicity in 1976 surrounding possible links between the pill and cardiovascular disease. While only 10 per cent of the women born between 1926 and 1930 surveyed in 1982 had been sterilised or had had sterilised partners by the time they were forty, the comparable figure for women born in the early 1940s was 50 per cent.[174] The growth in male sterilisation was particularly notable, especially after vasectomies were provided on the NHS from 1972. In other instances, the greater availability of abortion from 1967 liberated generations of Scottish women from the cruel trade of the back-street abortionist, if not from a lifetime of what-might-have-beens. In 1968, a year after the passage of the Abortion Act, 1,492 abortions were carried out in Scotland and this represented 2 per cent of live births that year.[175] But regional differences were marked. In the Northern

Hospital Board region, abortions amounted to 4.9 per thousand women while, in the Western Hospital Board area where more doctors stuck to the letter of the law, abortions amounted to 1.6 per thousand women.[176] Even in the seventies, many Glasgow women were forced to board the Glasgow–Liverpool train (nicknamed the 'Abortion Express') in the hope of treatment from a more liberal health board. (In 1968, abortions in England numbered 23,641 or 4.2 per cent of live births.)[177] Ultimately, the fate of the unborn child rested, for the most part, as it had always done, with the expectant mother. While there were more choices by the end of the century, guilt and responsibility attached to each and, in that sense at least, little had changed.

Like elsewhere in the world, in Scotland love was only one reason for getting married. Roderick Wilkinson recalls how his mother:

> left school in Clydebank at thirteen to work as a labouring girl in Singers' factory. Then she became a seamstress in a small back-street tailor's where she met Sadie Kerr who had a brother Jimmy who had a pal called Willie Wilkinson. And that was that. I believe my mother was mainly attracted to him because he didn't drink.[178]

As the century progressed, despite the continued popularity of traditional weddings, traditional marriages were becoming increasingly unpopular. In Liz Lochhead's poem, 'The Bride', the new wife muses in bed after the wedding:

> I lie beside you
> utterly content that I know for sure
> that this is never
> ever going to
> work.

Divorce became easier after 1969 and unhappy Scottish couples took full advantage of simplified ways of untying the knot – whereas only forty-four legal separations took place in Scotland in 1900, in 1999, 1,200 divorce actions were filed in the Scottish courts.[179] Cohabitation became common either as an end in itself or as a trial period before marriage – by the 1990s, the majority of couples in Scotland marrying for the first time had lived together before marriage and, in 1999, around 15 per cent of twenty-five- to thirty-four-year-olds were cohabiting.[180] Where all this left Scottish children was puzzling. By the end of the century, around 40 per cent of Scottish births were outside marriage although, in 70 per cent of cases, the parents of these children lived at the same address.[181] Teenage mothers – of which Scotland boasted amongst the highest numbers in Europe by the 1990s for a country of its size – were rarely in marriage relationships and, unlike a decade or so earlier, for most, marriage was seldom seen as a valuable response to their situation.[182]

The altered profile of the Scottish family, however, belied the continuity of a more traditional moral outlook on family matters. The 2000 Scottish Social Attitudes Survey showed Scots to be more tolerant of homosexuality than they had been in the 1950s when Scottish evidence before the Wolfenden Committee on Prostitution and Homosexual Offences was overwhelmingly opposed to the decriminalisation of homosexual acts between consenting adults.[183] But the 2000 Survey also indicated that a majority of the sample considered marriage to be the best kind of relationship, that people wanting children should marry and that levels of teenage pregnancy were problematic.[184] Aware of the moral minefield they were entering, the new Scottish Executive sought to distance itself from a judgemental approach in 2000. In a White Paper on family law from that year it noted:

> Marriage is the most widely recognised way in which a man and woman show their commitment to each other and lay the foundations of a stable family. Nevertheless, we recognise that not every couple chooses to marry and many stable families are not based on marriage.[185]

Day-to-day life in twentieth-century Scotland was an exercise in reconciling values and realities, traditions and modernity. The pace of change was seldom uniform and attitudes took time to catch up with circumstance – family was valued throughout the century but, by its end, family had changed and the traditional values invested in it were only seldom realised. The merits of the new family lay elsewhere – in its potential for change and its accommodation of different forms of relationship.

CONCLUSION

Both continuity and change of dramatic proportions marked different aspects of Scottish life in the twentieth century. Incomes rose but, as always, failed to keep pace with UK averages; consumption of the bric-a-brac of modernity increased but tastes were often doggedly traditional; and, while the welfare state offered a more comfortable safety net for those who fell foul of the new economic order, the poor remained. Scots also became increasingly reliant on the UK state as the century progressed but the administration of new welfare services often relied on distinctive Scottish agencies. Structures governing the National Health Service in Scotland were very different from those in the south; local councils were Scots' principal landlords for much of the century; and education still bore the hallmarks of its native origins. Given this state of affairs, the persistence of social problems in the north confuted arguments, growing in popularity as the century drew to its close, that devolution would inevitably result in social amelioration. Strangely, the twentieth century offered precious little reassurance that more devolution inevitably generated more effective policymaking. Society also maintained independent dynamics that were seldom governed by state influence from whatever quarter. Scottish social attitudes were, in many ways, more liberal and tolerant at the close of the century but, in their approach to women and the family, they frequently bore the hallmarks of the Victorian domestic ideal. Living in Scotland meant negotiating this maze of contradictions, this patterning of extremes.

SEVEN The Migrant Nation

FOR THE FUTURE
THE NATIONAL PARTY OF SCOTLAND
STANDS FOR
SCOTTISH REGULATION OF IMMIGRATION
AND THE
PRESERVATION OF SCOTTISH CHARACTERISTICS
NO OTHER PARTY DOES
                    National Party of Scotland (1928)

The National Party were not alone in fearing the influence of immigration in the 1920s. Earlier in the decade, the Scottish Unionists had turned the nationalist argument on its head and argued that, should home rule ever be granted, 'specious pledges on Socialistic lines' would impede any Scottish Parliament, swamped as it would be with Labour members who had been returned by voters who 'are not and were not Scotsmen, but a more ignorant type of Irish worker, Lithuanians, and other aliens, working in or about the mines and factories in the industrial areas of the West'. Home Rule would bring 'ALIEN RULE'.[1]

Scotland – a nation of migrants – frequently failed to embrace its own immigrant communities. Fears that 'Scottish-ness' was being eroded in the twentieth century by the incursion of mass popular culture and the decline of native mores were exacerbated, particularly in the interwar years, by concerns regarding growing immigrant communities which, in their 'difference', seemed a very visible threat to the safe uniformity that protected what remained of a Scottish way of life. Even Scottish emigrants were becoming defensive. By 1928, the Order of Scottish Clans, established in St Louis, Missouri, fifty years before, boasted 25,000 members, a newsletter entitled *The Fiery Cross* and a ladies' auxiliary organisation poetically styled the Daughters of Scotia, which visited 'the dear auld hameland' for the fourth time in its history in 1930, when they were met at Yorkhill Quay in Glasgow by a pipe band.[2] Members of the fraternal order had to be 'of Scottish blood, of Scottish parentage or Scottish descent . . . birth in Scotland by other than Scottish parents [did] not establish eligibility'.[3] 'New Scots' – Scots of Irish, English, European or colonial parentage – apparently failed the test of authenticity.

But Scottish identity was changing. During the course of the late nineteenth and early twentieth centuries, the ethnic profile of Scotland was transformed, as war and the decline of Empire recast Scotland as a land of opportunity for those facing economic, political and moral challenges in their own countries. Whether as final destinations or as stopovers on the way to North America, Scottish ports received countless human cargoes which were to add a new dynamic to Scottish society.

BECOMING SCOTS

Immigration had a long history but the twentieth century experience was different in terms of its scale, the diverse origins of the migrants themselves and the cultural influences that they brought. There is no singular immigrant's story. The long-established Irish community was joined by growing numbers of Italians and Lithuanians, while the distinctive Jewish population of Glasgow's south-side, by the end of the century, had largely dispersed and had given way to new immigrants from India, Pakistan and other Asian countries. Even the citizens of England were moving to the north in unprecedented numbers by the end of the century.

In 1901, 205,000 of the Scottish population were Irish-born.[4] Of all the immigrant groups, this was the largest at the time and they left the biggest imprint on both the culture of Scotland and its history. Distinguished by its lack of denominational homogeneity (Catholic and Protestant) and commitment to conflicting visions of Ireland's political future (Republican and Unionist), the Irish 'community' left a contradictory and confrontational legacy for urban Scotland in particular. By the early twentieth century, intermarriage between Catholic Irish immigrants and native Protestant Scots was less common than it had been for early nineteenth-century migrants. And – having been met with native hostility and suspicion since they arrived – the development of distinct and separate schools, charitable and voluntary organisations and social activities consolidated the isolation of the Catholic Irish settlers. The Protestant Irish, for the most part, integrated more effectively into Scotland – though, in their Unionist politics, Orange sympathies and marching culture, many were chronically out of step with the popular Liberalism of the early decades of the twentieth century.[5]

Growing Irish Catholic support for the Labour Party in Scotland after 1918 and the consolidation of the Irish Free State after 1922 went some way to reconciling Irish Catholics to the host community, though hostilities between the two groups continued on the streets and on the football terraces and, for a while in the 1930s, was articulated in the local politics of Glasgow and Edinburgh. (These issues will be addressed in more detail in Chapter 11.) Yet, while research is regrettably sparse for the 1940s and 1950s, it is clear that the onset of The Troubles in Northern Ireland – ignited by political tensions, inter-ethnic rivalries and the increasing British military presence in the Province from the 1960s – fuelled residual antipathies in Scotland for some time.[6] By the 1990s, however, secularisation, the decline of older associational cultures and shared hopes invested in the Northern Ireland peace process did much to reconcile Irish descendants both to one another and to Scotland as a whole. Indeed, by the end of the century, the Roman Catholic community – the identity of which had been re-formed through Irish immigration – was to the fore in campaigning for a devolved Scottish Parliament and had come to think of itself as Scottish (rather than or more than British) to an extent not matched by even its Protestant neighbours.[7]

The history of Scotland's Italian settlers is more uniform. In 1901, Italians in Scotland numbered around 4,000 and, having reached a peak of nearly 6,000 in 1961, settled at around 4,000 at the end of the century, when it was estimated that the wider Italian ethnic presence was approximately 30,000.[8] Chain migration dominated the community's profile and, as a result, throughout the century, the vast majority of Italian migrants in Scotland came from one of three Italian areas – Barga (Tuscany), Picinisco (Lazio) and Borgo Val di Taro (Emilia-Romagna).[9] The regional concentration of their origins was matched by the regional focus of their settlement patterns. In 1986, around two thirds of the Scottish Italian population were in Glasgow and Edinburgh, although there had been a sizeable Italian community in Dundee also from the 1920s.[10] Italians entered the wider political consciousness rarely and largely as a result of war in the first half of the century. There were many Fascist units in Scotland in the 1930s and Italian-born males were subject to arrest and internment during World War Two, although most were more at risk from the misplaced patriotism of native Scots than posing a risk to their adopted homeland. Piero Tognini recalls the night of 10 June 1940 at the Marina Café in Prestwick:

The glass front door of the café had been smashed and a crowd of people, mostly women, were milling around. They were systematically looting the shop! I stared in horror as large jars of sweets and bulky packs of cigarettes were handed out to accomplices, who made off with guilty haste. My heart was sick as I saw one time neighbours and even friends sneaking off into the growing darkness of a summer night. War had turned even law-abiding folk into a pack of scavenging wolves![11]

The major impact of the 'italo-scozzesi' was to be found mainly in the urban environment and in coastal resorts and, specifically, in their businesses. By 1911, Italian confectioners in Scotland numbered 1,683; in 1921, there were fifty-one Italian trades listed in Dundee alone; and, by 1931, there were 737 cafes under Italian management in Scotland.[12] Certainly, Scots Italians proved an important influence on the arts in Scotland – Sir Eduardo Paolozzi (1924–2005), Alberto Morrocco (1917–1998) and Richard Demarco (1930–) all contributed a refreshing international dynamic to their respective disciplines and exhibited a greater affinity for the avant-garde than many of their more conservative contemporaries. Yet the cultural reach of the many more Scots Italians who engaged with more domestic Scottish tastes ought not to be forgotten. Romeo Rinaldi of the Golden Arrow Fish and Chip Shop in Dumfries, the home of the Bard, offers this poetic reminder:

La patata oggi m'invita	The tattie noo invites me
A descrivere il destino	Tae describe tae ye ma life
Che mi lega per la vita	And the fate that means each morning
A pelarla ogni mattino	I must peel her wi' a knife
Nella notte un giovanotto	The young man sees his sweetheart
Sogna poi la fidanzata	In nocturnal reverie
Io mi sveglio a sei di botto	But I wake up in a cold sweat
Perché sogno – la patata	It's the tattie that I see![13]

Lithuanian immigrants in Scotland, largely working as waged labour, left a less visible impact on their host communities. Typically arriving at Scotland's eastern ports, by 1914, there were around 8,000 Lithuanians living in the industrial counties of Fife, West Lothian, Lanarkshire and Ayrshire and smaller numbers in Edinburgh and Dundee. Until mid century, these settlers maintained a vibrant cultural life supported by social events and community newspapers.[14] However, immigration restrictions, intermarriage and close associations with Scottish neighbours, the impact of two world wars and the dispersal of communities occasioned by changing public sector housing strategies encouraged assimilation. Migrants anglicised their surnames to less conspicuous appellations and, without the financial independence to sustain an alternative identity like the Italians, becoming Scots turned out to be their only option.

By the 1930s, the Italian, Lithuanian and Jewish communities in Scotland together numbered 40,000.[15] The Jewish community in Edinburgh preceded that of Glasgow and, by 1930, around 2,000 Jews lived in the capital.[16] But, in Glasgow, the Jewish population mushroomed following the impact of pogroms like those in Kishinev (1903) and Odessa (1905) and, from around 6,500 in 1902, Glasgow Jews, in 1935, numbered around 15,000.[17] Throughout the century, Scottish Jews developed a strong associational culture. Jews in Glasgow's Gorbals established a Hebrew School as early as 1895 and, leading on from the activities of earlier charitable organisations, in 1927, a Glasgow Jewish Board of Guardians was established. Zionism, from the 1890s, was the major political contribution of this immigrant group but, in a social context, its impact was more diverse – the Jewish Lads' Brigade, for example, boasted its own kilted pipe band, a Jewish Institute was formed in 1900 and a Jewish football team, the Oxford Star, competed in local leagues.[18] From the 1920s, however, signs of change were evident. Successful Jewish families increasingly moved out of city-centre communities into the suburbs, where the building of new synagogues denoted the dispersal of the community. Langside Synagogue and Queen's Park Synagogue, Glasgow, were built in 1926 and 1927 respectively.

Even for successful Jews, however, life in Scotland posed many challenges. Whilst Manny Shinwell (1884–1986) – Scotland's first Jewish MP – claimed in 1923 that there was no anti-Semitism in Scotland, others felt caught between two worlds, even though they regularly felt at home in each. As an adolescent in Edinburgh, David Daiches (1912–2005) had a 'proud sense of being lonely and different' and Leon Frederick Levison (1910–), the son of an immigrant Jewish Christian convert, was amused by his Jewish roots. Only at the age of twelve did he realise that 'there was something not quite Scottish about [his] family'.[19]

Earlier in the century, Glasgow Jews had scratched a living from peddling a variety of goods in the smaller Lanarkshire and Ayrshire towns and villages until they could afford their own small businesses.[20] As the century progressed, their places as itinerant salesmen were often taken up by fresh immigrants and, increasingly, these were young Indian males.[21] By the interwar years, Indian migrants to Glasgow numbered between fifty and one hundred and – other than students – Edinburgh and Dundee boasted Indian populations of less than ten per city.[22] However, estimates would suggest that, following the Second World War and the passage of the 1948 British Nationality Act that facilitated the granting of UK citizenship to Commonwealth citizens, numbers increased dramatically, particularly as unemployment on the Indian subcontinent restricted opportunities for the young and ambitious. Dundee's College of Technology, for example, recruited 133 overseas students between 1956 and 1967, of whom 121 were from Pakistan and India. They mainly registered for the Certificate of Jute Manufacture or a Diploma in Textiles and, in one Dundee jute mill alone, Asian employees on the payroll increased from three in 1952 to 100 in 1968.[23] By 1955, the total population of Asians in Scotland was about 1,300 – most of them Muslim.[24] As with the Irish, Italian and Jewish settlers, Asian migrants concentrated in Glasgow – by 1960, Glasgow's Asian population numbered around 3,000 and many were abandoning earlier traditions of selling door-to-door for waged or salaried employment. Two hundred Pakistani men, for example, were employed as bus conductors and drivers.[25] Thereafter, the later 1960s saw a new trend, with large numbers of Asian immigrants from England moving north, though this was to peter out by the 1980s, when 24,900 Indo-Pakistanis were recorded by Scottish Office officials as residing in Scotland.[26] Tangible evidence of the impact of this group was to be found throughout the country – in almost 24-hour convenience stores, restaurants and takeaways, managed and staffed by Indian, Bangladeshi and Pakistani families; in colourful temples and mosques whose minarets enlivened areas razed by earlier city planners; in vigorous and diverse religious cultures the health of which was in sharp contrast to indigenous faiths; and in the contribution of Asian health professionals, entrepreneurs and academics to public service. But did they feel part of the society they were helping to create? Studies of Pakistani children in the 1990s indicated that the younger generations eschewed Scottish identity in favour of their religious, typically Muslim, identity and favoured the bicultural term 'Scottish-Pakistani' to describe their ethnicity.[27] Scottishness was not enough.

By the end of the century, former colonial subjects from other Asian, African and West Indian provinces and asylum seekers from war-torn Eastern Europe and the Gulf also contributed to the immigrant profile of modern Scotland. In 1953, there were only three Chinese families in Glasgow but, between 1951 and 1985, the Chinese population in Scotland grew from 837 to around 10,000, the vast majority of them originating in Hong Kong.[28] By 1981, there were 1,100 Vietnamese settlers in Scotland and 1,500 Africans and 1,000 West Indians contributed further to Scotland's ethnic profile.[29] Also, in the four years following the 1999 Asylum and Immigration Act, around 9,000 asylum seekers were dispersed to Glasgow and, by June 2003, around 80 per cent of their asylum applications had been successful.[30] Despite various experiences of harassment in the city, around 50 per cent of them decided to stay, for the short term at least.[31]

By 1921, the English had overtaken the Irish as the largest migrant group in Scotland.[32] Yet, over the course of the century, Scotland arguably had a greater impact on the identity of the English who settled there than the settlers had on the Scotland they inhabited. The numbers of English settlers in Scotland, while large – they amounted to 222,161 in 1951 and 408,948 in 2001 – never matched the hordes of Scots resident in England – 565,828 in 1951, and 796,049 in 2001.[33] Although they were concentrated in the Central Belt (164,174 English residents were to be found there in 1961), they did not form a coherent community. Rather, they occupied a variety of occupations and classes, and linguistic and cultural similarities with Scottish neighbours made differences pale into insignificance at most times – save for periods of heightened political interest and international football competitions.[34] While English migrants were statistically significant, culturally they were less so – except, ironically, where they formed a conspicuous and vocal minority in marginal rural areas, where they became known as 'white settlers'. Until 1997, what the English did in England, where they were in a position to influence – nay, determine – governments, was always more important than what English exiles did in Scotland.

The considerable English minority in Scotland, nevertheless, draws particular attention to the limits of Scottishness as a vehicle for absorbing migrant groups even at the end of the century. Many of the English in Scotland found their identity challenged rather than accommodated in their new surroundings and were, at times, reluctant to 'cry' themselves English in the north, preferring instead spurious claims to adopted Scottish status or some sort of ill-defined Britishness.[35] Scottishness appeared too exclusive to accommodate even the citizens of the nation's Union partners.

To Lewis Grassic Gibbon, the Gorbals of the 1930s was:

incredibly un-Scottish. It is loudly and abominably and delightfully and hideously un-Scottish. It is not even a Scottish slum. Stout men in beards and ringlets and unseemly attire lounge and strut with pointed shoes: Ruth and Naomi go by with downcast Eastern faces, the Lascar rubs shoulder with the Syrian, Harry Lauder is a Baal unkeened to the midnight stars.[36]

Aside from the undercurrent of anti-Semitism evident here, the depiction of 'the foreign' as alien to Scottishness is telling.[37] By the end of the century, nearly 2 per cent of the Scottish population were from a non-white minority ethnic group and qualifications to vote for the new devolved Parliament rested on little more than Scottish residence.[38] On the surface, this suggests the emergence of an inclusive nation. Yet racism was widespread – in 1991, 72 per cent of Asian and Black Fife residents surveyed by researchers reported that they had been victims of racist incidents.[39] In popular culture, 'being Scots' still meant something more than one's current place on the planet and those not fitting the stereotype regularly suffered the consequences. Diversity proved far harder to harness as a characteristic of nationhood than the convenient tartan-wrapped paraphernalia of a more homogeneous mythic past. By the end of the century, Scotland was a multicultural nation but one is tempted to suggest that this was mainly because celebrating differences within its borders was the only option for a country that had failed to accommodate them in a more inclusive rendering of Scottishness.

LIVING ANCESTORS?

Glasgow is like the sea; a greater sea
Than that which surges about my native isles,
Less calculable and more cross-currented.
A man could know those waters like his hand,
But who gauges Glasgow's endless wiles,
    Who understands?

Nor are we fixed Hebrids here ourselves,
But waves, each of us, that in this ceaseless tide
Change shape and colour in countless ways and yet
Keep our identity through all;
Our lives in this vast whirlpool ride
    Well-reined withal!

It is one thing to gauge the waters
And know the set a sailing boat must have
And all the bearings of the wind and weather.
We islanders never weary of such lore
– But another to be oneself a wave
    And know no more.

'Glasgow is Like the Sea: A Hebridean Speaks'[40]
Hugh MacDiarmid

Leaving home was an experience that many Highlanders in Glasgow shared with immigrants from furth of Scotland and, having little to return to, together they made the most of the 'Dear Green Place', then made it their own. In the process, the city (every Scottish city) could remake the Highlander who – far from the twitching curtains of neighbours and the eyes of family and out of earshot of a hundred pulpit admonishments – could take comfort in the best of his culture, while relishing the city's anonymity. Nevertheless, like other migrants' tales, it is regret that dominates the written histories of Highland migration. Tragedy – and Highlanders are traditionally most suited to this genre – has no place for happy endings.

The answer, at least in part, lies in a convention which reads the history of the Highlander in what he leaves behind, rather than in what he takes with him, and privileges his environment over his ambition.

sa bhaile seo	in this village
chan eileas a' siubhal ach an aon uair	people only travel once
's na clachan a rinn ballaichean	and the stones that made
a' dol 'nan cairn	walls
	become cairns[41]

It is strange how those who leave, rather than those who stay behind, are typically blamed for what happens after their departure.

The history of the Highlands in the twentieth century bears the scars of many academic and literary conventions that frequently leave it stranded between two implicit yet resilient traditions. On the one hand, the Highlands have been considered an exceptional area in the sense that, more so than any other region, they have been defined in terms of their pre-1900 past. In the 1940s, for example, Adam Collier identified the population of the Highlands as 'the last, and perhaps least changed representatives of that peasantry which at one time inhabited much of Britain' and reflected that, on 'surveying' the Highlands, 'the most vivid of all the observer's impressions is a sense of remoteness . . . It is more than a mere sense of remoteness in space that strikes him; it is a sense also of remoteness in time.'[42] This must be contrasted with the perspectives of others who, like the Earl of Home (1903–95), as Secretary of State for Scotland in 1953, rejected the idea of a unique 'Highland Problem' but instead emphasised that 'the Highlands do not differ from the rest of the country in the multiplicity of problems which confront them'.[43] Associated with these positions were popular beliefs that the Highlands were either under threat in the late twentieth century or simply reluctant to adapt and marginal to national developments in any case. In the middle of the Second World War, the SNP's Donnachadh Mac'Illedhuibh claimed that 'for two centuries the Highlands [had] been bleeding to death'; in

1970, David Turnock concluded that 'crofting is symbolic of the incompleteness of the agricultural revolution in the Highlands'; and, in 2000, James Hunter, Chairman of Highlands and Islands Enterprise (HIE), the government's foremost development agency in the north, would claim that the Highlands had been marginalised for much of the twentieth century.[44]

Such perspectives, united in their cynicism if little else, have succeeded in distorting much of our knowledge regarding the manner in which the Highlands have always interacted with and continue to participate in wider economic changes. A far more useful model of twentieth-century progress was suggested by J. I. Prattis, who highlighted the fact that the problems, which were evident in the Highland economy, had emerged not through lack of integration with the wider world but as a result of the nature of integration.[45] The marginality of the Highland economy and the 'peasantness' identified in the culture of the area were the result of exposure to modern market forces and expressed the manner through which the area had been integrated into the economic system of the wider society from an initial position of inequality and relative disadvantage.[46]

The outcome of economic and social progress in the Highlands in the twentieth century was clearly different but the processes through which such a state of affairs emerged were far from exceptional. Industrial change was clearly evident in the Highlands as was the growth in central government intervention – at its most basic there was little here to distinguish the area from many other parts of Scotland. However, the chronology of change differed from that of the south and industrial progress was generally less dependent on the human capital of the Highland area than on its natural resources. Partly as a consequence, the aims and objectives of government policy in the north frequently deviated from those evident in the Lowlands. As a further consequence, Highland society remained distinctive.

While the Lowlands emerged from the nineteenth century with a relatively highly developed economic infrastructure, the topography of the Highland area and its continued reliance in many parts on subsistence agriculture had resulted in more rudimentary road and sea links and sparse coverage by utilities. Indeed, in the first decades of the century, there were few signs of improvement. In 1928, the problems were only too apparent, with piers being allowed to fall into decay and sea freight charges high. According to Peter Morrison, a former sub-commissioner of the BoAS, 'The freights for all commodities are now so exorbitant that trade is stifled on every hand. Passengers' fares are so prohibitive that hundreds desirous of visiting the Islands cannot afford the present charges.'[47] Lewis District Committee warned, 'So long as the present inadequate services remain, so long must the earning capacity of the people be limited and industry depressed.'[48]

The next few years brought some relief. A hard surface was applied to the 'Road to the Isles' between 1930 and 1938; government grants amounting to £1.5 million were made to support road building in the Highlands during the early 1950s alone; and improvements were recorded on other 'spine' roads, notably the route between Invergarry and Cluanie and the Glenfinnan–Lochailort road in the early 1960s.[49] Fewer mainland communities were forced to rely on sea travel as new roads and rail links opened up isolated townships; bus services made travel easier for locals and tourists alike, particularly after 1918; and car ferry services to the isles were improved with the aid of government subsidies from the 1960s. The Scottish Transport Group, a government agency, was established in 1969 and took over the ferry and haulage services of the Caledonian Steam Packet Company and the interests of David MacBrayne. Then, in 1973, ferry services to the Clyde ports and the Western Isles were consolidated under Caledonian MacBrayne Ltd (CalMac) and, in 1990, the Scottish Secretary (later the Scottish Executive) became its sole shareholder. In the seventies and eighties, despite complaints regarding CalMac's monopoly grip on sea travel into and out of many island communities, progress was marked, particularly in the carriage of motor vehicles to the isles – while 359,000 cars had used CalMac services in 1969, in 1989, 1,231,000 cars had travelled on CalMac's modern ferry fleet.[50] Progress was also recorded in the provision of services: between 1945 and 1960, the proportion of farms and crofts connected to an electricity supply increased from 7 to 80 per cent, and County Councils were spending around £700,000 per annum on water facilities alone in the early 1950s.[51]

The character and timing of industrial developments in the Highlands inevitably diverged at times from the Lowland pattern. As the growth of industrial production in the south appeared to be slowing down at the beginning of the twentieth century, it seemed that the Highlands were embarking on a period of significant transformation. In the Hebrides, the Harris Tweed industry was booming, as the number of looms in Lewis grew by more than fivefold to 300 in the first decade of the new century.[52] By 1900, aluminium production in Foyers stood at around 1,000 tons per year and, by 1909, production at Loch Leven made up a third of total world output.[53] Meanwhile, the activities of the Forestry Commission (established in 1919) seemed to promise a period of prosperity in many marginal agricultural communities, as this new body sought to counter rural decline while, at the same time, building up a national strategic reserve of timber.[54] Popular tourism was also taking its first tentative steps in the area, exploiting cheaper transport links and the popularity of all things 'Scotch' which had been encouraged by Queen Victoria's romance with Balmoral. In Highland communities, tweed-clad hunting parties annually greeted the 'Glorious Twelfth' and each summer heralded an 'invasion' of hikers, 'vigorous, youthful, multi-hued, noisy, cheerful, vulgar, and every year more numerous'.[55]

Yet the promise of these years turned to despair in many communities between the wars. Lord Leverhulme's visionary schemes for developing a fishing and fish processing industry on his Lewis and Harris estates (acquired in 1918 and 1919 respectively) had proved costly and unsuccessful even before his Hebridean dreams died with him in 1925 and, in 1936, the unemployment rate in the Highlands and Islands was around 35 per cent.[56] The tweed industry in the southern Hebrides was in decline from the 1930s, as production became centralised and controlled by the mills of Lewis, and the collapse of the herring fleet after 1918 led to severe economic problems for many coastal communities in the interwar years. In Tomintoul meanwhile, where work in local distilleries and 'on the roads' was generally seasonal, the writer and diplomat Sir Robert Bruce Lockhart (1887–1970) judged that the 'smartest boy in the village' appeared to be the one who got on the dole quickest. Elsewhere, only the 'anaesthesia of doles, pensions and cheap amusement' sustained what remained of townships and villages diminished already by the urge to emigrate.[57]

War and its aftermath overtook the 'Highland Question' for a time. Thereafter, despite signs of change encouraged by electrification and the development of agricultural grants from the 1940s, fresh hopes of regeneration invested in afforestation, industry and other activities were dashed, one by one. Experience was to prove that there was no single panacea for the problems of the Highland economy. Forestry ventures only employed around 9,000 workers by the 1960s (and declined even further thereafter, as the environmental agenda came to challenge production priorities); and the boost to employment facilitated by the siting of an aluminium smelter in Invergordon in 1968 came to an abrupt end in 1981 when its closure was announced.[58] The high cost of electricity had made the production of aluminium in the north uncompetitive and there seemed little the Scottish Office could do about it.[59] The hi-tech employment offered by the atomic reactor at Dounreay in Caithness from 1954 proved similarly short-lived, as did the 1,000 jobs which came with the pulp and paper mill at Corpach, Fort William, in 1966 – over the years, both industries cut back their workforces until only decommissioning work sustained labour on the Caithness site into the twenty-first century.[60] New fish-farming ventures, which took off in the late 1970s, were also facing stagnation in many areas less than twenty years later, due to overproduction, imports and disease. Tourism itself was a mixed blessing. While 10–12 per cent of British tourists visiting Scotland between 1973 and 1978 headed north to the Highlands and spent money at roughly the same rate per day as they did elsewhere in UK areas, tourism in the Highlands was 'markedly more seasonal than in Scotland or Britain as a whole'.[61] Half the annual ferry traffic to the Western Isles, for example, was concentrated in a twelve-week period during the summer.[62] Tourism in these areas also relied more heavily on younger holidaymakers using caravans and tents for accommodation. Revenue from this source was thus much less than was anticipated in earlier years and resulted in few permanent, non-seasonal, highly paid jobs.

As early as 1956, John Rollo – himself a successful entrepreneur with manufacturing interests in Bonnybridge, Easdale and Wick – reflected:

To the average industrialist the thought of a factory in a remote part of the Highlands raises nightmares of remote control, dreadful transport and the much repeated but despicable slander of the 'lazy Highlander' as well as the pre-determined certainty that such a venture could result only in loss.[63]

The success of Highland e-commerce, alongside profitable glass, pottery, whisky and food production, in the final decades of the century challenged such preconceptions, as did a business start-up rate some 25 per cent higher than the Scottish average by 2000.[64] But Rollo's caricature took time to fade and considerable government investment was required to change the outlook of Scottish business.

Throughout the century, the Highland environment and traditional land use proved the area's most valuable resource and its biggest liability. The limits of the initial advantages which the Highlands had offered to aluminium manufacturers in the first decades became increasingly apparent in the second half of the century, as Canada's hydro-electricity resources overwhelmed what was possible in Scotland. The agricultural subsistence offered by crofting supported the rise of the tweed industry and supplemented incomes from fishing but was often a serious impediment to efficient land use. Giving evidence to the Taylor Commission in 1954, the Scottish Agricultural Organisation Society argued that the security of tenure for crofters, enshrined in legislation of 1886, had engendered a 'complacency and a disregard of the need to move with the times' which made many crofting townships 'among the most backward of farming communities'.[65]

Also, while landscape and scenery were seen as the working capital of tourism in the Highlands, their protection could inhibit industrial development.[66] By 2000, almost half of Scotland's officially recognised Sites of Special Scientific Interest (SSSI) were in the Highlands and Islands and it was clear that the long-awaited development of national parks in Scotland at the end of the century would have a disproportionate impact on Highland communities.[67] Over the years, environmentalists and local communities frequently clashed over important development programmes – insensitivity from the conservation lobby was often matched by the suspicion of Highland residents who associated the environmental cause with obstructionism.[68] The stalemates which ensued generally lay with government to resolve and there were few happy endings. A planning proposal by Redland Aggregates Plc for a superquarry at Lingerbay on the Island of Harris, for example, led to one of the longest public inquiries in Scotland in 1991. Delays and appeals meant that it was not until April 2004 that the company finally withdrew their application, by which time the proposal had divided the local community, aroused lasting suspicions of conservation agencies and compromised trust in both the Scottish Office and, latterly, the Scottish Executive. On most occasions, however, government intervention sought a road between competing interests. It was notable that the national parks legislation of 2000, governing Scotland, incorporated an explicit commitment to socio-economic development as part of their remit. Tension had marked earlier attempts to preserve parts of the Cairngorms (the site for one of the two national parks identified in 2000) in the 1960s and government bodies were determined not to re-ignite old arguments.[69]

Overall, priorities quite different from and frequently at odds with those followed in the Lowlands were regularly pursued by governments in the north. The environmental and cultural context of the Highlands partly explains this but history also played a part. Over the course of the century, guilt about the Highland Clearances, perpetrated by landowners and enforced by law generations before, proved a powerful, if regularly misplaced, motive behind government policy. Politicians from all parties proved susceptible to the myth of a Highland idyll destroyed by capitalist forces that would have been best kept within an urban setting.[70] 'For two hundred years,' remarked Willie Ross (1911–88), the Secretary of State for Scotland in 1965, 'the Highlander has been the man on Scotland's conscience.' At various times, governments of all political persuasions defended the terms of the 1886 Crofters Holdings (Scotland) Act which dictated important differences in land use north and south of the 'Highland Line'.[71] The maintenance of the crofting 'system' was considered intrinsic to the perpetuation of what remained of a distinct Highland way of life that was worth preserving. Historical, as much as economic, arguments were therefore drawn upon to defend crofting and an appreciation of Highland society as worthy of nurture shaped many government priorities. The 'ferm touns' of the Lowlands and the children of their former residents dispersed throughout Scotland enjoyed no such privileges. While they had suffered similar fates at the hands of 'progress', they had no debts to call in and no sense of collective guilt to exploit. It was a very selective historic sense that privileged the Highlands at the expense of the rest of Scotland.

It was within this environmental, cultural and historical context that regional policy developed, initially under the aegis of the Scottish Office and later as part of wider European schemes. In the years following the Great War, 'successive governments faced with grave post-war problems preferred to turn a blind eye to an area where there was little political capital to be gained' and, during this period, intervention in the Highlands focused almost exclusively on land settlement, partly in response to land raids undertaken by ex-servicemen.[72] The 1919 Land Settlement (Scotland) Act created over 1,500 new holdings in the Highlands and the enlargement of a further 1,200.[73] It was not enough. Sir Alexander MacEwen (1875–1941), a former Provost of Inverness, suggested, in 1939, that 'the government had no policy with regard to the Highlands, but a policy of palliatives' and it acted like a 'traveller in a foreign country who may toss coins to a group of children but bestows no thought on their welfare or education'.[74]

The Second World War, however, left a very different legacy. The Hydro-Electric Development (Scotland) Act of 1943 established the North of Scotland Hydro-Electric Board, thus initiating several major schemes providing work for thousands in the Highlands and improving the area's infrastructure. The late 1940s and 1950s were also marked by several inquiries and important if limited developments: in 1946, an Advisory Panel on the Highlands and Islands was established to instruct the Secretary of State for Scotland on economic and welfare issues in the north; in 1948, the Highlands became a Development Area; the 1955 Crofters (Scotland) Act reconstituted the Crofters Commission; and a White Paper, in 1959, committed the government to improving services, amenities and employment in the Highlands.

However, the formation of the Highlands and Islands Development Board (HIDB) in 1965 must be regarded as the major turning point in government policy in the north and it reflected the confidence of the Labour government at the time that even the Highlands could not resist the compelling logic of planned development. The HIDB was given powers to prepare and promote measures aimed at improving the economic and social welfare of the Highlands and Islands and, in its first annual report, announced that it would be 'judged on its achievements in the remote and fragile areas'.[75] Nevertheless, in its first years, it focused almost overwhelmingly on the area around the Moray Firth that quickly entered a period of prosperity due to the discovery of North Sea oil and the North West Highlands and Islands were largely neglected. In its first twelve years, the HIDB pumped £38 million into the Highlands and attracted an additional £57 million from private investment but, in the Western Isles, the Board proved unable to halt depopulation and the economic impediments of an ageing community.[76] Overall, the HIDB was continually restricted by inadequate funding and limited compulsory land purchase powers but proved at least partly successful throughout its lifetime in encouraging indigenous manufacturing, fishing and tourist ventures.[77]

Government interest in the Highlands, however, did not stop there. The operations of the HIDB, which, from 1991, became known as Highlands and Islands Enterprise (HIE), coincided with a period of greater government investment in agriculture. In the second half of the century, government grants, subsidies and loans to crofters and small farmers grew dramatically – together, by the 1990s, the agricultural grant scheme in the crofting counties and housing grants and loans to crofting households amounted to an annual expenditure of around £2 million.[78] Infrastructural improvements were also receiving attention although it was not invariably of the most positive kind. The Skye Bridge ('the concrete rainbow') was opened by Michael Forsyth (1954–), the Conservative Secretary of State for Scotland, in October 1995. Initial wide public support for a bridge had died quickly as it became apparent that tolls would be charged at rates comparable to the existing ferry prices. An effective protest group, Skye and Kyle Against Tolls (SKAT), was organised and the arrests of key activists for the non-payment of tolls were well publicised. In the end, local anger appeared vindicated when the Committee of Public Accounts concluded that serious mistakes had been made in the planning of the bridge – one of the first infrastructural projects to be carried out under an innovative private finance initiative. Philip Hope, a member of the inquiry team, noted:

> We see a project where there was no proper quantifiable risk, no proper test of the external financing arrangements, a very high return to equity investors, no systematic financial comparisons

either in public sector projects or to maintain the ferry service and a failure to set budgets for price ceilings on various aspects of the project. It seems to me that in effect the Department [the Scottish Office Development Department] and now the taxpayer have been turned over.[79]

Land reform was also back on the agenda by this time. Few crofters had exploited new opportunities made available in 1976 to own their own crofts (had they done so, they would no longer have been eligible for most crofting grants) but, by the 1990s, it was clear that the legal framework governing land ownership in the north of Scotland was not meeting contemporary demands. Community buyouts – in Assynt (1992); Borve and Annishader, Skye (1993); Eigg (1997); and Knoydart (1999) – and the purchase of the 4,500 acre Orbost estate by Skye and Lochalsh Enterprise (1997) suggested that crofting was now appreciated as a popular and valuable means for supporting families on marginal land whose main occupations typically lay elsewhere. These schemes allowed the crofters to remain tenants but with a community landlord. In 2003, the Land Reform (Scotland) Act made it the right of private citizens in a crofting community on a collective basis similarly to acquire the land they lived on.[80] It was a radical innovation although it remains to be seen whether it does more than simply salve the collective conscience perennially disturbed by Clearance memories.

Still, other governments now had a stake in the Highlands. In the early 1980s, the European Community introduced a five-year Integrated Development Programme (IDP) – or 'I Don't Pay' in the popular local parlance of the time – in the Outer Hebrides which invested heavily in infrastructural improvements. As the years passed, similar programmes addressed improvements in the Northern Isles, Lochaber, Wester Ross and Sutherland, bringing around £100 million into the economy of the north of Scotland.[81] Yet problems remained. In 1983, a European Parliament Committee Report emphasised that the economy of the Highlands and Islands, despite public sector investment, remained 'precarious', 'over dependent on primary industry and on seasonal employment' and 'more exposed to the effect of adverse economic circumstances'.[82] Investment in the 1980s tackled some of these concerns but real incomes in the Highlands still lagged behind the rest of the country. In response to significant pressure for assistance from Highland Members of the European Parliament and local Regional and Island Authorities, in 1994, the Highlands and Islands were 'awarded' Objective 1 status by the EU, the highest category of assistance administered by the Union through its structural fund for communities with a

GDP of less than 75 per cent of the EU average. Within two years, around £250 million was invested in schemes intended to promote communications and services, community development, tourism and culture, business development, the environment and the primary sector.[83] It seemed that something of a renaissance beckoned.

To consider the Highlands simply in terms of their historical 'victim' status or, alternatively, to ignore the obvious challenges they pose to broader Scottish patterns, is too simple. Rather, it is clear that the main features that have distinguished the Highlands throughout their history – ostensibly the area's topography and climate and the culture of its dispersed population – remained the determining features of Highland progress in the twentieth century. What was new in these years was the way in which these features were appreciated and how this way of under-standing the Highlands was considered sufficient justification for treating the area as exceptional in Scotland when, at times, differences were more apparent than real. Industrial dislocation, poverty, crime, poor housing, emigration and immigration: the Highland story is but one version of a tale that was repeated throughout the country. The timing, nature and extent of social change may have been distinctive but the most important difference governing Highland history in these years was, ironically, still to be found in its past – in emotive episodes that remained powerful enough to shape the future of the area by pricking the conscience of the political elite while partly absolving natives of the blame for problems that were often just as much of their making.

Conclusion

> History, climate, social conditions, and the national beverage have all combined . . . to make the Scot an individualist, fighting for his own hand.
>
> *The House with the Green Shutters*, 1901
> G. Douglas Brown (1869–1902)

The individualism beloved of Victorian Liberals offered little guidance to twentieth-century Scots. Much the same could be said of the collectivism preached by turn-of-the-century Socialists. Yet the uneasy accommodation of both traditions in the social fabric of the nation determined much that was unique to Scottish society after 1945. Little separated the ethos of self-improvement intrinsic to the culture of Edwardian Scots from the consumerism of the post-war decades bar the former's sensitivity to ostentation and its abhorrence of waste. Wealth, if not greed, had, for some time, been a measure of worth in Scotland – after all, the elect were typically known as much by their possessions as by their deeds. In an increasingly secular society, it was but a small step to the debt-fuelled acquisitiveness of the final decades. Alongside all this, however, was a tendency to seek social amelioration through the offices of the state. This was not collectivism in the truest sense of the word – the individual had to invest little but his taxes and sacrifice nothing of his time. Indeed, throughout the century, society's reliance on an increasingly professionalised and centralised welfare state largely eroded the keen sense of a shared enterprise that had greeted the foundation of the welfare state in 1948. What remained was toleration of government agencies (many of them Scottish) on which many relied but towards which few felt any sense of responsibility. A culture of entitlement had evolved.

Scottish society created, relied on and was, in turn, shaped by an increasingly bloated state apparatus over the course of the twentieth century. But regional, class, gender and ethnic social dynamics resisted the uniformity implied by this state of affairs. The changing profile of Scottish criminality, the evolution of the Scottish family and the growing contribution of immigrant groups to Scottish society all point to important changes the state alone did not determine. The Scottish people still governed their own futures, still made of Scottishness what they willed.

PART THREE

'The Instinct for Freedom' –
Twentieth-century Politics

Prologue

This is a moment anchored in our history.

Today, we reach back through the long haul to win this parliament, through the struggles of those who brought democracy to Scotland, to that other Parliament dissolved in controversy nearly three centuries ago.

Today, we look forward to the time when this moment will be seen as a turning point: the day when democracy was renewed in Scotland, when we revitalised our place in this, our United Kingdom.

This is about more than our politics and our laws. This is about who we are, how we carry ourselves. There is a new voice in the land, the voice of a democratic Parliament. A voice to shape Scotland as surely as the echoes from our past:

> the shout of the welder in the din of the great Clyde shipyards;
> the speak of the Mearns, with its soul in the land;
> the discourse of the Enlightenment, when Edinburgh and Glasgow
> were a light held to the intellectual life of Europe;
> the wild cry of the Great Pipes;
> and back to the distant cries of the battles of Bruce and Wallace. . . .

A Scottish Parliament. Not an end: a means to greater ends . . .

Wisdom. Justice. Compassion. Integrity. Timeless values. Honourable aspirations for this new forum of democracy, born on the cusp of a new century.

Donald Dewar (1937–2000)
Opening of the Scottish Parliament, 1 July 1999[1]

The neat coincidence of the passage of the old – century and style of governance – and the emergence of the new – millennium and Parliament – was perhaps enough to determine that the foundation of the Scottish Parliament in 1999 would be identified by its architects as the realisation of older dreams and ambitions. But the compelling logic of time was deceptive. As much as devolutionists sought 'closure' in the Parliament, those who sought an independent Scotland resisted claims that the 'settled will' of the nation would be expressed in this devolved legislature – in April 1999, polls indicated that around 45 per cent of Scots would vote for independence if offered the option in a referendum.[2] In contrast, many unionists confidently awaited confirmation that, for Westminster, power devolved was in fact power retained and that devolution had, ironically, preserved the status quo, save for a few cosmetic changes. But 1999 was a year poised for novelty, as the world anticipated millennial excess at its close. Even the historian of this time finds it hard to resist the seductive 'happily ever after' of the Parliament's foundation. Nevertheless, while that Hogmanay gave birth to a new year (pedants would claim the twentieth century had one more year to run), it is yet to be confirmed that the Parliament played midwife to a new Scotland.

EIGHT

Political Territories

Without a unique Scottish legislature, territorial questions alternately mediated and confounded the political voice of the nation. The sociologist David McCrone has suggested that, from as early as the 1960s, 'Scotland' was 'an ideological category offering an alternative framework for interpreting the political world'. But this 'Scotland' (beyond administrative offices on the site of an old Edinburgh jail and an unpopular seat in Cabinet) was not grounded in the material world of politics.[1] Unique Scottish institutions sustained it – for example, the law, the church, the education system, the health service and local government – and its power as an idea (or an ideal) cannot be disputed. But such bodies boasted no legislative assembly. As a result, the voice of 'Scotland' sought expression in chambers where Scotland itself had no elected representative – in local government, where councillors represented 'wards'; in the Scottish Office, whose senior official was a UK government appointee; in the UK Parliament, where MPs spoke for constituencies rather than nations; and in Europe, where Scotland had regional status. In 1998, this amounted to 1,222 members of thirty-two local councils, several thousand civil servants supporting one cabinet minister, seventy-two UK MPs and eight members of the European Parliament (MEPs).[2] Not surprisingly, the voice of Scotland emanating from such bodies was discordant and frequently out of tune.

PROVOSTS, PARISHES AND POLL TAX

Local government was transformed in the twentieth century. In 1900, local government in Scotland was the outcome of the operations of thirty-three county councils, 200 burgh councils, 869 parish councils, over 1,000 school boards and a host of other commissions, committees and boards. In the years that followed, rationalisation was relatively fast if less than wholesale. In 1918, provision of education became the responsibility of thirty-eight education authorities and, after the 1929

Local Government (Scotland) Act was passed, parish councils, district committees and some types of burgh government were abolished and authority became largely invested in thirty-three county councils, four city councils, 196 district councils and 198 burgh councils that regularly worked together in the provision of services.[3]

Despite (or because of) this bewildering array of offices, local government throughout the early part of the century was closer to the priorities and pre-occupations of ordinary Scots than the machinations of Parliament. After all, in these years, basic amenities, health services, education and public welfare were largely the responsibility of local politicians. The consolidation of elected offices, while encouraging greater efficiencies, did not necessarily encourage greater participation. Thomas Mitchell, Lord Provost of Aberdeen from 1939, was elected to the City Parish Council in Aberdeen in 1908 and later bemoaned its passing:

> The duties of the Parish Council were numerous and in my opinion far more important than Town Council . . . We had to care for the poor, the sick, the mentally deficient and those who were mentally ill, and had to administer relief to the destitute. That to my mind was a more satisfying work than debating whether a water pipe should be 3/4 inch thick, or 1 inch thick, as I was later to do on the Town Council.[4]

Local public office declined in both popularity and prestige as the century progressed.

Nine out of the first ten twentieth-century Lord Provosts of Edinburgh were knighted for their services to the local community and belonged to the mercantile elite of that city.[5] Meanwhile, in Aberdeen's Lord Provost Henry Alexander, who held the post from 1932 to 1935, we are offered a model of the archetypal public-spirited employer and councillor. 'Throughout all his service,' noted Bailie Duncan in 1936, 'he has displayed characteristic humility and yet retained that reserved dignity which has always commanded the genuine respect of his fellow citizens. Mr Alexander is one of Nature's Gentlemen.'[6] But men like Alexander were to become a rare breed as the century progressed. Party politics slowly infiltrated local government – an arena traditionally hostile to party appellations and loyalty other than that to the community. Labour candidates were first to contest seats as party representatives in urban constituencies (from the 1880s), while the Liberals and the Unionists (that is the Conservatives) only slowly came round. This was particularly the case in rural areas where they often stood as either independents or, in the latter case, 'Progressives' until as late as the 1970s.[7]

But even party colours failed to develop public interest and actually eroded the good will of many who considered politics to have no role in the service owed to the public. James Gibson, for example, resigned from various Liberal committees on becoming Edinburgh's Lord Provost in 1906. As early as 1939, William Marwick commented on the 'general apathy and low polls' that marked local council elections.[8] True, the local franchise was often more inclusive than the parliamentary vote – Scotswomen could vote in local council elections twenty years before they secured the parliamentary franchise and, from an early date, assumed elected office on school boards whose eager members were elected by proportional representation. Yet the public showed increasing disregard for local politics – Dundee's Lord Provost from 1940 to 1946 was Garnet Wilson and he complained that 'democracy does not flourish on a 50 per cent poll (or less) or on a roll of municipal candidates drawn from a fraction of the electorate'.[9] By the 1970s, nearly 70 per cent of seats in local government in Scotland were not contested in elections and turnouts averaged 47 per cent.[10] As the role of the Scottish Office grew and central government took on additional social responsibilities, the remit of local government bodies in Scotland diminished and the allure of elected office declined. After 1918, as central government grants to local authorities increased as a proportion of their overall revenue, local government's relationship with the state became closer and more contested. Its relations with the public, meanwhile, lost their earlier intimacy.

Despite increasing responsibilities in housing and education, declining local autonomy was to be the price for increasing state benefaction. As the doctrine of planning came to dominate economic policy in Scotland and as responsibility for key health, infrastructural and welfare matters passed to administrative agencies and central government departments in the immediate post-war years, independent local government initiative and influence in Scotland declined and, increasingly, local government became a principal means for delivering and administrating central government policies.[11] From only 6 per cent in 1881–82, central government grants to local authorities rose to over one third of their budgetary resources by 1947–48 – more than the revenue from local rates in that year.[12] By the 1950s, Robert Baird would conclude that rates had 'ceased to be the main source of finance and have almost come to be local subventions in aid of Imperial services'.[13]

In 1969, a Royal Commission on Local Government in Scotland, the Wheatley Commission, published its report. In stark terms, it emphasised that 'something is seriously wrong with local government in Scotland' and went on to record the problems, weaknesses and inefficiencies in a system that was marred by limited democratic participation, duplication of effort, uneven resourcing and government interference.[14] Largely as a consequence of its recommendations, local government was re-organised from May 1975, when a two-tier system of nine regional and fifty-three district councils was instituted and three all-purpose island authorities were created. The regions were the larger of the new authorities and their responsibilities covered strategic planning, education, social work, the emergency services and civil registration. Meanwhile, the districts had obligations for housing, leisure, licensing and environmental health.

The public response to local government reform was alternately muted and outrightly hostile. Aspects of Wheatley's plans were amended during the various parliamentary stages largely as a consequence of popular outrage and the sensitivities of the incoming Conservative government that had inherited these radical plans. After a popular campaign by residents of 'the Kingdom' ('Fight for Fife'[15]), Fife, instead of being divided between Lothian and Tayside, became a region in its own right; Scottish Borders Region was created out of the southern-most areas of Lothian; and the island authorities (Western Isles, Orkney and Shetland) were detached from Highland Region.[16] But other interests were not appeased. Aberdeen had opposed the changes to its status during the consultation period before the Act and 'repeatedly argued for all purpose status for Scotland's four main cities'.[17] Regardless, the City of Aberdeen District Council was established in 1975. Others lamented the passing or radical reform of local offices, including that of bailie, which had been closely associated with Scottish traditions. John Gray, one of Edinburgh's last bailies of the old type, appointed for one year in 1974, noted:

> Change was necessary, but surely not the wholesale destruction of institutions which were part of the history and culture of our nation: they have all gone. The Counties, the Burghs, the Bailies, the Provosts, the Town Clerks, and Chamberlains, the 'Kirkings', the Guild Brethren, the Dean of Guild and Burgh Courts – every centre of local power and independence. The guts have been ripped out of our national life. All can now be controlled either administratively or politically. The new system is a paradise for the civil servant and the politician as well as being costly and remote.[18]

There were certainly problems with the new structures. Regions were of uneven sizes and influence – Strathclyde, incorporating Glasgow and much of the heavily populated west-central belt of Scotland, contained

over 40 per cent of Scots, while Highland Region was sparsely populated but covered a third of the Scottish land mass.[19] Many citizens were
confused about the responsibilities of the various district and regional
offices, and the overlapping and duplication of services also remained a
problem. As an exercise in encouraging participative democracy, the
consequences of the Wheatley reforms were also contradictory – they
placed least power with the bodies closest to the people and did little to
tackle complaints about the restrictive practices of council cliques.[20] In
1976 Dundee's former Progressive Lord Provost, Alex MacKenzie,
complained that 'unsavoury, distasteful things take place behind the
scenes' and criticised the power of 'cliques comprised of a few "power-
drunk" amateur politicians'.[21] Certainly, the role and presence of
parties in Scottish local government became even more pronounced
after May 1975.

Changes to the politics inside Scottish council chambers were soon to
be matched by changes in political approaches to local government. In
1944, Scottish Unionists defended the freedoms of local authorities:

> In our consideration . . . our guiding principle throughout has been
> the preservation of the democratic ideal and the extension to Local
> Authorities of the fullest possible control over their own affairs
> without undue interference from Government departments. This is
> held to be of the highest importance in view of the very large
> measure of control which has been exercised by government offi-
> cials during the war years. We think that the maintenance and
> extension of local control is vital and that the good government of
> Scotland depends on it.[22]

Thirty-five years later, with Margaret Thatcher in Downing Street, the
perspective of many Scottish Tories had changed. Now concerns with
efficiency overwhelmed the 'democratic ideal' and Scottish local councils (many of them, like Stirling and Edinburgh, Labour-controlled)
were major obstacles in the way of reform. By prioritising reductions in
public expenditure, increasing central control of local government
finances, promoting council house purchase schemes and encouraging
competitive tendering for public service contracts, the Conservative
governments of the 1980s and 1990s directly challenged the autonomy
of local authorities as well as traditions of civic provision that had
developed since the nineteenth century. From a high point of 75 per cent
of local government expenditure in 1975–76, central government
grants had fallen to a little over 55 per cent by 1990–91. (In 1992, this
amounted to £7.5 billion.) With such cuts, there was little political

capital to be made in claims that Scotland still maintained her relative advantage over England and Wales when it came to rate support funding.[23] Further difficulties experienced in collecting and administering the unpopular community charge ('poll tax') from 1988 also exacerbated local authority funding shortages at a time when central government extended its powers to claw back rate support grants from authorities that spent above government guidelines.[24] The balance of power had clearly shifted to the centre. Not even the protests of the Convention of Scottish Local Authorities (COSLA), the principal voice of local government in these years, could effect a return to the consensus of the past, although it is notable that, in the late 1980s, COSLA proved a driving force behind the Scottish Constitutional Convention (SCC) and its demands for devolution.

During its first years in office, the Conservative administration did little more than 'tinker' with the local government structures bequeathed them from the 1970s.[25] However, following successive local government defeats – the Conservatives held no regions at all after losing Lothian, Tayside and Grampian in 1986 and failed to retain Edinburgh, their last major city council, in 1984 – and despite a lack of overwhelming public support, the Conservatives returned Scottish local government to a single-tier system of twenty-nine unitary and three island authorities following the passage of the 1994 Local Government (Scotland) Act. Arguments, strangely evocative of the 1970s, that the current system was inefficient, misunderstood and remote were employed by the Secretary of State for Scotland Ian Lang (1940–) to explain the need for change. But memories of countless Tory battles with Labour Regions such as Strathclyde were too fresh in the public mind not to rule out the possibility of more self-serving interests on the part of the government. Tory claims that the reforms would pass decision making downwards were also treated with suspicion – after all, since the raft of Conservative reforms in the 1980s, there appeared to be little power left in local government and, as a consequence of introducing market principles into local government, citizens were now more readily styled consumers or clients than the arbiters of local democracy.[26] The development of associated Scottish Office agencies and the increase in statutory joint boards involving both Scottish Office and local membership also raised doubts about the Tories' commitment to local democracy – a whole new tier of (largely unaccountable) secondary local government had been created that owed little to local initiative.[27] After 1995, Scottish local government still rested on far fewer units of authority in relation to population than any other country in western Europe with the exception of England.[28]

In April 1995, the first elections were held for the new unitary councils and, in March 1996, after a changeover period, regional and district councils were abolished. The Conservatives failed to win control of any of the new unitary authorities and, three years later, won fewer seats than the Liberal Democrats in the local bodies they themselves had created.

By the end of the century, Scottish local government was not as close to its citizens as it had been and its scope and responsibilities had changed. Yet, while it had different obligations, it was not necessarily more independent. Indeed, the encroachment of central government was the dominating theme in its history in the previous hundred years. As the Scottish Office grew, local government paid the price and, as the new Scottish Executive (later, the Scottish Government) asserted its presence after 1999, local government's Cinderella role in the drama of national politics appeared guaranteed. Glasgow Councillor, Charles Gordon, was despondent when he observed that 'Members of the Scottish Parliament (MSPs) seem to think that the creation of the new Parliament was a "year zero", which invalidated all hitherto accepted knowledge, especially in other levels of governance'.[29] While slow to legislate on local government, the new Parliament was not slow to interfere, with various initiatives encouraging new management approaches, modernisation and effective leadership. After all, 40 per cent of the Scottish Executive's budget was earmarked for local government. Even under the new order, local government would remain a hostage to the fortunes of competing conservative and modernising tendencies in Scottish politics over which it had little control.[30]

THE SCOTTISH OFFICE – A LOGICAL ABSURDITY?

It has been suggested that the Scottish Office gave *meaning* to Scotland in the twentieth century at a time when its constitutional status was under pressure.[31] Alternatively, as William Miller put it in 1981, the Scottish Office was simply one of those 'logical absurdities' with which the whole of British government was 'riddled' but which worked well enough in practice until the 1970s.[32]

Founded in 1885 and based initially at Dover House in Whitehall, the Scottish Office was created largely to ensure that due attention was paid to Scottish interests when legislation was being shaped at Westminster.[33] During its first years, however, progress was slow and the volume of Scottish legislation going before the House remained paltry. From 1892, the Scottish Secretary acquired a seat in Cabinet but, even in 1904, Reginald MacLeod of Macleod, 27th Chief of the Clan MacLeod, would jocularly congratulate P. J. Rose (1878–1959), Private Secretary to the Scottish Secretary 1909–1912 and later Assistant Under-Secretary 1921–1942, on the passage of an Act protecting 'the smallest of God's creatures – the St Kilda wren'. 'Well, Rose,' he said, 'we have passed *one* Scottish Act this Session.'[34]

Nevertheless, the Scottish Office would accumulate an important portfolio by acquiring responsibility for law and order in 1887, agriculture in 1912 and health and housing in 1918, in addition to its original obligations in education. Reflecting on her husband's time from 1905 to 1912 as Secretary for Scotland, Lady Pentland, wife of the Liberal, the Rt Hon. John Sinclair, Lord Pentland (1890–1970), commented:

> Sinclair had to advise the Sovereign in all matters regarding the Royal prerogative, including appointments; he was the ministerial head of the Scottish Education Department, the President of the Local Government Board for Scotland ... and the Chairman of the Congested Districts Board. He was responsible to Parliament for the Fishery Board, the Prison Commission, the Registrar-General's Department, the Board of Lunacy, the Board of Trustees of the National Galleries of Scotland. All these subjects had to be mastered by studying boxes full of papers; by endless correspondence, interviews, deputations, meetings, and journeys to Scotland. After finding out what to do he had to get it done; officials, Cabinet colleagues, Parliament had to be convinced; time and money had to be obtained for the smaller and poorer country, and, should Scotland be ready for it, the right to advance alone.[35]

Robert Munro (1868–1955), the Coalition Liberal Scottish Secretary from 1916 to 1922, also acknowledged the diverse responsibilities of the job and the Secretary's anomalous position relative to his peers when he returned to Scotland as Chief Justice Clerk in 1922:

> The duties of the Secretary for Scotland are at once multifarious, responsible, and exacting – more multifarious indeed than those of any other member of the Government except the Prime Minister, the Foreign Minister, or the Chancellor of the Exchequer. The office involves the control and direction of many boards and departments in Scotland. It comprises the responsibilities of three English departments, each of which is controlled by a Cabinet Minister – Agriculture, Education and Health. The Secretary of Scotland, moreover, represents a nation. And yet he is not a Secretary of State, and his emoluments remain those of a minor Minister.[36]

In 1926 some of Munro's concerns were addressed when the then Scottish Secretary, the Unionist Sir John Gilmour (1876–1940), was elevated to the position of Secretary of State. But, as the duties of the ministry grew, administration from London and a branch office in Edinburgh became increasingly difficult, particularly as the Scottish Boards, over which the minister, at least theoretically, had authority, were notoriously independent and wedded to administrative practices quite out of step with the English civil service. Board membership was addressed in 1928 when career civil servants acquired a more prominent role in the renamed departments of Health, Agriculture and Prisons which joined the established Department of Education. Then, following pressure from senior Scottish politicians and the recommendations of the Gilmour Report (1937), the Scottish Office departments were rationalised once more in 1939 into four units – Health, Home (incorporating the former Local Government Division, the Prisons Department and the Fisheries Board), Education and Agriculture – each fiercely defensive of their remit and identity.[37] When, in 1939, the Office's new Scottish home at St Andrew's House on Calton Hill in Edinburgh was opened, the Scottish Office resembled 'a microcosm of a complete British Government in the field of functions'.[38]

War accelerated rather than interrupted change at the Scottish Office and encouraged more collaborative ways of working across the component departments. During the years of conflict, Labour's Tom Johnston, Secretary of State from February 1941, arranged for Scottish MPs to meet in Edinburgh and, as Scotland's 'strong man in the Cabinet', he did much to elevate the status and powers of the Scottish Secretaryship of State.[39] He was a man known for getting things done and was keen to exploit the potential of reconstruction.[40] He instituted various committees during the war years to shape a distinctly Scottish post-war vision. Among the most important of these was the Council of State, the membership of which was made up of all previous Scottish Secretaries, and its offspring, the Scottish Council on Industry (see Part One). Throughout, he also sought to keep Scottish needs to the fore in the concerns of his cabinet colleagues. The status of the Forestry Commission and the development of factory space in the north, for example, both came under his critical gaze.

Importantly, Johnston's period in office set the tone for the immediate post-war years. In the late forties, he reflected on the necessity for increased economic power for the Scottish Office:

Sometimes the Scottish nation . . . is administered as if it were a branch post office: sometimes as if it were an animal disease . . .

Personally I am now and always have been in favour of public ownership of essential industries, and public direction of essential services, but public ownership to me never meant a vesting of the control in some department or Board 400 miles away . . .

[F]or years past I have been convinced that while the political forms were being discussed it was essential we should get economic control . . . It will avail us little if we got a Parliament and inherited little with it but a gigantic poorhouse and an emigration scheme.[41]

More responsibilities were added to those of the Secretary of State in 1954, including the appointment of JPs and responsibility for roads, ferries and bridges. But it is by no means clear that all Scottish Secretaries of these years shared Johnston's enthusiasm for a wider Scottish Office remit. James Stuart (1897–1971), Churchill's man in the north from 1951, was a reluctant occupant of Johnston's old office – '[T]he Scottish Office had never been one of my ambitions,' he claimed – although, as an influential cabinet member and confidant of the Prime Minister, he would have been better placed to argue Scotland's case than many that had gone before him.[42] He wrote:

It is an arduous job being Secretary for Scotland, involving constant travelling from and to London. Regularly my timetable involved leaving the Commons for King's Cross about midnight on Thursday, so as to be at work in St Andrews House, Edinburgh, about 10am on Friday. I would often have to spend a night in Glasgow before returning to London on the overnight train on Sunday night. Even worse, the week-end would involve not only Thursday and Sunday nights in the train, but also one of the intervening nights in a cold, strange bed in Glasgow and the other in, say, Aberdeen.[43]

Perhaps it is not surprising that Stuart was the Scottish Secretary who got Cabinet approval for the Forth Road Bridge! In other respects, however, Stuart effected few changes in the Scottish Office, beyond the addition of an undersecretary and a Minister of State, and saw little merit in innovative practice when the current system was generally adequate for the job.

Nevertheless, growth of the Scottish Office seemed unremitting – from employing just 2,400 civil servants in 1937, by 1970, 8,300 civil servants staffed Scottish Office corridors.[44] In 1962, the Scottish Home and Health Departments were amalgamated and a Development Department was established and, in the later 1960s and the 1970s, Scottish Office responsibilities in industry developed significantly (see Part One). After 1964, the presence of Willie Ross as Labour's Secretary of State for Scotland further enhanced the role of the Scottish Office, as increasing amounts from the public purse were expended north of the Border. (Ross was the longest-serving Scottish Secretary, holding the office between 1964 and 1970 and again between 1974 and 1976.) Public expenditure in Scotland rose by 900 per cent between 1964 and 1973.[45] In the early sixties, a Treasury official offered a poetic interpretation:

> In matters of money the fault of the Scots
> Is asking too often and asking for lots.[46]

In these years, a Secretary's success was largely judged by the monies he could extract from the Treasury, though it could just as easily have been suggested that the persistent need for preferential treatment in Scotland was a confession that, quite simply, governments were failing to deliver meaningful improvements or, more drastically, that the current constitutional set-up was failing Scotland. However, Ross held firmly entrenched expectations that his role was to be principally that of a lobbyist, willing to be as abrasive and forceful as Scotland's interests required.[47]

But the political environment was changing. In 1978, the introduction of the Barnett Formula – a transparent means for calculating Scotland's entitlement in relation to UK-wide public expenditure – restricted the Secretary's ability to negotiate deals behind the scenes in Scotland's favour. Had Labour been successful in the 1979 general election, it is doubtful that even a politician as experienced as Ross could have promised Scots as much as he had done in the past. But Labour did not win in 1979. Instead, memories of the 'Years of Plenty' became a useful tool for Labour in opposition during the last two decades of the century.

Margaret Thatcher found little in Scottish interests and claims to exceptional status to warrant disproportionate support for the Scottish Office – indeed, she identified within the Office a culture at odds with her vision of the Union. Under George Younger (1931–2003) – her first Secretary of State for Scotland – the Scottish Tories' traditional patrician take on the Secretary's role continued for a while but, in the years which followed, major changes were wrought. By the late nineties, 374 extra-governmental agencies were connected to the Scottish Office with up to 3,800 appointees operating within them – around three times the number of Scotland's elected local councillors.[48] None of these were government departments or necessarily parts thereof but they were accountable to Scottish ministers.[49] The Conservatives had found that the only way to influence Scottish politics was to remake its offices. The range of these 'quangos' was remarkable and included bodies as diverse as the National Museums of Scotland and Scottish Homes, Highlands and Islands Enterprise and the General Teaching Council for Scotland, the Scottish Valuation and Rating Council and the Horse Race Betting Levy Appeal Tribunal.

Until the 1980s, the Scottish Office had often been appreciated as a corrective to a legislative process that refused to acknowledge Scottish difference in its most fundamental sense. However, in the last two decades of the century, the multiplication of quangos and the emergence of high-profile non-elected bodies in the administration and policy process in Scotland reinforced feelings that Scotland's place in the UK system – dominated as it was by a party for whom Scots had little time – was being further eroded by unaccountable bodies attached to the very office that should have protected Scottish interests. For many, it seemed that Scotland had reached the end of the autonomy that could be 'effected by bureaucratic means'.[50]

'Administrative devolution' was a phrase apparently invented by a civil servant in the 1930s to describe the process whereby an increasing number of responsibilities fell to the Scottish Office and an increasing number of decisions regarding the implementation of policy in Scotland came to be made north of the Border.[51] Initially, this process was intended to soothe the frustrations of the nationalists in the early decades of the century and respond to calls for more efficient administration. Facing the challenge of the nationalist Convention Movement in the 1940s, Arthur Woodburn (1890–1978), Labour's Secretary of State for Scotland from 1947 to 1950, was advised by officials in the Scottish Home Department that:

> there is something to be said for re-examining the extent to which it would be possible to assign to a Scottish Minister additional responsibility for administering in Scotland the functions of Central Government. The widest possible extension of the range of Scottish ministerial responsibility might go a long way to meet those who, without wishing a separate Parliament, feel that Scottish affairs should be as far as possible in Scottish hands.[52]

But it was a double-edged sword:

> The fullest development of administration in Scotland under Scottish ministers might well be welcomed also by many who favour a Scottish parliament as a means of building up the administrative machinery which such a parliament would require.[53]

The process of administrative devolution had paradoxical consequences for the status quo that the Establishment intended to perpetuate. As the historian Michael Lynch notes, '[T]he organ of government designed to dissipate Home Rule agitation had, by the 1960s, become the most important single reason for the perpetuation of the distinctively Scottish nature of Scottish politics.'[54] By 1979, Scots had become used to looking to the Scottish Office to articulate Scottish grievances. It was seen as an agency of government defending Scotland from the harmful encroachment of unsympathetic UK (or English) interests. But it was inherently flawed and encouraged expectations far beyond what it could realistically deliver.

The sheer scope of Scottish Office responsibilities meant that ministers had little time to initiate new policies for Scotland. In the early 1980s, it was estimated that the Scottish Office had responsibilities equivalent to around eleven Whitehall Departments.[55] The territorial remit of the Office also meant that policies for application to the UK as a whole were very unlikely to emerge from this stable. As a consequence, Scottish interests were most readily appreciated in terms of the defence of established groups and native institutions. It was a state of affairs reinforced by the fact that ministerial control of the Scottish Office had always been at one remove. The remit of ministers in St Andrew's House typically straddled departments, leaving the way open for senior civil servants to be the principal arbiters of how measures would be implemented in practice.[56] In turn, the common social and educational backgrounds of Scottish Office civil servants and their restricted knowledge of other Whitehall Departments further limited the scope for modernising Scottish Office operations and tempered any desire to do so.

For much of the century, none of this seemed to matter much. While public spending in Scotland was high and Scottish interests were protected, the Scottish Office generally failed to excite public opinion. By the 1990s, however, the public purse was not as generous as it had been and established Scottish interest groups were either under attack from the Scottish Office itself or from emerging new interests. It was only then that the lack of democratic accountability at the heart of Scottish government proved a galvanising force for change. It may be a little cynical but nonetheless true to say that some of the roots of devolution were grounded in the same defensive self-interests that had generated and perpetuated the very office home rule sought to refashion. After all, ever since 1707, what was left of patriotism had commonly expressed itself in defending what was left of the civic and political offices of state that were still in Scottish hands.

In the end, the predictions of Woodburn's anonymous civil servant in 1949 were correct. In 2000, the apparatus of government supporting the Scottish Executive was essentially that of the old Scottish Office. For example, the Scottish Office Information Directorate simply became the Scottish Executive's Information Directorate and, as devolution approached, there was little evidence of a cultural change within the organisation.[57] Similarly, there was no 'bonfire of the Quangos' – instead, as in the realm of economic policy, the incoming coalition government in Scotland did not unpick Thatcher's legacy. While the Scottish Parliament was self-consciously novel in its operations, it was supported by a structure which still bore the imprint of tradition and the conventions of past. For the most part, the civil servants under the old regime retained their posts but they had new masters who were more familiar with the forms and features of local government than Whitehall. It would take some time for a new order to emerge and, in the meantime, with a Labour-led coalition in Scotland for the first eight years, the evolving New Labour model in Whitehall would prove difficult for the Executive to resist. Spin doctoring was not solely the preserve of London's chattering classes.

AT THE COURT OF KING JAMES

> Suggestions of apathy on the part of the women voters were not supported by the evidence of the polling booths, for everywhere they showed a determination to record their votes, one way or another. This feature was specially noticeable in the towns. Women of all social positions took their part in the election. The working man's wife, often carrying the youngest child, was much in evidence at some of the Glasgow polling booths.
>
> *The Scotsman* (16 December 1918)

The extension of the electorate marked the history of most western democracies in the twentieth century and, in this, Scotland, as part of the UK, was no exception. However, despite the adoption of comparable qualification and registration procedures, the parliamentary electorate that emerged after 1918 retained many regional peculiarities.

Largely as a consequence of the 1918 Representation of the People Act, the Scottish parliamentary electorate grew from around 760,000 in 1910 to 2.2 million in 1921 and, by the end of this period, 79.2 per cent of Scottish women of thirty years or more were enfranchised, alongside over 94 per cent of Scottish men.[58] The population of the urban Central Belt also became better represented as constituency boundaries were redrawn at the expense of the rural hinterland and many Irish migrants enjoyed the franchise for the first time. Michael Dyer has suggested that, for Scotland, the 1918 Act was 'the highest point in the assimilation of its electoral system within the United Kingdom'.[59]

Yet a standardised system had far from uniform consequences. In the Borders, the legislation of 1918 increased the total parliamentary electorate by 161 per cent in comparison to 1910, while the increase in Dundee was 252 per cent. Glasgow's male franchise holders rose by 109 per cent over the same period whereas, in the Borders, the increase was just 40 per cent. In Dundee, 45 per cent of the parliamentary electorate was female in 1921, compared to a little over 39 per cent in the Highlands.[60] In terms of female and first-time voters, constituencies clearly experienced contrasting fates and this would go some way to ensuring that the impact of the legislation on party fortunes in Scotland would have a peculiar regional dynamic.

There may not have been a 'typical' Scottish voter or constituency after 1918 but distinctive Scottish voting patterns were clearly emerging, marked by Labour's ascendancy in the urban Central Belt and the retreat of Liberalism to the periphery – typically the Highlands and the Borders. Liberal Inverness, for example, resisted the advances of other suitors until 1950 whereupon, after a relatively brief Conservative interlude, the constituency returned to its Liberal loyalties in 1964.[61] And, in the city of Aberdeen, the North and South constituencies betrayed their class composition for much of the century in their contrasting Labour and Unionist preferences.[62] Yet not all constituencies were as predictable. In four successive elections between 1918 and 1924, candidates from four different parties, including one Communist and an Orange MP, were returned to Parliament for Motherwell, an erstwhile Liberal stronghold until 1900.[63]

Still, in the House of Commons – if population is our guide – Scotland was overrepresented for most of the twentieth century, thus further compromising the standardisation achieved in 1918.[64] (Scotland had seventy-four MPs at the turn of the century and retained seventy-two at its close.) Public justification for this inequity rested on Scotland's distance from London, Scotland's significant numbers of large sparsely populated constituencies (often of particular environmental or cultural interest) and Scotland's 'special status' within the Union.[65] Privately, it suited many (principally Labour) Prime Ministers to maintain Scotland's disproportionate advantage.

With so many Scottish voices, it may not surprise anyone to discover that parliamentary debates on Scottish issues were often dominated by MPs from the north. Yet there were more important reasons than mere numbers for the Scottish representatives holding sway. Scottish issues generally failed to attract public or prime ministerial attention except in the event of crises – memorable careers were seldom made in the minutiae of Scottish affairs. By the 1960s, it could be said as something of a rule, with little fear of contradiction, that 'Scottish debates are not usually dramatic. Giants do not clash on the floor of the House over matters which seem unlikely to overthrow governments.'[66]

As a consequence, Scottish MPs, aside from some notable exceptions throughout the century, were often considered parochial and pedestrian, even by Scots themselves. To Hugh MacDiarmid, writing in the 1930s, Scottish politics were 'still to be created' and Scotland's MPs were 'futilitarians, openers of bazaars and star-turns at the Band of Hope'.[67] To Moray McLaren fifteen years later, the Scottish MP was a man for whom Scotland had been 'but an instrument by which he has levered himself into a petty position in a more powerful foreign country'.[68] Writing with fellow students in 1972, even Gordon Brown (1951–), later Chancellor of the Exchequer from 1997 and Prime Minister from 2007, bemoaned that Edinburgh's MPs were 'either ambitious advocates, gentlemen of land and leisure or aging trade unionists', while its local councillors were 'either less successful or up and coming versions of the same'.[69]

Scots were also known for the chilly reception they accorded the southern perspectives of English colleagues on Scottish questions. Vernon Bogdanor has argued that something of a Scottish 'sub-system' operated at Westminster, at least in the immediate pre-devolution years, and non-Scottish MPs taking an interest in Scottish affairs were often regarded as 'intruders'.[70] The Committee system, while offering a forum in which Scottish issues could be more fully addressed also often reinforced impressions that Scottish affairs were the exclusive concerns of Scots. The Scottish Grand Committee became a permanent feature of government from 1907 and included all Scottish MPs (non-Scottish representation within its ranks was removed in 1964); in 1957, a Scottish Standing Committee was established to take over the Committee stage of Scottish bills; and, in the years 1968–1972 and 1979–1987, a Select Committee on Scottish Affairs was in operation, with power to scrutinise government administration in Scotland and question ministers and civil servants.[71] What emerged from all this was 'the idea of a distinct Scottish sphere of public policy', which was characterised by the Scottish origins of its participants and their generally narrow experience of Westminster as a whole.[72] It was an environment in which Scottish national claims could thrive and the homogenising impulses of Union were compromised.

The party-political mosaic which overlaid the constituency map of Scotland further reinforced claims of difference, and generated a party bias at Westminster among Scotland's MPs which at times was quite at odds with that of the representatives of other UK nations. The rise of Labour, the emergence of the post-war consensus, the rise to power of Thatcherism and the New Right, and the middle ground identified in Blairism and New Labour were trends which were expressed differently in Scotland and often left contrasting legacies north and south of the border.

In the last quarter of the twentieth century, the balance of power between the political parties in Scotland seldom coincided with that evident in England and Wales but it had exhibited many parallels before then. Edwardian Liberalism had been a political faith shared by a significant proportion of voters north and south of the Border and, in these years, Labour in Scotland fought a relatively unsuccessful campaign to win converts. The Liberal Party in Scotland thereafter survived the First World War in somewhat better health than its parallel body in the south, achieving thirty-three seats in the election of 1918 in comparison to the Unionists' thirty.[73] However, hindsight confirms that Labour's 22.6 per cent share of the vote in this year would prove an omen of future developments although, at the time, few would have seen it that way. The Unionists – the Scottish Conservatives were officially the Scottish Unionist Party until 1965 – made significant progress in the interwar years, largely as a result of their involvement in the Coalition and National governments and their absorption of much Liberal support.

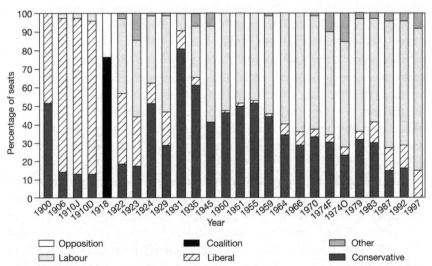

Figure 8.1 General Election Results (Scotland), 1900–1997 (seats). Key to letters on horizontal axis: J January; D December; F February; O October.
Source: D. Butler and G. Butler, *Twentieth Century British Political Facts* (8th edition, London, 2000, pp. 240–1).

In 1931, they recorded their highest share of the vote (49.5 per cent) since 1832.

However, 1945 found Labour in power for the third time in its history, this time with a majority of seats in Scotland but only 6 per cent more votes than the Unionists. As elsewhere, the Liberal Party was now a pale reflection of its former self, securing only 5 per cent of the vote and no seats north of the Border. Thereafter, the 1950s marked a period of Unionist resurgence in Scotland, as the party secured the majority of the Scottish vote in the 1951, 1955 and 1959 general elections and proved the only party to win over 50 per cent of the vote in a general election in Scotland in 1955.

As recession set in after the late 1950s, however, Labour proved transcendent. From 1964 onwards, Labour won the highest proportion of the Scottish vote in general elections and, from 1959, secured a majority of Scottish seats. As in England and Wales, the 1960s also marked the beginning of a period of growth for the Liberal Party in Scotland. From having two MPs in 1950, the party in the north more than doubled its representation in the Commons in 1966. In Scotland, however, a fourth party was asserting its presence during these years – the Scottish National Party (SNP).

From achieving only 1.2 per cent of the popular vote in 1945, the SNP's fortunes slumped further in the 1950s, only to pick up again in 1964 when 2.4 per cent of the vote went nationalist. By 1970, the SNP was outperforming the Liberals, gaining over twice their share of the popular vote but losing out on MPs due to the first-past-the-post (FPTP) system. Nevertheless, the general elections of 1974 proved to be a turning point in the nationalists' fortunes – in the February election, the party won seven Scottish seats and, in October, had enough MPs if insufficient sporting talent to field a football team. While this momentum was not maintained into the 1980s, following the disaster of the 1979 devolution referendum, it was clear that Scottish politics, in the final decades of the twentieth century, were resolutely at odds with those of England.

Scotland failed to echo quite as resoundingly to the cries of the New Right that greeted the Conservatives' rise to power in 1979 under Margaret Thatcher. Indeed, Conservative fortunes in the north after 1979 tell a tale of near unremitting decline. From twenty-two Scottish MPs in 1979, Conservative representation fell first to twenty-one in 1983 and then to ten in 1987. The party managed a slight revival in 1992, with eleven seats, but there was little cause for celebration. Many Scots were becoming disillusioned with politics and their inability to change things. The feminist magazine, *Harpies and Quines*, noted,

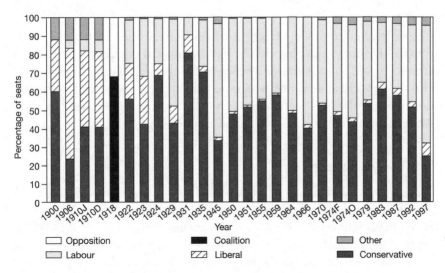

Figure 8.2 General Election Results (UK), 1900–1997 (seats). Key to letters on horizontal axis: J January; D December; F February; O October.
Source: D. Butler and G. Butler, *Twentieth Century British Political Facts*
(8th edition, London, 2000, pp. 240–1.

'Change means risk. Loss of security. These last 13 years have meant depression. Loss of confidence. Put those together and you get a demoralised people who can hardly believe change will bring anything better.'[74] And yet, five years later, a renewed sense of confidence expressed itself at the polls when, at the general election of 1997, Scotland returned no Conservative MPs whatsoever.

Between 1979 and 1997, executive control at Westminster had been in the hands of a party that did not have the support of the majority of Scottish voters and, by the mid 1990s, arguably did not even have their confidence. Similarly, years before, Labour's dominance in Scotland had helped deliver Labour administrations that had only marginal support in vast swathes of southern England. Not surprisingly, few Scottish voices then had been raised in opposition to the democratic and constitutional mechanisms that resulted in such a state of affairs. In the 1980s and 1990s, the constitution was as it had always been throughout the twentieth century. What was different was the fact that key Scottish interests were being threatened by the same voting system that had sustained them for decades and that perceptions of national identity were increasingly receptive to Scottish claims and were more inclined to sacrifice British loyalties to attain them. It remains to be seen whether the Scots' new-found commitment to democracy will go as far as supporting proportional representation at Westminster (as in Holyrood) where such a move would undoubtedly challenge Labour's near monopoly of Scottish seats. Certainly, the reduction of Scottish MPs at Westminster from seventy-two to fifty-nine following devolution did little to correct the imbalance created by the foundation of a separate Scottish legislature in 1999 and effected few changes to the traditional character of Scottish representation at Westminster – forty of the fifty-nine Scottish MPs elected in 2003 were Labour.

SCOTLAND IN EUROPE

The imperial legislature lost much of its lustre in a century when Empire lost its commanding influence. Arguably, this meant the Mother of Parliaments had greater time for her more unruly northern child but, for Scots – traditionally keen imperialists – it made many question their place in the world and, in the long term, encouraged them to turn their attention to Europe.

Scotland's voice in Europe following British entry into the EEC in 1973 was largely that of the eight Members of the European Parliament representing Scottish constituencies and lobbying groups, such as Strathclyde Regional Council, Highlands and Islands Enterprise and Scottish Enterprise, whose interests were seldom truly national in scope. The Scottish Office also played a major role in emphasising the importance of Scottish issues; the Scotland Europa organisation in Brussels from 1991 did much to lobby on behalf of a variety of Scottish interests; and the Secretary of State in cabinet frequently drew attention to a Scottish perspective on European questions.

But Scotland itself was often at best ambivalent. When EEC membership was put to the vote in the 1975 referendum, the Western Isles and the Shetland Isles both rejected continued membership, while the overall Scottish vote in favour of remaining within the European body was only 58.4 per cent, compared to a UK average of 67.2 per cent.[75] Scots were suspicious of Tory claims that Scottish futures lay in Europe – at that time, they were the principal party supporting British membership and sold the Community as a modern form of Union:

> In some ways it is easier for us to contemplate the partnership which the membership of the European Community would involve for we ourselves inherit the experience and benefit of a political and economic community set up in 1707 – not, one should add, with universal support from the public opinion polls of the day. Our ability to retain our identity and evolve our institutions within this wider patriotism is not irrelevant in the debate.[76]

By contrast, many Scots feared that Community membership would merely add another level of bureaucracy that was remote from Scottish interests. As the sceptical Conservative journalist, Michael Fry, pointed out in 1979, 'Seen from Scotland, Brussels rule is only an extension, a modified form, of London rule.'[77] In any case, while there were thirty European controlled manufacturing companies and eleven European non-manufacturing companies with interests in Scotland in January 1973 (eleven had been set up within the last year in anticipation of UK entry into the EEC), such investment was dwarfed by the American presence – at the end of 1972, there were 118 US companies in Scotland.[78] Many Scots remained to be convinced that old colonial ties had withered entirely.

However, the harsh realities of an economy highly dependent on foreign capital, the political disaster of the 1979 devolution referendum for both the Labour and Scottish National parties and the failure of oil revenue to engender an economic renaissance in Scotland came together in the 1980s and encouraged Scots to re-assess their attitudes towards Europe. (By 1980, European nations were Scotland's biggest customers, absorbing 40 per cent of exports.[79]) At much the same time English nationalism took on an increasingly 'anti-Euro' complexion – a true sign, many thought, that there must be something in it for the Scots.[80] In the 1980s, the SNP also found in Europe a new context within which independence could be appreciated without the taint of isolationism or separatism. 'Independence in Europe' had a pleasing sound to it and proved popular in opinion polls – while, in 1988, around 35 per cent of Scots supported independence, when offered the option of independence combined with full participation in the European Community, support increased to nearly 53 per cent.[81] But the European Community was not a static phenomenon and resting claims to nationhood on such a body was risky, especially as regionalism and enlargement altered the nature of the Community itself.

The birth of the Committee of the Regions (CoR) in 1994 confirmed welcome particularising tendencies in Community practice, which became more attuned to regional affairs following the Maastricht Treaty (1991) and the Amsterdam Treaty (1997). Scotland had ten representatives in the CoR – initially all local councillors – and, while protests were regularly heard from Scotland regarding agriculture and fisheries policies, Scotland did relatively well out of European Union Funds. Between 1973 and 1983, for example, Scotland, boasting around 10 per cent of the UK population, averaged 25 per cent of grants and loans coming into the UK from Europe. Scottish regional councils also benefited far more than English county councils from both European Regional

Development and European Investment Bank funding, due, in part, to their responsibility for water and sewerage.[82] Overall, Europe increasingly became valuable as a forum where Scotland was less impaired by Union commitments in expressing a view on non-domestic affairs. But things were not that simple.

After 1999, some areas over which the EU had influence, such as the environment and agriculture, were matters devolved to the Scottish Parliament. Yet the EU was a matter retained by Westminster. No Scottish Minister for Europe joined the Scottish Executive line-up under Scotland's first First Minister, Donald Dewar, or his successor. Although a European Committee of the Scottish Parliament was created in May 1999, its influence in the first years of the Parliament, beyond raising awareness of EU issues, was negligible.[83] Even Winnie Ewing (1929–), former MEP, grande dame of Scottish nationalism and one of the Committee's first members, considered it 'a waste of time'.[84] Indeed, Scottish Executive Ministers were generally conspicuous by their absence at meetings of the European Council of Ministers.[85] Instead, following devolution, Scotland's new government relied on the activities of five Executive representatives in the CoR – five local councillors were made to step aside – and of Scotland House in Brussels (established in 1999)[86] to influence EU decision-making through diplomatic and promotional activities.[87] Continuity rather than change, therefore, marked Scotland's role in the EU after the first term of the Scottish Parliament. Among the political and administrative elites who shaped Scotland's role in Europe during this time, the consensus seemed to be that while greater potential existed for more 'democratically legitimate and discernible participation', they 'did not expect Scotland to exert greater influence on legislative outcomes'.[88]

Meanwhile, the SNP continued to complain that, even after devolution, Scotland's voice was constrained by its place within the Union state. Unfavourable comparisons with the international reach of small European nations such as Ireland, Denmark and Luxembourg were made to emphasise the subservient status of 'Europe's oldest nation'. (Denmark, with roughly the same population as Scotland, had sixteen seats in the European Parliament in comparison to Scotland's eight.) But the imperial legacy was still compelling. Scots, according to Ian Lang, the Secretary for State for Scotland in 1991, had more influence within the EU rather than less as a consequence of their partnership with the other UK nations.[89] In any case, Scots showed a remarkable lack of interest in Europe at the polls – turnout for the Scottish European elections in 1999 was a mere 24.7 per cent.[90] Scots were not quite ready to trade influence, won in an age of Empire, for the status of a marginal European state.

In Robert Garioch's poem 'Scottish Scene', Scottish voices are dissonant and contradictory. It is a description easily applied to the 'political scene' of the twentieth century.

> They're a gey antithetical folk are the Scots
> jurmummelt thegither like unctioneers' lots
> or a slap-happy family of bickeran brats;
> the scrauch of their squabbles wad gie ye the bats.[91]

Territorial arrangements – local, regional, national and European – mediated the expression of the Scottish body politic and constrained both its power and the nature of its influence. In the legislative practice and administrative offices which these forums sponsored, Scotland failed to speak with one voice – if it spoke at all – and, on occasion, particularly in the 1980s and early 1990s, many Scots wondered whether anyone was listening anyway.

NINE   Parties and Players

One thing . . . we retain in a more marked degree in Scotland than anywhere else in Britain – a determination that political differences shall not prevent our grasping the opportunity which time and circumstance have given us.

Arthur Woodburn, Secretary of
State for Scotland
St Andrews Day, 1948[1]

Whether or not his sentiments were true at the time, Woodburn's statement – viewed from the perspective of the 1990s – at best revealed only a partial truth. Certainly, the legacy of Tom Johnston's tenure of the Scottish Office and the recent experience of war had encouraged corporate and consensual tendencies in the Scottish administration. Indeed, the small size of the Scottish political community made this not only desirable but – importantly – possible. It might also be suggested that the ethical approach to local government that presided in these years and the embattled nature of Scottish politics generally in a Union state together challenged the more partisan tendencies in party politics. However, the political culture of Scotland changed remarkably during the course of the twentieth century. Both collaboration and confrontation were the hallmarks of political parties in Scotland in the twentieth century – their common endeavours were always tempered by their commitment to values and principles that were generally at odds with their rivals. In addition, all major parties, bar the SNP, were the Scottish manifestations of British parties and, at times, they were under pressure to adopt a party line less in keeping with Scottish sensitivities than might otherwise have been the case had they been free of the whip's office. To understand the impact such a state of affairs had on Scotland it is important to consider each party in turn.

LIBERALISM – 'NO TROOPS AND FEW OVERT SUPPORTERS'

Between 1832 and 1918 Liberalism was more than an ideology in Scotland – it was a living faith. Its doctrines of free trade, land reform and self-improvement and its charismatic leaders – most notably William Ewart Gladstone (1809–1898) and the Fifth Earl of Rosebery (1847–1929) – reflected the beliefs of a society shaped by progress and profit, philanthropy and thrift. The Great War, the democratisation of the franchise and the Depression of the interwar years, however, shattered Liberalism's hold on Scotland, as the party itself suffered internal fragmentation due to feuding in its leadership ranks and declining membership.[2] The party split over the efficacy of continued support for Lloyd George's Coalition government after 1918 and the reunion that was secured in 1923 failed to heal bitter divisions within the ranks. It was too late to save the Liberals from becoming the third party in politics. The party entered the 1924 general election with 158 MPs but it emerged with only forty – a paltry eight Scottish seats were secured.[3]

The creation of a National government intended to meet the challenge of the Depression in 1931 further complicated the political environment. Again, Liberal associations up and down the country were divided. While some accepted that long-standing free-trade principles should be sacrificed for the greater social good and joined with Unionists as National Liberals, others maintained their independence even at the cost of their seats. Pacts with the Unionists were to be a persistent feature even after 1945, when unity in the face of the threat from socialism was the primary motivating force. In 1950, John MacLay (1905–1992) – a National Liberal who would secure the office of Secretary of State for Scotland in a Conservative administration between 1957 and 1962 – emphasised:

> It is quite clear that if we are to avoid the danger of losing everything we value, Liberals and Conservatives alike must sacrifice some independence, recognise that their basic beliefs are identical and present a united front.[4]

But such a relationship merely seemed to confirm the party's Establishment status and the abandonment of its earlier radical identity – neither of which would endear it to a more diverse electorate, particularly in Scotland. Liberalism doggedly resisted the interest politics of both Labour and the Unionists and it shunned class rhetoric in favour of loyalty to the 'commonweal' but suggested few meaningful political alternatives.[5] Indeed, these years seemed to confirm the general observation that '[i]n a democracy there is nothing more logical and more doomed than a centre party. Everybody applauds it and nobody joins.'[6] In Dundee, average annual subscriptions for the local Liberal Association dropped from a lowly £79 in 1951 to a debilitating £27 in 1955 and candidatures across Scotland fell from forty-one to five between the 1950 and 1955 elections.[7] It is hardly surprising that, in a 1958 Liberal pamphlet adorned with engravings of 'Mirth' and the 'Dance of Albion' and quotations from Milton, the Liberal Party leader openly confessed that 'Liberals are not expecting to form a government after the next election'.[8] The once all-powerful party of Gladstone appeared to be out of touch and could no longer even maintain the pretence of power.

Between 1951 and 1964, the Liberal Party in Scotland boasted only one MP, Jo Grimond (1913–1993), Liberal Party leader from 1956 to 1967, as the National Liberal vote was effectively absorbed by the Unionists. Grimond's charismatic leadership and John Bannerman's enthusiastic re-awakening of Liberalism's Highland heritage in the early 1960s, however, saved the party from oblivion, although electoral success proved elusive. Grimond, MP for Orkney and Shetland, the son of a Dundee jute manufacturer and the husband of a granddaughter of Herbert Asquith – the last Liberal Prime Minister to sit for a Scottish constituency (Paisley) – sought a radical realignment in party politics in these years to undermine the stranglehold of the two-party system. In an era dominated by 'planning', however, his belief that, in a healthy society, government should have a comparatively narrow field claimed comparatively little support.[9] Few could see a place in politics for a progressive alternative to the Labour Party. Meanwhile, Bannerman (1902–1969), Scottish Liberal Party Chairman for a decade after 1955, never achieved a Commons seat but, as Lord Bannerman of Kildonan, his Westminster career was shaped in the Lords after 1967. Later in life, he reflected on his unsuccessful candidature for Argyll in 1945:

> Some crofters would not wish it to be known that they attended a political meeting which did not have the approval of the laird . . . The revolution which I was prepared to start at Westminster for comprehensive redress of the complex Highland problems never got off the ground. I was a revolutionary with no troops and few overt supporters.[10]

Even rural constituencies traditionally sympathetic to the Liberal message seemed to have turned their back on the party.

Growing economic discontent and a Conservative Party wracked by scandal in the early 1960s, however, encouraged some electors to look again at a third option in British politics. In 1966 the Liberals in Scotland took five seats – a high watermark for the party since 1931 that would not be matched again until 1983 and then only with the assistance of Social Democratic Party (SDP) votes. New life had been breathed into the party in 1965 following the election of David Steel (1938–) for Roxburgh – at twenty-six, he was the youngest MP in the Commons. In his autobiography, the elder statesman reflected:

> What we had succeeded in doing was infusing the areas of traditional Liberalism . . . with fresh zeal and renewed efficiency. But in general and in Scotland in particular, we had not had much impact in urban, especially Labour areas.[11]

In typically Liberal fashion, both Grimond and Steel were keen to meet the Labour challenge and effect political realignment through cross-party collaboration.[12] Indeed, as early as 1955, Jo Grimond had addressed his constituents with the words, 'I make no claim that all wisdom resides with the Liberal Party and I am always ready to co-operate with other parties in your interest and that of Britain.'[13] For Scottish Liberals facing the challenge of a fourth party in the north (the SNP), the tactic made sense, even if it won few plaudits. Grimond, for example, was enthusiastic about an SNP-Liberal pact in the 1960s but the proposal was repeatedly rejected by the party in the north.[14]

Throughout the 1970s, the Liberals maintained only three seats in Scotland and between 8 and 9 per cent of the vote after February 1974. This decade also saw Steel's rise to the leadership of the UK party in 1976 and the eventual realisation of the co-operative tactic when, in 1978, a short-lived Lib-Lab pact was brokered with James Callaghan's ailing administration. It did little to boost Liberal fortunes in the north – at the 1979 general election, only three Liberals were returned for Scottish seats. The collaborative strategy, however, had not been exhausted and, from 1981, the Scottish Liberal Party shared in the UK-wide alliance with the SDP – an offshoot of the Labour Party – which inspired David Steel to encourage Liberals at the annual conference in Llandudno to 'go back to your constituencies and prepare for government'. It was not to be. While associating the Liberals with the remarkable victory of Roy Jenkins at the Glasgow Hillhead by-election in March 1982, the pact did little to boost Liberalism's profile in Scotland – the SDP's Scottish branches were the smallest in the country – and drew the party into the destructive breakup of the Alliance in the aftermath of the 1987 general election.[15]

But breakup eventually resolved itself in remarriage when, in 1988, members recorded their approval of the Liberal-SDP merger which created the Liberal Democrats. In the years that followed, the new party would gain widespread recognition as an influential voice within the Scottish Constitutional Convention and as the most consistent supporter of home rule in Scotland. For the Liberals, it was a commitment that reached back into the nineteenth century and had been reaffirmed in their response to the SNP challenge. David Steel, for example, had been a long-standing critic of the 'democratic vacuum' created in Scottish politics by the Scottish Office.[16] Ironically, therefore, it was this very traditional Liberal shibboleth that re-invigorated the party at a time when other traditional features were holding it back. Even in the 1990s, for example, the Liberal Party continued to suffer in electoral terms due to its over-reliance on the personal reputations of their local councillors and MPs. Grimond had earlier approved of this state of affairs, saying, 'The Liberal Party since the war has to a large extent depended for its successes on local personalities . . . As a believer that communities must fashion their own growth . . . I find this encouraging.'[17] But, by the 1990s, such 'local heroes', it was suggested, prevented the party establishing a coherent corporate identity in an age that regularly worshipped style over substance.[18]

The arrival of the Scottish Parliament was to deliver the Lib Dems their first taste of executive power in several generations.

Table 3.1　Result of the Elections to the Scottish Parliament, 1999

Party	Constituency		Regional List		Total Seats
	Votes (%)	Seats	Votes (%)	Seats	
Conservative	15.6	0	15.4	18	18
Labour	38.8	53	33.6	3	56
Lib. Dem.	14.2	12	12.4	5	17
SNP	28.7	7	27.3	28	35
Other	2.1	1	11.3	2	3

Source: B. Morgan, 'Scottish Parliament Election, 6 May 1999', *House of Commons Research Paper* (99/50, 8 September 1999), p. 7.

The outcome of the first elections to the new legislature failed to produce a majority administration. As a consequence, the Liberal Democrats stood as potential arbiters of the complexion of the future administration as they formed the most obvious allies for Labour in a coalition government. Also, with Sir David Steel as Presiding Officer of the Parliament, Liberal values and approaches to governance infused early decisions on parliamentary rules and conduct.

The coalition agreement with Labour was eventually signed one week after the elections, on 14 May 1999. With the Liberal Democrat Jim Wallace (1954–) as Deputy First Minister, the party, in the Scottish context at least, seemed to have experienced something of a modern Gladstonian revival in those early days. The subsequent day-to-day compromises involved in coalition government, however, would soon dull the glamour of office. Although some important concessions were wrought by Labour's coalition partners – the abolition of tuition fees for undergraduate students, for example – the Liberal voice in the new coalition was relatively muted. With home rule won, early land reform anticipated and proportional representation the voting mechanism that had elevated them into a position of power, there was little left in the traditional Liberal arsenal that the Lib Dems could offer the Scottish public that was now uniquely their own. Having maintained a lonely guard over the middle ground in Scottish politics for most of the twentieth century, the Liberals – now led by another Scot, Skye and Lochalsh MP Charles Kennedy (1959–)[19] – found it a very crowded place to be.

UNIONISM – 'INDICTED . . . AS THE PARTY OF NO COMPASSION'

> Come, gie's a sang, the Major cried–
> Amen! the Unionists replied–
> Ye needna langer try tae hide
> Your turn'ed Toryorum;
>
> Whig an' Tory now agree,
> Whig an' Tory, sic a story!
> Whig an' Tory now agree
> An' every hall a Forum.
>
> *Paisley Daily Express* (30 May 1891)[20]

The split in the Liberal Party in 1886, caused by Gladstone's declaration in support of Irish home rule, established a Liberal Unionist presence in Scottish politics that finally amalgamated with the Scottish Conservatives in 1912 to create the Scottish Unionist Association (SUA). This Liberal rump within the Scottish right exerted a significant influence in Scotland in the early years of the twentieth century that was far out of proportion to that evident in the south.[21] The reforming zeal that was thus injected into Conservatism arguably resulted in it being better placed than it might otherwise have been to challenge Labour in the interwar years in Scotland. In any case, the self-destructive tendencies in Liberalism almost guaranteed that the Unionists would be the nation's main proponents of anti-socialist rhetoric. A SUA pamphlet from 1918 warned that 'WHAT

BOLSHEVIST SOCIALISM HAS DONE FOR RUSSIA IT WOULD LIKE TO DO FOR YOU' – namely, 'ANARCHY, ROBBERY, MURDER'.[22]

In the 1930s, the Scottish Unionists proved adept at gauging the mood of the Scottish nation, maintained a well-organised constituency structure and an enthusiastic membership and proved proficient at exploiting new modes of political propaganda.[23] The creation of a National government in 1931 had 'blurred distinctions' on the centre-right and brought National Liberals into the arms of the Unionists who, under Baldwin's leadership, were experienced at exploiting Scottish sensitivities.[24] As we have seen earlier, the role of the Scottish Office was significantly enhanced in the 1930s and its status was reinforced during the incumbency of Unionists like Walter Elliot. In any case, both Scottish Liberals and Unionists had a long tradition of working together in local government. In contrast to the Labour Party, whose support was becoming concentrated in industrial and urban areas, the Unionists also had a truly 'national constituency'.[25] Predictably, the Unionists proved popular in the agricultural counties – Argyll, Berwickshire, Moray and Roxburgh were reliable seats for them. But the Unionists also held Aberdeen South throughout the interwar years and, in the capital, only Edinburgh East resisted their advances. In Glasgow, the Unionist strongholds of Hillhead and Kelvingrove were joined by less predictable constituencies as Cathcart, Partick, Pollock and the Central constituency all went Tory in the thirties.

By 1945, however, the Unionists had lost many of their most secure urban constituencies. They were coming to rely precariously on the last vestiges of National Liberal support and were acquiring 'something of a grouse moor image', not helped by a growing reluctance among party members to canvas in working-class areas.[26] But, when it came to policy, Unionism in the north still managed to assert a popular form of Scottish nationalism within the Union in the 1940s and beyond. Importantly, the party made regular attacks on the centralising tendencies of the Attlee government and styled nationalisation as a threat to Scottish interests. For a time, it seemed to work, as Unionist successes at the polls in the 1950s make clear – the Unionists matched the Labour total of thirty-five Scottish seats in the general election of 1951 and won two more than their main rivals in 1955.

In 1965, however, the re-organisation of the party in the north, as the Scottish Conservative and Unionist Party, seemed to herald the end of the distinctive history of Scottish Unionism. The Conservatives came to abandon the most profitable areas of the middle ground in Scotland which, until then, had made them both distinctive and successful. They found it difficult to recruit among young electors and, despite a short-lived pro-devolution period in the late sixties, initiated by Edward

Heath's 'Declaration of Perth' in 1968, they increasingly adopted candidates from among the 'anglicised upper classes' who showed little sympathy with Scottish peculiarities.[27] The change of name and closer links with the English party from the 1970s, however, neither immediately nor comprehensively undermined the relative ideological autonomy which had always been evident in the party in the north. While Nicholas Fairbairn (1933–1995), MP for Kinross and West Perthshire, ridiculed the 'tide of Nationalist dementia tartanica' in 1974, many in the party supported devolution for Scotland in the 1970s – among them the popular Alick Buchanan-Smith (1932–1991), MP for North Angus and Mearns.[28] Others encouraged the party to adopt a greater social conscience in the face of industrial dislocation in that decade. During the work-in at Upper Clyde Shipbuilders in 1972, 'SCOTORY' – an anonymous pamphleteer sponsored by the 'Thistle Group' within the party – pleaded with the government to restore 'the compassion and humanity that are so much of the Tory philosophy' and predicted that, if Gordon Campbell (1927–2005), the Conservative Secretary of State for Scotland, did not alleviate present unemployment:

> his other achievements will be forgotten in the rightful indignation of the Scottish people. And the Conservative Party will stand indicted not only for the present unemployment, but as the party of no compassion, of callous indifference, and of the jungle law of the survival of the fittest.[29]

The 1980s would prove such predictions correct, although it is worth noting that the Tory vote was declining in Scotland long before Mrs Thatcher entered Number Ten. As early as 1976, Michael Forsyth, later Secretary of State for Scotland, David McLetchie, later leader of the Conservatives in the Scottish Parliament, and Douglas Young, then Vice-Chairman of the Scottish Young Conservatives, considered their party weak and its constituency associations too obsessed with bridge evenings and coffee mornings to attract a broad membership. Significantly, they insisted that 'new measures to boost the Scottish personality of the Party [were] vital'.[30] Even on the morning of her victory in May 1979, the *Glasgow Herald* warned Margaret Thatcher not to imagine that the expected collapse of the SNP vote meant that politics in the north had suddenly lost their 'Scottish dimension'. It also warned that, if no account was taken of the constitutional question, 'then in five years the tide of nationalism could once again have turned'.[31]

Thatcherism, while successful in leading the party to electoral victory in the south in the 1980s, succeeded in making the party in the north nigh on un-electable. For many, the 'New Right', with which Mrs Thatcher was so closely associated, was a 'southern English metropolitan phenomenon' shared by a 'small coterie of like-minded individuals and organisations centred around the home counties'.[32] It lacked the flexibility of traditional Scottish Unionism and was unsympathetic to its claims. In its identification of a dependency culture at the heart of Scottish society and in its attacks on the nationalised industries and aspects of the welfare state that had reinforced Scotland's commitment to the Union in the immediate post-war years, Thatcherism – and, by implication, the Conservatives – earned the reputation of being anti-Scottish.[33] Even the activities of the Scottish Tory Reform Group (STRG), established in the mid 1980s, could not seem to effect a change in this widely held impression. Malcolm MacKenzie, Vice-Chairman of the STRG, despaired in 1988, saying:

> Scottish Toryism has somehow become displaced in Scottish consciousness. It has been afflicted by the near-lethal twin problems of being marginalized and of being perceived as inimical to Scottish culture . . . The task facing Scottish Toryism is to change perception, to create a new reality, a task which will not be achieved by the endless repetition of statistics or reprimands on the subject of 'cultural dependence' by visiting English Ministers.[34]

Even after Mrs Thatcher's resignation in November 1990, the ensuing Major terms of office failed to signal any fundamental change in outlook beyond desperate attempts at cultural nationalism in their final days – the Stone of Destiny was returned in 1996, a lion rampant was adopted as the party's new logo and the slogan 'Fighting For Scotland' signalled a change in presentation, if not substance, as the Conservatives remained resolutely anti-devolutionist. To Tom Nairn, this seven-year regime was composed of 'fag ends and left-overs' that failed to convert many new voters.[35] Certainly, few in Scotland would have agreed with former Conservative Secretary of State for Scotland Malcolm Rifkind (1946–), in 1996, that the Conservatives had delivered 'increasing prosperity' and 'national self-confidence'.[36] Indeed, one year on, the electorate's judgement was made clear when the Scottish Conservatives failed to return any MPs to Westminster.

The Scottish Conservatives survived beyond the end of the century largely as a result of party reforms (see the Strathclyde Commission Report, 1998) that followed the disaster of 1997 and rebuilt the party in the north as a far more autonomous body. Thereafter, their engagement with the new Scottish Parliament – a body which many of the eighteen

Conservative MSPs in 1999 had opposed most fervently only two years before – provided them with a much-needed forum in which to recreate themselves in public and differentiate themselves from an English party that was suffering from bitter infighting, a lacklustre leadership and some of the worst defeats in its history. Only the passage of time will determine whether this rebirth will convince Scots that the Conservatives are a viable party of government in either Holyrood or Westminster. Certainly, even in the last days of the century, there was cause for some optimism – in its commitment to the values of self-improvement and entrepreneurship, there was much in simple Tory philosophy that resonated with Scotland's traditional self-image. Yet, in the 1980s, these values appeared to have been turned against Scotland and had underpinned the Conservatives' attack on Scottish industry and welfare. It will take time for those years to be accommodated in a sympathetic rendering of Unionism – it will take time for those same Tory values to acquire a comfortable Scottish guise again.

LABOUR – 'FALL INTO LINE'

What-might-have-beens are generally of little use to the historian but are usually present somewhere, even if unacknowledged, in the most engaging historical debates and so it is with the rise of the Labour Party in Scotland. Without Scotland's Labour MPs, the Labour Party, in a UK bereft of its northerly province, would have won an overall majority of seats in only three elections in its history – 1945, 1966 and 1997.[37] The twentieth century might have been very different.

By the end of the century, Labour dominance in Scotland – while some way from being the hegemonic creed of turn-of-the-century Liberalism – was treated as a given and accepted as a fundamental feature of the political landscape in most political discussions, even though the party had never secured more than 50 per cent of the vote in a general election. Why and how had this come to pass?

In many ways, Labour in Scotland was a reluctant offshoot of radical Liberalism, offering little to distinguish it in its early days from the Liberal progressives than its determination to elect workingmen rather than members of the Scottish bourgeoisie. Yet the Labour Party in Scotland, evolving in the late 1880s, originated in a party and support structure in the north that was distinct and separate from that in England and, in its commitment to Scottish home rule, its enthusiasm for housing and land reform and its passionate moralising tone, it heralded a new era in Scottish politics. The Scottish Labour Party (established in 1888, following Keir Hardie's defeat as an independent working-class candidate in Mid Lanark), the Scottish United Trades Councils' Labour Party (established with the support of the Aberdeen and Falkirk trades councils and led by Chisholm Robertson after 1891), the Scottish Trades Union Congress (STUC) (established in 1897, following the expulsion of trades councils from the TUC) and the Scottish Workers' Representation Committee (SWRC) (established six weeks before the Labour Representation Committee (LRC) in January 1900), together formed the distinctive heritage of the Labour Party north of the Border. By 1909, however, the SWRC had effectively amalgamated with the LRC and Scottish Labour was, for the most part, absorbed within a British party. Thereafter, no separate Scottish co-ordinating body within the Labour Party was created until the Scottish Advisory Council (SAC) was established in 1914. Increasingly, the Scottish party's early commitment to home rule became provisional. At the end of the day, its status was dependent on immediate electoral considerations and the priorities of a party leadership that at times appeared distant from the concerns of the constituencies. Labour was a unionist party with a centralising agenda operating in the parliamentary context of a Union legislature. Scotland was part of that Union but was accorded regional status by the party both in terms of organisation and ideology.

Distinctive features nevertheless persisted – the role of the trade unions, the prominent position of the Independent Labour Party (ILP) and the lasting influence of the iconic 'heroes' of the Red Clyde ensured that homogenising tendencies within the party would take some time in realising their ambitions of a truly integrated party machine.

In the late 1930s, Tom Johnston, using the politically incorrect idioms common in these years, reflected that, without the trade unions and their activities, 'Scotland might today be a coolie plantation'.[38] Trade unionism had a marked impact on both Scotland and Scottish Labour, producing many of Labour's most notable leaders and its most valuable resources, in terms of finance and membership. 'The trade unions were . . . the backbone of the Labour Party,' noted Tom Fraser (1911–88), Labour MP for Hamilton from 1943 to 1967, at the STUC Congress in 1961.[39]

In 1900, Scotland boasted 150,000 trade unionists. At about 4 per cent of the population, this was around 1 per cent less than the English figure. The organisation of unskilled workers in the Edwardian period and the radicalising impact of war, however, convinced many more that there was 'strength in unity' and, by the mid 1920s, over 536,000 Scots were union members – around 40 per cent of the insured population.[40] As time went by, however, increasing numbers joined UK-wide unions and the influence of uniquely Scottish associations declined as more and more of them amalgamated with English-based bodies. By the end of 1922, for example, the North of Scotland Horse and Motormen's

Association, the Scottish Union of Dock Labourers, the Greenock Sugar Porters' Union and the Dundee Flax and Jute Stowers' Society had all amalgamated with the Transport and General Workers Union (TGWU). By 1947, just over 15 per cent of trade unionists in Scotland were members of exclusively Scottish unions.[41] Nevertheless, a distinctive Scottish voice was still to be found in the STUC which, by 1951, boasted a membership of 730,000, rising to 1.07 million by 1980. But concentration was marked here also and, over the same period, the number of unions affiliated to the Scottish Congress declined from eighty-five to seventy-three, with just eleven of these accounting for over 70 per cent of the total membership in Scotland.[42]

For Scottish Labour, the affiliation of such a large body of workers was of great significance – as early as 1947, Labour boasted over 470,000 union affiliates – and, at various times, the political activities of the Scottish Congress did much to sustain Labour's profile in Scotland when the party was out of office. This was particularly apparent in the eighteen years of Conservative rule during the last decades of the century when the STUC undertook broad-based campaigning against a range of anti-union laws, the poll tax and privatisation. Under Campbell Christie (1937–), the Congress became adept at building consensus among a range of interest groups and moulding a distinctive Scottish political vision.[43] But such benefits were not without associated problems. In Scotland, the longer-lasting dominance of heavy industry and the manner in which this affected the complexion of the trade unions tied Labour to partners whose dependence on state subsidy was increasing by mid century and whose priorities, later on, appeared somewhat old-fashioned in an era lit by the 'white heat' of technology. In 1969, for example, the STUC vehemently opposed the Labour government's economic policy in Scotland. At that year's Congress in Rothesay, STUC President Enoch Humphries, of the Fire Brigades Union, complained:

> In their central economic strategy the Government has adopted the advice of the orthodox economists and opted for policies which regard unemployment as a legitimate regulator. They have gone flat out in favour of the wrong economic policies, and we all know it.
>
> This Government exhibits to its own supporters a marked lack of courage to act on its own convictions, on the very points of policy which we claim distinguishes us from our opponents.[44]

The Labour Party was less than conciliatory. John Reid of the Labour Party's Scottish Council responded that, while the President was right in encouraging the government to listen to its friends, 'the Government had the same right'. The following year, with the party facing a general election, Labour's tone was somewhat different. At the STUC Congress in Oban, a representative from the Scottish Council flattered his union comrades. He appealed to Congress, saying:

> [A]s they were the leaders of the working class in Scotland and as they were the people that the people turned to for guidance and advice . . . they could influence 800,000 Trade Unionists and their wives for better or worse. The enthusiasm of their appeal could make or break the Government. They had too much at stake to differ now.[45]

Labour's relations with the unions were clearly not as straightforward as they might first appear – there was a delicate equilibrium to be maintained and, by the end of the century, others, such as the SNP, were competing for the union vote.

Partly as a consequence of slow trade union recruitment and the financial impediments this created at the turn of the century, Labour, in its early years, was forced to rely on the activities of the Independent Labour Party (ILP), established by Keir Hardie in Bradford in 1893.[46] While initially far weaker than the party in the south in terms of branches and membership, the Scottish ILP, particularly in the west Central Belt, came to dominate the early history of Labour in Scotland and provided most of its remarkable personnel.[47] Ramsay MacDonald (1866–1937), the Prime Minister of Labour's first minority government in 1924; John Wheatley (1869–1930), MacDonald's Health minister; James Maxton (1885–1946), charismatic leader of the ILP between 1926 and 1931 and again between 1934 and 1939; and Patrick Dollan (1885–1963), Glasgow Lord Provost between 1938 and 1941, all entered the Labour Party via the ILP.[48] By 1925, the ILP in Scotland boasted 297 branches and, in the 1929 general election, sixty-seven out of Labour's sixty-eight candidates in Scotland were ILP members.[49]

By the 1920s, while the Labour Party recorded significant advances at the ballot box, its constituency associations remained rudimentary, riven by factionalism and frequently non-existent. In 1927, the Scottish membership of the party stood at 11,000, out of a UK total of 300,000.[50] Instead, ILP branches regularly fulfilled the role of 'keeping the Labour interest alive'.[51] Such reliance on this semi-autonomous organisation was dangerous. Arthur Woodburn, Secretary of the Scottish Council of the Labour Party between 1932 and 1939, reflected on the advantages the ILP had over Labour:

Its branches were enthusiastic individuals who worked together as a team, socially friendly, and with their interests centred in their branch. The Labour Party is a federal party and when a Constituency Party meets it is a group of delegates from branches of trades unions, local labour parties and ward committees. The power of the Labour Party is therefore exercised by delegates who have only a periodic association. The ILP was small and intimate. The Labour Party by its very size could not have this advantage.[52]

In 1932, the ILP disaffiliated from the Labour Party largely as a consequence of Ramsay MacDonald's formation of a National government in 1931, although a breach had been rumoured for some time by then. In all, nineteen Scottish ILP branches left the Labour Party.[53] Labour in Scotland felt the impact of ILP disaffiliation more acutely than the party in the south, particularly as men like Maxton, who had epitomised the radical sentiments of Labour's Red Clyde interlude of the war years, were lost to the party and former areas of significant support were disrupted – seven ILP councillors in Glasgow left the Labour Party.[54] More significantly, ILP members who remained within the Labour Party – organised under Patrick Dollan as the Scottish Socialist Party (SSP) – were a persistent obstacle for Labour Party organisers. Woodburn noted that 'the existence of the SSP meant that Labour Party workers were divided and that the work was duplicated in many towns and villages'.[55] Labour may have 'grown up', as Woodburn put it, but it was still paying for the mistakes of its earlier years into the 1940s and beyond.

The legacy of the past was further evident in the 'working-class heroes' who peopled the party in the north and who, at times, could appear bigger than the party itself. The Red Clyde, in the period 1914–1919, had given birth to many of them. James Maxton attracted public attention for anti-war activities that led to his imprisonment during the war; Emmanuel Shinwell, while later Minister of Fuel and Power (1945–1947), Secretary for War (1947–1950) and Minister of Defence (1950–1951), was himself imprisoned for five months in 1919 on account of his activities in relation to the forty-hours strike campaign of that year; and George Buchanan (1890–1955), a future Under-Secretary of State for Scotland (1945–7) and Minister of Pensions (1947), had been a well-known anti-war protestor during the Great War. The legacy of these personalities would remain with the party long after they themselves had died.

During the war years, an explosion of working-class radicalism had – at least in the popular imagination – coloured the Clyde red. Rent strikes, industrial militancy and a strong pacifist tradition drew the politics of the Clyde to the attention of national politicians and the official censor's pen.

But jail sentences and the closure of newspapers failed to stem the radical-ising tide. In the immediate post-war years, many Red Clyde participants achieved elected office and those who reached the Commons formed a distinctive and irreverent cohort. John Bannerman would recall, 'They were true Scottish rebels whose socialism had the needs of Scotland as its base and the cruel unemployment of Clydeside in the 'thirties as its spur.'[56] They gifted Labour a powerful radical past from which to draw inspira-tion in future years but they also promoted ideals which were not neces-sarily in the gift of a parliamentary democracy to deliver. Their passion was attractive and their rhetoric, at times, inspiring but Westminster had little room for revolutionaries of this ilk.

Scots who found the parliamentary road to socialism a slow and unrewarding affair, however, had alternatives. The Communist Party of Great Britain had notable Scottish leaders, such as Willie Gallacher (1881–1966), an MP for Fife in the 1930s and 1940s, and could draw on the example of men like John MacLean (1879–1923), Soviet Russia's first consul in the UK and a charismatic disciple of a heady faith that combined Scottish nationalism and socialism. Matt McGinn's 'Ballad of John MacLean' sketches the popular image:

> The leaders o' the nation made money hand o'er fist
> By grinding down the people by the fiddle and the twist,
> Aided and abetted by the preacher and the Press –
> John called for revolution and he called for nothing less.

But MacLean inspired more literary tributes than tangible political gains.[57] In the late 1930s, Labour itself adopted a more pragmatic approach and more managerialist political organisation – it lacked the fire of the righteous indignation that fuelled the Communist Left but at least it seemed to be getting the job done.

Planned economic development and a corporate style of policymaking and administration became the hallmarks of the Labour Party in Scotland in the 1940s and 1950s. In such a climate – boosted by the vision of a shared destiny that wartime patriotism had encouraged – such strategies were most effectively comprehended on a truly national scale. Seen in these terms, the Union was to be defended and Scottish idiosyn-crasies put firmly in their place. The opening lines of the Scottish Labour Party's Policy for Post-War Scotland (1941), recorded, 'We recognise the first broad principle that . . . Scotland is a nation with its own traditions, customs and law and with problems not encountered or understood outside its borders.' But it was also 'part of the island of Great Britain' and separation was roundly rejected. If Scottish voting patterns at the elections of the 1940s and 50s offer any indication, most Scots shared such views as the vast majority of votes went to unionist parties.

Nevertheless, by the 1960s, Labour Party membership in the north still accounted for much less than 10 per cent of the national total and the corrupting influences of machine politics in some cities did little to encourage new members or indeed reform until the 1970s. Labour in Scotland came increasingly to resemble the party in the south to an extent unknown in the pre-war years. Centralisation did much to ensure compliance but not all were happy to follow orders. As early as 1950, Sir Patrick Dollan complained that:

> [i]t was high time our people in London, whether connected with the Government, newspapers, trade unions and other organisations, consulted local officials in Scotland in matters affecting our side of the border. There is far too much done in London on the assumption that we will be glad to fall into line with anything they may want done. They strain one's loyalty almost to the breaking point.[58]

Yet, for most, an increasing commitment to the Union state and the prizes which the national party could deliver from it were enough to ensure that protests would be relatively muted until the 1970s. For most Scots, housing, employment and health were, in any case, more immediate concerns than the constitution. Even history, of a sort, could be employed to ground this unionist vision. In 1955, Woodburn noted in the Commons:

> Up to 1707, Scotland never had peace. The people of Scotland never had an opportunity to develop their agriculture or to do anything to give them that accumulation of prosperity which makes a nation rich. From 1707 onwards, Scotland went ahead by leaps and bounds. It never looked back until we came to the slump of the interwar years.[59]

Not surprisingly, in 1968, the Scottish Labour Conference rejected home rule for the first time in its long career. And still, in 1977, its *Industrial Strategy for Scotland* placed the emphasis squarely on UK-wide solutions. But this was by no means the party's final word on the 'national question'.

In the 1970s, the threat from the nationalists led Labour to tentatively embrace devolution once more and to address organisational failures that had been evident for some time. For members like Jim Sillars (1937–), a recent convert to devolution in the 1970s, the party did not go far enough. In 1976, he formed the short-lived Scottish Labour Party, before joining the SNP.[60] But, for others, Labour captured the mood of the times and did enough in promoting the devolution referendum of 1979 to retain Scottish loyalties. A new generation of activists rose to the fore, among them John Smith (1938–1994), a future Labour leader; Donald Dewar, the Scottish Parliament's first First Minister; Robin Cook (1946–2005), a future Labour Foreign Minister and Leader of the Commons; George Robertson (1946–), a future NATO Secretary General (1999–2003); and Gordon Brown, a future Labour Prime Minister. These were not trade union leaders but university-educated professionals and clearly of cabinet calibre.[61] They interrupted a long succession of lacklustre Scottish Labour politicians in the Commons – indeed, between 1951 and 1964, despite Scotland's loyalty to the party, only one Scottish MP, Tom Fraser, sat in Labour's shadow cabinet.[62] Even before 'New Labour' was invented, Scottish Labour was re-inventing itself. At much the same time, whether as cause or conse-quence of this reforming strategy, union affiliations in Scotland rose, largely among service sector unions; the party proved increasingly adept at securing the middle-class vote; and a youthful presence, radicalised by global events in the 1960s, came to influence policy and reshape the image of the party, particularly after the Scottish conference permitted debate on non-Scottish subjects after 1972.[63]

In general terms, Labour in Scotland avoided the most damaging divi-sions caused by the emergence of the extreme left which rent the English party in the eighties – the Militant Tendency had important successes in the Provan and Pollok areas of Glasgow but was effectively expelled in 1986. Similarly, any hopes the SDP may have had to challenge Labour's influence in Scotland died eight days after Roy Jenkins won the Hillhead by-election in 1982 when Argentina invaded the Falkland Islands and the Home Front rallied round their earlier familiar party preferences.[64] Rather, this period was used to consolidate the reforms of the seventies and reinforce Labour's position in Scotland as the guardian of the traditional values that Thatcherism sought to undermine. For all their 'New Labour' credentials and despite obvious ideological differences over the years, John Smith, Robin Cook, Donald Dewar and Gordon Brown shared strong Presbyterian backgrounds that they brought with them into the Labour Party. A commitment to social justice and a moral approach to public service united them and reinforced distinctive Scottish qualities in the north that had their roots in the Christian socialism of Labour's founding fathers, if not in the history of the Reformation itself.[65] This was not an intoxi-cating cocktail of theoretical socialism and nor was it a new 'Third Way'. This was not even nationalism. But it did engender a more enthusiastic endorsement of devolution and a more collaborative approach to constitutional reform in the 1990s.

The Labour Party of the 1990s – at least for a time – eschewed its traditional partisanship. Instead of closing ranks, it revisited more consensual approaches in the Scottish Constitutional Convention (SCC) in order to avoid the inter-party difficulties that had effectively killed devolution in 1979. It was idealism fused with pragmatism – in office, Labour had done little to rein in the undemocratic tendencies of the Scottish Office but now home rule seemed the only way of breaking the constitutional stalemate that had condemned them to eighteen years on the opposition benches at Westminster.

In 1994, Labour's Scottish Conference voted to change the name of the Scottish Council to the Scottish Labour Party and, for the rest of the decade, was vociferous in calling for greater autonomy for the party in the north. Indeed, the Scottish Conference was known for passing more radical resolutions than the national body. In 1995, however, while Scotland contributed 18 per cent of the parliamentary Labour Party, the country was home to only 8 per cent of the party's members.[66] At this time, in terms of grass-roots membership support, the Scottish Nationalists seemed to be eclipsing the party that had dominated Scottish politics for decades. But Labour Party membership was growing too and, in any case, membership did not necessarily reflect popular support.

In the 1997 general election, the SNP doubled its number of seats at Westminster to six but its share of the popular vote rose by less than 0.5 per cent. In contrast, Labour, with 56 seats, secured nearly 46 per cent of the popular vote – an increase of around 7 per cent and the party's best performance since 1966. However, while the New Labour government that emerged in 1997 boasted six Scottish Labour MPs in its first cabinet, it owed little to Scottish loyalties – beyond that which it had come to expect – for securing office. The votes of middle England, the unpopularity of John Major's last Conservative administration and the novelty of a New Labour Party shorn of its socialist credentials had generated the Tory wipeout. While the assumption cannot be tested, it is highly likely that Labour would have been elected in 1997 even without a commitment to the immediate formation of devolved assemblies. Looked at from one perspective, 1997 proved that the Union state was working – an unpopular government had been replaced. One wonders if a Blairite Scottish Office would have felt very different to the Scottish Executive that emerged in 1999. Nevertheless, the Labour government was quick to deliver the referendum on Scottish devolution that it had promised in its manifesto, with the surprise addition of a second question on tax-raising powers. Would Scotland's Labour allegiance really have been much challenged had it not done so? The SNP vote did not seem to suggest a significant rise in nationalist tendencies. But the momentum behind devolution was, by this stage, unstoppable. The irony of it all was that only a unionist party with a truly national UK reach could have unseated the Tories in 1997 – only a party resolutely committed to the integrity of the Great Britain could have set Scotland free, at least in part.

In 1999, the Scottish Labour Party, led by Donald Dewar, became the major partner in the coalition that would form the first Scottish Executive. For Scottish Labour, this reflected the realisation of long-standing ambitions and confirmation of its unique position in Labour's past. For Tony Blair's government, it was merely one aspect of a constitutional reform process which, by reshaping the union, would ensure its survival well into the new century. The rigorous selection procedure that produced Labour's Holyrood hopefuls effectively barred 'Old Labour' discontents from office (or emboldened them to stand as independents, Dennis Canavan (1942–), for example) in favour of politicians more sympathetic to Blair's modernising agenda. In the end, the class profile of Labour MSPs was even more middle class than the parliamentary Labour Party at Westminster. The development of the Scottish Policy Forum (SPF, established in 1998) – a body of delegated Labour Party members, trade unionists and elected politicians whose reports and policy recommendations came to effectively dominate the Scottish Conference – stifled debate and reduced the ability of constituency Labour Parties to influence policy outwith SPF processes. For a party committed to devolution, inclusion and empowerment, Labour remained doggedly centralist – and was becoming more so – in its own operations. The party that delivered Scottish home rule was not prepared to accord similar privileges and responsibilities to its Scottish comrades in their own operations. A partial consequence of this was that Scottish voters were increasingly inclined not to trust them either. In the first year of the new Parliament, it became clear that many traditional Scottish Labour supporters were sceptical of New Labour's commitment to its working-class constituency and, indeed, to Scottish interests in general.[67]

NATIONALISTS – 'SPIRITS CONGENITALLY FACTIOUS'

Scottish Independents consisted mainly of spirits congenitally factious, of a small minority, mostly young, who had read history and considered the economic problem in some detail and with an open mind, of remaining Jacobites, of a few Liberals who remembered the early doctrines of their party, of some eccentric ladies, and of an insecure

working-class element, more susceptible to sentiment than their bourgeois neighbours, and who further believed that any change from the
existing order of society would of necessity be for the better. Vested
interests were openly hostile to the movement, and the great majority
of middle-class people were indifferent to it with the calm indifference
of ignorance.

Magnus Merriman
Eric Linklater

It was not until 1928 that the various groups which had, until
then, comprised the main agents pushing for home rule – the Scottish
Home Rule Association, the Scottish National League, the Scottish
National Movement and the Glasgow University Scottish Nationalists
Association – came together in a separate party, the National Party of
Scotland (NPS). The public viewed it alternately with mild amusement and
suspicion. Eric Linklater, standing as a nationalist in the East Fife parliamentary by-election in 1933 noted, 'In certain quarters the policy of the
National Party of Scotland is said to be revolutionary in its
intention, narrow in outlook and likely to be dangerous in practice.'[68] Six
years after its foundation, having been purged of its more extreme elements
under the calculating gaze of leader John MacCormick (1904–1961), the
NPS joined with the smaller moderate-right Scottish Party that had been
established in 1932 and was committed to limited home rule. From the
beginning, the new Scottish National Party (SNP) lacked ideological coher-
ence and struggled to keep its disparate interests united.[69] Its 'Ten Points
for Propagandists', published in 1938, give some insight into the very basic
lessons that the party was trying to learn in these years:

1. Don't force your Nationalism upon people. They will avoid
   you next time.
2. Don't bore them with long arguments in which they show
   little interest.
3. Don't embarrass them by loud controversy in tram-cars and
   public places. (Especially in Edinburgh where people travel
   silent.)
4. Don't use dishonest arguments. There are plenty of honest ones.
5. Don't use facts or figures you are not sure of. Be accurate.
6. Don't give the impression that you are a monomaniac about
   Nationalism. You will exert more influence if you have an
   intelligent interest in the world at large.
7. Don't talk with dislike or contempt of England. That is silly;
   it misrepresents Scottish Nationalism, and it does no good.

8. Don't treat other people or their arguments with scorn or assume that they are actuated by bad faith.
9. Don't take up a factious attitude within the Party. Grave harm has been done in the past by the publicity which a malicious press has given to our disagreements – often over trifles.
10. Don't be discouraged if the walls of Jericho do not fall at the first blast of the trumpet.[70]

Despite such 'wise words', by the end of the 1930s, according to the historian Richard Finlay, the SNP had 'degenerated into a plethora of factions and cliques'.[71] Beyond its commitment to a fuzzy rendering of home rule, its aims and objectives were unclear and imprecise. In many ways, it acted more like a pressure group than a conventional political party – ordinary members, for example, were permitted to hold the membership of other parties and regular pacts with like-minded Liberals only succeeded in confusing the electorate even further. At any rate, the party was small. 'In those days, to meet another Nationalist was almost as unusual as the Livingstone/Stanley encounter in Africa,' wrote Donald Stewart (1920–1992), SNP MP for the Western Isles from 1970 to 1987.[72]

In 1939, war intervened and served to enhance such confusion. In 1942, MacCormick established the Scottish Convention with the aim of galvanising cross-party pressure on the government to deliver a devolved legislature and 'educate the people of their country in the principles of good citizenship'.[73] This left a more radical rump to dominate the Scottish National Party and reaffirm the party's commitment to independence. For example, the SNP's chairman in these years, Douglas Young (1913–1973), took a determined stance on the ineligibility of the Westminster government to impose conscription in Scotland, pushing the case all the way to the law courts. His determination was admired by many in the party but was opposed by most members of the public committed to the war effort.

In 1945, light relief from internal party squabbling was offered by the SNP's first victory at a by-election in Motherwell but it did not last long. The Motherwell victor, Robert McIntyre (1913–1998), had benefited from the lack of Conservative and Liberal opposition, had the services of a small but enthusiastic local party branch, at a time when other party machines were moribund, and had offered a pragmatic nationalist message, eschewing the romanticism that usually drew derision.[74] But ambitions were dashed when the seat was lost to Labour at the general election a few months later and the popularity of Labour's nationalisation and welfare policies became apparent. McIntyre appealed to the people of Motherwell, saying, 'I stand for the democratic freedom of the

Scottish people to run their own affairs. We must develop the resources of our country for the benefit of all our people.'[75] But the electorate were more easily convinced that Scottish resources would be most effectively harnessed for the common good in a union state that had recently proved itself strong enough to defeat the global Fascist threat to democracy. Of the nine Scottish National Party candidates who stood for election in 1945, seven forfeited their deposits and the party received only 30,854 votes – a high point in their electoral experience so far but still only 1.27 per cent of the poll.[76]

Away from the polling booths, however, popular enthusiasm for Scottish home rule appeared to be growing, although the British Establishment and the other Scottish parties stood resolutely immune to its influence. The first years following the martial victory in 1945 were paradoxical – Scots in huge numbers voted for Attlee's nationalising Labour government, one of the most centralising administrations in the history of the country, whilst expressing nationalist sympathies to an extent unheard of in previous decades. Robert Garioch summed up the nationalist perspective on this dilemma in his 1954 play, *Masque of Edinburgh*:

> Makar: In Seventeen-oh-seeven
> the Parliament an aw
> were wafted sooth frae Edinbro
> an coffined in Whitehaa . . .
>
> Donald: An sin they nabbed oor Parliament
> the rest is nae surprise;
> they come nae mair a-reivin,
> noo they simply nationalise.

In 1949, the Scottish Convention gathered around two million signatures for its petition, the Scottish Covenant, in support of Scottish home rule. Its signatories affirmed:

WE, the people of Scotland who subscribe this Engagement, declare our belief that reform in the constitution of our country is necessary to secure good government in accordance with our Scottish traditions and to promote the spiritual and economic welfare of our nation.

WE affirm that the desire for such reform is both deep and wide spread throughout the whole community, transcending all political differences and sectional interests, and we undertake to continue united in purpose for its achievement.

WITH that end in view we solemnly enter into this Covenant whereby we pledge ourselves, in all loyalty to the Crown and within the framework of the United Kingdom, to do everything in our power to secure for Scotland a Parliament with adequate legislative authority in Scottish affairs.[77]

Despite massive popular support, the Covenant failed to persuade the other parties to make home rule a priority and the SNP itself failed to exploit this arousal of public interest.

The following year, the remarkable theft of the Stone of Destiny from Westminster Abbey similarly grabbed popular attention. The unlikely student prank dominated the press for weeks but Labour's Secretary of State for Scotland, Hector McNeil (1907–1955), simply bided his time, as the police scoured the country in a comedic manner evocative of a Compton Mackenzie (1883–1972) novel. Eventually the Stone returned to Scotland – ironically, part of it enjoyed the northwards journey from London in an HP (Houses of Parliament) Sauce box. Press attention turned to other matters and the publicity of prosecution was denied the culprits and their cause.[78]

Such public stunts failed to generate significant electoral successes for the SNP and could have worked against the party – in the 1950 general election, all six nationalist candidates lost their deposits and, in the election a year later, the idea of a Scottish Assembly was hardly mentioned.[79] Instead, the Nationalists' campaigning style drew the derision of its critics – in 1949, the *Inverness Courier* styled the 'Scots Nats' as 'comic opera Covenanters'.[80] The Nats, however, were partly responsible for one ministerial scalp in these years. Arthur Woodburn's mishandling of the Nationalist challenge – he accused them of guerrilla tactics – cost him the Scottish Office. The popular press enjoyed the spectacle:

> They mock you, Arthur, laughing when you bleat
> Of tartaned types with bombs in Downing Street.
> They bid you have a care lest the display
> Of Scotland's saltire on St Andrew's Day
> Be but a cover for some fiendish trick
> Of sending Southward Haggises that tick.[81]

Controversy further dogged the nationalist cause when, in 1953, many Scots, including MacCormick, strongly objected to the coronation of the new queen as Elizabeth II because she was the first monarch of the United Kingdom to bear that name. Postboxes bearing the 'EIIR' cipher were attacked and MacCormick raised an (unsuccessful) action in the Court of Session but little in the way of real progress was made.

Under the leadership of Robert McIntyre, the SNP leader from 1947 to 1956, however, party discipline was stiffened in the 1950s. The party came to focus on rural areas where it had more of a chance of attracting wavering Conservative and Liberal support and membership grew to around 100,000 by the mid 1960s. But it took the onset of economic recession to translate popular enthusiasm into votes. In the 1960s, John Herdman, a novelist and short-story writer, joined the SNP in Edinburgh, and he recalled:

> In the early sixties nationalism in Scotland seemed to be the preserve of literary intellectuals, folk singers and fiery students, and I embraced it more as an expression of quixotic dissent from the established British order than from any confident conviction that there was a realistic prospect of eventual constitutional change.[82]

In the 1964 general election, the SNP contested fifteen seats and twelve candidates lost their deposits. Two years later, twenty-three seats were contested and 5 per cent of the vote was secured but, still, ten deposits were lost. It was hardly an edifying record.

However, by the early 1970s, neither of the major parties was offering imaginative solutions to Scotland's ills and the Liberal Party was too weak to influence policy. Various factors were to determine that the SNP would prove adept at filling this vacuum. After thirty-three years, the SNP secured its second seat in the Commons when Winnie Ewing won the Hamilton by-election of 1967 and, a year later, 100 SNP municipal councillors were elected, having secured 30 per cent of the vote. Though the ideal of its slogan 'Free by 73' was not realised, by 1974, the party boasted first four (February) and then seven (October) more MPs in Scotland than the Liberals and became Labour's most serious opponent in a number of constituencies. In forty-two constituencies, the SNP had come second place at the polls. The SNP's 'It's Scotland's Oil' campaign was influential in convincing Scots that they could go it alone successfully and so too was the party's appeal in Scotland's New Towns, where electors were less wedded to old party affiliations than elsewhere and were often more aspirational. Colourful campaigning and tabloid-friendly slogans also shouted the arrival of a 'new' presence in Scottish politics.

Nevertheless, later developments in the 1970s proved that the SNP was not prepared for success.[83] Slogans could not mask continued divisions over policy evident in conflicting statements from the party leadership or prevent the splits in the party which paralysed its operations after the debacle of the 1979 referendum.[84] It took the party at least three years to rid itself of the Celtic romanticists of 'Siol Nan Gaidheal' and the left-leaning '79 Group', during which time the embarrassing escapades of such factions had threatened to undermine the progress of earlier decades. In October 1981, for example, six nationalists led by Jim Sillars, then SNP Vice-Chairman for Policy, occupied the debating chamber of the Scottish Assembly building in Edinburgh before being escorted to Gayfield Square Police Station and charged with vandalism.[85] SNP fortunes waned – in 1983, the SNP polled only 11.7 per cent of the vote in the general election and was rewarded with only two MPs. Facing another Thatcher term in office, Scots had returned to their traditional Labour sympathies, now enlivened by a talented new generation. By comparison, the SNP was less convincing as a champion against the New Right.

Developments in the later 1980s, however, brought renewed optimism as the Conservative administration did much to reinforce the nationalists' message that Scotland would be better off without its southern neighbour. In 1985, Rory Watson observed a 'new confidence, aggression and enthusiasm . . . permeating the party'.[86]

The SNP's 'Independence in Europe' policy – a volte-face from its Euro-scepticism of the 1970s – grew in strength between 1983 and 1988 and seemed to strike an immediate chord with many in the Scottish electorate. Jim Sillars had been an early advocate of the strategy, noting, in 1985, that 'Scottish nationalism has an opportunity within the European context to widen its vision and reputation'.[87] Certainly, Europe played a major role in Sillars' own victory at the Govan by-election in November 1988. Thereafter, the grip of Alex Salmond (1954–) on the party leadership in the 1990s tightened. Organisation was streamlined and his advocacy of gradualist left-of-centre policies and devolution as a step to independence, while losing him the sympathies of many party hardliners, attracted wide support both within and outwith the party.[88] Not only did the SNP seem a serious rival to Labour in the run up to the 1997 general election, but the party had also secured 33 per cent of the vote at the European elections of 1994 and over 26 per cent of the votes during the Unitary Council elections in 1995.

As it turned out, the 1997 general election was to prove a grave disappointment for the SNP and its consequences for the party were profound. Labour's election victory guaranteed that Scotland was to have a parliament of sorts and, from 1999, the SNP joined the ranks of the opposition parties in the Scottish Parliament, alongside the Conservatives, the Scottish Green Party and the Scottish Socialist Party. With thirty-five seats, they were the largest single non-governmental group and, from early on, were seen by most Scots and the media – both reluctant to abandon familiar Westminster models – as the Executive's 'shadow'. There were, however, problems inherent in such a high profile for a party whose official policy remained an independent Scotland. In the short term at least, the only prospect of forming a government in Scotland would be as part of a coalition or as a minority government and a commitment to independence did not make the SNP an attractive marriage partner for any would-be suitors. Alternatively, the longer the party remained committed to making devolution work, the greater the credence that was added to views that devolution was enough. At the end of the century, devolution proved to be a trap for the party that it was ill equipped to escape. And seven years on, its ascendance into government at the 2007 election, as a minority administration with forty-seven seats, compared to Labour's forty-six, did little to resolve these dilemmas.

The Scottish electoral and party-political landscape clearly changed dramatically over the course of the twentieth century. Hindsight lends one's interpretation of change an air of inevitability but some major outcomes, such as Labour's rise to dominance and the decline of both Liberal and Conservative fortunes, could not have been reasonably predicted in Scottish tea leaves in 1900. Nor was the foundation of the Scottish Parliament somehow pre-ordained by the Scottish political elite – it took the determination of a sympathetic UK government, elected by voters across the British Isles, to undo 1707 in a very British coup. Those who lived through it know just how close things came to being very different.

TEN   Difference and Devolution

As a teenager, Gordon Brown won a prize of £200 in a competition sponsored by the *Scottish Daily Express* for an essay describing Britain in the year 2000. The Fife schoolboy's focus was close to home:

> A new generation is being born . . . By 2000, Scotland can, for the first time in history, have found her feet as a society which has bridged the gaps between rich and poor, young and old, intellectual and labourer. The inheritance of a respect for every individual's freedom and identity, and the age-long quality of caring, both transmitted through our national religion, law and educational system and evident in the lives of countless generations of our people, makes Scotland ideal for pioneering the society which transcends political systems.[1]

It is a revealing glimpse of the values that shaped the young politician but also suggests that national identity acted as a prism through which Scots came to understand and evaluate broader social and economic dynamics. Put simply, being Scottish was important.

The Scottish Parliament neither created nor transformed Scottish politics and the political community, at least in the short term. Even in the old Union state, sharing Parliament and parties with the other component nations of the UK, there was something one could call 'Scottish politics' in the twentieth century. Though its origins and characteristics were often complex and contradictory, four principal arguments – or combinations of them – have traditionally been used to define this phenomenon. Many have pointed to distinct Scottish political traditions shaping general responses to UK patterns and have highlighted a set of values, generally characterised by their collective nature, which partly determined contrasting electoral geographies north of the Border.[2] Others have highlighted the legacy of the Union settlement of 1707 in shaping a distinct Scottish 'body politic'.[3] A third perspective points to the existence of separate authorities and organisations which have dictated that politics took place in a Scottish 'arena',[4] while an associated viewpoint has stressed the importance of the distinctive political culture which this arena nurtured.[5] One might also appeal to constitutional change itself – with the establishment of a Scottish Parliament, mandated by a convincing referendum vote in favour of devolution, there seemed little reason to doubt the importance of a distinct political will in 1999. Yet how did this will express itself in the days before devolution?

Throughout the twentieth century, attempts to understand the persistence of a distinct Scottish political dynamic, in the face of the homogenising influences of democratisation, centralisation and modernisation, looked to aspects of Scottish identity to explain apparent differences. In the process, class, religion and tradition would all be called upon to interpret Scotland's unique place in the politics of the Union. Whether they amounted to more than the sum of their parts is open to debate.

DEFENCE OR DEPENDENCY? – CLASS AND SCOTTISH POLITICAL CHANGE

Only for a relatively short interlude in mid-century politics did objective class measures appear to shape party fortunes in Scottish elections. In the early years of the century, both Conservatives and Liberals had already become adept at manipulating their core message to attract different class groups in various areas and, following the First World War, Labour was successful in attracting disaffected middle-class Liberal voters with more radical leanings. Nevertheless, between the 1930s and the 1970s, class more readily translated directly into political affiliation in many constituencies – middle class and Conservative, working class and Labour became almost synonymous terms in some political analyses. (In such an environment, the SNP were described as 'a bourgeois party without a bourgeoisie'.[6]) Yet this classic model of voting behaviour was not to last.

At mid century, it seemed plausible to explain Labour's hold on Scottish electoral politics in terms of the northern nation's overwhelming working-class profile and the Scottish economy's dependence on manufacturing industry. Quite simply, there were more working-class and fewer middle-class constituencies in Scotland than in England.[7] This made it easy for working-class interests in Scotland to be readily equated with the public good and class to be used to castigate Labour's enemies even when their opposition rested on ideas far more complex than sectional interests. The small size and electoral weakness of the middle classes did little to discourage this. By the end of the century, however, class seemed to offer little in the way of an explanation for the continued dominance of the

Labour Party in Scotland.[8] Scotland's class profile had moved increasingly closer to that of Britain as a whole during the twentieth century. In 1991, while 41 per cent of Scottish households could be termed 'manual working class' in comparison with 36 per cent of British households, Scotland had comparable proportions in intermediate classes (24 and 23 per cent respectively) and only 6 per cent separated the proportion of households of middle-class status in Scotland (31 per cent) from those in Britain as a whole (37 per cent).[9]

Yet a closer look at electoral results shows that class still mattered. The potential of the class argument is enhanced if one points to class consciousness, rather than to structural and economic measures. Despite a recorded rise in the number of middle-class households, a decline in manual occupations and an increase in home ownership, the percentage of Scots identifying themselves as 'working class' actually rose from 68 per cent to 74 per cent between 1974 and 1992. At the same time, similar social trends in England more predictably resulted in a decline in those identifying themselves as working class (from 65 per cent to 57 per cent).[10] Scots seemed to identify more readily with a proletarian image of themselves and their nation and this, more so than their incomes, seemed to influence their political choices.[11] While Labour benefited, the Conservatives suffered at the polls in Scotland at the same time as their message delivered success in English constituencies. A 'Scottish' dynamic was clear and it was anti-Conservative.[12] Why?

The voters who grew to maturity in the 1960s were the first generation that, 'from the cradle', had benefited from the post-war welfare state. They were also more dependent on public-sector employment than their forebears and increasingly relied on the health of traditional industries that, by then, were being sustained by the subsidies which nationalisation generally guaranteed. As the children of a generation who could readily measure the difference such changes had made to their families and communities, the collective memory served to remind these young adults of their debts to both the Union and to Labour. In Scotland, the social amelioration which the expansion of central welfare provision and nationalisation wrought had a fundamental impact on how Scots appreciated the role of the state and, hence, their electoral priorities. Until the early 1980s, Scottish working-class voters found little in nationalist alternatives to tempt them from their commitment to both the Union and to Labour but, by the nineties, the health, education and housing opportunities that, for many, had facilitated greater social mobility were under attack. Social mobility actually declined in the final years of the century and increasing numbers of Scots remained in the same class as their parents.[13] For many, it became increasingly apparent that the Union state in its current form no longer seemed able to reflect the preferences of Scottish voters or guarantee the continuity of central funding that had sustained Scottish society and supported Scottish economic interests since 1945. That, over the years, more Scots had risen into the middle class did not seem to matter or, at least, this was certainly not attributed to recent Conservative policies. Something more fundamental was at stake.[14]

By the end of the century, Scottish support for devolution was as defensive as the nation's earlier commitment to the Union status quo had been – it was a means of preserving social institutions and services upon which many Scots relied and a vehicle for delivering economic growth in much the same way as planning had sought to do a generation before.[15] Changes within the Union by the end of the century guaranteed that such interests were less distinguished by class than by their specific relevance to Scotland. On paper, Scotland may have become a more middle-class nation than it had been at mid century but its reliance on collective solutions to its ills suggested that it was taking time to get used to the fact and, in any case, understood what had got it there.

RELIGION – 'THE MARKS OF ORIGIN'

In 1904, Peter Hume Brown (1850–1918), one of Scotland's most preeminent historians, reflected on the importance of the Reformation to the nation and the national character of the Scots.

> The Reformation supplied the special class of questions in which the nation found its chief concern, but it did not determine the spirit in which these questions were regarded . . . While to the Reformation we must ascribe the immense service of awakening the Scottish nation to a conscious life and a sense of its own destinies, it would be inconsistent with the evidence of history to say that we equally owe to it our type of national character. [Nevertheless, it] was in the paroxysm produced by the rejection of one religion and the adoption of another that Scotland emerged into national life, and, whatever may be the modifying influences of time, she can never wholly lose the marks of her origin.[16]

By 2000, Scotland was neither as Protestant nor as religious a country as the nation in which Brown wrote and religious controversies – particularly those of several hundred years before – seemed of little relevance to all but a small minority of Scots. But, for most of the century, religion had been a persistent feature of Scottish society. (This will be addressed further in the following chapter.) In 1947, for example, the author George Blake (1893–1961) noted, 'The influence of the Kirk in Scotland may be dwindling sadly today, but the influence of the religious struggles on the Scottish temperament, and the sense of *difference* or *separateness* they fostered, should never be underrated.'[17] In terms of Scottish politics, religious values and affiliations declined in appreciable influence only in the last thirty years of the century.

At the turn of the century, Liberalism and Unionism won significant electoral capital from their avowed commitment to the Reformation settlement in Scotland and benefited from party loyalties won during ecclesiastical battles in the late nineteenth century. While support for disestablishment attracted many to the Liberal Party, the preservation of the established status of the Church of Scotland attracted others to the Scottish Unionists. Even Labour identified its inheritance in the ethos of Presbyterian democracy in these years and used the rhetoric of the pulpit to highlight just how far, under capitalism, Scotland had drifted from its destiny as a godly commonwealth for all workers. Socialist Sunday Schools, replete with 'hymns' – for example, 'An Offering to the Shrine of Power our Hands will Never Bring' – and 'readings' – such as 'The Unity of Labour is the Hope of the World' – similarly enticed a new generation of young radicals into the Labour Party at the turn of the century. For the nationalists, religion was likewise an obvious means of identifying their movement with uniquely Scottish institutions and could, on occasion, be used to suggest divine endorsement of their ambitions. At the Scottish 'Independence Day' ceremony in Arbroath in April 1933, for example, SNP voices were raised in song in the hymns 'O God our Help in Ages Past' and, more predictably, 'The Land which Thou Gavest unto our Fathers'.[18]

By mid century, however, religion had largely lost its power to compromise material self-interest in the polling booths. By then, with Irish independence as complete as it would ever be in the century, Labour had secured the working-class Catholic vote. Once the guarantor of many Liberal seats in the major cities, the Catholic vote now became the foundation of Labour's northern fiefdom. Meanwhile, protestant religiosity was in decline and, as a consequence of disestablishment and greater church unity, there seemed few pressing ecclesiastical battles to be fought through the offices of the state and few church members willing to fight them. Nevertheless, sectarianism remained a powerful political weapon in some areas – in the interwar years, many Unionists and Protestant church leaders raised the threat that Irish Catholic immigration posed to native Scottish qualities and interests in an attempt to secure the wavering sympathies of working-class Protestants. Thereafter, the traditional Unionist sympathies of the Scottish Orange Lodges perpetuated this association into the 1970s. By the 1990s, however, in all but a few constituencies (mainly in Lanarkshire), sectarianism had declined in political importance as ecumenical understanding developed, the peace process in Northern Ireland gained momentum and, in an increasingly multicultural and secular society, political parties sought to avoid exclusive associations with minority religious interests regardless of their native or historical origins.

The remnants of religious influence at the end of the century became increasingly contested and therefore less and less powerful. In the 1990s, the Catholic vote remained anti-Conservative but now it was less attached to Labour than in previous years. The SNP had started to make inroads. By the end of the century, Scottish Catholics were less ambivalent about the symbols of Scottish nationhood than they had been a generation before and, if polls are to be believed, they were even slightly more likely to support home rule than Protestants.[19] Meanwhile, the Conservatives generally maintained a Protestant image – more often out of habit than intent as it meant little in terms of policy. By the century's close, the Protestant working class were 'no longer a cohesive political force' and, in any case, were less likely to vote Conservative than previously.[20] By this time, Labour felt able to celebrate the Presbyterian roots of many of its leading lights, such as John Smith, Donald Dewar and Gordon Brown, without fear of alienating voters. Aspects of Scottish Presbyterianism had been accommodated as an inoffensive feature of a Scottish identity it was in Labour's interests to cultivate.

Religion fails to deliver neat explanations for Scotland's distinctive political history in the twentieth century. Throughout this time, its influence waxed and waned and tended to be regionally specific, contradictory and secondary to other socio-economic interests. Secularising tendencies elsewhere in society did much to blunt its political influence. Yet Presbyterianism at least evoked a sense of identity that was integral to the devolution agenda. Independently, the churches were, to all intents and purposes, a spent political force by the end of the century. Acting in alliance with other civil institutions within a context of a resurgent sense of nationhood, however, they underpinned the case for home rule with moral, historical and sentimental claims on the sympathies of many voters.

TRADITION – 'VESTIGIAL RELICS STILL REMAIN'

In 1953, a columnist in a Scottish Covenant newsletter reflected on 'Scotland – that Distressed Area' in prose which could hardly contain the complexities he wished to sketch:

Scotland, the Scottish people, the Scottish culture, are all the outcome of the interaction of converging forces. The collision of a set of racial and cultural energies within a narrow, well-defined, geographical and climatic environment, modified through time by the impingement of certain philosophical influences and by a series of fertilising contacts with other peoples and cultures, created a human type, not altogether agreeable, perhaps, but nevertheless vigorous in expression and powerful in outline. Created more than that – for example, a culture, a political organisation of which the vestigial relics still remain, a church, a philosophy, a tradition, stubbornly sprouting, frequently threatened and firmly defended, and appealed to on countless occasions throughout the centuries in an ardent and successful demand for sacrifice on its behalf. It would be impossible to repeat, in any other area of the globe or with any other amalgam of people, the coincidence of these factors and their result. Scotland, like every other true nation, is something whole, something grounded, complete and therefore it cannot be repeated. It is a unit, it is unique.[21]

Tradition was a powerful factor shaping Scottish political choices in the twentieth century. As the site where history frequently met polemic, however, it was notoriously difficult to evaluate and impossible to measure. It was open to accommodation by all political persuasions, prone to manipulation and, as we see above, exaggerated to the point that its meaning and influence was largely obscured.

Much was made in the final years of the twentieth century of the persistence of a civil society in Scotland which, surviving the Union in the education system, local government, the legal Establishment and the Church, did much to preserve traditions and a sense of Scottishness that otherwise might have come to grief on the anglicising 'rocks' of Union.[22] True, Scots law met seemingly unending challenges to its authority – exemplified in tendencies to refer to English decisions and increasing appeals to the House of Lords – and other Scottish institutions with, at times, limited success in the course of the twentieth century sought to maintain traditions, values and conventions distinct from those of their counterparts in the south.[23] In the SCC, such bodies had a powerful voice. But it is open to serious doubt whether, in the final years of the century, Scottish voters had the protection of a faceless judiciary in mind when they recorded their votes for pro-devolution parties. In the end, it was their votes, rather than the machinations of lawyers, civil servants, teachers and local councillors (who had already had nearly 300 years to change things), that delivered a Scottish

Parliament; and their understanding of Scottish identity was not the tame creature of civil Scotland. One might even suggest that, in part, popular support for devolution paradoxically reflected a wide distrust of the very officials who were the architects of the devolution settlement itself. After all, it was supposed to make them accountable.

Traditions rooted in a sense of place, rather than pale institutionalised conventions, offered fertile sources of identity for both politicians and voters alike. But how was the influence of such identity to be measured, and how could it be judged?

For much of the century Scottish traditions appeared comfortable within the Union state and Scottish identity readily complemented rather than competed with British loyalties. The nineties changed all that. Political commentators at the close of the century interpreted the divergence in voting behaviour between Scotland and England as the expression of a renewed sense of Scottish identity. 'Separate scales of values have now developed north and south of the Border, which simply fail to integrate,' noted Christopher Harvie (1944–) in 1989.[24] Having rested on this sense of 'otherness' in their analyses of Scottish political culture, however, writers tended to resist any temptations they might have had to define Scottishness in favour of measuring responses to it.[25] They similarly diverted attention from the invented-ness of much that made up Scottish traditions and the contradictory nature of identity by looking for 'Scottish values' in the policy preferences of Scottish voters. Principally through the mechanisms of polls and surveys, they came to conclude that, during the course of the Conservative administrations in the 1980s and 1990s, increasing numbers of Scots came to prioritise their Scottish identity over their British identity. In a poll of over 800 Scots in 1997, 23 per cent considered themselves 'Scottish not British' and 38 per cent '[m]ore Scottish than British'.[26] Also, if offered a range of options, it appeared that Scots, by the end of the century, tended slightly more than their English counterparts to opt for collective or socialistic responses to social problems and to exhibit more liberal values.[27] According to Lindsay Paterson, Scots had a 'utopian inclination'.[28]

Such studies went some way to addressing the values that inspired end-of-the-century Scots and how these Scots viewed themselves. But by leaving definitions of 'Scottish' (and 'British') wide open, they left much unsaid. Across the decades, Scottish 'identity' resisted generalisations. In this sense, it offered little to those seeking to explain political phenomena that were national in scale. But somehow it remained meaningful – Scots (and 'outsiders') still spoke of it in impassioned terms with the confident assumption that those who listened would know what they meant and even felt the same way. It survived contradiction and even thrived on being contested. In the end, it explained much but resisted explanation itself. If only for that reason alone, it was valuable political territory.

The distinctiveness of Scottish politics in the twentieth century clearly drew heavily on tradition but also owed much to contemporary manifestations of Scottish 'difference' that were increasingly drawn into sharp relief by the attitudes and policies of central government. Much may be made of class, religion and tradition but twentieth-century Scotland was overwhelmingly shaped by the conflicting dynamics of centralisation and regional autonomy. 'Scottish politics' formed at this interface but, at times, it had few sources of legitimisation beyond history, principle and a certain language of rights to sustain it. At any one time, its salience was principally determined by the wider interests of political parties within a Union state and its character was shaped in assemblies that changed over time. It is not surprising that creating these assemblies anew became the focus of many who sought an environment where Scottish politics could thrive.

FROM 'NO' TO 'YES YES'

Christopher Harvie's *Scotland and Nationalism* was first published in 1977 and is infused with the confidence of the immediate pre-referendum years and the enticing unfamiliarity of a future that, whatever else, was to be resolutely 'Scottish'.

> Whatever it is called during the process of legislation, the Scots will unquestionably call the Assembly in the Royal High School their parliament and the leader of its majority party their prime minister. Will it be a stepping-stone on the road to independence or a terminus?[29]

Over twenty years later, an older and more cynical Scotland boasted a Parliament which met for the first time in rented accommodation in the Church of Scotland's Assembly Hall – the old 'High' on Calton Hill was rejected in favour of quarters near the Palace of Holyroodhouse, as yet un-built but, the public were assured, more fitting the nation's new aspirations. A First Minister, rather than a Prime Minister, supervised an Executive,[30] rather than a government, but Harvie's final question remained unanswered.

Both continuity and change marked the referenda of 1979 and 1997 – the underlying principles behind them were basically the same but what was on offer and the terms of the offer were very different.

Table 3.2 Devolution Referenda (Scotland): 1979, 1997

Referendum	Turnout (% electorate)	Option	Response	Votes (% turnout)	(% electorate)
1979	63.8	Support for a Scottish Assembly	Yes	51.6	32.9
			No	48.4	30.8
1997	60.4	Support for a Scottish Parliament	Yes	74.3	44.7
			No	25.7	15.5
	60.2	Support for tax-raising powers	Yes	63.5	38.1
			No	36.5	21.9

Source: D. Denver et al., *Scotland Decides: The Devolution Issue and the 1997 Referendum* (London, 2000) pp. 23, 133.

While only the second poll was successful in delivering devolution, both referenda were important episodes in Scotland's modern history.

In the late 1970s, socio-economic pressures and a fresh confidence founded on the discovery of North Sea oil engendered widespread support for constitutional change but clear objectives were largely absent. A Labour Royal Commission on the UK Constitution had reported in favour of an elected Scottish Assembly in 1973 but, in February 1978, the passage of the Scotland Act – which specified the remit and character of the Assembly and the referendum required to endorse it – was marked by the disunity of Scottish MPs.[31] Both within and across the parties, differences of opinion were evident and proved the undoing of the legislation. The Act itself, navigated through the Commons by Labour's John Smith, was described later by Sir David Steel as 'unsatisfactory'. It offered Scotland an Assembly elected by the first past the post (FPTP) system – a guaranteed boon for the Labour Party – with no power to raise or lower taxation and a range of legislative powers which could have been regularly vetoed by the Secretary of State for Scotland – an ominous state of affairs had the Secretary been the nominee of a Westminster government of a different political persuasion to that in Edinburgh. Yet these provisions would never be tested. The famous Cunningham amendment, named after George Cunningham, the Scots-born MP for Islington who had proposed it, demanded that over 40 per cent of the Scottish electorate endorse constitutional changes of such magnitude and effectively sealed the Act's ignominious fate. Every vote not cast effectively counted as a rejection of home rule and this meant that, for example, the votes of 28,000 students each with two votes, due to the vagaries of registration, would count for naught if only one vote per person was cast in favour of devolution.[32] Also, the registers on which the referendum was based were seriously out of date, meaning the silence of the dead regularly annulled the votes of those in the polling booths.

The referendum campaigns of the early spring of 1979 found the Scottish public increasingly fed up with the whole thing and both sides seriously divided and exhausted following Britain's 'winter of discontent'. Indeed, many voters used the referendum simply as a means to record their disillusion with the Callaghan government which itself had refused funding for referendum campaigning.[33] Labour, under Gordon Brown's guidance, ran a 'Labour Movement Yes' campaign, although many in the party hierarchy were opposed to it and refused to co-operate with Nationalists in joint campaigning for fear of being tainted with separatism. Meanwhile, Labour unionists, led by Tam Dalyell (1932–), the West Lothian MP, announced 'Labour Says No'. Dalyell was adamant in his defence of the constitution for both historic and pragmatic reasons. In *Devolution: The End of Britain*, he considered that, since the Union of 1707, 'Scotland has successfully retained her own very distinctive identity while enjoying the benefits of a wider political association'.[34] In another publication sponsored by 'Labour Against Assemblies', he attacked home rule as an unnecessary and costly challenge to the role of local government:

> It is difficult to think of sufficient urgent Scottish legislation on devolved subjects that would justify the full-time activity of 150 Assembly-men in Edinburgh, unless they are to spend a lot of time meddling in what hitherto has been universally agreed to be the business of councillors and local authorities, performing tasks which are better carried out on a local basis.[35]

The SNP were also cautious about what devolution might bring. While the party launched its own 'Yes' offensive, devolution was styled alternately as an end in itself and a step on the road to complete independence. The Tories, meanwhile, embarked on a well-funded 'Scotland Says No' campaign, carefully avoiding the stain of being unpatriotic by claiming they were resisting the model of devolution laid out in the Scotland Act, rather than devolution per se.[36] Yet some of their number – Alick Buchanan Smith, for example – muddied the waters by declaring in favour of home rule. There were also cross-party lobbies, both supporting and opposing devolution, which contributed to making the whole affair a study in chaos and confusion.[37] For a Scottish electorate attuned to recognisable party agendas after sixty years of democratic government, the referendum campaigns uneasily attempted to affirm familiar party identities while pointing the way forward to a new type of Scottish politics. In the end, 52 per cent of the 64 per cent of Scots eligible to vote who braved the inclement weather on the polling day, voted for a devolved Assembly. This represented 33 per cent of the electorate – too little, according to the statistical challenge of the Cunningham amendment, to carry devolution forward.

In Scotland, the fallout from the devolution experiment was immediate. Neal Ascherson (1932–), a reporter on the *Scotsman* in 1979, remembered twenty years later how:

> [t]wo months after the March referendum, the political mail and handouts I received on my desk had shrunk to about a third of the volume of a year before. For many of my friends and colleagues, who had grown used in the last few years to the idea of a bright future for themselves in a self-governing, self-reforming Scotland full of new ideas and initiatives, the world grew too dark to bear. More than I like to count fell into clinical depression or alcoholism, or withdrew into themselves. Many left Scotland for ever.[38]

For those left behind, the future lay in the hands of the Conservatives, as a parliamentary no-confidence motion, supported by the SNP, brought down the Callaghan administration and necessitated an election which installed the first elected mistress of 10 Downing Street in her new London residence.

As discussed elsewhere, the eighteen years of Conservative government that followed clarified the limitations of administrative devolution and refined party policies regarding constitutional change by providing a context within which legal and constitutional distinctions bore heavily on the lived experiences of Scots. Factory closures, rocketing unemployment, welfare cuts, the 'Poll Tax', attempts to privatise water utilities and insensitivity towards Scottish traditions in education and the law distilled the emotive sentiments of the 1970s into clear policy objectives, coherent party programmes and organised cross-party collaboration.

It took some time, however, for the wounds of 1979 to heal and the recriminations to grow faint and certainly, by 1997, Scottish parties did not share identical constitutional objectives. But, after three consecutive election defeats, it was clear that Labour could no longer go it alone in Scotland and through bodies such as the SCC (established in 1989), a new generation of activists joined older campaigners from the seventies to seek the unified voice on devolution that had been absent in 1979 and plan, ahead of time, an agreed constitutional settlement.[39] In a way, they had learned a lesson forecast by Jo Grimond as early as 1976 who said, '[W]e must start with the Scottish people and ask what sort of government they should create. We must not start from Westminster and ask what powers it should delegate.'[40] The SCC borrowed much from the legacy of Conventions that had been called by nationalist groups in the 1920s and 1940s and the Scottish Covenant of 1949 but it operated under very different conditions. In the 1980s, central government was 'implacably hostile' to home rule and 'rather than seeing itself as supplementing the work and authority of Parliament' – as many of the earlier bodies had done – the SCC saw itself as challenging Westminster's authority.[41] In very practical terms, this was a useful strategy for groups whose differences were more evident than their similarities. Attacking Westminster was also a lot easier and less divisive than looking a bit more closely at native bodies whose mere Scottishness was, for the time being, an adequate defence against the grander designs of the Convention. Asserting a concept of popular sovereignty, which it claimed as a Scottish tradition dating back to the Declaration of Arbroath (1320), the SCC drew on the support of the majority of Scotland's MPs, MEPs, Regional and District Councils and the major political parties in the north – excluding the Conservatives and the Scottish Nationalists. It also secured the support of the STUC, the Scottish churches and a variety of prominent cultural and business interest groups.[42] It was civic Scotland in miniature, blended with a few more colourful rogue elements. While some sought an emboldened and inclusive new Scotland, others in the Convention would have been content to simply turn the clock back to the pre-Thatcher years of the 1970s, when established Scottish interests had been allowed more independence from Whitehall. For the latter, greater accountability was the price they had to pay for collective defence of their interests. From past experience, they had little to fear – Westminster, for long enough, had listened to their claims for special treatment. A Scottish Parliament would surely be just as easy to convince, would it not?

It is possible to exaggerate the unity and power of this body in the run-up to the referendum of 1997. After all, its members had major disagreements on the franchise that would elect the new Assembly, for example, and, in the end, it was Westminster that dictated what aspects of the Convention's work would find their way on to the statute book. But its influence was clear in many of the clauses of the Scotland Bill that followed the Referendum in 1998 and the collaborative style of the '97 'Yes' campaign. In two key publications, *Towards Scotland's Parliament*

(1990) and *Scotland's Parliament, Scotland's Right* (1995), it offered the beginnings of a blueprint on which Labour would build after 1997.

Under the umbrella organisation Scotland Forward, the 'Yes' campaign included the Labour, Liberal Democrat and (from July 1997) the Scottish National Parties which, while maintaining their own campaign operations, as a group, co-ordinated their individual activities up and down the country.[43] Devolution was variously styled as efficient and effective, the realisation of long-standing national ambitions, a defence against the recurrence of the traumas of the Thatcher years and an expression of cultural difference. Ceilidhs were held to raise money for the 'Yes' campaign – 'reel with Rothesay and Rowerdennan – jig with Johnston and Jedburgh! Birl with Brora, Ballachulish and Balmoral! Have a hooch in the Highlands,' one pamphlet exhorted.[44] Whisky was bottled to mark the occasion – 'Make mine a double – a double yes in the referendum on September 11th'.[45] And the STUC cautioned:

> REMEMBER . . . how we were treated for nearly 20 years by a Government we didn't elect, stuffing policies we didn't want down our throats – from health service privatisation to water quangos – at an extra cost to the tax payer of one billion pounds.
> REMEMBER . . . the Poll Tax.[46]

By contrast, the Conservative 'Think Twice' campaign was as half-hearted as its ambivalent slogan and lacked both confidence and effective resources on the ground. There were, of course, some campaigners on both sides who refused to toe official party lines but, unlike 1979, these were a very small minority who failed to compromise their party's overall message. Labour's Tam Dalyell, for example, was consistent in his opposition to devolution in both 1979 and 1997. All in all, party members generally voted in line with their party's stance on devolution in 1997 so that there was a more straightforward overlap of party and national loyalties.[47] Given the outcome of the general election that had heralded it, the outcome of the referendum surprised no one, though few could have predicted it even a year before.

As Scotland existed for most of the twentieth century as a nation without a state legislature of its own, one cannot easily mark and measure its politics by the administrations of successive governments. Indeed, Scottish politics throughout the twentieth century were more fluid and resist simple periodisation. However, two dates do stand out – 1979 and 1997. Neither were simple turning points as neither dramatically altered Scottish political culture overnight. But both mark important beginnings and endings and point to trends that changed how Scotland understood itself as both part of the United Kingdom and as a nation in its own right.

'THERE SHALL BE A SCOTTISH PARLIAMENT'

The front-page headline of *The Scotsman* on 6 May 1999, the first polling day for the new Scottish Parliament, screamed 'Scotland makes history'. Below it, a photograph of Dryburgh's statue of William Wallace confirmed the fact that, in reaching forward, the Scots were looking back. This new Parliament was determined to reject the conventions of Westminster but its very self-conscious novelty at times seemed a deliberate claim on history – an attempt to prove that something distinctive, something different, something Scottish, had in the past been silenced and now at last could speak. It was a pity that 40 per cent of the electorate had better things to do than vote that Thursday.

In 1998, a Consultative Steering Group was established to formulate the standing orders and working processes of the Parliament in advance of its birth. Much influenced by the democratic ethos which had guided the SCC, the values it identified as its governing principles were instructive and set the tone for the preparations for devolution:

- the Scottish Parliament should embody and reflect the sharing of power between the people of Scotland, the legislators and the Scottish Executive;
- the Scottish Executive should be accountable to the Scottish Parliament, and the Parliament and Executive should be accountable to the people of Scotland;
- the Scottish Parliament should be accessible, open, responsive and develop procedures which make possible a participative approach to the development, consideration and scrutiny of policy and legislation;
- the Scottish Parliament in its operation and its appointments should recognise the need to promote equal opportunities for all.[48]

In the first year of the new Parliament, novel constitutional features were matched by novel political outcomes but the passions of the first months soon dulled. Day-to-day operations may have borne the mark of history in the early days but were not designed to endlessly make and remake it.

Scotland's place in the 'new-improved' Union which devolution sought to achieve was defined more by what the new Parliament could not do, rather than by what it could. The Scotland Act of 1998 – passed *following* the referendum, unlike in 1979 – defined the powers retained by Westminster rather than those devolved to Holyrood and left areas of dispute to the respective governments and their legal officers to resolve. Much was left unsaid and, for all the Act's prescriptive content in other areas, in the end, 'convention' – that much prized and most ambiguous of traditional British constitutional features – would largely determine when Westminster could legitimately override the legislative competence of the new Parliament in some contested areas.[49] Popular sovereignty clearly did not make major inroads into the relationships between the Union's component nations – the sovereignty of Westminster was enshrined in the Scotland Act.

More innovative, however, was the new system of proportional representation – which was originally designed by the SCC – the Committee structure of the Parliament and the working practices of the MSPs. The Scottish Parliament was composed of 129 members, seventy-three of whom were elected through the FPTP system and fifty-six through eight regional lists. It was a system that almost guaranteed coalition or minority administrations and placed a premium on collaborative inter-party practices. In 1999, it yielded the Labour–Lib Dem coalition, a phenomenon largely unknown in peacetime Britain and still described as a 'delicate flower' after one year in office.[50] The Committee Structure of the new Parliament placed further emphasis on a non-combative style of approach – eight subject committees were established to reflect the new departments of the Executive[51] and eight mandatory committees covered Subordinate Legislation, Europe, Equal Opportunities, Finance, Audit, Procedures, Standards and Public Petitions. These were to be the motor of a new politics.[52] The Committees combined the duties typical of both the select and standing committees of the Westminster model. In other words, they both scrutinised the conduct of the government and considered new legislative proposals.[53] Without a second chamber to revise bills, the Committees were of critical importance and, as a less public forum for debate, party rivalries proved less of an impediment to effective parliamentary practice. In the first year of the Parliament, the Committees generated sizeable workloads for MSPs and experienced a few teething troubles but, as time passed, they were to grow in authority and confidence. For the MSPs themselves, business hours of work generally encouraged a workman-like approach to government – late-night sittings were ruled out in the new Parliament which sought a more family-friendly approach to representative office. Gone also were the 'Honourable' titles of the Commons and other colourful yet costly ceremonial. In many ways, this really was a departure from the old – Scots making history by refusing to follow precedent. But did such operational practices really deliver anything more than a rather unimaginative common-sense approach to getting things done? The first session of the new Parliament was described by David Steel as 'a pale imitation of Westminster'.[54]

New structures, nevertheless, could deliver controversial outcomes. The role of women in Scottish politics was greatly enhanced by their participation in the new Parliament and, as a consequence of proportional representation (PR), many small parties came to be represented in a legislative Assembly for the first time.

For most of the twentieth century, female participation in politics in Scotland had been largely out of public view, concentrated in pressure group activities and support roles in the major parties or else focused on the arena of local government. Yet Scottish women had been deeply involved in the female suffrage campaigns at the turn of the century.[55] Edinburgh, Glasgow and Dundee had all been influential centres for suffragette activity and 'Scots wha Hae wi Wallace Bled' was a rousing song for militants, even though one of their number, Ethel Moorhead, actually smashed a glass case containing the Wallace Sword housed in Stirling's Wallace Monument in September 1912 as part of a campaign of militant activities.[56] Nevertheless, between 1945 and 1992, only seven women at most had represented Scottish constituencies in the course of a parliamentary session and, in 1979 – over fifty years since female emancipation had been secured on the same terms as men – there was only one female Scottish MP.[57] In local government, things were slightly better – around 20 per cent of councillors were female in the 1990s – but, by European standards, female representation in Scotland was poor.[58] By contrast, forty-eight women MSPs – 37 per cent of all MSPs – entered the Parliament on the Mound in 1999. This was well short of the 50 per cent many women's campaigners had desired but a point had been made.[59] Equal representation had been a major focus of debate in the SCC but, in the end, the individual parties had either adopted contrasting means to ensure greater female participation or had refused to get involved in any positive discriminatory practices at all – the Scottish Conservatives, for example. Only the Labour Party managed to achieve equal representation of men and women among their MSPs in the Parliament's first session although, in its first ministerial team, less than a quarter of the offices went to women. High expectations that greater female involvement in parliamentary business would underpin the more consensual aspirations of the Parliament's founders remain the focus of debate – a distinctively 'female' approach to government certainly failed to evolve in the first year at least. Nevertheless, the new structures of government and the values that underpinned them had created a forum in which the female voice would be heard louder than before. Other under-represented groups in Scottish politics, however, could not boast the same influence – for example, the Scottish Parliament in 1999 was an all-white affair.[60]

For the smaller parties, proportional representation opened the door to parliamentary participation. The Green Party and the Scottish Socialist Party (SSP) are cases in point. In 1999, Robin Harper (1940–) in the Lothians secured 22,848 votes for the Scottish Greens to win a seat in the Parliament. Over the next few years, he styled his role as that of the 'green conscience' of the Parliament and benefited from the more consensual approach to Committee operations by becoming the first chairperson of the Transport and Environment Committee – an important lever for such a small party. Meanwhile, in the west, Tommy Sheridan (1964–), having finished in third place in the Pollok constituency in 1999, attracted 18,581 votes in the Glasgow region for the SSP and became his Party's first MSP. Sheridan had risen to prominence during the anti-Poll Tax disturbances and sought to align his party with the long lineage of radical protest in Scotland which he felt Labour had abandoned.[61] He recounted:

> From draughty village halls in remote corners of the Highlands to fortified community centres in run-down city housing schemes, I had travelled thousands of miles and spoken to thousands of people. Socialism is supposed to be dead and buried with its ashes scattered to the four winds. Yet people were turning out in droves to these meetings, not to discuss some immediate pressing issue that affected their everyday lives, but to hear the general case for a socialist Scotland.[62]

Both Harper and Sheridan made effective use of the Parliament's liberal facilities for private members' bills and, as was confirmed in 2003, started a trend in politics that threatened the stranglehold of the major parties in areas and among groups that felt increasingly out of touch with traditional party politics. Seven Green and six SSP MSPs were elected in that year, not to mention two independents and two further fringe candidates.[63]

Yet, seven months after the opening of the Parliament, Murray Ritchie (1941–), *The Herald*'s Scottish political editor, observed a growing cynicism in Scotland toward the new legislature. '[T]here is something peculiarly Scottish about the eagerness of a sullen minority to discredit the new order,' he recorded.[64] After a year, verdicts on the Parliament were mixed. Legislative activity on Scottish issues had clearly increased – in the first term of the Scottish Parliament, sixteen Acts were passed, compared to an average of six per term at Westminster between 1979 and 1999.[65] Distinctive policy outcomes had also been achieved in education – Scottish students studying in Scottish universities, from the academic session 2000–2001, would no longer pay tuition fees and the Parliament had adopted a more liberal line on educating Scottish pupils on homosexuality than was the case in England and Wales, which, of course, now boasted its own devolved Assembly. But the Executive appeared inept in its handling of errors in examination marking and certification endorsed by the Scottish Qualifications Authority in the autumn of 2000 and the enfolding crisis drew attention to persistent problems of accountability in Scottish governmental agencies that had not been resolved through the process of devolution.[66] Dewar's sacking of his Policy Unit's chief-of-staff attracted further bad publicity and the reputation of Scottish politics in general suffered as a result of what came to be known as 'Lobbygate' – allegations surrounding the working practices of the son of the Secretary of State for Scotland, Dr John Reid (1947–).[67]

Disillusionment was common – polls recorded more than 50 per cent agreement among Scots that 'it doesn't really matter who is in power' and journalists bemoaned the low calibre of the new political class.[68] Early on, partisanship had obstructed the speedy realisation of a 'new politics'. David Simpson (1926–), successful electronics entrepreneur and founding director of the Fraser of Allander Institute at the University of Strathclyde, regretted that the politics of the 'general good' had soon been defeated by the 'self-serving behaviour of a majority of MSPs'.[69] And an audit of the first year of the Scottish Parliament indicated that 'the centrality of political party involvement and competition within the Parliament has ensured a more adversarial, less consensual Parliament than was suggested by some of the more idealistic rhetoric of the "new politics" '.[70] There were also signs that the 'new order' would be as keen to defend old interests as the Scottish Office had been. The voice of civil Scotland tended to dominate Committee business, just as it had guided Scottish Office ministers, and established public-sector interests remained the principal point of contact between the Parliament and the wider public when it came to consultation. This led many to suspect that 'the institutional elite dominance of Scottish public life has, in fact, become more pronounced under devolution'.[71]

Tragedy exacerbated the problems of the infant Parliament when, in October 2000, Donald Dewar, Scotland's First Minister and the principal architect of the new constitutional environment, died suddenly.[72] Scotland lost an experienced politician and a man whose integrity had grounded the Parliament in something more solid than an uneasy consensus. Neither his successor, Henry McLeish (1948–), who left office in November 2001 under the shadow of alleged financial irregularities in his constituency affairs, nor Jack McConnell (1960–), who followed after, was of Dewar's calibre or boasted his experience. What is more, the high turnover of ministers and special advisors such changes necessitated merely created further instability.[73]

The founding principles of the Parliament had relied overwhelmingly on collective sentiments and said little or nothing about leadership. It was an omission that the Parliament now felt acutely. Many would have agreed with Naomi Mitchison that:

> Scotland will need to be led,
> But never by one man only,
> of whatever wrongs a righter:
> Not that for any excuse!
> Those days are dead,
> Dead with Wallace and Bruce.[74]

But time had not been on Scotland's side – a new politics was yet to be fully formed and the Parliament, taking its first steps to maturity, had lost the 'Father of the Nation'. Leadership was at a premium but there was no consensus on preferred style and substance and there were few successful models in modern Scottish politics to follow.

The Scottish Parliament of 1999 was not the resumption of the old Scottish Parliament, the expression of a century committed to devolution or a predictable consequence of democracy's strained accommodation within the Union. It was, rather, a pragmatic response to a particular set of circumstances that owed much to familiar Scottish claims for 'special treatment', to trends across the UK as a whole and to foreign models of devolved governance – Catalonia and Quebec, for example – in a postmodern age.[75] Constitutional change, by its very gravity, encourages analyses more rooted in high-sounding principles than party. Yet, even taking the most charitable perspective, constitutional motivations tend to be more pedestrian (and less principled) than one would suppose. In Scotland, the constitutional question has been manipulated by party interests for centuries – devolution is merely the most recent chapter in a very long story and most probably not the happily-ever-after that its architects hoped it would be. Rather, devolution left to the future many dilemmas rooted in Scotland's Union relationships and further confused the country's role outwith the bounds of the British Isles. In the Parliament, Scotland was no longer 'an imagined community' but a material political entity and, through it, Scotland both shaped and was shaped by its citizens. Scottish politics, however, remain bigger than the Parliament itself. We must be cautious not to create a convenient fiction that equates what goes on in the Parliament with the *real* politics of Scotland, while judging that which happens outwith its chambers to be but a peripheral concern.

With the Parliament won, the political consensus that heralded it was soon no longer the priority it once was. In a way, the logic of parliamentary government necessitates the undoing of such consensus. It is too early to judge whether, as a consequence, Scottish politics will ever prove able to realise the 'timeless values [and] honourable aspirations' – 'Wisdom. Justice. Compassion. Integrity.' – which, on 1 July 1999, the First Minister set as the Parliament's ultimate test.

Conclusion

Roch the wind in the clear day's dawin
Blaws the cloods heelster-gowdie owre the bay
But there's mair nor a roch wind blawin
Through the great glen o' the warld the day
                          'The Freedom Come Aa Ye'
                          Hamish Henderson (1919–2002)

In the course of the twentieth century, politics in Scotland seldom
matched the poetic imagination of the nation's makars (poets). Local
government became increasingly distant from local communities despite
an emerging rhetoric of participative democracy that sought to trans-
plant unfashionable notions of service. Try as it might, it would never
recreate the intimacy of parish government. In the century's dying
moments, a devolved Parliament provided the forum in which the claims
on which it rested would be debated but it did not ensure that a new
politics more fitting Scotland's traditions and aspirations would emerge
or that Scots shared a common understanding of these. Throughout,
Westminster remained the ultimate prize and, for much of the century,
Scots were over-represented in this legislature. Through the Scottish
Office, Scotland was also the only British nation that occupied a seat in
cabinet although, even among those whom this suited, few could often
muster a rationale for this beyond immediate self-interest.[1] Claims to
colonial status are therefore hard to sustain, as are excuses as to why
such influence was not more skilfully exploited by the very civil institutions that claimed to defend much that was distinctive in Scotland's
political culture. Europe offered some the prospect of a new political
environment in which an 'instinct for freedom' might one day be realised
but such freedom would only come at a cost. Few Scots were willing to
trade the familiarity of the Union relationship for the uncertain promise
of new continental alliances. Indeed, it pays to be reminded that, even
in the twentieth century, Scotland's role in the Union state was just as

significant and more tangible a feature of the nation's history and identity than more romantic claims on its sympathies. In 2000, many Scots still awaited the realisation of Hamish Henderson's vision, 'Freedom Come Aa Ye', but, for the time being, rested comfortably in the embrace of an enduring constitutional compromise.

PART FOUR

Cultural Extremes

Prologue

As a rule, for most of the twentieth century, the Scottish cultural elite – or perhaps those who shouted loudest – generally regretted the impact of the Reformation on the development of Scottish culture and identified the Presbyterian tradition as a brake on the Scottish imagination. Writing in 1927, Christopher Grieve (he was yet to transform himself as Hugh MacDiarmid) was damning:

> There has been no religious poetry – no expression of 'divine philosophy' – in Scotland since the Reformation. As a consequence Scotland today is singularly destitute of aesthetic consciousness. The line of hope lies partially in re-Catholicisation, partially in the exhaustion of Protestantism.[1]

In a rare coalescence of opinion, MacDiarmid's erstwhile adversary, Edwin Muir, was similarly sceptical about the impact of the Reformation on Scottish creative talents and, in the novels of the 1920s, the Reformed Church was regularly depicted as being 'the lethal antagonist of Celtic tradition' and an inhibitory influence on the development of the individual.[2] Even those supportive of the reforming impulse regretted its destruction of a deeper Celtic spirit – the artist J. D. Fergusson (1874–1961), for example, attacked the misuse of Calvinist principles that had detached Scotland from *l'esprit Gaulois* that could have nurtured its art as part of a wider European tradition.[3] In 2000, little appeared to have changed as the novelist Andrew O' Hagan (1968–) noted that the 'dominant culture, whether it means it or not, whether it chooses to see it or not, is washed and dried in Protestant values, and the depredations of Calvinism on Scottish art are evident to this very hour'.[4]

For good or ill, the influence of the reformed tradition on Scottish culture provided many of the characteristics from which the arts in the twentieth century derived their identity as expressions of a national imagination. In literature, the central role that fear played in many well-known novels – James Barke's *Land of the Leal* (1939) is a case in point – has been identified by Cairns Craig as being directly connected to Scotland's Calvinist legacy. Religion also seemed to make Scottish authors more comfortable exponents of certain genres. In this regard, crime fiction, engaging with issues of justice and punishment, and the gothic, exploring society's darkest imaginings, spring to mind. Indeed, the formative impulse of Calvinism, according to Duncan Petrie, was most powerfully evidenced in Scottish writers' 'indigenous Gothic impulse'.[5] In modern Scottish art, an emphasis on figurative work has been interpreted as symptomatic of the emphasis in Protestant theology on the individual.[6] And in music, the works of Peter Maxwell Davies (1934–), through the incorporation of church music with songs from the local folk canon, explored the impact of reformed religion on Orcadian traditions and the resulting conflict between piety and paganism.[7] Similarly, William Sweeney's musical interpretation of the verse of Aonghas Macneacail – 'salm an fhearainn' – relied heavily on the stark simplicity of traditional psalm tunes.[8]

In all genres, it seems that, four hundred years on, the artistic imagination bore the indelible mark of the Reformation. But more than this, as Cairns Craig has noted, there was a tendency in twentieth-century Scottish writers to view the imagination itself in metaphysical terms, as a 'diabolic antagonist rather than spiritual representative' of divine truths.[9] The relationship was no less productive for all that but the creative impulse certainly appeared more straightforward for those without this inherent tension with their muse. Would the arts in Scotland have been more pregnant with promise had religion helped rather than hindered artistic conception? We will never know. They would certainly have been different. The contemporary Scottish poet, Robert Crawford (1959–), however, offers an alternative insight into this uneasy alliance. He identifies the iconoclasm of the Protestant faith as 'an important impulse within modern creative processes' and denies the claims of Whiggish commentators that the Church necessarily inhibited engagement with the arts.[10] In sum, the reformed religion was (or was at times) empowering for modern artists by emphasising the direct personal connection of the individual with God – or, at least, a greater being – and its very origins suggested a critical discontent with the world that, in turn, encouraged an aspirational outlook and a very immediate engagement with 'big ideas'. Thus, religion was both one way of engaging with national identity and a principal reason for rejecting conventional renderings of the nation itself. In the imagination, Scotland could always be both better and worse than it really was. In this realm, the influence of extremes was profound.

ELEVEN

Columba to Carfin – Scottish
Christianity

Iona of my heart, Iona of
my love,
Instead of monks' voices there
shall be lowing of cattle
But ere the world comes to
an end
Iona shall be as it was.

Attributed to St Columba[1]

Here, in one of the most
hideous stretches of countryside in an industrial region
festering with poverty and
unemployment, a flourishing
shrine has grown up in a few
years.

Edwin Muir[2]

In the years of peace which were little more than a repose between
conflicts, Father Thomas Taylor (1873–1963), Carfin, and Rev. George
MacLeod (1895–1991), Govan, initiated ventures which would create
sites of pilgrimage for the Scots of the twentieth century. One a Marian
shrine in industrial Lanarkshire, the other a picturesque island Abbey
with roots in a Columban monastery dating from the seventh century,
they both bore the marks of their birth or rebirth in the Depression
years. The hands of unemployed workmen erected these monuments to
faith and hope through the 'Fellowship of Labour' during a time when
both were in short supply.[3] In the 1920s, many fellow Scots were sceptical about the primacy of the spirit when life itself seemed little more
than a game of chance.

Yet it is strangely fitting that the development of the Carfin site,
modelled on the Grotto at Lourdes, actually benefited from the economic
tensions of the twenties, as striking miners married collective effort with
individual religious commitment to complete the grotto in time for the
feast day of Our Lady of the Rosary in October 1922. This was, in many
ways, a memorial to the power of human devotion rather than the
outcome of divine intervention – Father Taylor eschewed any temptation
to associate the site with apparitions or supernatural occurrences.[4]
Nevertheless, it would not be long before rumours of the healing powers
of the waters of the grotto's Mary Well circulated. In 1923, Mrs Holmes,

a Coatbridge resident, was said to have been cured of her rheumatoid arthritis and, in 1934, Mary Traynor of Chapelhall found relief from a variety of maladies after taking the waters and being blessed with a relic of St Thérèse.[5] But Presbyterian Scotland was uncomfortable with such modern miracles despite the fact that even desperate Protestants were seeking solace at Carfin's shrines. Rose bushes adorning the garden of the statue of the 'Little Flower', for example, were gifted by a grateful Protestant family whose child had recovered from a serious illness.[6] As Edwin Muir noted, Carfin 'was part of a world of which most of Scotland [knew] nothing'.[7] Carfin was part of a European Catholic tradition that was stubbornly resisted by most Scots who preferred their miracles reassuringly bound by the leather covers of family bibles, and its emergence on Scottish soil was sufficient to fuel age-old suspicions. In June 1924, a planned Eucharistic procession in Carfin was prohibited when it was proposed that processing clerics in vestments could be threatened with fines and prison sentences under an Act of 1829. It took two years for this legislation to be reformed.[8] Scottish Roman Catholics had no choice but to engage with the prejudices of the society around them – for them, to be in the world was to be of it. Even Carfin offered no escape.

In May 1939, *The Coracle*, the journal of the Iona Community, struggled to establish Iona's place in this religious environment that seemed most comfortable with the straightforward oppositions of the sixteenth century. It emphasised that the Community 'is not a return to Rome ... is not a pacifist Community ... is not a visionary movement ... and ... is not a one-man enterprise!'[9] Yet, five years later, in the midst of 'Total War', George MacLeod felt compelled to make the case again:

> [O]ur movement is not an attempt to reassert Romanist devices or imitate nineteenth-century Anglican ways ... [Rather] the Iona Community is ... a small assertion of the full intended Catholic recovery of the Reformers, which our Church has largely lost.[10]

As politicians spoke of reconstruction, MacLeod sought recovery. It was to be as 'loyal children of the Reformation' that the Community's members sought to rebuild the Abbey and re-awaken the latent influence of the Celtic Church in the everyday life of the Church of Scotland. But, as Taylor had found at Carfin, suspicions were hard to break down.

In 1938 George MacLeod, having bypassed the conservative reservations of the Kirk's General Assembly and having received a £5,000 donation from Sir James Lithgow, Scotland's pre-eminent battleship manufacturer, set about the restoration of the Iona Abbey complex with a group of young ministers and unemployed craftsmen. Dressed in blue serge suits, their days were structured with military precision and combined the sweat of hard labour with the discipline of regular worship.[11] After three months on the island, ministers would embark on mission work in the challenging circumstances of inner-city parishes and be replaced by a new cohort who, on the island, sought modern solutions to contemporary social ills in ancient surroundings while practising the sacraments with a regularity that appeared positively excessive (if not heretical) to many in the General Assembly.

Yet the community was not, in many ways, the radical departure from restrictive social conventions that conservatives claimed. The original members were all bachelors and married male members were not permitted to bring their wives to the island until 1970. Meanwhile, women were not admitted to full membership until 1969. The Community also eventually arrived at an understanding with the General Assembly when, in 1951, the joint Iona Community Board was established. MacLeod himself eventually became Moderator of the General Assembly in 1957 and, a decade later, the Celtic visionary was raised to the peerage as Lord MacLeod of Fuinary.

Both the Carfin Grotto and the Iona Community highlight the importance of both collective and personal expressions of faith in Scotland during the 'secular century' and encourage us to examine both institutional and individual responses to religion. Yet they also emphasise the weight of the past in the lives of modern Scottish Christians – both were novel responses to the challenges of the interwar years and struggled to find their place in the religious environment of the times but both rested on historical understandings of faith. Taylor and MacLeod sought to distil the essence of their belief and harness the legacy of a past and a Christian community (whether of saints or Celtic monks) that, in comparison to their own times, seemed closer to God. Carfin reminded Scots of their Catholic inheritance while Iona reached further back to the Celtic Church. But Iona was not 'as it was'.

Edwardian Scotland recorded high levels of church attendance and membership and, during the Great War, the churches' support for the war effort coincided with a rise in church membership. Church of Scotland membership rose by 1.3 per cent between 1913 and 1918 and United Free Church membership by 3.3 per cent over the same period.[12] Thereafter, as historian Callum Brown has highlighted, 'despite the economic dislocation and high unemployment of both the 1920s and 1930s, adult Protestant Church connection only fell slightly overall'.[13]

Yet some, even in these years, identified worrying portents of the future. John Buchan (1875–1940), author and Unionist MP, lamented that, in the two foremost Presbyterian Churches, membership encompassed less than half the Scottish population and, between them, there were '200 congregations with less than 50 members and nearly 500 with less than a hundred each'.[14]

In the 1950s, the Church of Scotland, the Methodist Church, the United Free Church and the Scottish Episcopal Church reached peaks in membership and, in comparison to England and Wales, church membership in Scotland remained more pronounced – while 22.9 per cent of the population of the southern nations were church members, in Scotland the figure was 57.8 per cent in 1950.[15] A decade hence, however, decline had become particularly acute.[16] The Church of Scotland, the Congregational Union, and the Baptist and Episcopal Churches began to experience serious problems in the late 1950s.[17] By 1960, only 26 per cent of the adult population of Scotland regularly attended church services and this number included a mere 22.8 per cent of Church of Scotland members.[18] Between 1961 and 1990, the number of baptisms in the Church of Scotland fell from 51,767 to 17,164 and similarly, between 1956 and 1994, the number of children enrolled in Church of Scotland Sunday Schools declined from 325,200 to 60,936.[19] By 1994, Church of Scotland membership stood at only 717,930 and, in 2002, the Church of Scotland alone owned over 1,000 redundant buildings – many of them churches.[20]

For the Roman Catholic Church, decline came later. In the sixties and seventies, the baptised Catholic constituency at times exceeded 800,000 – in Clydebank alone, the Catholic population of the burgh increased sixteenfold between 1900 and 1960.[21] But, by 1995, Roman Catholic Church 'membership' stood at 743,000[22] and, on the day of the 1994 Church Census, Roman Catholic attendance at Mass totalled only 245,990.[23]

All major churches seemed to be losing their young – in both the Church of Scotland and the Roman Catholic Church declining child attendance patterns were evident. Between 1990 and 1994, 74 per cent of the decline recorded in attendance in the Church of Scotland could be accounted for by a drop in numbers of children and 32 per cent of the decline in the Roman Catholic Church could be explained by a loss of children in the congregations.[24]

Declining church engagement seemed to confirm the victory of secularisation in an increasingly cynical, post-industrial age. But it was a far from linear process and neither was its momentum unrelenting. Declining church attendance came relatively late to Scotland, long after the process of urbanisation with which this trend is often closely associated.[25] And church decline was not uniform in its geographical concentration or in the manner

'It cam wi a lass . . .': Margaret Thatcher with Scottish Conservative MPs in Perth, 1979. By 1997 the haemorrhage of Conservative support was reflected in abysmal election results that yielded no Tory MPs north of the Tweed. © The Scotsman Publications Ltd. Licensor www.scran.ac.uk

Michael Forsyth, in his second period in office as Secretary of State for Scotland in the mid-1990s, demonstrates some of the symbolic consequences of Scottish separatism, namely, a Union flag bereft of Saltire. © Scottish media Newspapers Ltd. Licensor www.scran.ac.uk

Above. **Looking for Messiah:** The debris of a trade union rally rests on the walls of the Usher Hall in 1974, partly obscuring publicity for Handel's Messiah. © The Scotsman Publications Ltd. Licensor www.scran.ac.uk

Right. **Political apprenticeship:** Gordon Brown, the future Prime Minister, was an active student politician and was elected rector of Edinburgh University in 1972. University-educated and a son of the manse, he was one of a promising generation in Scottish Labour politics who had not, like many before them, emerged from the trade union movement, but who rose to prominence during the party's years in opposition after 1979. © The Scotsman Publications Ltd. Licensor www.scran.ac.uk

A brush with destiny: Glasgow University students masterminded the theft of the Stone of Destiny in December 1950 from Westminster Abbey. The stone was eventually 'returned' to Arbroath Abbey, as seen here, after weeks of a well-publicised national search. © Newsquest (Herald & Times). Licensor www.scran.ac.uk

The Royal Mail: Postboxes bearing the EⁱⁱR cipher, such as this one in the Inch Housing Estate, were attacked in 1953 – the coronation year. Anger was aroused because the new monarch's formal title failed to reflect that she was in fact only the first Queen Elizabeth of the United Kingdom. © The Scotsman Publications Ltd. Licensor www.scran.ac.uk

Above. **'The Long Goodbye':**
After the Conservative victory
at the 1992 general election, a
group of campaigners kept a
vigil on Calton Hill in
confident anticipation of the
successful achievement of
devolution . . . eventually.
© National Museums Scotland.
Licensor www.scran.ac.uk

Right. **Yes Yes No No:** The
referendum of 1997 recorded
the electorate's support for
devolution and tax-raising
powers for a new parliament,
and was witness to some
colourful campaigning.
© Colin McPherson. Licensor
www.scran.ac.uk

The First Scottish Cabinet, 1999: In 1999 Donald Dewar (front, centre) became Scotland's first First Minister of a Coalition administration. His Deputy was Jim Wallace of the Liberal Democratic Party (back row, left).
© The Scottish Executive. Licensor www.scran.ac.uk

In the minority? The SNP's Alex Salmond became the first First Minister of the Scottish Parliament not to emerge from the Labour fold when he took office in 2007 as the leader of a minority administration pledged to a referendum on the question of Scottish independence. © David Black. Licensor www.scran.ac.uk

Right. **A waning force:** An Orange rally at Kelvingrove Park (Glasgow) in 1980 is reminded of the religious roots and obligations of the movement. By the end of the century the working-class protestant vote no longer held much promise for the Conservative Party. © The Scotsman Publications Ltd. Licensor www.scran.ac.uk

Below. **Remember the Sabbath Day . . .:** In 1965 Rev. Angus Smith was carried off by the police, having led a demonstration against the introduction of a Sunday ferry service. © Newsquest (Herald & Times). Licensor www.scran.ac.uk

Above. **Lord of the Isle:** Lord MacLeod of Fuinary maintained his activism for social justice into later life. He is most famous – as Rev. George MacLeod, Govan – as the founder of the Iona Community. © The Scotsman Publications Ltd. Licensor www.scran.ac.uk

Left. **Father Taylor's Mission:** The Carfin Grotto owed much to Father Thomas Taylor, the local priest, who modelled Scotland's very modern site of pilgrimage on the Shrine of Our Lady of Lourdes. Here weary pilgrims rest at the feet of St Pius in 2004. © Gerry McCann. Licensor www.scran.ac.uk

Right. **Portrait of George Douglas Brown by William Strang:** Brown's novel *The House with the Green Shutters* (1901) exposed the darker side of rural life neglected in the Kailyard literature that was popular at the time. © Scottish National Portrait Library. Licensor www.scran.ac.uk

Below. **Image and reality:** Hugh MacDiarmid, leader of the Scottish Renaissance in the arts in the inter-war years, and Scottish nationalist. © The Scotsman Publications Ltd. Licensor www.scran.ac.uk

Below. **Look Left:** James Kelman, Alasdair Gray and Tom Leonard exemplify the quality and variety of late twentieth-century Scottish literature. © Gerry McCann. Licensor www.scran.ac.uk

The bardic tradition: Somhairle MacGill-Eain (Sorley MacLean), seen here in 1991, was the leading figure in bringing Gaelic verse into the vanguard of modern Scottish poetry. © Roddy Simpson. Licensor www.scran.ac.uk

'I am someone who is very interested in colour . . . bright colour, gay colour': Anne Redpath, artist, was a well-known figure of the 'Edinburgh School' of the inter-war years. © The Scotsman Publications Ltd. Licensor www.scran.ac.uk

A very modern chronicler: Hamish Henderson was to the forefront in early efforts to record and conserve the Scottish folk tradition. Here he is recording Ailidh Dall in 1958. He himself was a talented makar in his own right. © The School of Scottish Studies. Licensor www.scran.ac.uk

The boy band phenomenon is a thoroughly modern Scottish 'first'. The Bay City Rollers' effect on young female fans in the 1970s finds a ready echo in the boy bands of the final decades of the century. The tartan 'thing' is harder to explain. © Scottish Media Newspapers Ltd. Licensor www.scran.ac.uk

First and last among minstrels: Sir Harry Lauder, seen here rehearsing at Glasgow's Alhambra in 1930, was a music hall artist with a global reach whose songs provide an evocative soundtrack to the events and attitudes of the first decades of the twentieth century. © The Scotsman Publications Ltd. Licensor www.scran.ac.uk

A Festival first!: Tyrone Guthrie's adaptation of *Ane Satyre of the Threi Estatis* was staged during the second Edinburgh International Festival in 1948 to much public and critical acclaim. © Scottish Theatre Archive. Licensor www.scran.ac.uk

Left. '**I always liked the pictures**': An innovative and sensitive director, Bill Douglas blended biographical, dramatic and documentary styles to powerful effect in his *Trilogy* in the 1970s. © The Scotsman Publications Ltd. Licensor www.scran.ac.uk

Below. **The first DG:** Sir John Reith of Stonehaven, shown here in a portrait by Sir Oswald Birley dating from 1933, was the BBC's first Director General. © Scottish National Portrait Gallery. Licensor www.scran.ac.uk

Above. **Slamannan Bluebell Football Club, 1900:** Scotland's amateur football tradition survived the century but failed to maintain the popularity it had attracted in the opening decades. © Falkirk Museums. Licensor www.scran.ac.uk

Right. **Home Internationals:** Scotland–England games were among the most eagerly anticipated fixtures of the sporting year throughout the twentieth century. Here Matt Busby leads out the Scotland team, while the English side is captained by Joe Mercer. © Newsquest (Herald & Times). Licensor www.scran.ac.uk

Above. **Not all football . . . :** Curling was popular in the Lothians and, as this photograph of Inveresk shows, it was a sport in which both men and women regularly participated, although not always at the same time. © Grier Collection, East Lothian Library Service. Licensor www.scran.ac.uk

Left. **Glasgow Central, Glasgow Fair:** Paul Flannigan sits on his luggage while waiting to go on holiday. Like many Scottish holiday makers until the 1960s, he travelled by train to his holiday destination. © The Scotsman Publications Ltd. Licensor www.scran.ac.uk

Crossing the Border: Road and rail signs marked the line of the English–Scottish border in a variety of colourful and definitive ways. © The Scotsman Publications Ltd. Licensor www.scran.ac.uk

in which it affected the various denominations. At the end of the century, the Church of Scotland retained a high profile in the Western Isles, where one adult in eleven was a practising member, but was weak in the cities of Aberdeen, Dundee and Glasgow, where only 5 per cent of the adult population attended its churches.[26] The Episcopal Church, meanwhile, remained strong in the Borders and in Edinburgh but was weakest in the area covered by Strathclyde Region, where the Roman Catholic Church proved strongest. In Motherwell and Monklands, for example, nearly 17 per cent of the population attended Mass on Sunday in the mid 1990s.[27]

Differences were evident also in the gender, age and class composition of the denominations. In 1994, 28,000 fewer men were recorded by the churches in comparison to 1984 and, while male attendance at Mass remained higher than that at the weekly Protestant services, men still only represented 43 per cent of Roman Catholic congregations. The church-going population in Scotland was also overwhelmingly biased towards the over-thirties as the churches failed to keep awkward adolescents in the pews.[28] It was a problem that had been evident early in the century – in 1929, the United Free Church, for example, drew attention to the 'serious situation caused by the lapsing of adolescent boys and girls from regular religious instruction'.[29] Thereafter, things only got worse. Roughly speaking, of the 115,150 teenagers between ten and nineteen years who attended church in 1984, only 59,710 remained in 1994 – a haemorrhage of 48 per cent.[30]

Evidence would also suggest that the Church of Scotland attracted more members from professional and skilled worker groups than the Roman Catholic Church.[31] This was clearly a by-product of the ethos of evangelical respectability that had marked Presbyterian communities in the nineteenth century and the relative social disadvantage of Catholic immigrant groups that had established themselves in Scotland at the same time. Yet the persistence of such social distinctions speaks volumes about how slowly the churches kept pace with the changing social environments within which they operated. As Sissons reflected in the 1970s, 'It is the social world of the Church of Scotland which is both its strength and its weakness.'[32]

Over the course of the century, popular culture evidenced the declining role of the church in the lives of the Scottish population as a whole – sabbatarianism became less pronounced, styles of worship lost their distinctive qualities and the associational and material culture of the churches lost much of its social influence.

At the start of the twentieth century, the arrival of the Sabbath (Sunday) was heralded by distinctive sights and sounds – 'the rustle of Sabbath gowns and the squeak and tip tap of new shoes filled the streets'.[33] For most young Presbyterian Scots, the call to worship was almost compulsory, though often sweetened by parental customs. Alec Cairncross's experience is near to typical in this regard.

> Every Sunday we set out at 10.50am and took our seats in the backmost pew. My father, equipped with a 'poke' of imperial mints which he sucked along with the sermon, counted the attendance and reported the same at lunch.[34]

So confident were clerical interests at mid century of Scotland continuing to keep the Lord's Day holy that it was considered unnecessary to include the northern nation in the provisions of the Shops Act of 1950 that restricted Sunday opening.[35] But six years earlier, George MacLeod had already introduced a note of caution, declaring quite simply that 'sabbatarianism is dead'.[36] The first Sunday newspapers had been sold on Scotland's streets during the First World War and, during the Second World War, restrictions on the Sunday opening of theatres and cinemas had been lifted. Sporting competitions regularly took place on Sundays by the second half of the century and licensing laws were also liberalised. As an increasingly affluent society sought new ways of spending its wealth, traders responded by extending shop hours and, between 1977 and 1988, there was a fourfold increase in the proportion of shops trading on Sundays – that is from 12.5 per cent to 49 per cent.[37] Nevertheless, Sunday remained 'special' – a day set apart from the rest of the week. Like previous generations, it was a day marked by family traditions – a Sunday roast was still enjoyed by a large proportion of the population as late as the 1980s.[38] But, for most, church services no longer punctuated the day of rest.[39]

Whether because or in spite of falling attendances, inside the churches, things were changing. Baptismal fonts made their first appearance in many Presbyterian churches in the interwar years as older practices of baptism at home declined; it became increasingly common for Presbyterian congregations to say the Lord's prayer together, though many traditionalists sat in stubborn silence; communion cups replaced the shared chalice in the interests of hygiene and efficiency in many Protestant churches; and, in the Catholic Church, fasting before Communion, which was now typically delivered in English rather than Latin, was relaxed.[40]

Theology, on occasion, was also made to bow before sentiment and modern demands in a way it had seldom done in the past. During the First World War, high Scottish casualties – estimates vary between

74,000 and 110,000 – and the grief of a nation encouraged some Scottish Presbyterian clergymen to offer prayers for the dead and preach sermons which came dangerously close to suggesting that death in battle ensured salvation.[41] In the years that followed, similar attempts to reconcile public sentiment, clerical traditions and calls for reform were marked in the most influential publications of the Church of Scotland. The process encouraged the church to reflect on the core principles of its faith but also brought to light tensions between the various traditions that made up the church which appeared anachronistic – the final remnants of debates that, even in the late nineteenth century, were going out of fashion. The 1940 *Book of Common Order*, like earlier editions, detailed suggested forms of worship and the conduct of the sacraments but departed from established practice by drawing explicitly on a wide heritage of devotional literature and increasing the materials available for the different seasons of the Christian year.[42] It was controversial. The National Church Association complained that the 'whole atmosphere of the book is too liturgical . . . alien to the tradition of the Reformed Church in general and to the spirit of the Scots people in particular'.[43] In practice, however, it shaped the life of the church for two generations until it was superseded in 1979 by another controversial edition – attacked by some church members as the product of 'Scoto Catholics' in the church – and again, in 1994, with the publication of the last *Book of Common Order* of the century. On the eve of a new millennium, it was a volume that spoke to a constituency that still sought meaning in its past. The introduction claimed that the *Book* reflected 'the common heritage of prayer and devotion of the whole church, drawing from the orthodox wellsprings of liturgy and from the lay heritage of Celtic spirituality originating in these shores'.[44] Even when moving forward, the church was being called back. Tensions were further manifest in the musical traditions of the church. The *Revised Church Hymnary* (1928) was overhauled in 1973 to produce the *Third Edition of the Church Hymnary*.[45] Partly as a consequence, the cadences of popular music and the strains of the guitar were now to be heard in kirks across Scotland alongside stirring organ accompaniments to psalms that would have been familiar to earlier evangelicals.[46] It was an uneasy mix.

Some regions, nevertheless, clung to tradition. In the Highlands, by the century's close, sermons remained longer on average in the Presbyterian churches, preaching in Gaelic still claimed supporters, if diminishing audiences, and the Communion season was doggedly defended. John Bannerman reflected on Communion week in Applecross at the start of the twentieth century:

The little church on the headland could not hope to contain the invasion, so at eleven o'clock the scene was set on the hill among the bracken. Five or six hundred people ranged themselves in tiers as in an amphitheatre, and on the level ground below us was the white-clothed communion table. It held at one sitting only 30 or 40 people. They came in relays – indeed a marathon service . . . Prayers were lengthy, sonorous and earnest, and sighs of assent and groans of remorse rose from the congregation.[47]

While admirable in their tenacity, supporters of tradition nevertheless frequently failed the church they sought to defend. As early as the 1930s, missionaries customarily looked after the religious needs of dwindling Hebridean congregations. The broadcaster, Finlay J. Macdonald, remembering church services as a young boy in Harris at this time, wrote, 'Thirty self-conscious souls in a miniature cathedral, frozen to the marrow and bored to extinction' alternately struggled to stay awake or worried about Sunday lunches burning on blackened ranges.[48] In the Highlands, conventions rooted in custom rather than biblical precedent also frequently discouraged believers from the gift of communion. In *Highland River*, Neil Gunn (1891–1973) delicately highlights the personal impact of this state of affairs:

Kenn's mother did not go to communion on the Sabbath of the Sacrament simply because she believed she was not worthy. Never in her life did she sit at communion table, never broke the bread nor drank the wine. She had done nothing to make herself unworthy. She was seen in her life as a good woman and without reproach.

Yet she believed herself unworthy . . .

It was a humility that was never confessed, as if the core of it were shyness delicate as the compassion of Christ.

Neither . . . did her husband, who attended church regularly, go to communion. When the tables were being 'fenced' by the ministers, he and his brother seamen remained in their seats, worshipping with prayer and praise . . . They knew their lives in the past had not contained enough solemnity of holiness to justify them in going forward to the tables. They were in act and fact not good enough.[49]

Both reform and a reliance on tradition could, in different ways, discourage potential new believers and they could also circumscribe the spiritual lives of the faithful. It was a balance the churches arguably never quite got right.

This can be seen in the associational culture of the churches over the course of the century. The Boys' Brigade (established in 1883) remained one of the most popular uniformed children's organisations until mid century. Yet, with a membership of over 111,000 in 1933, the Brigade's jubilee year, only around 3,500 went on annually to become members of the church.[50] Similarly, the Church of Scotland's Women's Guild (established in 1887 and gender-neutered to form 'The Guild' in 1997) was as much a feature of church life at the close of the twentieth century as it had been in earlier decades.[51] But membership of both the Guild and the Brigade declined in the second half of the twentieth century, as children were increasingly lost to the churches and leisure time increasingly became a private affair, resistant to the discipline and compromise of associational bodies.

Change was even marked in the church buildings themselves. Sir Robert Bruce Lockhart visited a Cromdale church in 1937:

[The] church has become a village hall. As I stopped to go in I saw a notice on the door: 'Saturday, March 6 Whist Drive and Dance'.

I felt a pang of regret and remorse. There was a symbol in the conversion of that church to a dance hall. It marked the end of a generation of men and women who, however narrow their views may have been, were self-reliant and as severe to themselves as they were to others. They set themselves a high standard of frugality and hard work, and from this standard they rarely departed. This was a life that seemed to yield little, but I wonder if they were unhappier than a generation which wants more from God and man and gives less to both.[52]

The churches had clearly changed in the twentieth century but so, evidently, had Scotland.

Little remained at the end of the twentieth century of the social gospel which had been integral to the evangelicalism of the mid nineteenth century – a time when the church's role in poor relief and education reinforced its spiritual message with material power. The churches' retreat from their secular responsibilities in society, however, was not total and nor was it entirely enforced by pressures from 'outside'.

Central to the changing social position of the churches in the twentieth century was the growing power of the state and the institutionalisation in a secular context of a doctrine of collective responsibility that had once been the call to arms of reforming churchmen themselves. John Buchan emphasised this in 1930:

[T]he whole conception of the State has changed, Whig individualism had given place to a deeper and more organic conception of
the part of the State in the communal life . . .

This richer conception of the state is accompanied by a quicker
conscience in the individual. We no longer believe that human
misery is the result of some mysterious decree of Omnipotence; we
realise that it is mainly the consequence of human bungling.[53]

It was therefore partly as a consequence of the success of the evangelical
message that the church was compelled to step aside from the social
agenda that had inspired the civic morality of the late Victorian era.
From the interwar period, the Church of Scotland increasingly abandoned areas of its social reform agenda as the state asserted a more interventionist role. Incrementally, the church's social influence declined in
education from 1918 (Education (Scotland) Act) and in a variety of local
welfare areas from 1929 (Local Government (Scotland) Act) onwards.

Yet government legislation that marked these years only offers a
partial explanation for the church's retreat into the spiritual.[54] Under
the leadership and influence of Rev. John White (1867–1951),
Moderator in 1925 and 1929, the General Assembly of the Church of
Scotland in the years after the Great War withdrew from its earlier
commitment to intervention and social criticism and increasingly
adopted a policy of non-interference.[55] United in such social conservatism, the long-awaited union of the United Free Church and the
Church of Scotland in 1929 was little more than a fait accompli. In
the midst of self-congratulatory pageantry that year, White made it
clear that:

[w]e are not called on to elaborate any scheme of social economics
or politics; but we are required to declare that the teaching of the
Kingdom of God, when applied to the problems of to-day brings into
prominence two governing principles of human value and human
comradeship – viz, the equal and infinite value of every personality
in the sight of God, and the brotherhood of man . . . History shows
that there never is any sustained and successful social effort apart
from the vision of the Kingdom of God.[56]

White sought the solution to the problems of the 1920s in the transformation of personal morality and the protection of the Scottish nation
from the contaminating influences of Irish (or simply Catholic) immigration. In part, this new vision was articulated through the Forward
Movement.[57] Aimed at revitalising the parish system with a renewed

sense of collective responsibility and personal initiative, in much the same sense as Rev. Thomas Chalmers had intended in Glasgow during the early nineteenth century, the Forward Movement failed to revitalise the membership of the new united church. Undaunted, another 'borrowing' from the nineteenth century was launched in 1931, with the inauguration of a Church Extension Programme, but this fared much the same as earlier initiatives, taking five years to reach its initial goal of raising £180,000 for the erection of new churches.[58] By 1939, the Church of Scotland had succeeded in building seventeen new church buildings and many other new halls as a result of the Extension scheme but little enthusiasm had been engendered for it.[59] At root, the problem was not necessarily the number of buildings that the church provided but what was happening inside them and in their senior executive offices.

Many who had watched the country decline into economic catastrophe became infuriated with the inaction of Scotland's 'national church'. During the 1926 General Strike, for example, the Church of Scotland opted for conciliation rather than overt support for either side and offered little more than palliative concern for the unemployed in halls set aside for their recreation and in instructional centres where training was offered free of charge.[60] The Free Church, meanwhile, condemned the unions' attempts to hold the country to ransom.[61]

The Church of Scotland, which prided itself on neutrality at a time when the country was being torn apart and condemned MacLeod's Iona experiment as fanciful folly, chose instead to focus temporarily on the Catholic enemy within as the root cause of the country's woes and to draw attention to racial as opposed to class divisions. In its infamous publication, *The Menace of the Irish Race to Our Scottish Nationality* (1923), Irish Catholic immigrants were identified by the Kirk as a contaminating alien influence on the Scottish race and a principal cause of the country's descent into economic chaos. While founded on little more than bigotry and fuelled largely by a need to find a scapegoat for Scotland's decline, the report nevertheless offered an analysis that struck a chord with many in the urban Central Belt in the Depression years. During the early 1930s, anti-Catholicism entered the political agenda as populist Protestant candidates like Alexander Ratcliffe (1888–1947), councillor for Denniston in 1931, and John Cormack (1894–1978), a Leith councillor from 1934, were elected to local public office.[62] At best, Catholics were viewed by such militant Protestants as dupes, 'ready victims of priestcraft'.[63] At worst, they were second only to the Jews in corrupting native purity. In his 1943 publication, *The Truth About the Jews*, Ratcliffe emphatically recorded, 'The Jews are clever;

they are keen, and ever minding Number One. They are clannish, and keep themselves to themselves. They do not seek marriage union with Gentiles, except in their interests of filthy lucre.'[64] The interwar years were unedifying to say the least for the Church of Scotland and drew it into associations (whether intentionally or otherwise) in the public mind with racial rhetoric and causes that were to be totally discredited in the fight against Fascism.

Yet the Second World War would change church priorities. In keeping with the passions for planning and reconstruction popular in these years, in 1942, the Baillie Commission (The Commission for the Interpretation of God's Will in the Present Crisis) recommended an overt social role for the Church of Scotland in the post-war world. Similarly, the Roman Catholic Church, through the Archdiocesan Council of Social Action from 1948, encouraged Catholic involvement in schemes of social improvement. Such enthusiasm, however, had come too late and proved somewhat out of date when, in 1945, a Labour government was elected with a mandate to create the world anew. In the 1950s and 1960s, the Church of Scotland proved slow to locate churches in the new post-war housing estates which were emerging on the peripheries of the major Scottish cities and took time to adjust to an emergent teenage culture which placed value in rebellion.[65] In 1996, the Church of Scotland remained the country's largest non-state social work agency, employing over 1,600 people.[66] But, by professionalising this aspect of its Scottish mission – by taking the pursuit and control of its social goals out of the hands of its congregations – it moved further away from the aims of the nineteenth century evangelicals and created a bureaucracy from which many members felt alienated.

There is no guarantee that church influence would have been greater had its social role been less impeded by the encroachment of the state. After all, the direct involvement of the Roman Catholic Church in state education ironically lasted longer than that of the Kirk – typically identified as the standard-bearer of Scottish educational traditions – but its legacy was mixed.

The provision of education by the Roman Catholic Church in Scotland in the nineteenth century established a precedent in denominational education which continued throughout the twentieth century, assisted by the granting of state patronage in the 1918 Education (Scotland) Act.[67] Strained church budgets had meant that primary education had been prioritised over secondary schooling in the nineteenth century and it took some time for provision for older children to be adequately addressed. This certainly did not help the upward social mobility of a community already disadvantaged as a result of prejudice and poor housing. But falling attendance at Mass among the young during the late twentieth century suggests that the role of the church in education did not necessarily guarantee adherence in later life and the persistence of denominational education guaranteed that sectarianism would always have a political dynamic.[68]

In 1929, the parishioners of St John's Roman Catholic Church in Port Glasgow celebrated the centenary of Catholic Emancipation and noted in a souvenir publication that, over the years:

> [o]ur non-Catholic fellow-countrymen have learned to respect our Faith and to leave us to practise it in peace. The keynote of the modern religious spirit is toleration, but our aim must be something higher, something infinitely nobler, that we may enrich, as well as maintain, the traditions of the past.[69]

Despite such high hopes, sectarianism persisted long after the interwar years and was most marked in the west Central Belt of Scotland where football helped to perpetuate and colour-code divisions that, elsewhere in life, were becoming increasingly ambiguous and dependent upon Northern Irish events for their contemporary relevance.[70] By the 1950s, Ratcliffe was dead and Cormack's influence was largely confined to Leith where his limited following was more personal than ideological. (He retired in 1964.) In 1979, however, the journalist Douglas Rae still considered Glasgow's Old Firm matches 'an institution', part of the 'psyche of a city if not a nation'. 'The contest is not readily isolated from its context in society,' he noted, 'and that society is as schizoid as the contest.'[71]

Indeed, the Pope's visit to Scotland in 1982 was to be marred (if not overwhelmed) by sectarian tensions. A Catholic school bus was attacked on its way back to Glasgow from the Edinburgh festivities, train stations were daubed with sectarian graffiti and anti-Catholic demonstrations addressed by well-known figures, such as Pastor Jack Glass (1937–) and Northern Ireland's Rev. Ian Paisley (1926–), were held to coincide with the Pope's address to the crowds that greeted him at Bellahouston Park.[72] By the final decade of the century, however, it was clear that, while ugly sectarian incidents regularly accompanied Saturday football crowds, the social disadvantages experienced by the first generations of Irish Catholics had become a thing of the past.[73] Despite high-profile claims to the contrary – the composer James MacMillan (1959–), for example, considered Scotland a land of 'sleep-walking bigotry' in 1999 – at the end of the century, Scottish anti-Catholicism was overwhelmingly 'unsystematic and unstructured' and more alive in populist rhetoric, alternative comedy and the urban imagination than in civic institutions.[74] That did not mean that religious divisions no longer mattered – only that they mattered less and mattered in a different way.

Throughout the century, the churches maintained a political role in Scotland though only in the latter years did they seem to speak with anything resembling a united voice. As we have seen, in 1926, the Church of Scotland remained aloof from the General Strike but, in 1971, Kirk and Roman Catholic clergy in Clydebank together assisted in the success of the work-in at Upper Clyde Shipbuilders.[75] The role of the churches in Scottish politics changed over the course of the twentieth century and was far from a tale of unremitting decline. Religion clearly lost its *determining* significance in the electoral choices of most Scots, as we discovered in Part Three, but, on a number of occasions, the churches worked in tandem with the popular political will of the nation.

The party-political profile of Church of Scotland members consistently showed a high proportion of Unionist sympathisers in the 1950s and early 1960s but, by the 1980s, the Scottish churches played an important role in galvanising support for constitutional reform through the SCC, with the Church of Scotland's role being particularly significant as one of the three pillars of civic society left relatively intact since 1707. The cold reception which was accorded to Mrs Thatcher's famous 'Sermon on the Mound', when she addressed the General Assembly of the Church of Scotland in 1988, was also significant. '[It] is not the creation of wealth that is wrong, but love of money for its own sake,' she informed the assembled clergy before going on to say:

> Any set of social and economic arrangements which is not founded on the acceptance of individual responsibility will do nothing but harm. We are responsible for our own actions. We cannot blame society if we disobey the law. We simply cannot delegate the exercise of mercy and generosity to others.
>
> (*Observer*, 22 May 1988)

To a country whose collective sense of being was growing and whose economy and public services had suffered since Mrs Thatcher's rise to power, such sentiments succeeded in highlighting her insensitivity to Scottish susceptibilities and, in contrast, the church's greater understanding of Scottish traditions. The Church of Scotland clearly did not have a mandate to represent the will of the multicultural and increasingly secular Scottish population in the 1990s but it, at least, generally failed to regularly antagonise popular opinion and, on occasion, could still appear as Scotland in miniature. A week before her visit to the General

Assembly, Mrs Thatcher had been greeted by a sea of red cards, distributed by Health Service trade unionists and held aloft by a 74,000-strong Scottish Cup Final crowd at Hampden. The cards bore the words:

> Enjoy the match.
> But
> Let's make Thatcher
> Realise that Scotland's
> United against the
> Tories.[76]

There were no red cards on the Mound the following week but the sentiments of both 'congregations' were closer than they had been for some time.

Paradoxically, Scottish churches have generally been least successful in shaping public opinion when they have been at their most vocal. The Roman Catholic Church's determined – and increasingly overtly political – stance against abortion frequently attracted criticism in the late twentieth century. A 1992 campaign leaflet, 'Facing the Crossroads: A Special Message From the Bishops of Scotland', appealed to believers to pay particular regard 'for the moral standards espoused by the candidates and their parties' and was uncompromising in its suggestion that 'the ultimate in powerlessness is to be destroyed before birth'.[77] Similar overt propaganda was evident at the general election five years later when 'right to life' issues were again prioritised by the Roman Catholic Church in public forums.[78] Yet most research would seem to indicate that the church's voice on these matters had little resonance amongst its adherents, particularly the young.[79] From the 1920s, the Catholic community had used the ballot box to assert its socio-economic priorities rather than its religiosity and was overwhelmingly characterised by its left-leaning values and its tendency to vote Labour (the party in power when the 1967 Abortion Act was passed) – the church could do little to alter this, even if it had wanted to.[80]

Over the course of the century, congregations of all persuasions grew increasingly reluctant to adhere to church-sponsored conventions that had little to do with Christian principles and appeared out of touch with popular culture. The 'Dornoch Dance Case' in 1935 is a case in point. In December 1934, Provost John Murray of Dornoch and his wife held a Christmas party at their home, during which local children danced. In the summer of the following year, however, the couple's membership of Evelix Free Presbyterian (FP) Church was suspended by the Kirk Session on account of their allowing such unseemly behaviour in their home. In protest, John Murray held regular opposition services at the local Birichen

School, taking the majority of the church members with him – including a ninety-year old man who had to walk four miles to get there – and took issue with the unconstitutional behaviour of the Kirk Session and the Northern Presbytery which supported the local minister. But the church authorities were unrepentant and Murray's name was erased from the church roll. Defiantly, the Free Presbyterian Church declared, 'If the Free Presbyterian Church were dependent on the favourable verdict of the world there never would have been a Free Presbyterian Church at all.'[81]

In the years that followed, opposition to drinking and attacks on the high profile of light entertainment in the government's public service campaigns during the Second World War earned the Scottish churches a puritanical image which was going out of fashion.[82] This persisted into the post-war period when, in the late 1940s, the Church of Scotland maintained its support for temperance and, from the 1950s, television was identified as a major contributor to falling church attendance. In 1961, the Church of Scotland's Church and Nation Committee maintained that plays and films which questioned the sanctity of marriage should not be broadcast and that blasphemy should be banned from the airwaves along with anything which would serve to encourage gambling or drinking.[83] In the same decade, raffles were banned in the Church of Scotland and the FP Church held fast to its belief that football pools were a 'cancer that threatened to spread like a festering disease through the nation'.[84]

Clearly, on occasion, Scottish churches stubbornly resisted changes evident around them but Scottish churchgoers frequently exemplified such change in their faith and practice – a silent revolution in the pews gathered speed as the century progressed. By the 1980s, Scots associated with both the Church of Scotland and Roman Catholic Church prioritised the loving nature of God over a more judgemental image. For both denominations, prayer remained important, though less than 40 per cent of those claiming connection with the Church of Scotland prayed every day. Less than 25 per cent regularly watched religious programmes on TV – the figure was 16.2 per cent among Roman Catholics surveyed.[85] A little over 73 per cent of those attached to the Church of Scotland believed in the Resurrection and the corresponding Catholic figure was 91.5 per cent. And, despite clerical protestations, less than 45 per cent of Catholics surveyed agreed that abortion was always wrong while the corresponding Church of Scotland figure was 6.4 per cent.[86]

At times, the churches proved adept at using popular media to get their message across. BBC Radio broadcast religious programmes almost from its inception and launched a series of evangelistic crusades as early as the late 1940s. Billy Graham's 'All Scotland Crusade' in 1955 developed the churches' use of both radio and television – over 2,600,000 attended his Glasgow meetings – as did the Pope's visit to Scotland in 1982.[87] However, as Alan Gilbert has shown, audiences across Britain for religious radio programmes declined by two thirds between 1945 and 1955 and by a further 50 per cent in the 1960s.[88] Indeed, religious revivalism was not universally popular and could still point to the church being out of touch. In Hugh MacDiarmid's *Voice of Scotland* journal, Hugo Moore offered a 'Billy Graham Autopsy':

> If Dr Graham's first sermon had declared for the slums instead of being all too obviously addressed to the suburbs; if, having come to save Scotland, he had tried to save it from exploitation; from squalor; from cultural benightedness; from the scribes of the Press and the Pharisees of the Presbytery; from the cunning of the businessmen and the callousness of the politicians: then, he would have been assured of at least a little influence and a little authority in the affairs of the nation, if not his £5,000 a year.[89]

As congregations dwindled it seemed to matter little that the churches' message lent itself to a variety of media – increasingly the message itself was the focus of criticism.

And, yet, the churches' responses to the changing parameters of popular morality do not present a uniform or predictable picture either across denominations or between similar issues of importance. The General Assembly of the Church of Scotland maintained, in 1963, that 'chastity before marriage and fidelity after marriage remain the true ideal for the Christian' but, at much the same time, supported the liberalisation of the divorce laws. In 1966, its Social and Moral Welfare Committee recommended conditions for abortion very close to those which found their way into the new Abortion Act and, in 1969, the church's Temperance and Morals Committee decided that the 'mechanical means' possessed by mankind to limit births should be welcomed as 'a divine call'.[90] Needless to say, the Church of Scotland was at odds with the Roman Catholic Church on these matters.

Nevertheless, on other issues, the churches seemed to coincide. The Church of Scotland's opposition to the recommendations of the 1957 Wolfenden Report on Homosexual Offences was shared by most other churches north of the Border. For example, the Report's recommendation that homosexual acts between two consenting adults should be legalised was attacked by the Synod of the Free Presbyterian Church which considered such acts to be a 'sin which is contrary to the law of God and abominable in the eyes of all right-minded persons'.[91]

The Church of Scotland, meanwhile, held out for a 'complete cure' and compromise proposals, advocating support for the decriminalisation of homosexual activity, were repeatedly rejected by the General Assembly.[92]

In other respects, however, the churches came increasingly into line with changing Scottish values. By the end of the century, the clergy of the Church of Scotland commonly came from urban backgrounds – in sharp contrast to the small-town preachers of previous church generations – and women gradually secured ordination in the Protestant churches from 1929. (The Congregational Union was first to ordain women in Scotland.)[93] The churches also contributed to the tempering of sectarian tensions in their greater commitment to ecumenical understanding.

Change had been evident since the late nineteenth century when Charles Wordsworth (1806–1892), Bishop of St Andrews, observing a new temper in the Church of Scotland, wrote, 'Presbyterian Scotland is ceasing to love ugly churches, extempore prayers, long sermons, and pseudonymous Fast Days ... I see no reason for doubting that Presbyterian Scotland will receive Episcopacy when the proper time comes.'[94] In the 1920s, 1940s, 1950s and again in the 1960s, it appeared, at times, that relationships between the reformed faith groups had softened to the extent that the intercommunion (and even union) of the Church of Scotland and the Episcopal Church of Scotland (or even the Church of England) seemed a possibility and the introduction of Bishops as permanent moderators of the presbyteries of the Church of Scotland appeared to be a real prospect.[95] The spectre of the Covenanters (helped by the protestations of Ian McColl (1915–2005), the editor of the *Scottish Daily Express* in 1966) was, however, enough to temper the resolve of the ecumenicals in the 1960s. The General Assembly was reminded of the Presbyterian traditions over which it was the principal guardian and its fundamental role in grounding what was left of Scottish nationhood.[96] The proposals came to nothing.

Nevertheless, change was evident elsewhere. Inter-marriage between Catholics and Protestants became more common in the second half of the century, the Church of Scotland reacted positively to the Pope's visit in 1982 and Cardinal Winning (1925–2001) visited the Assemblies of both the Church of Scotland and the Free Kirk in the mid 1990s. The churches also proved capable themselves of raising moral eyebrows. In 1996, the 'Roddy Wright' affair pointed to lapses in the clerical discipline of the Scottish Catholic clergy when the Bishop of Argyll and the Isles was identified as a father in the tabloid press and, in the 1990s, damaging personal allegations of sexual harassment and courtroom drama centring on the figure of Professor Donald Macleod, Principal of the Free Church College, led to some of the most unedifying schisms in the history of the Presbyterian Church in Scotland.[97]

Nevertheless, the history of the Scottish churches in the twentieth century is far from a tale of unremitting decline or of the evasion of social responsibility. By the century's end, the Scottish churches were more diverse organisations than they had been at its beginning and they still offered valuable spiritual guidance and support to Scottish citizens, even if many of these citizens resolutely ignored the call to worship in the traditional churches. It is interesting to note that non-Christian faiths in Scotland and non-institutional interpretations of faith increased in popularity in the late twentieth century – as did the small churches, in contrast to their larger contemporaries.[98] The churches may have lost their way at times but religion in Scotland – in some sense, at least – had not entirely lost its relevance.

TWELVE Cultural Spaces

In a global age, it pays to reject homogeneity. There is value in difference and reputation to be made in rebellion. So it was that the internationalisation of communications encouraged a greater focus on contrasting national traditions in the twentieth century and, ultimately, on the local and the personal experiences that compounded them. Scotland, as part of the British Empire and a small European nation in its own right, was both central and marginal to the major cultural forces of the age and seemed to like it that way. Scotland challenged the foremost players at their own game while simultaneously attempting to change the rules of engagement. Not surprisingly, the outcome of such cultural entanglements with international forces produced a contradictory legacy. Globalisation determined that Scottish culture would be forged in the relationships between popular images ascribed from 'outside' the nation – at first by Scottish émigré writers and then by Hollywood and international tourism – and conflicting identities emerging indigenously. Such discourse, at different times, both retarded and nurtured innovation in the arts, perpetuated conventions borrowed from English literature or drove writers to seek new voices in vernacular Scottish dialects. It animated Kailyard icons on screen while simultaneously undermining them in 'serious' literature. In this sense, the iconographic Robert Burns of the tourist trail and the Burns who inspired generations of twentieth-century poets to reject a 'borrowed tongue' represent two faces of the same process of cultural expression.

No' wan in fifty kens a wurd
  Burns wrote
But misapplied is a'body's property,
And gin there was his like alive
  the day
They'd be the last a kennin' haund
  to gi'e–

In Robert Burns's house at
  Dumfries
I saw the words 'The Poet
  died in this bed'

Translated into thirty
  languages.

Croose London Scotties wi' their
  braw shirt fronts
And a' their fancy freen's, rejoicin'
That similah gatherings in
  Timbuctoo,
Bagdad – and hell, nae doot – are
  voicin'

Burns' sentiments o' universal love,
In pidgin' English or in wild-fowl
  Scots,
And toastin' ane wha's nocht to
  them but an
Excuse for faitherin' Genius wi
  their thochts.

'A Drunk Man Looks at the Thistle'
Hugh MacDiarmid

He'd take a can of petrol
  to his verses and letters,
Torch them, and scatter
  the acrid ashes
In a shopping mall, for
  self-respect.

'The Declaration of
Arbroath'
Robert Crawford

Across many aspects of Scottish culture in the twentieth century – from literature to art, music to drama – Scotland occupied this contradictory 'space' and took from it lessons which encouraged both assimilation and distinctiveness, diversity and homogeneity. What emerged was a vibrant cacophony of competing voices each speaking of Scotland if not for it, and none claiming unconditional support. If the century sought to recapture the culture of Burns, lost in the smog of nineteenth-century industry, it failed. If it sought to be more honestly itself, it came close.

LITERATURE

The supposed homogenisation of British culture at the turn of the twentieth century – commonly attributed to the emergence of modern media, Britain's imperial mission and the final stages of industrialisation – typically led to the siting of Scottish cultural difference in the Scottish past. As a result, traditional images of Scotland were reinforced which tended to caricature and sentimentalise the nation and, for the most part, ignore her industrial present. A complex matrix of images was generated, only partly encapsulated in tartanry and Kailyard writings identified by Tom Nairn, amongst others, as the essence of Scotland's distorted national identity in the twentieth century.[1] Rather – borrowing from the playwright James Bridie – the imagery was a sophisticated though inexact blending of 'Wallacethebruceism, Charlieoverthewaterism, Puirrabbieburnsism, Bonniebonniebanksism, Myainfolkism and Laymedoonandeeism', which proved an innovative combination of the maudlin and the comic guaranteed to appeal to early twentieth-century tastes.[2]

Popularity and financial profitability ensured the longevity of these images in an increasingly commercial age, when journals such as the *British Weekly* fed the public's desire for nostalgic renderings of more polite times. But fame came at a cost. Nineteenth-century Scottish authors who sought to engage with the urbanised nation they saw around them were eclipsed by the stars of the Kailyard and tended to publish their work in serial form in regional journals with limited circulations that were, in any case, under threat from the new journalism and distribution networks of the popular national press as the new century opened.[3] In their stead, the Kailyard tradition embedded Scottish literature in the restrictive sentiments of an imagined past and offered little to offset the encroaching conventions of English critical orthodoxies.[4] A Saltire pamphleteer, J. M. Reid, reflected in 1945:

> Nineteenth-century Scotland was one of the chief centres of the industrial world. Its society was complex and curious enough to feed and excite any keen observer of human nature. Yet there is no Scottish Balzac or Dickens, not even any Scottish Thackeray or Trollope. Scottish writers and their readers both inside the country and elsewhere preferred Scott-land to Scotland.[5]

The publication of George Douglas Brown's *The House with the Green Shutters* (1901) neatly coincided with the beginning of the new century and suggested that Scottish literature would not be in the thrall of sentiment for much longer. Set in the small town of Barbie, it offered an alternative and far darker rendering of Scottish parish life in which greed, pride and tragedy replaced the couthy neighbourliness of Kailyard 'happily-ever-afters'. Indeed, in a letter to the political theorist Ernest Barker (1874–1960), Brown reflected that '[e]very clachan in Scotland is a hot-bed of scandal and malevolence'.[6] But this was to be Brown's first and last novel of note and, in the short term, no one else took up his standard.[7]

And yet, somewhat paradoxically, in the long term the ultimate rejection of the Kailyard did not, as many had anticipated, liberate an imprisoned sense of nationhood more in keeping with the realities of the age. The illusion that something deeper lay behind it was confirmed in this silence. Indeed, it could be argued that the ultimate legacy of the Kailyard was not the corpus of literature it produced but a regrettable tradition in literary criticism which sought in vain the distilled essence of Scotland in the works of Scottish writers and undervalued difference in its search for the unified national voice which had apparently eluded Scotland at the turn of the century. Scottish studies were marked by their 'urge for essentialism'.[8] In the interwar years and beyond, it was too often assumed that literature's task was to shape a singular national culture rather than record the conflicting expressions of Scots who, as poets, novelists or dramatists, sought to sketch the parameters within which – as Scots – they could express *themselves*. This tension between the individual and the collective will and this weight of expectations bore more heavily on Scottish writers than on most others in the United Kingdom. Even in the final decades of the century, there remained the remnants of the lingering illusion that there could or should be a more cohesive rendering of Scottish identity than that being produced at the time. The poet Edwin Morgan made a refreshing case for greater honesty in 1972 when he said, 'Scottish writers must simply write as well as they can, and leave it to others to decide whether their provenance stands out, and what value infuses into their work.'[9]

Another poet, Douglas Dunn (1942–), has noted that 'Scottishness' is a 'quality open to crass exaggeration as well as more subtle forms of garbled excess'.[10] Others, meanwhile, suggest that the 'national dimension of "Scottish" literature has never been, and presumably will never be conclusively defined'.[11] Regardless, wherever one stands, the identities evident in the works of the writers of the twentieth century lend themselves to few generalisations – or to a problem-free national appellation, for that matter – and the literary styles adopted and adapted by the wordsmiths, during the course of the century, do not tend to any unified approach.

It took time for the writers who sought distance from their Kailyard antecedents to abandon the themes and motifs of the school altogether. Among Scottish novelists of the first decades of the twentieth century, such trends are most explicit. Frequently, their most radical departures consist of little more than a defence of traditions under threat or a harkening back to an age of supposed greater wisdom. In this regard, their reliance on Scottish history's more colourful moments is notable but it is qualified. The wind that 'beats through the glen', in *The Gowk Storm* (1930) by Nancy Brysson Morrison (1907–1986), is 'like the coming of the Campbells'.[12] But, in *Highland River*, the city appears devoid of history – rather, Neil Gunn shows a contempt for the urban environment that would have found a ready echo in the prejudices of Kailyard sentiment.[13]

It was a Saturday night, and the scene, for Kenn's fresh country senses, one of nightmare horror. The figures in the dim close, the smash of a fist on flesh, the sexual oaths, the scurrying feet, the dark stairway, the stinking common lavatory, the blousy women, the filthy room with its rags and sheets of newspapers.[14]

For some, looking further back to a time when Scotland was peopled with contrasting 'tribes' was the corrective to such a present but it is doubtful whether they found anything different there. Brysson Morrison again:

> By the time we were half-way to Barfingal, papa, under Julia's influence, was talking with animation about the tribes of ancient Scotland, the 'smeared people' of the far north, the 'hunters' of Galloway, the Caledonians of our own and neighbouring shires, the 'horsemen' of Argyll, and the squat, dark, unbekent people found sometimes in the Hebrides who are believed to be either relics of the Lost Ten Tribes or descendants of sailors wrecked from the Spanish Armada.[15]

A longer historical reach merely confirmed in history the fragmentation all too evident in the contemporary scene and the absence of a singular cultural dynamic. Yet, for many, it appeared that modernity had detached Scotland from its past and, in so doing, had made self-knowledge impossible.[16] In response, ancient loyalties were clung to and the redemptive balm of a lost innocence allowed writers to blame others – whether capitalists, landowners or the English – for Scotland's depressed state, for their own inability to soar beyond its narrow horizons, or at least for the reluctance of others to join them.

Fionn MacColla (1906–1975) clearly shared the early commitment of his protagonist, Maighstir Sachairi, to the lifestyle of the pre-Clearance Highlands in his novel *And the Cock Crew* (1945):

> The life of the glenpeople in its yearly round and seasons possessed in his eyes a harmony; it appeared as a natural work of completion of unassisted Nature, on which it rested as on a base properly proportioned to it and with which it formed a single, ordered, intelligible whole. To destroy it seemed an outrage and violation, the triumph of chaos over order. For Maighstir Sachairi had no feeling but repulsion for what was to succeed it. He could not contemplate that more crudely pastoral life of the sheep men without a deep sense of the incomplete, of frustration. It meant the forcible pushing back of completed Nature into infertility. It involved the senseless dehumanisation of a whole countryside.[17]

'Progress' was about to make organic Scotland inaccessible, set apart from the present, just as that earlier fissure in Highland history – the failed Jacobite rebellion of 1745 – had, once and for all, detached the nation from its freedom. Looking back, Fearchar, the glen's bard, is despondent when he says, 'The end of all is that our nation is helpless.'[18] The veiled politicised message may be new but, forty years on, there is only a thin disguise on the familiar melodrama of Jacobitism and the literary edification of a lost rural idyll that had beguiled the Kailyard authors of Edwardian Scotland.

Nonetheless, after 1914, departures from familiar sentiments *were* notable. Some commentators have stressed certain writers' rejection of the parameters of high and low culture and their fusion of the mundane and the philosophical – in the words of Colin Milton, 'the traditional Scots habit of linking the exalted and the homely' – as characteristic of a refreshed Scottish approach.[19] This tendency is fundamental to the pathos of many of Compton Mackenzie's tragicomic characters, for example.[20]

In a sense, this is a symptom of 'Caledonian Antisyzygy' – a condition to which Scots, according to Gregory Smith in 1919, were particularly prone:

> Does literature anywhere, of this small compass, show such a mixture of contraries as [the Scot's] outlook, subject, and method; real life and romance, everyday fact and the supernatural, things holy and things profane, gentle and simple, convention and 'cantrip', thistles and thistledown?[21]

In like fashion, one might also point to the significant use of legend, allegory, ritual and symbol in Scottish writing – these are worked powerfully in the poetry and prose of Naomi Mitchison and Lewis Grassic Gibbon, for instance.[22] In the end, it is surely diversity rather than a unity of expression and style that characterises Scottish literature in the later twentieth century – a diversity which globalisation in many ways accelerated.

The earliest battleground in Scotland's confrontation with the homogenising tendencies of globalisation and its Anglicising and Americanising variants was on the linguistic plane – principally in the medium rather than the content of the work of Scottish writers and particularly in their use and abuse of English. The threat which writers at the start of the twentieth century perceived to native Scots, Scottish dialects and Gaelic was one of the key motive forces shaping the commitment to indigenous languages evident in the literary renaissance of the 1920s. Indeed, as early as 1899, it occurred to R. B. Cunninghame Graham (1852–1936) that:

To be a Scotchman nowadays is to fill a position of some difficulty and trust.

It is expected that when he takes pen in hand that he must write, no matter what his predilections, antecedents, or education may have been, a language which no Englishman can understand. It is vain to plead that all our greatest writers in the past have written what they hoped was English.[23]

Many Kailyard authors had experimented with Scots, while many other successful Scottish writers followed Sir Walter Scott (1771–1832) in writing in a conventional English medium. Among the latter category were Robert Louis Stevenson (1850–1894), Edwin Muir and John Buchan who, according to James Kelman, was 'an assimilated member of British society'.[24] However, it is largely in the linguistic tension evident in the writing of those who felt compelled to reject Standard English as a medium that a principal dynamic of the literature of the twentieth century is to be found.

Hugh MacDiarmid clearly was not the first to exploit the poetic treasure chest of the Scots vernacular. The 'Book of Genesis' was published in Scots in 1921 – 'I' the ingang God schuppit the hevin and the erd.'[25] But MacDiarmid politicised the Scots tongue through his association with Scottish nationalism and he sought to expose its power to express the subconscious denied writers by their English enthralment. He noted in his autobiography of 1943 that, '[his] job in Scotland was to discredit and hustle off the stage a . . . poetry . . . of mawkish doggerel . . . into which the Burns tradition had degenerated.'[26] Instead, braid Scots offered writers 'a peerless directness of utterance'.[27] The so-called Scottish Renaissance (Renascence) – the phrase dates from 1924 and was ascribed by a Frenchman – was the outcome of this commitment to refashion and rescue Scottish literature. Its disciples included Lewis Grassic Gibbon, Lewis Spence (1874–1955), William Jeffrey (1896–1946) and many others, and their influence was evident in a subsequent generation of makars in the middle decades of the century, among them, Sydney Goodsir Smith (1915–1975) and Edinburgh's Robert Garioch. Like their predecessors, the past bore heavily on the work of these individuals, much of it written in Lallans, and on their ideals. Douglas Gifford has explored this dynamic in the fiction of these years and has identified its components. He is worth quoting at length:

Past defines present; roots are deep and tenacious; contemporary individuals are powerless to resist the effects of tradition, and they will only successfully realize themselves if they move with the grain of 'Scottish' experience. Standing stones, earth houses, brochs and cairns, 'speak' to their human descendants; ruined castles and graveyards hold aristocrats and peasants who still have the power to communicate with the present and to insist on the significance of their ancient ideology.[28]

Touching at times on arguments rooted in ethnic or racial determinism, these were sentiments very much of their time. As we have discovered already, even the Church of Scotland was not immune. But these ideas were hardly radicalising and – for all their proponents' claims regarding the democratisation of culture – they failed the post-war litmus test of egalitarianism. In the harsh light of a post-Holocaust world, they would have fewer unquestioning followers. At any rate, MacDiarmid's increasing bitterness in his later years, the loss of the passion and lyricism that had marked some of his most successful early works and the growing frustrations and acrimony within the political nationalist movement together guaranteed that the Renaissance years failed to galvanise a new sense of nationhood. In 1927, even MacDiarmid had to confess that the Renaissance movement had failed to 'set the heather on fire'.[29] Scots were resistant to the claims and styles of these new prophets and – like the Scottish novelist Frederick Niven (1878–1944), whose favourite literature in his early years included *Deadwood Dick: The Outlaw of the Black Hills* – the Scots typically sought literary stimulus in less challenging works and foreign imports.[30] It is hardly surprising. Poetry in Lallans, by necessity supplied with a glossary, hardly reflected the reality of most Scots' lives and nor did it provide them with a straightforward escape to another one. For a literary movement that sought to empower a nation, it spoke in a language that merely created a new cultural elite as detached from the majority of Scots as the metropolitan elite they sought to replace. In subsequent decades, the use of Scots and Scottish dialects became almost de rigueur in the Scottish literary Establishment and, for a time, language lost its subversive intent. At the end of the day, the Scots tongue was less imbued with a persecution complex from which others could effect a rescue than Gaelic. Alone it would not effect the revolution in letters that many had hoped.

Instead, a fundamental sense of place – usually regional rather than national – emerged as the hallmark of some of Scotland's most successful writers. Edwin Morgan, George MacKay Brown (1921–1996) and Iain Crichton Smith exemplify this tendency in their respective landscapes of Glasgow, Orkney and the Outer Hebrides.[31] Focusing on a community below the national, these authors spoke more of the human condition that was transnational rather than a unique national psyche per se. Yet their cities, islands and villages were Scottish and could be read, on occasion, at a symbolic level as representative of the nation as a whole. In the process, the interface between the regional, the national and the global was blurred.

Realism rather than symbolism, however, asserted the most powerful influence over the writers of the 1960s and beyond and language and place became tools in the pursuit of a more prosaic understanding of the writer's environment rather than necessarily ends in themselves. Such social realism encouraged the unease many felt with the Renaissance project and, with it, a commitment to the creation of a literary canon more evocative of the times and more in keeping with popular, largely urban, concerns. It is hardly surprising, therefore, that there emerged a left-leaning tendency in the works of these years that can be seen clearly in the poetry of Tom Leonard and others. Realism came to be closely aligned with a class agenda that seemed to reaffirm commonly held notions of Scottish egalitarianism and traditional political radicalism. In this sense, at least, it was defensive. The test of realism seemed to be how close one could get to a working-class perspective on contemporary social ills whilst remaining true to the conventions of the literary Establishment. It may have been liberating for some – William McIlvanney became the pre-eminent exponent of Clydesideism around this time – and the activism implied in literary production gave the arts a laudable purpose. But, for others, it was restrictive. The role of women in Scottish society was underplayed and undervalued and the redemptive promise of a socialist Scotland was quickly losing both resonance and supporters as industry died and the Labour Party continually failed to usher in a new commonweal. The poet Kenneth White (1936–) found that 'flat realism began to look like the remains of last night's fish-supper'.[32]

This new environment called for a literature shorn of ideals rather than posing solutions, open to the nihilism of post-industrial society without harking back to working-class communities, critical of authority without promoting material alternatives and alive to individuals without making claims about their typicality. Abroad, two Scots – Alexander Trocchi (1925–1984) and the aforementioned Kenneth White – had embraced such dynamics years before.[33] As a leading figure in the counter culture of Paris in the 1950s and later in New York, Trocchi flatly rejected the 'turgid, petty, provincial . . . stale porridge, bible-class nonsense' he identified in the Scottish arts in the early 1960s, choosing instead the dissolution of the self and the transcendence of nationalism and a restrictive literary Establishment afforded him in a heady cocktail of heroin addiction and post-structural cultural resistance.[34] His novels

Young Adam (1957) and *Cain's Book* (1961) are reminders of this literary thread only recently woven into the story of Scottish literature.[35] By contrast, White sought the same distance from fixed social categories in emerging personal theories of geopoetics and nomadism but, unlike Trocchi, he did so from the relative comfort of a professorial office at the Sorbonne.[36] Like earlier generations, prophets of a new order were not necessarily accorded the warmest welcome in their own country – MacDiarmid referred to Trocchi as 'cosmopolitan scum'. And, having been freed from the paternal stranglehold of one messianic literary figure (MacDiarmid died in 1978), Scottish authors were not about to sign up to another literary manifesto, especially as White was identified by many as an 'outsider' and many of his literary outpourings were in French.[37]

Cue the novelist James Kelman and others. With novels set in recognisable, if largely nameless spaces, Kelman 'refuse[d] to adopt a narrative voice whose cadences [were] in any significant way different from the demotic utterance of his characters'.[38] Authorial intent was clear – Kelman argued emphatically, in 1998, that 'my culture and my language have the right to exist' – but the author was largely missing from this work.[39] Now there was no omnipotent creator, no saving message, no grand plan, no singular Scotland. Rather, in the work of Kelman, Alasdair Gray and Iain Banks (1954–), confident experimentation took the place of predictable intent in terms of narrative structures and language and made the reader work for her 'story'.[40] Scott-land had clearly been eclipsed. In its stead, Scotland was appreciated as an idea, a 'spectrum of possibilities', a place where only myth might offer meaning – and then only until you reached the last page.[41]

In 1956, Edwin Muir suggested that 'the distinguishing mark of Scottish literature is conservatism'.[42] In the 1990s, few would have agreed. By tackling disturbing themes, experimenting with styles and voices and pushing back the limits of genres, writers such as Irvine Welsh, Iain Banks, Liz Lochhead and others fiercely resisted convention. In their work, meanings were heteroglot and insurgent.[43] By dint of birth, residence or sympathy, they might well have been exemplars of, in Muir's words, a 'Scottish imagination more powerful than the individuality of any Scottish poet or novelist can be'.[44] But most were guided by more than one muse and sought to shape as much as follow the Scotland that gave them life.

LANGUAGE

Changes in language partly necessitated changes in the country's literature but more than just time separated the language of MacDiarmid from that of Irvine Welsh. Linguistic change was a feature writ large in the everyday life of twentieth-century Scotland though, at times, it largely went unnoticed. It was influenced by changing tastes, new experiences and altered social mores. Even Dundee sweet-makers appreciated its significance. In the early twentieth century, the makers of 'Love Hearts' – confectionery dating back to 1793 bearing mottoes such as 'Time will unite us' and 'Guid folk are scarce' – added 'Cupid's Whispers' to their range. These sweets – similar in most respects to the more traditional alternatives – announced in an American accent, 'Say, kid, I like your style' and 'Gee, but you're some baby'. They were sold in towns with cinemas, whereas the older sweets still occupied space on shop counters in more remote areas.[45]

Scotland spoke with different accents and, as the century progressed, more were heard in public forums and more appeared in the printed word. Americanisms entered popular speech across the country as intellectuals mourned the erosion of 'true' Scots.[46] Meanwhile, Glaswegian made it on to the Scottish stage and was nourished decades later by popular TV dramas set in the industrial west of Scotland – *Tutti Frutti*, *Taggart* and *Rab C. Nesbitt* are cases in point. In 1983, Glasgow's poet, Edwin Morgan, noted:

> The acceptable emergence of Glasgow speech, both as an object of linguistic study and as a medium for serious writing, is recent and still has much headway to make, but one can say today with some confidence that the long-ingrained attitudes – linguistic, social, aesthetic – which hindered that emergence have lost the almost automatic respectability they once enjoyed.[47]

Received pronunciation, the 'Queen's English' and an insistence on 'speaking properly' gave way to the celebration of accent, dialect and linguistic diversity in the last thirty years of the century, as if an invading army of letters had been conquered by indigenous forces in speech and sound.

Yet, in the north of Scotland, this phenomenon coincided with the commodification of the Doric[48] – it survived the century largely as a comedic medium and a reminder of an older agricultural community more alive in tourist brochures and folk songs than in reality – and 'the virtual disappearance' of the monoglot Gael.[49] While over 250,000 Scots, at the turn of the century, were fluent in Gaelic, by its end, less than 100,000 could even 'understand' the language and, of these, the vast majority were concentrated in Lochalsh, Skye and the Outer Hebrides.[50] Some innovative reforms had been introduced to sustain the language. A

Chair in Celtic was founded in the University of Edinburgh as early as 1883, An Comunn Gàidhealach (known largely for its sponsorship of the annual Gaelic cultural festival, the Royal National Mòd) was founded in 1891, Gaelic was an option leading towards the award of the Leaving Certificate in Scottish schools from 1904 and the 1918 Education Act made the teaching of Gaelic compulsory in Gaelic-speaking areas.[51] (By the 1930s, Gaelic was being taught to 7,129 pupils in 284 schools across Scotland.[52]) But there was worrying evidence that younger Gaels were abandoning the language as the century progressed – in 1972–73, around 56 per cent of youngsters in Harris used Gaelic regularly in play, whereas the figure had been over 91 per cent around fifteen years earlier.[53]

Gaelic radio broadcasting dated back to 1926 and, by the 1970s, around three hours a week were devoted to Gaelic radio programmes and around fifteen minutes of TV airtime. The introduction of VHF broadcasting enhanced this service and the foundation of the BBC's Radio nan Eilean, based in Stornoway, did much to add a local touch to Gaelic on the airwaves. Gaelic publishing benefited immensely from the foundation of the Gaelic quarterly *Gairm*, which appeared in 1952, and the poetry of writers such as Somhairle MacGill-Eain (Sorley MacLean, 1911–1996), Iain Mac a' Ghobhainn (Iain Crichton Smith), Fearghas MacFhionnlaigh and Aonghas MacNeacail proved an important and, in many ways, a unique feature of Scotland's cultural development in which native and cosmopolitan influences were intertwined. A Gaelic college was established in Skye in 1973 (Sabhal Mór Ostaig) and the proceedings of the new Western Isles Council (Comhairle nan Eilean, established in 1975) were partly conducted in Gaelic from its early days. Still, in the 1980s, the number of Gaelic speakers was declining.

Assisted by several million pounds from an uncharacteristically generous Conservative cultural strategy, Gaelic became a focus of public attention in the last two decades of the century. In 1985 a national development agency for Gaelic, Comunn na Gàidhlig, was established and Gaelic-medium education was seized on as Gaelic's last hope for revival.[54] By now, even the churches were finding it difficult to recruit and retain sufficient numbers of Gaelic-speaking clergy who were confident enough to use the language in the pulpit and instituted their first ever course in Gaelic preaching in 1994 at the University of Aberdeen.[55] By 2003, in Highland Region alone, 45 schools with more than 1,100 pupils and 74 teachers were involved in Gaelic medium education, and an additional 54 schools with more than 1,300 pupils were teaching Gaelic as a subject of study.[56] Across the Highlands and Islands, the Fèis movement sought, in the 1990s, to resuscitate traditional Gaelic crafts, sports and music and the Scottish

Arts Council invested more money than ever before in 'Gaelic arts'.[57] At much the same time, new bilingual road signs confused natives and tourists alike in their sojourns in the Hebrides and, on television, Gaelic programmes self-consciously targeted the young in their attempts to appear more relevant. But, still, the numbers of Scots speaking Gaelic declined – between 1991 and 2001, despite the initiatives outlined above, the number of Gaelic speakers fell by 11 per cent, to 58,650. Gaels themselves were notoriously resistant to the political activism and intellectualism associated with attempts at Gaelic revival – they typically appreciated their language in the context of local relations, not national initiatives or grand cultural designs and, for most, it was not seen as the sole defining element of their identity.[58]

Only time will tell if such developments and the plethora of Gaelic strategies that emerged in the first years of the Scottish Parliament will eventually go beyond identifying the character of Gaelic's decline to halting it.[59] If this is achieved, then maybe Gaelic's modern history will be told in the language itself rather than through the narrative of the bodies that sought to 'rescue' it.

PICTURES WITHOUT WORDS – SCOTTISH ART

[W]e observed in almost every part of Scotland, except Edinburgh, that we were reminded ten times of France and Germany, for once of England.

> *Recollections of a Tour Made in Scotland* (1803)
> Dorothy Wordsworth

The care with which general statements are made regarding Scotland's art is testament to the fact that Scottish roots did not necessarily point to a national style or shared approach in the twentieth century.[60] Still, there were a number of features that were distinctive, though not necessarily distinctively Scottish. Accomplished painterly technique and skilful artistic draughtsmanship were qualities valued throughout the century and these in turn rested on the rigorous training of the art schools of Glasgow and Edinburgh[61] whose, at times, antagonistic relationship contributed a healthy competitiveness to what was a relatively small academic artistic community.[62] In part, this was symptomatic of a regional dynamic in the art itself that echoed the sense of place that inspired many Scottish novelists. For example, the seascapes of William McTaggart (1835–1910) created on the eve of the twentieth century are clearly Atlantic pieces and their execution reveals an instinctive Gaelic sensitivity. And, yet, Scottish artists were far more akin to the nation's poets when it came to their emotive intent. Just as Scottish poets generally eschewed the epic and, in preference, chose far shorter verse as their canvas, so artists typically sought to capture a fleeting moment or condense complex ideas through symbol in works that strained within the confines of gilt-edged frames. As Ian Finlay noted of the 'Glasgow Boys' of the first decades of the century, '[T]hey chase the impalpable.'[63]

Yet the artists of the twentieth century were a diverse lot and, in a very real sense, painted on international canvasses – Scotland was but one of many influences. In this, they exemplify a common cultural tendency – the 'conjunction of the national and the international' has been seen as characteristic of the Scottish cultural tradition.[64] That tradition itself also encouraged diversity: beckoning some to follow ('tradition has sought them out'), while others resolutely rejected its entreaties to adopt the paths established by previous generations.[65] In sum, Scotland's art in the twentieth century was forged in the spaces where the international met the national, and tradition and resistance were fused. Pastiche and imitation were the dangers inherent in these respective dynamics avoided only by those whose art bore witness to a strong sense of individualism. (Another throwback to religion?) Is it any wonder that a 'Scottish School' failed to emerge?

The 'Glasgow Boys' of the turn of the century – James Paterson (1854–1932), R. M. Stevenson (1854–1952), John Lavery (1856–1941), George Henry (1858–1943), James Guthrie (1859–1930) and Arthur Melville (1855–1904) (the list is not exhaustive) – were clearly influenced by the work of the American artist James McNeill Whistler (1834–1903) who was awarded an honorary doctorate by the University of Glasgow in 1903 and whose portrait of Thomas Carlyle was the first of his works to be purchased for a public gallery when the Corporation of Glasgow bought it in 1891. Japanese and Impressionist influences are also clear in their works, although the Glasgow palette was often more vibrant than that of the French. These artists owed much to the city whose name they bore. Art dealers, John Forbes White (1831–1904) and Alexander Reid (1854–1928), were the principal conduits of the European influences that infused the works of these artists but Scottish capital and Scottish scenes rooted this school firmly in their native environment. Their long-term legacy for Scottish art, however, was perhaps in their emphasis on design – a feature most evident in the work of their contemporary, Charles Rennie Mackintosh (1868–1928) who, alongside Margaret Macdonald (1863–1933), Frances Macdonald (1874–1921) and Herbert MacNair (1868–1955) ('The Four'), explored the insights offered by modernism in painting, the decorative arts and architecture from a perspective still alive to the draw of myth and history more associated with their forebears.[66]

The Scottish Colourists, following after them, similarly drew heavily on continental and avant-garde influences. S. J. Peploe (1871–1935) explored the insights into form offered by Cubism and, in the work of his friend J. D. Fergusson, the vortex of cultural and philosophical dynamics that shaped Paris in the years before the Great War is evident. But their borrowing was taken only so far. Fergusson, in particular, claimed a Celtic inspiration and, for most, their modernism had conservative tendencies at best.[67] The insights into colour gleaned from Matisse and other French fauvists nevertheless inspired the Colourists' passion for the rich palette of the Mediterranean which, in turn, influenced the 'Edinburgh School' of Anne Redpath (1895–1965) and others from the 1930s onwards. She herself remarked, 'I am someone who is very interested in colour – and by that I mean bright colour, gay colour.'[68] Their approach to art, however, was less intellectual than that of their forebears, more concerned with technique and strongly subjective – making them hard to categorise and thus too easy to dismiss.[69] They were a soft target for post-war artists seeking a purpose for their craft beyond the decorative – as was the London-based Scot Duncan Grant (1885–1978) of the Bloomsbury Group – although it took some time for that purpose to emerge.[70] In the interim, the neo-romanticism evident in the early works of Kilmarnock's Robert Colquhoun (1914–1962) and the debt his later work owed to the influence of Picasso identify him as an important transitional figure in Scottish art, whose figurative works presage the interests of subsequent generations of Scottish artists.[71]

It was, however, to be expressionism that would guide Scottish artists in the years following the Second World War. This is clearly evident in the work of artists such as adopted-Scot Robin Philipson (1916–1992),[72] most notably in his cock-fighting series.[73] Here the painter's emotive response to the scenes and objects he depicts was to the fore – Philipson's technique and use of colour were tools in this process of expression rather than ends in themselves. Similarly, abstract expressionism offered Joan Eardley (1921–1963) the freedom to reflect the intensity of the North Sea as seen from her home in Catterline. But expressionism too readily found its echo, if only a quiet one, in the art of earlier Scottish artists – the elder McTaggart's *The Storm* (1890) springs to mind – to effect a radical shift in the Academy. Instead, in the 1960s it was institutional rather than, or at least as much as, intellectual change that empowered Scottish artists to redefine their art. The opening of the Scottish National Gallery of Modern Art in Edinburgh in 1960 and the foundation of the Scottish Arts Council in 1967 offered Scottish artists valuable resources that would sustain a revolution in both the status and the direction of modern art.

The work of John Bellany (1942–) heralded the re-emergence of realism and figurative art after decades during which abstraction seemed to have claimed the sympathies of the art Establishment and still lifes and landscapes were the preferred canvasses on gallery walls. Strongly allegorical, his paintings told stories of his sea-soaked childhood and his religion – they were not that easy on the eye and required a cerebral as much as a sympathetic response from their audience. But it was the first indication that something rather different was happening. In the years that followed, a radical approach to figurative painting became the hallmark of a new generation of Glasgow painters who – like the 'Boys' of two generations earlier – found a ready global clientele while retaining something of the city in their work. *Glasgow Triptych* (1986) by Ken Currie (1960–) borrowed heavily from the legacy of Mexican mural artist Diego Rivera and proved that the reach of Scottish artists could stretch to epic proportions and their brushes could tell stories and reveal histories as well as capture a momentary insight or reveal a certain sensuality. Like the Clydeside literary school, this was art with intent – it was political, it was polemical and it offered an alternative socialist narrative to the bleak post-industrial / post-'79-referendum anxieties that pre-occupied the nation.[74] Yet not all his contemporaries shared Currie's confidence and his own early certainties became increasingly qualified as the century drew to a close. Bold figurative works and powerful symbolism were dominant tendencies in the work of Steven Campbell (1953–2007), Peter Howson (1958–) and Adrian Wiszniewski (1958–) but the confidence of their technique and the vigour of their imagination were not wedded to a definitive 'message'.[75] Instead, their visual language was poetic, ambiguous and often contradictory. Similarly, while the central concern of Currie's later works is undoubtedly morality, little can be said beyond this. In his studies of heads, torsos and death masks, man is no longer seen in or saved by the mass – even the body is denied its wholeness. The nihilism of the novels of Kelman and Gray find their artistic shadow in Currie's silent witnesses – in both cases, only symbols retain any meaning as reality is revealed as contested and confused.

Despite a tendency to explore the limits of realism, these artists were not chroniclers. Euan McArthur has written that what one found in Steven Campbell's work was 'a realism based on the exposure of dogmas . . . It amounts to an attempt to depict the condition of knowledge as fragmented, multiple, and synchronous.'[76] These artists did not recreate Scotland or Scottishness on canvas and nor did they necessarily believe that it could have been done even if it was desirable. For the most part, their art also failed to find a ready audience among everyday Scots. At the end of the century, domestic interiors were not typically enlivened by Peter Howson's challenging canvasses which took issue with modern masculinity but more commonly embraced the reassuring pastels of impressionist prints or the photographic landscapes of a new generation of Scottish postcard artists.[77] Art, therefore, did not straightforwardly reveal Scotland's history in these years. And, yet, changing over time, responsive to international stimuli and intimately bound by a marketplace and institutions funded by British capital, Scottish art exemplified Scotland's twentieth-century condition. So did Scotland's music.

MUSIC – WHERE NATIVE AND FOREIGN COLLIDE

It is relatively easy to identify the most obvious indigenous influences on Scotland's musical heritage in the twentieth century – the sound of the great pipes, the traditions of island fiddlers, the rhythm of the Border ballads, the poetry of Scotland's bards and landscapes and the pulse of history can be found in the works of many Scottish composers. Yet their treatment of these themes changed as the century wore on as contemporary imperatives encouraged Scotland's composers to reassess their significance for each generation. On the eve of the twentieth century, Greenock-born Hamish MacCunn (1868–1916) set Scotland to music in overtures such as 'Land of the Mountain and the Flood' (1887) and exploited the treasure trove of Sir Walter Scott's novel *The Heart of Midlothian* in his opera *Jeanie Deans* of 1894.[78] Meanwhile, his contemporary, John Blackwood McEwen (1868–1948), a Principal of the Royal Academy of Music in London (1924–1936), was inspired by Scotland's borderlands in *The Solway Symphony* (1911), first performed by the Bournemouth Symphony Orchestra in 1922. These works were characteristic of late-Victorian romanticism and spoke to well-established popular tastes for all things recognisably 'Scotch'.

After 1918, however, modernist impulses increasingly influenced the treatment of conventional Scottish themes in much the same way as they informed new literary and artistic insights into national identity. But they did not destroy their popularity. An important contributor to the interwar Renaissance in the Scottish arts, F. G. Scott (1880–1958) (at one time teacher of the Langholm schoolboy Christopher Grieve), looked to Scottish flora for inspiration in his 1932 song 'Milkwort and Bog

Cotton' and relished the texture of Grieve's language in his treatment of the poet's 'The Eemis Stane' in 1924.[79] Erik Chisholm (1904–1965), meanwhile, blended modernism with the ancient strains of pibroch in works such as his first piano concerto, premiered in Amsterdam in 1933. And bagpipes again were to be heard in Edward McGuire's (1948–) searching symphonic poem *Calgacus* (1976), where they counterpoint explosive percussion, and triumphantly and hilariously in *An Orkney Wedding, with Sunrise* (1984) by Peter Maxwell Davies – the northern isles' modern Mendelssohn.[80] For many of these later composers, their muse encouraged a more critical and contemporary rendering of tradition. William Sweeney (1950–) would weld jazz saxophone and orchestra with the motifs of the Gaelic musical tradition in his work *An Rathad Ur* (1988). And, two years later, James MacMillan's *The Confession of Isobel Gowdie* (1990) offered a belated requiem for a victim of the seventeenth-century witch-hunts. The composer noted:

> On behalf of the Scottish people the work craves absolution and offers Isobel Gowdie the mercy and humanity that was denied her in the last days of her life. To do this I have tried to capture the soul of Scotland in music.[81]

Both Sweeney and MacMillan were motivated by strong social and, in the case of MacMillan, religious convictions which, while not prescriptive, impart to their work a moral seriousness that commands attention and mirrors the concerns of some of their literary and artistic contemporaries.[82] (Sweeney's orchestral work, *Sunset Song* (1986), was commissioned by the STUC.)

In their treatment of Scottish themes, then, and in their adoption of Scottish instruments – the pipes were to music what Scots was to poetry – Scottish composers were certainly rooted in a particular Scottish cultural environment. But the Scottish classical tradition also had an international dynamic. Erik Chisholm was affectionately known as 'MacBartok' owing to the influence of the Hungarian pianist and composer on his own compositions.[83] And in 1948–49, Chisholm composed his second concerto, based on Hindustani themes. Similarly, while Edinburgh's Thea Musgrave (1928–) was clearly in debt to the nation of her birth in her 1977 opera, *Mary, Queen of Scots*, other works – including the opera *The Voice of Ariadne* (1972); the concerto *Journey through a Japanese Landscape* (1994), based on a series of haiku; the opera *Símon Bolívar* (1993); and 'Voices from the Ancient World', commissioned by the Scottish Flute Trio in 1998 – explore much more diverse and truly international influences.[84]

One could also point to anglicising tendencies in Scotland's recent musical past. The sanitisation and conservative choral arrangements imposed upon much of the early Scottish folk canon robbed Scotland of some of its most authentic oral styles and arrangements. Marjory Kennedy-Fraser's arrangements of Hebridean songs collected by Father Allan MacDonald of Eriskay (1859–1905) and others attempted to standardise and harmonise Gaelic melodies into forms more in keeping with conventional tastes. Her *Songs of the Hebrides* was published in 1905 to popular acclaim but, by the century's end, most regretted her legacy.[85] The Gaelic Establishment did not escape such influence. Ailie Munro records:

> A wit from the island of Lewis writing in the *Stornoway Gazette* in the 1950s, protests none too subtly: 'To win at the Mod, ye singers, leave the natural airs at home, then go to some professor of the musical arts who will train you in Eyetalian airs and the taafetiffies and the doramifasosos till such a time as you can hold a note from Queen Street to Mallaig.[86]

In the later twentieth century, most appreciated that Scotland sang best in its own accent and to its own rhythm. That others listened was a bonus born of a revolution in communications that also allowed Scotland to hear the voice of others.

This musical 'space' created where native and foreign collide and coalesce was evident to the majority of Scots in the development of the nation's folk and pop music. Both academic and political dynamics inspired the rediscovery of Scottish 'folk' in the 1950s – the foundation of the School of Scottish Studies in 1951 and the remarkable song collections of Hamish Henderson and Norman Buchan (1922–1990) offered inspiration to singers and instrumentalists alike seeking an echo of their own voice in Scotland's past. A growing folk-club scene, new BBC radio broadcasts in these years and the legendary People's Festival Ceilidhs in Edinburgh, beginning in 1951, enhanced the profile of Scotland's native song traditions further. Then, in the civil rights protests and anti-nuclear campaigns of the sixties and seventies and the industrial protests and nationalist resurgence of the eighties and nineties, Scotland's folk musicians created something of a 'democratic muse'.[87] Hamish Henderson's 'Freedom Come All Ye' became an unofficial anthem asserting a distinctively Scottish egalitarian agenda with a global reach. Meanwhile, when it came to performance, bands such as The Corries, Silly Wizard, The Battlefield Band, The Whistlebinkies (counting Edward McGuire among their number) and Capercaillie came to boast an international following, as did soloists such as Dougie MacLean (1954–) and the dynamic pairing of Aly Bain (1946–) and Phil Cunningham (1960–).[88] Yet, for Scotland's songsmiths, folk remained a very personal vehicle to record their passions and their place in a Scotland that had gone bad, gone wrong or had simply gone. Archie Fisher and Bobby Campbell's 'The Shipyard Apprentice' is a hymn to the lives which were made and unmade by the changing fortunes of Scottish shipbuilding.

> I was born in the shadow of a Fairfield crane,
> And the blast of a freighter horn
> Was the very first sound that reached my ears
> On the morning I was born.
> I lay and listened to the shipyard noise
> Coming out of the big unknown,
> And was sung to sleep by the mother tongue
> That was to be my own . . .
>
> For I sat and listened tae my father tell
> Of the Clyde that he once knew
> Where you either sweated for a measly wage
> Or joined the parish queue.
> Where life grew harder day by day
> Along the riverside
> Oh it's oft I've heard my mother say
> It was tears that made the Clyde.[89]

Song may have offered consolation but could suggest few solutions. Socialism and nationalism variously harnessed Scottish songs for political purposes but little in the way of a revolution would be rhymed into melody. By the 1990s, Scottish folk music was as commercially inspired as other musical genres but it was far from the tame creature of market forces.

Emerging in the 1950s as rock'n'roll, Scottish pop music represented a reaction against the polite predictability of Scotland's ballroom orchestras and the repetitive strains of Scottish country-dance bands. In the thirties and forties, however, the 'Big Bands' held sway – Louis Freeman, the musical director of Green's Playhouse, was a household name in Glasgow, as was Andy Lothian, the band leader of Dundee's Palais who had led the musical entertainment at the Empire Exhibition in 1938.[90] For more Scottish tastes, there was Auchtermuchty's Jimmy Shand, Kirriemuir's Jim Cameron and Bobby MacLeod from Tobermory whose radio broadcasts attracted toe-tapping audiences both young and old from the late-forties.[91] It took some time for Scots to abandon band-leaders for 'pop stars'.

Nevertheless, individual Scots – many of them inspired by American rhythm and blues artistes and early Motown hits – made important contributions to the new order, thought by most to be nothing more than 'another passing fad, a momentary madness' in the 1950s.[92] Glasgow-born Lonnie Donegan (1931–2002), offered a Celtic twist to skiffle in memorable numbers such as 'Rock Island Line'; Alex Harvey (1935–82) – in various guises – followed suit, having won a competition to find Scotland's 'Tommy Steele' in 1957 and, in 1958, Scotland's own kilted 'Elvis' – Jackie Dennis – took 'Le Da Da' into the 'Top 5'.[93] In the early days, imitation rather than innovation marked the Scottish scene. However, by the 1960s, Alex Harvey had abandoned skiffle for soul and the 1963 Polydor recording of *Alex Harvey and His Soul Band* has since gone down as Scotland's first rock album – even though it was not recorded by the Soul Band line-up.[94] Across Scotland, town and village halls were commandeered and dance halls and cinemas made way for pop venues of various kinds. In 1960, this offered sufficient scope for Johnny Gentle to tour the Highlands with a relatively unknown support band – The Silver Beatles. After gigs in Alloa, Inverness and Fraserburgh, the performers reached Nairn where:

> [b]eyond the girls hugging the stage couples jived and girls danced together whilst the unattached lads leant against the wall at the back, puffing on cigarettes and trying hard to look like they didn't really want to be there.[95]

Even a major Scottish tour in 1963, when The Beatles this time topped the bill, left little in the way of an immediate impression on the local music scene.[96]

Much was to change, however, in the next couple of years. On 15 June 1965, twenty fainting cases and twenty-five arrests at Glasgow's Odeon venue were followed the next day by a heavy police presence at the Usher Hall as The Rolling Stones continued a four-day Scottish tour with two gigs in the capital. *Edinburgh Evening News* reporter, John Gibson, looked on in disbelief at scenes that were to become only too familiar at pop concerts over the next three decades:

> For hysteria, bedlam and sheer idle [sic] worship both the Stones' shows . . . beat every pop promotion staged in Edinburgh so far.
>
> The hairiest and reputedly ugliest group in the business out-Beatled the Beatles.
>
> The screaming, stamping, storming hordes never gave the Stones a chance to make their earthy jungle music heard above the din . . .

[Mick Jagger's] every gyration in 'The Last Time', 'Route 66', and 'Little Red Rooster' had the teenagers in an uncontrollable frenzy.[97]

When it came to local talent, groups such as Lulu and The Luvvers represented Scotland's principal contribution to the conventional pop scene of the sixties, when they reached No. 7 in the hit parade in 1964 with The Isley Brothers' 'Shout'. The Scottish diaspora also played its part in developing popular music worldwide, when three emigrant Scots – Glaswegians Angus and Malcolm Young and Kirriemuir's Bon Scott – came together in Australia as the rock group AC/DC in 1974.[98] But Scottish bands in the old country generally made little impression on the music scene beyond their local communities – the big record labels, the major promoters and the most influential radio stations were all based in London. There were exceptions, of course. Glasgow's Donovan exploited the rising interest in folk music in the mid 1960s, Dunfermline band, Nazareth, entered the top ten after the launch of their third album *Razamanaz* in 1973 and Tayside's Average White Band, after relocating to New York, went to No. 1 in the US album charts in 1974. Back home, however, the pop sensation which was The Bay City Rollers – Britain's first 'boy band' – blanketed teenage Britain in tartan in the early 1970s to the accompaniment of catchy if unremarkable hits such as 'Shang-A-Lang' (No. 2, 1974) and 'Bye Bye Baby' (No. 1, 1975).[99] Of more substance, if initially less commercially successful, was the Fife band, The Skids, and Jim Kerr's Simple Minds which, having signed with Virgin Records in 1981, made it to the No. 1 spot in America with 'Don't You (Forget About Me)' in 1985. Success also beckoned for bands such as Clydebank's Wet Wet Wet whose version of The Troggs' single 'Love is All Around' spent fifteen weeks at No. 1 in the British charts in 1994. Fife's Proclaimers also tackled linguistic and aesthetic pop conventions in the 1980s and 1990s as these bespectacled Scottish nationalists, in hits such as 'Letter from America' and 'I'm Gonna Be (500 miles)', proved the potency of native dialect and raw talent in an otherwise saccharine pop scene. At much the same time, Runrig's folk-rock albums *Heartland* (1985) and *The Cutter and the Clan* (1987) introduced the cadences of Gaelic song into the hit parade to popular acclaim and commercial success. By then, football stadia across Scotland – at one time the reserve of silence during the close season – had become favoured venues for major international acts and more home-grown talent.

Even international Scottish artistes, however, carried with them the mark of their origins. The Eurythmics were named by their lead singer, Aberdonian Annie Lennox (1954–), after her music and movement classes at school and, along with Midge Ure (James Ure, 1953–) – lead singer with 1980s' band Ultravox and one-time apprentice engineer – they and others emerged from communities whose identities were being ripped apart by economic depression. (Lennox's communist father had worked in Aberdeen's shipyards and on the railway and the singer's last summer job before entering London's Royal Academy of Music was at the local fish-processing factory.) For both Lennox and Ure, local musicians were instrumental in introducing them to music. Lennox's father was a piper and she herself was a keen visitor to Aberdeen's Beach Ballroom.[100] Ure, meanwhile, was introduced to playing in public when Adam McNaughton – Ure's teacher and himself a major figure in the Scottish folk revival – encouraged him to play guitar in the Rutherglen folk club.[101]

Across Scotland, however, these years saw the decline of the amateur musical tradition. Participation in Scotland's choral and amateur orchestral traditions waned – after touring war-ravaged Germany in 1946, the world-famous Glasgow Orpheus Choir sang its last encore in 1951 – and alternative attractions and access to a variety of media diverted Scots from local concerts and recitals.[102] Music had become a commercial enterprise to an extent unknown in the first half of the century and its associational dynamic suffered in much the same way as church-centred activities paid the price for the privatisation of leisure. Technological change made it possible to listen to orchestral works and international 'names' in the privacy of one's home but made it more likely that fewer amateur orchestras could be sustained and that local talent would aspire to celebrity rather than necessarily musicianship.

STAGE AND SCREEN

We went to the Gaiety Theatre in Leith every week . . . and the Theatre Royal and the Empire about once a month and we loved it. The Gaiety was very popular and I went there a lot during the war years and I didn't pay any attention to who was playing, you just went along to that week's show and they were all good. The small local shows would have singers, jugglers, comedians, and four or six dancers. We saw all kind of acts: animals, acrobats, and contortionists, maybe two or three double-jointed men, doing incredible things.

Ina Howden (1921–), theatregoer[103]

In 1900, Scotland boasted thirty-two theatres and, a decade later, fifty-three theatres were in operation. The larger theatres in the major Scottish cities were already features of the urban skyline when the century opened but, in the heady days of Edwardian entertainment, smaller Scottish towns built their own variety theatres. The Gaiety in Ayr opened in 1902, Dundee and Greenock both boasted an Empire a year later and, in 1904, the King's opened its doors in Kirkcaldy.[104] Theatres, in turn, encouraged leisure developments in surrounding areas – Annovazzi's Fish Restaurant and the ice-cream parlour of Moncogni & Co were well placed to attract the audiences of Glasgow's Tivoli Variety Theatre, which opened in 1899.[105] War, however, was to turn many of these pleasure palaces into recruiting offices and stages became the vehicles of patriotism and propaganda. At much the same time, cinema also challenged the theatre as the focus of light entertainment and, by 1920, the number of Scottish theatres had dropped to forty-five and fell further, to thirty, a decade later.[106] Even innovations like the successful 'Half Past Eight Shows', sponsored by the Howard and Wyndham company in the early thirties to encourage the development of summertime urban theatre audiences, and popular Scottish talent – Sir Harry Lauder (1870–1950), Rikki Fulton (1924–2004), Johnny Beattie (1927–), Stanley Baxter (1928–) and Walter Carr (1926–1998) all made a name for themselves on Scotland's variety stages – failed to save these havens of the last Scottish minstrels.[107] It was not only the British Empire that died after the Second World War – the Glasgow Empire, the second largest variety theatre in Britain, made way for the developers in March 1963, the Clydebank Empire was reduced to ashes in a fire in June 1959 and even a licensed bar from 1954 could not save Greenock's Empire, which staged its last performance in May 1957.[108]

In 1937, the playwright James Bridie (1888–1951) confessed that 'Scottish theatre is still young and immature' and, until the 1950s, variety and music hall were pretty much all there was of a popular theatrical tradition in Scotland.[109] 'Serious' theatre was largely represented by a few 'short-lived professional organizations and long-running amateur groups.'[110] As early as 1929, the actor Duncan Macrae (1905–1967) bemoaned this sorry state of affairs and highlighted the risks it posed for the nation's native theatrical sensibility:

The Art of the Theatre is the art of conceiving a play as acted in a particular style in a particular place. Without this approach Scottish Drama will continue to waver indeterminately following the lead of the West End in a vicious Piccadilly Circus.[111]

Alfred Wareing's Glasgow Repertory Company (established in 1909) had, by this time, tried and failed to buck the trend that cast Scottish theatre as a provincial interest. Although it was the first British company to stage a Chekhov play – it produced *The Seagull* in 1909 – it failed to make a profit and ceased business in 1914.[112] Similarly, The Scottish National Players were launched in 1921 with the explicit aim of encouraging the development of distinctive Scottish drama.[113] However, despite boasting the production talents of Tyrone Guthrie (1900–1971) over two seasons, the Players failed to do for Scotland what the Abbey Theatre had achieved for Ireland and had petered out by 1947.[114] Scotland's amateur talents, meanwhile, were corralled in the Scottish Community Drama Association (SCDA, established in 1926) and were enlivened by that organisation's annual festival of one-act plays. But, from a high point of 500 entries in 1951, the festival attracted only a little over 200 applications by 1961.

In the aftermath of the Second World War, the impetus behind theatre in the main urban centres became more radical and more proletarian. In Glasgow, the Citizen's Theatre (established in 1943) and the Unity Theatre group (established in 1941) seized the moment. More conservative bourgeois tastes retreated to the provincial theatres or sought solace in dependable renditions of classic works.[115] Indeed, James Bridie regretted, in 1942, how the stage tended to 'insulate itself against contemporary life'.[116] Nevertheless, increasingly Scots was to be heard on stage and new Scottish works were being staged at a rate and of a quality hitherto unknown. In the 1930s, the work of John Brandane (1869–1947) – for example, *The Glen Is Mine* (1923) – Joe Corrie (1894–1968) – for example, *In Time o' Strife* (1928) – Robert McLellan (1907–1985) – for example, *Jamie the Saxt* (1937) – and James Bridie – for example, *The Anatomist* (1930) – grew in popularity, bringing historic characters and contemporary concerns with industrial relations and Highland landownership on to the Scottish stage. And something of a renaissance seemed to beckon when Tyrone Guthrie's production of Robert Kemp's edition of *Ane Satyre of the Thrie Estaitis* (1552) by Sir David Lindsay (c.1490–c.1555) with music by the Scottish composer Cedric Thorpe Davie (1913–1983) attracted substantial audiences at Edinburgh's second International Festival in 1948. (The first had eschewed any engagement with indigenous works.) On stage, new Scottish talents were attracting attention from further afield – Duncan Macrae starred in his first feature film, *The Brothers*, in 1947; after 1965, Walter Carr became a household name as Dougie, the mate in the long-running BBC TV series *The Vital Spark*; and Russell Hunter (1925–2004), having begun his stage career with the Unity Theatre after an apprenticeship in a Clyde shipyard, first appeared on the silver screen in the film version of *The Gorbals Story* in 1950.[117] More experimental styles in the 1960s, however, failed to attract big box-office profits and central government grants encouraged a safe reliance on popular plays. (Macrae himself had moved into variety in 1950.) But the century's last three decades saw something of a theatrical renaissance in Scotland, as local talent was supported through new commissions, innovative direction – Giles Havergal (1938–) arrived at the Citizens Theatre in 1969 and stayed until 2003 – and, eventually, greater devolved control over Arts Council resources. (Responsibility for the Scottish Arts Council eventually passed to the Scottish Office in 1994.) In 1968, the Traverse Theatre in Edinburgh set out to radicalise Scottish drama (and came pretty close); in 1978, seventy Scottish theatre companies appeared on the Edinburgh Festival Fringe; and, as the Scottish Parliament opened its doors, it seemed only a matter of time before the dream of successive theatrical generations – a Scottish National Theatre – would become a reality.[118] (Its first performances took place in the spring of 2006.) Progress had been slight and stuttering at times but, in the final decades of the century, Scottish theatre was transformed.

Even in the latter half of the twentieth century, however, variety had its place and a peculiar Scottish take on this most British of theatrical institutions was still evident. Tyrone Guthrie considered the annual Christmas pantomime at the Princess Theatre in Glasgow's Gorbals, starring Tommy Lorne (1890–1935), as 'one of the most impressive pieces of real native theatre in Glasgow . . . true and lively folk art'.[119] Scots took panto seriously. Scottish panto runs were typically longer than those in other UK theatres and reputations could be made or broken when comedians donned the frock of a panto dame. Moreover, from the 1960 Alhambra pantomime, *A Wish for Jamie* – a tartan extravaganza with the singer Kenneth McKellar (1927–) in the lead role and Rikki Fulton as the dame – to the very contemporary pantos of Forbes Masson (1963–) at Glasgow's Tron Theatre, Scots were susceptible to panto with a self-consciously Scottish twist. Scottish performers were also quick to identify the particular characteristics of their home crowd – Walter Carr suggested that the 'key traditions of Scottish comedy lie in homeliness'; Johnny Beattie emphasised that 'Glasgow has a very down-to-earth sense of humour'; and Stanley Baxter pointed to 'language' as the 'elusive thing' which made Scottish comedy.[120] Others broke the mould: Chic Murray's (1919–1985) humour was variously described as abstract and surreal, while the mature Billy Connolly (1942–) moved, comedically and (almost) literally, a million miles from the stair-heid humour that had been the hallmark of his early career.

Common theatrical forms clearly lent themselves to very local interpretations, suggesting that the authorship of Scottish plays was but a poor indicator of the health of Scottish theatre. For as long as it lasted, Scottish variety did much to sustain Scottish theatrical traditions in a way that was meaningful to a great proportion of Scots – those who ignored it in the search for a more intellectual treatment of Scotland on stage were destined to relearn its lessons. It was no coincidence that some of the most popular works of the modern Scottish theatre blended song and story – John McGrath's (1935–2002) *The Cheviot, the Stag and the Black, Black Oil (1973)* and Liz Lochhead's *Mary Queen of Scots Got her Head Chopped Off* (1989), for example. That was what Scottish theatre had always been about.

Scots were enthusiastic filmgoers from an early stage in the development of the medium in the UK, when the 'moving pictures' were little more than fairground attractions. Cinema settled in more permanent venues in the 1890s and, on the eve of the First World War, even small towns in Scotland, particularly seaside resorts, often boasted their own cinemas. In 1913 alone, three such cinemas opened – The Star Picture House in Portobello, The Picture House in Dunoon and La Scala in Saltcoats.[121] By the twenties, picture palaces fed the popular imagination. Glasgow's Playhouse Cinema on Renfield Street (established in 1927) had seating for 4,200 and space for a full size orchestra; children's Saturday clubs coaxed pocket money from little fingers; and, by 1930, 634 cinemas were operating in Scotland.[122] By 1951, Scots averaged thirty-eight cinema visits a year in comparison to the British average of twenty-nine.[123] The Scottish director Bill Douglas (1934–1991) offered an insight into why the Scots flocked to the 'flicks':

> For as long as I can remember I always liked the pictures. As a boy I spent so much time in cinemas, a friend suggested I take my bed with me. I would have had it been possible. That was my real home, my happiest place when I was lucky enough to be there. Outside, whether in the village or the city, whether I was seven or seventeen, it always seemed to be raining or grey and my heart would sink to despairing depths. I hated reality.[124]

Cinema auditoriums, as much as the imaginative realm of the films that they showcased, offered an escape in the 1930s. Thereafter, improved housing, an increased standard of living and the arrival of television, however, encouraged more Scots to stay indoors and, as production declined in Hollywood, Scots had less choice in their cinema diet. From the 1960s, attendances fell and increasingly cinemas across Scotland were transformed into bingo halls or left to decay. A resurgence in cinema-going from the 1980s, fed by special effects, big-budget productions and media hype, took time to reach the north of Britain but, by 1994, the number of Scots who attended the cinema at least once a year stood at 73 per cent – nearly 20 per cent more than in 1991.[125] In 1996, there were over ten cinema seats for every 1,000 people in Scotland, compared to 8.6 the previous year and, between 1995 and 1998, the total number of cinema seats in Scotland rose from 44,262 to 66,432.[126] The wooden benches of the 'flea pits' of the interwar years had made way for the cushioned comforts of multi-screen complexes – now Scots could escape in style.

Film-making in Scotland originated in local initiatives dating from the 1890s that recorded significant community events and, by 1917, interest in such material could sustain a regular newsreel, *Scottish Moving Picture News*.[127] Despite such promising beginnings, however, over the course of the century, Scotland failed to develop both the infrastructure and influence necessary to support a vigorous independent film industry. As Hollywood produced the world's first talking pictures, the few Scottish production companies that managed to survive the Depression – for example, the Thames and Clyde Film Company, Campbell Harper Films and Zest films – concentrated on promotional and educational films. Maybe, as Forsyth Hardy (1910–1994), a leading exponent of state-sponsored cinema, suggested, film-making was a business to which the Presbyterian mind was not attuned – rationally there could be no market for make-believe (could there?) and, in any case, the Americans were already ahead of the game.[128] Whatever the truth of such arguments, Scottish film-making emerged through the genre of the documentary – a more laudable endeavour, one supposes, than mere entertainment – and, almost from its birth, this capital-intensive artistic enterprise relied on state subsidy.

In 1934, a Scottish Film Council, supported by the British Film Institute, was established to encourage educational, social and amateur interests in film as a medium. (Glasgow had hosted Britain's first amateur film festival in 1933.) Four years later, the Empire Exhibition of 1938 offered an ideal opportunity for the state – in this case, the Scottish Office under the secretaryship of Walter Elliot – to harness the medium of film for its own promotional purposes. The first Films of Scotland Committee was established, boasting such members as Perthshire's pioneering documentary film-maker John Grierson, the novelist Neil Gunn and the playwright James Bridie, and benefited from a £5,000 donation from Sir John McTaggart (1867–1956), a Glasgow industrialist. Seven Exhibition films were made, among them films depicting Scotland's industries (*Wealth of a Nation*), history (*The Face of Scotland*), agriculture (*They Made the Land*) and education (*The Children's Story*). They signalled the beginning of film's long-running relationship with the government and guaranteed that, more perhaps than any other artistic discipline, Scottish film-making would always be judged in terms of its national relevance and its impact on nationality. As Grierson emphasised, the Films of Scotland Committee was 'founded in a deliberate attempt to use film for national purposes'.[129] To varying degrees, Scottish film-makers have been labouring under this patriotic imperative ever since.

With the onset of war in 1939, the Films of Scotland Committee was effectively wound up and, in its stead, the initiative passed to the Ministry of Information which targeted Scottish audiences through films such as *Highland Doctor* (1943), raised hopes of reconstruction in *Power for the Highlands* (1943) and gave a voice, if only a limited one, to the rural periphery in *The Crofters* (1944). It took until 1954 for the Scottish Office to revisit the unfinished business of the Films of Scotland Committee. In that year, it established a second committee bearing the same name, this time partly funded by a generous donation from Hugh Fraser (1903–1966) but intent on attracting further business sponsors as well as public sector interest. Grierson again was a member and Forsyth Hardy took on the role of director. Over twenty-seven years, the second Films of Scotland Committee was involved in the production of 160 films ranging from the Oscar-winning industrial documentary *Seawards the Great Ships* (1960), featuring the Clyde shipyards, to travelogues such as *Walkabout Edinburgh* (1970) and cultural documentaries like *Practical Romantic, Sir Walter Scott* (1969).[130] To meet statuary UK government quotas on the exhibition of home-produced films, documentaries such as these were twinned with more popular box-office hits in cinemas throughout the country. *Seawards*, for example, came as part of a double bill in Rank cinemas with *Tunes of Glory* (1960), an adaptation of the novel of the same name by the Scottish author James Kennaway (1928–1968) that featured Alec Guinness (1914–2000). With the exception of the one-off feature-length productions *The Duna Bull* (1972) and *The Great Mill Race* (1975), the Films of Scotland Committee itself eschewed fiction and tended to produce short films. Its influence, therefore, has to be qualified. As Duncan Petrie has emphasised, its productions were little more than extended commercial advertisements or neatly packaged variations on familiar Scottish themes and stereotypes.[131] They certainly proved to be the training ground for a generation of Scottish cinematographers who resisted the brighter lights of London or Californian sunshine but, when theatrical distribution of their films became impossible to sustain, the Committee limped into retirement in 1982.

In the end, the renaissance in Scottish cinema identified in the last decade of the century was not to be delivered by a singular state institution. No one could have realistically predicted the upsurge in interest in Scotland on screen in the nineties and the way in which it emerged spoke of an independent dynamic, supported yet untamed by the grand designs of the cultural patricians of the Scottish Office. From 1994 onwards, more than ten feature films a year were being produced in Scotland and Scotland had earned itself an enviable reputation in the production of shorts.[132] The short film *Franz Kafka's It's a Wonderful Life* (1993), for example, won Peter Capaldi (1958–) an Oscar. Public funds were made available to promote commercial film production in Scotland for the first time (through the Scottish Film Production Fund) after 1982; monies from the National Lottery certainly encouraged projects that might otherwise have struggled for finance; fresh opportunities also opened up as a consequence of the Glasgow Film Fund after 1992; and the consolidation of funding, support and educational services under Scottish Screen in 1997 strengthened the voice of the film community in Scotland.

But this is only part of the story. The emergence of the Channel Four Television Corporation as a powerful cultural force commissioning new and challenging works greatly assisted young producers and screenwriters. Fresh Hollywood and new Bollywood interest in Scotland – *Kuch Kuch Hota Hai* (1998), for example – exploited the technological infrastructure and skills resources emerging in the Scottish industry. The high profile of a new generation of Scottish actors and writers also drew attention to the industry in the north. At the end of the century, however, much remained to be done. A report commissioned at the request of the Scottish Office in 1996 reaffirmed that there was scope for Scotland to increase its share of the global film industry but highlighted major obstacles, among them insufficient training resources, a lack of capital and the constraints imposed on Scottish developments by the metro-centricity of the British scene.[133]

The health of the Scottish film industry was, however, but one measure of Scotland's influence on this creative medium and its significance for the wider life of the nation. Scots (and Scotland) proved an abiding interest both on and off the silver screen. As scriptwriters, producers and directors, Scots made a valuable contribution to the development of cinema both in the UK and abroad and they shared much in common with others in the arts. Orkney's Margaret Tait (1918–1999) was one of the most influential independent female cinematographers of the twentieth century in Britain. In short works, such as *Where I am is Here* (1964), and her only feature-length work, *Blue Black Permanent* (1992), she was experimental in her approach to the medium and eschewed the role of a straightforward chronicler in films such as *Rose Street* (1956) and *Aspects of Kirkwall* (1981) in the search for something more revealing than simple documentary.[134] In similar fashion, according to Andrew Noble, the film-maker Bill Douglas rejected factualism for a more intense realism in his partly autobiographical trilogy *My Childhood* (1972), *My Ain Folk* (1973) and *My Way Home* (1978) – works largely forgotten by those who decry the provincial couthiness of Scottish cinema.[135] John Grierson, meanwhile, exploited the academic qualities of documentary and graced them with humanity to realise their reforming social potential. Variously as Film Commissioner for Canada, Director of Mass Communication for UNESCO and Controller of the Films Division of the Central Office of Information, his reach was truly global and his influence profound.[136] Frank Lloyd (1889–1960), however, found his way in the world of film rather differently. The Glasgow-born son of music-hall entertainers, he made his first appearance as an extra in a movie in 1913, after a career in vaudeville on America's west coast. Yet it was ultimately as a director that he made his name, winning his first Oscar in 1929 for *The Divine Lady* and directing such classics of early cinema as *Cavalcade* (1933) and *Mutiny on the Bounty* (1934). Years later, screenwriter Alan Sharp (1934–) followed Lloyd in outdoing American cinematographers at their own game. *The Hired Hand* (1971), *Ulzana's Raid* (1972) and *Billy Two Hats* (1974) rank as three of the most influential westerns of the 1970s. Some Scots were clearly adept at producing Americana (Sharp preferred to call it pastiche). But it is telling that, at the close of the century, Sharp was better known for his screenplay for *Rob Roy* (1995) than his early seventies successes.

Cinema's romance with Scotland has been a long one. Five versions of the Mary, Queen of Scots epic were produced in France between 1908 and 1913.[137] Ivor Novello and Gladys Cooper starred in Gaumont's 1923 production, *Bonnie Prince Charlie*, and, thereafter, the interwar years were marked by film adaptations of Kailyard classics. Audiences crowded to see *Beside the Bonnie Brier Bush* in 1921 and, in 1934, Katherine Hepburn starred in RKO's *The Little Minister*. Scotland's landscape as well as its history and literary canon also played a part. In *The Edge of the World* (1937) and *I Know Where I'm Going* (1945), the English director Michael Powell (1905–1990) established a trend for siting filmic Scotland at its extremes – in island communities apart from the rest of the world.[138] Still, the lure of history's more dramatic moments tended to hold sway – yet another version of *Bonnie Prince Charlie* hit the screens in 1948, this time with David Niven in the leading role, and Disney's interpretation of *Rob Roy: The Highland Rogue* emerged five years later. British producers were similarly entranced by Scottish narratives that owed little to Scotland's urban and industrial twentieth-century experiences. The most notable examples, perhaps, appeared in the late 1940s and 1950s under the direction of Alexander Mackendrick (1912–1933) – the comedies *Whisky Galore* and *The Maggie* (1949, 1953) both focused on the rural periphery of Scotland.[139] These were communities peopled by characters who hammed up Scottish stereotypes for comic effect. (Over the years, cultural critics have taken them too seriously.) Meanwhile, across the Atlantic, Hollywood's interest seemed unrelenting. Both Orson Welles and Roman Polanski filmed versions of *Macbeth* and Burke and Hare's story was told several times over the years through the performances of classic horror actors, among them, Boris Karloff, Bela Lugosi and Peter Cushing. Even at the end of the century, Scottish legends remained hits at the box office – *Chariots of Fire* (1981), *Chasing the Deer* (1984), *Highlander* (1986), *Rob Roy* (1996) and *Braveheart* (1996) put Scotland's past (if not always necessarily Scotland or Scots) in front of the camera.

Hollywood, Pinewood and Ealing studios all exploited seriocomic, historical, fantastical and mythical representations of Scotland and, over the years, undeniably did much to perpetuate unrepresentative images of the nation. But they also made audiences laugh, cry and criticise. One ought not to assume that film-makers are necessarily obliged to be chroniclers or offer 'discourses' adequate for 'the historical and contemporary reality of Scotland'.[140] Margaret Tait offered the following assessment of her work:

> I'm not really interested in 'recording for posterity'. That's an incidental, or accidental, value that my films might have, not what I'm making them for. I make my films for audiences who are there at the time – for a response, at the time.[141]

Too often twentieth-century Scottish critics revealed more about their own values than those of the discipline when they bemoaned depictions of Scotland on screen. Reflecting on *Rockets Galore* (1958), a film which found a group of island Scots get one over on the Ministry of Defence, Colin MacArthur noted, 'With a nod, a wink and a dram, the Scots once more triumph at the level of the imagination while in the real world their country gets pulled out from under them.'[142] Maybe so – like so many things in the cinema it depends how you look at it – but this was only one version of Scotland on screen.

Floodtide (1949), starring the Scottish actors, Jimmy Logan (1928–2001) and Gordon Jackson (1923–1990), did much to create images of contemporary Scotland for popular consumption as did director Bill Forsyth's (1946–) later successes with *That Sinking Feeling* (1980), *Gregory's Girl* (1981) and the big-budget *Local Hero* (1983). In the following decade, the powerful and popular work of Ken Loach – *My Name is Joe* (1998), for example – took issue with adulatory Clydesideism without abandoning its social intent. It was a trend echoed in Gillies MacKinnon's *Small Faces* (1996), a film that explored gang culture in Glasgow and the meaningless violence of the post-industrial 'hard man'.

> Malky: Do you know what mental is, son?
> Lex: No.
> Malky: Mental's nothing gets in your way. You know what I mean? . . . Mental's doin time for murder 'cos you don't give a fuck. Do you think you could do that, son? Do *you* think you could be mental?
> Lex: Aye.

Other films such as *Shallow Grave* (1994), *Trainspotting* (1996) and Lynne Ramsay's *Ratcatcher* (1998) signalled that, when it came to film at least, the Kailyard was wilting under the heat of studio lights. Scottish actors were also beginning to make a name for themselves in Hollywood in roles for which their accent and their nationality was seen as neither an obstacle nor an essential requirement – few were now typecast to quite the same extent as previous generations. The 'Scot Pack' of the 1990s – it was as inclusive or as exclusive as one cared to make it – included both old and new faces, although its founding father was undoubtedly Edinburgh's Sean Connery (1930–), whose various performances as James Bond had made him a household name furth of Fountainbridge. Of the next generation, Ewan McGregor (1971–), Robert Carlyle (1961–), Robbie Coltrane (1950–), Peter Mullan (1960–) and Kelly MacDonald (1976–) easily made the transition from actor to star – few Scottish performers before them achieved so much so quickly.

Over the course of the twentieth century, both the stage and the screen proved unreliable vehicles for those wishing to communicate national identity in Scotland. Actors played roles driven by a foreclosed narrative and were usually required to leave their nationality at the stage door. In this sense, unlike writers, artists and musicians, they made for awkward national heroes. Financial considerations and popular tastes also regularly mattered more than academic rigour and elite endorsement to investors in costly productions. At the end of the day, tartan stereotypes were popular even, nay particularly, amongst Scots – was it really the job of entertainers to challenge them at every opportunity? Both disciplines were as vulnerable to the vagaries of funding bodies and fashions as their artistic and musical peers and both laboured on the periphery of creative industries that took their cue from London or Los Angeles. It is to their credit that the image of Scotland that remained was as recognisable as it was – and that we are still laughing.

CONCLUSION

Pictures painted in melody and colour, lyric and form, captured the imagination of generations of Scots in the course of the century. Tastes changed – the new sound of one generation quickly became the classic tracks of the next and radical artists were transformed into Establishment figures as the years passed. But, throughout, Scottish culture faced common problems that were shared by successive generations.

Lack of finance was a perennial complaint of artists of all media. And, in a small country, this was further exacerbated by the limited domestic market for their 'products'. Over the years, many would suggest that Scotland hardly nourished the talent in its midst. While the Scottish National Orchestra was established in 1891, it was part-time until 1951 and it took a century for it to gain its regal appellation as the Royal Scottish National Orchestra. Similarly, while the BBC's Scottish Orchestra (established in 1935) was the first full-time professional orchestra in Scotland, it took until 1967 for it to achieve full symphony status, though even that did not guarantee a secure future.

In the post-war decades the arts in Scotland became dangerously reliant on state subsidy and hampered by an immature commercial infrastructure that lacked sufficient influential agents, promoters and publishers to challenge the cultural dominance of London.[143] In art, this frequently encouraged an 'investigative' style that spoke to social issues of relevance to government – a state of affairs that hardly encouraged commercial success.[144] Indeed, it seemed, at times, that even artistic rebellion required a subsidy – by 2002, 7 per cent of the Scottish Arts Council budget propped up literary magazines whose pages frequently bemoaned various governments' cultural strategies.[145] Put simply, over the course of the century, a robust critical community failed to develop – there were few outlets where the arts could be seriously discussed, though plenty of opportunities in those that did exist to offend the sensitivities of the tight-knit artistic world in Scotland whose very intimacy, while a useful bulwark against the metropolitan elite, could be a disincentive to healthy debate.

Nevertheless, in the late twentieth century, culture was at a premium – the Edinburgh International Festival (established in 1947) was joined by Aberdeen's International Festival of Youth Orchestras (later the Aberdeen International Youth Festival) in 1973, Glasgow's Mayfest in 1981 and, in 1990, Glasgow became European City of Culture. Dundee opened a new Contemporary Arts Centre in 1999 and, in 1996, the Gallery of Modern

Art – known in fashionably lower-case circles as 'goma' – opened in Glasgow's Royal Exchange Square. Elsewhere new venues suggested that the performing arts would soon reap the benefits of more modern public spaces – Edinburgh's Festival Theatre opened it doors in the nineties, Stirling made good use of the MacRobert Centre at the local university and Inverness's Eden Court Theatre offered a welcome home to the performing arts in the north. The arts clearly offered Scotland new world exports and important vehicles of self-expression. But, existing as they did between the commerce and vocabulary which increasingly defined them as industries and the creativity which was their capital, the arts ended the century at an awkward impasse between the poverty of principle and the profits (and perils) of state patronage.

It is not surprising, therefore, that Scottish culture at the end of the twentieth century offered little to those who sought to replant the Kailyard with delicacies more palatable for nationalism. Globalisation had fostered the growth of an international cosmopolitan sensibility, rather than a 'longing for uniformity', although the icons of the past remained some of the few things Scots could still recognise as theirs.[146] (That did not mean they had to like them – kail itself is something of an acquired taste, after all.) Scottish culture, as a consequence, bore the scars of twin processes best summarised as internationalism and localism. It was a state of affairs not helped by late-twentieth-century attempts to provide a stable cultural essence to underpin the unity implied in popular support for constitutional reform. Repeatedly thwarted, such designs added an urgency to the cultural project which frequently produced more heat than light.

Throughout the century, Scottish culture had stubbornly resisted temptations to anchor political nationalism or, indeed, the pretensions of intellectuals and critics who sought its essence. Rather, Scottish cultural life in the twentieth century paid testament to the fact that, in the postmodern world, quoting Zygmunt Bauman (1925–), 'the only consensus likely to stand a chance is the acceptance of heterogeneity and dissensions'.[147] In literature, art, music, theatre and film, the Scottish people seldom expressed a 'settled will'. Supported and restrained by state subsidy while driven by market forces, modernised by an unrelenting technological and commercial revolution while in debt to traditional approaches and popular historic narratives, beholden to metropolitan cultural arbiters yet the great hope of separatists, resting regularly on the whim of fashion yet measured against timeless standards, Scottish cultural life was the product of extremes. There was no alternative.

THIRTEEN

Hobbies, Holidays and
Headlines

What Scots in the twentieth century got up to when history was not
looking can be as important as their contributions to the institutions and
formal events that marked their nation's progress. Scotland was, perhaps,
made as much in periods of repose as through hard work. And, as 'doing
nothing' became big business and sport evolved as a substitute for
national achievement in other areas of life, it was the media – faceless
facilitators – that increasingly acted as the necessary intermediaries
through which Scots came to experience their leisure hours. Just as, at the
turn of the century, community networks were regularly replaced by
formal associational bodies, so too were voluntary organisations increasingly challenged at the century's end by the privatisation of leisure and
virtual social networks made possible by technology. In this way, Scots
became more aware than ever before of the choices that life offered them
in the twentieth century and yet it was widely regretted that, while
knowing more, Scots did less. Ironically, with more leisure hours to spend
and greater affluence, Scots were more often to be found watching the
news as others made it. It was simple – the same media that made possible
a revolution in information set new standards in leisure that were scornful
of the amateur ethos and the homespun characteristics of community
activities. The glamour of professional sports and the provisions of a more
sophisticated service sector, in turn, encouraged the Scot to await gratifi-
cation from others rather than doing much about it himself. Is it any
wonder that voyeurism increasingly challenged participation and local
heroes were abandoned in favour of national celebrities?

A SPORTING CHANCE

Sport both unified and divided Scotland in the twentieth century. In this
respect, Eric Linklater's fictional vision of Edinburgh, on the day when
a rugby international and local football derby coincide, is telling. The
rugby supporters, enjoying the morning spring sunshine on Princes

Street, are 'tall men from the Borders, brave men from the North, and burly men from the West who have made their names famous in school or university, in county and burgh, for prowess in athletic games', while the more talkative football crowd 'had not the athletic look' of the rugby fans – 'They were another order, socially inferior to the devotees of Rugby, and they had not been seen on Princes Street in the morning sunlight because they had been at work.'[1] Once both games start, however, the crowds are united, at least in part. When the spectators at Murrayfield cheer, they 'were wild as their poorer neighbours who, some mile or two away, were cheering their paid teams with coarser tongues'. Linklater comments, 'Now all Scotland was at one, united in its heat, and only the most sour of moralists would decry that heat because it had been lighted by a trivial game.'[2] United as ninety-minute patriots, divided by game of choice; united as voyeurs, divided as fans for opposing sides; united as sportsmen, divided by class – sport contributed significantly to Scotland's contradictory cultural life in the twentieth century.[3] Over the course of a hundred years, a national distraction was raised to the status of a science and gave a nation, traditionally fond of heroes, peaceable twentieth-century alternatives to historic martial icons.

As elsewhere in Europe, sport in Scotland was formalised, codified and professionalised in the course of the twentieth century; competition became increasingly international in scope and commercialisation made winning big business. Amateur sports clubs were popular – 227 teams played for the Scottish Junior Football Cup in 1939. But, over the course of the century, Scots were more likely to be armchair enthusiasts than keen participants – the Scottish Junior Football Cup attracted fewer and fewer teams after 1951.[4] Season after season of lacklustre performances on inhospitable pitches could destroy the resilience of even the keenest amateur players and their fans. Robin Jenkins' fictional Drumsagart Thistle Junior Football Club is a case in point:

> The team had been at the bottom of the League for three seasons in succession, a record in shamefulness. It had also been knocked out of the Scottish Junior Cup in the first round. Glory, without a fragment of which no faith can survive, was as scarce as whisky at a poorhouse Ne'erday. Former glory, such as being runners up in the League in 19- and reaching the final round of the Cup in 18-, was now quite used up: there was no substance in it any longer: faith could gnaw on that dry bone no more.[5]

It is hardly surprising that, as the stadiums housing the glamour of the professional game got bigger and more comfortable with each sporting generation, spectating at these new temples of commercialism or watching the 'geme' on the 'box' would triumph over the trials of competing in or even supporting local league football.

The Scottish Football Association (SFA) had already been formed in 1873 (ten years behind the English FA), and twenty years later (eight years behind England) professionalism was legalised in the Scottish game (although Queens Park remained aloof). By the 1900s, there were around twenty Scottish teams that played for the SFA's cup and the league championship. (The League was instituted in 1890 and, by the eve of the Great War, there was an unofficial Second Division.) In this new professional environment, Glasgow Rangers and Celtic dominated the sport, although Rangers failed to win the Scottish Cup for twenty-five years on the trot, breaking this ignominious record only in 1928 with a 4–0 win over Celtic in the cup final. At the national level, internationals between Scotland and England were a much-anticipated feature of the game's calendar of events. In 1928, Rangers' luck rubbed off on the national squad when Scotland overwhelmed the England side in a 5–1 victory at Wembley. The Scottish team – including eight players contracted to English and Welsh clubs – became known as the 'Wembley Wizards'.[6] Other international performances, however, were not so commendable – in 1931 Scotland were beaten 5–0 by Austria and 3–0 by Italy during one of their first European tours. (One wonders if such things were remembered at the Battle of Monte Cassino in 1944.) Indeed, war took many of the game's best players into the forces and the Scottish League was suspended for the duration. After 1945, however, Scottish football's problems persisted – in 1950, Scotland went down to their first defeat by a foreign team (Austria, again) on home soil and, between 1953 and 1962, managed to beat England only once in nine games.

For the home teams, fortunes were also mixed. Edinburgh's Hibernian challenged the dominance of the western giants in the immediate post-war years and Dundee stole the League Cup from Rangers in 1952 with an impressive performance from Tommy Gallacher who had begun his career with the Gordon Highlanders when stationed in Aberdeen during the war.[7] Footballing history, however, was made in the 1960s when the Celtic squad, managed by Jock Stein (1922–1985), became the first British team to win the European Cup, defeating Inter Milan 2–1 in Lisbon in 1967, with a squad dominated by home-grown talent – the Lisbon Lions. It was a remarkable season for the club – in a matter of months, the team captain, Billy McNeil (1940–), had held aloft the League Cup, the Scottish Cup and the Glasgow Cup. Not to be outdone, in 1972 Rangers, managed by Willie Waddell (1921–1992), with Jock

Wallace (1935–1996) as coach, took the European Cup Winners' Cup, beating Moscow Dynamo 3–2 in Barcelona. The hat-trick of Scottish European successes was completed in 1983 when Aberdeen too, managed by Alex Ferguson (1941–), won the European Cup Winners' Cup. After beating Real Madrid 2–1 in Gothenburg, the team were greeted on their return to Scotland's north-east by a crowd several thousands strong.[8] The last decades of the century, however, were again to see the main battles for hearts, minds and trophies in Scotland taking place between Rangers and Celtic. Yet, in contrast to the first decades of the century, Scotland was now importing players rather than exporting its keenest talents – losing matches had come to have commercial consequences too grave to rest on the promise of Glasgow schoolboys.[9] Those who could remember regretted the passing of a distinctive and dramatic Scottish style of play and its substitution with a relatively risk-free game that only seemed guaranteed to please clubs' shareholders.[10] In such a climate, it is perhaps not surprising that club managers, as much if not more so than the nation's players, became a source of Scottish pride. Stretching a point to incredible lengths, through the efforts of Scots such as Matt Busby (1909–1994), manager of Manchester United, Bill Shankly (1913–1981), manager of Liverpool, Kenny Dalglish (1951–), Liverpool player and manager, and Alex Ferguson, manager of Manchester United from 1986, Scots even felt they earned a share in the success of English teams.

In contrast to football, Scottish rugby, formally organised under the Scottish Football (later Rugby) Union (SFU) from 1873, maintained its commitment to the amateur ethos of the game until 1996 – although cracks had begun to appear in SRU policies far earlier, particularly after the introduction of the Rugby World Cup in 1987. Still, its defence of gentlemanly conduct withstood various commercial pressures – only in the mid thirties, for example, were numbered jerseys officially endorsed and it took until 1971 for the national team to acquire its first coach.[11] Indeed, in 2005, one-time Scottish international Jim Telfer (1940–) would admit that, even then, some people were 'only beginning to accept that professional rugby [was] here to stay'.[12] For most of the century, Scottish rugby relied on the hothousing of talent in the schoolboy and local leagues and sponsorship in the game came relatively late.[13] (National leagues were not introduced until 1973.) It is not, therefore, surprising that, on the international stage, Scotland's fortunes were mixed. Under the eyes of around 70,000 spectators, Scotland secured its first Grand Slam victory in 1925 with a 14–11 victory over England, at Scottish rugby's new Murrayfield Stadium, and went on to win the Triple Crown twice in the 1930s. A grudging

Scotsman reporter in 1925, however, recorded that the national team's play was 'not by any means above criticism'.[14] He may have been more generous had he known that, in the 1950s, four years and seventeen games would pass without Scotland recording a single victory and a second Grand Slam for Scotland would not be achieved until 1984 (though it was followed quickly by a third, in 1990).

Team sports more easily galvanised national interest (and media criticism) than the endeavours of individuals – more seemed to ride on collective effort, as if teams represented Scotland in miniature. Yet Scotland's pride in a variety of sporting successes speaks of a nation that still valued exceptional individuals. Currie's Dougal Haston (1940–1977) dominated British climbing in the 1960s and 1970s, ascending the north face of the Eiger in 1966 and recording the first ascent of Mount Everest by the south-west face in 1975.[15] In motor racing and rallying, Scotland boasted four world champions during the course of the century – Jim Clark (1936–1968), Jackie Stewart (1939–), Colin McRae (1968–2007) and Louise Aitken Walker (1960–). On two wheels, Graeme Obree (1965–) broke the world cycling record in 1993 and again in 1994 and was the individual pursuit world champion in 1993 and 1995, pedalling bikes he engineered himself.[16] In boxing, Scottish champs included Benny Lynch (1913–1946), Jim Watt (1948–) and Pat Clinton (1964–). On the athletics field, Eric Liddell (1902–1945) and Allan Wells (1952–) won Olympic gold, as did David Wilkie (1954–) in the pool. And, in golf, Scots dominated the British Open championship in the first years of the century: Fife joiner, James Braid (1870–1950) won golf's ultimate prize five times in 1901, 1905, 1906, 1908 and 1910. In such successes, there was much to celebrate and much to unify the country – they also seemed to endorse claims to a distinctive national character that was salient even in the twentieth century.

Yet sporting disasters of various kinds could equally harm national sentiment and morale. In April 1902 and again in January 1971, Rangers' Ibrox Stadium was the scene of tragedy on the terraces. Twenty-five fans died in 1902 as wooden terracing gave way during a Scotland–England game and, in 1971, sixty-six died on Stairway 13 as a wave of spectators crushed the life from bodies who minutes before had been cheering their sporting heroes. On the field, pride rather than lives were at stake and Scotland regularly paid the price for reaching too high. The 1978 World Cup Championships were a humiliating disaster for the Scottish football team and challenged the nation's self-image as an international sporting force. According to the memorable team song and *Football Magazine*'s 'Guide to the World Cup '78', Scotland went to Argentina 'confident they can win the world cup'. But such unreasonably high hopes of victory were ignominiously dashed, when a despondent Tartan Army looked on as the squad lost to Peru, drew with Iran and failed to score enough goals against the Netherlands to get them past the opening round. *The Times* headline said it all – 'Scotland back from the dead only to see hopes expire'.[17] Over the course of the century, Scotland qualified for the World Cup Finals on eight separate occasions but were victorious in only three matches.[18] Even success, however, seldom came untarnished. Rangers' victory in the 1972 European Cup Winners' Cup Final in Barcelona was followed by crowd trouble, as fans invaded the pitch, threw bottles, ripped seats from the terracing and were met with the batons of the Spanish police. To avoid inflaming the situation further, the presentation of the cup to the team captain, John Greig (1942–), was made in private and Rangers were banned from competing in international competition for a year. The victors could not even defend their title. Back home, most of the time England–Scotland games offered Scots little, either on the pitch or off it, to cheer about and repeated instances of football violence and hooliganism after 1960 brought these 'friendlies' to an end in 1989.[19] Individual clubs had their own problems – football 'casuals' brought the game into disrepute in the 1980s, as Saturday final whistles became a call to arms for hooligans intent on trouble. C. S. Ferguson, a Hearts supporter between 1981 and 1986, felt like 'part of an invading army' when he followed his team to Dunfermline for the first time and he relished the violence that accompanied a local derby testimonial game in Edinburgh:

> As we turned into Easter Road, the riot started in general. There were over a thousand of us rampaging up the road, smashing fuck out of anything that got in our way. Cars were trashed, shop and house windows put in. It was mental.[20]

Meanwhile, in Glasgow, sectarianism had turned an early healthy rivalry between the city's two most successful teams into something far darker and left a permanent scar on Scotland's self- and international image.[21] Sport may have been a pastime for many Scots but it was also a serious business.

Over the years, sport overwhelmed many other measures of national vitality to an extent that would have appeared faintly ridiculous in the opening decades of the century. Yet, when other sources of pride waned – Scotland's industrial strength is a case in point – sport and sportsmen (it was typically men who grabbed the headlines) took on added importance in ways that allow us to gauge the values that they came to represent.[22] Scots were clear, if somewhat fickle, when it came to identifying sporting heroes. Hard work was valued as much on the sports field as on the shop floor and, in Jock Stein, Kenny Dalglish and Alex Ferguson, Scots celebrated the work ethic.[23] Football journalist Archie Macpherson (1937–) eschewed more elaborate imagery and effusive praise when, in his biography of Stein, he celebrated the iconic Celtic manager as 'a journeyman', 'a grafter' – a man who knew the game from the bottom up.[24] And, yet, for Scots, plodding resilience was not enough. The initiative and style of footballer Willie Waddell, the dramatic play of Denis Law (1940–), the mercenary footballing talent of Jim Baxter (1939–2001), the individual gait of runner Eric Liddell, the resilience of climber Dougal Haston and the single-minded determination of rally driver Colin McRae variously echoed qualities and values that the nation claimed as its own.[25] McRae reflected in 1997:

> I like to win, I push as hard as I can to win and I know I can win. I would rather be the way I am than be a driver who finished second and third regularly and won once in a blue moon.[26]

Overriding all else, however, was popular appreciation of instinctive humility and a sense of home. Scottish sporting heroes were never allowed to 'get above themselves' and were cherished all the more if they had overcome adversity in the course of their lives. The poverty from which managers such as Matt Busby and Bill Shankly emerged and the physical challenges that faced Jackie Stewart, Graeme Obree and Denis Law were as much a part of their greatness as their podium appearances.[27] Maintaining a loyalty to the land that begat them also seemed to confirm the native roots of genius. Jim Clark, world champion racing driver (1963 and 1965), maintained a keen interest in the prices being fetched at the Kelso ram sales throughout his career and is described on his gravestone at Chirnside – he died during a race at the Hockenheim track – as a farmer first.[28]

Sporting heroes allowed Scots to personify what was good about the nation and, in turn, by following them, Scots did much to internationalise a popular image of Scottishness. The Tartan Army – an appellation typically accorded football and rugby fans in the last decades of the century but extended to just about any collection of fans who watched Scots compete in sports at an international level – took the kilt out of the retirement to which it had been assigned over the years and made public relations their game away from the action on the field, pitch and track. Reporting on their activities became a necessity for the media and, even in defeat, the Tartan Army's endearing, if often drunken, exploits off the field were seized on as a sign that the nation had at least done itself proud when it came to international diplomacy. Scots celebrated as they outdid the English – stereotypically cast as a nation of gentlemen and sportsmen – at their own game. The journalist Tom Shields recounted the scene in Saint-Étienne following Scotland's defeat by Morocco in the 1998 FIFA World Cup:

> Outside the stadium, the Wee-ist Pipe Band in the World are putting our World Cup campaign decently to rest. Fans gather silently in a circle, some of them weeping, as piper Kevin plays 'The Floo'ers o' the Forest'. The band finish their lament, pause for a respectable moment, then lead the retreat from the stadium playing 'Scotland the Brave'.[29]

ASPECTS OF LEISURE

It would simply be impossible to chart the changes to all Scottish leisure pursuits over the course of the twentieth century. Yet there are themes common to all that reflect many of the major social and cultural changes encountered so far. Most notably, in amateur sports and social drinking, changing social mores regarding gender, religion and respectability are writ large. Women were slow to gain full membership of a range of amateur sporting associations. Only in 1962, for example, did Corstorphine Curling Club allow women members – and only then corralled in a Ladies Section.[30] Meanwhile, in Partick, female membership of the Curling Club was still being discussed in 1970, despite having first been raised for discussion in 1929.[31] The determination of sportsmen to uphold the Scottish tradition of Sabbath observance, however, was more quickly undermined than their hostility to their sporting sisters. Baberton Golf Club in Edinburgh permitted Sunday play from 1926, although the membership of the Lothianburn Club three years later voted down a recommendation by their Council to allow the clubhouse bar to open on the Lord's Day.[32] Up and down the country, curling clubs boasted their own chaplains who would annually preach a service in which the whole range of Christian metaphor would be utilised in an endeavour to ground the game in biblical precedent. Rev A. Gordon Mitchell of Killearn reminded the curlers in Woodside Parish Church in 1936 that from 'the sacred narrative of what a stone accomplished in Old Testament history we may learn what a curling-stone can do in the difficult and dangerous times through which we are passing.'[33]

There was a determination in all these efforts to assert a social doctrine of respectability and to distinguish what was best in the amateur ethos from the rough culture of the streets. This was not surprising – in Presbyterian Scotland, there was a need to prove, in explicit terms, that secular leisure pursuits did not encourage licentious lives. Alcoholism was a perennial concern, particularly in the early decades of the century when the temperance lobby won some notable legislative successes to curtail licensing hours and the sale of intoxicating liquor, and organisations such as the Band of Hope and the Scottish Temperance Alliance encouraged teetotal activities and savings schemes.[34] But the dichotomy of rough and respectable leisure is artificial – leisure still bore a strong regional dynamic and reflected the fragmented and contested nature of social change throughout the country. We should also not take for granted the views of those who knew little about the lives they sought to reform. Jean Stevenson's reign at the Bull Inn in Paisley highlights how duty and responsibility did not cease at the door of the public house:

> Men coming in at 5 o'clock on pay day were allowed only one drink. They were then sent home to hand over the housekeeping and have a meal before returning for their night's drinking. Miss Stevenson, while looking after the wives' interests, would not, however, allow any women into the premises.[35]

Leisure preferences resist generalisation but the longevity of one such activity was marked. Until the 1960s, evenings after the 'big geme' would have been frequently spent in Scotland's many dance halls. Indeed, in Edinburgh the relationship between dance and sport was so close that its popular Heart of Midlothian Football Club (established in 1874) took its name from a dance hall off the Royal Mile. The typical arena of courtship, gossip and the vogues of fashion, the dance hall recorded the slow encroachment of international tastes on Scottish leisure. At the turn of the century, American dances like the Bunny Hug and Turkey Trot were becoming increasingly popular in Edinburgh's dance halls and, by the 1930s, it was suggested that, in Tomintoul, 'the last local piper ha[d] put away his pipes' and his son had taken up the saxophone – 'In the dance halls the young men and women sway[ed] to the languorous notes of a modern waltz, and in the square the boys whistle[d] "Goodnight my Love" and the Broadway tunes of the previous year.'[36] Others, however, resisted the sounds and dances of a new generation. The Albert Ballroom in Glasgow maintained a commitment to older dances like the waltz and the quadrille until the 1920s and the Palais de Danse in Aberdeen insisted on a formal dress code well into the thirties.[37] Scottish country dancing itself was not left untouched – in 1923, the rasping chords of the Yahoo Jazz Sextet at the Northern

Meeting in Inverness seemed to signal the end of what was left of 'traditional' Scottish dance.[38] Yet the foundation of the Scottish Country Dance Society in the same year ensured that country dancing would have stout defenders as the century progressed and an international influence when it came to competitive dance.[39]

The impulse behind dance, however, became more informal as the decades wore on. Swing music began making an impact in Scottish dance halls on the eve of World War Two and American involvement in the war brought new dances, such as the jitterbug, as well as servicemen to the dance halls of Scotland. Dress codes were relaxed as fashions changed, liquor licenses became increasingly common and the improvised nature of bebop and rock-and-roll brought the revolution in dance to its ultimate conclusion and marked the end of ballrooms. Even the Highland scene had to bow to the inevitable – dance repertoires narrowed, music became infused with influences from jazz and pop genres and ceilidhs increasingly replaced more formal get-togethers.[40] At the end of the century, disco neon and the strobe lights of raves in disused warehouses burned as brightly as the ballroom lights that had twinkled prettily in the evening gloom of generations past. In many respects, they whispered the same promise to courting couples who went there not just to dance – perhaps only the music had changed.

For most, days out and annual holidays were the only time when relief from work and the domestic routine was real and not just the product of imaginings stolen in the course of a time-bound life of toil. Mary Brooksbank, the Dundee jute-worker, socialist and songsmith, recalled:

> the golden threads woven into the grey fabric of our existence. There were the rambles to Windmill Park at Newport. The drives by horse brake to Kirrie, Monikie, Longforgan, Blair, Carnoustie, and once at least as far as Perth.[41]

Improvements in transport made travel easier and, by the twenties, local 'fairs' (holidays) emptied Scotland's industrial towns of all but their poorest and oldest citizens on an annual basis, as whole populations headed to coastal resorts or back to Highland townships that had once been home. Indeed, from as early as the 1880s, it was said that Oban 'existed simply for tourists'.[42] In Scotland's major urban centres, 'railway hotels', such as Edinburgh's iconic North British and Caledonian Hotels (completed in 1902 and 1903 respectively), offered shelter to the well-heeled weary rail traveller, while cheap excursion rail fares on Scotland's coastal routes meant a speedier journey to seaside resorts for Glasgwegians than the trip 'doon the watter' on crowded paddle steamers. Yet holidays were not necessarily an escape from it all.

In 1934, James Bridie revisited that bane of every schoolboy's career, the holiday essay, and, in a piece for the *Glasgow Herald*, focused on the exhaustive preparations more familiar to middle-class parents than their impatient offspring or, indeed, their less well-off contemporaries. He wrote:

> We write to the telephone people. We arrange with the post-office. We instruct the newsagent, the milkman, the baker, the grocer to stop supplies. We come to an agreement with the cook about her future movements. We see the policeman. We visit the railway station. We pack and pack and strain at the luggage straps. We cover the furniture with sheets and the pictures and ornaments with *Glasgow Heralds*. We hand over our silver to the neighbours or to the bank. We live for a day and a night in a state of desolation on boiled eggs and tea. We find a good home for the parrot, the cat, and the India-rubber plant. We turn off the gas, the water, and the electric light. We lock the doors and dispose of the keys. Distraught, subdued, and anxious we crowd into a taxicab. We are off. We hope for the best. Give to us the life we love, let the lave go by us.[43]

Urban Scots took the social divisions of the city to the seaside along with their luggage. The author, David Daiches, remembered Edinburgh's seaside customs:

> The great middle-class thing was to go to the seaside in August and places were classified according to income groups. You went to such-and-such a place if you were lower down the scale, and a little further up you went to another place and so on. Aberdour was lower down the scale than Crail. A lot of Glasgow people came to Crail, well-to-do, middle-class people. But the system of going as a family throughout the month of August, renting a house by the seaside, was pretty universal in those days.[44]

The economic privations of the 1920s did little to stop the development of popular holiday culture but distinctions remained and the thirties were to be a difficult decade for Scottish tourism.[45] The car replaced the train for middle-class travellers who were assisted in their explorations by guidebooks such as *Scotland for the Motorist* (1910) and *Motoring in Scotland* (1931). For others, charabanc trips and bus tours opened up

Scottish rural areas that had not been webbed by rail links earlier. The royal blue coaches of the Alexander bus company in Falkirk became a familiar sight on Highland roads in the 1930s and, after the Beeching rail reforms of the early 1960s, bus services such as these sustained tourism in the north at a time when foreign travel was beginning to make serious inroads into domestic tourism.[46]

Nevertheless, with increased holiday entitlement, Scots had more time and were now more able to explore the sites and scenery of their own country. And Scotland's heritage – at least, its stately homes, battlefields and formal gardens – became more widely accessible, proving popular destinations for the growing armies of day trippers.[47] The National Trust for Scotland, for example, was established in 1931 and, by 1993, boasted an annual income of £15 million. By the end of the century, the Scottish Museums Council supported more than 300 local museums. Between 1986–97 and 1992–93 state spending on the National Museums of Scotland rose by 250 per cent and, by the century's close, 'heritage [was] proportionately more important North of the Border than in the UK generally'.[48]

From 1969, Scotland boasted a National Tourist Board and, in the 1980s, it became the major body marketing Scotland's attractions overseas, with a budget (for 1998–99) of nearly £20 million.[49] But, even in the 1970s, Scotland's tourist income was largely dominated by Scots and English visitors and, of the Scots, 40 per cent in these years stayed with relatives when on holiday.[50] The Scottish tourist also had an unfavourable image in an era driven by the demands of youth. A survey in the 1960s indicated that the 'typical holiday maker in Scotland' was visualised as 'older rather than younger; middle class rather than working class; fond of beautiful scenery, of touring and of strenuous (and sometimes rather upper class) outdoor activities'.[51] The grouse-moor image was hard to shake. Poor weather prospects were also identified as an impediment to Scottish tourism and poor quality accommodation was another concern the further north you travelled.

Given these factors, it is far from surprising that, when faced with cheaper air fares to continental and trans-Atlantic locations, the greater availability of direct flights from Scottish airports and the development of 'package holidays', many Scots opted to holiday abroad. (In a classic piece of understatement, even a Scottish Office researcher had to admit, in 1966, that 'Scotland cannot hope to compete with Italy or Spain for a sunshine holiday'.[52]) Aircraft had flown out of Prestwick since 1913 but a revolution in transport and aspirations had transformed this site into Scotland's trans-Atlantic gateway by at least March 1960 when Elvis Presley stopped off en route to America, after completing his national service in Germany. By the 1980s, however, Glasgow Airport (Abbotsinch) was attracting the major airlines with its modern facilities and larger capacity – by the end of the century, annual passenger numbers were around five million. Edinburgh's airport too grew in these years, its runway becoming the busiest in Scotland by the end of the century – a remarkable transformation in the Turnhouse site that had begun the century as an RAF base and only started running commercial flights in 1947. Between 1977 and 1980, visits abroad by UK residents grew by 52 per cent at a time when overseas visitors to the UK grew by only 1 per cent.[53] By 1998, it was estimated that people living in Scotland made 2.7 million visits abroad annually, of which more than two thirds were for holiday purposes. Glasgow Airport co-ordinated the bulk of this traffic. Sixty-three per cent of holidays abroad were package holidays and the most favoured destinations for Scots were on Spain's Balearic Islands.[54] Back home, the spa towns and coastal resorts favoured by earlier generations fell silent and their fabric became neglected – Strathpeffer's main pump room was demolished in the 1950s, the Picture House on Ayr's High Street, which had opened in 1921, closed in 1968 and Portobello's open-air swimming pool was demolished in 1988.

At ease, Scots at the century's close had much in common with their grandparents' generation but greater wealth and the transformation of transport on a global scale offered a wider choice of places where leisure hours, of which there were more, could be spent. Given the option, one assumes earlier Scots would have made much the same choices.

REPORTING SCOTLAND – THE PRESS, RADIO AND TV

If any nation on the face of the earth has reason to be satisfied with the character of its public journals, that nation is Scotland. The Newspaper press of Scotland spurns the cringing servility which characterises many of the English provincial journals; it expresses its honest opinion on subjects of importance either to the nation or to individuals, free from outrageous violence of language and coarseness of expression peculiar to the majority of Irish newspapers; and there are few of the similarly scurrilously personal and hyperbolic American papers which would not be flattered by being put upon a par, in point of veracity or gentlemanliness of tone, with the most obscure of our country newspapers.

Scottish Newspaper Directory and Guide to Advertisers (1855)

The confidence of the Scottish newspaper press in the nineteenth century gave way to concerns regarding outlook and ownership in the twentieth century. Somewhere between the status of a national fourth estate and a collection of local 'rags', the Scottish press exemplified Scotland's changing and ambiguous relationship within the Union – were its successful dailies merely provincial organs or the foremost expressions of national sentiment and a distinct political will? For some in the mid twentieth century, the future seemed bleak. The nationalist, Duncan Ferguson, remarked in 1946:

> To those who wish to see Scotland served by newspapers which are Scottish in interest and character, capable of expressing Scottish thought (not echoing the sentiments of a distant suzerain) and championing Scottish interests the outlook is disturbing.[55]

By the end of the twentieth century, the near saturation coverage of newspapers produced in Scotland was the strongest argument supporting the contention of a distinct Scottish newspaper culture. In 1988, average sales of the *Daily Record* amounted to 769,000 and the *Scotsman* and the *Glasgow Herald* – Scotland's 'quality' dailies – were purchased by around 156,000 and 125,000 citizens respectively on a daily basis.[56] One in seven Scots read the *Daily Record* at this time and the coverage of the 'English' dailies was paltry in comparison – the *Daily Mail* sold around 30,600 copies in Scotland and even the Scottish edition of the *Sun* managed only around 262,000. If readership distinguished a national press, then the press in the north was distinctively 'Scottish'.

The dominance of the Scottish press in the north had been guaranteed in the nineteenth century by transport and distributive problems which meant news hot off the press in London arrived cold and well after breakfast to many Scottish readers. By the mid twentieth century, however, other dynamics ensured the perpetuation of the dominance of Scottish journals in the north. For a start, Scottish titles kept pace with innovations in the industry. In 1928, for example, the *Scotsman* became the first paper to own and operate a picture telegraph system and, despite retaining only advertisements and notices on its front page until 1957, it scored another notable first in 1962 when it became the first newspaper in Britain to introduce a separate Saturday magazine supplement.[57] Such reforms regularly refreshed and strengthened the trans-generational reading preferences of Scottish families that proved hard to break down over the course of the century. Scottish newspapers also focussed their attention on Scottish stories[58] – largely human-interest stories – and news from their surrounding area to secure their readers' loyalty.[59] For example, while limited column inches in Fleet Street were devoted to Glasgow's Cheapside Street Fire of 1960, which cost the lives of nineteen fire- and salvage-men, or indeed the 'great storm', which battered that city's tenements in 1968 and cost the lives of twenty citizens, local daily, evening and weekly papers kept readers up to speed with pictures and stories of survivors and regular updates on the actions of the relevant authorities. The decentralised nature of the Scottish press – Aberdeen, Dundee, Glasgow and Edinburgh all boasted popular dailies – made localism even more pronounced.[60] And this was, in turn, encouraged by close networks of journalists who shared similar apprenticeships in the newsrooms of the Scottish presses. Jack Campbell (1913–) began his life in print as an office boy in the Albion Street works of the Glasgow-based *Scottish Daily Express* and ended up that paper's managing editor.[61] Meanwhile, for Harry Conroy (1943–) and Jack Webster (1931–), Albion Street was to be but an intermediary stage in careers that took them on to success in other Scottish papers – in their cases, the *Daily Record* and the *Glasgow Herald* respectively.[62] At times, even the east–west divide would be crossed in careers that would shape Scotland's media history. As its new editor, Alastair Dunnet (1908–1998) brought a new enthusiasm to the *Scotsman* in 1956 along with the insights he had gleaned during his time as editor of the *Daily Record*.[63] All things considered, it is surely no wonder that the Scottish press continued to develop a distinct identity.

In terms of political complexion, the maintenance of everyday editorial independence in all but a small minority of the Scottish print rooms over the years meant that Scotland's newspapers came increasingly to reflect the political priorities of the majority of Scots at a time when these were diverging from British norms. While this ensured public acclaim for editorials at election times and appreciation for a subtle bias in reporting which translated into healthy sales, it also meant that, by the 1990s, the vast majority of Scotland's newspapers sold in Scotland shared a similar vision which, if not pro-Labour, was at least anti-Tory.[64] The Unionist dominance which was evident in the Scottish press in the 1950s had been destroyed. Cracks had appeared from as early as the late 1960s when readership of the solidly Unionist *Scottish Daily Express* began to decline (its last Glasgow edition 'went to bed' in 1974) and these trends were further exacerbated when both the *Glasgow Herald* and the *Scotsman* opted for devolution in the late 1970s.[65] Thereafter, Thatcherism dispelled any remnants of sympathy that might have survived 1979. (*Scotland on Sunday* greeted her departure in November 1990 with the headline 'Good Riddance'.) Yet not all in the industry considered this a good thing. In 1994, Magnus Linklater (1942–), editor of the *Scotsman* between 1988 and 1994, reflected:

This relative uniformity of view presents the weakness as well as the strengths of Scottish journalism. It is undoubtedly a drawback that there is, save in the enclave of Dundee and amongst English-based papers, no widely-read right-wing press. That may reflect the mood of the times, but it means that far too many received ideas about the state of the nation go by unchallenged.[66]

Over the course of the twentieth century, the ownership of Scottish newspapers became concentrated in fewer hands and increasingly those hands were not necessarily Scottish. Provincial presses amalgamated and came under the control of larger newspaper companies. In the 1970s, for example, the interests of Johnston Newspapers, established in Falkirk in 1767, included twenty-six weekly Scottish newspapers from the *Cumnock Chronicle* to the *Kirriemuir Herald*.[67] More troubling to those who feared the southward drift of ownership in industry, however, was the encroachment of English interests in Scotland. For some time during the century, only the D. C. Thomson empire – most famously known for the *Sunday Post*, the *Scots Magazine* and the *Beano* – was an exclusively Scottish concern. Scotland's most widely read daily, the *Daily Record*, had been created with the capital of Britain's foremost media moguls, Lords Rothermere and Northcliffe, in the nineteenth century and was in the hands of Robert Maxwell (1923–1991) – arguably the twentieth century's most notorious media baron – at the end of the century, as part of the Mirror Group, later Trinity Mirror. (The Mirror Group acquired the title in 1956.) In the east, the *Scotsman*'s story was more complex. The title was sold to Canadian Roy Thomson in 1953 and then – after ten years in the hands of the millionaire media magnates, the Barclay Brothers (London-born sons of Scottish parents) – it returned to Scottish ownership in 2005 when it was purchased by the Johnston Press. The *Glasgow Herald*'s progress similarly told the story of a title subject to the whims of a global media marketplace. After a number of years under the multinational Lonrho company, the *Glasgow Herald* only returned to Scottish ownership in 1992, although it was to be a brief respite from non-native control – in 2002, the *Herald*, rebranded in 1992, and its sister titles, the *Sunday Herald* and the *Evening Times*, were sold by the Scottish Media Group to the, appropriately named, US Gannett corporation.[68]

From as early as the 1940s, concerns were expressed that 'no Scottish-owned paper of any kind enters a large number of Scottish homes, especially in the Clyde valley'.[69] At a time when new London media could invisibly reach Scotland via radio waves, the Scottish press was worried. Time would prove that their fears were well founded. By 2002, 'only

18 per cent of papers sold in Scotland [were] owned in Scotland' and new forms of media were challenging the printed word as the principal arbiters of politics and fashion.[70] Attempts to buck this trend repeatedly proved futile. A workers' co-operative had sought to retain newspaper production at the Albion Works of the *Scottish Daily Express* when they faced closure in 1974. Nevertheless, within a matter of months, their new title, the *Daily News*, folded as readers were lost, disputes among the new management (which included Robert Maxwell) led to weak leadership and government grants proved inadequate to sustain the new paper.[71] Scotland's media future was being shaped elsewhere.

The tower room of the Port Dundas power station in Glasgow, a wooden hut in the quadrangle of Edinburgh University's Old College and the Caldrum Jute Works in St Salvador Street in Dundee were instrumental in the history of broadcasting in Scotland as, at various times in the 1920s, each of these locations hosted BBC transmitters for the Corporation's new Scottish radio service.[72] Public service broadcasting in Scotland began in March 1923 with the BBC's first Scottish radio station in Glasgow and, a year later, an Edinburgh station opened. In 1930, the BBC opened its new Scottish Headquarters in Edinburgh's Queen Street in a building formally occupied by, in succession, the synod of the Secession Church, Free Church splinter groups and latterly the New Embassy Night Club and Dance Hall. The diversity of the building's former occupants was reflected in the output of the new studios. Confined initially to broadcasting in the evenings, the Scottish stations attempted to cultivate a distinctive Scottish voice on the airwaves, which was initially attempted through an uneasy blend of maudlin religious reflections and the 'hits' of the Scottish variety stage.[73] Education and entertainment, however, were to be uneasy bed fellows, particularly given the high moral tone that the Corporation's influential founding Director General, the Scotsman John Reith, set for the new medium.

When war intervened in 1939, centralised Home Service programming curtailed the development of the Scottish stations for a while but, in the later 1940s, the range of Scottish output increased and a Gaelic news broadcast even went on air once a week. In the first three months of 1947, for example, the works of Scottish literary stars such as Neil Gunn and James Bridie were broadcast by the Scottish Home Service and the BBC was actively sponsoring a radio play competition north of the Border. Scottish news bulletins, by this time, were aired every weekday night at 6.10 p.m. and the service also offered a special weather forecast for herring fishermen in the north-west of Scotland during the season.[74] By now, the number of radio licences in the UK had increased to over 10 million and further innovations in the medium guaranteed the future of the wireless in Scotland.[75] VHF transmission reached Scotland in 1956 and, by 1960, over 1,800 hours of radio broadcasting were produced by the BBC in Scotland annually.[76]

But competition was emerging. Scotland's first 'pirate' radio station, Radio Scotland, began broadcasting from a refitted boat anchored off Dunbar in 1965 (one year after England's more famous Radio Caroline) and, at its height, claimed an audience of over two million listeners.[77] But a move to Troon and the development of programming more suited to tartan slippers than teenage fashions encouraged a slump in the station's audience and the station closed in 1967 – the victim of the Marine Offences Act (1967). Scotland's first licensed commercial station, Radio Clyde, began broadcasting six years later and, by 1982, it had been joined by five more. In the interim, Scotland acquired its first national radio network when BBC Radio Scotland was launched at Glasgow's Kelvin Hall in 1978. In the years that followed, the BBC opened more local stations, among them Radio nan Eilean (1979), Radio Tweed and Radio Solway (both, 1983).

TV reached Scotland in 1952, when the opening speeches greeting the arrival of this new medium were followed by a display of Scottish country dancing.[78] Interest in 'the box' was slow to grow in the north, however, and it took national events, such as the coronation in 1953, to persuade Scots that maybe it was a thing worth having. In the early years, there were no TV studios in Scotland (the first became operational in 1955) and, as a result, Scottish contributions to TV schedules were dominated by outside broadcasts. BBC Scotland's commemoration of the 1400th anniversary of St Columba's arrival in Scotland is typical of this period – six hours of television were produced over sixteen days on location on Iona in 1963.[79] The arrival of commercial TV stations, however, encouraged the BBC to develop its Scottish output further – following the Television Act (1954), Scottish Television were awarded the contract for central Scotland and set up home in the Theatre Royal in Glasgow where, despite budget constraints, it attracted new local audiences with popular programmes such as the *One O'Clock Gang* (axed in the interests of good taste in 1965) and *Scotsport*, the longest running sports programme in the world.[80] By 1964, four hundred hours of the BBC's total programme output was produced in Scotland and, in 1967, the first colour broadcasts (on BBC2) were transmitted in Scotland (a full colour service from STV was operational from 1973).[81] As part of a UK operation that was heavily weighted towards metropolitan concerns and investment in a centralised infrastructure, BBC Scotland did as well as could be expected as a regional outpost of a nationwide corporation. But, like all Scottish arms of nationalised industries, it lacked sufficient independence and funds to truly meet the needs of its home market.[82]

Responses to such new media were mixed. In the early days, radio and television were little more than a distraction from the popularity of cinema but, as they asserted their hold on the leisure time of Scots, complaints resounded about their deleterious impact on the morals, language and industry of youth. By the late nineties, most Scottish homes boasted more than one television and cable and satellite services brought a mesmerising selection of channels to around 40 per cent of households across the UK. In Scotland, adults watched more television per week than the residents of other UK viewing regions – around twenty-six hours a week – and radio still broke the silence of Scottish households for between sixteen and nineteen hours a week.[83] Such media gave Scots more excuses for staying at home but still did not explain their desire to do so. It is still to be resolved whether TV killed the wider active life of many communities or whether such communities were already failing when TV began to light up front parlours across Scotland.

By the end of the century, the technological and distributive impediments that had restricted the reach of the media in the early years had all but vanished – daily newspapers could arrive in the most remote destinations well before noon and colour TV facilitated by satellite and cable offered Scots miles from transmitters the promise of clear 'moving pictures' in their own homes. Scotland's media was at once more 'Scottish' and less 'Scottish' than it had ever been – cartoon characters now spoke in Gaelic but the owners of the Scottish press were typically based outside the country. By the 1990s, the media appeared responsive to Scotland's diverse audiences but still perpetuated images of more homogenous Scottish communities in dramas evoking the legacy of Compton Mackenzie. (The BBC dramas *Hamish Macbeth* – a tale of a Highland policeman and his quirky community – and *Monarch of the Glen* – replete with gullible ghillie and aristocratic buffoonery – are cases in point.) Like Scottish culture as a whole, the media moved with the times but, too frequently, rested in the past. As the main arbiter of taste in the north, however, the onus on it to do more regularly animated critical circles and energised the public at least once a year in their, typically negative, analysis of various Hogmanay entertainments. Yet a lack of consensus over what exactly should change merely reflected the diverse nature of cultural tastes and the variety of leisure preferences that the media itself had encouraged. It was a vicious circle that even the most adept cultural escapologist would find hard to disentangle.

Conclusion

There is no singular observation that, for the sake of literary convenience, would neatly conclude this exploration of Scottish culture. No encompassing metaphor is offered – there is no picture in words, no simple melody or grand orchestration to draw it all together. To offer such simplicity would be to act against the very dynamics that have proved to be the most enduring impulses behind Scottish culture – the fragmentation, the multiplicity of voices, the contradictions, the regional dynamics, the personal and spiritual passions and the global reach and response of its most alluring protagonists. How all this was played out in the religious, artistic and leisured moments of Scottish lives is the story of culture in the twentieth century and, like most things about lives lived rather than written, an ending, while awaited, will likely not emerge – at least not as one would expect.

Cultural developments call on the observer to acknowledge their constant state of becoming and ending – the renewing generational dynamic that, while willing change, exists only as a consequence of the efforts of past generations. A century is a clockmaker's whim when measured against changes that, owing more to timeless values – faith, beauty, laughter and pride amongst them – resist history's calendar.

Place is also problematic in this sense. While Scotland asserted a hold, it was not by necessity the country that laid claim to loyalty. History, institutions, traditions, localities, landscapes, languages, heroes and habit moved Scots to both create and criticise, celebrate and resist. Those who have sought an essence in all of this have typically come unstuck – Scotland remained a country where its own prophets were generally without honour and cultural manifestos were made only to be broken, bent and shaped in environments that did not thole, far less support, other-worldly aspirations – except in church or chapel and only then in the abstract. Scotland was also but one influence on Scots in the twentieth century: the surprise is that having the choice of many tongues, alternative sounds, and brighter colours from a global palette, so many chose to remain rooted in, if not entirely true to native sentiments.

Is this a unique story? It is doubtful. But this version is Scotland's and it is the one the twentieth century bequeathed to now.

Epilogue: Bridges, Borders and Frontiers

Royal Tweed (1928), Kincardine (1936), Forth (1964), Tay (1966), Kingston (1970), Erskine (1971), Bonar (1973), Ballachulish (1974), Kessock (1982), Dornoch (1991), Skye (1995) – road bridges were a very modern expression of the twentieth century's improving impulse which, in denying the limits set by geography, sought to refashion popular understandings of the place called Scotland by facilitating movement while, at the same time, providing permanent memorials to artifice. The sentiment is beautifully evoked in Douglas Dunn's musings on the Tay Bridge:

> Conjectural infinity's outdone
> By engineering, light and hydrous fact,
> A waterfront that rises fold by fold
> Into the stars beyond the last of stone,
> A city's elements, local, exact.

Reaching to infinity, we return invariably to the local – to a renewed sense of self. In a very real sense, bridges unified Scotland in a more straightforward way than the machinations of legislatures or intermittent calls of patriotism but that did not mean Scots were any more united. By the century's close, Scotland's bridges were taken for granted. They were important largely for what they facilitated – speed, convenience and commerce – rather than for what they were – attempts to make as one what Nature had ordained to keep separate. That this grand design has gone largely unnoticed does not make it any less remarkable.

The second half of the twentieth century recorded the greatest change in this regard – by the 1970s, there were 14,390 road bridges in Scotland and, of these, 868 on the major trunk roads had been erected since the

Second World War.[2] By the century's end, as motorists approached the country's widest estuaries, journeys were no longer punctuated by ferry travel or compromised by the whims of tidal charts. The *Queen Margaret* made her final crossing of the Forth in 1964 and the half-hourly ferry service between Newport and Dundee ended in 1966 with the opening of the Tay Road Bridge.

Bridges – grand feats of collective endeavour – ironically encouraged the privatisation of travel. They certainly facilitated communication between communities separated by a shared waterway. But familiarity, more often than not, merely confirmed differences between people. These were engineering paradoxes which, in allowing Scots to know their country more intimately, made them less respectful of its challenging topography and, while drawing attention to regional difference, did not necessarily guarantee greater understanding.

In all this, they are fitting monuments to the complexities of the age and metaphors in concrete for many of the themes encountered throughout this book. Yet we would be mistaken to assume that they are any more permanent than this literary sleight of hand. Indeed, the century's dawn was heralded by the urgent preservation of a bridge of the past – the auld brig o' Ayr – that itself had rightly predicted the demise of its new neighbour in Burns' famous poem.[3]

> AULD BRIG
> Conceited gowk! Puff'd up wi' windy pride!
> This monie a year I've stood the flood an' tide;
> And tho' wi' crazy eild I'm sair forfairn,
> I'll be a Brig when ye're a shapeless cairn!
> 'The Brigs o' Ayr' (1787)
> Robert Burns

No less than the Earl of Rosebery warned the country in 1906 of the 'ineradicable shame' should 'this twentieth century of ours' allow the bridge to be 'wiped out of existence'. The call to arms was duly honoured and charitable endeavour protected for the future a bridge to the past consecrated by poetry.[4]

Yet neither engineered nor poetic bridges could overwhelm constitutional and political realities. Scotland's southern border scarred the organic unity of Great Britain, undoing the logic of Nature with the map-maker's precision and limiting the bridge-builder's remaking of community by dictating the parameters within which nationhood was set.

BORDERS

> It is not easy for the Scot who is travelling southward to decide at what point of his journey he has reached an environment and an atmosphere that are truly and typically English. And if, instead of travelling by train he makes his entry by means of that modern equivalent of the stage coach, the motor bus, and if he chooses the bus route across the Cheviots – the route of the Roman legionary – he finds the problem at once more insistent and more difficult.
>
> *The Study of Local History and Other Essays* (Edinburgh, 1932)
> George Pratt Insh (1883–1956)

At the turn of the twentieth century, when the Union seemed secure and its future almost guaranteed by imperial dominions and world trading dominance, the English–Scottish border marked little more than a line distinguishing two halves of mainland Britain – a line commemorating past encounters rather than current concerns. According to Sir Walter Scott, the grand design of King James VI and I had been realised many years before – the Marches were no more, the Border was little more than an administrative convenience and, from lands that were once the extremities of two warring nations, the 'middle shires' had been fashioned, making the Borders the heart of the new island kingdom.[5]

Indeed, even nature seemed to conspire to limit the Border's relevance, as on neither side of it did landscape and topography suggest anything other than continuity. In the 1930s, having crossed the Border marked and colour-coded by signboards ('one with a background of light blue, the other with a background of mustard yellow'), historian and author George Pratt Insh looked ahead 'at the far stretching uplands' and saw 'little variation in the landscape to confirm the emphatic suggestion of the roadside monitors'.[6] Similarly, over forty years later, TV journalist Robert Langley – having walked the Border's 110 miles, starting at the Solway – was only a short distance from his destination in the east but had to ask where the borderline actually ended.[7]

The Border was real enough but, in the twentieth century, its meaning was disputed and, at times, it seemed to exist more powerfully in the minds of both nations than in the land itself. The Border was the site of historic memory and fantasy and these often overwhelmed its more mundane reality. For Langley, the Border was 'all about gory deeds, fierce loyalties and even fiercer treacheries' and, even in the 1970s, he felt as though he 'would be stepping back into its past . . . recapturing some of the colour and tradition that made it such a romantic and fascinating locality'.[8] But, when he turned up late at night in Carlisle, he was met with a very different scene:

> Drunken singing echoed between the shiny fronts of modern department stores. Cars hissed by, their tyres making sucking noises on the gleaming asphalt. Mist hung like streamers between the streetlamps. This was Carlisle, Gateway to the Border, and it had seemed to me the ideal jumping off spot to begin my journey. At that moment it seemed like the last place on earth.[9]

For others, the Border was allowed to persist in the imagination no matter how much the reality of the place – settled as the boundary between the two nations since the sixteenth century – suggested otherwise.

In the 1880s, George Eyre-Todd visited the Scottish Borders and fell under the spell of the hills of Yarrow that seemed 'peculiarly reminiscent of the past'.[10] Two decades later, however, Mr and Mrs William Platt had to admit that '[t]oday the Border presents scenes of peaceful cattle-farming', although 'Romance [was] still in the air, hang[ing] about the fine, breezy moorlands and beautiful dales.'[11] Similarly, while the novelist George Macdonald Fraser (1926–) admitted that motoring offences rather than cattle-rustling typically occupied the local Border police courts in the 1970s, he easily indulged a 'sentimental imagination' with thoughts of the spirits of long-dead reivers speaking through the Cheviot wind and casting shadows beneath a hunter's moon.[12] Even esteemed bodies such as the Royal Automobile Club sponsored route books of the Borders that regularly resorted to fantasy:

> Betwixt Tweed and Forth lies a strip of Scotland compact of enchantment. This Borderland which has inspired a wealth of ballad lore unsurpassed even in Scotland, is a kingdom in itself, true territory of faerie, with a mysterious pensive charm which makes it a memory and a song in the heart for ever.[13]

Travel writers perpetuated such Border imagery and often compromised history in the process. Best-selling author H. V. Morton (1892–1979) referred to the Border as 'a wide and persistent wilderness' – 'that No Man's Land between England and Scotland'. It had 'a spirit of its own':

> These very rocks thrusting their sharp jaws from the brown moorland sheltered the Picts, who sat in the heather listening to the bees that made their honey-wine as they gazed southward to the far

smoke and the occasional heliograph of a brazen shield which
marked the western limit of the Roman world. This side of the Wall
was never tamed. It has known many playmates but no masters. It
has made many songs but no laws.[14]

Despite the honesty of the landscape and the reality of three hundred years
of reasonable stability, writings such as these styled the southern border as
a 'queer compromise between fairyland and battle-field'.[15] It was as much
a frontier in time as a border between two nations and, as such, is best
appreciated as both a spatial and temporal frontier. As Kenneth White
noted in the poem 'On the Border', 'these Borders border on more than
England'. It was a fitting frame for Scotland in the twentieth century which
for many was most real as an 'imagined community'.[16]

FRONTIERS

In 1893, historian Frederick Jackson Turner (1861–1932) developed his
frontier thesis of modern American history:

> American social development has been continually beginning over
> again on the frontier. This perennial rebirth, this fluidity of
> American life, this expansion westward with its new opportunities,
> its continuous touch with the simplicity of primitive society, furnish
> the forces dominating American character.[17]

In Scotland, the Border was less a place of beginnings than a place where
things ended – the Border marked the end of Scottish independence and
its 'closure' in the sixteenth century had inspired a defensive rather than
an aggressive national spirit by the twentieth century. Yet the Union of
the Crowns in 1603 and the consolidation of the parliamentary Union
after 1707 had ushered in a period of success for Scotland, just as the
extension of the frontier westward continually added to the resources of
America in the nineteenth century. Nevertheless, whereas the American
frontier guided that society further from European influences, the
Scottish Border 'tied' Scotland to London dominance.[18] While America
was made at its frontier and it, in turn, became a symbol of the future,
Scotland was 'unmade' at its border – a symbol of the past. Crossing the
Border in the 1960s, the poet Norman MacCaig noted:

> I sit, being helplessly
> lugged backwards
> through the Debatable Lands of history.[19]

Yet change affected both countries over the course of the twentieth century and recast their frontiers in light of fresh contemporary challenges. In America, the Pacific Ocean overtook the moving frontier line as America's western boundary and encouraged Americans to look for other frontiers – imaginative and real – where America might create itself anew. Meanwhile, in Scotland the Border reasserted its political meaning that had been submerged in the vocabulary of North Britishness since the eighteenth century. In 1970, Hugh MacDiarmid reflected:

> If I am asked when I think I got my first idea about Scotland, I can only reply that I don't think I was ever unaware of it. As a Border man, *living on the frontier*, I was always acutely conscious of the difference between the Scots and the English and I had from the start a certain anti-English feeling.[20]

Thirty years later, contemporary circumstances styled the Border as a frontier with the future – a line distinguishing differences that time had reinvigorated and choices that seemed to grow increasingly insistent. Only time will tell whether that line will act as bridge or fissure between auld enemies and truly modern partners.

In the twentieth century, the southern border of the nation without a state was, at times, most powerful as an imagined landscape subsuming tradition and fantasy. It is a fitting place to end this account of a century on the cusp of memory and history. And yet Scotland was clearly something more than the belief in a community imagined; something other than the affective commitment of its self-appointed members; something beneath the spectacular outbursts of togetherness which conditioned public Scotland in the twentieth century.[21] Scots in their actions and experiences created the parameters of the collective imagination and the Border was an important manifestation of difference.

This book has sought to sketch this Scotland while attempting to understand its fictive boundaries and dreams. Scotland was certainly an imagined community but it also boasted an economy, a society, a body politic and many cultures which together influenced the country's dreamers, bounded the country's imaginings and determined which vision of the nation was most dominant over time. Scotland was experienced as well as imagined and lived as intensely as it was rhymed into poetry. Change and continuity marked Scotland's identity and its relationships with England and the wider world, but at no time was the twentieth century free to create Scotland anew. The legacy of the past and the responsibilities owed to the present restricted its imaginings. Its final achievement was to secure the trappings of statehood that had confounded it since 1707 and its gift to the future was a desire on the part of many for more. Even the future was made to echo to the claims of the past in this debatable land, this country of extremes.

Notes

INTRODUCTION

1. W. Fyfe, *Holiday Sketches and Work-a-day Essays, Being Notes of Holiday Tours and Sentiments on Social Subjects* (Dundee, 1880), pp. 55–6.
2. W. Winter, *Gray Days and Gold: in England and Scotland* (London, 1893), pp. 253–4.
3. *The Epistles of Peggy: Written From Scotland* (1910), p. 32.
4. A. A. MacGregor, *Wild Drumalbain or, the Road to Meggernie and Glen Coe* (London, 1931), p. 1.
5. *Summer Tours in Scotland's Wonderland by the Royal Route Through the Western Highlands and Islands by MacBrayne's Swift Passenger Steamers* (n. d.), p. 34.
6. John R. Gray, *Memories of a Tour in the Scottish Highlands* (Elgin, 1938), p. 28.
7. *Bonnie Scotland: A Handbook for Visitors* (London, 1894), p. 33.
8. G. Eyre-Todd, *Scotland: Picturesque and Traditional – A Pilgrimage with Staff and Knapsack* (New York, 1907), p. 341.
9. R. D. Anderson, *Education and the Scottish People, 1750–1918* (Oxford, 1995), p. 230.
10. Winter, *Gray Days*, p. 324.
11. R. Bruce Lockhart, *My Scottish Youth* (Edinburgh, 1993 edition), p. 196.
12. I. Hamilton, *Scotland the Brave* (London, 1957), p. 162. Hamilton's book describes a childhood in 1930s Renfrewshire.
13. J. Urry, 'Globalisation, Localisation and the Nation State', *Lancaster Regionalism Group Working Papers* (40, November 1990), p. 1.
14. See M. Guibernau, *Nations Without States: Political Communities in a Global Age* (Cambridge, 1999), p. 48.
15. See S. Hall, 'The Local and the Global: Globalization and Ethnicity', in A. D. King, *Culture, Globalisation and the World System: Contemporary Conditions for the Representation of Identity* (Basingstoke, 1991), pp. 19–140.
16. See P. G. Cerny, 'Reconstructing the Political in a Globalising World: States, Institutions, Actors and Governance', in F. Buelens (ed.), *Globalisation and the Nation State* (Cheltenham, 1999), pp. 91–2.
17. Hall, 'The Local and the Global', p. 28.

18. Ibid., p. 28; R. Robertson, *Globalization: Social Theory and Global Culture* (London, 1991), p. 172.

19. T. Spybey, 'Modernity, Globalisation and the End of History', *Plymouth International Papers* (4, 1996), p. 12.

20. Hall, 'The Local and the Global', p. 34.

21. D. McCrone, *Understanding Scotland: The Sociology of a Stateless Nation* (London, 1992), p. 218.

22. Urry, 'Globalisation', p. 22.

23. See T. M. Devine, *Scotland's Empire, 1600–1815* (Penguin Allen Lane, 2003) and M. Fry, *The Scottish Empire* (East Linton, 2001).

24. See Urry, 'Globalisation', p. 23.

PART ONE: PROLOGUE

1. 'Official Guide' (Glasgow, 1938).

2. *Scottish Pavilions: Official Guide* (Glasgow, 1938), p. 7. See also B. Crampsey, *The Empire Exhibition of 1938: The Last Durbar* (Edinburgh, 1988).

CHAPTER ONE: SCOTLAND IN CONTEXT – COINCIDENCE AND CONTRASTS

1. A. Midwinter, M. Keating and J. Mitchell, *Politics and Public Policy in Scotland* (London, 1991), pp. 17, 18.

2. A. K. Cairncross, 'Introduction', in A. K. Cairncross (ed.), *The Scottish Economy* (Cambridge, 1954), p. 1.

3. R. L. Mackie, 'The Survival and Decline of Locally-based and Family Firms in the Kirkcaldy Area, 1900–1960' (unpublished PhD thesis, University of Edinburgh, 1995), p. 11.

4. C. Lee, *Scotland and the United Kingdom: the economy and the Union in the twentieth century* (Manchester, 1995), pp. 24–6.

5. R. Steward, 'To Keep the Highlander at Home: the Story of A1 Welders', *Scottish Industrial History* (14–15, 1992), pp. 13–17.

6. S. McKendrick, F. Bechhofer and D. McCrone, 'Is Scotland Different? Industrial and Occupational Change in Scotland and Britain', in H. Newby et al. (eds), *Restructuring Capital* (Basingstoke, 1985), p. 81.

7. See Mackie, 'The Survival and Decline of Locally-based and Family Firms', p. 13.

8. Sir E. Geddes, *Mass Production: The Revolution which Changes Everything* (London, 1931), p. 3.

9. Lee, *Scotland and the United Kingdom*, p. 125.

10. N. Buxton, 'The Scottish Economy, 1945–1979: Performance, structure and problems', in R. Saville (ed.), *The Economic Development of Modern Scotland, 1950–1980* (Edinburgh, 1985), p. 54.

11. G. McCrone, *Scotland's Economic Progress, 1951–1960: A Study in Regional Accounting* (London, 1965), p. 28, Table II.

12. Rt. Hon. W. Elliot, *What Sort of Warriors?* (Address delivered to the Students of the University of Glasgow, 6 February 1948), p. 9.

13. McCrone, *Scotland's Economic Progress*, p. 28, Table II.

14. J. Scouller, 'Made in Scotland', in K. P. D. Ingham and J. Love (eds), *Understanding the Scottish Economy* (Oxford, 1983), p. 22. In terms of GDP, the UK recorded growth rates of just over 2 per cent in the 1970s, when France reached nearly 4 per cent and Japan exceeded 5 per cent. (Buxton, 'The Scottish Economy, 1945–1979', p. 50.) By the 1980s, Britain's share of world trade in manufactures had fallen to just 7 per cent – in the late 1940s, this had been 25 per cent. See A. Cairncross, *The British Economy Since 1945* (Oxford, 1992), p. 286.

15. This report bears the name of its author, John Toothill, and was sponsored by the Scottish Council (Development and Industry) to investigate problems in Scotland's economy and to promote growth and diversification in industry.

16. *Inquiry into the Scottish Economy, 1960–1961: Report of a Committee Appointed by the Scottish Council (Development and Industry) under the Chairmanship of J. N. Toothill* (Paisley, 1961), p. 21.

17. Buxton, 'The Scottish Economy, 1945–1979', p. 53.

18. Ibid., p. 51.

19. J. Johnstone, 'Scotland Through the Looking Glass', St Andrew's Day Lecture, BBC Radio Scotland, 1981, p. 3.

20. See C. Harvie, *No Gods and Precious Few Heroes: Twentieth Century Scotland* (Edinburgh, 1998), pp. 169–72.

21. S. Wakefield, 'Economic Development', Scottish Parliament Information Centre (14 June 1999); C. Harvie, 'Scotland after 1978: From Referendum to Millennium', in W. W. J. Knox and R. A. Houston (eds), *The New Penguin History of Scotland: from the Earliest Times to the Present Day* (London, 2001), p. 503.

22. D. Wight, *Workers not Wasters: Masculine Respectability, Consumption and Unemployment in Central Scotland* (Edinburgh, 1993), pp. 236, 210.

23. Buxton, 'The Scottish Economy, 1945–1979', notes that the structure of Scottish production moved more 'closely into line with that of the UK as a whole', p. 60.

24. Cairncross, *The British Economy Since 1945*, p. 282.

25. The rise of the 'service trades' is noted in C. E. V. Leser, 'Production', in A. K. Cairncross (ed.), *The Scottish Economy* (Cambridge, 1954), p. 65; see also P. L. Payne, 'The Economy', in T. M. Devine and R. J. Finlay (eds), *Scotland in the Twentieth Century* (Edinburgh, 1996), p. 23.

26. In terms of gross value added. Scottish Executive Information Directorate, *New Figures on the Service Sector in Scotland, 1997* (24 November 1999), p. 2.

27. J. Foster, 'A Proletarian Nation? Occupation and class since 1914', in A. Dickson and J. H. Treble (eds), *People and Society in Scotland, Vol. III, 1914–1990* (Edinburgh, 1992), p. 203, Figure 1.

28. R. Saville, 'The Industrial background to the Post-War Economy', in R. Saville (ed.), *The Economic Development of Modern Scotland, 1950–1980* (Edinburgh, 1985), pp. 6–9.

29. Buxton, 'The Scottish Economy, 1945–1979', p. 49.

30. *The Times* (28 January 1982).

31. T. C. Smout, 'Introduction', in Edwin Muir, *Scottish Journey* (London, 1985 ed.), p. xvii; O. and C. Checkland, *Industry and Ethos: Scotland 1832–1914* (Edinburgh, 1989), pp. 172–3; T. M. Devine, *The Scottish Nation, 1700–2000* (London, 1999), pp. 249–72.

32. Checkland, *Industry and Ethos*, pp. 172–3.

33. Smout, 'Introduction', p. xvii. See also P. L. Payne, 'The Economy', in T. M. Devine and R. J. Finlay (eds), *Scotland in the Twentieth Century* (Edinburgh, 1996), pp. 14–16; W. W. Knox, *Industrial Nation: Work, Culture and Society in Scotland, 1800–Present* (Edinburgh, 1999), pp. 132–6.

34. *The Scotsman* (14 October 1904).

35. *The Scotsman* (9 September 1908).

36. *The Scotsman* (24 December 1908).

37. *The Scotsman* (21 March 1908).

38. *The Scotsman* (27 December 1909).

39. See Mackie, 'The Survival and Decline of Locally-based and Family Firms', *passim*.

40. 'William Beardmore', *Dictionary of Scottish Business Biography, Vol. I* (Aberdeen, 1986), p. 92.

41. H. Walker, 'The Rise and Fall of Dunfermline Linen', *Scottish Industrial History* (16, 1993), pp. 31–8.

42. A. Slaven, *The Development of the West of Scotland, 1750–1960* (London, 1975), p. 183.

43. H. V. Morton, *In Scotland Again* (London, 1949), pp. 141–2.

44. Devine, *The Scottish Nation*, p. 272; R. B. Weir, 'Structural change and diversification in Ireland and Scotland', in R. Mitchison and P. Roebuck (eds), *Economy and Society in Scotland and Ireland, 1500–1939* (Edinburgh, 1988), p. 299.

45. R. Saville, 'The Industrial Background to the Post-war Scottish Economy', in Saville (ed.), *The Economic Development of Modern Scotland*, p. 4. Taking 1907 as a base (i.e. 1907 = 100), Scottish production slumped to 99 in 1924 and rose to only 107 by 1935. By comparison, UK production over the same period recorded a rise in 1924 to 111 and in 1935 to 147. See Harvie, *No Gods and Precious Few Heroes*, p. 37, Table 2.1.

46. Saville, 'The Industrial Background to the Post-war Scottish Economy', pp. 6–9.

47. Slaven, *The Development of the West of Scotland*, p. 183.

48. Mackie, 'The Survival and Decline of Locally-based and Family Firms', p. 185.

49. C. A. Oakley, *Scottish Industry Today: A Survey of Recent Developments Undertaken for the Scottish Development Council* (Edinburgh, 1937), p. 129.

50. See A. Muir, *Nairns of Kirkcaldy: A Short History of the Company* (Cambridge, 1956).

51. E. H. L. MacAskill, 'Holm Woollen Mills, 1798–1984', *Scottish Industrial History* (7 : 2, 1984), pp. 36–44.

52. 'William Beardmore', *Dictionary of Scottish Business Biography, Vol. I*, p. 93.

53. As quoted in I. Johnston, *Beardmore Built* (Clydebank, 1993), p. 146.
54. See T. L. Johnston, N. K. Buxton and D. Mair, *Structure and Growth of the Scottish Economy* (London, 1971), p. 72.
55. M. French, 'Organisation and Profitability in Exporting: Albion Motors Overseas, 1920–1956', *Scottish Industrial History* (14–15, 1992), pp. 1–12.
56. Saville, 'The Industrial Background to the Post-war Scottish Economy', p. 10.
57. N. K. Buxton, 'Economic Growth between the Wars: The Role of Production Structure and Rationalization', *Economic History Review* (33, 1980), p. 554.
58. *The Scotsman* (19 November 1930).
59. Oakley, *Scottish Industry Today*, p. 137.
60. M. Spark, *The Prime of Miss Jean Brodie* (London, 1961).
61. Knox, *Industrial Nation*, p. 190.
62. Harvie, *No Gods and Precious Few Heroes*, p. 47.
63. Slaven, *The Development of the West of Scotland*, p. 184.
64. *The Scotsman* (4 February 1935).
65. M. Jamieson, 'Old Paisley Collections', *Scottish Industrial History* (4, 1981), pp. 14–15.
66. W. Ferguson, *Scotland: 1689 to the Present* (Edinburgh, 1987), p. 363.
67. D. Charman (ed.), *Glengarnock*, A Report on the Manpower Services Commission Conservation Projects Sponsored by the British Steel Corporation and Cunninghame District Council, in Association with the SDA (Netherlands, 1981), p. 80.
68. Ferguson, *Scotland*, p. 373.
69. 'Ex-Soldier', *Queen Mary* (c.1936).
70. *The Daily Telegraph* (Supplement, 25 May 1936).
71. Slaven, *The Development of the West of Scotland*, pp. 210–11.
72. Muir, *Nairns of Kirkcaldy*, pp. 132–3.
73. C. H. Lee, 'Silk Weaving in Lochwinnoch', *Scottish Industrial History* (8:2, 1985), pp. 15–19.
74. Devine, *Scottish Nation*, p. 551.
75. Slaven, *The Development of the West of Scotland, 1750–1960*, pp. 210–11.
76. C. A. Oakley (ed.), *Scottish Industry: An Account of What Scotland Makes and Where She Makes It* (Edinburgh, 1953), p. xv.
77. Buxton, 'The Scottish Economy, 1945–1979', p. 51.
78. McCrone, *Scotland's Economic Progress*, p. 28.
79. Payne, 'The Economy', p. 22.
80. Harvie, *No Gods and Precious Few Heroes*, p. 144.
81. Buxton, 'The Scottish Economy, 1945–1979', pp. 51–2; Johnston, Buxton and Mair, *Structure and Growth of the Scottish Economy*, pp. 58–9.
82. Knox, *Industrial Nation*, p. 256.
83. Buxton, 'The Scottish Economy, 1945–1979', pp. 52–3.
84. J. Doherty, 'Dundee: A Post Industrial City', in C. A. Whatley (ed.), *The Remaking of Juteopolis* (Dundee, 1992), pp. 24–39.
85. Knox, *Industrial Nation*, p. 254.
86. Ibid., p. 254.

87. Buxton, 'The Scottish Economy, 1945–1979', pp. 57–9; Harvie, *No Gods and Precious Few Heroes*, p. 166.
88. Devine, *Scottish Nation*, pp. 595–6.

CHAPTER TWO: MANUFACTURING SCOTLAND – TRADITIONAL
INDUSTRIES

1. Lavinia Derwent was the *nom de plume* of Elizabeth Dodd who became the first woman president of Scottish PEN. Her first job, remembered here, was with the Collins publishing house in Glasgow.
2. For an interesting discussion on the persistence of family enterprises in Scotland, see B. Dunn, 'Success Themes in Scottish Family Enterprises' *Family Business Review* (8:1, 1995), pp. 17–28.
3. As quoted in Charman (ed.), *Glengarnock*, p. 74.
4. T. G. Velek, 'Industrial and Commercial Efficiency: The Role, Reform and Development of Scottish Technical and Commercial Education, 1895–1914' (unpublished PhD thesis, University of Edinburgh, 1996), pp. 52, 307, 221.
5. A. Carnegie, *A Rectorial Address Delivered to the Students in the University of Aberdeen, 6 June 1912* (New York, 1912), p. 10.
6. Saville, 'The Industrial Background to the Post-war Scottish Economy', Table 2.
7. Buxton, 'The Scottish Economy, 1945–1979', p. 62, Table 6.
8. Cairncross, 'Introduction', p. 4.
9. *Inquiry into the Scottish Economy, 1960–1961*, p. 30.
10. Buxton, 'The Scottish Economy, 1945–1979', p. 60; Saville, 'The Industrial Background to the Post-war Scottish Economy', Table 2.
11. *Inquiry into the Scottish Economy, 1960–1961*, p. 34.
12. C. Levy and the Ardrossan Local History Workshop, *Ardrossan Shipyards: the Struggle for Survival, 1825–1983* (WEA, 1983), p. 27.
13. D. Hunter, *Girvan Valley Coalfield* (Ayr, 2003), p. 19.
14. P. L. Payne, 'The Decline of the Scottish Heavy Industries, 1945–1983', in Saville (ed.), *The Economic Development of Modern Scotland*, p. 80.
15. Devine, *Scottish Nation*, p. 267.
16. E. D. Hyde, *Coal Mining in Scotland* (Edinburgh, 1987), p. 13.
17. Benarty Mining Heritage Group, *No More Bings in Benarty* (Glenrothes, 1992), pp. 32–3.
18. R. Watt, *History of Coal Mining Round Dunfermline* (Carnegie Dunfermline Trust Project, November 1997), pp. 30–4.
19. R. Duncan, *Steelopolis: The Making of Motherwell, c.1750–1939* (Motherwell, 1991), p. 166
20. Slaven, *The Development of the West of Scotland*, p. 210.
21. R. S. Halliday, *The Disappearing Scottish Colliery* (Edinburgh, 1990), pp. 50, 73.
22. Slaven, *The Development of the West of Scotland*, p. 213; Johnston, Buxton and Mair, *Structure and Growth of the Scottish Economy*, pp. 109–10; Payne, 'The Decline of the Scottish Heavy Industries, 1945–1983', p. 88.

23. Johnston, Buxton and Mair, *Structure and Growth of the Scottish Economy*, pp. 109–10.
24. Payne, 'The Decline of the Scottish Heavy Industries', p. 90.
25. Benarty Mining Heritage Group, *No More Bings in Benarty*, p. 93.
26. Ibid., p. 129.
27. See G. Hutton, *Coal Not Dole: Memories of the 1984–5 Miners' Strike* (Catrine, 2004).
28. Section 53 of the Coal Industry Act (1994) imposed heavy environmental duties on the coal industry and planning authorities and Scotland's two main coal-fired power stations are due for closure in 2015. Scottish Planning Policy (SPP16), *Opencast Coal: Consultation Draft* (Revised, August 2004), pp. 7, 2.
29. Geddes Thomson, 'In Ayrshire Now', *Chapman* (25, Autumn 1979), p. 18.
30. This industrial epic poem is reproduced in full in *Chapman* (30, Summer 1981).
31. Slaven, *The Development of the West of Scotland*, p. 170.
32. Ibid., p. 171.
33. Ibid., p. 195.
34. Ibid., p. 184.
35. G. Thomson, 'The Iron Industry of the Monklands', *Scottish Industrial History* (5:2, 1982), pp. 27–40. See also J. R. Harris, *The British Iron Industry, 1700–1850* (Basingstoke, 1988), p. 44.
36. P. L. Payne, *Colvilles and the Scottish Steel Industry* (Oxford, 1979), p. 54.
37. Ibid., p. 102.
38. Ibid., p. 81.
39. Ibid., pp. 130, 133.
40. Slaven, *The Development of the West of Scotland*, p. 193.
41. Ibid., p. 192.
42. See P. L. Payne, 'Rationality and Personality: A Study of Mergers in the Iron and Steel Industry, 1916–1936', *Business History* (19, 1977), pp. 162–91.
43. S. Tolliday, 'Tariffs and Steel, 1916–1934: The Politics of Industrial Decline', in J. Turner (ed.), *Businessmen and Politics* (London, 1984), p. 51.
44. H. A. Brassert & Co. (Chicago), *Report to Lord Weir of Cathcart on the Manufacture of Iron and Steel* (16 May 1929), pp. i–ii.
45. Duncan, *Steelopolis*, p. 165.
46. *The Scotsman* (28 January 1935).
47. Slaven, *The Development of the West of Scotland*, p. 215.
48. *Report of Speech by the Rt Hon. Sir Andrew Duncan GBE MP, in the House of Commons, Wednesday 17 November 1948* (British Iron and Steel Federation, 1948), p. 19.
49. Payne, *Colvilles and the Scottish Steel Industry*, p. 350.
50. Payne, 'The Decline of the Scottish Heavy Industries', p. 95.
51. Ibid., p. 96; Slaven, *The Development of the West of Scotland*, p. 218.
52. Payne, *Colvilles and the Scottish Steel Industry*, p. 392.
53. Payne, 'The Decline of the Scottish Heavy Industries', p. 100.
54. P. L. Payne, 'The End of Steelmaking in Scotland, c. 1967–1993', *Scottish Economic and Social History* (15, 1995), p. 78.

55. F. Martin, 'A Profile of the Scottish Iron Foundry Industry, 1969–1984', *Scottish Industrial History* (9 : 1 and 9 : 2, 1986), p. 64.

56. Committee on Scottish Affairs, *The Steel Industry in Scotland* (December 1982), p. 5.

57. The ore terminal at Hunterston was taken over by the Clydeport Management Company and, from 2003, plans were afoot for its redevelopment as a container port.

58. Arthur D. Little, *Options for Steel in Scotland*, Executive Summary and Presentation of Interim Findings to the Scottish Development Agency, 24 January 1991.

59. STUC, *The Scottish Steel Industry* (Typescript, n. d.)

60. Payne, 'The End of Steelmaking in Scotland', p. 82.

61. J. Kelman, *Fighting for Survival: The Steel Industry in Scotland* (Glasgow, 1990), p. 12.

62. A. Slaven, 'Scottish Shipbuilders and Marine Engineers: the Evidence of Business Biography, 1860–1960', in T. C. Smout (ed.), *Scotland and the Sea* (Edinburgh, 1992), p. 182.

63. Slaven, *The Development of the West of Scotland*, p. 178.

64. Levy, *Ardrossan Shipyards*, p. 10; A. I. Bowman, *Kirkintilloch Shipbuilding* (Strathkelvin District Libraries and Museums, 1983).

65. A. Borthwick, *Yarrow & Company Ltd (1865–1977)* (Glasgow, 1977), pp. 43–6.

66. Slaven, *The Development of the West of Scotland*, p. 184.

67. M. Northcott, *Hood: Design and Construction* (London, 1975); A. Coles and T. Briggs, *Flagship Hood: the Fate of Britain's Mightiest Warship* (London, 1985).

68. P. J. Telford, *Donaldson Line of Glasgow* (Kendal, 1989).

69. A. A. McAlister, *H. Hogarth & Sons Ltd: Baron Line* (Kendal, 1976), p. 7.

70. A. Slaven, 'Management and Shipbuilding on the Clyde, 1919–1976' (SSRC Report, 1980), p. 8.

71. H. V. Morton, *In Search of Scotland* (London, 7th edn, 1930), p. 246.

72. Borthwick, *Yarrow & Company Ltd*, pp. 50–1.

73. A. Slaven, 'A Shipyard in Depression: John Browns of Clydebank, 1919–1938', *Business History* (19, 1977), p. 194.

74. 'Sir James Lithgow', *Dictionary of Scottish Business Biography, Vol. I*, p. 224.

75. Slaven, *The Development of the West of Scotland*, p. 189; 'Management and Shipbuilding on the Clyde', pp. 9–12.

76. Payne, 'The Decline of the Scottish Heavy Industries', p. 101.

77. Oakley, *Scottish Industry Today*, p. 97. Tonnage launched on the Tay in 1936 was 26,000 (18,000 in 1913). Tonnage launched on the Forth in 1936 was 29,000 (20,000 in 1913).

78. Mackie, 'The Survival and Decline of Locally-based and Family Firms', pp. 205–21.

79. M. S. Moss and J. R. Hume, *Workshop of the British Empire: Engineering and Shipbuilding in the West of Scotland* (London, 1977), pp. 103–7.

80. Ibid., p. 101.

81. I. Bowman, 'The Grangemouth Dockyard Company', *Scottish Industrial History* (1 : 2, Spring 1977), pp. 4–11.

82. D. C. E. Burrell, *Scrap and Build* (Kendal, 1983), p. 10.

83. S. Tolliday, *Business, Banking and Politics: the Case of British Steel, 1918–1939* (London, 1987), p. 90.

84. Ibid., p. 11. See also H. B. Peebles, *Warshipbuilding on the Clyde: Naval Orders and the Prosperity of the Clyde Shipbuilding Industry, 1889–1939* (Edinburgh, 2000), p. 145.

85. Borthwick, *Yarrow & Company Ltd*, p. 75.

86. Ibid., p. 75.

87. Ibid., p. 79.

88. F. E. Hyde, *Cunard and the North Atlantic, 1840–1973* (London, 1975), p. 283. See also McAlister, *H. Hogarth & Sons Ltd*.

89. Borthwick, *Yarrow & Company Ltd*, p. 96.

90. McAlister, *H. Hogarth & Sons Ltd*, p. 10.

91. Payne, 'The Decline of the Scottish Heavy Industries', p. 107.

92. Geddes, *Mass Production*, p. 9.

93. Payne, 'The Decline of the Scottish Heavy Industries', p. 105.

94. Fairfield's had been temporarily saved by an innovative public–private partnership.

95. See F. Heron, *Labour Market in Crisis: Redundancy at Upper Clyde Shipbuilders* (London, 1975).

96. F. Broadway, *Upper Clyde Shipbuilders* (Centre for Policy Studies, London, 1976), p. 17.

97. As quoted in C. Barnet, *The Audit of War: the Illusion and Reality of Britain as a Great Nation* (London, 1987), p. 119.

98. Broadway, *Upper Clyde Shipbuilders*, p. 37.

99. Payne, 'The Decline of the Scottish Heavy Industries', p. 106.

100. Broadway, *Upper Clyde Shipbuilders*, p. 49.

101. Payne, 'The Decline of the Scottish Heavy Industries', p. 106.

102. Heron, *Labour Market in Crisis*, p. 182.

103. Morton, *In Search of Scotland*, p. 246.

104. Payne, 'The Decline of the Scottish Heavy Industries', p. 107.

105. See ibid., pp. 79–113 and *Growth and Contraction: Scottish Industry, c.1860–1990* (Economic and Social History Society of Scotland, Dundee, 1992); Slaven, *The Development of the West of Scotland*, p. 190.

106. Lee, *Scotland and the United Kingdom*, p. 35.

107. Borthwick, *Yarrow & Company Ltd*, p. 117.

108. R. H. Campbell, 'The North British Locomotive Company Between the Wars' *Business History* (20, 1978), pp. 201–34. See also Moss and Hume, *Workshop of the British Empire*.

109. Rt Hon. W. Elliot, *Adventurers' Coast: or The Two Sides of the Tay* (Edinburgh, 1954), p. 11.

110. J. Doherty, 'Dundee: A Post Industrial City', in Whatley (ed.), *The Remaking of Juteopolis*, p. 24.

111. Whatley, 'The Making of Juteopolis', in Whatley (ed.), *The Remaking of Juteopolis*, p. 13.

112. D. C. D. Pocock, 'Economic Renewal: The Example of Fife', *Scottish Geographical Magazine* (86, 1970), p. 123.

113. Ibid., p. 132. (The phrase comes from the *Financial Times*, 10 October 1966.)

114. Payne, 'The Economy', p. 14, Table 1; Foster, 'A Proletarian Nation', p. 203, Figure 1. Similarly, while in 1988 agriculture in Scotland contributed 2.69 per cent of Scotland's GDP, the comparable proportion for the UK as a whole was 1.44 per cent. Payne, 'The Economy', p. 25, Table 2.

115. Scottish Council (Development and Industry), *Industrial Change in Scotland: An Agenda for Progress* (Edinburgh, October 1981); Scottish Trades Union Congress, *Scotland: A Land Fit for People* (Glasgow, 1987), p. 21.

116. NFU (Scotland), *A Sustainable Future for Scottish Agriculture* (September 1999), p. 2.

117. Grampian Regional Council: Economic Development and Planning Department, *The Importance of Fishing to Grampian Region* (1993), p. 5.

118. A Farmer's Wife, *Notes on Farming* (Aberdeen, 1905), pp. 7, 75. (The Scots word 'fashed' means bothered.)

119. A. D. Hall, *A Pilgrimage of British Farming* (London, 1913), pp. 384–5.

120. Scottish Liberal Federation, *Report of the Scottish Liberal Land Inquiry Committee, 1927–1928* (Glasgow, 1928), p. 5.

121. Ibid., p. 7.

122. J. Littlejohn, *Westrigg: The Sociology of a Cheviot Parish* (London, 1998 [1963]), pp. 150, 148.

123. Hall, *A Pilgrimage of British Farming*, pp. 137, 141.

124. T. B. Franklin, *A History of Scottish Farming* (1952), p. 162; J. A Symon, *Scottish Farming: Past and present* (Edinburgh, 1959), p. 220.

125. Symon, *Scottish Farming*, p. 247. For the First World War, see R. Anthony, *Herds and Hinds: Farm Labour in Lowland Scotland, 1900–1939* (East Linton, 1997).

126. Scottish Liberal Federation, *Report of the Scottish Liberal Land Inquiry Committee*, p. 26.

127. G. F. B. Houston, 'Agriculture', in Cairncross (ed.), *The Scottish Economy*, p. 85; J. Bryden, 'Scottish Agriculture, 1950–1980', in Saville (ed.), *The Economic Development of Modern Scotland*, p. 150. Note that the high proportion of marginal land in Scotland tended to encourage this trend.

128. Anthony, *Herds and Hinds*, p. 16.

129. Bryden, 'Scottish Agriculture', pp. 149, 147.

130. Scottish Agricultural College, *The Changing Borders Countryside* (Edinburgh, 1991), p. 23; Scottish Office (Agriculture and Fisheries Dept.), *Agriculture in Scotland: Report for 1994* (Edinburgh, July 1995), p. 5.

131. Houston, 'Agriculture', p. 86.

132. Bryden, 'Scottish Agriculture', p. 150.

133. Houston, 'Agriculture', p. 88.

134. A. Gray, *White Gold? Scotland's Dairying in the Past* (Melksham, 1995), p. 393.

135. Bryden, 'Scottish Agriculture', pp. 151, 153; Johnston, Buxton and Mair, *Structure and Growth of the Scottish Economy*, p. 106.

136. Johnston, Buxton and Mair, *Structure and Growth of the Scottish Economy*, p. 107.

137. L. Moar, 'Farming Today', in Ingham and Love (eds), *Understanding the Scottish Economy*, p. 81.

138. *Agriculture in Scotland: Report for 1994*, p. 27.

139. National Farmers' Union (Scotland), *A Sustainable Future*, p. 2.

140. Scottish Executive (Environment and Rural Affairs Department), *Farm Incomes in Scotland, 2000–2001* (May 2002), pp. 4–5.

141. Anthony, *Herds and Hinds*, p. 18.

142. Houston, 'Agriculture', p. 98.

143. J. McEwen, *Who Owns Scotland* (Edinburgh, 1981), p. 9. See also A. Wightman, *Who Owns Scotland* (Edinburgh, 1996).

144. Houston, 'Agriculture', pp. 102, 104, Table 50.

145. Bryden, 'Scottish Agriculture', p. 160. See also Johnston, Buxton and Mair, *Structure and Growth of the Scottish Economy*, p. 101.

146. From J. R. Allan, *Farmer's Boy* (1935), as quoted in I. Carter, *Farm Life in North East Scotland, 1840–1914: The Poor Man's Country* (Edinburgh, 2003), p. 122.

147. Scottish Liberal Federation, *Report of the Scottish Liberal Land Inquiry Committee*, p. 17.

148. Anthony, *Herds and Hinds*, p. 38. See also T. M. Devine (ed.), *Farm Servants and Labour in Lowland Scotland, 1770–1914* (Edinburgh, 1984), p. v.

149. R. Munro, 'Foreword', *Scottish Journal of Agriculture* (1 January 1918), p. 1.

150. Symon, *Scottish Farming*, p. 250; Anthony, *Herds and Hinds*, p. 47.

151. Symon, *Scottish Farming*, pp. 250–1.

152. W. Elliot, 'Changing Scotland' (3 March 1942), in *Long Distance* (Glasgow, 1943), p. 185.

153. Bryden, 'Scottish Agriculture', p. 159.

154. Jean Leid, in I. MacDougall, *Bondagers: Eight Scots Women Farm Workers* (East Linton, 2000), p. 142.

155. Ibid., p. xi.

156. Morton, *In Scotland Again*, p. 314.

157. M. Gray, *The Fishing Industries of Scotland, 1790–1914: A Study in Regional Adaptation* (Oxford, 1978), p. 149.

158. See J. R. Coull, 'The Scottish Herring Fishery in the Interwar Years, 1919–1939: Ordeal and Retrenchment', *International Journal of Maritime History* (2:1, June 1990), pp. 55–81.

159. P. Anson, *The Sea Fisheries of Scotland* (Edinburgh 1939), pp. 5, 15.

160. Ibid., p. 27.

161. P. F. Anson, *Fishing Boats and Fisherfolk on the East Coast of Scotland* (London, 1971 [1930]), p. 129.

162. A. Martin, *Fish and Fisherfolk: Of Kintyre, Lochfyneside, Gigha and Arran* (Colonsay, 2004), p. 17.
163. J. R. Coull, *The Sea Fisheries of Scotland* (Edinburgh, 2003).
164. J. Miller, *Salt in the Blood: Scotland's Fishing Communities Past and Present* (Edinburgh, 1999), 138.
165. Ibid., p. 160.
166. Scottish Office, *Sea Fishing Industry in Scotland* (Fact Sheet 33, HMSO, 1988), p. 2.
167. Ibid., p. 89; Gray, *The Fishing Industries of Scotland*, pp. 157, 167.
168. Anson, *Sea Fisheries*, pp. 15–16.
169. John Robb, in Miller, *Salt in the Blood*, p. 126.
170. *Inquiry into the Future of the Scottish Fishing Industry* (Royal Society of Edinburgh, 2004), p. iii.
171. Gray, *The Fishing Industries of Scotland*, p. 149.
172. J. and L. Taylor, *Fraserburgh Means Fish* (Fraserburgh, 1993), p. 8.
173. Anson, *The Sea Fisheries of Scotland*, p. 17.
174. *Inquiry into the Future of the Scottish Fishing Industry*, p. iii.
175. Anson, *The Sea Fisheries of Scotland*, p. 21.
176. Leser, 'Production', pp. 70–1.

CHAPTER THREE: THE NOVELTY OF THE NEW

1. Cairncross, 'Introduction', p. 3.
2. T. Burns and G. M. Stalker, *The Management of Innovation* (London, 1961), pp. 49, 140. See also *Inquiry into the Scottish Economy*, p. 53.
3. Buxton, 'Economic Growth in Scotland between the Wars', p. 549, Table 6.
4. Saville, 'The Industrial Background to the Post-war Scottish Economy', p. 31.
5. Ibid., pp. 31, 37.
6. Slaven, *The Development of the West of Scotland*, p. 206.
7. Saville, 'The Industrial Background to the Post-war Scottish Economy', p. 38.
8. Ibid., p. 38.
9. G. Oliver, *Motor Trials and Tribulations* (Edinburgh, HMSO, 1993), pp. 40, 75.
10. McCrone, *Scotland's Economic Progress*, p. 131.
11. A. Buchanan and M. Unsworth, *The Electricity Industry in Scotland* (London, Smith New Court Research, 1992), p. 9.
12. *Inquiry into the Scottish Economy*, pp. 75–6.
13. R. Johnston, *Highland Development* (Edinburgh, 1964), pp. 14–15.
14. J. B. Gardyne, *Scotland to 1980* (London, 1975), p. 52.
15. Lee, *Scotland and the United Kingdom*, p. 34.
16. Johnston, Buxton and Mair, *Structure and Growth of the Scottish Economy*, p. 132.
17. N. Hood and S. Young, *Multinationals in Retreat: The Scottish Experience* (Edinburgh, 1982), p. 67.
18. W. W. Knox and A. McKinlay, 'Working for the Yankee Dollar: American Inward Investment and Scottish Labour, 1945–1970', *Historical Studies in Industrial Relations* (7, Spring 1999), p. 17.

19. J. Henderson, 'Semiconductors, Scotland and the International Division of Labour', *Urban Studies* (24, 1987), p. 399.
20. Lord Thomson of Fleet, *After I was Sixty: A Chapter of Autobiography* (London, 1975), pp. 41–3.
21. W. T. Jackson, *The Enterprising Scot: Investors in the American West After 1873* (London, 1968), p. 297.
22. Ibid., p. 268.
23. J. Scott and M. Hughes, *The Anatomy of Scottish Capital: Scottish Companies and Scottish Capital, 1900–1979* (London, 1980), pp. 70, 81.
24. S. McKendrick et al., 'Is Scotland Different?', p. 75.
25. Slaven, *The Development of the West of Scotland*, p. 223.
26. Hood and Young, *Multinationals in Retreat*, p. 5.
27. Johnston, Buxton and Mair, *Structure and Growth of the Scottish Economy*, p. 88; C. Lythe and M. Majmudar, *The Renaissance of the Scottish Economy?* (London, 1982), p. 153.
28. Henderson, 'Semiconductors, Scotland and the International Division of Labour', p. 397.
29. Saville, 'The Industrial Background to the Post-war Scottish Economy', p. 32.
30. K. Ingham, 'Foreign Firms', in K. P. D. Ingham and J. Love (eds.), *Understanding the Scottish Economy* (Oxford, 1983), p. 225.
31. Buxton, 'The Scottish Economy, 1945–1979', pp. 56–7.
32. Hood and Young, *Multinationals in Retreat*, pp. 4–5.
33. Ibid., pp. 43–55.
34. *The Times* (7 October 1963).
35. S. Wakefield, *Economic Development* (Scottish Parliament Information Centre, June 1999), p. 3.
36. O. Brown, *Scotland: This Wealthy – and Poor – Country* (SSP, 1948), p. 8.
37. *Scotland in 1957: A Political and Economic Review* (SNP, 1957).
38. A. Hargrave, *A Nation of Labourers?* (Glasgow Fabian Society, 1964), p. 5.
39. See Lee, *Scotland and the United Kingdom*, pp. 110–13.
40. J. Scouller, 'Made in Scotland', in Ingham and Love, *Understanding the Scottish Economy*, p. 24.
41. Scottish Economic Planning Department (Highlands and Islands Development Board), 'Closure of the Invergordon Smelter: Impact and Action Programme' (March, 1982), p. 4. See also J. B. Sewell, 'Immediate Local Reactions to the Invergordon Smelter Closure' (SSRC Report, September 1982).
42. Kelman, *Fighting for Survival*, p. 12.
43. Locate in Scotland, *Scotland: Europe's Centre of Electronics Excellence* (1992), p. 1.
44. Scottish Enterprise, *Electronics Manufacturing in Scotland* (July 1997), p. 1.
45. N. Phelps, 'From Local Economic Dependence to Local Development?: The Case of the Scottish Electronics Industry', *Papers in Planning Research*, University of Wales, (136, 1992), p. 8.
46. Henderson, 'Semiconductors, Scotland and the International Division of Labour', p. 396.

47. M. Danson, 'The Scottish Economy: Revisiting the Development of Under-development', *Economics and Management Working Papers: Paisley College* (17, 1990), pp. 15, 25; Wakefield, *Economic Development*, p. 2.
48. Hood and Young, *Multinationals in Retreat*, p. 17.
49. R. H. Campbell, 'The Scottish Society of Economists: The Scottish Economic Society, 1897–1997', *Scottish Journal of Political Economy* (44:4, 1997), p. 365.
50. Lee, *Scotland and the United Kingdom*, p. 118; Johnstone, *Scotland Through the Looking Glass*, p. 1.
51. Henderson, 'Semiconductors, Scotland and the International Division of Labour', p. 393.
52. Payne, 'The Economy', pp. 27–8.
53. Phelps, 'From Local Economic Dependence to Local Development?', p. 16.
54. Danson, 'The Scottish Economy', p. 15.
55. As quoted in I. Turok, 'Linkages in the Scottish Electronics Industry: Further Evidence', *Regional Studies* (31:7, 1997), p. 710.
56. W. J. Pike, 'The Impact of North Sea Oil and Gas on the Economic Bases of Scotland and the Netherlands: A Comparison', in G. G. Simpson (ed.), *Scotland and the Low Countries, 1124–1994* (East Linton, 1996), p. 209.
57. *Black Oil and the Silver City: The Oil Revolution in Aberdeen and the North of Scotland, 1965–2000* (Balmoral Group, Aberdeen, 2000), pp. 25, 27.
58. Ibid., p. 31.
59. S. McDowall, 'Coal, Gas and Oil: The Changing Energy Scene in Scotland, 1950–1980', in Saville (ed.), *The Economic Development of Modern Scotland*, p. 301; I. McNicoll, 'North Sea Oil and Gas', in Ingham and Love, *Understanding the Scottish Economy*, pp. 228–9.
60. *Glasgow Herald* (27 February 1964).
61. *Glasgow Herald* (15 May 1964).
62. McDowall, 'Coal, Gas and Oil', p. 308.
63. Lee, *Scotland and the United Kingdom*, p. 103.
64. M. G. Lloyd and G. Newlands, 'Aberdeen: Planning for economic change and uncertainty', *Scottish Geographical Journal* (105, 1989), pp. 94–100.
65. *Black Oil and the Silver City*, p. 36.
66. *Estimates of Local Economic Output (GDP) in Scotland: 2000* (MacKay Consultants, Inverness, June 2001), pp. 2, 3.
67. Interview with Jonathan Wills, in T. Kidd and T. Morton, *Black Gold Tide: 25 years of Oil in Shetland* (Lerwick, 2004), p. 21.
68. Ibid., p. 22.
69. McDowall, 'Coal, Gas and Oil', p. 311.
70. See C. Harvie, *Fool's Gold: The Story of North Sea Oil* (London, 1994).
71. Ibid., p. 306.
72. Pike, 'The Impact of North Sea Oil and Gas', pp. 207–20.
73. C. Harvie and S. Maxwell, 'Scottish Nationalism and North Sea Oil', in T. C. Smout (ed.), *Scotland and the Sea* (Edinburgh, 1992), p. 218.
74. Lee, *Scotland and the United Kingdom*, p. 103.

75. Pike, 'The Impact of North Sea Oil and Gas', p. 213. As was the case in the electronics industry, much of this contribution has been non-specialised and thus easily replaceable. See pp. 213–14.

76. J. McGrath, *The Cheviot, the Stag and the Black, Black Oil* (London, 1981 edition), pp. 63–4.

77. See A. G. Kemp and L. Stephen, 'The Hypothetical Scottish Shares of Revenues and Expenditures from the UK Continental Shelf 2000–2013' (University of Aberdeen, June 2008).

78. See D. Hann, *Government and North Sea Oil* (Basingstoke, 1986).

CHAPTER FOUR: INTERESTS, INSTITUTIONS AND INTERFERENCE

1. Johnston, Buxton and Mair, *Structure and Growth of the Scottish Economy*, p. 254.

2. Ibid.

3. A. Cameron, 'Banking Mergers in Twentieth Century Scotland' in M. Pohl (ed.), *A Century of Banking Consolidation in Europe* (Aldershot, 2001), p. 180.

4. C. W. Munn, 'Bank Mergers and the Social Consequences, 1920–1950: The Case of the Clydesdale Bank', in Pohl (ed.), *A Century of Banking Consolidation*, pp, 146–77.

5. See S. G. Checkland, *Scottish Banking: A History, 1695–1973* (London, 1975).

6. M. Gaskin, 'The Scottish Financial Sector', 1950–1980', in Saville (ed.), *The Economic Development of Modern Scotland*, p. 117.

7. M. Moss and A. Slaven, *From Ledger Book to Laser Beam: A History of the TSB in Scotland, 1810–1990* (Edinburgh, 1992), pp. 84, 124.

8. For example, the Royal Bank of Scotland took over New England's Citizens Financial Group in 1988 and, between 2000 and 2005, established an alliance with Spain's Banco Santander.

9. Cameron, 'Banking Mergers in Twentieth Century Scotland', p. 187.

10. Scott and Hughes, *The Anatomy of Scottish Capital*, pp. 20–1, 72, 80–1, 83, 137, 207, 223.

11. Slaven, *The Development of the West of Scotland*, p. 203.

12. See N. Earnshaw, 'The Establishment of Scottish Industrial Estates: Panacea for Unemployment?', *Scottish Industrial History* (19, 1999), pp. 5–20.

13. Scottish Economic Committee, *Scotland's Industrial future: The Case for Planned Development* (1939), p. 46. See also Saville, 'The Industrial Background to the Post-War Scottish Economy', p. 15.

14. G. Walker, *Thomas Johnston* (Manchester, 1988), p. 153.

15. R. H. Campbell, 'The Committee of Ex-Secretaries of State for Scotland and Industrial Policy, 1941–1945', *Scottish Industrial History* (2:2 and 2:3, 1979), pp. 1–10.

16. Saville, 'The Industrial Background to the Post-war Scottish Economy', pp. 23–6.

17. Walker, *Thomas Johnston*, pp. 156, 167, 168.

18. This was the conclusion of George Pottinger (1979), as quoted in R. Galbraith, *Without Quarter: A Biography of Tom Johnston* (Edinburgh, 1995), p. 244.

19. Sir Steven Bilsland, *Industrial Estates* (Edinburgh, 1947), p. 3 (my emphasis).
20. Slaven, *The Development of the West of Scotland*, p. 222.
21. Bilsland, *Industrial Estates*, p. 7.
22. G. McCrone, 'The Role of Government', in Saville (ed.), *The Economic Development of Modern Scotland*, p. 196.
23. See J. Tomlinson, *The Labour Governments, 1964–1970* (Manchester, 2004).
24. Cabinet Economic Committee on the Future of the Shale Oil Industry, 19 February 1958, as quoted in I. Levitt, *The Scottish Office: Depression and Reconstruction, 1919–1959* (Edinburgh, 1992), pp. 222–3.
25. E. M. Wills, *Livingston: the Making of a Scottish New Town* (Livingston, 1996).
26. C. J. Carter, 'The Scottish New Towns: Their Contribution to Post-War Growth and Urban Development in Central Scotland' (Occasional Paper 9, Duncan of Jordanstone College of Art, n.d.)
27. D. Cowling, *An Essay for Today: The Scottish New Towns, 1947–1997* (Edinburgh, 1997).
28. I. Sutherland, *Dounreay: An Experimental Reactor Establishment* (Wick, 1990), p. 41.
29. McCrone, 'The Role of Government', pp. 210–11.
30. R. Boyle, 'Changing Partners: The Experience of Urban Economic Policy in West Central Scotland, 1980–90', *Urban Studies* (30:2, 1993), p. 316.
31. Harvie, *No Gods and Precious Few Heroes*, p. 170.
32. See J. Mitchell, *Conservatives and the Union: A Study of Conservative Party Attitudes to Scotland* (Edinburgh, 1990).
33. Harvie, *No Gods and Precious Few Heroes*, p. 171.
34. Following 1999, the Scottish Executive's economic policies were guided by the Development Department and the Enterprise and Lifelong Learning Department, as well as a host of quangos.
35. R. Marsh and F. Zuleeg, 'The Scottish Public Sector: Does Size Matter?' (Hume Occasional Paper No. 69, David Hume Institute, September 2006), p. 26.
36. A. Cumbers and K. Birch, 'Adding Value: Public Sector Spending and Scotland's Economic Development' (Report Commissioned by UNISON Scotland, January 2006), p. 18.
37. N. Fraser, 'Scotland in Europe', in Ingham and Love (eds), *Understanding the Scottish Economy*, pp. 245, 249.
38. *Extracts from a speech by Mr George Younger MP, Secretary of State for Scotland* (30 April 1984).
39. E. A. Cameron, 'The Scottish Highlands', in Devine and Finlay (eds), *Scotland in the Twentieth Century*, p. 156. See also L. Leneman, *Fit for Heroes? Land settlement in Scotland after World War I* (Aberdeen, 1989).
40. Symon, *Scottish Farming*, pp. 246–7.
41. Ibid., p. 260.
42. Elliot, 'Changing Scotland', pp. 186, 187.
43. B. A. Holderness, *British Agriculture Since 1945* (Manchester, 1985), p. 12.

44. Following the recommendations of the Balfour Committee, the Scottish Office finally consolidated its control over agriculture by acquiring responsibility for animal health after 1954.

45. Johnston, Buxton and Mair, *Structure and Growth of the Scottish Economy*, p. 103.

46. G. Sprott, 'Lowland Country Life', in Devine and Finlay (eds), *Scotland in the Twentieth Century*, p. 183.

47. Sprott, 'Lowland Country Life', p. 183.

48. E. A. Cameron, 'The Modernisation of Scottish Agriculture', in T. M. Devine, C. H. Lee and G. C. Peden (eds), *The Transformation of Scotland: The Economy Since 1700* (Edinburgh, 2005), p. 202.

49. H. McHenry, P. Chapman, M. Shucksmith and M. Henderson, *Rural Scotland Today: People, Perceptions, and Policies* (Rural Forum Scotland, February 1997), p. 13; *Extracts from a speech by Mr George Younger MP, Secretary of State for Scotland* p. 1.

50. McHenry et al., *Rural Scotland Today*, p. 14.

51. John N. Gray, *At Home in the Hills: Sense of Place in the Scottish Borders* (New York, 2000), p. 76.

52. *Inquiry into the Future of the Scottish Fishing Industry*, p. 5.

53. William West, in Miller, *Salt in the Blood*, p. 219.

54. Grampian Regional Council, *The Importance of Fishing*, p. 1.

55. Ibid., p. 3.

PART TWO: PROLOGUE

1. W. McIlvaney, 'Where Greta Garbo Wouldn't Have Been Alone', in *Surviving the Shipwreck* (Edinburgh, 1991), p. 184.

2. R. B. Lockhart, *My Scottish Youth* (Edinburgh, 1993 [1937]), p. 57.

3. L. G. Gibbon, 'Glasgow', in L. G. Gibbon and H. MacDiarmid, *Scottish Scene, or the Intelligent Man's Guide to Albyn* (London, 1934), p. 115.

4. Edwin Muir, *Scottish Journey*, pp. 9, 10; A Tramp, 'A Walk along the East Coast', in *Wayside Musings in Prose and Verse* (Brechin, 1901), p. 106.

5. W. Elliot, 'Presidential Address: Sir Walter Scott Club of Edinburgh' (18 January 1951), p. 1. (He was from Lanarkshire.)

6. Muir, *Scottish Journey*, p. 4.

7. H. MacDiarmid, 'Edinburgh', in Gibbon and MacDiarmid, *Scottish Scene*, pp. 70–1.

8. R. Garioch, *The Masque of Edinburgh* (Edinburgh, 1954).

9. Muir, *Scottish Journey*, pp. 160–1.

10. Ibid., pp. 103–4.

11. McIlvaney, 'The Courage of Our Doubts', in McIlvaney, *Surviving the Shipwreck*, p. 157.

12. T. Leonard (1944–), 'Dripping with Nostalgia', in *Intimate Voices* (London, 1995), p. 137.

13. 'Weedjie' is a colloquial term used in Edinburgh for Glasgow or a Glaswegian. Note: Irvine Welsh (1958–).

14. Moray McLaren to James Bridie, 'Letter' (2 March 1949), in J. Bridie and M. McLaren, *A Small Stir: Letters on the English* (London, 1949), p. 125.
15. P. Harris, *Aberdeen Since 1900* (Aberdeen, 1988), p. vi.
16. C. McKean and D. Walker *Dundee: An Illustrated Architectural Guide* (Edinburgh, 1993), p. 4.
17. Alexander Small, 'A Small Town', *Chapman* (42, 1985), p. 45; Roy Gill, 'Edinburgh', *Critical Quarterly* (42:4, 2000), p. 50.
18. Tom Pow, 'In a Small Town . . .', *Chapman* (32, 1982), p. 61.
19. I. Scott, *The Life and Times of Falkirk* (Edinburgh, 1994), p. 178.
20. I. C. Smith, 'Me and the Little White Rose', *Cencrastus* (36, 1990), p. 28.
21. Tramp, 'Modern Scottish Nationality', in *Wayside Musings*, pp. 121, 124.
22. Muir, *Scottish Journey*, p. 226.
23. I. Rankin (1960–), 'Auld Lang Syne', in *The Complete Short Stories* (London, 1992), p. 145.
24. W. Elliot, 'The Endless Adventure: a rectorial address delivered at Aberdeen University on 18th January, 1934' (London, 1934), pp. 36–7.
25. A. Gray, 'Portrait of a Playwright', in *Lean Tales* (London, 1995), pp. 249–50.
26. James Bridie to Moray McLaren, Letter (29 July 1948); Bridie to McLaren, Letter (21 November 1948), in Bridie and McLaren, *A Small Stir*, pp. 1, 50–1.
27. David McCrone, *Understanding Scotland*, pp. 1, 3.

CHAPTER FIVE: HEALTH AND HEARTH – SCOTLAND'S PEOPLE

1. See W. Ferguson, *Scotland: 1689 to the Present* (Edinburgh, 1987), p. 70.
2. M. Flinn (ed.), *Scottish Population History from the Seventeenth Century to the 1930s* (Cambridge, 1977), p. 301.
3. M. Anderson, 'Population and Family Life', in A. Dickson and J. H. Treble (eds), *People and Society in Scotland, Vol. III* (Edinburgh, 1992), p. 12.
4. Ibid., p. 12.
5. Stationery Office, *Scotland* (London, 1997), pp. 10–11.
6. Scottish Women's Group on Public Welfare, *Our Scottish Towns: Evacuation and the Social Future* (Edinburgh 1944), p. 1.
7. D. J. Robertson, 'Population Growth and Movement', in Cairncross (ed.), *The Scottish Economy*, p. 9.
8. Anderson, 'Population and Family Life', pp. 14–16.
9. C. E. V. Leser, 'Births and Deaths', in Cairncross (ed.), *The Scottish Economy*, p. 22, Table 8.
10. *Scottish Abstract of Statistics*, 25 (HMSO, 1996), p. 20.
11. P. Boyle. D. Exeter and R. Flowerdew, 'The role of population change in widening the mortality gap in Scotland', *Area* (36:2, 2004), p. 165.
12. *Scottish Abstract of Statistics*, 25 (HMSO, 1996), p. 15.
13. Leser, 'Births and Deaths', p. 31.
14. Anderson, 'Population and Family Life', p. 34.
15. Ibid., p. 33.

16. One Parent Families Scotland, *Teenage Pregnancy in Scotland Factfile*, http://www.opfs.org.uk/factfile/teenpreg.html, accessed 13 September 2006.
17. Anderson, 'Population and Family Life', p. 25.
18. Flinn, *Scottish Population History*, pp. 322–3, 326–7. Low nuptiality was a long-standing feature in the Scottish crofting counties and was evident from as early as 1871. See M. Anderson and D. J. Morse, 'High Fertility, High Emigration, Low Nuptiality: Adjustment Processes in Scotland's Demographic Experience, 1861–1914, Part Two', *Population Studies* (47, 1993), pp. 319–43.
19. P. Hanlon et al., *Chasing the Scottish Effect* (PHIS, 2001) p. 12.
20. SNP, 'Beware of Emigration' (New Series No. 7, c. 1948), p. 1.
21. E. Linklater, *The Lion and the Unicorn: Or what England has meant to Scotland* (London, 1935), p. 133.
22. Lythe and Majmudar, *Renaissance of the Scottish Economy?*, p. 10.
23. Ibid., p. 10; M. Harper, *Emigration from Scotland Between the Wars: Opportunity or Exile?* (Manchester, 1998), p. 6.
24. Harper, *Emigration from Scotland Between the Wars*, p. 7.
25. Johnston, Buxton and Mair, *Structure and Growth of the Scottish Economy*, p. 67.
26. Ibid., p. 96; Robertson, 'Population Growth and Movement', p. 18; Harvie, *No Gods and Precious Few Heroes*, p. 150.
27. Johnston, Buxton and Mair, *Structure and Growth of the Scottish Economy*, p. 245.
28. Anderson, 'Population and Family Life', p. 14.
29. F. Niven, *The Transplanted* (1944), pp. 9–10.
30. A. Herman, *The Scottish Enlightenment: The Scots' Invention of the Modern World* (London, 2003), p. 401.
31. See J. Stewart, 'This Injurious Measure: Scotland and the 1906 Education (Provision of Meals) Act', *Scottish Historical Review* (78, 1999), pp. 76–94.
32. Moss and Slaven, *From Ledger Book to Laser Beam*, p. 80.
33. A. Woodburn, 'An Open Letter to Every Scottish Household on Your New Health Service!' (1948).
34. T. T. Paterson, 'Health', in Cairncross (ed.), *The Scottish Economy*, p. 212.
35. G. G. Robertson, *Gorbals Doctor* (London, 1970), p. 177.
36. See J. Brotherston and J. Brims, 'The Development of Public Medical Care: 1900–1948', in G. McLachlan (ed.), *Improving the Commonweal: Aspects of Scottish Health Services, 1900–1984* (Edinburgh 1987), pp. 35–102.
37. See J. Jenkinson, 'Scottish Health Policy, 1918–1948: Paving the Way to a National Health Service', in C. Nottingham (ed.), *The NHS in Scotland: the Legacy of the Past and the Prospect of the Future* (Aldershot, 2000).
38. Brotherston and Brims, 'The Development of Public Medical Care: 1900–1948', pp. 65–9.
39. Jenkinson, 'Scottish Health Policy, 1918–1948', p. 10.
40. Ibid., p. 12.
41. Levitt (ed.), *Government and Social Conditions in Scotland*, p. 62. The peculiarities of the Scottish scheme vis-à-vis that of England and Wales have been

the focus of much attention. See, for example, I. A. G. MacQueen, 'Differences in the National Health Services in England and Scotland', *British Journal of Preventative Social Medicine* (7, 1953), pp. 94–8; D. McTavish, 'Scottish and English Health Policy from 1948 to the 1973 Reforms: Management through a UK Prism?', *Scottish Affairs* (51, Spring 2005), pp. 59–75; J. Stewart, 'The National Health Service in Scotland, 1947–1974: Scottish or British?', *Historical Research* (76, August 2003), pp. 389–410.

42. Brotherston and Brims, 'The Development of Public Medical Care: 1900–1948', p. 106.
43. M. McCrae, *The National Health Service in Scotland: Origins and Ideals, 1900–1950* (East Linton, 2003), pp. 232, 234–5.
44. Ibid., p. 234; Brotherston and Brims, 'The Development of Public Medical Care: 1900–1948', p. 109.
45. Scottish Home and Health Department, *The Health Service in Scotland: The Way Ahead* (Edinburgh, 1976).
46. *Scottish Abstract of Statistics*, p. 46.
47. Stationery Office, *Scotland*, pp. 86–9.
48. *Scottish Abstract of Statistics*, p. 45; Stationery Office, *Scotland*, p. 89.
49. Smout, *A Century of the Scottish People*, p. 122; D. Kemmer, 'Investigating Infant Mortality in Early Twentieth Century Scotland Using Civil Registers', *Scottish Economic and Social History* (17:1, 1997), p. 1.
50. N. Mitchison, *Among You Taking Notes* (London, 1985 edition), pp. 72–3.
51. N. P. A. S. Johnson, 'Scottish 'Flu: the Scottish Experience of Spanish 'Flu', *Scottish Historical Review* (83, 2004), p. 226.
52. Edinburgh, National Library of Scotland (NLS), 6.287, Dr L. MacKenzie, Extracts from Diaries . . . in regard to visitations made by commissioners . . . in connection with the Royal Commission on the Housing of the Industrial Population of Scotland, Rural and Urban (28–9 September 1913).
53. Smout, *A Century of the Scottish People*, p. 120, Table 4.
54. Brotherston and Brims, 'The Development of Public Medical Care: 1900–1948', p. 82.
55. J. Boyd Orr, *Food, Health and Income: Report on a Survey of Adequacy of Diet in Relation to Income* (London, 1937), p. 8.
56. Smout, *A Century of the Scottish People*, p. 120, Table 4.
57. Paterson, 'Health', p. 214.
58. *Scottish Abstract of Statistics*, p. 17.
59. A. Bold, 'An Open Letter on the Closed Mind', *Chapman* (July 1983), p. 3.
60. NLS, MacKenzie, Extracts from Diaries (11 March 1914, 12 March 1914, 4 June 1914).
61. A. Spence (1947–), *Changed Days: Memories of an Edinburgh Community* (London, 1988). First staged on 1 November 1988 at Muirhouse Parish Church Hall.
62. E. McAlister, *Shadows on a Gorbals Wall* (Glasgow, 1986), p. 8.
63. *Return Showing the Housing Conditions of the Population of Scotland* (1908).

64. D. Niven, *The Development of Housing in Scotland* (London, 1979), p. 26.

65. Parliamentary Paper Cmd. 8731, *Report of the Royal Commission on the Housing of the Industrial Population of Scotland Rural and Urban* (1918), p. 104.

66. Niven, *The Development of Housing in Scotland*, pp. 26–7.

67. Mary Brooksbank, *No Sae Lang Syne: A Tale of this City* (Dundee, n. d.), p. 25.

68. Smout, *A Century of the Scottish People*, p. 54; Niven, *The Development of Housing in Scotland*, p. 29; R. D. Cramond, 'Housing Policy in Scotland, 1919–1964: A Study in State Assistance' (University of Glasgow, Social and Economic Studies, Research Paper No. 1, 1966), p. 26.

69. Cramond, 'Housing Policy in Scotland', p. 26.

70. C. Johnstone, 'Housing and Class Struggles in Post-War Glasgow' in M. Lavalette and G. Mooney (eds), *Class Struggle and Social Welfare* (London, 2000), pp. 142–3.

71. Smout, *A Century of the Scottish People*, p. 54.

72. D. Glenday, *Anderston as It Was* (Glasgow, 1992), p. 9.

73. C. Smith 'Pull Doon the Chimneys' (sung to the tune of 'The Bonnets of Bonnie Dundee'), in N. Gatherer, *Songs and Ballads of Dundee* (Edinburgh, 1985), p. 154, chorus.

74. Jim Reid, 'Catherine Street', in Gatherer, *Songs and Ballads of Dundee*, p. 153, stanza 2.

75. Harvie, *No Gods and Precious Few Heroes*, p. 72.

76. Cramond, 'Housing Policy in Scotland', p. 30.

77. Norris, 'Poverty in Scotland', p. 35; see *Scottish Special Housing Association: A Chronicle of Forty Years, 1937–1977* (Edinburgh, 1977).

78. A. Gibb, 'Policy and Politics in Scottish Housing Since 1945', in R. Rodger (ed.), *Scottish Housing in the Twentieth Century* (Leicester, 1989), p. 167.

79. G. McCrone, 'Scottish Housing in a European Perspective' *Urban Studies* (32:8, 1995), p. 1269.

80. Gibb, 'Policy and Politics in Scottish Housing Since 1945', pp. 167–8.

81. R. Crammond, 'The National Housing Drive' in M. Glendinning (ed.), *Rebuilding Scotland: the Post-war Vision* (East Linton, 1997), p. 62.

82. Midwinter et al., *Politics and Public Policy in Scotland*, p. 18.

83. A. Murie and Y. P. Wang, 'The Sale of Public Sector Housing in Scotland, 1979–1991' (Heriot Watt University, Edinburgh College of Art, Research Paper No. 3, 1992), p. 11.

84. Ibid., p. 9.

85. Ibid., p. 17.

86. Ibid., p. 28.

87. *1991 Census: Monitor for Strathclyde Region* (GRO Scotland, 1992), p. 2; *1991 Census: Monitor for Tayside Region* (GRO Scotland, 1993), p. 2.

88. Craig, *Poverty and Anti-Poverty Work in Scotland*, p. 9. See also R. Carr Hill, 'Impact of housing conditions upon health status', in *The Wider Issues of Housing* (Hume Papers on Public Policy, 8:4, 2001), p. 22.

89. Cohen and Long, *Little or Nothing*, p. 5.

90. Gibb, 'Policy and Politics in Scottish Housing Since 1945', p. 179.

91. H. Third, 'Researching Homelessness and Rough Sleeping in the Scottish Context', *Social Policy and Administration* (34 : 4, 2000), p. 450.
92. Ibid., p. 454.
93. J. Cathcart, 'One Completed Day', in J. Kelman (ed.), *An East End Anthology* (Glasgow, 1988), p. 12.

CHAPTER SIX: LIVING IN SCOTLAND

1. Linklater, *The Lion and the Unicorn*, pp. 99–100.
2. *The Scotsman* (30 January 1935).
3. *The Scotsman* (21 October 1935).
4. *The Scotsman* (29 April 1935).
5. Tollcross Local History Project, *Waters under the Bridge: Twentieth Century Tollcross, Fountainbridge and the West Port* (Aberdeen, 1990), p. 8.
6. A. D. Campbell, 'Income', in Cairncross (ed.), *The Scottish Economy*, p. 50, Table 25; T. C. Smout, *A Century of the Scottish People, 1830–1950* (London, 1988), p. 109.
7. Harvie, *No Gods and Precious Few Heroes*, p. 35.
8. Buxton, 'The Scottish Economy, 1945–1979', pp. 52–3.
9. Harvie, *No Gods and Precious Few Heroes*, p. 166.
10. *Scottish Abstract of Statistics* 25 (HMSO, 1996), p. 189.
11. L. G. Gibbon, 'Aberdeen', in Gibbon and MacDiarmid, *Scottish Scene*, pp. 204–5.
12. D. J. Oddy, 'The Paradox of Diet and Health: England and Scotland in the Nineteenth and Twentieth Centuries', in A. Fenton (ed.), *Order and Disorder: the Health Implications of Eating and Drinking in the Nineteenth and Twentieth Centuries* (East Linton, 2000), pp. 49–50.
13. J. E. Burnett, 'Glasgow Corporation and the Food of the Poor, 1918–1924: A Context for John Boyd Orr', in Fenton (ed.), *Order and Disorder*, p. 22.
14. D. J. Robertson, 'Consumption', in Cairncross (ed.), *The Scottish Economy*, pp. 172, 175.
15. Littlejohn, *Westrigg*, p. 65.
16. N. Mitchison, 'The Talking Oats', *Chapman* (27–8, 1980), pp. 10–20.
17. C. Harvie, 'Scotland after 1978: from Referendum to Millennium', in Houston and Knox (eds). *New Penguin History of Scotland*, p. 513.
18. M. Blades, 'An Examination of Data on the Scottish Diet', *Nutrition and Food Science* (34 : 6, 2004), p. 249.
19. J. Inchley, J. Todd, C. Bryce, C. Currie, 'Dietary trends among Scottish school-children in the 1990s', *Journal of Human Nutritional Dietetics* (14, 2001), pp. 208, 212.
20. Blades, 'An Examination of Data on the Scottish Diet', p. 250.
21. A. Cairncross, *Living with the Century* (Fife, 1998), p. 12.
22. Ibid., p. 21.
23. P. H. Scott, *A Twentieth Century Life* (Argyll, 2002), p. 29.
24. A. J. Durie, 'The Impact of Motor Traffic on the Roads System of Central Scotland', *Scottish Economic and Social History* (17 : 2, 1997), pp. 94, 95; R. Grieves, *Scotland's Motoring Century* (Paisley, 1999), p. 2.

25. T. C. Smout, 'Patterns of Culture', in Dickson and Treble (eds), *People and Society in Scotland*, p. 263.

26. Stationery Office, *Scotland*, p. 70; Harvie, 'Scotland after 1978', p. 513.

27. Harvie, *No Gods and Precious Few Heroes*, p. 140.

28. Gardyne, *Scotland to 1980*, p. 3.

29. V. Carstairs and R. Morris, *Deprivation and Health in Scotland* (Aberdeen, 1991), p. 223.

30. N. Mitchison, 'Then', Stanza 2, *Cleansing of the Knife and Other Poems* (Edinburgh, 1978), p. 21

31. C. Hardyment, *From Mangle to Microwave: the Mechanisation of Household Work* (Cambridge, 1988).

32. L. MacNeice, *Crossing the Minch* (London, 1938), p. 58.

33. City of Glasgow District Council, *Modern Homes Exhibition '75* (1–18 October 1975), p. 7.

34. Fiona Black, 'Scot Couture', *Modern Homes Exhibition '94* (7–23 October 1994), p. 9.

35. E. Kilgour, *A Time of Our Lives*, p. 76.

36. C. P. Aitken, *Retailing Change in Stirling Town Centre: A Study of Trends through the 1970s* (Stirling, 1981), p. 77.

37. J. A. Dawson, 'Review of Retailing Trends: With Particular Reference to Scotland' (Scottish Office, Central Research Unit, 1994), pp. 27–8.

38. S. Barron, *A History of Shops and Shopping in Scotland* (Hamilton, 2002).

39. R. McMillan (1923–1979), *All in Good Faith* (Glasgow, 1979).

40. S. McPhee, *In the Red: Debt – the Evidence of CAB Clients in Scotland* (Edinburgh, June 1995), pp, 3, 4.

41. M. Adler and R. Sainsbury, *Personal Debt in Scotland: A Report for the Scottish Consumer Council* (Edinburgh, February 1988), p. 10.

42. McIlvanney, 'Being Poor', in McIlvanney, *Surviving the Shipwreck*, p. 35.

43. R. Wilkinson, *Memories of Maryhill* (Edinburgh, 1993), p. 20.

44. Parliamentary Paper Cd. 5075, Vol. LII, 1910, C. T. Parsons, 'The Condition of the Children Who are in Receipt of Various Forms of Poor Relief in Certain Parishes in Scotland', in I. Levitt (ed.), *Government and Social Conditions in Scotland, 1845–1919* (Edinburgh, 1988), pp. 102–10.

45. See I. Levitt, 'Scottish Poverty: the Historical Background', in G. Brown and R. Cook (eds), *Scotland: the Real Divide* (Edinburgh, 1983), pp. 66–75.

46. McIlvanney, 'Being Poor', Brown and Cook (eds) *Scotland: the Real Divide*, p. 34.

47. STUC, *Scotland – A Land Fit for People* (STUC, 1987), p. 7.

48. I. Levitt, 'Poverty in Scotland', in G. Brown (ed.), *The Red Paper on Scotland* (Edinburgh, 1975), pp. 318, 319.

49. Ibid., p. 317.

50. G. Norris, 'Poverty in Scotland: An analysis of official statistics', *Discussion Papers in Social Research 17* (University of Glasgow, 1977), p. 30.

51. G. Craig, *Poverty and Anti-Poverty Work in Scotland: A Review of Policy, Practice and Issues* (Scottish Poverty Network, Glasgow, 1994), p. 6.

52. *Scottish Abstract of Statistics* 25 (HMSO, 1996), p. 45.
53. *Glasgow Herald* (23 March 1993). As quoted, Craig, *Poverty and Anti-Poverty Work in Scotland*, p. 8.
54. R. Cohen and G. Long, *Little or Nothing: A Report on the Social Fund in Greater Pilton* (London, 1996), p. 6.
55. Scottish Poverty Information Unit, 'Women, Family and Poverty' (Briefing Sheet 3, March 1998), p. 1; G. Bramley, S. Lancaster and D. Gordon, 'Benefit Take-up and the Geography of Poverty in Scotland', *Regional Studies* (34:6, 2000), p. 516.
56. Smout, *A Century of the Scottish People*, p. 115.
57. Scottish Council (Development and Industry): Committee on Industrial and Social Conditions, 'Scotland's Employment Prospects: A Commentary on the Public Policy Issues Raised by the Sustained High Level of Unemployment in the early 1980s' (Edinburgh, June 1983), p. 3.
58. T. Davies and A. Sinfield, 'The Unemployed', in Brown and Cook (eds), *Scotland: the Real Divide*, p. 95.
59. Knox, *Industrial Nation*, p. 261.
60. Elliot, 'The Endless Adventure', p. 34.
61. *Disinherited Youth: A Survey, 1936–1939* (Carnegie UK Trust, Dunfermline, 1943), pp. 5–6.
62. Muir, *Scottish Journey*, p. 138.
63. J. Mack, 'Crime', in Cairncross (ed.), *The Scottish Economy*, pp. 227–44.
64. P. Young, *Crime and Criminal Justice in Scotland* (HMSO, Edinburgh, 1997), p. 16.
65. D. J. Smith and P. Young, 'Crime Trends in Scotland Since 1950', in P. Duff and N. Hutton (eds), *Criminal Justice in Scotland* (Aldershot, 1999), p. 19.
66. Ibid., p. 20.
67. Ibid., p. 21.
68. A. Davies, 'Sectarian Violence and Police Violence in Glasgow during the 1930s', in R. Bessel and C. Emsley (eds), *Patterns of Provocation: Police and Public Disorder* (Oxford, 2000), p. 46.
69. R. Jeffrey, *Gangland Glasgow: True Crime from the Streets* (Edinburgh, 2005), p. 24.
70. A. Davies, 'Street Gangs, Crime and Policing in Glasgow During the 1930s: The Case of the Bee-hive Boys', *Social History* (23:3, 1998), p. 266.
71. J. Boyle, *A Sense of Freedom* (Edinburgh 1977), p. 23.
72. Mack, 'Crime', in Cairncross (ed.), *The Scottish Economy*, p. 237.
73. Scottish Office Statistical Bulletin (Criminal Justice Series), 'Children and Crime, Scotland: 1989' (October 1991), pp. 1, 2.
74. *The Scotsman* (11 June 1946).
75. Ibid.
76. *The Scotsman* (8 August 1946).
77. *Measurement of the Extent of Youth Crime in Scotland* (Scottish Executive, 2005), p. 1. (Executive Summary, Paragraph 4.)

78. B. Whyte, 'Responding to Youth Crime in Scotland', *British Journal of Social Work* (34, 2004), pp. 395–411.
79. W. Fraser, 'Post-War Police Developments: Retrospect and Reflections' (James Smart Lecture, Glasgow, 8 October 1981), pp. 2–3.
80. J. Pieri, *The Big Men: Personal Memories of Glasgow's Police* (Glasgow, 2001), pp. 33–4.
81. P. Laughlin, 'Police Management of Public Drunkenness in Scotland', *British Journal of Criminology* (25:4, 1985), p. 357.
82. Mack, 'Crime', p. 231.
83. *Scottish Abstract of Statistics*, p. 107.
84. 'Children and Crime, Scotland: 1989', p. 6; A. Stewart, *Where is She Tonight?: Women, Street Prostitution and Homelessness in Glasgow* (Glasgow, c. 2000), p. 21.
85. For further details on local approaches to prostitution, see N. Georghiou and F. McCallum, *Prostitution Tolerance Zones (Scotland) Bill* (SPICE Briefing, 12 December 2002) and 'Report of the Expert Group on Prostitution' (Scottish Executive, 16 December 2004).
86. Stationery Office, *Scotland*, pp. 25, 28, 29; J. Cameron, *Prisons and Punishment in Scotland* (Edinburgh, 1983), p. 202.
87. Angus MacKay, S1W–515, Written Answers, Scottish Parliament (26 July 1999).
88. Drugs Misuse Information Strategy Team, *Drugs-related offences and proceedings*, http://www.drugmisuse.isdscotland.org/publications/04dmss/offen.htm, accessed 13 September 2006.
89. A. Buchan, Address to Fishing Conference (3 June 1999).
90. B. Keen, *Easy Money* (Edinburgh, 1991), p. 11.
91. *Being Outside: Constructing a Response to Street Prostitution (A Report of the Expert Group on Prostitution in Scotland* (Scottish Executive, Edinburgh, 2004).
92. Stewart, *Where is She Tonight?*, p. 14.
93. *Being Outside*, p. 15.
94. Strathclyde Regional Council, 'Multiple Deprivation' (October 1976), p. 3.
95. B. Holman, *Faith in the Poor* (Oxford, 1998), p. 98.
96. M. Keating, *The City that Refused to Die: Glasgow – the Politics of Urban Regeneration* (Aberdeen, 1988), p. 17.
97. C. Jones, 'Population Decline in Cities', in C. Jones (ed.), *Urban Deprivation and the Inner City* (London, 1979), pp. 194, 196.
98. A. Middleton, 'Glasgow and its East End', in D. Donnison and A. Middleton (eds), *Regenerating the Inner City: Glasgow's Experience* (London, 1987), p. 8.
99. Keating, *The City that Refused to Die*, p. 23.
100. Ibid., p. 23.
101. See M. Pacione, 'Multiple Deprivation and Public Policy in Scottish Cities: An Overview', *Urban Geography* (18, 1987).
102. See R. Boyle, 'Changing Partners: The Experience of Urban Economic Policy in West Central Scotland, 1980–1990', *Urban Studies* (30:2, 1993), pp. 309–24.
103. Jones, 'Population Decline in Cities', p. 200.

104. I. M. L. Robertson, 'Access to the Health Services', in Donnison and Middleton (eds), *Regenerating the Inner City*, p. 169; J. Forbes, 'A Strategy for Education', in Donnison and Middleton (eds), *Regenerating the Inner City*, p. 249.

105. H. Crummy, *Let the People Sing* (Edinburgh, 1992), p. 25.

106. Norris, 'Poverty in Scotland', p. 36; V. Cable, 'Glasgow: Area of Need', in Brown (ed.), *The Red Paper on Scotland*, p. 243.

107. J. English, 'Access and Deprivation in Local Authority Housing', in Jones (ed.), *Urban Deprivation and the Inner City*, pp. 119–24.

108. A. McGregor, 'Urban Deprivation and Unemployment: A Case Study' (University of Glasgow, Discussion Paper No. 20, May 1976), p. 1.

109. A. Mackay, 'Social Indicators for Urban Sub-Areas: The Use of Administrative Records in the Paisley Community Development Project' (Discussion Paper 5, University of Glasgow, May 1974), pp. 12, 17.

110. G. McLaren and M. Bain, *Deprivation and Health in Scotland: Insights from NHS Data* (Edinburgh, 1998), p. ix.

111. S. C. Ofori, 'Partnership in Urban Housing and Environmental Regeneration in the Peripheral Estates of Castlemilk and Ferguslie Park' (University of Central England in Birmingham, School of Planning, Working Paper Series No. 59, 1996); R. Tarling et al., 'An Evaluation of the New Life for Urban Scotland Initiative' (Scottish Executive Central Research Unit, Development Department, Research Findings No. 70, 1999), p. 2.

112. See J. McCarthy, 'Urban Regeneration in Scotland: An Agenda for the Scottish Parliament', *Regional Studies* (33 : 6), pp. 559–66; G. Lloyd, J. McCarthy and K. Fernie, 'From Cause to Effect? A New Agenda for Urban Regeneration in Scotland', *Local Economy* (16 : 3, 2001), pp. 221–35.

113. J. Wilson, *Tales and Travels of a School Inspector* (Stornoway, 1998), pp. 236–7.

114. P. Geddes, 'Scottish University: Needs and Aims', Closing Address at University College, Dundee, (Perth, 1890), p. 2.

115. R. Garioch, 'All Prizes, No Blanks', in *Collected Poems* (Manchester, 1980), p. 175.

116. Scottish Education Department, Circular 374, (16 February 1903), in H. Hutchison (ed.), *Scottish Public Educational Documents, 1560–1960* (Scottish Council for Research in Education, Series 3, No. 1), 1973, p. 152.

117. M. Liverani, from *The Winter Sparrows* (London, 1976), as quoted in D. Northcroft (ed.), *Scots at School* (Edinburgh, 2003), p. 205.

118. L. Paterson, *Scottish Education in the Twentieth Century* (Edinburgh, 2003), pp. 11–12.

119. H. M. Paterson, 'Incubus and Ideology: The Development of Secondary Schooling in Scotland, 1900–1939', in W. M. Humes and H. M. Paterson (eds), *Scottish Culture and Scottish Education, 1800–1980* (Edinburgh, 1983), p. 199.

120. See A. McPherson, 'Schooling', in Dickson and Treble (eds), *People and Society in Scotland*, pp. 80–107.

121. H. M. Knox, *Two Hundred and Fifty Years of Scottish Education, 1696–1946* (London, 1953), p. 210.
122. Paterson, 'Incubus and Ideology', p. 211; T. R. Bone, *School Inspection in Scotland, 1840–1966* (London, 1968), p. 203; Knox, *Two Hundred and Fifty Years of Scottish Education*, p. 213.
123. M. Lawn, 'The Institute as Network: the Scottish Council for Research in Education as a Local and International Phenomenon in the 1930s', *Paedagogica Historica* (40:5–6, October 2004), pp. 719–32.
124. Scottish Council for Research in Education, *Curriculum for Pupils of Twelve to Fifteen Years (Advanced Division)*, (ULP, 1931), in Hutchison (ed.), *Scottish Public Educational Documents*, p. 198.
125. Bone, *School Inspection in Scotland*, p. 210.
126. Ibid., pp. 202–3.
127. George Macdonald to Sir John Struthers, 1920, as quoted in Paterson, 'Incubus and Ideology', pp. 208–9.
128. See A. McPherson, 'An Angle on the Geist: Persistence and Change in the Scottish Educational Tradition', in Humes and Paterson (eds), *Scottish Culture and Scottish Education*, pp. 216–43.
129. J. M. Lloyd, 'The Second World War and Educational Aspiration: Some Scottish Evidence', *Journal of Educational Administration and History* (15, 1983), pp. 38–41.
130. Knox, *Two Hundred and Fifty Years of Scottish Education*, p. 227.
131. Bone, *School Inspection in Scotland*, p. 222.
132. As quoted in Northcroft (ed.), *Scots at School*, p. 226.
133. Bone, *School Inspection in Scotland*, p. 237; McPherson, 'Schooling', p. 92.
134. See D. Raffe, 'Education and Class Inequality in Scotland', in Brown and Cook (eds), *Scotland: the Real Divide*, pp. 192–3.
135. *Scottish Abstract of Statistics*, p. 136.
136. P. Munn, J. Stead, G. McLeod et al., 'Schools for the 21st Century: the National Debate on Education in Scotland', *Research Papers in Education* (19:4, December 2004), p. 446.
137. *Scottish Abstract of Statistics*, p. 125.
138. I. G. C. Hutchison, *The University and the State: The Case of Aberdeen, 1860–1963* (Aberdeen, 1993), pp. 1, 10, 23.
139. Ibid., p. 87.
140. Paterson, *Scottish Education in the Twentieth Century*, pp. 12, 156.
141. Hutchison, *The University and the State*, p. 100.
142. Scottish Executive (Information Directorate), 'Statistical Release' (13 June 2002), pp. 1, 5.
143. M. McVicar and S. Morris, 'Further and Higher Education in Scotland' (Scottish Parliament Information Centre, 3 August 1999), p. 2.
144. Ibid., pp. 3, 5.
145. L. Paterson, 'Trends in Higher Education Participation in Scotland', *Higher Education Quarterly* (51:1, January 1997), p. 32.
146. Ibid., p. 34.

147. Ibid., p. 33.

148. See Harvie, *No Gods and Precious Few Heroes*, p. 152, and L. Paterson, 'Liberation or Control: What are the Scottish Education Traditions of the Twentieth Century?', in Devine and Finlay (eds), *Scotland in the Twentieth Century*, p. 244.

149. L. Paterson, 'The Survival of the Democratic Intellect: Academic Values in Scotland and England', *Higher Education Quarterly* (57:1, January 2003), pp. 67–93.

150. A. McPherson and C. D. Rabb, *Governing Education: A Sociology of Policy Since 1945* (Edinburgh, 1988), p. 126; G. S. Osborne, *Scottish and English Schools: A comparative survey of the past fifty years* (London, 1966), pp. 17, 35.

151. M. I. Ogilvie, *A Scottish Childhood and What Happened After* (Oxford, 1952), p. 2.

152. See F. MacKay, 'A Slow Revolution?: Gender Relations in Contemporary Scotland', in G. Hassan and C. Warhurst (eds), *Anatomy of the New Scotland* (Edinburgh, 2002), pp. 277–84.

153. Joan Ure was a pseudonym for Elizabeth Thomson Clark (née Carswell), 1918–1978.

154. See T. Brennan, *Reshaping a City* (Glasgow, 1959).

155. A. McRobbie, *A Privileged Boyhood* (Glasgow, 1996), as quoted in Northcroft, *Scots at School*, p. 195.

156. NPS Pamphlet, No. 13, (May 1929).

157. Brooksbank, *No Sae Lang Syne*, p. 7.

158. J. Maxwell, *Sixteen Years On: A Follow-up of the 1947 Scottish Survey* (London, 1969), p. 6.

159. L. Jamieson, 'We all left at 14: boys' and girls' schooling, c.1900–1930', in J. Fewell and F. Paterson (eds), *Girls in Their Prime: Scottish Education Revisited* (Edinburgh, 1990), pp. 16–37.

160. 'Statistical Release', p. 1.

161. H. Kay, 'Women and Men in the Professions in Scotland' (Scottish Executive, Central Research Unit, 2000), pp. 1, 3.

162. S. McKendrick, 'Scotland, Social Change and Politics', in D. McCrone, S. McKendrick and P. Straw (eds), *The Making of Scotland: Nation, Culture and Social Change* (Edinburgh, 1989), p. 76.

163. McCrone, *Understanding Scotland*, p. 83; S. Livingstone, *Bonnie Fechters: Women in Scotland, 1900–1950* (Motherwell, 1994), p. 6.

164. Equal Opportunities Commission Scotland, 'Facts about Women and Men in Scotland, 2002' (Glasgow, 2002), p. 2.

165. A. McIvor, 'Gender Apartheid?: Women in Scottish Society', in Devine and Finlay (eds), *Scotland in the Twentieth Century*, p. 197, Table 3.

166. R. Mitchison, 'The Hidden Labour Force: Women in the Scottish economy since 1945', in Saville (ed.), *The Economic Development of Modern Scotland*, p. 184.

167. M. Brooksbank, 'The Spinner's Wedding', in Gatherer (ed.), *Songs and Ballads of Dundee*, p. 42. Stanza 1, extract.

168. Equal Opportunities Commission Scotland, 'Facts about Women and Men in Scotland, 2002', p. 1.

169. Livingstone, *Bonnie Fechters*, p. 9; E. Breitenbach, *Women in Trade Unionism in Scotland: A Study of Women's Employment and Trade Unionism* (Glasgow, 1982), p. 5.

170. Leonard, *Intimate Voices*, p. 106.

171. M. Bone, *Family Planning in Scotland in 1982: A Survey Carried out on Behalf of the Scottish Home and Health Department* (London, 1985), p. 63.

172. J. Aitken-Swan, *Fertility Control and the Medical Profession* (London, 1977), p. 18.

173. *The Benefits of Birth Control: Aberdeen's Experience, 1946–1970* (Birth Control Campaign, 1973), p. 14.

174. Bone, *Family Planning in Scotland*, p. 61.

175. G. Davis and R. Davidson, '"Big White Chief", "Pontius Pilate", and the "Plumber": The impact of the 1967 Abortion Act on the Scottish Medical Community, c.1967–1980', *Social History of Medicine* (18 : 2, August 2005), p. 286.

176. Ibid., p. 288.

177. Ibid., pp. 286–8.

178. Wilkinson, *Memories of Maryhill*, p. 67.

179. A. Barlow, 'Cohabitation and Marriage in Scotland: Attitudes, Myths and the Law', in J. Curtice, D. McCrone, A. Park and L. Paterson (eds), *New Scotland, New Society?: Are Social and Political Ties Fragmenting?* (Edinburgh, 2002), p. 65.

180. K. Hinds and L. Jamieson, 'Rejecting Traditional Family Building? Attitudes to Cohabitation and Teenage Pregnancy in Scotland', in Curtice, McCrone, Park and Paterson (eds), *New Scotland, New Society?*, pp. 34, 35.

181. Ibid., p. 35.

182. Ibid., p. 35.

183. R. Davidson and G. Davis, 'A Field for Private Members: The Wolfenden Committee and Scottish Homosexual Law Reform, 1950–1967', *Twentieth Century British History* (15 : 2, 2004), p. 183.

184. Hinds and Jamieson, 'Rejecting Traditional Family Building?', pp. 37, 38, 40.

185. Scottish Executive, 'Parents and Children: A White Paper on Scottish Family Law' (2000), as quoted in F. Wasoff and M. Hill, 'Family Policy in Scotland', *Social Policy and Society* (2002), p. 177.

CHAPTER SEVEN: THE MIGRANT NATION

1. Scottish Unionist Association, 'Scottish Home Rule' (Leaflet, New Series, No. 9, n. d.), pp. 7–8.

2. Order of Scottish Clans, 'Daughters of Scotia Ladies Auxiliary Fourth Biennial Excursion to Scotland' (1930).

3. Anon, 'No Folk Like Oor Ain Folk' (Mass., 1928).

4. B. Collins, 'Origins of Irish Immigrants to Scotland in the Nineteenth and Twentieth Centuries', in T. M. Devine (ed.), *Irish Immigration and Scottish Society* (Edinburgh, 1991), p. 1.

5. See W. S. Marshall, *The Billy Boys: A Concise History of Orangeism in Scotland* (Edinburgh, 1996).

6. See S. Bruce, T. Glendinning, I. Paterson and M. Rosie, *Sectarianism in Scotland* (Edinburgh, 2004).

7. A. Brown, D. McCrone and L. Paterson, *Politics and Society in Scotland* (Basingstoke, 1996), p. 202.

8. T. Colpi, 'Italian Migration to Scotland: Settlement, Employment and the Key Role of the Padrone' (Race, Curriculum and Employment Conference, Glasgow, 8 March 1986), pp. 1, 7.

9. A. E. H. Wood, 'Italian Immigration into Scotland' (Proceedings of the Fourth Annual Conference of the Scottish Association of Family History Societies, 1992), p. 17.

10. Colpi, 'Italian Migration', p. 3.

11. P. Tognini, *A Mind at War: An Autobiography* (New York, 1990), p. 17.

12. Colpi, 'Italian Migration', p. 29; J. Murray and D. Stockdale, *The Miles Tae Dundee: Stories of a City and Its People* (Dundee, 1990), p. 28.

13. Romeo Rinaldi, 'La Patata', translated by Giancarlo Rinaldi, *From the Serchio to the Solway* (Dumfries, 1998), pp. 50–1.

14. Devine, *Scottish Nation*, p. 508.

15. Ibid., p. 486.

16. Scottish Jewish Archives Centre, *Patterns and Images of Jewish Immigration in Scotland* (Glasgow, 1997), p. 17.

17. Gorbals Fair Society, *A Scottish Shtetl: Jewish Life in the Gorbals, 1880–1974* (Glasgow, 1974), p. 1.

18. M. Edward, *Who Belongs to Glasgow?* (Glasgow, 1993), p. 74.

19. D. Daiches, *Two Worlds* (Edinburgh, 1997), pp. 3, 118; F. Levison, *Christian and Jew: the Life of Leon Levison* (Edinburgh, 1989), p. ix.

20. K. E. Collins, *Glasgow Jewry: A Guide to the History and Community of the Jews in Glasgow* (Scottish Jewish Archives, 1993), p. 15.

21. T. H. Hollingsworth, 'Migration: A Study Based on Scottish Experience Between 1939 and 1994' (University of Glasgow, Social and Economic Studies, Occasional Papers, No. 12, 1970), p. 123.

22. B. Maan, *The New Scots: The Story of Asians in Scotland* (Edinburgh, 1992), pp. 105, 123, 126.

23. Murray and Stockdale, *The Miles Tae Dundee*, pp. 60, 62.

24. B. Maan, *The New Scots*, pp. 158, 160.

25. Ibid., pp. 161–2. See also S. Audrey, *Multiculturalsm in Practice: Irish, Jewish, Italian and Pakistani Migration to Scotland* (Aldershot, 2000), p. 63.

26. Ibid., p. 167.

27. A. Saeed, N. Blain, D. Forbes, 'New Ethnic and National Questions in Scotland: Post-British Identities among Glasgow Pakistani Teenagers', *Ethnic and Racial Studies* (22:5, 1999), pp. 821–44.

28. A. Chan, 'The Chinese in Scotland: Their Education, Employment and Social Needs in British Society in the Past Twenty Years' (University of Glasgow, 1987), p. 21.

29. Maan, *The New Scots*, p. 175.

30. Shelter Scotland, 'Dispersed?: Housing and Supporting Asylum Seekers and Refugees in Scotland' (December 2001), p. 19.

31. One Scotland, *Refugees and Asylum Seekers Today*, http://www.onescotland.com, accessed 13 September 2006.

32. M. Watson, *Being English in Scotland* (Edinburgh, 2003), p. 10.

33. Ibid., p. 28.

34. M. Watson, 'Using the Third Statistical Account of Scotland to Expose a Major Gap in Scottish Historiography', *Contemporary British History* (18 : 1, 2004), p. 111.

35. R. Keily, D. McCrone and F. Bachhofer, 'Whither Britishness? English and Scottish people in Scotland', *Nations and Nationalism* (11 : 1, 2005), pp. 65–82; A. M. Findlay, C. Hoy and A. Stockdale, 'In What Sense English? An exploration of English migrant identities and identification', *Journal of Ethnic and Migration Studies* (30 : 1, 2004), pp. 59–79.

36. Gibbon, 'Glasgow', p. 122.

37. There is plenty evidence to suggest that anti-Semitism was not confined to the Scottish literary elite. See B. Braber, 'The Trial of Oscar Slater (1909) and Anti-Jewish Prejudices in Edwardian Glasgow', *History* (88, 2003) pp. 262–79.

38. One Scotland, *Ethnicity Data*, http://www.onescotland.com, accessed 13 September 2006.

39. E. Kelly, 'Stands Scotland Where It Did?: An Essay in Ethnicity and Internationalism', *Scottish Affairs* (26, 1999), p. 94.

40. H. MacDiarmid, 'Glasgow Is Like the Sea', Stanzas 1–3, extract, from *Voice of Scotland* (4 : 4, June 1948), pp. 10–13. Originally published in the *Broughton Magazine*.

41. A. MacNeacail, 'gleann fadamach' (trans. 'remote glen'), in D. Dunn (ed.), *The Faber Book of Twentieth-Century Scottish Poetry* (London, 1992), p. 316.

42. A. Collier, *The Crofting Problem* (Cambridge, 1953), pp. 5, 6.

43. Rt Hon. Earl of Home, *Roads to Highland Prosperity* (Pamphlet, 1953), p. 1.

44. Donnachadh Mac'Illedhuibh, 'Death to the Highland Scot?: An Exposure of British Government Policies in Scotland' (Glasgow, 1944), p. 3; D. Turnock, *Patterns of Highland Development* (London, 1970), p. 115; J. Hunter, 'The Atlantic North West: The Highlands and Islands as a Twenty-first Century Success Story', *Scottish Affairs* (31, Spring 2000), p. 12.

45. J. I. Prattis, 'Economic Structures in the Highlands of Scotland', *Fraser of Allander Institute Speculative Papers* 7 (1977), p. 13.

46. Ibid., pp. 13, 31. See also J. I. Prattis, 'A Theoretical Perspective', in D. R. F. Simpson (ed.), *Island and Coastal Communities: Economic and Social Opportunities: Proceedings of a Conference Organised by the Fraser of Allander Institute, 26–28 April 1978* (Glasgow, 1980), pp. 9–39.

47. Peter Morrison, 'Précis of Evidence', *Report from the Select Committee on the Western Highlands and Islands of Scotland* (London, 24 July 1928), Appendix No. 3, p. 87.

48. Ibid., Lewis District Committee to the Select Committee, 6 June 1928, p. 90.

49. Turnock, *Patterns of Highland Development*, pp. 132–3; Earl of Home, *Roads to Highland Prosperity*, p. 8.

50. J. White, *Speed Bonny Boat: the Story of Caledonian MacBrayne Ltd under Scottish Transport Group, 1969–1990* (Edinburgh, 1990).

51. M. A. M. Dickie, 'The Crofting Counties – Problems and Prospects', published in pamphlet form from the *Transactions of the Royal Highland and Agricultural Society of Scotland* (1960); Earl of Home, *Roads to Highland Prosperity*, p. 9.

52. Turnock, *Patterns of Highland Development*, p. 154. See also J. Hunter, *The Islanders and the Orb* (Stornoway, 2001) and F. Thompson, *Harris Tweed: The Story of a Hebridean Industry* (Newton Abbot, 1969).

53. Ibid., p. 159.

54. R. F. Callander, *Forests and People in Rural Scotland: A Discussion Paper* (Perth, 1995).

55. Linklater, *The Lion and the Unicorn*, p. 90.

56. J. Hunter, *The Claim of Crofting: The Scottish Highlands and Islands, 1930–1990* (Edinburgh, 1991), p. 38.

57. Lockhart, *My Scottish Youth*, p. 228; Linklater, *The Lion and the Unicorn*, p. 104.

58. K. J. W. Oosthoek, 'An Environmental History of State Forestry in Scotland, 1919–1970' (unpublished PhD thesis, University of Stirling, 2001), p. 60.

59. R. E. Utiger, 'Never Trust an Expert: Nuclear Power, Government and the Tragedy of the Invergordon Aluminium Smelter', Business History Unit, LSE, (Paper 1, 1995).

60. See M. Brander, *The Making of the Highlands* (London, 1980).

61. Economist Intelligence Unit, *The Highland Region of Scotland: A preliminary study of economic resources and employment potential* (1979), pp. 54, 55, 58.

62. J. G. L. Adams and J. D. McCallum, *A Ferry Strategy for the Hebrides: A Report to Caledonian MacBrayne Ltd* (Glasgow, 1980), p. 58.

63. J. M. Rollo, 'Little Industries in Crofting Areas: Renaissance at a Profit', *Glasgow Herald* (12 March 1956).

64. Hunter, 'The Atlantic North West', p. 6.

65. Hunter, *The Claim of Crofting*, p. 77.

66. F. Fraser Darling, 'Ecology of Land Use in the Highlands and Islands', in D. S. Thomson and I. Grimble (eds), *The Future of the Highlands* (London, 1968), p. 51.

67. Hunter, 'The Atlantic North West', p. 8.

68. J. Hunter, 'Wilderness with People: Conservation and development in the Scottish Highlands', *John Muir Trust Paper* (1984), p. 7.

69. J. McCarthy, G. Lloyd and B. Illsley, 'National Parks in Scotland: Balancing Environment and Economy, *European Planning Studies* (10: 5, 2002), pp. 665–70; R. A. Lambert, 'A Hostile Environment: The National Trust for

Scotland, the Cairngorm Trust and Early Ski Developments in the Cairngorm Mountains, 1961–1967', *Northern Scotland* (21, 2001), pp. 99–120.

70. H. Lorimer, 'Ways of Seeing the Scottish Highlands: Marginality, Authenticity and the Curious Case of the Hebridean Blackhouse', *Journal of Historical Geography* (25 : 4, 1999), pp. 517–33.

71. See D. J. MacCuish, 'Crofting Legislation since 1886', *Scottish Geographical Magazine* (103, 1987), pp. 90–4; Cameron, 'The Scottish Highlands', pp. 153–69.

72. Brander, *The Making of the Highlands*, pp. 206–7. See also E. A. Cameron, *Land for the People: The British Government and the Scottish Highlands, 1880–1930* (Edinburgh, 1995).

73. E. A. Cameron, 'Unfinished Business: the Land Question and the Scottish Parliament', *Contemporary British History* (15 : 1, 2001), p. 91.

74. Sir A. MacEwen, 'Government's Highland Plan Under the Microscope', reprinted from *The Highland News* (26 August 1939).

75. J. Shaw Grant, 'Government Agencies and the Highlands since 1945', *Scottish Geographical Magazine* (103, 1987), p. 97.

76. Prattis, 'A Theoretical Perspective', p. 19.

77. A. S. Mather, 'Government Agencies and Land Development in the Scottish Highlands: A Centenary Survey', *Northern Scotland* (8, 1988), pp. 44–9.

78. Hunter, *The Claim of Crofting*, p. 213.

79. HC 348, *Minutes of Evidence Taken Before the Committee of Public Accounts* (17 November 1997), p. 9.

80. J. MacAskill, 'The Crofting Community Right to Buy in the Land Reform (Scotland) Act 2003', *Scottish Affairs* (49, Autumn 2004), pp. 104–33.

81. Ibid., p. 167.

82. *Report Drawn Up on Behalf of the Committee on Agriculture on the State of Agriculture in the Highlands and Islands of Scotland and Other Severely Disadvantaged Regions of the Community*, European Parliament Working Documents: 1982–3 (3 February 1983), p. 16.

83. *Twenty-One Years, 1975–1996: Highland Regional Council* (Inverness, 1996), p. 34.

PART THREE: PROLOGUE

The title of Part Three comes from David Lowe's *Souvenirs of Scottish Labour* (1919): 'The Scottish Labour Movement was not founded on materialism. The instinct for freedom and justice which animated the Covenanters and Chartists also inspired the nineteenth-century pioneers.'

1. There are many versions of this famous speech. The one offered here is that given in *Donald Dewar: A Book of Tribute* (HMSO, 2000), pp. 11–12.

2. P. Lynch, *Scottish Government and Politics* (Edinburgh, 2001), p. 181, Table 10.5.

CHAPTER EIGHT: POLITICAL TERRITORIES

1. D. McCrone, 'The Unstable Union: Scotland since the 1920s', in M. Lynch (ed.), *Scotland, 1850–1979: Society, Politics and the Union* (London, 1993), p. 47.

2. J. Fairley, 'Layers of Democracy: Making Home Rule Work', in A. Wright (ed.), *Scotland: the Challenge of Devolution* (Aldershot, 2000), p. 85.

3. G. Monies and G. Coutts, *Local Government in Scotland* (Edinburgh, 1989), pp. 3–4.

4. M. Johnston, *Ninety Wonderful Years, 1869–1959: The Biography of Sir Thomas Mitchell, Lord Provost of Aberdeen* (Aberdeen, 1960), p. 45.

5. *The Lord Provosts of Edinburgh, 1296–1932* (Edinburgh, 1932).

6. 'Presentation of Portrait to Henry Alexander Esq., Lord Provost of Aberdeen, 1932–35' (18 December 1936), p. 9.

7. A. Midwinter and C. Monaghan, *From Rates to the Poll Tax* (Edinburgh, 1993), p. 6.

8. W. H. Marwick, *Scottish Local Government: A Survey in Peace and War* (Fabian Society, Research Series, No. 46, November 1939), p. 22.

9. G. Wilson, *The Making of a Lord Provost: A Memory Book by Garnet Wilson* (Dundee, n. d.), p. 42.

10. K. Davidson and J. Fairley, *Running the Granite City: Local Government in Aberdeen, 1975–1996* (Aberdeen, 2000), p. 30.

11. G. Monies and G. Coutts, *Local Government in Scotland* (Edinburgh, 1989), p. 4.

12. R. Baird, 'Local Government', in Cairncross (ed.), *The Scottish Economy*, pp. 181–2.

13. Ibid., p. 186–7.

14. Scottish Local Government Information Unit, *The Guide to Scottish Local Government* (Glasgow, 1995), p. 17.

15. J. Dunlop, 'Fight for Fife' (Fife County Council, 16 February 1972).

16. A. Midwinter, *Local Government in Scotland: Reform or Decline?* (Basingstoke, 1995), p. 16. (Note that housing was also given to the district councils as their particular responsibility.)

17. Davidson and Fairley, *Running the Granite City*, pp. 25–6.

18. John G. Gray, 'Aince a Bailie: Or the Sad End of a Great Scottish Institution' (Edinburgh, April 1976), p. 7.

19. P. Carmichael, *Central-Local Government Relations in the 1980s: Glasgow and Liverpool Compared* (Aldershot, 1995), p. 116.

20. Davidson and Fairley, *Running the Granite City*, p. 31.

21. A. MacKenzie, *And Nothing But the Truth* (Dundee, 1976), p. 10.

22. Reconstruction Committee, Scottish Unionist Association, 'Scottish Local Government: Memorandum on the Problem of Post-War Reconstruction' (Edinburgh, 1944), p. 16.

23. Carmichael, *Central-Local Government Relations in the 1980s*, p. 96.

24. Scottish Local Government Information Unit, *The Guide to Scottish Local Government*, p. 20.

25. Monies and Coutts, *Local Government in Scotland*, p. 8.

26. K. Orr and M. McAteer, 'The Modernisation of Local Decision Making: Public Participation and Scottish Local Government', *Local Government Studies* (30:2, 2004), p. 136.

27. A. Midwinter, 'Developments and Issues in Scottish Local Government', in *Perspectives on Policy* (Universities of Glasgow and Strathclyde, 2000), p. 3.

28. G. Boyne, G. Jordan and M. McVicar, 'Local Government Reform: A Review of the Process in Scotland and Wales' (Joseph Rowntree Foundation, 1995), p. 101. In 1995, the average population size of Scottish local authorities was 92,000. In England, this figure was 127,000 while, in France (the western European country with the lowest population to authority ratio), this figure was 1,500.

29. C. Gordon, 'From War of Attrition to Roller-Coaster Ride: Local and Central Government in Scotland', in *Public Money and Management* (April–June 2002), p. 8.

30. G. Kerevan, 'City States and Local Governance', in G. Hassan and C. Warhurst (eds), *Anatomy of the New Scotland: Power, Influence and Change* (Edinburgh, 2002), pp. 37–45.

31. McCrone, *Understanding Scotland*, p. 23.

32. W. L. Miller, *The End of British Politics? Scots and English political behaviour in the seventies* (Oxford, 1981), p. 260.

33. I. Levitt, 'Introduction', in Levitt (ed.) *The Scottish Office and Reconstruction, 1919–1959* (Edinburgh, 1992), p. 1.

34. P. J. Rose, 'The Office of the Secretary of State for Scotland', pp. 30–1 (my emphasis). This was the 1904 Wild Birds Protection (St Kilda) Act.

35. Lady Pentland, *The Right Honourable John Sinclair, Lord Pentland, GCSI: A Memoir* (London, 1928), pp. 81–2.

36. R. Munro, *Looking Back: Fugitive Writings and Sayings* (London, n. d.), pp. 345–6.

37. J. S. Gibson, *The Thistle and the Crown: A History of the Scottish Office* (Edinburgh, 1985), p. 89.

38. C. Coote, *A Companion of Honour: The Story of Walter Elliot* (London, 1965), p. 188.

39. R. J. Finlay, 'Scottish Nationalism and Scottish Politics, 1900–1979', in Lynch (ed.), *Scotland, 1850–1979*, p. 22.

40. G. Pottinger, *The Secretaries of State for Scotland, 1926–1976: Fifty Years of the Scottish Office* (Aberdeen, 1979), p. 89.

41. NLS, Acc. 5862 Johnston MS, typed MS (c.1949).

42. J. Stuart, *Within the Fringe: An Autobiography* (London, 1967), p. 161.

43. Ibid., p. 167.

44. Pottinger, *The Secretaries of State for Scotland*, p. 22.

45. A. Clements, K. Farquharson and K. Wark, *Restless Nation* (London, 1996), p. 44.

46. J. Stewart, 'The National Health Service in Scotland, 1947–1974: Scottish or British?', *Historical Research* (76, 2003), p. 404.

47. J. M. Ross, 'The Secretary of State for Scotland and the Scottish Office', in *Studies in Public Policy* (87, 1981), (University of Strathclyde, Centre for the Study of Public Policy), p. 12.

48. Bennie et al., *How Scotland Votes*, p. 33.
49. Ibid., p. 33; G. Lloyd, 'Quasi-government in Scotland – A Challenge for Devolution and the Renewal of Democracy', in Wright (ed.), *Scotland: The Challenge of Devolution*, p. 102.
50. McCrone, 'The Unstable Union', p. 44.
51. A. Midwinter, M. Keating and J. Mitchell, *Politics and Public Policy in Scotland* (Basingstoke, 1991), p. 61.
52. NLS, Woodburn MS, Acc. 7656/16/1, typed MS, Scottish Home Department, 'Proposals for Scottish Home Rule or Devolution' (14 December 1949).
53. Ibid.
54. M. Lynch, 'Introduction', in Lynch (ed.), *Scotland, 1850–1979*, p. 10.
55. J. Mitchell, *The Invention of Administrative Devolution* (Basingstoke, 2003), p. 1.
56. M. Keating and A. Midwinter, 'The Scottish Office in the United Kingdom Network', *Studies in Public Policy* (96, 1981), (University of Strathclyde, Centre for the Study of Public Policy), p. 3.
57. P. Schelsinger, 'The Reinvention of Scotland', *Political Communication* (17, 2000), p. 317.
58. M. Dyer, *Capable Citizens and Improvident Democrats: The Scottish electoral system, 1884–1929* (Aberdeen, 1996), pp. 113, 114; I. G. C. Hutchison, *A Political History of Scotland, 1832–1924: Parties, Elections and Issues* (Edinburgh, 1986), p. 285.
59. Dyer, *Capable Citizens and Improvident Democrats*, p. 122.
60. Ibid., p. 114.
61. J. Miller, *Inverness* (Edinburgh, 2004).
62. See M. Dyer, 'Twentieth-century Politics', in W. H. Fraser and C. Lee (eds), *Aberdeen 1800–2000* (East Linton, 2000).
63. R. Duncan, *Steelopolis: The Making of Motherwell* (Motherwell, 1911), p. 141.
64. Dyer, *Capable Citizens and Improvident Democrats*, p. 122.
65. Bennie et al., *How Scotland Votes*, p. 26.
66. Coote, *Companion of Honour*, pp. 80–1.
67. H. MacDiarmid, 'Politicians', in MacDiarmid and Gibbon, *Scottish Scene*, pp. 214, 216.
68. Moray McLaren to James Bridie (2 March 1949), in Bridie and McLaren, *A Small Stir*, p. 135.
69. G. Brown, B. Campbell, B. Wright, 'Alternative Edinburgh' (Edinburgh University Student Publications Board, 1972), p. 146.
70. V. Bogdanor, 'The Start of a New Song', *Hume Occasional Paper* (55, 1998), p. 10.
71. Midwinter et al., *Politics and Public Policy*, pp. 65–9.
72. Ibid., p. 69.
73. This includes the seats of both the Coalition and Independent Liberals. In England, the Liberals won 107 seats in comparison to the Conservatives' 315.
74. *Harpies and Quines* (May–June 1992), p. 2.

75. K. J. Nagel, 'Transcending the National/Asserting the National: How Stateless Nations like Scotland, Wales and Catalonia React to European Integration', *Australian Journal of Politics and History* (50:1, 2004), p. 66.

76. 'Introduction', *Scotland and Europe: Seven View Points* (Scottish Conservative Central Office, Edinburgh, June 1971), p. 5.

77. M. Fry and J. Cooney, *Scotland in the New Europe* (Dublin, 1979), p. 5.

78. 'A Survey of European Investment in Scotland' (Scottish Council, Development and Industry, Edinburgh, March 1973).

79. 'Scotland', Commission of the European Communities (November 1982), p. 3.

80. See J. Mitchell, 'Scotland in the Union, 1945–1995', in Devine and Finlay (eds), *Scotland in the Twentieth Century*, p. 99.

81. C. Harvie, 'Europe and the Scottish Nation', Scottish Centre for Economic and Social Research (1, 1992), p. 2.

82. N. Waters, 'Scottish Local Government and the European Communities', *The Planning Exchange Research Paper, No. 9* (Glasgow, 1983), p. 3.

83. From January 2002 the onus was placed upon the other Subject Committees to explore EU matters relevant to their own interests. The European Committee warned other Subject Committees of long- and short-term changes in EU policy and practice relevant to their remits but could also take the initiative in exploring other areas of European concern.

84. W. Ewing (with M. Russell), *Stop the World: The Autobiography of Winnie Ewing* (Edinburgh, 2004), pp. 297–8.

85. Nagel, 'Transcending the National/Asserting the National', p. 67.

86. Scotland House combined the activities of Scotland Europa and the Scottish Executive's European Office.

87. See Lynch, *Scottish Government and Politics*, pp. 156–63.

88. A. Sloat, 'Scotland in the European Union: Expectations of the Scottish Parliament's Architects, Builders and Tenants', *Scotland Europa Papers* (22 March 2001), p. 19.

89. 'The Power of Small Nations in the New Europe', Scottish Centre for Economic and Social Research (September 1994), p. 3.

90. A. Ichijo, *Scottish Nationalism and the Idea of Europe: Concepts of Europe and the Nation* (London, 2004), p. 79.

91. Garioch, *Collected Poems*, p. 181.

CHAPTER NINE: PARTIES AND PLAYERS

1. NLS, Woodburn MS, Acc. 7656, notes for an address by the Rt Hon. Arthur Woodburn MP, Secretary of State for Scotland, to press correspondents in the Savoy Hotel, London, (November 1948).

2. See Hutchison, *A Political History of Scotland*, Ch. 10.

3. R. Winfield, *Liberals in Parliament: An Electoral History, 1924–1994* (Aberystwyth, 1992), p. 4.

4. J. S. MacLay, 'Liberalism and the Present Situation' (London, 1950), p. 6.

5. C. M. M. Macdonald, *The Radical Thread* (East Linton, 2000), p. 281.

6. Coote, *Companion of Honour*, p. 48.

7. I. G. C. Hutchison, *Scottish Politics in the Twentieth Century* (Basingstoke, 2001), pp. 79, 81.

8. J. Grimond, *The New Liberalism* (London, 1958), p. 16.

9. Ibid., p. 8.

10. In John Fowler (ed.), *Bannerman: The Memoirs of Lord Bannerman of Kildonan* (Aberdeen, 1972), pp. 104–5.

11. D. Steel, *Against Goliath: David Steel's Story* (London, 1991), p. 71.

12. P. Bartram, *David Steel: His Life and Politics* (London, 1981), p. 43.

13. J. Grimond, *Why I Claim Your Support* (Stromness, 1955).

14. M. McManus, *Jo Grimond: Towards the Sound of Gunfire* (Edinburgh, 2001).

15. Hutchison, *Scottish Politics in the Twentieth Century*, p. 144.

16. D. Steel, 'Out of Control: A Critical Examination of the Government of Scotland' (Vanguard Publication, January 1968), p. 7.

17. J. Grimond, *Memoirs* (London, 1979), p. 179.

18. Bennie et al., *How Scotland Votes*, p. 94.

19. He was soon to be followed by yet another Scot, the aging Sir Menzies Campbell (1941–), MP for North-east Fife and Lib Dem leader from 2006 to 2007.

20. The major referred to here is Major McKerrel, the Unionist candidate at the upcoming general election.

21. Hutchison, *A Political History of Scotland*, pp. 207, 226–7.

22. SUA Pamphlet, G.E.S. Series, No. 1 (1918).

23. I. G. C. Hutchison, 'Scottish Unionism between the Two World Wars', in Macdonald (ed.), *Unionist Scotland*, pp. 73–99.

24. M. Dyer, 'The Evolution of the Centre-right and the State of Scottish Conservatism', *Political Studies* (39, 2001), p. 40; G. Ward-Smith, 'Baldwin and Scotland: More than Englishness', *Contemporary British History* (15 : 1, 2001), p. 65.

25. Dyer, *Capable Citizens and Improvident Democrats*, p. 150.

26. Midwinter et al., *Politics and Public Policy in Scotland*, p. 23; Hutchison, *Scottish Politics in the Twentieth Century*, p. 110.

27. Fry, *Patronage and Principle*, p. 199. See also D. Seawright, *An Important Matter of Principle: The Decline of the Scottish Conservative and Unionist Party* (Aldershot, 1999).

28. N. Fairbairn, *A Life is Too Short* (London, 1989), p. 332.

29. SCOTORY, 'Unemployment' (Thistle Group, 1972), p. 5.

30. M. Forsyth, D. McLetchie and D. Young, 'The Scottish Conservatives: the Way Ahead' (1976), pp. 7, 8, 11.

31. *Glasgow Herald* (4 May 1979).

32. D. McCrone, 'The New Right and Scotland', *Cencrastus* (19, 1984), p. 12.

33. J. Mitchell, 'The Myth of Dependency', *Scottish Centre for Economic and Social Research, Forward Series* (3, 1990).

34. M. L. MacKenzie, 'Scottish Toryism, Identity and Consciousness: a personal essay' (May 1988), p. 3.

35. T. Nairn, 'Virtual Liberation or British Sovereignty Since the Election', *Scottish Affairs: Understanding Constitutional Change* (Special Issue, 1998), p. 14.

36. M. Rifkind, 'Conservative Britain in the 21st Century' (Centre for Policy Studies, 1996), p. 15.

37. Bennie et al., *How Scotland Votes*, p. 46.

38. NLS, Johnston MS, Acc 6862 (7), T. Johnston, typescript article on Trade Unionism in Scotland (c. 1937), p. 12.

39. STUC, *Annual Report* (1961), p. 349.

40. NLS, Johnston MS, Acc 6862 (7), T. Johnston, typescript article on Trade Unionism in Scotland (c. 1937), p. 12.

41. Knox, *Industrial Nation*, p. 280.

42. Ibid., p. 281.

43. K. Aitken, *The Bairns o' Adam: The Story of the STUC* (Edinburgh, 1997), pp. 265–6, 297.

44. STUC, *Annual Report* (1969), pp. 203–4.

45. STUC, *Annual Report* (1970), p. 395.

46. See J. J. Smyth, 'The ILP in Glasgow, 1888–1906: the struggle for identity', in A. McKinlay and R. J. Morris (eds), *The ILP on Clydeside, 1893–1932: From Foundation to Disintegration* (Manchester, 1991), pp. 20–55.

47. Hutchison, *A Political History of Scotland*, pp. 247–8.

48. See W. W. Knox (ed.), *Scottish Labour Leaders, 1918–1939* (Edinburgh, 1984).

49. Anon., *The Independent Labour Party in Scotland* (Glasgow, 1925), p. 5; Knox, *Industrial Nation*, p. 239.

50. J. J. Smyth, *Labour in Glasgow, 1896–1936: Socialism, Suffrage and Sectarianism* (East Linton, 2000), p. 117.

51. Hutchison, *A Political History of Scotland*, p. 296.

52. NLS, Woodburn MS., Acc 7656/4/3, 'Recollections' (draft form), pp. 76–7.

53. I. Donnachie, 'Scottish Labour in the Depression: the 1930s', in I. Donnachie, C. Harvie and I. S. Wood (eds), *Forward! Labour Politics in Scotland, 1888–1988* (Edinburgh, 1989), p. 61; Hutchison, *Scottish Politics in the Twentieth Century*, p. 65.

54. See W. W. Knox and A. McKinlay, 'The Re-making of Scottish Labour in the 1930s', *Twentieth Century British History* (6, 1995), pp. 174–93; Hutchison, *Scottish Politics in the Twentieth Century*, p. 65.

55. Hutchison, *Scottish Politics in the Twentieth Century*, p. 70.

56. Fowler (ed.), *Bannerman*, p. 45.

57. A selection of these must include J. McGrath's play, *The Game's A Bogey: 7:84's John MacLean Show* (Edinburgh, 1975) and a variety of poems including: S. G. Smith 'John MacLean, martyr', *The Voice of Scotland* (2:2, 1945), p. 23; 'A new ballant of John MacLean', *Cencrastus* (14, 1983), p. 16; Thurso Berwick, 'Til the citie o John MacLean', *Chapman* (7:2, 1982), p. 19; and John Kincaid, 'On John MacLean', *The Voice of Scotland* (4:1, 1947), p. 41. See also T. S. Law and T. Berwick (eds), *Homage to John MacLean* (EUSPB, 1979) for works on this theme by MacDiarmid, Hamish Henderson, Edwin Morgan and others.

58. NLS, Woodburn MS, Acc 7656/6/4, Sir Patrick Dollan to Arthur Woodburn (9 March 1950).

59. NLS, Woodburn MS, Acc 7656/16/1, A. Woodburn, House of Commons (1 February 1955).

60. H. Drucker, *Breakaway: the Scottish Labour Party* (Edinburgh, 1977).

61. This replicates a trend noted among local Labour councillors in Glasgow. See M. Keating, R. Levy, J. Geekie and J. Brand, 'Labour Elites in Glasgow', *Strathclyde Papers on Government and Politics*, No. 61 (Glasgow, 1989).

62. G. Hassan, 'A Case Study of Scottish Labour: Devolution and the Politics of Multi-level Governance', *Political Quarterly* (2002), p. 149.

63. See Hutchison, *Scottish Politics in the Twentieth Century*, p. 134.

64. See B. McLean, 'Labour in Scotland Since 1945: Myth and Reality', in G. Hassan (ed.), *The Scottish Labour Party* (Edinburgh, 2004), p. 44.

65. See G. Brown and J. Naughtie, *John Smith: Life and Soul of the Party* (Edinburgh, 1994); M. Stuart, *John Smith: A Life* (London, 2005); J. Kampfer, *Robin Cook* (London, 1998); *Donald Dewar: A Book of Tribute* (Stationery Office, 2000), p. 39.

66. Bennie et al., *How Scotland Votes*, pp. 48–9.

67. L. Paterson, 'Scottish Democracy and Scottish Utopias: the First Year of the Scottish Parliament', *Scottish Affairs* (33, Autumn 2000), p. 46.

68. E. Linklater, 'East Fife Parliamentary Bye-election' (NPS, 1933).

69. See R. J. Finlay, *Independent and Free: Scottish Politics and the Origins of the Scottish National Party, 1918–45* (Edinburgh, 1994).

70. D. Watson and I. MacRae, *Your Job in Scotland's Crisis* (Edinburgh, 1938), p. 37.

71. Finlay, 'Scottish Nationalism and Scottish Politics', p. 22.

72. D. Stewart, *A Scot at Westminster* (Nova Scotia, 1994), p.14.

73. J. M. MacCormick, 'Experiment in Democracy: A Convention Publication' (n. d.), p. 1. Note that MacCormick had tried a similar initiative in 1939 before war intervened.

74. D. Douglas, *At the Helm: The Life and Times of Dr Robert McIntyre* (Buckie, 1995), pp. 47–8.

75. 'To the Electors of Motherwell and Wishaw from Dr Robert McIntyre' (July 1945).

76. Scottish Unionist Association, *The Year Book for Scotland* (1955), p. 307.

77. 'Preamble', Scottish Covenant, 1949.

78. P. Gerber, 'Kay Matheson and the Stone of Destiny', *Chapman* (77, 1994), pp. 55–8.

79. I. Levitt, 'Britain, the Scottish Covenant Movement and Devolution, 1946–50', *Scottish Affairs* (22, 1998), p. 34.

80. *Inverness Courier* (18 November 1949).

81. Harold Stewart, 'Calling Mr Woodburn', *Daily Record* (26 November 1949). Woodburn, in a debate in the Commons, rejected an inquiry into Scottish devolution and commented disparagingly on potential bomb threats from the Nationalists.

82. J. Herdman, *Poets, Pubs, Polls and Pillar Boxes: Memoirs of an Era in Scottish Politics and Letters* (Kirkcaldy, 1999), p. 14.

83. See J. Mitchell, 'From National Identity to Nationalism', in H. T. Dickinson and M. Lynch (eds), *The Challenge to Westminster: Sovereignty, Devolution and Independence* (East Linton, 2000), p. 159.

84. See R. Levy, 'The Search for a Rational Strategy: the Scottish National Party and devolution', *Political Studies* (34, 1986), pp. 236–48.

85. *79 Group News* (October, 1981).

86. R. Watson, 'The Scottish Political Juncture 1985', *Cencrastus* (20, 1985), p. 16.

87. J. Sillars, 'Scotland: Moving On and Up in Europe. The case for Scottish independence within the European Community' (June 1985), Introduction.

88. See P. Lynch, *SNP: The History of the Scottish National Party* (Cardiff, 2002), pp. 191–219.

CHAPTER TEN: DIFFERENCE AND DEVOLUTION

1. See P. Routledge, *Gordon Brown: The Biography* (London, 1998), p. 36.

2. See M. B. Dickson, 'Scottish Political Culture: Is Scotland Different? – A Preliminary Investigation', *Strathclyde Papers on Government and Politics* 108 (Glasgow, 1996), pp. 14–15.

3. See M. Fry, *Patronage and Principle: A Political History of Modern Scotland* (Aberdeen, 1991), Ch. 1 and, for a more contemporary approach, J. Mitchell, 'Contemporary Unionism', in C. M. M. Macdonald (ed.), *Unionist Scotland, 1800–1997* (Edinburgh, 1998), pp. 117–39.

4. L. Bennie, J. Brand and J. Mitchell, *How Scotland Votes: Scottish Parties and Elections* (Manchester, 1997), p. 44.

5. Dickson, 'Scottish Political Culture', p. 1.

6. T. Gallagher, 'National Identity and the Working Class in Scotland', *Cencrastus* (33, 1989), p. 15.

7. J. G. Kellas and P. Fotheringham, 'The Political Behaviour of the Working Class', in A. A. MacLaren (ed.), *Social Class in Scotland: Past and Present* (Edinburgh, n. d.), p. 154.

8. A. Brown, D. McCrone and L. Paterson, *Politics and Society in Scotland* (London, 1996), pp. 141–2; Midwinter et al., *Politics and Public Policy in Scotland*, p. 45; Bennie et al., *How Scotland Votes*, p. 100.

9. D. McCrone, 'We're A' Jock Tamson's Bairns: Social Class in Twentieth Century Scotland', in Devine and Finlay (eds), *Scotland in the Twentieth Century*, p. 111.

10. Bennie et al., *How Scotland Votes*, p. 102.

11. A. Brown, D. McCrone, L. Paterson and P. Surridge, *The Scottish Electorate: the 1997 General Election and Beyond* (Basingstoke, 1999), p. 60.

12. See D. McCrone and F. Bechhofer, 'The Scotland–England Divide: Politics and Locality in Britain', *Political Studies* (XLI, 1993), pp. 96–107.

13. C. Lanneli and L. Paterson, 'Moving Up and Down the Social Class Ladder in Scotland' (CES Briefing No. 33, Centre for Educational Sociology, University of Edinburgh, May 2005), p. 1.

14. See S. Kendrick and D. McCrone, 'Politics in a Cold Climate: The Conservative Decline in Scotland', *Political Studies* (XXXVII, 1989), pp. 589–603.

15. Brown, McCrone, Paterson and Surridge, *The Scottish Electorate*, p. 151.

16. P. Hume Brown, *Scotland in the Time of Queen Mary* (London, 1904), pp. 207–8, 209.

17. G. Blake, 'Scottish Affairs', *Current Affairs* (Bureau of Current Affairs, 34, 1947), p. 8.

18. 'Scottish Independence Day Celebrations' (Arbroath, 15 April 1933).

19. Gallagher, 'National Identity and the Working Class in Scotland', pp. 16, 17.

20. Bennie et al., *How Scotland Votes*, p. 8; David Seawright wrote in 1999 that 'the Conservatives are still a Protestant party, simply not a very successful one', *An Important Matter of Principle*, p. 197.

21. Covenant News Letter (Vol. 2, No. 2, 1953), p. 1.

22. See G. Morton, *Unionist Nationalism: Governing Urban Scotland, 1830–1860* (East Linton, 1999); J. Breuilly, *Nationalism and the State* (Manchester, 1993).

23. See Stair Society, *An Introduction to Scottish Legal History* (Edinburgh, 1958) and D. M. Walker *The Scottish Legal System: An Introduction to the Study of Scots Law* (Edinburgh, 1981), pp. 149, 150.

24. C. Harvie, 'Democracy or Tribalism?', *Cencrastus* (34, 1989), p. 3.

25. Some initial attempts have been made to address this dilemma. See F. Bechhofer, D. McCrone, R. Kiely and R. Stewart, 'Constructing National Identity: Arts and Landed Elites in Scotland', *Sociology* (33:3, 1999), pp. 515–34; R. Kiely, F. Bechhofer, R. Stewart and D. McCrone, 'The markers and rules of Scottish national identity', *Sociological Review* (2001), pp. 33–55; R. Haesly, 'Identifying Scotland and Wales: types of Scottish and Welsh national identities', *Nations and Nationalism* (11:2, 2005), pp. 243–63.

26. D. McCrone, 'Who Are We?: Understanding Scottish Identity', in C. Di Domenico, J. Skinner and M. Smith (eds), *Boundaries and Identities: Nation, Politics and Culture in Scotland* (Dundee, 2001), p. 18. See also R. Bond and M. Rosie, 'National Identities in Post-Devolution Scotland', *Scottish Affairs* (40, 2002), pp. 34–53.

27. McCrone, 'Who Are We?', pp. 29–30. See also L. Paterson, 'Scottish Social Democracy and Blairism', in Hassan and Warhurst (eds), *Tomorrow's Scotland*, pp. 116–29.

28. Paterson, 'Scottish Democracy and Scottish Utopias', p. 60.

29. C. Harvie, *Scotland and Nationalism: Scottish society and politics, 1707–1977* (London, 1977), p. 280.

30. The Scottish Executive was rebranded as the Scottish Government in 2007.

31. See Harvie, *Scotland and Nationalism*, pp. 260–71.

32. Ewing, *Stop the World*, p. 161.

33. Ibid., p. 158.

34. T. Dalyell, *Devolution: The End of Britain?* (London, 1977), p. 1.

35. T. Dalyell, 'Why not all Scots support proposals for an Edinburgh Assembly' (Edinburgh, n. d.), p. 6.

36. J. H. Proctor, 'Lessons from the Scottish Referendum on Devolution', *Journal of Constitutional and Parliamentary Studies* (16, 1982), p. 5.

37. See Clements et al., *Restless Nation*, pp. 72–82.

38. N. Ascherson, 'The Yes Road: *A* Reflection on Two Devolution Campaigns' (Welsh Political Archive Lecture, National Library of Wales, 1998), p. 9.

39. See J. Mitchell, 'Constitutional Conventions and the Scottish National Movement: Origins, agendas and outcomes', *Strathclyde Papers on Government and Politics* (78, 1991).

40. J. Grimond, *A Roar for the Lion* (London, September 1976), p. 1.

41. Mitchell, 'Constitutional Conventions', p. 12.

42. See B. Taylor, *The Road to the Scottish Parliament* (Edinburgh, 2002).

43. See D. Denver, J. Mitchell, C. Pattie and H. Bochel, *Scotland Decides: The Devolution Issue and the 1997 Referendum* (London, 2000), pp. 51–77.

44. NLS, Pamphlets and Materials from the Scotland Forward Campaign.

45. Ibid.

46. Ibid.

47. D. Denver, 'Voting in the 1997 Scottish and Welsh devolution referendums: Information, interests and opinions', *European Journal of Political Research* (41, 2002), p. 840.

48. D. Millar, 'Scotland's Parliament: A Mini Westminster, or a Model for Democracy?', in Wright (ed.), *Scotland: The Challenge of Devolution*, p. 15.

49. See N. Burrows, 'Unfinished Business: The Scotland Act 1998', *Modern Law Review* (62:2, 1999), p. 260.

50. M. Ritchie, *Scotland Reclaimed: The Inside Story of Scotland's First Democratic Parliamentary Election* (Edinburgh, 2000), p. 219.

51. These were Justice and Home Affairs, Enterprise and Lifelong Learning, Health and Community Care, Rural Affairs, Social Inclusion, Housing and the Voluntary Sector, Local Government, Education, Culture and Sport, and Transport and the Environment. These changed over time under successive administrations.

52. D. Arter, 'The Scottish Committees and the Goal of a "New Politics": A Verdict on the First Four Years of the Devolved Scottish Parliament', *Journal of Contemporary European Studies* (12:1, 2004), p. 73.

53. J. Convery, *The Governance of Scotland: A Saltire Guide* (Edinburgh, 2000), p. 220.

54. Arter, 'The Scottish Committees and the Goal of a "New Politics"', p. 81.

55. L. Leneman, *A Guid Cause: The Women's Suffrage Movement in Scotland* (Edinburgh, 1995) and *Martyrs in our Midst: Dundee, Perth and the Forcible Feeding of Suffragettes* (Dundee, 1993).

56. Leneman, *Martyrs in our Midst*, p. 15. See also N. Watson, *Dundee's Suffragettes* (1990), L. M. Brewster, *Suffrage in Stirling: the Struggle for Women's Votes* (Stirling, 2002).

57. Bennie et al., *How Scotland Votes*, p. 13.

58. A. Brown, 'Women in Scottish Politics' (Unit for the Study of Government in Scotland, University of Edinburgh, November 1990), p. 5.

59. A. Brown, 'Taking Their Place in the New House', *Scottish Affairs* (28, 1999), p. 44.

60. G. Hassan and C. Warhurst, 'New Scotland? Policy, Parties and Institutions', *Political Quarterly* (72:2 2001), p. 216.

61. T. Sheridan, *A Time to Rage* (Edinburgh, 1994).

62. T. Sheridan and A. McCombes, *Imagine: A Socialist Vision for the 21st Century* (Edinburgh, 2000), p. xiii.

63. See L. G. Bennie, 'Exploiting New Electoral Opportunities: the small parties in Scotland', in G. Hassan and C. Warhurst (eds), *Tomorrow's Scotland* (London, 2002), pp. 98–115.

64. Ritchie, *Scotland Reclaimed*, p. 211.

65. M. Keating, L. Stevenson, P. Cairney and K. Taylor, 'Does Devolution Make a Difference? Legislative Output and Policy Divergence', *Journal of Legislative Studies* (9:3, 2003), p. 112.

66. E. Clarence, 'Ministerial Responsibility and the Scottish Qualifications Agency', *Public Administration* (80:4, 2002), pp. 791–803.

67. See P. Schlesinger, D. Miller and W. Dinan, *Open Scotland? Journalists, Spin Doctors and Lobbyists* (Edinburgh, 2001), pp. 226–44.

68. L. Paterson, A. Brown, J. Curtice, K. Hinds, D. McCrone, A. Park, K. Sprotston and P. Surridge, *New Scotland, New Politics?* (Edinburgh, 2001), p. 53; Schlesinger et al., *Open Scotland?*, pp. 89–90.

69. D. Simpson, 'Foreword', in A. Salmond, 'The Economics of Independence' (University of Strathclyde and *The Scotsman*, 2003), p. 11.

70. B. Winetrobe, *Realising the Vision of a Parliament with a Purpose: an audit of the first year of the Scottish Parliament* (Constitution Unit, University College London, 2001), p. 2.

71. Hassan and Warhurst, 'New Scotland?', pp. 215, 217.

72. See R. McLean, 'Gallant Crusader or Cautious Persuader? Donald Dewar's role in Securing Scotland's Parliament', *Scottish Affairs* (34, 2001), pp. 1–10.

73. D. Fraser, 'New Labour, New Parliament', in G. Hassan (ed.), *The Scottish Labour Party* (Edinburgh, 2004), p. 138.

74. N. Mitchison, 'The Cleansing of the Knife, 1941–1947' (IV, What are you doing?), from *The Cleansing of the Knife* (Edinburgh, 1978).

75. See M. Keating, *Nations Against the State: the New Politics of Nationalism in Quebec, Catalonia and Scotland* (Basingstoke, 2001).

PART THREE: CONCLUSION

1. The Wales Office was established in July 1999.

PART FOUR: PROLOGUE

1. C. M. Grieve, *Albyn: Or Scotland and the Future* (London, 1927), p. 30.

2. J. Schwend, 'Calvin Walker – Still Going Strong: The Scottish Kirk in Early Twentieth-Century Scottish Fiction', in J. Schwend and H. W. Prescher (eds), *Studies in Scottish Fiction: Twentieth Century*, Publications of the Scottish Studies Centre of the Joahnnes Gutenberg Universität Mainz in Gemersheim (Frankfurt, 1990), p. 338.

3. J. D. Fergusson, *Modern Scottish Painting* (Glasgow, 1943), p. 69.

4. A. O'Hagan, 'Into the Ferment', in T. M. Devine (ed.), *Scotland's Shame* (Edinburgh, 2000), p. 25.

5. D. Petrie, *Contemporary Scottish Fictions: Film, Television and the Novel* (Edinburgh, 2004), p. 135.

6. B. Hare, 'Past and Present: An Historical View of Scottish Art in the 1980s', in B. Hare, *Contemporary Painting in Scotland* (East Roseville (Australia), 1992), p. 3.

7. J. Warnaby, 'Peter Maxwell Davies' recent music, and its debt to his earlier scores', p. 88, and A. Whittall, 'A Dance of the Deadly Sins: the Beltane Fire and the rite of modernism', p. 145, both in R. McGregor (ed.), *Perspectives on Peter Maxwell Davies* (Aldershot, 2000).

8. A. Riach, *Representing Scotland in Literature, Popular Culture and Iconography* (Basingstoke, 2005), p. 137.

9. C. Craig, *The Modern Scottish Novel* (Edinburgh 1999), pp. 35, 205.

10. R. Crawford, 'Presbyterianism and Imagination in Modern Scotland', in T. M. Devine (ed.), *Scotland's Shame: Bigotry and Sectarianism in Modern Scotland* (Edinburgh, 2000), pp. 188, 189, 194.

CHAPTER ELEVEN: COLUMBA TO CARFIN – SCOTTISH CHRISTIANITY

1. Verse noted by Rev. Norman MacLeod (*Caraid nan Gaidheal*), great-grandfather of George MacLeod, 1828. As quoted in R. Ferguson, *George MacLeod: Founder of the Iona Community* (London, 1990), p. 142.

2. Muir, 'Carfin', *Scottish Journey*, p. 176.

3. *The Coracle* (November 1939).

4. S. McGhee, *Monsignor Taylor of Carfin* (Glasgow, 1972), p. 180.

5. S. McGhee, *The Carfin Grotto: The First Sixty Years* (Motherwell, 1981).

6. Monsignor Thomas N. Canon Taylor, *The Carfin Grotto* (Glasgow, 1952), p. 11.

7. Muir, *Scottish Journey*, p. 176.

8. McGhee, *The Carfin Grotto: The First Sixty Years*, pp. 7–10.

9. *The Coracle* (May 1939).

10. G. MacLeod, *We Shall Re-Build: the work of the Iona Community on mainland and on island* (Glasgow, 1944), p. 6.

11. R. Ferguson, *Chasing the Wild Goose: the story of the Iona Community* (Glasgow, 1998), p. 69.

12. C. G. Brown, *Religion and Society in Scotland Since 1707* (Edinburgh, 1997), p. 139. See also C. G. Brown, *Death of Christian Britain: Understanding Secularisation, 1800–2000* (London, 2001). In this second text, Brown notes that, in Scotland, the peak year for church attendance was reached in 1905.

13. Brown, 'Religion and Secularisation', p. 51.

14. J. Buchan, *The Kirk in Scotland* (Dunbar, 1985 [1930]), p. 108.

15. J. Highet, 'Scottish Religious Adherence', *British Journal of Sociology* (IV, 1953), p. 144.

16. Brown, *Religion and Society in Scotland*, p. 162.

17. C. A. Piggott, 'Population Change and the Churches in Scotland, 1951–1971', Research Discussion Paper No. 14, Department of Geography, University of Edinburgh (October 1977), p. 6.

18. J. Highet, *The Scottish Churches: a review of their state 400 years after the Reformation* (London, 1960), p. 61.

19. Brown, *Religion and Society in Scotland*, pp. 159–60. By the 1980s, only around 13 per cent of Scotland's children attended Church of Scotland Sunday Schools – a drop of nearly 25 per cent since 1951. See T. M. Phillips, *All God's Children: The Sunday School in Scotland* (Milngavie, 1988), p. 40.

20. P. Brierley, '"Christian" Scotland: What the 1994 Scottish Church Census reveals', in P. Brierley and F. MacDonald, *Prospects for Scotland 2000* (National Bible Society of Scotland, 1995), p. 15. H. Reid, *Outside Verdict: An Old Kirk in a New Scotland* (Edinburgh, 2002), p. xxix.

21. C. Brown, 'Religion', in J. Hood et al., *The History of Clydebank* (Carnforth, 1988), p. 195.

22. Brown, *Religion and Society in Scotland*, p. 161.

23. Brierley, '"Christian" Scotland', p. 15.

24. Ibid., p. 17.

25. C. G. Brown, 'Secularisation: a theory in danger?', *Scottish Economic and Social History* (11, 1991), pp. 52–8, and 'Religion and Secularisation', in Dickson and Treble (eds), *People and Society in Scotland*, pp. 48–79.

26. Brierley, '"Christian" Scotland', p. 33.

27. Ibid., pp. 34, 42.

28. Ibid., pp. 25, 46, 48. See also R. Gill, 'Who Goes to Church in Scotland?: A further sociological perspective', *Liturgical Review* (May 1976), pp. 48–53.

29. *The Scotsman* (25 May 1929).

30. Brierley, '"Christian" Scotland', p. 23.

31. P. Sissons, *The Social Significance of Church Membership in the Burgh of Falkirk* (Edinburgh, 1973), p. 284.

32. Ibid., p. 290.

33. F. Niven, *Coloured Spectacles* (London, 1938), p. 86.

34. Cairncross, *Living with the Century*, p. 16.

35. R. P. Lang, *Scotland's Sunday Under Pressure: Survey of the Extent and Growth of Sunday Trading in Scotland, 1977–1988* (March 1989), p. 4.

36. MacLeod, *We Shall Re-Build*, p. 48.

37. Lang, *Scotland's Sunday Under Pressure*, p. 1.

38. C. D. Field, '"The Secularized Sabbath" Revisited: Opinion Polls as Sources for Sunday Observance in Contemporary Britain', *Contemporary British History* (15:1, Spring 2001), pp. 1–20.

39. C. D. Field, '"The Haemorrhage of Faith?" Opinion Polls as Sources for Religious Practices, Beliefs and Attitudes in Scotland since the 1970s', *Journal of Contemporary Religion* (16:2, 2001), p. 162.

40. D. Forrester, 'Worship Since 1929', in D. Forrester and D. Murray (eds), *Studies in the History of Worship in Scotland* (Edinburgh, 1984), pp. 159, 160.

41. E. W. McFarland, 'A Coronach in Stone', in C. M. M. Macdonald and E. W. McFarland (eds), *Scotland and the Great War* (East Linton, 1999), p. 1; J. L. MacLeod, 'Greater Love Hath No Man Than This: Scotland's Conflicting Religious Responses to Death in the Great War', *Scottish Historical Review* (81, April 2002), pp. 84, 86–7.

42. *Book of Common Order* (1940).

43. National Church Association, *The Book of Common Order of 1940 Examined* (1940), p. 4.

44. *The Book of Common Order of the Church of Scotland* (Edinburgh, 1994), p. x.

45. The major Presbyterian Churches in Scotland had shared a joint hymnal since 1898.

46. In 1988, a supplement to the 'hymn book', *Songs of God's People*, reinforced these trends.

47. Fowler (ed.), *Bannerman*, p. 41. See also D. E. Meek, 'The Language of Heaven?: The Highland Churches, Culture Shift and the Erosion of Gaelic Identity in the Twentieth Century', in R. Pope (ed.), *Religion and National Identity* (Cardiff, 2001), pp. 307–37.

48. F. J. Macdonald, *Crotal and White* (London, 1991), pp. 37–8.

49. N. Gunn, *Highland River* (Edinburgh, 1996 [1937]), p. 93.

50. *The Scotsman* (11 September 1933). This total excludes over 52,000 Life Boys.

51. In 1929, Guild membership stood at 57,500, registered in 970 branches. See *Church of Scotland's Women's Guild, 1887–1937* (1937), p. 21.

52. Lockhart, *My Scottish Youth*, p. 202.

53. Buchan, *The Kirk in Scotland*, p. 129.

54. See Brown, *Religion and Society in Scotland*, pp. 137, 140; also, S. J. Brown, 'The Campaign for the Christian Commonwealth in Scotland, 1919–1939', in W. M. Jacob and N. Yates (eds), *Crown and Mitre: Religion and Society in Northern Europe Since the Reformation* (Woodbridge, 1993), pp. 203–21, and D. C. Smith, *Passive Obedience and Prophetic Protest: Social Criticism in the Scottish Church, 1830–1945* (New York, 1987).

55. Brown, 'The Campaign for the Christian Commonwealth in Scotland', p. 129.

56. *The Scotsman* (3 October 1929).

57. The roots of the Church's anti-alien policy were long-standing. In *Social Advance: Its Meaning, Method and Goal* (London, 1912), David Watson (later Convenor of the Church and Nation Committee of the Church of Scotland), noted, 'It is bad enough to lose our best who go [abroad]; but it is worse to have their places filled by the off scourings of Europe.' This is quoted in B. Aspinwall, 'Baptisms, Marriages and Lithuanians: or "Ghetto? What Ghetto?", some reflections on modern Catholic historical assumptions', *Innes Review* (51, 2000), p. 60.

58. Brown, 'The Campaign for the Christian Commonwealth', p. 215.

59. Ibid., p. 216.

60. G. I. T. Machin, *Churches and Social Issues in Twentieth-Century Britain* (Oxford, 1998), pp. 28, 48.

61. *The Scotsman* (19 May 1926).

62. S. Bruce, *No Pope of Rome: Anti-Catholicism in Modern Scotland* (Edinburgh, 1985). See also T. Gallagher, *Edinburgh Divided: John Cormack and No Popery in the 1930s* (Edinburgh, 1987).

63. A. Ratcliffe, 'An Exposure of the Margaret Sinclair Fiasco' (Edinburgh, September 1928), p. 1.

64. A. Ratcliffe, 'The Truth About the Jews' (Glasgow, July 1943), p. 17.

65. In comparison, the Roman Catholic Church responded quickly to the new residential patterns which emerged, creating forty-one new parishes between 1951 and 1960. See Brown, *Religion and Society in Scotland*, p. 164, and G. Paterson, 'New Church Building', *Liturgical Review* (May 1976), p. 45.

66. Brown, *Religion and Society in Scotland*, p. 171.

67. See J. H. Treble, 'The Development of Roman Catholic Education in Scotland, 1878–1978' *Innes Review* (29, 1978), pp. 111–39.

68. J. C. Conroy, 'A Very Scottish Affair: Catholic Education and the State', *Oxford Review of Education* (27, 2001), pp. 543–58. See rejoinder from Steve Bruce, 'Catholic Schools in Scotland', *Oxford Review of Education* (29, 2003), pp. 269–77.

69. *Souvenir of Catholic Emancipation* (1929), p. 1.

70. See J. M. Bradley, *Football, Religion and Ethnicity: Irish Identity in Scotland* (University of North London Irish Studies Centre, Occasional Papers Series, 1996), p. 16.

71. *The Times* (29 December 1979).

72. *The Times* (2 June 1982).

73. S. Bruce, T. Glendinning, I Paterson and M. Rosie, *Sectarianism in Scotland* (Edinburgh, 2004), pp. 155, 157. See also L. Paterson, 'The social class of Catholics in Scotland', *Journal of the Royal Statistical Society* (163, 2000), pp. 363–79.

74. M. Rosie, *The Sectarian Myth in Scotland: Of Bitter Memory and Bigotry* (Basingstoke, 2004), p. 31. See also I. Paterson, 'Sectarianism and Municipal Housing in Glasgow', *Scottish Affairs* (39, 2002), p. 50.

75. C. G. Brown, 'Each take their several way?: The Protestant churches and the working classes in Scotland', in G. Walker and T. Gallagher (eds), *Sermons and Battle Hymns: Protestant Culture in Modern Scotland* (Edinburgh, 1990), p. 82.

76. Extract. (The final score was Celtic 2, Dundee United 1.)

77. 'Facing the Crossroads: A Special Message From the Bishops of Scotland', *Election 92: Shaping the Future* (1992).

78. P. Lynch, 'Catholics, the Catholic Church and Political Action in Scotland', in R. Boyle and P. Lynch (eds), *Out of the Ghetto: The Catholic Community in Modern Scotland* (Edinburgh, 1998), pp. 56–7.

79. Ibid., p. 55.

80. See D. McCrone and M. Rosie, 'Left and Liberal: Catholics in Modern Scotland', in Boyle and Lynch (eds), *Out of the Ghetto*, pp. 67–94.

81. *The Scotsman* (2 September 1935). See also *History of the Free Presbyterian Church of Scotland: 1893–1970* (Inverness, c.1970), p. 169.

82. Brown, *Religion and Society in Scotland*, p. 162. See also Machin, *Churches and Social Issues*, p. 122.

83. Machin, 'British Churches and Moral Change in the 1960s', in Jacob and Yates (eds), *Crown and Mitre*, p. 231.

84. Ibid., pp. 226–7; *History of the Free Presbyterian Church*, p. 172.

85. See Church of Scotland Board of Social Responsibility, *Lifestyle Survey* (Edinburgh, 1987).

86. Ibid., pp. 26, 35.

87. *The Times* (2 May 1955).

88. A. D. Gilbert, 'Secularisation and the Future', in S. Gilley and W. J. Sheils (eds), *A History of Religion in Britain: Practice and Belief from Pre-Roman Times to the Present* (Oxford, 1994), pp. 512–13.

89. *Voice of Scotland* (VI, October 1955), p. 15.

90. Machin, 'British Churches and Moral Change', pp. 234, 238, 236.

91. *History of the Free Presbyterian Church*, p. 257.

92. Brown, *Death of Christian Britain*, pp. 179–80. See also R. Davidson and G. Davis, '"A Field for Private Members": The Wolfenden Committee and Scottish homosexual law reform, 1950–1967', *Twentieth Century British History* (15 : 2, 2004), pp. 174–201.

93. Brown, 'Each take their several way?', p. 83; C. G. Brown and J. D. Stephenson, 'Sprouting Wings?: Women and Religion in Scotland, c.1890–1950', in E. Breitenbach and E. Gordon (eds), *Out of Bounds: Women in Scottish Society, 1800–1945* (Edinburgh, 1992), p. 98.

94. C. Wordsworth, *Church Union: Steps to Promote It. A charge delivered at the Diocesan Synod held in Perth, 1 September 1887* (Edinburgh, 1887), p. 22.

95. See I. Henderson, *Power Without Glory* (London, 1967).

96. T. Gallagher, 'The Press and Protestant popular culture: a case-study of the *Scottish Daily Express*' in G. Walker and T. Gallagher (eds), *Sermons and Battle Hymns* (Edinburgh, 1990).

97. See F. Macdonald, 'Scenes of Ecclesiastical Theatre in the Free Church of Scotland, 1981–2000' *Northern Scotland* (20, 2000), pp. 125–48.

98. See Brierley and MacDonald, *Prospects for Scotland 2000*.

CHAPTER TWELVE: CULTURAL SPACES

1. T. Nairn, *The Break-up of Britain: Crisis and Neo-Nationalism* (London, 1977).

2. James Bridie to Moray McLaren (21 November 1948), in J. Bridie and M. McLaren, *A Small Stir, Letters on the English* (London, 1949), pp. 50–1.

3. W. Donaldson, *Popular Literature in Victorian Scotland: language, fiction and the press* (Aberdeen, 1986), pp. 148–9.

4. B. Dickson, 'Foundations of the Modern Scottish Novel', in C. Craig (ed.), *The History of Scottish Literature, Vol. 4: Twentieth Century* (Aberdeen, 1987), p. 51. For insights into the role of English literary criticism on Scottish literature, see also R. Crawford, *Devolving English Literature* (Oxford, 1992).

5. J. M. Reid, 'Modern Scottish Literature', *Saltire Pamphlets* (5, 1945), p. 13.

6. Quoted in James Veitch, *George Douglas Brown* (London, 1952), Part 4.

7. Brown died in 1902.

8. E. Bell, *Questioning Scotland: Literature, Nationalism, Postmodernism* (Basingstoke, 2004), p. 3.

9. E. Morgan, 'The Resources of Scotland', *Times Literary Supplement* (28 July 1972), as quoted in E. Morgan, *Crossing the Border: Essays on Scottish Literature* (Manchester, 1990), p. 19.

10. D. Dunn, 'Language and Liberty', in Dunn (ed.), *The Faber Book of Twentieth-Century Scottish Poetry*, p. xxxvii.

11. S. Hagemann, 'Introduction', in S. Hagemann, *Studies in Scottish Fiction: 1945 to the Present*, Publications of the Scottish Studies Centre of the Johannes Gutenberg Universität Mainz in Gemersheim (Frankfurt, 1996), p. 1.

12. N. Brysson Morrison, *The Gowk Storm* (Edinburgh, 1997 [1933]), Book One, Chapter Three, p. 18.

13. See Craig, *The Modern Scottish Novel*, pp. 131–2.

14. Gunn, *Highland River*, Chapter Sixteen, p. 183.

15. Brysson Morrison, *The Gowk Storm*, Book One, Chapter Five, p. 25.

16. C. Craig, 'The Fratricidal Twins: Scottish Literature, Scottish History and the Construction of Scottish Culture', in E. J. Cowan and D. Gifford (eds), *The Polar Twins* (Edinburgh, 1999), pp. 25–7.

17. F. MacColla, *And the Cock Crew* (Edinburgh, 1995 [1945]), Chapter Two, p. 27. Note that MacColla was the pseudonym for Thomas Douglas MacDonald.

18. Ibid., Chapter Seven, p. 113.

19. See C. Craig, 'Twentieth Century Scottish Literature: An introduction', and C. Milton, 'Modern Poetry in Scots before MacDiarmid', in Craig (ed.), *The History of Scottish Literature,* Vol. 4, pp. 3, 24.

20. See A. Linklater, *Compton Mackenzie: A Life* (London, 1987).

21. G. Smith, *Scottish Literature: Character and Influence* (1919), as cited in K. Buthlay, 'Introduction', in H. MacDiarmid, *A Drunk Man Looks at the Thistle* (Edinburgh, 1987), p. xxiii.

22. See J. Calder, *The Nine Lives of Naomi Mitchison* (London, 1997).

23. R. B. Cunninghame Graham, 'A Survival', in *The Ipané* (1899), pp. 62–7. See J. Walker (ed.), *The Scottish Sketches of R. B. Cunninghame Graham* (Edinburgh, 1982), p. 62.

24. J. Kelman, 'Elitism and English Literature, Speaking as a Writer', in Kelman, *'And the Judges Said . . . : Essays* (London, 2002), pp. 58–9. See also A. Hagan, *Urban Scots Dialect Writing* (Oxford, 2002).

25. H. P. Cameron, *Genesis in Scots* (Paisley, 1921), p. 13.

26. H. MacDiarmid, *Lucky Poet* (London, 1994).

27. Grieve, *Albyn*, pp. 23–4.

28. D. Gifford, 'Imagining Scotlands: the return to mythology in modern Scottish fiction', in Hagemann (ed.), *Studies in Scottish Fiction*, p. 20.

29. Grieve, *Albyn*, p. 5.

30. Niven, *Coloured Spectacles*, p. 107.

31. See M. Lindsay, *History of Scottish Literature* (London, 1992), pp. 406–9.

32. K. White, 'The Re-mapping of Scotland', *The Consignia Lecture 2001* (Edinburgh, 2001), p. 9.

33. See G. Bowd, *The Outsiders: Alexander Trocchi and Kenneth White* (Kirkcaldy, 1998).

34. A. Campbell and T. Niel, *A Life in Pieces: Reflections on Alexander Trocchi* (Edinburgh, 1997), pp. 154–7.

35. A. M. Scott, *Alexander Trocchi: the Making of the Monster* (Edinburgh, 1991).

36. See K. White, 'The Shaman Dancing on the Glacier', in *Burns, Beuys and Beyond, Supplement to ArtWork* (50, 1991), p. iii.

37. In this regard, see J. Kelman, *Tantalising Twinkles: some thoughts on a first order radical thinker of European standing* (Stenness, 1997).

38. R. Watson, 'Dialectics of "Voice" and "Place": Literature in Scots and English from 1700', in P. H. Scott (ed.), *Scotland: A Concise Cultural History* (Edinburgh, 1993), p. 121.

39. E. Kelly, 'Stands Scotland Where it Did?: An Essay in Ethnicity and Internationalism', *Scottish Affairs* (26, 1999), pp. 85–6.

40. C. March, *Rewriting Scotland: Welsh, McLean, Warner, Banks, Galloway and Kennedy* (Manchester, 2002), p. 4.

41. Gifford, 'Imagining Scotlands', pp. 32, 37.

42. E. Muir, 'Preface', in G. Blake, *Annals of Scotland, 1895–1955* (BBC, 1956), p. 3.

43. J. Neubauer, *Literature as Intervention: Struggles Over Cultural Identity in Contemporary Scottish Fiction* (Marburg, 1999), p. 222.

44. Muir, 'Preface', p. 5.

45. H. V. Morton, *In Scotland Again* (London, 1936 [1933]), p. 340.

46. C. Matheson and D. Matheson, 'Languages of Scotland: Culture and the Classroom', *Comparative Education* (36:2, 2000), p. 216.

47. E. Morgan, 'Glasgow Speech in Recent Scottish Literature', in J. D. McClure (ed.), *Scotland and the Lowland Tongue* (Aberdeen, 1983), as quoted in Morgan, *Crossing the Border*, p. 312.

48. D. Knox, 'Doing the Doric: the institutionalization of regional language and culture in the north-east of Scotland', *Social and Cultural Geography* (2:3, 2001), pp. 315–31.

49. C. W. J. Withers, *Gaelic in Scotland 1698–1981: The Geographical History of a Language* (Edinburgh, 1984), p. 235.

50. Ibid., pp. 209, 215.

51. Ibid., p. 244.

52. Ibid.

53. Ibid., p. 245.

54. M. B. Sutherland, 'Problems in Policy and Practice: Celtic Languages in the United Kingdom', *Comparative Education* (36:2, 2000), pp. 199–209.

55. D. E. Meek, *The Scottish Highlands: The Churches and Gaelic Culture* (Geneva, 1996), p. 57.

56. B. Robertson (Highland Council), Evidence to Education, Culture and Sport Committee (Scottish Parliament), Gaelic Language Bill: Stage One (7 January 2003).

57. R. Hutchison, *A Waxing Moon: The Modern Gaelic Revival* (Edinburgh, 2005), p. 157; M. MacLean, 'Parallel Universes: Gaelic Arts Development in Scotland, 1985–2000', in G. McCoy Smith and M. Scott (eds), *Gaelic Identities: Aithne Na nGael* (Belfast, 2000), p. 112.

58. S. Macdonald, *Re-imagining Culture: Histories, Identities and the Gaelic Renaissance* (Oxford, 1997). See also S. Macdonald, 'The Gaelic Renaissance and Scotland's Identities', *Scottish Affairs* (26, 1999), pp. 100–18.

59. Note that in January 2003, the Scottish Executive established Bord Gaidhlig na h-Alba – a non-departmental public body to act as a Gaelic development agency. See J. Oliver, 'Scottish Gaelic Identities: Contexts and Contingencies', *Scottish Affairs* (51, 2005), pp. 1–24.

60. See J. Findlay, 'In My House: A short essay about art in Scotland', *Critical Quarterly* (42:4, 2000), pp. 31–8.

61. In total Scotland had four art schools – Glasgow, Edinburgh, Dundee (Duncan of Jordanstone College of Art and Design) and Aberdeen (Gray's School of Art).

62. Hare, *Contemporary Painting in Scotland*, p. 5. See also M. Campbell, *The Line of Tradition: Watercolours, Drawings and Prints by Scottish Artists, 1700–1990* (Edinburgh, 1993), p. 19.

63. I. Finlay, *Art in Scotland* (Oxford, 1948), p. 132.

64. M. Lynch, 'Scottish Culture in its Historical Perspective', in Scott (ed.), *Scotland: A Concise Cultural History*, p. 34.

65. D. Hall, 'Preface', *Twentieth Century Scottish Painting: Continuing the Tradition*, 369 Gallery, Exhibition Catalogue (July–September 1987), pp. ii, iii.

66. M. Macdonald, *Scottish Art* (London, 2000), p. 146.

67. J. Morrison, *Painting the Nation: Identity and Nationalism in Scottish Painting, 1800–1920* (Edinburgh, 2003), pp. 217–8. See also T. Normand, *The Modern Scot: Modernism and Nationalism in Scottish Art 1928–1955* (Aldershot, 2000).

68. G. Bruce, *Anne Redpath* (Edinburgh, 1974), p. 11.

69. D. MacMillan, *Scottish Art in the Twentieth Century, 1890–2001* (Edinburgh, 2001), p. 66.

70. S. Watney, *The Art of Duncan Grant* (London, 1990).

71. D. Mellor, *A Paradise Lost: The Neo Romantic Imagination in Britain, 1935–1955* (London, 1987) and M. Yorke, *The Spirit of Place: Nine Neo Romantic Artists and their Times* (London, 1988).

72. Philipson was head of the department of drawing and painting at the Edinburgh School of Art (1960–1982) and later President of the Royal Scottish Academy (1973–1983).

73. M. Lindsay, *Robin Philipson* (Edinburgh, 1976), pp. 9–15.

74. See T. Normand, *Ken Currie: Details of a Trilogy* (Aldershot, 2002).

75. *The Vigorous Imagination* was the name of an important art exhibition in Glasgow in 1987 that showcased the work of this promising generation.

76. E. McArthur, 'An Uncertainty Principle', in *Steven Campbell on Form and Fiction* (Glasgow, 1990), pp. 10–11.

77. Waldermar Januszczak noted of Howson's 1987 exhibition, *Saracen Heads*, that 'Howson's brooding men . . . represent a certain kind of dark masculinity, a primitive force, an animal inheritance, that has survived the cocktail-ification of modern life', *Saracen Heads Catalogue*, Angela Flowers Gallery, London (7–31 October 1987).

78. The former was also said to be partly inspired by Scott's *Lay of the Last Minstrel*.

79. J. H. Whyte (ed.), *Towards a New Scotland* (London, 1935), pp. 211–13. See also M. Lindsay, *Francis George Scott and the Scottish Renaissance* (Edinburgh, 1980).

80. See M. Seabrook, *Max: the Life and Music of Peter Maxwell Davies* (London, 1994).

81. J. MacMillan, *The Confession of Isobel Gowdie – Score* (London, 1992), p. i.

82. J. Purser, *Scotland's Music* (Edinburgh, 1992), p. 274.

83. In 1929, Chisholm established the Active Society for the Propagation of Contemporary Music in Glasgow and Bartok was one of many influential European performers attracted to the city under its auspices.

84. T. Musgrave, *Mary, Queen of Scots: An Opera in Three Acts* (Sevenoaks, 1977). See also D. L. Hixon, *Thea Musgrave: A Bio-Bibliography* (London, 1984).

85. J. L. Campbell, 'Songs of the Hebrides: A Reappraisal of Marjory Kennedy-Fraser', *Scots Magazine* (January 1958). See also Francis Collinson, *The Traditional and National Music of Scotland* (London, 1966), p. 73. Note Marjory Kennedy-Fraser (1857–1930).

86. A. Munro, *The Democratic Muse: Folk Music Revival in Scotland* (Aberdeen, 1996), p. 198.

87. See Munro, *The Democratic Muse*.

88. G. W. Lockhart, *Fiddles and Folk: A Celebration of the Re-emergence of Scotland's Musical Heritage* (Edinburgh, 1998).

89. Also known as 'The Fairfield Crane'. Munro, *The Democratic Muse*, p. 100, stanzas one and three. (This song dates from the mid 1960s.)

90. E. Casciani, *Oh, How We Danced!* (Edinburgh, 1994), pp. 73–6. See also J. Brown, *Glasgow's Dancing Daft!* (Ochiltree, 1994).

91. J. Helm, *Who's On the Dance Music Tonight?* (Ayr, 1998), pp. 22–3, 26, 32–3.

92. B. Hogg, *The History of Scottish Rock and Pop: All that ever mattered* (Middlesex, 1993), p. 16.

93. Ibid., p. 22. See also M. Kielty, *SAHB Story: The Tale of the Sensational Alex Harvey Band* (Glasgow, 2004).

94. Hogg, *The History of Scottish Rock and Pop*, pp. 27–8.

95. J. Gentle and I. Forsyth, *Johnny Gentle and The Beatles: First Ever Tour, Scotland 1960* (Runcorn, 1998), p. 70.

96. The Beatles also supported Roy Orbison at his gig at Glasgow's Odeon in June 1963.

97. *Edinburgh Evening News* (17 June 1965).

98. M. Huxley, *AC/DC: The World's Heaviest Rock* (London, 1966). The Youngs had already set Australia alight as The Easybeats – that country's answer to The Beatles.

99. See L. McKeown, *Shang-a-lang: Life as an International Pop Idol* (Edinburgh, 2003).

100. B. Sutherland and L. Ellis, *Annie Lennox: The Biography* (London, 2002).

101. M. Ure, *Midge Ure: If I Was . . . The Autobiography* (London, 2004).

102. H. Roberton, *A German Odyssey* (Glasgow, 1946).

103. V. Devlin, *Kings, Queens and People's Palaces: An Oral History of the Scottish Variety Theatre* (Edinburgh, 1991), pp. 177–8.

104. D. Hutchison, '1900 to 1950', in B. Findlay (ed.), *A History of Scottish Theatre* (Edinburgh, 1998), p. 207.

105. F. Bruce, *Scottish Showbusiness: Music Hall, Variety and Pantomime* (Edinburgh, 2000), p. 25.

106. Ibid., p. 218.

107. For an earlier period, see P. Maloney, *Scotland and the Music Hall, 1850–1914* (Manchester, 2003).

108. J. H. Littlejohn, *The Scottish Music Hall, 1880–1990* (Wigtown, 1990), pp. 12–13, 44.

109. J. Bridie, 'The Scottish Character as it was viewed by Scottish Authors from Galt to Barrie', The John Galt Lecture, Greenock Philosophical Society (1937), p. 21.

110. C. Craig and R. Stevenson, 'Introduction', in Craig and Stevenson (eds), *20th Century Scottish Drama: An Anthology* (Edinburgh, 2001), p. viii.

111. As cited in P. Barlow, *Wise Enough to Play the Fool: A Biography of Duncan Macrae* (Edinburgh, 1995), p. 16.

112. Hutchison, '1900 to 1950', pp. 210–12.

113. J. Forsyth, *Tyrone Guthrie: A Biography* (London, 1976), p. 69.

114. Hutchison, '1900 to 1950', p. 223.

115. See A. Scullion, 'Glasgow Unity Theatre: The Necessary Contradictions of Scottish Political Theatre', *Twentieth Century British History* (13, 2002), pp. 215–52.

116. James Bridie, 'O Philosophers!' (1942), in *Tedious and Brief* (London, 1944), p. 43.

117. See Hutchison, '1900 to 1950', *passim*.

118. M. Garattoni, 'Scottish Drama at the Edinburgh Fringe until the Seventies', V. Pogg and M. Rose (eds), *A Theatre that Matters: Twentieth-century Scottish Drama and Theatre* (Milan, 2000), p. 183.

119. Forsyth, *Tyrone Guthrie*, pp. 73–4.

120. Devlin, *Kings, Queens and People's Palaces*, pp. 183, 187. See also D. Goldie, 'Will ye stop yer tickling Jock?: Modern and postmodern Scottish comedy', *Critical Quarterly* (42:4, 2000), pp. 7–18.

121. J. McBain, *Pictures Past: Recollections of Scottish Cinemas and Cinema-going* (Edinburgh, 1985), p. 17.

122. Ibid., p. 24; D. Hutchison, 'Flickering Light: Some Scottish Silent Films', in E. Dick, *From Limelight to Satellite: A Scottish Film Book* (BFI/ SFC, 1990), p. 32.

123. D. J. Robertson, 'Consumption', in Cairncross (ed.), *The Scottish Economy*, p. 177.

124. B. Douglas, *Palace of Dreams: The Making of a Film-maker* (1978), p. 1.

125. D. Bruce, *Scotland the Movie* (Edinburgh, 1996), p. 6.

126. *Scottish Screen Data*, 'Cinemas and Film Exhibition' (1998), p. 38.

127. J. McBain, *Scottish Film Archive: A Companion to the Scottish Film Archive Catalogue* (Glasgow, 1996), p. 2. See also Scottish Film Council, *Scotscreen 100: The Centenary of Cinema in Scotland*, press release (9 April 1996).

128. F. Hardy, *Scotland in Film* (Edinburgh, 1990), p. 210.

129. As cited in D. Petrie, *Screening Scotland* (London, 2000), p. 103.

130. Ibid., p. 112.

131. Ibid., p. 119.

132. Ibid., p. 172.

133. Hydra Associates, *Scotland on Screen* (Commissioned by Scottish Enterprise and HIE, 1996), pp. 6, 9.

134. See P. Todd and B. Cook (eds), *Subjects and Sequences: A Margaret Tait Reader* (London, 2004).

135. A. Noble, 'Bill Douglas, 1934–1991: A Memoir', in E. Dick, A. Noble, D. Petrie (eds), *Bill Douglas: A Lanternist's Account* (London, 1993), p. 13.

136. See F. Hardy, *John Grierson: A Documentary Biography* (London, 1979).

137. F. Hardy, 'The Cinema', in Scott (ed.), *Scotland: A Concise Cultural History*, p. 270.

138. See M. Powell, *A Life in Movies: An Autobiography* (London, 1987).

139. C. McArthur, 'Scotland and Cinema: The Iniquity of the Fathers', in C. McArthur (ed.), *Scotch Reels: Scotland in Cinema and Television* (London, 1982), p. 47.

140. Ibid., p. 66.

141. Todd, *Subjects and Sequences*, p. 92.

142. McArthur, 'Scotland and Cinema', p. 49.

143. See D. McCrone, 'Cultural capital in an understated nation: the case of Scotland', *British Journal of Sociology* (56, 2005), pp. 65–82.

144. J. Calcutt, 'There and Then', in *Here and Now: Scottish Art, 1990–2001* (Dundee, 2001), p. 18. A memorandum submitted by the SAC to the Scottish Affairs Committee (11 December 1997) emphasised that the 'arts have a role to play in education, in health, in urban and rural regeneration, in economic development, in tourism, in job creation, in tackling social exclusion. There is no aspect of Scottish society which is not touched in some way by the arts.' HC442-i, Minutes of Evidence Taken Before the Scottish Affairs Committee (16 December 1997), pp. 4–5.

145. N. Spice, *The Funding of Literary Magazines by the Scottish Arts Council, 2001–2002* (January 2002), p. 14.

146. J. Urry, 'Globalisation, Localisation and the Nation State', *Lancaster Regionalism Group* (Working Paper 40, 1990), p. 21.

147. Z. Bauman, *Intimations of Postmodernity* (London, 1992), pp. 138–9.

CHAPTER THIRTEEN: HOBBIES, HOLIDAYS AND HEADLINES

1. Linklater, *Magnus Merriman*, pp. 113–15.

2. Ibid., p. 122.

3. See, for example, G. Jarvie and J. Burnett, 'Sport, Scotland and the Scots', in Jarvie and Burnett (eds) *Sport, Scotland and the Scots* (East Linton, 2000), pp. 1–18, and G. Jarvie and G. Walker, 'Ninety Minute Patriots?', in Jarvie and Walker (eds), *Scottish Sport in the Making of the Nation: Ninety Minute Patriots?* (Leicester, 1994), pp. 1–8.

4. *Junior Football Handbook* (*Evening Citizen*, 1959–1960), p. 96.

5. Robin Jenkins, *The Thistle and the Grail* (Edinburgh, 1983), p. 8.

6. *The Scotsman* (2 April 1928).

7. J. Hendry, *Dundee Greats* (Bristol, 1991). Tommy was the son of Celtic legend Patsy Gallacher.

8. A. Ferguson, *Managing My Life: My Autobiography* (London, 1999), p. 180.

9. Scottish players attached to English Football League sides in 1929 numbered 362, in 1965, numbered 258 and, in 1975, numbered 198. B. Crampsey, *The Scottish Footballer* (Edinburgh, 1978), p. 32.

10. See J. Rafferty, 'The decline and fall of Scottish Football', in M. Aitken (ed.), *When Will We See Your Like Again: The Changing Face of Scottish Football* (Edinburgh, 1977), p. 13.

11. A. Massie, 'Rugby', in Jarvie and Burnett (eds), *Sport, Scotland and the Scots*, p. 253.

12. J. Telfer with D. Ferguson, *Jim Telfer: Looking Back . . . for Once* (Edinburgh, 2005), p. 19.

13. See D. Douglas, *The Thistle: A Chronicle of Scottish Rugby* (Edinburgh, 1997); L. Speirs, *The Border League Story: One Hundred Years of the World's Oldest Rugby League* (Galashiels, 2000).

14. *The Scotsman* (23 March 1925).

15. See D. Haston, *In High Places* (Edinburgh, 1997).

16. See G. Obree, *The Flying Scotsman* (Edinburgh, 2004).

17. *The Times* (12 June 1978).

18. A. Bairner, 'Football', in Jarvie and Burnett (eds) *Sport, Scotland and the Scots*, pp. 98–9. Scotland first entered the World Cup competition in 1954, four years after England.

19. See H. F. Moorhouse, '"We're off to Wembley": The History of a Scottish Event and the Sociology of Football Hooliganism', in McCrone et al., *The Making of Scotland*, pp. 207–28. Note that, while the British Home Championships ended in 1984, an annual fixture between the 'auld enemies' continued until 1989 when the teams competed for the Rous Cup.

20. C. S. Ferguson, *Bring Out Your Riot Gear – Hearts Are Here!: Gorgie Aggro, 1981–1986* (Lockerbie, 1999), pp. 14, 33.

21. G. P. T. Finn, 'Faith, Hope and Bigotry: Case Studies of Anti-Catholic Prejudice in Scottish Soccer and Society', in Jarvie and Walker (eds), *Scottish Sport in the Making of the Nation*, pp. 91–112. See also J. M. Bradley, 'Abstruse and Insecure? Irish Identity in Modern Scotland', *Social Identities* (2 : 2, 1996), pp. 293–310; G. Walker, 'Identity Questions in Contemporary Scotland: Faith, Football and Future Prospects', *Contemporary British History* (15 : 1, 2001), pp. 41–60.

22. The SFA refused to recognise women's football until 1974–75.

23. See Ferguson, *Managing My Life* and S. F. Kelly, *Dalglish* (London, 1997).

24. A. MacPherson, *Jock Stein: the Definitive Biography* (Newbury, 2004), p. 7.

25. S. Halliday, *Rangers: the Waddell Years, 1938–1984* (Edinburgh, 1999), p. 15; D. Law, *The Lawman: An Autobiography* (London, 2001); D. P. Thomson, *Eric Liddell: The Making of an Athlete and the Training of a Missionary* (Glasgow, n. d.); D. Williams, *Colin McRae: Rallying's First Master* (Sparkford, 1997).

26. Williams, *Colin McRae*, p. 153.

27. R. Glanvill, *Sir Matt Busby: A Tribute* (London, 1995); B. Shankly, *Shankly* (London, 1976); T. Collings and S. Sykes, *Jackie Stewart: A Restless Life* (London, 2003).

28. G. Gould, *Jim Clark Remembered* (Cambridge, 1975), p. 97.

29. T. Shield and K. Gallagher, *Just the Three Weeks in Provence: Travels with the Scotland Squad and the Tartan Army in World Cup '98* (Edinburgh, 1998), p. 178.

30. D. Kyles, *Corstorphine Curling Club, 1829–1979* (Edinburgh, 1979).

31. J. Duncan Cran, *Partick Curling Club, 1842–1970* (Glasgow, 1971).

32. G. Grant, *Baberton Golf Club: the first hundred years* (Edinburgh, 1992), p. 42; W. Pritchard, *Lothianburn Golf Club Centenary, 1893–1993* (Edinburgh, 1993), p. 45.

33. A. Gordon Mitchell D.D., 'Sermon to Curlers' (15 November 1936), p. 1.

34. Important legislative enactments include the 1913 Temperance Act, the 1923 Intoxicating Liquor (Sale to Persons under Eighteen) Act and the 1920 Temperance (Scotland) Act.

35. T. Shields, *Great Scottish Pubs* (Gartocharn, 1977).

36. Casciani, *Oh, How We Danced*, p. 41; Lockhart, *My Scottish Youth*, p. 232.

37. Casciani, *Oh, How We Danced*, pp. 47, 66.

38. G. Emmerson, *A Social History of Scottish Dance: Ane Celestial Recreation* (London, 1972), p. 297.

39. H. Foss, *Notes on Evolution in Scottish Country Dancing* (Dumfries, 1973), p. 23.

40. G. W. Lockhart, *Highland Balls and Village Halls* (Edinburgh, 1997).

41. M. Brooksbank, *No Sae Lang Syne: A Tale of this City* (Dundee, n. d.), p. 7.

42. A. Durie and G. McPherson, 'Tourism and the First World War', *The Local Historian* (November 1999), pp. 240–55.

43. J. Bridie, 'Going on Holiday: a School Essay Rewritten', in Bridie, *Mr Bridie's Alphabet for Little Glasgow Highbrows* (London, 1934), p. 33.

44. D. Daiches, in C. Bell (ed.), *Scotland's Century: An Autobiography of the Nation* (Glasgow, 1999), p. 34.

45. A. Durie, *Scotland for the Holidays: Tourism in Scotland, 1780–1939* (East Linton, 2003), p. 196.

46. A. V. Seaton, 'The History of Tourism in Scotland: Approaches, Sources and Issues', in R. MacLellan and R. Smith (eds), *Tourism in Scotland* (London, 1998), p. 26.

47. See J. R. Gold and M. M. Gold, *Imagining Scotland: Tradition, Representation and Promotion in Scottish Tourism since 1750* (Aldershot, 1995).

48. D. McCrone, A. Morris and R. Kiely, *Scotland – the Brand: the Making of Scottish Heritage* (Edinburgh, 1995), p. 137

49. I. D. Duff, *The Tourism Industry and the Scottish Economy* (Scottish Council (Development and Industry), Briefing Note, 1998), Introduction, p. 3.

50. A. Hunt, *A Survey of Scottish Tourism* (survey carried out in 1964 for the Scottish Development Department, 1966), p. 7.

51. Ibid., p. 11.

52. Ibid., p. 12.

53. M. Brownrigg, 'Tourism', in Ingham and Love (eds), *Understanding the Scottish Economy*, p. 90.

54. *Social Statistics* (Scottish Executive National Statistics Publication, 2001), p. 163.

55. D. Ferguson, *The Scottish Newspaper Press* (Saltire Pamphlets, No. 6, London, 1946), p. 25.

56. A. Hetherington, *News in the Regions: Plymouth Sound to Moray Firth* (London, 1989), p. 194.

57. A. Morris, *Scotland's Paper: The Scotsman, 1817–1992* (Edinburgh, 1992), pp. 46, 57.

58. See J. MacInnes, 'The Press in Scotland', *Scottish Affairs* (1, 1992), pp. 137–48.

59. M. Macdonald, 'The Press in Scotland', in D. Hutchison (ed.), *HEADLINES: The Media in Scotland* (Edinburgh, n. d.), p. 15.

60. See P. Meech and R. Kilborn, 'Media and Identity in a Stateless Nation: the case of Scotland', *Media, Culture and Society* (2, 1992), p. 256.

61. J. Campbell, *A Word For Scotland* (Edinburgh, 1998), p. 13.

62. H. Conroy, *Off the Record: A Life in Journalism* (Glendaruel, 1997); J. Webster, *The Express Years: A Golden Decade* (Edinburgh, 1994) and *The Herald Years* (Edinburgh, 1996).

63. A. Dunnett, *Among Friends: An Autobiography* (London, 1984).

64. Seawright, *An Important Matter of Principle*, pp. 182–3.

65. Hutchison, *Scottish Politics in the Twentieth Century*, pp. 101–2.

66. M. Linklater, 'The Media', in L. Paterson (ed.), *The Anatomy of Scotland: How Scotland Works* (Edinburgh, 1994), p. 128.

67. F. Johnston, 'The Press in Scotland', in D. Campbell (ed.), *The British Press* (1978), pp. 44–5.

68. See Linklater, 'The Media', pp. 126–44. See also M. Smith, *Paper Lions: The Scottish Press and National Identity* (Edinburgh, 1994), pp. 148–72, 243–7. In 1996, these old Outram Press titles were taken over by Scottish Television and became part of the Scottish Media Group.

69. Ferguson, *The Scottish Newspaper Press*, p. 38.

70. J. Garside, 'The Scottish Media', in Hassan and Warhurst (eds), *Anatomy of the New Scotland*, p. 196.

71. A. Mackie, *The Trade Unionist and the Tycoon* (Edinburgh, 1992); R. McKay and B. Barr, *The Story of the Scottish Daily News* (Edinburgh, 1976). The six-month occupation of the Albion Street building by journalists that followed the collapse of the *News* merely postponed the inevitable.

72. W. H. McDowell, *The History of BBC Broadcasting in Scotland, 1923–1983* (Edinburgh, 1992), pp. 15, 18, 19.

73. *Broadcasting House, Edinburgh 1930–1990* (Edinburgh, 1990), p. 5.

74. *Scottish Broadcasts, January to March 1947* (BBC, 1947).

75. McDowell, *The History of BBC Broadcasting in Scotland, 1923–1983*, p. 43.

76. Ibid., p. 136.

77. Hogg, *The History of Scottish Rock and Pop*, p. 56.

78. McDowell, *The History of BBC Broadcasting in Scotland*, pp. 81–3.

79. R. Falconer, *Message Media Mission: the Baird Lectures, 1975* (Edinburgh, 1977), p. 27.

80. Grampian Television was established in 1961.

81. McDowell, *The History of BBC Broadcasting in Scotland*, p. 156.

82. I. Turok, 'Cities, Clusters and Creative Industries: The Case of Film and Television in Scotland', *European Planning Studies* (11 : 5, 2003), pp. 558–9.

83. *Social Statistics*, p. 155.

EPILOGUE: BRIDGES, BORDERS AND FRONTIERS

1. The description fits both the rail and road bridges, so I utilise authorial licence here to claim it for four-wheeled traffic.

2. L. Clements, 'The Scale and Nature of Bridge Maintenance in Scotland', Scottish Development Department, (Edinburgh, September 1978), p. 1.

3. The new bridge sustained serious flood damage in 1877.

4. *An Address Delivered by the Right Honourable the Earl of Rosebery . . . in Support of the Preservation of the Auld Brig of Ayr* (25 September 1906).

5. Walter Scott, *Tales of a Grandfather* (Second Series, London, 1923), p. 46.

6. G. P. Insh, *The Study of Local History and Other Essays* (Edinburgh, 1932), p. 152.

7. R. Langley, *Walking the Scottish Border* (London, 1976), p. 168.

8. Ibid., p. 14.

9. Ibid., p. 11.

10. G. Eyre-Todd, *Byways of the Scottish Border* (Selkirk, 1886), pp. 2, 3.

11. Mr and Mrs W. Platt, *Stories of the Scottish Border* (London, 1917), p. 11.

12. G. MacDonald Fraser, *The Steel Bonnets: the Story of the Anglo-Scottish Border Reivers* (London, 1971), pp. 380–1.

13. J. Inglis Ker, *The Land of Scott* (issued by the Royal Automobile Club, London, 1931), p. 6.

14. Morton, *In Search of Scotland*, pp. 2–3. See C. R. Perry, 'In Search of H. V. Morton: Travel Writing and Cultural Values in the First Age of British Democracy', *Twentieth Century British History* (10, 1999).

15. Morton, *In Search of Scotland*, p. 21.

16. B. Anderson, *Imagined Communities: Reflections on the origin and spread of Nationalism* (London, 1983). See, McCrone, *Understanding Scotland*, pp. 28, 30; D. McCrone, A. Norris and R. Kiely, *Scotland – The Brand: The Making of Scottish Heritage* (Edinburgh, 1995).

17. F. Jackson Turner, 'The Significance of the Frontier in American History', in *The Frontier in American History* (New York, 1953 edition), p. 2.
18. Ibid., p. 4.
19. N. MacCaig, 'Crossing the Border', *Collected Poems* (London, 1990), p. 174.
20. H. MacDiarmid, 'Satori in Scotland', in K. Miller (ed.), *Memoirs of a Modern Scotland* (London, 1970), p. 57 (my italics).
21. Bauman, *Intimations of Postmodernity*, pp. xix–xx.

Index

Aberdeen 62–5 *passim*, 76, 77–8, 82,
    104, 135, 144, 164, 165, 194,
    196, 207, 273, 310, 331
Aberdeenshire 56, 59
AC/DC 309
actors 320
    see also individual actors, cinema,
    drama, film-making, theatre
agriculture
    arable sector 57–8
    Board of Agriculture for Scotland
    (later Department of
    Agriculture) 92–3
    BSE 59–60
    Chernobyl disaster (1986) 59
    depopulation 113
    diversification 59
    employment 56, 62
    European Union 58, 60, 93–4,
    184–5
    Foot and Mouth Disease
    (2001) 60
    labour market 59, 62
    land-ownership 56, 60, 92,
    93, 184
    livestock production 58–9, 92
    mechanisation 61–2
    mixed farming 57–8, 360n
    state intervention 59, 65, 92–4, 183
    in World War One 23
    in World War Two 58, 61, 92–3
    see also highlands

air travel 334–5
alcohol 331, 407n
aluminium industry
    Foyers 16, 178
    Invergordon 73, 179
*Ane Satyre of the Thrie
    Estaitis* 312
Anti-Semitism 172, 174, 381n
Applecross 275–76
Argyll 218
Arrol, William 34–5
art 267, 300–4
    art dealers 301
    art schools 300
    Bloomsbury Group 302
    Edinburgh School 302
    emotive quality 301
    expressionism 302
    figurative painting 303
    galleries 302, 321–2
    Glasgow Boys 301
    and history 304
    international influences 301
    modernism 301
    neo-romanticism 302
    realism 303
    Scottish Colourists 302
    state subsidy 321
    see also individual artists
Ascherson, Neal 253
Average White Band 309
Ayr 311, 335